The History of American Literature on Film

THE HISTORY OF WORLD LITERATURES ON FILM

Series Editors:
Greg M. Colón Semenza
Bob Hasenfratz

Also Published in the Series
The History of British Literature on Film, 1895–2015
Greg M. Colón Semenza and Bob Hasenfratz

Forthcoming Volumes in the Series
The History of German Literature on Film
Christiane Schonfeld
The History of Russian Literature on Film
David Gillespie
The History of French Literature on Film
Kate Griffiths and Andrew Watts
The History of Sub-Saharan African Literatures on Film
Sara Hanaburgh

The History of American Literature on Film

Thomas Leitch

BLOOMSBURY ACADEMIC
NEW YORK • LONDON • OXFORD • NEW DELHI • SYDNEY

BLOOMSBURY ACADEMIC
Bloomsbury Publishing Inc
1385 Broadway, New York, NY 10018, USA
50 Bedford Square, London, WC1B 3DP, UK
29 Earlsfort Terrace, Dublin 2, Ireland

BLOOMSBURY, BLOOMSBURY ACADEMIC and the Diana logo
are trademarks of Bloomsbury Publishing Plc

First published in the United States of America 2019
This paperback edition published in 2021

Copyright © Thomas Leitch, 2019

For legal purposes the Acknowledgments on p. xiv constitute an
extension of this copyright page.

Cover design by Simon Levy
Cover images: Left, *Tarzan the Ape Man*, 1932,
Right, *The Scarlett Letter*, 1995 © Collection Christophel / ArenaPal

All rights reserved. No part of this publication may be reproduced or
transmitted in any form or by any means, electronic or mechanical, including
photocopying, recording, or any information storage or retrieval system,
without prior permission in writing from the publishers.

Bloomsbury Publishing Inc does not have any control over, or responsibility
for, any third-party websites referred to or in this book. All internet addresses given in
this book were correct at the time of going to press. The author and publisher regret
any inconvenience caused if addresses have changed or sites have ceased to exist,
but can accept no responsibility for any such changes.

Library of Congress Cataloging-in-Publication Data
Names: Leitch, Thomas M., author.
Title: The history of American literature on film / Thomas Leitch.
Description: New York : Bloomsbury Academic, 2019. | Series: History of world
literatures on film | Includes bibliographical references and index.
Identifiers: LCCN 2019007909 (print) | LCCN 2019012137 (ebook) |
ISBN 9781628923711 (ePDF) | ISBN 9781628923728 (ePub) |
ISBN 9781628923735 (hardback : alk. paper)
Subjects: LCSH: Motion pictures and literature. | American literature–Film adaptations.
| Film adaptations. | Motion pictures–History.
Classification: LCC PN1995.3 (ebook) | LCC PN1995.3 .L4255 2019 (print) |
DDC 791.43/6–dc23
LC record available at https://lccn.loc.gov/2019007909

ISBN: HB: 978-1-6289-2373-5
PB: 978-1-5013-9075-3
ePDF: 978-1-6289-2371-1
eBook: 978-1-6289-2372-8

Series: The History of World Literatures on Film

Typeset by Integra Software Services Pvt. Ltd.

To find out more about our authors and books visit www.bloomsbury.com
and sign up for our newsletters.

In memory of Laurence Raw

CONTENTS

List of Figures viii
Acknowledgments xiv

1 Introduction: American Cinema and American Literatures 1
2 1895–1915: The Attraction of Adaptation 31
3 1915–27: American Exotics 69
4 1927–39: Novel Impressions 111
5 1939–51: Invisible Adaptation 155
6 1951–67: Weaponized Best Sellers 199
7 1967–75: Counterculture Classics 231
8 1975–89: Screening the Silenced 267
9 1989–2007: Adapt or Die 301
10 2007–18: Entertainment for Me 339

Bibliography 379
Index 393

FIGURES

1.1 Howard Wakefield (Bryan Cranston) spies on his family from his self-imposed exile in his garage in *Wakefield* (2016) 2
1.2 James Franco's split-screen composition in *As I Lay Dying* (2013) presents both Vardaman (Brady Permenter) as Darl sees him and Darl himself (Franco) as he watches 5
1.3 Arthur Dimmesdale (Gary Oldman) and Hester Prynne (Demi Moore) in *The Scarlet Letter* (1995): a travesty, but not a fluke 18
2.1 Joseph Jefferson awakens to a second life in *Rip Van Winkle* (1896) 32
2.2 A credit in *The Adventure of the Hasty Elopement* (1914) not only identifies its literary source, but invites the audience to read it themselves after watching the movie 39
2.3 A high-spirited blackface dance in *Uncle Tom's Cabin* (1903) introduces the news that Eva is seriously ill 42
2.4 Before they get nestled all snug in their beds, the children in *The Night before Christmas* (1905) occupy themselves quite differently 47
2.5 A celebrated episode of Winsor McCay's *Dream of the Rarebit Fiend* provides a surprisingly detailed blueprint for Edwin S. Porter's 1906 adaptation 49
2.6 Porter's duplication of a single panel from McCay's strip in *The Dream of a Rarebit Fiend* (1906) 50
2.7 The Cowardly Lion greets the donkey Nickodemus in *The Magic Cloak of Oz* (1914) 57
2.8 Charlie Chaplin's heartbroken artist displays his grief by executing a comically amateurish drawing of his lost love in *The Face on the Barroom Floor* (1914) 60
2.9 *Ramona* (1910) directs attention to the scripts provided by both its literary source and its geographic locations 63
2.10 Questioned by a detective (Ralph Lewis), the Nephew (Henry B. Walthall) involuntarily recalls his murder of his Uncle (Spottiswoode Aitken) in *The Avenging Conscience* (1914) 66
3.1 The Ku Klux Klan prepares to execute summary justice against the would-be rapist Gus (Walter Long) in *The Birth of a Nation* (1915) 71
3.2 Edith Hardy (Fannie Ward) seeks desperately to hide her submissive relationship with her creditor Haka Arakau (Sessue Hayakawa) from her socialite friends in *The Cheat* (1915) 72

FIGURES

3.3 The orgy that never happens in *Manslaughter* (1922) 74
3.4 The name at the bottom of every intertitle in *Salomy Jane* (1914) leaves no doubt what the film considers its principal attraction to be 78
3.5 McTeague (Gibson Gowland, right) faces his nemesis Marcus Schouler (Jean Hersholt) in the Death Valley climax of *Greed* (1924) 82
3.6 *The Last of the Mohicans* (1920) balances its fear of miscegenation against the noble love between Cora Munro (Barbara Bedford) and Uncas (Alan Roscoe) 84
3.7 On her release from prison, Hester Prynne (Lillian Gish) is publicly shamed in *The Scarlet Letter* (1926) 86
3.8 Belgian Virginie Harbrok (Marguerite Courtot) begs American soldier Philip Landicutt (Raymond McKee), the hero of *The Unbeliever* (1918), to shoot her rather than allowing her to fall into the hands of the Germans 88
3.9 The calm before the storm: the Bernle family saying grace at dinner in the beginning of *Four Sons* (1928) 89
3.10 Owen (Rockliffe Fellowes) casts an appraising eye on the offscreen interlopers in his criminal underworld in *Regeneration* (1915) 96
3.11 An opening intertitle claims the right of *Where Are My Children?* (1914) to deal with a subject long considered off-limits for films 98
3.12 The final image of *The Vanishing American* (1925) sets the universal endurance of the physical world against the transience of the exotic people who inhabit it 103
3.13 The masked Zorro (Douglas Fairbanks) exults over his enemy and romantic rival Captain Juan Ramon (Robert McKim) in the climactic swordfight in *The Mark of Zorro* (1920) 107
4.1 His song finished, Jack Robin (Al Jolson) strikes up an impromptu conversation with his mother (Eugénie Besserer) in *The Jazz Singer* (1927) 115
4.2 A characteristically intimate moment between the ballerina Grusinskaya (Greta Garbo) and Baron Felix von Geigern (John Barrymore) in *Grand Hotel* (1932) 121
4.3 The dawn of a franchise romance: Tarzan (Johnny Weismuller) meets Jane (Maureen O'Sullivan) in *Tarzan the Ape Man* (1932) 124
4.4 David Harum (Will Rogers) protests that he can't possibly meet all the demands of Ann Madison (Evelyn Venable) in *David Harum* (1934)—even though it is clear that he will 126
4.5 Mr. Moto (Peter Lorre) accepts the greetings Charlie Chan's Number One Son (Keye Luke) brings from his father in *Mr. Moto's Gamble* (1938), a vehicle that began life as *Charlie Chan at Ringside* 129
4.6 William Powell as Nick Charles (right) greets William Powell as Philo Vance in MGM's trailer for *The Thin Man* (1934) 130
4.7 The title credit for *Song of the Thin Man* (1947) implies that the title character is Nick Charles, not an altogether different character who died in *The Thin Man* 131

4.8 Captain Spalding (Groucho Marx) steps forward from his fellow cast members in *Animal Crackers* (1930) long enough to indulge a "strange interlude" in a burlesque of Eugene O'Neill 139

4.9 *Birthright* (1938) establishes Tump Pack (Alec Lovejoy) and Peter Siner (Carman Newsome) as natural opposites 145

4.10 Wang Lung (Paul Muni) realizes at last that O-Lan (Luise Rainer), the wife he has neglected in his obsessive pursuit of land and wealth, has been the mainstay of his life in *The Good Earth* (1937) 147

4.11 Abandoned for good by Rhett Butler, Scarlett O'Hara (Vivien Leigh) is solaced by her still deeper ties to Tara in *Gone with the Wind* (1939) 150

5.1 The incorrigibly shiftless Lesters of *Tobacco Road* (1941): Jeeter (Charley Grapewin), Dude (William Tracy), Ada (Elizabeth Patterson), and Ellie Mae (Gene Tierney) 160

5.2 The title credit of *Northwest Passage* (1940) seems to promise a sequel that never materialized 164

5.3 The massively produced climactic number of *This Is the Army* (1943) promises both the characters and the audience that "This Time (Is the Last Time)" 168

5.4 James M. Cain's novel gets the star treatment in the title credit for *The Postman Always Rings Twice* (1946) 180

5.5 As he interrogates Brigid O'Shaughnessy (Mary Astor) in *The Maltese Falcon* (1941), does Sam Spade (Humphrey Bogart) already know that she has killed his partner? 182

5.6 The title characters of *The Killers* (1946) approach Henry's Diner in an opening scene whose blocking and lighting are both realistic and nightmarishly expressionistic 184

5.7 and 5.8 Authors' names get upstaged by producers' names or disappear entirely in the main titles of *Leave Her to Heaven* (1945) and *Black Angel* (1946) 189

5.9 The shattered mirror in *A Streetcar Named Desire* (1951) provides an elliptical representation of the rape of Blanche DuBois (Vivien Leigh) 194

5.10 The opening frame of *The Red Badge of Courage* (1951) introduces Stephen Crane's name and status even before those of director John Huston fade in beneath 196

6.1 Standing in for the author of *O. Henry's Full House* (1952), John Steinbeck reaches for the obligatory volume of O. Henry's stories 200

6.2 In *To Kill a Mockingbird* (1962), Atticus Finch (Gregory Peck) turns the defense of accused rapist Tom Robinson (Brock Peters) into an unforgettable film Universal advertised as not suitable for children as young as Finch's daughter Scout (Mary Badham), the film's principal identification figure 205

6.3 Cynthia Green (Ava Gardner) and Harry Street (Gregory Peck) enjoy one of the torrid sex scenes Darryl F. Zanuck was convinced were behind the success of *The Snows of Kilimanjaro* (1952) 208

6.4 Even during a rare domestic scene, Amber St. Clair (Linda Darnell) shows off to Bruce Carlton (Cornel Wilde) another of the plunging necklines she favors throughout *Forever Amber* (1947) 210

6.5 The petting party between Betty Anderson (Terry Moore) and Rodney Harrington (Barry Coe) in *Peyton Place* (1957) is about to turn out quite differently than it did in Grace Metalious's novel 215

6.6 *The Best of Everything* (1959) repeatedly frames newcomer Caroline Bender (Hope Lange) against the Seagram Building, her true home in New York 220

6.7 Transfixed by the shadow of Grace Caldwell (Suzanne Pleshette) as she undresses, Charlie Jay (Mark Goddard) will soon force himself on her in *A Rage to Live* (1965) 223

6.8 Trading in cultural cachet for materialistic excess: the chandelier striptease of Rina Marlowe Cord (Carroll Baker) in *The Carpetbaggers* (1961) 225

6.9 The classical sculpture behind the main title of *From the Terrace* (1960) assures the audience drawn by the promise of a scandalous adaptation that they will also enjoy some cultural uplift 226

7.1 The drama of the uneasy professional alliance between visiting Detective Virgil Tibbs (Sidney Poitier) and Sparta, Mississippi police chief Gillespie (Rod Steiger) propelled *In the Heat of the Night* (1967) past its Oscar competitors *Bonnie and Clyde* and *The Graduate* 232

7.2 The temptress Roxanne (Janice Rule) lets it all hang out in a timidly transgressive musical sequence in *The Subterraneans* (1960) 242

7.3 As a student demonstration boils around him, Harry Bailey (Elliot Gould) exultantly announces his final break with the academy he has long sought to fit into in *Getting Straight* (1970) 248

7.4 The demonic possession of Regan MacNeil (Linda Blair) in *The Exorcist* (1973) is consistently associated with the counterculture 251

7.5 Surrounded by competitors, Gloria Beatty (Jane Fonda) and Robert Syverton (Michael Sarrazin) drag themselves through the grueling dance marathon in *They Shoot Horses, Don't They?* (1969) 252

7.6 Jennie Cavilleri (Ali MacGraw) and Oliver Barrett IV (Ryan O'Neal) exchange vows in *Love Story* (1970) 253

7.7 *The Godfather* (1972) uses the Corleone family—Sonny (James Caan), Vito (Marlon Brando), Michael (Al Pacino), and Fredo (John Cazale)—to redefine both the crime family and the role of the family in shaping American culture 260

7.8 Adventurer Quint (Robert Shaw), Police Chief Martin Brody (Roy Scheider), and oceanographer Matt Hooper (Richard Dreyfuss) join forces to kill the shark that has terrorized visitors to Amity Island in *Jaws* (1975) 262

8.1 Detectives Grave Digger Jones (Godfrey Cambridge) and Coffin Ed Johnson (Raymond St. Jacques) take a break from the carnival of *Cotton Comes to Harlem* (1970) to question Iris (Judy Pace) 270

8.2 John Shaft (Richard Roundtree), aglow with racial charisma, doing what he does best in *Shaft* (1971) 272

8.3 Dorothy (Diana Ross) is surrounded by the friends she has met in *The Wiz* (1978): the Scarecrow (Michael Jackson), the Lion (Ted Ross), and the Tinman (Nipsey Russell) 275

8.4 *Yentl* (1983) constantly trades on the discomfort of its eponymous heroine (Barbra Streisand) in her cross-dressing role as a yeshiva student smitten by her mentor Avigdor (Mandy Patinkin) 279

8.5 James Leeds (William Hurt), who teaches at a school for the deaf, and custodian Sarah Norman (Marlee Matlin) struggle to overcome the obstacles *Children of a Lesser God* (1986) has placed between them 281

8.6 The disabling of the renegade computer HAL 9000 by Dave Bowman (Keir Dullea) provides a surprisingly touching moment in the generally chilly *2001: A Space Odyssey* (1968) 283

8.7 As Donald (Frederick Combs) looks on, Michael (Kenneth Nelson), Bernard (Reuben Greene), Emory (Cliff Gorman), and Larry (Keith Prentice) break into a performance of "Heat Wave" in *The Boys in the Band* (1970) 285

8.8 A typical morning in *Ordinary People* (1980) reveals Calvin (Donald Sutherland), Conrad (Timothy Hutton), and Beth (Mary Tyler Moore) already quietly but imperviously estranged from each other 289

8.9 The care God has lavished on the pigeons he has just shot helps assure David Kern (Christopher Collet) about the prospect of his own immortality in *Pigeon Feathers* (1988) 296

9.1 Carl (Rod Steiger) is haunted by his own history and fantasies the illustrations—they're not tattoos—all over his body represent in *The Illustrated Man* (1969) 305

9.2 The Los Angeles of *Blade Runner* (1982) is full of garish commercial signs, dreary weather, and echoes of film noir 307

9.3 Throughout *Superman* (1978), Lois Lane (Margot Kidder) clings with a variety of emotions to Superman (Christopher Reeve) 310

9.4 Batman (Michael Keaton) confronts the Joker (Jack Nicholson), a villain as mythically compelling as he is, in *Batman* (1989) 313

9.5 In the most notorious scene in *The Portrait of a Lady* (1996), Isabel Archer (Nicole Kidman) fantasizes her simultaneous embrace by three suitors: Caspar Goodwood (Viggo Mortenson), Lord Warburton (Richard E. Grant), and Ralph Touchett (Martin Donovan) 323

9.6 In *The Age of Innocence* (1993), passion flares decorously but realistically between Ellen Olenska (Michelle Pfeiffer) and Newland Archer (Daniel Day-Lewis) 325

9.7 Driven by the adventures of Texas Rangers Gus McCrae (Robert Duvall) and Woodrow Call (Tommy Lee Jones), *Lonesome Dove* (1989) led to a resurgence of the television miniseries 328

9.8   The baleful figure of Anton Chigurh (Javier Bardem) sets the tone for the pitch-black comedy of *No Country for Old Men* (2007)   329

9.9   Robert Kincaid (Clint Eastwood) begins his adulterous affair with Francesca Johnson (Meryl Streep) in *The Bridges of Madison County* (1995) with one of the most traditional of courtship rituals   334

10.1 and 10.2   Audiences for *The Human Stain* (2003) could not accept the premise that the young Coleman Silk (Wentworth Miller), who is teaching Steena Paulsson (Jacinda Barrett) to box, would grow up to become the older Silk (Anthony Hopkins), shown here with his lover Faunia Farley (Nicole Kidman)   345

10.3   The subdued graphics and an unusually brooding Batman (Christian Bale) help *Batman Begins* (2005) in marking a new era in superhero franchise adaptations   350

10.4   *Spider-Man* (2002) puts a superhero spin on the otherwise conventional teen romance between Spider-Man (Tobey Maguire) and Mary Jane Watson (Kirsten Dunst)   353

10.5   Because it is a reboot rather than a sequel, *The Amazing Spider-Man* (2012) can choose to include very much the same material in new guises, like this moment between Spider-Man (Andrew Garfield) and Gwen Stacy (Emma Stone)   355

10.6   *The Avengers* (2012) faces the challenge of integrating the stories of Black Widow (Scarlett Johansson), Thor (Chris Hemsworth), Captain America (Chris Evans), Hawkeye (Jeremy Renner), Iron Man (Robert Downey, Jr.), and the Hulk (Mark Ruffalo)   356

10.7   Carrie White (Sissy Spacek) is pressed by her fundamentalist mother Margaret (Piper Laurie) to join her in prayer moments before the two try to kill each other in *Carrie* (1976), the film that introduced Stephen King to Hollywood   371

10.8   The iconic moment in *The Shining* (1980) when the madness that has claimed Jack Torrance (Jack Nicholson) leads him to attack his wife and son   371

10.9   Skeptics complained that the new Academy Award category for Best Popular Film was created as a consolation prize for movies like *Black Panther* (2018)   374

ACKNOWLEDGMENTS

I hope it will not sap the confidence of readers who begin reading this volume with this page to admit that I was not eager to take on the work of writing it. As a theorist by training and something of a gadfly by temperament, I did not look forward to the sustained and systematic research that writing a history of screen adaptations of American literature would entail and was far from certain that I possessed, or could develop, the gifts to complete it successfully. Readers who persist past these opening remarks will judge for themselves how successful I have been. But first I'd like to take a moment to thank a few of the many friends and colleagues without whose encouragement and example I wouldn't have taken on the project in the first place.

Out of all the film historians whose work I've read over the years and returned to, once I had committed to the project, with an interest suddenly much more sharply and jealously focused, I'm particularly grateful to Peter Lev, whose work had always inspired me and whose genial but often highly critical responses to my trial balloons at several crucial points, from preliminary ideas to draft chapters, were invaluable. Apart from the obligatory citations of some of my earlier work in adaptation studies, none of this book has appeared in print in any previous form. But I could not have completed it if I had not had the opportunity to test-drive many parts of it at symposia and conferences across the country and sometimes even farther afield. Of the colleagues who invited me to give presentations that must sometimes have seemed perversely narrow in their focus, I'd particularly like to single out April Kendra, whose invitation to talk about Poe movies with the University of Delaware chapter of Sigma Tau Delta first got me thinking about many of the problems this book pursues, and Daniel Gunn, of the University of Maine in Farmington, whose remarkably generous and open-ended invitation to give a paper that served as an early draft of my opening chapter showed me how I wanted to frame my subject and served as a magic key that went far to unlock the rest of the work. I'd like to thank Katie Gallof and Erin Duffy at Bloomsbury and Vinu Vijayamurugan and the staff at Integra Software. Out of all the many people who gave me technical assistance, I'm especially grateful to Nico Carver, of the University of Delaware Multimedia Center, whose expertise is exceeded only by his patience.

My greatest debt, however, is to Greg M. Colón Semenza and Bob Hasenfratz, the general editors of this series, who first persuaded me that I was a perfectly reasonable candidate for this task, then gave me unstinting help in writing my formal proposal, answered a long series of questions with saintly patience, indulged my changing whims about what I could safely exclude and how to organize the material I could not possibly exclude, and gave me exactly the right kinds of feedback I needed to bring the project to a close. If it is not the success they hoped for, the responsibility is mine alone.

1

Introduction: American Cinema and American Literatures

Off the grid

A suburban lawyer arrives home from New York City late one spring evening because his commute was accidentally extended when the last car of his train, the car he was sitting in, got mysteriously uncoupled from the rest of the train and did not move for an hour and a half. Arriving home in the middle of a local power outage in a thoroughly bad mood, he sees the shadow of a raccoon near his garage, chases the animal away, and then discovers a family of raccoon cubs in the attic over the garage. Chasing them as well, he uses the light of his cell phone to find a rocking chair, plops down in exhaustion, and falls asleep. He wakes up the next morning replaying an argument he had had with his wife of fourteen years about her alleged flirting with another man. Feeling too embarrassed, disgruntled, and unwilling to face his angry wife when he enters his home after his night in the garage, he instead urinates in a stand of bamboo, forages for food in his own trash bin, finds the supper he never ate the night before, and takes it back to the garage to eat. Thus begins a period of several months he passes by spying on his wife and twin daughters through a set of conveniently placed windows, wandering the streets of his neighborhood each night for food, and reflecting on the remarkably ordinary life he has led and the circumstances that have led him to abandon his family and concluding that he hasn't left his family; he has left himself (see Figure 1.1). Determined to stay off the grid and give no sign that this abandonment had been planned, he decides not to drive his car, use his credit cards, or make himself known to anyone who might recognize him in his increasingly scraggly state. Circumstances bring him into a violent confrontation with a crew of scavengers trying to snatch away a pair of shoes he has removed from a neighbor's garbage can and into a closer relationship with two mentally challenged teenagers under

FIGURE 1.1 *Howard Wakefield (Bryan Cranston) spies on his family from his self-imposed exile in his garage in* Wakefield *(2016).*

the residential care of a neighboring physician who discover his lair but do not reveal it to anyone else. In general, however, he succeeds in remaining under the radar long after his family has given him up for dead, until the coming of winter threatens his comfort in his unheated attic and he sees his wife entertaining a male dinner guest, the former boyfriend from whom he had stolen her many years ago. Laboriously making himself first presentable enough to get a shave and shop for new clothes, then attired in clothing he has purchased from his usual Madison Avenue haberdashery, he returns home to see his family decorating a Christmas tree and enters the house.

The man who abandons his home with such a scandalous lack of premeditation, stays away for no obvious reason even though he could return at any moment, and then suddenly does return as abruptly as he departed is Howard Wakefield, the improbable hero of Robin Swicord's 2016 film *Wakefield*. The film would seem to have had all the ingredients, if not for mainstream success in a contemporary cinema increasingly dominated by action and comic book franchises, at least for the modest commercial success that awaited films successfully marketed to niche audiences. Its director had made a name for herself as the screenwriter of such varied adaptations as *Little Women* (1993), *Matilda* (1996), *Practical Magic* (1998), *Memoirs of a Geisha* (2005), and *The Curious Case of Benjamin Button* (2008), and had directed *The Jane Austen Book Club* (2007) from her own screenplay based on Karen Joy Fowler's novel. Wakefield was played by Bryan Cranston, whose star turn as meth-cooking chemistry teacher Walter White in the television series *Breaking Bad* (2008–13) had secured his reputation across

America, and his wife by Jennifer Garner, whose leading role in the television series *Alias* (2001–06) had made her a star as well. The film was based on a 2008 short story of the same name by E.L. Doctorow, whose well-regarded novels *Welcome to Hard Times* (1960), *Ragtime* (1975), *The Book of Daniel* (1971), and *Billy Bathgate* (1989) had all been filmed before his death in 2015. The film, an adaptation of a recent story by a highly regarded American novelist directed by a noted adaptation specialist and featuring two well-known stars, seemed to have all the ingredients for success. And it was indeed to a great extent successful with reviewers and critics: the online aggregator Rotten Tomatoes gave it an approval rating of 75 percent and summarized the critical consensus in these terms: "Thanks to a committed, powerhouse performance by Bryan Cranston, *Wakefield* is a fascinating character study of a decidedly unpleasant character."[1]

Yet the film, which premiered at the Toronto Film Festival in 2016, enjoyed only a limited commercial release, earning box-office receipts totaling $259,412 as of July 14, 2017, barely registering in the American consciousness before going online at Amazon Prime. Perhaps a film containing no overt action of any kind was too slow-moving or minimalist for audiences. Cranston's copious voiceover narration may have put some people off. Certainly the character he played, a self-absorbed loner less suited for love than for endless self-justification, was not calculated to appeal to a wide audience. And many members of the audience who did watch the movie complained about its ending, which they found unmotivated and frustratingly arbitrary. These audience members would have been even more disturbed had they looked beyond Doctorow's 2008 *New Yorker* story, whose major events (or non-events) the film follows surprisingly closely, to that story's own source. For Doctorow's story was itself a freely updated and expanded adaptation of Nathaniel Hawthorne's even more tantalizingly elliptical 1835 story "Wakefield," which had already been adapted at least twice before in the French short film *Wakefield* (2009) and the Italian short *The Wakefield Variation* (2013).

Unlike Doctorow's story, which roots Wakefield's bizarrely unmotivated behavior in a wealth of closely observed detail about his new habits, his voiceover accounts of his day-by-day feelings, and even his clothing, Hawthorne's story is remarkable for saying virtually nothing about the motivations of its eponymous hero and the circumstances of his much longer absence from his wife (he has no children in Hawthorne). The story, a curiosity even among Hawthorne's distinctively curious oeuvre of short stories, begins on a remarkably tentative note:

> In some old magazine or newspaper, I recollect a story, told as truth, of a man—let us call him Wakefield—who abstracted himself for a long time, from his wife. [...] The wedded couple lived in London. The man, under pretence of going on a journey, took lodgings in the next street to his own

house, and there, unheard of by his wife and friends, and without the shadow of a reason for such self-banishment, dwelt upwards of twenty years.[2]

Hawthorne poses his story frankly in hypothetical terms. "What sort of a man was Wakefield?" he asks. "We are free to shape out our own idea, and call it by his name."[3] His account of Wakefield's whimsical plan ends equally whimsically some twenty years later, when getting caught in a sudden rainstorm makes Wakefield think, "shall he stand, wet and shivering here, when his own hearth has a good fire to warm him, and his own wife will run to fetch the gray coat and small-clothes, which, doubtless, she has kept carefully in the closet of their bed-chamber? No!"[4] and provokes his otherwise unmotivated return home. Hawthorne's story, less than ten pages long, contains no dialogue, and its access to its hero's thoughts is marked by a veiled tentativeness unusual even for Hawthorne, who regularly chastises his hero—"Poor Wakefield! Little knowest thou thine own insignificance in this great world!"[5]—addresses his reader directly—"Would that I had a folio to write, instead of an article of a dozen pages!"[6]— and makes it clear at every point that his account of this "Outcast of the Universe"[7] is not so much a story as a story about a story that can be freely reshaped by the author's own whims, as when he introduces a chance meeting between Wakefield and the wife who no longer recognizes him with the exultant announcement: "Now for a scene!"[8]

Hawthorne's tale, stripped of all the circumstantial detail Doctorow's update reassuringly restores, is certainly a classic American short story, but a story of a peculiarly marginal sort. The idiosyncratic stance toward the events it recounts that makes it unique in Hawthorne's career has also marginalized it in the history of American literature, a body of work on which it has had no discernible impact. It remains a largely unread classic within the American canon, eclipsed not only by *The Scarlet Letter* and *The House of the Seven Gables*, but by such ambiguous but less elliptical short stories as "My Kinsman, Major Molineux," "Young Goodman Brown," and "Rappaccini's Daughter." No wonder this clearly unadaptable story waited 180 years for its Hollywood debut.

Yet Hawthorne's "Wakefield" is more than a sport or an outlier. It is on its own strange terms the most characteristic American literary text imaginable, one that exemplifies and explains as well as any other the leading subject of this volume: the remarkable marginalization of American literature by world cinema, particularly the cinema of its homeland. This marginal status applies not only to "Wakefield," or even to Hawthorne. Even when a well-connected filmmaker like the Oscar-winning actor James Franco undertakes an adaptation of a well-regarded American novel, the film sinks without a trace. Franco's adaptation of William Faulkner's 1930 novel *As I Lay Dying* (2013) is a case in point. The novel's famously fractured narrative is parceled out in fifty-nine short chapters assigned to fifteen different narrators who grieve the imminent death of Addie Bundren, then, once she has died, do everything they can to bury her despite a host of natural and human obstacles that make their homely task rise to an epic level even as it reveals deep fractures within the family. The narrators include Addie's indifferent husband Anse, her daughter Dewey Dell, her pragmatic son Cash, her idealistic son Darl, her furiously laconic son Jewel, her youngest son Vardaman, several neighbors and friends, and even Addie herself, who narrates one unforgettable section after she has died. Franco's film seeks to recreate Faulkner's kaleidoscopic approach to harshly elemental realities by its liberal use of voiceover narration and its presentation of a series of split-screen visuals (see Figure 1.2). Sometimes it follows Faulkner closely, as in its period setting and the thirteen reasons Cash gives, now in voiceover, for constructing his mother's coffin on a bevel; sometimes it seeks to naturalize or Hollywoodize him, as when the police officers who come to arrest Darl, whose dreamy idealism has tipped over to full-blown madness, for arson ask him: "Are you Darl Bundren?" Neither approach is entirely successful, and the alternation between the two suggests a discomfort with the material that has infected Franco's other adaptations and kept audiences away.

As I Lay Dying, neither a success nor an embarrassment, did poorly with reviewers—its Metascore on the internet aggregator Rotten Tomatoes is 50; its rating on the Internet Movie Database (IMDb) 5.4 out of 10—and at the box office, where it returned $15,000 of its modest $5.4 million budget before going to video. Undeterred, Franco followed it with his even more

FIGURE 1.2 *James Franco's split-screen composition in* As I Lay Dying *(2013) presents both Vardaman (Brady Permenter) as Darl sees him and Darl himself (Franco) as he watches.*

poorly reviewed 2014 period adaptation of Faulkner's celebrated 1929 novel *The Sound and the Fury* (which earned a Metascore of 39 and an IMDb rating of 4.8) and John Steinbeck's 1936 Depression-era tale of a labor union's attempt to organize California fruit packers, *In Dubious Battle* (Metascore 43; IMDb 6.1). Despite their respectful attitude toward the distinguished literary texts that inspired them, these adaptations helped establish their director and star as a self-styled Renaissance man of the cinema who used the American literary canon to promote his career, not the other way around. In this regard they have followed a long tradition of film adaptation that has seen American literature as a collection of variously useful raw material rather than a lodestar of aesthetic value.

The absence of American literature from American cinema

We might search the studio vaults in vain for a substantial backlist of films based on the work of any of the great writers of the American Renaissance, or any American writers of the nineteenth century. Compared to the torrent of Dickens and Austen adaptations that have been produced on both sides of the Atlantic, remarkably few films have been based on the work of Charles Brockden Brown, James Fenimore Cooper, Herman Melville, Henry James, William Dean Howells, Stephen Crane, Kate Chopin, or Sarah Orne Jewett. Of the nineteenth-century American classics, only Edgar Allan Poe and Mark Twain have been comprehensively served by movies. By contrast, minor British writers like Robert Louis Stevenson and Arthur Conan Doyle have spawned not only individual adaptations more numerous than those of Hawthorne and more reverential than those of Poe, but cinematic dynasties that have given them vigorous afterlives as franchises.

If we move forward to the twentieth century, we find more films, but not all that many more, based on the novels of Edith Wharton, Sherwood Anderson, Willa Cather, Sinclair Lewis, F. Scott Fitzgerald, Ernest Hemingway, William Faulkner, Ellen Glasgow, Nathanael West, Henry Miller, Saul Bellow, Norman Mailer, Eudora Welty, Flannery O'Connor, Kurt Vonnegut, Philip Roth, and Don DeLillo. American playwrights from Eugene O'Neill to Tennessee Williams have fared somewhat better, but none of them has generated a series of adaptations for either the cinema or television comparable to the BBC's Shakespeare, Austen, or Dickens, and none of them has been the subject of an ongoing cinema or television project. To the extent that Hollywood has been interested in them at all, that interest has focused on individual novels like *Moby-Dick* or *The Great Gatsby* rather than authorial careers. Judging from the way Hollywood has treated Melville and Fitzgerald, in fact, it is hard to see any interest at all in

Melville or Fitzgerald as such; the interest is limited almost exclusively to Jay Gatsby and the Great White Whale.

The 2013 film *Austenland* explores the Jane Austen industry in a way that has no parallel in American literature because filmmakers do not think of any American novelists as having generated industries or distinctive lands—with the notable exception of Poe, whose land is both cinematic and sub-literary. Fitzgerald, himself a notoriously unsuccessful screenwriter, once observed, "there are no second acts in American lives";[9] he might have added, "there are no Hollywood afterlives for great American authors."

It is not obvious that a greater number of movies have been based on British than American novels and plays. But it is certainly obvious that British television has helped Shakespeare, Austen, and Dickens establish themselves as central figures in the wider British culture in ways that no American novelist or playwright, or American literature in general, has been equally well served. American literature simply does not occupy the same position in American cinema that British literature occupies in British cinema. It might be argued that the long-standing attraction British literature has held for British cinema and especially British television stems not from a sense of cultural superiority but from an implicit acknowledgment that British cinema has been obliged to fall back on constant adaptations of its national literary classics, adaptations that might well be regarded as niche films if they were produced in Hollywood, because it cannot compete more directly with the blockbusters that have become the leading attraction of American cinema. For whatever reason, however, the two national literatures occupy very different positions in their corresponding national cinemas, and indeed within Hollywood, which has always been more interested in the cultural cachet of British than of American literature, whose stance toward its own national culture, if it is not exactly oppositional, it is certainly insurgent, marginal, and contested.

The flagship volume of the series in which this volume appears, Greg M. Colón Semenza and Bob Hasenfratz's *The History of British Literature on Film, 1895–2015* (2015), focuses on film adaptations of what the authors call "Brit-Lit," a label whose "slightly flippant tone [...] has the admirable effect of deflating the pretensions and cultural claims of 'British literature,' while at the same time preserving the affection of a student nickname for the classic works of British literature that we, and the movies, seem always to return to: *Wuthering Heights, Oliver Twist, Pride and Prejudice, Nineteen Eighty-Four,* and so forth."[10] They "focus on adaptations of 'canonical' British literature for the simple reason that we believe such films have the most to reveal about the larger historical development of literary adaptations."[11] This plan may be unexceptionable and even self-evident, but it would be much more challenging to organize a parallel volume around adaptations of Am-Lit because Am-Lit does not occupy anything like the central role in its creators' national cinema, or even in their national culture, that Brit-Lit does—a discrepancy that begins with the fact that the tag itself is in much less common use.

Reviewing Semenza and Hasenfratz's book, Deborah Cartmell, who finds its "'restriction' to British literature [...] artificial and misleading," has observed that "we can and should pigeonhole adaptations within historical periods, but it is not so easy to group adaptations within nationalities, authors, or even literature."[12] The present book springs from a deep agreement with the belief that it is not easy to organize adaptation study around adaptations of a particular national literature and an attempt to rise to that challenge anyway, not on the assumption that national literatures provide a definitive or even a privileged context for the study of adaptation, but in the hope that they may provide new perspectives that have been otherwise neglected.

Instead of tracing the smoothly triumphal progression of American literature through Hollywood history, it will focus instead on Hollywood's repeated, inconsistent, often contradictory attempts to come to terms with American literature, sometimes by ignoring it, sometimes by picking low-hanging fruits like *The Great Gatsby* and *Moby-Dick,* sometimes indulging in flings with Poe or Hemingway or Philip Roth that have rarely lasted, and along the way generating a whole series of American literatures—varied, contested, and often incompatible ways of thinking about American literature that might themselves have lasting value even for readers who rarely go to the movies. Hence a more exact title for this volume might be *The History of American Literatures on Film* or *The Histories of American Literature on Film,* for there is no single history to trace.

The downside of American literature's marginal relationship with the movies, from the literary establishment's point of view, is that cinema in general and Hollywood in particular seem to have some special trouble taking American literature seriously on anything like a sustained basis. Hollywood has never recognized Am-Lit as a meaningful category. No matter how many American-based adaptations it produces, American literature as such does not exist for American cinema, or indeed for any other national cinema. The upside of this startling neglect is that American cinema has shown a remarkably evergreen power to shape and reshape American literature, not merely by presenting new film versions of classics and best sellers, but by proposing radically different notions of American literature as such that have been surprisingly influential.

The problems posed by Hollywood's oscillation between ignoring and recreating American literature are deeply illuminating, not just for American literature but by implication for other national literatures as well. To a great extent, the history of American literature on film is a history of the many different ways Hollywood has addressed two questions: "What is American literature?" and "What good is American literature?" These questions have an obvious resonance even for literary scholars and citizens who are not interested in questions of cinematic adaptation. Hollywood studios and producers have rarely articulated these questions explicitly—indeed their absence from the discourse of Hollywood adaptation is one of the defining features of the adaptation industry in America—but their practice allows us to consider cinema as a medium of presentation, as a series of industries, and as what Gérard Genette would call a second-order signifying practice about literature.[13] Even when American cinema has ignored American literature as a conceptual category, the different ways it has ignored it speak volumes about the nature of American literature and about the problems of defining American literature.

Fifteen reasons why

There are many possible explanations why cinematic adaptations of American literature have been so difficult to achieve, why their status has been so fraught with problems, and why American literature has occupied such a marginal and contested place in American cinema compared with British literature in particular. Some of these explanations are doubtless more important or more convincing than others. Nor is any list likely to be exhaustive. Any discussion of the question, however, is likely to include at least the following reasons:

1. The United States has a younger literary culture than England, younger than virtually any European or Asian country. The United States has no Austen or Dickens, no Shakespeare or Wilde or Shaw, and the closest it has come to Wordsworth and Tennyson is Walt Whitman and Emily Dickinson. In particular, there is no widely preserved American theatrical heritage dating back before 1900. The emergence of Eugene O'Neill around 1920 therefore seems like a supernova without any background context. A relatively new literary culture, however high its achievements may reach, naturally provides a less rich sense of historical tradition than its obvious counterpart, British literature.

2. American literary culture has been more marginal to public life than English literary culture for several reasons. American writers enjoy no special status, at least not any positive status. English poets who are successful in their lifetimes can hope to be named Poet Laureate; those whose fame survives them can hope to be buried in the Poets' Corner of Westminster Abbey. Although there have been American Poets Laureate since 1985, neither their official title—the Poet Laureate Consultant in Poetry to the Library of Congress— nor the recent endowment of the position gives it anything like the resonance of the British post, whose honorees include John Dryden,

William Wordsworth, and Alfred, Lord Tennyson. Given the general lack of public funding or support for authors, few of them seek such status. With a few obvious exceptions like Philip Roth, American writers have rarely been celebrities unless, like Tina Fey and Madonna, they achieved celebrity status in some other field before they became writers. To the extent that American writers have enjoyed a public life at all, the anti-intellectualism and anti-elitism Richard Hofstadter identified as endemic to the United States half a century ago[14] have often recast this fame as notoriety, so that writers and literature are held up to skeptical scrutiny by everyone from Rufus Griswold, the literary executor who buried Poe for fifty years, to the Coen brothers, who satirize Clifford Odets in the clueless persona of Barton Fink.

3 There have been few screen biographies of American authors, and those that have been released have done little to rekindle interest in their subjects' work, still less in their position as avatars of American literature, because they have emphasized their status as variously deviant celebrities rather than their relation to either their own writing or an American literary tradition. It may be unfair to restrict this observation to American cinematic portraits of American writers, since apart from *Shakespeare in Love* (1997) and *Bright Star* (2009), cinematic portrays of English writers from *Devotion* (1946) to *Iris* (2001) take equally little interest in either their writing process or their finished work, and *Becoming Jane* (2007) is more an effect than a cause of the cinematic fashion for all things Austen. But Hollywood's gallery of American authors from D.W. Griffith's *Edgar Allen [sic] Poe* (1909) to Philip Kaufman's *Henry and June* (1990), David Cronenberg's *Naked Lunch* (1991), Bennett Miller's *Capote* (2005), Rob Epstein and Jeffrey Friedman's *Howl* (2010), and Kaufman's *Hemingway & Gellhorn* (2012) is a remarkable freak show. Taken as a group, these films, which present their heroes and heroines as barely functional, seem intended to raise the question of how each of these authors could possibly make breakfast, let alone pursue a successful writing career. Such films are hardly likely to sustain a serious interest in their subjects' writing, or in writing generally. It is hard to have a significant positive impact on the nation's public life when you have no public profile or are forced to operate under a cloud.

4 American literature has emerged only quite recently as part of university curricula. English literature began to supplement the classics of ancient Greece and Rome in British universities in the 1880s; it was not until the 1940s that American literature became a subject of study in American universities. A difference of sixty

years would not be that significant if it did not so precisely coincide with the invention and rise of the cinema, which found in English literature a far more institutionalized model than American literature offered. Guerric DeBona has recounted David O. Selznick's largely successful attempt to link the 1935 release of *David Copperfield* to study units of the novel for high school curricula that would generate a larger and better prepared audience for the film.[15] No such documents survive for any contemporaneous attempt to link the film adaptations *Moby-Dick* (1930) or *The Age of Innocence* (1934) or *The Good Earth* (1937) to American classrooms because none of the novels they adapted was being studied in those classrooms. It would be another generation before Hollywood could rely on American universities' investment in American literature to market Jack Clayton's adaptation of *The Great Gatsby* (1974).

5   Partly, though not exclusively, because of its relative delay in entering university curricula, what we now regard as the canon of American literature was also slow to emerge. Of the great nineteenth-century American novelists, only Washington Irving, J. Fenimore Cooper, and Mark Twain were hailed as classics within their lifetimes. In a 1940 series of "Famous American" postage stamps, these three writers were joined in the Authors series by Ralph Waldo Emerson and Louisa May Alcott. The poets featured in a parallel series of five postage stamps were Henry Wadsworth Longfellow, John Greenleaf Whittier, James Russell Lowell, Walt Whitman, and James Whitcomb Riley; not even Henry David Thoreau or Emily Dickinson had cracked the graybeard pantheon. Poe's reputation was overshadowed for years by Rufus Griswold's slanderously dismissive obituary. The United States Post Office first displayed his face in a supplementary stamp issued nine years after the Famous Americans series to commemorate the centennial of his death. The critical focus on writers of the American Renaissance dates only from 1941, when F.O. Matthiessen's monumental study of that title was published. Henry James and Stephen Crane have been even more recent entrants to the canon.

Since the consensual inauguration of the current American literary canon in the 1940s, demands for canonical revision in the name of greater inclusiveness have been much more pervasive and successful in the United States than in the United Kingdom. The rapid supplementation of a largely white male canon by women writers and writers of color has further destabilized what has increasingly become a canon of works that are largely unreadable, like *The Last of the Mohicans,* or unread, like *The Ambassadors.* The result has been a canon that is widely perceived as in flux, under construction, or subject to constant renegotiation, a canon in which membership is no longer conferred forever but granted only until the next round of revisions is mandated. Such a non-canonical view of the canon may well be less invidious than the forbiddingly timeless aura formerly cast by such worthies as Irving, Whittier, and Lowell, but its appeal to the movie industry is bound to be more muted.

6   The highly influential wave of émigré filmmakers who came to the United States in the 1920s and 1930s had little interest in American literature. Ernst Lubitsch, who drew on European plays for so much of his material, often featured Americans abroad but did not show them in their homeland until *Heaven Can Wait* (1943), a characteristically American transposition of a Hungarian play. Fritz Lang, whose films were much more likely to be on American subjects, favored original screenplays over adaptations of the American novels and plays that served as the basis for *Western Union* (1941), *Clash by Night* (1952), and *While the City Sleeps* (1956). The first decade of Alfred Hitchcock's American films is divided between adaptations of British novels like *Rebecca* (1940), *Suspicion* (1941), *Spellbound* (1945), *The Paradine Case* (1947), *Rope* (1948), *Under Capricorn* (1949, a film whose source was an Australian novel), and *Stage Fright* (1950) and projects like *Foreign Correspondent* (1940), *Saboteur* (1942), *Shadow of a Doubt* (1943), *Lifeboat* (1944), and *Notorious* (1946) that did not present themselves as adaptations. Not even *Strangers on a Train* (1951), based on Patricia Highsmith's deeply American novel, set a new pattern of adapting American fiction to American cinema. Instead, Hitchcock's later career alternated between foreign-set projects—*I Confess* (1952), *Dial M for Murder* (1953), *The Man Who Knew Too Much* (1956), *Frenzy* (1972)—non-American fiction transposed to American settings—*Vertigo* (1958), *The Birds* (1963), *Marnie* (1964), *Family Plot* (1976)—adaptations focusing on foreign nationals or Americans abroad—*To Catch a Thief* (1955) and *Topaz* (1969)—and original screenplays—*North by Northwest* (1959) and *Torn Curtain* (1966). Of Hitchcock's later films, only *Rear Window* (1954), *The Wrong Man* (1957), and *Psycho* (1960) are adaptations of American originals set in America.

7   The monumental and widely publicized failure of two important early cinematic adaptations of notably ambitious American novels—*Greed* (1924) and *An American Tragedy* (1931)—served as vivid cautionary examples that discouraged filmmakers from tackling similar projects. The most financially successful Hollywood silent features, *The Birth of a Nation* (1915), *Ben-Hur* (1925), and *The Big Parade* (1925), were all adaptations of American literary

sources, but they presented themselves as historical epics, heavy on spectacle, that were only incidentally literary adaptations rather than adaptations that sought to replicate the probing psychology of *McTeague* and *An American Tragedy.*

8   American classics do not meld with history as readily as English classics to produce heritage nostalgia. Brockden Brown, Cooper, Hawthorne, Melville, Crane, and John Steinbeck cannot match the heritage appeal of Jane Austen and E.M. Forster because the several American pasts they record amount to a series of times and places most Americans have difficulty revisiting, partly because America's national mythology is almost exclusively progressive, partly because the past memorialized in their writing is not especially pleasant, since American fiction does not valorize its social history as English fiction does. To the extent that Americans celebrate their history, they do so in the ideational terms associated with slogans like "Tippecanoe and Tyler Too" or "Remember the *Maine*" rather than the spatial, scenic terms invoked by heritage cinema. The great exception, the Hollywood Western, invokes a spatial past that is both highly visual and highly schematic, a past genre fans are more interested in memorializing than returning to, except under the reassuring aegis of Walt Disney's Frontierland, and in such variously elegiac adaptations as *Shane* (1953), *The Searchers* (1956), and *Little Big Man* (1970). So the museum aesthetic of British heritage cinema and television must fight to establish a beachhead on American literature, not only because the visual tableaux most memorably enshrined in American history involve the genocidal conquest of the national frontier rather than the interiors of country houses whose architecture bespeaks classical models, grandeur, and permanence, but because most Americans' attitude toward their nation's past is nostalgic only in the most broadly conceptual terms. It is no wonder that the title of the magazine *American Heritage,* which for over sixty years presented articles about American history for a general public, carries a much different charge than the label of heritage cinema.

Hence adaptations of quasi-heritage classics, like *The Great Gatsby* (1974) and Terence Davies's *The House of Mirth* (2000), place the audience's longing for self-celebratory nostalgia in conflict with their representation of social arrangements of which Fitzgerald and Edith Wharton are deeply critical. The resulting ambivalence is charted in detail in the American adaptations of Ismail Merchant and James Ivory, who are best known for the English and postcolonial settings of adaptations like *Heat and Dust* (1983), *Howards End* (1992), and *The Remains of the Day* (1993). When

Merchant Ivory turns to American literary properties, its choices are revealing: Joseph Moncure March's poem "The Wild Party" (1975), Henry James's *The Europeans* (1979) and *The Bostonians* (1984), Tama Janowitz's *Slaves of New York* (1989), and Evan Connell's *Mr. and Mrs. Bridge* (1990). Each of these properties evokes some corner of an American culture, either a contemporary cultural moment or an iconic past, that the films can treat as nostalgic even as they seek to analyze it critically. In the case of *The Wild Party*, the film emphasizes the poem's Americanness by changing the party's setting from Greenwich Village to Hollywood; in later adaptations like *Jefferson in Paris* (1995), *A Soldier's Daughter Never Cries* (1998), *The Golden Bowl* (2000), and *Le Divorce* (2003), Merchant Ivory focuses on Americans abroad in order to preserve the balance of nostalgia and critique so distinct from the generally self-celebratory tone of British heritage cinema.

9   The lack of a close and comfortable nexus between American history and American literature is exacerbated by the status of so many classics of American fiction marked as outliers or one-offs. Writers like Margaret Mitchell, Flannery O'Connor, Ralph Ellison, and Harper Lee have left little fodder for Hollywood adaptations because their oeuvre, however celebrated, has been slender. And no matter how copious their output, writers like Hawthorne, Melville, Fitzgerald, Crane, and Chopin are often identified with a singular masterpiece rather than a coherent oeuvre or a fully developed career. But even writers like Poe, Hemingway, Faulkner and Roth who are less closely associated with a single delimiting work rarely command attention because their representations of American social culture carry nothing like the weight of *Vanity Fair*, *Little Dorrit*, or *Middlemarch*. As Richard Chase argued sixty years ago in *The American Novel and Its Tradition*:

> The English novel [...] has been a kind of imperial enterprise, an appropriation of reality with the high purpose of bringing order to disorder. By contrast [...] the American novel has usually seemed content to explore, rather than to appropriate and civilize, the remarkable and in some ways unexampled territories of life in the New World and to reflect its anomalies and dilemmas. It has not wanted to build an imperium but simply to discover a new place and a new state of mind.[16]

As Chase acknowledges, the American novel in a fundamental sense has no tradition because the great American novels—*The Scarlet Letter*, *Moby-Dick*, *The Portrait of a Lady*, *The Adventures of Huckleberry Finn*, *The Red Badge of Courage*, *A Farewell to Arms*, *The Sound and the Fury*—are outliers that have chosen to avoid majoritarian American society as their subject in order to focus on self-reflexive studies of unmoored individuals or, as Charles Feidelson observes, on "their attitude toward their medium—that their distinctive quality is a devotion to the possibilities of symbolism."[17] Compared especially to the great nineteenth-century British novels from Sir Walter Scott to Thomas Hardy, American novels, as Chase points out, are more like *Wuthering Heights,* which "proceeds from an imagination that is essentially melodramatic, that operates among radical contradictions and renders reality indirectly and poetically,"[18] because American novels, and indeed American plays, do not seek to offer a coherent account of American society or a coherent model for American literature, which keeps getting defined and redefined in terms of exceptionalism, oppositionality, and what Russell Reising has called an unusable past.[19] The fact that *Wuthering Heights* has itself been repeatedly and successfully adapted indicates that adapting American novels that echo its oppositional stance toward their own social culture is certainly not impossible. The process simply presents challenges quite different from those of Brit-Lit adaptations.

The disconnect between American literature and American cinema is no bad thing. It presents a far more provocative situation, pregnant with more stimulating questions and possibilities, than the cozily incestuous relationship between British literature and British cinema, which exempts either oeuvre from the need to submit to closer examination on its own. What is tonic for scholars of American literature and cinema is precisely the failure of American literature to present a single consensual myth of social cohesion of the kind that has made English literature readily marketable to a mass audience.

10 Classic American novels are not notable for the kind of dialogue Hollywood has traditionally sought in its source material. The dialogue in Fenimore Cooper's Leatherstocking Tales is preposterous, and although Poe's dialogue has an undeniable declamatory power, it is far too stylized to transfer comfortably to a cinema that aims at representational realism. *The Scarlet Letter, The Confidence Man,* and *The Red Badge of Courage* are all great novels, but none of them is full of great dialogue. Henry James writes memorably opaque dialogue, full of veiled hints, insinuations, attacks, and counterattacks, but James's well-documented failure to write a successful play is only the most obvious indication that he does not write the kind of dialogue the movies seek, and *The Heiress* (1949), the first successful film based on a James novel,

takes every opportunity to punch up his dialogue and literalize the conflicts James keeps lurking beneath a decorous surface. Mark Twain is the only important nineteenth-century American novelist and Hemingway the only important twentieth-century novelist capable of writing anything like Hollywood dialogue. Film adaptations of Hemingway routinely and imprudently attempt to improve on his dialogue, but the opening twelve minutes of Robert Siodmak's 1946 film *The Killers,* which replicates the dialogue of Hemingway's 1927 short story almost verbatim, show how well it plays onscreen.

Not surprisingly, American plays have provided dialogue easier for Hollywood to adapt than American novels. Yet apart from the reliably comic Neil Simon, even the most widely adapted American playwrights—Eugene O'Neill, Elmer Rice, Clifford Odets, Thornton Wilder, William Saroyan, Sidney Howard, Robert E. Sherwood, Tennessee Williams, Arthur Miller, William Inge, Edward Albee—have been more notable for their original theatrical concepts, their subjects, themes, and ideas about staging, than for their dialogue, and few Americans, I suspect, could recite half a dozen lines of dialogue from any American play that was not *A Streetcar Named Desire.* Because the United States lacks both a strong native theatrical tradition and a canon of novels whose dialogue is memorable, Hollywood filmmakers who have sought to produce new adaptations of American literature have by and large had to commission new dialogue to support it. Adding insult to injury, the talkies swept Hollywood with a demand that stars affect a transatlantic diction that made them sound more deracinated and less American unless they were playing specifically ethnic types like Little Caesar or Charlie Chan.

11 Even movies that do adapt American literary texts do not commonly consider them their primary source. Instead of anointing them inviolable source texts, as literature teachers assume they should, they consider them one among many generative contexts that also include stars, screenwriters, directors, genres, market research into the demographics of specific target audiences, and the history of earlier adaptations of a given property, all of which play important roles in positioning and marketing movies. This process inevitably devalues the films' avowed literary sources by demoting them to the status of one hypotextual script among many—a lesson that adaptation specialists have embraced in principle, but one that has been slow to percolate through adaptation study in practice. Ever since Robert Stam argued that "notions of 'dialogism' and 'intertextuality' [...] help us transcend the aporias of 'fidelity' and of a dyadic source/adaptation model which excludes not only all sort

of supplementary texts but also the dialogical response of the reader/
spectator,"[20] adaptation scholars have agreed that adaptations spring
from many scripts in addition to the literary sources they identify.
Despite the best efforts of theorists from Gérard Genette to Patrick
Cattrysse, however, no one has come up with an entirely satisfactory
way to describe the relationship among these different scripts.

In the course of wrestling with this vexing question, I have
suggested that adaptation specialists inquire more closely into
the distinctions most of them make "between [source] texts and
contexts,"[21] an inquiry that Simone Murray has pursued in much
greater detail following her call for "a *sociology* of adaptation,"[22]
and have proposed that adaptation scholars consider "defining
adaptation as a genre with its own rules, procedures, and textual
markers"[23] instead of defining it as a transgeneric practice, and
regarding adaptations as members of hybrid genres that combine
the generic markers of adaptation with those of musicals or
Westerns or films noirs. Adaptations of American literature
suggest still another possible tactic. In accord with Rebecca
Schneider's observation that it is *"precisely the logic of the archive
that approaches performance as of disappearance"* [emphasis in
original] and her suggestion to "think of the ways in which the
archive depends upon performance,"[24] Hollywood's consistent
attitude toward an American canon it defines in remarkably
inconsistent terms suggests that it considers adaptation a mode of
performance rather than a plundering of the archive. Accordingly,
I use the word *scripts* instead of sources or genres or hypotexts to
describe the progenitor texts and contexts that engender particular
adaptations and sustain the practice of adaptation in general. I
prefer "scripts" to "sources" or "genres" or "hypotexts" because in
the plural form, it already implies both a forward impetus lacking
in "sources" and a hybridity that has to be smuggled into each of
the other terms through inadequately theorized appeals to multiple
sources or contexts. It is no accident that "scripts" is closely related
to screenplays, or more precisely to screenplay drafts, because
everyone knows that the screenplays that serve as more proximate
sources for movies than their avowed novels or plays or stories
commonly go through many drafts, none of which has absolute
authority. Even the optimistically identified shooting script, as
countless on-set anecdotes attest, is less a recipe than an incitement,
and it can always be overridden by the whims of the director, the
performers, or the weather.

In other words, the scripts provided by what are commonly
called source texts are legitimate sources for the movies that adapt
them, but no more legitimate than the demands of performers,

directors, budgets, genres, screenplays, and the numberless vagaries of collaborative filmmaking that provide the jostling scripts that constantly compete with them for respectful attention. Loyalty or textual fidelity is certainly one kind of this attention, but it is hardly the only kind, and Stam has urged adaptation studies to take at least some of those other scripts just as seriously as the presumed demands of authors who, even if they are still alive, generally lose their legal and moral control over the films based on their works as soon as they sell the adaptation rights. Teachers who use film adaptations without thinking about their provenance, and even some adaptation scholars who ought to know better, assume that they are publicized by using posters that look like the one for *Lolita*, which gives pride of place to a question—"How did they ever make a film of *Lolita*?"—that emphasizes the film's status as an adaptation. But many more movies are advertised by posters that indicate the authors or properties they are adapting in tiny print, if they mention them at all.

A quintessential example of this second approach to adaptation is Roland Joffé's notorious *The Scarlet Letter*, a 1995 film whose advertising posters said nothing about Nathaniel Hawthorne or adaptation. Nearly everyone who reviewed this movie, citing an unforgettable scene featuring Hester Prynne (Demi Moore) in a hot tub, treated it as a travesty of Hawthorne. But although it may be a scandalously unfaithful adaptation of its source novel, *The Scarlet Letter* is no fluke (see Figure 1.3). Its identification of Roger Chillingworth (Robert Duvall) with the Indians and its climactic

FIGURE 1.3 *Arthur Dimmesdale (Gary Oldman) and Hester Prynne (Demi Moore) in* The Scarlet Letter *(1995): a travesty, but not a fluke.*

Indian attack, which struck most observers as coming out of deep left field, is a logical product of its determination to restore the film's story to a more recognizable historical matrix—the shifting relations between the Salem colonists and the Native Americans around them—that Hawthorne had chosen to ignore. The anachronistic feminism that motivates Hester's wildly improbable moments of wisdom and independence faithfully recuperates the past as the forerunner of the present, another pattern common to Hollywood. And its insinuating lead-in to Hester's sexual encounter with Arthur Dimmesdale (Gary Oldman), an affair that ends before Hawthorne begins his narrative, is calculated to update *The Scarlet Letter* by giving the audience exactly what Hawthorne withholds, from the soft-core embraces of the lovers to the shot of Hester's servant Mituba (Lisa Joliffe-Andoh) sympathetically masturbating in the next room. *The Scarlet Letter* may be a travesty, but it is an exemplary travesty, a perfectly reasonable mashup of sex, feminism, and period drama that may have been ridiculous in its individual details but would be equally ridiculous to judge as a failed attempt to follow the script provided by Hawthorne's novel, which Demi Moore assured interviewers could safely be ignored because "it had been a very long time since people had read it."[25]

12 Because the scripts provided by the canon of nineteenth-century American classics seem both more demanding and more remote than the other scripts movies typically elect to follow, Hollywood has almost from the beginning been less interested in classic American literature, however defined, than in more recent novels and plays. Until very recently, however, not even modern American literature offered any authorial franchises with the staying power of Shakespeare, Austen, or Dickens. The apparent exceptions, Poe and Hemingway, provide textbook examples of how not to sustain a franchise. Except for a brief period around the time he won the Nobel Prize for Literature in 1954, Hemingway adaptations, however frequent, have been scattershot, and of the most highly regarded of them, Frank Borzage's *A Farewell to Arms* (1932), Howard Hawks's *To Have and Have Not* (1944), Robert Siodmak's *The Killers* (1946), and John Sturges's *The Old Man and the Sea* (1958), only the last, a tranquilly meditative film dominated by Spencer Tracy's voiceover, was released during the period surrounding Hemingway's Nobel Prize, a period more typically associated with Henry King's Technicolor spectacles *The Snows of Kilimanjaro* (1952) and *The Sun Also Rises* (1957) and Charles Vidor's equally overblown *A Farewell to Arms* (1957).

Although Poe has been by far the most frequently adapted of all American writers, with over 350 adaptations to date, these films have almost without exception been marketed and marginalized as non-literary. Consider the two best-known Poe franchises. The mashup approach of the Universal cycle of Poe adaptations including Robert Florey's *Murders in the Rue Morgue* (1932), Edgar G. Ulmer's *The Black Cat* (1934), and Louis Friedlander's *The Raven* (1935) is best illustrated by the third of these, which, "suggested by Edgar Allan Poe's immortal classic," borrows virtually nothing but its title directly from Poe but owes a great deal to Universal's *The Black Cat*. The cast is headlined by Boris Karloff and Bela Lugosi, whose last names, their only identifiers, are set in capital letters and given the biggest type in the credits. *The Raven* recycles the improbably innocent lovers from the earlier film and invites them, all unwitting, to spend the night in a house of horrors, where the villains plan to keep them in what looks like the very same basement dungeon as the one that awaited their counterparts in *The Black Cat*. The torture devices Dr. Richard Vollin (Lugosi) has prepared for his unwilling guests are taken from "The Pit and the Pendulum." Karloff's pitiable Edmond Bateman, who insists querulously that "I don't want to get into no more trouble," is forced into helping Vollin with his agenda of "torture and murder" by a hideous physical transformation and the promise of a second corrective transformation that recalls his adventures with Frankenstein, his physical deformation, and his essential innocence, especially in *The Bride of Frankenstein,* which had been released less than three months earlier.

The film is less an adaptation of Poe's story than a story about Poe as a second-order signifier. Vollin, a famous surgeon, is also a fan of Poe who collects torture devices. "It's *more* than a hobby," he tells Jean Thatcher (Irene Ware), the dancer whose life he saved after she was critically injured in an auto accident. To thank Vollin, Jean dances "The Spirit of Poe" to the accompaniment of excerpts recited from "The Raven." When Jean's fiancé Jerry Halden (Lester Mathews), driving Jean off in the film's last shot, offers to "finish the job" of crushing her, she responds, "So you're the big bad raven, huh?" In a pivotal scene halfway through the film, Jean asks Vollin, "What is your interpretation of 'The Raven'?"—a question rarely heard in movies of any kind—and he hypothesizes that Poe's ambitious plans were dashed by his loss of his beloved Lenore, and that the torture her death inflicted on him led to his own fascination with torture. Vollin's explanation at once collapses Poe and the narrator of "The Raven," uses the events of the poem to explain the characteristic concerns of Poe's fiction, and assumes that both Poe and "The Raven" are topoi to be discussed, not originals to be adapted. So it makes perfect sense for Vollin to cry exultantly as walls of his torture chamber close in on Jean and Jerry: "Poe only conceived it. I have done it, Bateman." Poe provides nothing more than a blueprint the Universal franchise has the job of fleshing out.

A more influential model for Poe adaptations is represented by the series of adaptations Roger Corman directed for Universal–International beginning in 1960 with *House of Usher*. These widescreen color spectaculars are once again palimpsests, prequels, and mashups, though their attitude toward their credited sources is very different from earlier mashups, and sometimes from each other. According to its credits, for example, Corman's 1963 film *Edgar Allen [sic] Poe's The Haunted Palace* is "based on the poem by Edgar Allen Poe and a story by H.P. Lovecraft," a deft use of articles that demotes Lovecraft to the status of studio hack. Although the film nowhere identifies the 119-page novella, *The Case of Charles Dexter Ward*, that supplies the film's story, the full name of Lovecraft's title character, here played by Vincent Price, is uttered at least a dozen times in the dialogue, congratulating readers familiar with the story on their knowledge but leaving the uninitiated in the dark.

When Dr. Erasmus Craven (Price) asks the Raven in Corman's 1963 *The Raven* whether he will ever again see his lost Lenore, the Raven replies, in the voice of Peter Lorre: "How the hell should I know? What am I, a fortune teller?"—a startling departure that reframes the film as a burlesque mashup of Poe's poem and a fairy tale focused on freeing Dr. Adolphus Bedlo (Lorre) from his malign transformation and pitting the two unlikely heroes and their even more unlikely sidekick Rexford Bedlo (Jack Nicholson) against the common enemy, Dr. Scarabus (Boris Karloff), who stole Lenore (Hazel Court) and enchanted Bedlo, a name borrowed from "A Tale of the Ragged Mountains."

The 1964 *Masque of the Red Death* provides a convenient anthology of Corman's most characteristic adaptational strategies. The Universal–International films invent backstories to motivate the climactic tableaux they borrow from Poe. They add nubile young actresses like Jane Asher, Elizabeth Shepherd, and most often Hazel Court. They invent psychological motivations to explain incidents whose causality Poe shrouds in obscurity, in this case a combination of implicit lust and explicit Satan-worship. They append an ending that is at least marginally happy, this time courtesy of six mostly unseen survivors. And more often than not, they add material from other stories, often but not always by Poe, like the casual subplot the dwarf Hop-Toad (Skip Martin) borrows from "Hop-Frog" and injects into *The Masque of the Red Death,* to create their distinctive but utterly characteristic mashups.

Entries in both the Universal and the Universal–International Poe franchises are less adaptations of the stories whose titles they borrow than remakes of earlier franchise entries with the same trademark stars, a set of stories that are remarkably similar to one another—and not simply because they are Poe stories—an audiovisual design that remains consistent within each franchise, and the promise of similar pleasures that are peculiar to the two franchises but quite different from each other. Of the stars these franchises cast, Bela Lugosi, whose screen persona is variously suave malignancy, is not a particularly close fit for Poe. Boris Karloff, whose persona is grotesque pathos, is considerably closer. But Price, whose persona is cultivated, reticent codependency rather than malevolent agency, is still closer. Price, who like Christopher Lee is generally cast as a tormented self-victim rather than a cackling villain, is the single most Poesque aspect of Corman's Universal–International films.

The goal of films in these franchises, and of Poe films generally, is not to adapt specific texts but to return their audience to Poeland, a place that is conceived theatrically, imagistically, and spatially. Like the theme park the film title *Austenland* satirizes, this space is host to a variety of narrative potentialities. But it is a space, not a story, itself. The stories it promises are coextensive and simultaneous, each story only a single attraction in the theme park the audience has come to visit, as when an adaptation of some other canonical author is pronounced Shakespearean or Dickensian. What Poe offers the cinema is not a collection of adaptable stories but a franchise like those associated with Sherlock Holmes, James Bond, and Harry Potter. The best known hero of this franchise may be Vincent Price, but he is frequently joined by Poe himself, who regularly crosses textual boundaries to inhabit films conceived and marketed in antiliterary terms.

If the cinema has subverted classic American writers from Poe to Hemingway to its own ends, it was shown scant interest in contemporary literary novelists like Thomas Pynchon and Don DeLillo. The leading vector, in fact, points in exactly the opposite direction. As Gabrielle Temblay-Leduc has noted in conversation, DeLillo's novels, like those of John Dos Passos two generations earlier, suggest that the American novel has a greater appetite for assimilating and exploiting the tropes of American cinema—not so much specific movies as the tropes of cinema in general—than American cinema has shown for the American novel. The contemporary American writers who have enjoyed most consistent success in providing fodder for Hollywood films are comic book writers like Stan Lee and Neil Gaiman who have created durable franchise heroes and novelists like Robert James Waller, Nicholas Sparks, Stephenie Meyer, Suzanne Collins, and George R.R. Martin whose work falls into an established, broadly appealing popular genre like sentimental romance or fantasy epic which provides a script for adaptation more potent than any single instance of the genre.

13   Even though it has proved more appealing to Hollywood than nineteenth-century American fiction, twentieth-century American fiction presents problems of its own. Although the first wave of high modernism is more closely associated with English and Irish authors like T.S. Eliot, James Joyce, and Virginia Woolf, modern American fiction has been even more determined than contemporaneous British fiction to scorn popularity, challenge accessibility, and cultivate literariness even at the cost, and sometimes apparently in the pursuit, of the kinds of obscurantism that discourage offers from Hollywood. Contemporary critics routinely bemoan the fact that *Gone with the Wind* beat *Absalom, Absalom!* for the 1936 Pulitzer Prize for the Novel, but Margaret Mitchell's victory is hardly surprising given that William Faulkner's novel was greeted by critical bemusement and indifferent sales. Certainly no one ever expected *Absalom, Absalom!* to be made into a movie, and not even James Franco has tried to do so. MGM cherry-picked American modernist writers like O'Neill and Faulkner for material the studio could turn into mass entertainment in adaptations like Clarence Brown's *Ah, Wilderness!* (1935) and *Intruder in the Dust* (1949) by choosing the least despairing and formally radical of the authors' properties. John Steinbeck could become the most successfully adapted of modernist American novelists because his modernism was less stylistic than thematic, taking the form of a deeply felt social critique that could readily be pruned back in films like *Of Mice and Men* (1939) and *The Grapes of Wrath* (1940). Hollywood's flirtations with writers of the Harlem Renaissance have been brief and generally unavailing, and although filmmakers have been consistently respectful of Zora Neale Hurston, Richard Wright, James Baldwin, Maya Angelou, and Toni Morrison, that respect has translated into only a handful of film projects: Darnell Martin's TV movie *Their Eyes Were Watching God* (2005), Pierre Chenal's *Native Son* (1951), Stan Lathan's *Go Tell It on the Mountain* (a 1985 segment of the TV series *American Playhouse*), Fielder Cook's *I Know Why the Caged Bird Sings* (1979), and Jonathan Demme's *Beloved* (1998).

14   When Americans thirst for literary cachet in their popular culture, they routinely turn to adaptations of English, not American, literature to slake that thirst. Ever since *David Copperfield* in

1935 and *Romeo and Juliet* the following year, Hollywood has spelled culture using British, not American, spelling. The television series *Masterpiece Theatre,* whose productions were chosen from BBC offerings, ran on American television for forty-two seasons, beginning in the same year as *Upstairs, Downstairs* (1971–5) and continuing long enough to see in the opening seasons of *Downton Abbey* (2010–15). There has been no comparable attempt to put American theater on television since the 1950s. Of the fourteen plays filmed for theatrical release in the 1973–5 series *American Film Theatre,* only five are by American playwrights. The American project that comes closest to imitating in native terms the Anglophilia of *Masterpiece Theatre—The American Short Story,* a series of twenty-one forty-five-minute adaptations of stories from Hawthorne's "Rappaccini's Daughter" to Hortense Calisher's "The Hollow Boy" (1976–91)—suggests that the short story, not the novel or play, is the single most innovative and influential mode in American literature, and this mode does not lend itself easily to feature film adaptations. American audiences seem to persist in thinking of American literature as exceptional in precisely the opposite way they think of American history or American democracy or the American form of government as exceptional. Even the Americans most likely to think of their country as uniquely gifted or privileged among all the nations of the world are unlikely to think of American literature in the same terms, for American literature continues to be a minority taste even among Americans. It is hard to imagine an introductory credit parallel to the credit "Based on the celebrated novel by Victor Hugo" in William Dieterle's 1939 adaptation of *The Hunchback of Notre Dame* introducing a film based on an American novel. Hollywood in particular has rarely used the cachet of American literature to sell movies to audiences largely indifferent to the larger project of American literature, and often disdainful, dismissive, or hostile to it, even if they are not entirely clear about what it takes exception to.

15 Although American literature is less congenial to screen adaptation than English literature, that contrast takes on different valences on different screens. The predominance of canonical English literary adaptations over canonical American literary adaptations depends largely on three figures: Shakespeare, Austen, and Dickens. Shakespeare's great contemporaries were largely neglected by early cinema—there are no silent film adaptations, and precious few sound adaptations, of any plays by Christopher Marlowe or Ben Jonson—and although Sergei M. Eisenstein found in Victorian novelists like William Makepeace Thackeray, George Eliot, Anthony

Trollope, George Meredith, and Thomas Hardy "the first shoots of American film esthetic,"[26] all these writers have been much less well served by the cinema than Austen or Dickens. To date there has been only one feature film adaptation of Meredith, Denison Clift's *Diana of the Crossways* (1922), and one of Trollope, Henry Herbert's *Malachi's Cove* (1973). Movie adaptations of Sir Walter Scott and the Victorian novelists, more widely prevalent on the silent screen, slowed to a crawl with the coming of synchronized sound. What kept these authors alive in the popular imagination were adaptations for television rather than the cinema: episodes and miniseries adapting Scott's Waverley novels, Trollope's Barsetshire and Palliser novels, and Hardy's Wessex novels. Nineteenth-century American novelists like Hawthorne, Melville, and Crane lent themselves much less obviously to miniseries; only Henry James has enjoyed anything like his Victorian contemporaries' television afterlife, largely courtesy of the non-American television series *Affairs of the Heart* (UK, 1974–5) and *Nouvelles de Henry James* (France/West Germany/UK, 1974–6). The relative neglect of American literature on the big screen is both reflected and to a surprising extent exacerbated by its even greater neglect on the small screen.

What has limited the usefulness of American literature to American cinema is not a dearth of accomplished authors or accomplished works but rather a dearth of tentpole figures like Shakespeare, Austen, and Dickens who can serve as the basis for cinematic and televisual franchises. Twain's output is too varied, Faulkner's too opaque, and James's too un-American to be homogenized for a mass audience as readily as the BBC has homogenized Shakespeare, Austen, and Dickens.

Despite all these obstacles, a significant number of American novels and plays and stories have been adapted to the screen, and the success of these adaptations offers several lessons about the history of American literature—or about the series of sharply revised histories of American literature, or the history of American literatures, generated and promulgated by the movies. The following chapters present a series of attempts the movies made to use American literature for sustenance, and through the different choices they made in those attempts to imply new definitions of American literature that have repeatedly challenged earlier categorical definitions and now encourage us to ask still other questions they do not ask themselves. Consider one such hypothetical example. Literary/historical analyses of American literature, like cognate analyses of Irish literature, typically define American literature both within and against the unmarked model offered by English—actually British—literature. What would happen if instead we defined American literature within the context of Anglophone literature, or European literature, or literature of the Americas, or world literature? Hollywood adaptations of American literature do not ask questions like this. But thinking about what is at stake in adapting American literature invites us to consider them in ways that can only renew the study of national literatures, national cinema, and adaptation as an exercise in defining, policing, and crossing national borders.

Things to come

This book aims to consider the leading ways the film industry, mostly the American industry headquartered in Hollywood, has used adaptations of specific, often highly tendentious scripts in the hope of padding its bottom line, in the process generating a surprisingly diverse series of ideas about and versions of American literature and American culture. Precisely because these ideas and versions have been so diverse, the methodology behind the book invites further comment in lieu of the obligatory chapter summaries with which introductions like this one so often end.

Readers anticipating a series of close readings of the ways in which particular adaptations do and do not honor our present-day readings of *The Last of the Mohicans* or *The Age of Innocence* should be warned that I have made no attempt to emphasize adaptations of canonical literary texts, to provide close readings of the films I choose to discuss, or to focus my remarks primarily on their relations to those specific texts. I am more interested in what the films I have chosen to consider say about American literature and American culture generally than on their readings of their literary scripts. Although I have often criticized one-to-one text-to-screen adaptations in the past, I find considerable value in that approach, which has inspired such useful volumes as Stephen Pendo's *Raymond Chandler on Screen* (1976), Bruce F. Kawin's *Faulkner and Film* (1977), Gerald Peary and Roger Shatzkin's *The Classic American Novel and the Movies* (1977) and *The Modern American Novel and the Movies* (1978), Frank M. Lawrence's *Hemingway and the Movies* (1981), John Orlandello's *O'Neill on Film* (1982), Gene D. Phillips's *Hemingway and Film* (1980) and *Fiction, Film, and Faulkner* (1988), William Luhr's *Raymond Chandler and Film* (1991), Laurence Goldstein's *The American Poet at the Movies* (1994), Barbara Tepa Lupack's *Nineteenth-Century Women at the Movies* (1999), John C. Tibbetts and James M. Welsh's *Encyclopedia of Novels into Film* (1998, 2005) and *Encyclopedia of Stage Plays into Film* (2001), Barbara Wyllie's *Nabokov at the Movies* (2003), Laurence Raw's *Adapting Henry James to the Screen* (2006) and *Adapting Nathaniel Hawthorne to the Screen* (2008), R. Barton Palmer's *Nineteenth-Century American Fiction on Screen* (2007) and *Twentieth-Century American Fiction on Screen* (2007), Parley Ann

Boswell's *Edith Wharton on Film* (2007), Jason P. Vest's *Future Imperfect: Philip K. Dick at the Movies* (2007), William Robert Bray and R. Barton Palmer's *Modern American Drama on Screen* (2013), Candace Ursula Grissom's *Fitzgerald and Hemingway on Film* (2014), Peter Lurie and Ann J. Abadie's *Faulkner and Film* (2014), Susan M. Griffin's *Henry James Goes to the Movies* (2015), and William H. Mooney's *Dashiell Hammett and the Movies* (2015). But exactly because that approach has been well represented in adaptation studies ever since George Bluestone's pioneering *Novels into Film* (1957), I have felt no need to organize this book as if it were an anthology of material drawn from those volumes.

Semenza and Hasenfratz's emphasis on Brit-Lit adaptations gives their history a welcome thematic and methodological coherence at the cost of omitting a large number of adaptations of British scripts. My own decision to cast a wider net incurs problems of its own. Because I define my subject more broadly, I have found it impossible to cover it comprehensively. Instead of applying a single global principle of selection, I have been obliged to make innumerable selections on a smaller scale, inevitably limiting my discussion to a small number of examples each representing a much larger corpus and omitting any extended analysis, and sometimes even passing mention, of any number of adaptations readers might feel were essential to any such history as this one, from *The Grapes of Wrath* (1940) and *To Kill a Mockingbird* (1962) to *The Silence of the Lambs* (1991) and *Angels in America* (2003). After devoting several pages to adaptations of Henry James, I dispose of Edith Wharton adaptations in a single subordinate clause. My greatest concern has not been to highlight the best novels and plays and stories made into movies, or the best movies that happen to have been based on material first presented in another medium, but on the adaptations that best illustrate the story I am presenting.

This book organizes that story into chapters that describe dramatically different approaches American cinema has taken to American literature. These approaches crest and ebb at different time periods, but at any given moment they are all theoretically possible and available, and the topical organization of the book has often encouraged me to interpret its chronological organization very loosely indeed. Readers will find many flashbacks and a smaller number of flashforwards in most of my chapters as I try to describe the roots and provide the leading contexts for each approach I discuss.

In addition, I have chosen to focus almost entirely on mainstream Hollywood adaptations of American literature at the expense of most independent productions, television productions, and foreign productions. Pausing to note foreign adaptations at the different times they appeared in my story would make that story more discontinuous and harder to tell. Cinematic and televisual adaptations of American literature outside Hollywood are less likely to fit the categories into which I have chosen to organize this history. And at any event, American literature as such has had even less impact abroad than at home. For a nation often accused of cultural hegemony, the United

States has been very little inclined to treat its own literature as an export quantity, and indifferently successful when it has done so.

Finally and most disconcertingly, my assumptions about what counts as American literature vary, often wildly, from chapter to chapter, and sometimes within chapters. I can only plead that the resulting inconsistencies in defining American literature are rooted in the cinema's own protean definitions of its subject. Any history that begins with an adaptation of *Rip Van Winkle* and ends with Stephen King and the Marvel Universe must either impose a single definition of American literature that will often be remote from Hollywood practice or do its best to trace the many different phases and fashions in the (mostly American) industry's view of its material. In choosing the second of these alternatives and organizing each of my individual chapters around a different approach American cinema has taken to American literature, I have committed, for better or worse, to place the resulting inconsistencies at the center of my own project. Instead of defining American literature, I have been more concerned to let the film industry define it through its selection and treatment of material, so that American literature means *Gone with the Wind* in the 1930s, *Peyton Place* in the 1950s, *Superman* in the 1970s, and *The Bridges of Madison County* in the 1990s.

The inevitable results of all these methodological and procedural decisions have been to omit any serious consideration, sometimes even any mention, of what readers might well feel are indispensable adaptations of American literature, from *Moby-Dick* (1930) to *The Natural* (1984). The history I have to tell is not definitive but tendentious. Although its approach to the history of American literature, or American literatures, on screen is consistently shaped by themes and ideas, those themes and ideas naturally shift from chapter to chapter, and so do its emphasis and, to a lesser but still significant extent, its terminology, as Hollywood's changing notions of American literature and the examples that best illustrate those changing notions demand. Whether the particular, perhaps idiosyncratic and highly personal, history I have written justifies all these omissions, compromises, and inconsistencies in chronology, selection, and terminology is something I leave to my readers to decide and, if they are so inclined, to supplement, complicate, and correct with their own histories.

Notes

1. "Wakefield," *Rotten Tomatoes*, https://www.rottentomatoes.com/m/wakefield.
2. Nathaniel Hawthorne, *Tales and Sketches* (New York: Library of America, 1982), p. 290.
3. Hawthorne, *Tales and Sketches*, p. 291.
4. Hawthorne, *Tales and Sketches*, p. 297.

5   Hawthorne, *Tales and Sketches*, p. 292.
6   Hawthorne, *Tales and Sketches*, p. 295.
7   Hawthorne, *Tales and Sketches*, p. 298.
8   Hawthorne, *Tales and Sketches*, p. 295.
9   F. Scott Fitzgerald, "The Last Tycoon," in *Three Novels of F. Scott Fitzgerald* (New York: Scribner, 1957), p. 163.
10 Greg M. Colón Semenza and Bob Hasenfratz, *The History of British Literature on Film, 1895–2015* (New York: Bloomsbury, 2015), p. 12.
11 Semenza and Hasenfratz, *The History of British Literature on Film*, p.12.
12 Deborah Cartmell, "Review of Greg M. Colón Semenza and Bob Hasenfratz, *The History of British Literature on Film, 1895–2015*," *Adaptation* 9.2 (August 1, 2016): 258.
13 See Gérard Genette, *Palimpsests: Literature in the Second Degree*, trans. Channa Newman and Claude Doubinsky (Lincoln: University of Nebraska Press, 1997).
14 See Richard Hofstadter, *Anti-Intellectualism in American Life* (New York: Knopf, 1963).
15 See Guerric DeBona, *Film Adaptation in the Hollywood Studio Era* (Urbana: University of Illinois Press, 2010), pp. 37–63.
16 Richard Chase, *The American Novel and Its Tradition* (Garden City: Doubleday, 1957), pp. 4–5.
17 Charles Feidelson, *Symbolism and American Literature* (Chicago: University of Chicago Press, 1953), p. 4.
18 Chase, *The American Novel and Its Tradition*, p. 4.
19 See Russell Reising, *The Unusable Past: Theory and the Study of American Literature* (New York: Methuen, 1986).
20 Robert Stam, "Introduction: The Theory and Practice of Adaptation," in *Literature and Film*, ed. Robert Stam and Alessandra Raengo (Malden, MA: Wiley-Blackwell, 2004), p. 27.
21 Thomas Leitch, "The Texts behind *The Killers*," in *Twentieth-Century American Literature and Film*, ed. R. Barton Palmer (New York: Cambridge University Press, 2007), p. 40.
22 Simone Murray, *The Adaptation Industry: The Cultural Economy of Contemporary Literary Adaptation* (New York: Routledge, 2013), p. 4.
23 Thomas Leitch, "Adaptation, the Genre," *Adaptation* 1 (Fall 2008): 106.
24 Rebecca Schneider, *Performing Remains: Art and War in Times of Theatrical Reenactment* (New York: Routledge, 2011), p. 99.
25 Hal Rubenstein, "New Again: Demi Moore," *Interview*, March 2, 2017, https://www.interviewmagazine.com/culture/new-again-demi-moore.
26 Sergei M. Eisenstein, "Dickens, Griffith, and the Film Today" (1944), in Eisenstein, *FilmForm*, ed. and trans. Jay Leyda (New York: Harcourt, Brace, 1949), p. 195.

2

1895–1915: The Attraction of Adaptation

A second life

As the lights come up in a darkened exhibition space in 1896, audience members talk excitedly about the four-minute film they have just seen. It's great to see so many of the highlights from such a familiar story, says one of them. Another remarks how powerfully the film evokes the stage presentation whose star has toured in the role for many years. His companion, who has never seen the stage play, is transfixed by the lifelike movements of America's most famous actor. A fourth marvels in particular at the completeness of the hero's transformation over the space of a single cut after which he is leading a completely different second life: his appearance, his stance, his gait, and his gestures all those of a much older man. Another, less impressed, complains that the picture has left out any hint of the hero's domestic life or his return home or, for that matter, the thunderous sound of a divine bowling ball scattering the pins. Still another expresses his delight at being able to see the film—actually eight short films averaging some thirty seconds each—compiled and screened in a single public exhibition available to all his friends instead of having to watch them in private one at a time on a series of eight mutoscopes several months ago. Despite the variety of their responses, and despite the film's absence of credits identifying its source—it would be seventeen years before the release of Cecil B. DeMille's *The Squaw Man,* the first American film to carry production credits—none of them has any trouble following the story because they all know it so well. And none of them seems aware of what a momentous chapter in American entertainment is beginning.

Their conversation is imaginary, but the film itself is real: *Rip Van Winkle,* directed by William Kennedy Laurie Dickson for the American Mutoscope Company, a vehicle for Joseph Jefferson, who had long been acknowledged as the most famous actor in the United States largely for playing the same role on hundreds of different stages. Traveling to Jefferson's summer home in Buzzards Bay, Massachusetts, Dickson and his assistant, Billy Bitzer, captured eight separate excerpts from the five-act 1865 theatrical adaptation Jefferson and Dion Boucicault had produced of Washington Irving's 1819 short story about the Dutch New York colonist who wandered off into the hills outside his village, lay down to sleep, and awoke twenty years later in a new nation that had been engendered by the American Revolution (see Figure 2.1). In the first of Dickson's films, *Rip's Toast*, the hero is animated, assertive, and free-spirited in raising a celebratory glass with a friend. The second, *Rip Meeting the Dwarf*, finds him suspicious but undeniably interested in a stranger he meets in the forest, played by a bearded man of normal height stooped over and wearing a peaked hat. In *Rip and the Dwarf*, the hero is already beginning to slow down as he agrees to hoist the other man's keg onto his shoulders and follows him into the woods. *Rip Leaving Sleepy Hollow* introduces the hero to the location in which he will remain for the rest of the story and allows Jefferson to display the widest range of his emotions: pleasure at arriving with his heavy load, sudden shock at seeing among the bearded men around him a particularly dominant figure in a cape, and acceptance of his new mates. *Rip's Toast to Hudson*

FIGURE 2.1 *Joseph Jefferson awakens to a second life in* Rip Van Winkle *(1896)*.

and Crew echoes his opening toast at a much slower pace and ends with his beginning to sink to the ground in response to whatever he has drunk. His fainting spell continues in *Rip's Twenty Years Sleep* as his drinking companions watch him briefly before abandoning him. In *The Awakening of Rip,* perhaps the single most striking of the eight individual films, the hero is suddenly older—much more than twenty years older, it would seem from his long white beard and cautious, rusty movements—and *Rip Passing Over Hill* shows him tentatively beginning to climb the rise he had descended so easily twenty years earlier.

Compared even to *The Life of an American Fireman* and *The Great Train Robbery,* two narrative films released in 1903, *Rip Van Winkle* is undeniably primitive in terms of its length, its simplicity, and its use of the technology of the infant medium. Yet it retained enough interest for American Mutoscope to copyright it for the first time in December 1902 and re-release it shortly thereafter. Its power evidently rests in something other than its storytelling, since it does not begin at the beginning of Rip's story, end at the end, or present most of what transpires in between. It is a stellar example of what André Gaudreault and Tom Gunning christened the cinema of attractions, a series of early films produced throughout the first ten years of cinematic exhibition that differ in crucial and perhaps deliberate ways from the more extended narratives that would gradually replace them. In Gunning's formulation, the cinema of attractions "sees cinema less as a way of telling stories than as a way of presenting a series of views to an audience"; it is "a cinema that displays its visibility, willing to rupture a self-enclosed visual world for the chance to solicit the attention of the spectator."[1] Hence "the filmmaker of early cinema appears as a *monstrator,* one who shows, a showman."[2]

Gunning's account of the cinema of attractions as a series of monstrations has been enormously influential in rehabilitating early cinema on its own terms rather than as a series of variously misbegotten baby steps toward the narrative cinema that largely succeeded it. His argument has led to a radical revision of early film history and film history in general. Adaptations like *Rip Van Winkle* suggest that Gunning's account can be further sharpened by revisiting the assumptions it makes, not about the cinema of attractions, but about the narrative cinema Gunning poses as its alternative and successor.

As Gunning acknowledges, narrative cinema did not so much oppose as absorb the cinema of attractions. Even today, no one sits through animated shorts or pornographic features in search of original or compelling narratives. Obligatory attractions are of paramount importance in gangster films (shootouts between the gangsters and the police or each other), Westerns (the more ritualized conflicts like the gun duel that forms the climax of adaptations of Owen Wister's 1902 novel *The Virginian* and countless imitators), and science-fiction films (glimpses of alien beings the human heroes will have to battle or contain). Indeed, it is hard to think of a popular Hollywood genre that is not organized around its attractions, an insight perhaps best expressed in Raymond Chandler's remark that in the early days of hardboiled detective fiction, "the scene outranked the plot, in the sense that a good plot was one which made good scenes. The ideal mystery was one you would read if the end was missing."[3] One might argue that genre itself is a narrative codification of attractions, a compact with the audience that the film they are about to see will contain a full measure of gunfights, musical numbers, amusingly animated physical transformations, or action sequences. Some filmgoers will find pleasure in seeing a maximum integration of these attractions into a coherent narrative, but very few will take pleasure in a coherent narrative that omits them altogether.

The audience Gunning postulates for the earliest cinema of attractions is "not primarily gullible country bumpkins, but sophisticated urban pleasure seekers, well aware that they were seeing the most modern techniques in stage craft."[4] The cinema directed at this audience was marked by "a trompe l'oeil play of give-and-take, an obsessive desire to test the limits of an intellectual disavowal—I know, but yet I see."[5] Gunning aptly notes: "In the earliest years of exhibition the cinema itself was an attraction. Early audiences went to exhibitions to see machines demonstrated, [...] rather than to view films."[6] The early film audiences Gunning describes are moved by both rational skepticism about magic and delighted astonishment when confronted by magical effects. They know that the attractions they are seeing are not real, but they are willing to react to them as if they were real. Like Japanese audiences in the 1920s, who were willing to pay a premium to sit in theater seats close to the movie projector, they are capable of attending simultaneously to the specifics of the films at hand, the direct address of those films, and the exhibition situations represented by discontinuous performances and opulent picture palaces.

Narrative cinema itself depends on an unending series of disavowals of its own. Movie audiences who take the time to admire particular performances, witty lines of dialogue, or memorable visual compositions are all displaying different modalities of meta-awareness that are constantly at odds with narrative immersion. The ability to identify heroes and villains as such in order to root for or against them, the ability to recognize structures like scenes and jokes in order to laugh at them or realize that they are over, the ability to distinguish appropriate times to laugh or gasp or weep from times when none of them is appropriate, even the saving ability to remember that the painful suspense they may be feeling is being produced by nothing more threatening than a movie—all these skills may seem natural and innate, but they are all analytical and learned, though the apparatus of narrative cinema, along with the terms on which it is marketed and exhibited, may well encourage audiences to disavow the learned nature of their narrative competence and their meta-narrative skills. Audiences for even the simplest films attend to them in many different and often logically incompatible ways, whether they are making rapid-fire guesses about where a quickly unfolding story is headed or approving the technique of the very performances that are moving them to laughter or tears. And the variety of these ways is multiplied still further for any audience watching a film adaptation who knows that it is an adaptation.

Adaptation as attraction

Adaptations like *Rip Van Winkle* present a particularly apt test case for theories of both early cinema and classical narrative cinema because they depend on their audiences' irreducibly double awareness. As Linda Hutcheon puts it:

> If we do not know that what we are experiencing actually *is* an adaptation or if we are not familiar with the particular work that it adapts, we simply experience the adaptation as we would any other work. To experience it *as an adaptation*, however [...] we need to recognize it as such and to know its adapted text, thus allowing the latter to oscillate in our memories with what we are experiencing. In the process we inevitably fill in any gaps in the adaptation with information from the adapted text.[7]

Hutcheon's last sentence might have been written in direct response to *Rip Van Winkle*, whose full enjoyment depends on the audience's ability to supplement its narrative hints from their more comprehensive knowledge of Washington Irving's story or Jefferson and Boucicault's stage adaptation. But it is the second sentence of this passage that is pivotal. The audience's awareness of any adaptation as an adaptation requires a constant oscillation between their acceptance of the adaptation on its own terms and their variously informed knowledge of its relationship to an earlier text or texts. It is ironic but entirely understandable that even adaptation scholars who evaluate specific adaptations as if they were *substitutes* for the texts they adapt, and whose leading features they were therefore obliged to replicate as best they could, almost invariably theorize these adaptations as if they were *supplements* for adapted texts the audience already knew well enough to provide comparative touchstones.

Hutcheon's model only begins to describe the complexity of audiences' responses to adaptations. The audience I have imagined watching *Rip Van Winkle* in 1896 is on the whole aware that it is an adaptation, but the oscillation Hutcheon describes indicates only two dimensions of a response that is normally far more multivalent. Irving's story provides what humor theorist Victor Raskin calls a "script"[8] for both the filmmakers and the audience, but so do Jefferson and Boucicault's play, Jefferson's star persona, his performance in the films at hand, and the experience of watching a public projection as opposed to the experience of peering into a series of mutoscopes. As Kathleen Murray has argued in her discussion of Howard Hawks's 1945 film adaptation of Ernest Hemingway's 1937 novel *To Have and Have Not,* which "needs to be thought of as a Warners picture, a Hawks film, a Hemingway adaptation, a Faulkner screenplay, a response to *Casablanca,* and a Bogart/Bacall vehicle simultaneously,"[9] a given adaptation may well offer its audience multiple scripts. The primary script for film adaptations, as Jack Boozer has pointed out, "is the screenplay, not the source text."[10] The script the nominal source text provides is only one of many competing scripts, a lesson adaptation scholars who limit their purview to comparisons between film adaptations and the sources they explicitly identify would do well to take to heart. Kyle Meikle provides the logical conclusion: "Any adaptation involves the collision of differing scripts"[11] in both its creation and its reception: audiences who watch a given adaptation as an adaptation, in Hutcheon's terms, are equally likely to watch it as a star vehicle, an auteur director's creation, a showcase for visual effects or pop music, a genre piece, or simply a pretext for a night out.

Like the early cinema Gunning describes as a monstration, *adaptation itself is an attraction* that adds its own distinctive menu of attractions to those the cinema already offers its audience. The adaptation of a narrative the cinema audience already knows supplements these attractions with an extensive new menu of additional attractions: the anticipation of seeing a familiar story retold, the anticipation of recognizing familiar elements from a given story in a new mode of presentation, the opportunity to compare the adaptation to whatever scripts the audience recognizes, the dimensions of performance and visual design distinctive (though by no means unique) to cinema, the astonished pleasure at the cinema's perceived ability to bring lexical worlds to life, the crushingly self-righteous sense of dismay that the adaptation has missed the boat. All these pleasures depend on both the immersive recognition of narrative and adaptive tropes and the meta-narrative ability to recognize them as tropes. Just as the actualités of the Lumière brothers are not narratives but monstrations—or, as I will more often call them, displays[12]—that exhibit visual spectacles for the audience's delight, adaptations are monstrations simultaneously capable of conferring a second (or third or tenth) life on a familiar story and pointing self-consciously to the fact that they are enshrining or reproducing that story. One sign of monstration in early films is the expository intertitles that serve explicitly to introduce characters and performers, instead of gathering all this information into opening credits. Another is the prominence of the live presenters who introduce so many programs of these films, a function assumed by many a later ringmaster. Horror-film auteur William Castle outfits his low-budget features with extradiegetic features like "Emergo," "Percepto," "Illusion-O," and the "Fright Break." Director Robert Altman parades dozens of stars in cameo appearances through *The Player* (1992). Advertisers of the 1950s invite television audiences to the cinema to experience films in widescreen or Cinerama. Publicists develop high-concept publicity campaigns for *Sharknado* (2013) and its sequels and a grassroots campaign for *The Blair Witch Project* (1999). Like these other figures, the cinematic adapter also functions as both a storyteller inviting audiences to immerse themselves once more in a familiar story and "a fairground barker"[13] framing the adaptation as an adaptation by calling attention to the fact that it is being presented as such.

Although all adaptations frame themselves as attractions, there are several reasons why it is hard to generalize confidently about the specific menu of attractions the earliest film adaptations of American literature offered their audiences. Early cinema did not make such comparisons available to mass audiences for the first time, because the ubiquitous theatrical adaptations of novels to the stage had accustomed nineteenth-century audiences to the practice. Many of these early adaptations' sources have fallen into an obscurity rooted in profound differences between the canon and the cultural status of American literature now and a century ago. The fact that none of Herman Melville's fiction was adapted to the screen until 1926 and that Melville's screen debut, Millar Webb's *The Sea Beast* (1926), used Captain Ahab's monomaniacal pursuit of the white whale Moby-Dick as a background to a romantic rivalry between Ahab Ceeley (John Barrymore) and his brother Derek (George O'Hara) for the favors of minister's daughter Esther Harper (Dolores Costello) does not mean that early cinema was not interested in adapting American literature, but that its ideas about what constituted American literature were as remote from our own as its ideas about what constituted adaptation. The ability of producers before 1909 to borrow material from prior sources without paying for adaptation rights and the absence of credit sequences from all films before 1913 can make it surprisingly tricky to identify exactly which films are adaptations and which are not, an ambiguity any number of early filmmakers presumably intended to foster.

Nor do contemporaneous reviews offer consistent help in identifying adaptations. In its columns during a single year, 1908, the trade journal *Moving Picture World* accurately describes D.W. Griffith's Biograph film *After Many Years* as presenting "a subject on the lines of [Tennyson's poem] Enoch Arden,"[14] calls Pathé Frères's *Puss in Boots* an "interesting little fairy tale,"[15] and identifies Pathé Frères's *L'Arlesienne* as an adaptation of "the story of L'Arlesienne, as written by the famous French writer, Alfonse Daudet."[16] Going further in a column titled "Dickens in Pictures," it hails the release *A Christmas Carol* as the first in a series of Essanay adaptation of Dickens films that will prove that "the new art of photographic actions is the domain wherein the pictorial possibilities of Dickens shall achieve its finest results."[17] But in reviewing three other 1908 films, Edison's *The Face on the Barroom Floor*,[18] Biograph's *For the Love of Gold*,[19] and Biograph's *The Lady or the Tiger*,[20] *Moving Picture News* nowhere mentions the sources of these films, or even notes that they are adaptations.

A final and potentially fatal obstacle to generalizations about early film adaptation is the shocking number of early films that have not been preserved. The Library of Congress estimates that 75 percent of silent films have not survived to the present day. Martin Scorsese's Film Foundation suggests even more pessimistically that 90 percent of films made before 1929 have been lost. The unavailability of an overwhelming majority of silent films to modern researchers poses a grave a problem for adaptation scholars and indeed for all film scholars who deal with the silent era. Many films that have survived are available only in incomplete prints that cannot be compared to an authoritative negative or master positive. But the unavailability of a given film for comparative analysis or possible compromises in its surviving prints does not diminish its most important feature as an adaptation: that it chose to adapt a given property in the first place. Given the unprecedented capital-intensiveness of motion pictures, to know that a given property was ever selected for adaptation is to know the single most important fact about the adaptation as an adaptation.

Even if most of the adaptations based on his work have not survived, it is clear that the American author whose work was adapted to the screen most often between 1896 and 1915 was James Oliver Curwood, a journalist/adventurer in the mold of Jack London who was paid more by the word for his writing than any contemporaneous author in the world.[21] Curwood's tales of outdoor adventure, often set, like London's, in the Yukon territory of Canada, were adapted eighty-one times between 1910 and 1915, sixty more times before his death in 1927, and sixty-one times thereafter, most notably in Jean-Jacques Annaud's *The Bear* (1988) and *Aventures dans le Grand Nord,* a 1995 French television series.[22] The second most frequently adapted American author of the period was columnist/playwright George Ade, a writer of brief, facetious fables satirizing American social types in the manner of Mark Twain that were adapted seventy times during 1914 and 1915, practically all of them by Essanay, and a total of ninety-nine times, from *The Fable of the Brash Drummer and the Nectarine* to *The Fable of the Girl Who Took Notes and Got Wise and Then Fell Down* between 1914 and 1917.

Throughout the first twenty years of the cinema, no other American author was adapted nearly as often as Curwood or Ade. Their closest competitors were far behind: Frederick Burr Opper with twenty-six adaptations; Henry Wadsworth Longfellow with twenty-four; Richard Harding Davis with twenty-two, all for Edison; Washington Irving with twenty-two, seventeen of them of "Rip Van Winkle"; O. Henry and Bret Harte with nineteen each; Cyrus Townsend Brady and Bud Fisher with eighteen each; Roy Norton, James Oppenheim, Richard Felton Outcault, and Jack London with fifteen each; Frederick Arnold Kummer, otherwise known as Arnold Fredericks, with fourteen, including twelve featuring the private detective Octavius; Hal Reid, Rex Ellingwood Beach, and Edgar Allan Poe with thirteen each; David Belasco with twelve; Mary Imlay Taylor, George Randolph Chester, Clyde Fitch, George Bronson Howard, and Hal Meredith, aka Harry Blyth, tied at eleven; and Daniel Carson Goodman, Rudolph Dirks, Nick Carter, and Booth Tarkington with ten each.

Most of these writers were still alive and of current interest when their works were filmed. Belasco was the most celebrated theatrical producer and impresario of his day, and the work of many of the others continued to appear virtually alongside the films based on their stories in popular newspapers or magazines (see Figure 2.2). Unlike William Shakespeare, Charles Dickens, and Sir Walter Scott, whose respective canons were adapted seventy-five, sixty, and twenty-three times over this period, American literature did not

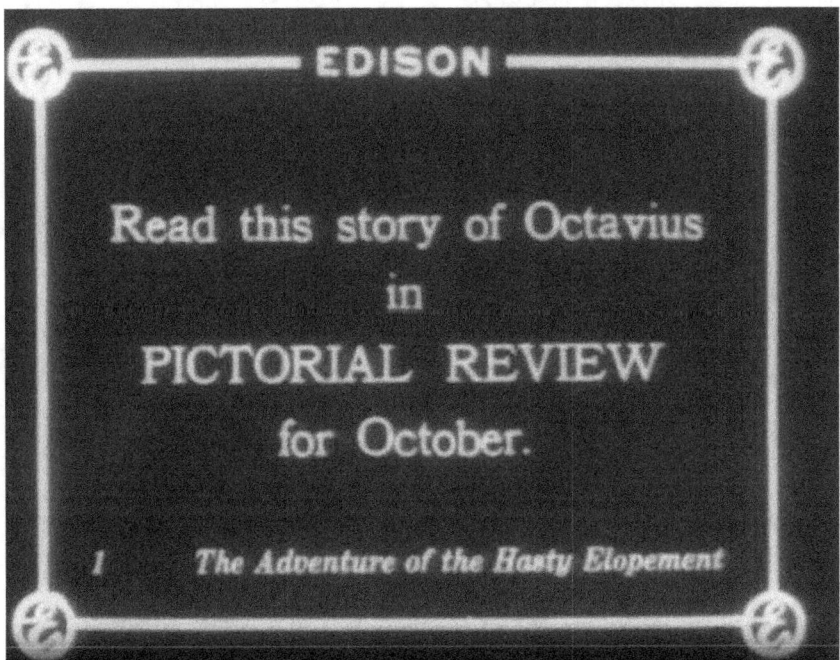

FIGURE 2.2 A credit in The Adventure of the Hasty Elopement *(1914) not only identifies its literary source, but invites the audience to read it themselves after watching the movie.*

offer nearly as attractive a backlist to early filmmakers. Only Irving, Poe, Harte, Henry, London, and Tarkington have continued to hold even a marginal place in contemporary histories of American literature, and only Irving and Poe had achieved anything like the status of literary classics at the time their stories were first filmed.

Monstrations, monsters, and minstrelsy

Why did early filmmakers have so little interest in filming classic American novels and plays? The obvious explanations are that the classic American novels from *Wieland* to *Moby-Dick* were long, dense, unwieldy, obscure, and therefore difficult to adapt, and there were no American plays widely recognized as classics; classic American writers were poets like Longfellow, John Greenleaf Whittier (whose poems were adapted seven times between 1986 and 1915), and Rose H. Thorpe (whose poem "Curfew Shall Not Ring Tonight" was adapted five times over the same period). The cinema paid homage to Mark Twain not only by basing seven different films on six different Twain stories during this period, but by filming the great man himself at his Connecticut home in 1909, an attraction presumably as appealing as any adaptation. When early filmmakers turned to adaptation, they favored adventure stories set in spectacular locations, franchises whose heroes had already achieved popularity and name recognition in comic strips (as attested by twenty-six adaptations of Frederick Burr Opper's Happy Hooligan, eighteen of Bud Fisher's Mutt and Jeff, fourteen of Richard Felton Outcault's Buster Brown, and ten of Rudolph Dirks's Katzenjammer Kids) or other sources (fourteen of Frederick Arnold Kummer's detective Octavius, ten of Nick Carter's dime detective), or other texts that had already become well known through theatrical adaptations. Fifteen different companies produced adaptations of *Rip Van Winkle* before 1916, and eight produced adaptations of *Uncle Tom's Cabin*.

Harriet Beecher Stowe's celebrated anti-slavery novel, originally serialized in 1851–2 and published under separate cover in 1852, had rapidly become the best-selling American novel of the nineteenth century. George L. Aiken's six-act stage adaptation enjoyed a similar success in England and America, and Stowe's refusal to license Aiken's adaptation or any other left the field open to many more unauthorized adaptations, making the story familiar to two generations of audiences before Edwin S. Porter first filmed it for Edison in 1903, launching the Hollywood career of the single most important work of American literature for the movies. The importance of *Uncle Tom's Cabin* depends not on its repeated adaptations—although its twelve adaptations make it the American novel most frequently filmed throughout the silent era, it has been filmed only seven times since the coming of synchronized sound—but on the fact that more than any other widely adapted text, it reveals the unique problems and opportunities that faced adapters since the earliest days of cinema, especially the status of adaptation as an attraction.

Although modern audiences may feel that Porter's film barely scratches the surface of Stowe's novel, its nineteen minutes constituted a monumental length for its time. Presenting selected scenes from an unidentified traveling troupe's performance of the play, it comprises fourteen shots, each introduced by a title that explains what is to come (sometimes with unintentional irony, since the saintly slave Uncle Tom is still alive at the beginning of the scene headed "MARKS AVENGES DEATH'S OF ST. CLAIR AND UNCLE TOM," though it is in this scene that he receives the wounds that will lead to his death). Plunging into the action in its first scene, "ELIZA PLEADS WITH TOM TO RUN AWAY," the film shows no interest whatsoever in the exposition of plot or character. Assuming that its audience is already familiar with its people and their story, it never pauses to explain who Uncle Tom and Eliza are or identify by name Stowe's two most memorable characters, the high-spirited slave girl Topsy and the cruel plantation owner Simon Legree. The film does not focus on what Brian McFarlane, following Roland Barthes, has called the "cardinal functions" in the novel, those that "open up alternatives of consequence to the development of the story."[23] Nor does it present sharply individuated characters or even, except through perfunctory hints and the casting of white performers in the leading African American roles, the racial stereotypes that had made Stowe's novel notorious. Instead, the film presents itself, as if with a nod to Raymond Chandler, as a collection of noteworthy scenes rather than a coherent story. Many of the scenes it displays are spectacles borrowed from Stowe (the escape of Eliza over an icy river and the deaths of Eva and Uncle Tom, each one vouchsafed a vision of heavenly redemption), narrative turning points counterpointed by incongruously cheerful group dances starkly at odds with Stowe's tale of cruelty and injustice (like the one that introduces the scene in which Tom realizes that Eva is seriously ill, or the one that introduces the sale of Tom and St. Clair's other slaves), or incidents imported into the story from other sources—most notably the race between the steamboats *Robert E. Lee,* carrying Eva and her father, and *Natchez,* adding the explosion of the latter to accounts of a famous 1870 race between the *Natchez* and the *Robert E. Lee,* which was not even built until 1866, three years after the Emancipation Proclamation ended slavery (see Figure 2.3).

Contemporary audiences may consider Porter's film less an adaptation than a highlights reel of Stowe's novel. But there is no reason to assume that audiences in 1903 would have welcomed a more comprehensive

FIGURE 2.3 *A high-spirited blackface dance in* Uncle Tom's Cabin *(1903) introduces the news that Eva is seriously ill.*

adaptation, especially of a 500-page novel that remains to this day more widely debated than read. Renata Kobetts Miller has noted that nineteenth-century theatrical dramatizations of novels like *Nicholas Nickleby* "make no attempt to provide a coherent narrative, but instead present a series of scenes without interstitial connections" long before the arrival of the cinema.[24] More specifically, the film inherited the associations of Stowe's novels with a long tradition of blackface minstrelsy, a performative mode of monstration that may have been based on

> European folk rituals that involved blacking up, such as mummers' plays, callithumps, and impromptu shivarees. In these practices, blackened faces signaled that the activity was metaphorical, performative, or ritual. This resonance later translated into minstrelsy's strong associations with burlesque, where blackface was the sign that something was being travestied. In America, however, blackface also took on racial connotations, so that by the 1820s it was sometimes known as "Ethiopian delineation."[25]

What is most telling about the film is not its status as a series of spectacular displays clearly inspired by the tableaux vivants that had counted *Uncle Tom's Cabin* among their most popular subjects even before the invention of the cinema, but its attempt to marry monstration and narration through a series of paradoxical moves. The first of these, which has been well documented, is the close relationship it assumes between monstration and the monstrous. If the pioneering films of Auguste and Louis Lumière, from *Workers Leaving the Lumière Factory* to *Baby's Breakfast* (both 1895) had valorized scenes from everyday life, *Uncle Tom's Cabin* emphasizes deviant or otherwise remarkable figures, actions, and tableaux, from the incongruous ensemble of blackface dance performers to the monstrous Simon Legree.

In addition, these dance sequences establish a close connection between monstration and minstrelsy, connecting the film to both nineteenth-century minstrel show stereotypes on which Stowe herself had drawn and the much older tradition that defined minstrels as musical performers who entertained their audiences by singing of distant places. A stellar instance of this connection is Stowe's initial presentation of Topsy introducing herself to Ophelia by accepting Augustus St. Clare's invitation to "show us some of your dancing":

> The black, glassy eyes glittered with a kind of wicked drollery, and the thing struck up, in a clear shrill voice, an odd negro melody, to which she kept time with her hands and feet, spinning round, clapping her hands, knocking her knees together, in a wild, fantastic sort of time, and producing in her throat all those odd guttural sounds which distinguish the native music of her race; and finally, turning a summerset or two, and giving a prolonged closing note, as odd and unearthly as that of a steam-whistle, she came suddenly down on the carpet, and stood with her hands folded, and a most sanctimonious expression of meekness and solemnity over her face, broken only by the cunning glances which she shot askance from the corners of her eyes.[26]

Topsy is clearly meant to be both appealing and monstrous. If the patronizing detail with which Stowe describes her performance did not make this point, her three iterations of the word "odd" would do so. Lacking any authentic core self that would make it possible to identify with her as a fully human character, Topsy can only monstrate herself through a performance by turns responsive, energetic, sanctimonious, cunning, and furtive.

Building not so much on Stowe's narrative as on its gallery of monstrous monstrations, Porter's film sets the pattern for countless later film adaptations, whether or not they deal explicitly with slavery, blackface minstrelsy, or any other aspect of white audiences' perceptions of the African American experience, by establishing its own adaptation as both monstration and minstrelsy. Julie Grossman has argued that "*any* adaptation might be considered 'monstrous,' that is, isolated from its predecessors because it is born of new concerns, new desires to express ideas in a different medium, with a changed-up narrative reflecting shifting cultural priorities."[27] Adaptations are most likely to be perceived as monstrous by audiences who already know and value the scripts they monstrate, from which they derive both their inspiration and their point of departure. In addition, many audiences, even if they would never dream of using this term, continue to perceive all film adaptations as examples of what might be called intertextual minstrelsy, performances of new texts that can never truly be the same as the texts they adapt.

All these connections involve paradoxical modes of disavowal. Monstrating the monstrous involves domesticating it by bringing it into a safe and familiar exhibition space, perhaps even rendering it as sympathetic as the grotesque creature in Mary Shelley's endlessly adapted *Frankenstein* (1818), while preserving enough of its monstrosity to guarantee a frisson of astonishment and fear. Audiences may see in these monstrations avatars of a radical Other familiar to white Americans from countless previous stereotypes that root their disavowals of both racism and pan-racial identification in the disavowals with which audiences had greeted the self-conscious performances of medieval minstrels. Adaptation's promise to be both the same and different as the scripts it adapted conjoins and powerfully amplifies the disavowals of both monstration and minstrelsy for audiences seeking to immerse themselves in performances—of monstrous stereotypes, of racial Others, of familiar scripts—that they know perfectly well are performances.

Porter's reliance on tropes of minstrelsy assumes an audience at once eager to see a familiar story retold and self-consciously aware that they are watching a show, and indicates the rationale behind the particular scenes chosen for inclusion. Although these scenes include several pivotal moments in the novel's plot, they exclude many others, from Arthur Shelby's decision to settle his debts by selling Eliza and Tom, a decision that sets the plot in motion, to the escape of Cassy and Emmeline from Legree, an action that leads to Tom's death when he refuses to tell Legree where they have gone. Instead, the film's Legree kills Tom for his refusal to beat Emmeline, just as it had earlier achieved a remarkable economy by showing Legree killing St. Clair for his defense of Tom in a saloon, making Legree indirectly responsible for the sale of Tom after St. Clair's death. Many of the film's tableaux, most of them group scenes filmed in long shot, are spectacular attractions. Many of them showcase operatic emotional moments in the lives of Eliza, George, and Eva. Even more important than the outsized emotions that the characters are shown feeling, however, are the sentiments the film aims to provoke in the audience. Unlike Stowe's novel, whose subtitle, *Life among the Lowly*, was intended to move Northern audiences to pity and outrage on behalf of a slave culture they might never have experienced directly, the film's subtitle, *Slavery Days*, recalls a comfortably remote historical period whose outrages can be used to tug at the audience's heartstrings without asking them to do anything in particular. The principal attraction consistently on display throughout Porter's version of *Uncle Tom's Cabin* is not the emotional sentiments of the characters but those of the audience, aroused not through a coherently developed narrative but through individual moments of heightened intensity that appeal directly to a reaction that is at once empathetic, condescending, self-conscious, and self-congratulatory. Instead of preaching that slavery is evil, a hotly contested argument when Stowe advanced it in 1852, the film congratulates its audience on already knowing that slavery is evil, an entrance requirement, like its previous knowledge of the story, that will allow its members to enjoy the spectacle of their own moral outrage. Like all adaptations, it frames these reactions as the same but different, already familiar through the audience's memory of the earlier texts it adapts but rendered different through the display of the old story as a vehicle for adaptation in a new medium.

Early-film historian Charles Musser has argued that Porter is "the first filmmaker to sketch out a vision of American society."[28] A briefer look at three other early adaptations Porter directed for Edison reveals the ways this vision depends on different versions of an essentially similar dynamic involving individual, often added, attractions, and the attraction of displaying an adaptation of an earlier text. By the time Porter and Wallace McCutcheon filmed *The Miller's Daughter* (1905), its dramatic source, Steele MacKaye's 1880 play *Hazel Kirke*, already remembered as the longest-running American play of its time, had enjoyed a New York run of 486 performances, and, because MacKaye was a pioneer in organizing touring companies, a total of 2,000 performances in Philadelphia, Baltimore, and Washington, DC, through 1883. This first cinematic adaptation of a theatrical property that would be adapted again in 1916 depends much more completely than *Uncle Tom's Cabin* on developing a sustained narrative continuity across cuts. The thirteen shots of the prints that survive stand far less completely on their own as tableaux than the individual shots in *Uncle Tom's Cabin*. Even so, it is hard to imagine a contemporaneous audience who did not already know it being able to follow this story of a young woman who favors the romantic overtures of an artist over those of a farmer, elopes with the artist only to suffer abandonment and humiliation when the appearance of his wife and child reveals that he is already married, descends into poverty when the father who has favored the farmer turns her away, and attempts suicide, only to be rescued and married by the farmer. The film quickly and surely establishes the artist and the farmer as rivals in its opening two shots and shows the artist advancing his suit over a series of shots that show the artist painting the miller's daughter, joining her in a barn dance, and kissing her hand as she sits astride a horse whose saddle girth he is adjusting just before her father chases him away. But it is much less clear when he arrives at her home, throws a stone at her door, and then leads her off on another pair of horses that he plans to elope with her. And although the cryptic but helpful intertitle "WIFE AND CHILD OF ARTIST" identifies the woman who comes to another door in the following shot and drives off in a cart with a man who indicates that the artist is not at home, the absence of dialogue at the beginning of the following shot, which shows the miller's daughter standing outside a church as the artist approaches with a minister who waves his hands dismissively, makes it far more challenging for the audience to interpret than the corresponding scene in MacKaye's play until the arrival of the wife and child send the miller's daughter into a fainting fit that makes it clear what this moment means to her.

Along the way, the film takes care to supply distinctively American attractions of its own, from the waterfall behind the miller's daughter as the artist paints her picture to the exuberant antics of one of the other three couples at the barn dance, who repeatedly upstage the two leads throughout the longest and most gratuitous shot in the film without threatening their narrative prominence. As Hazel, rejected by her father and unable to support herself as a seamstress, totters along a wintry city street, she reaches out imploringly to a vision of her father that appears above her, but it vanishes just as quickly. Most strikingly, the shot in which the miller's daughter, against a glaringly two-dimensional painting of a bridge that still allows a more explicit presentation of a suicide attempt than the stage would allow, throws herself into a river and is rescued by the farmer, is divided into three by two remarkably long moments—an eight-second pause between the time she disappears from the frame and the farmer's entrance, and a nine-second pause after he disappears into the river before he emerges again clutching her—that daringly extend the time during which nothing is happening onscreen. More clearly than anything else in the film, these two prolonged moments indicate that the principal attraction it offers is the audience's ability to enjoy the suspense of waiting to see their expectations fulfilled as they feel, and at some level feel themselves feeling, the same emotions they have felt before in response to earlier versions of this familiar story.

If *The Miller's Daughter* adds American attractions like the extended barn dance sequence to MacKaye's familiar story and intensifies the melodrama of its heroine's suicide attempt in order to encourage the audience to enjoy a stressful yet familiar emotional response, Porter's *The Night before Christmas* (1905) plays with Clement Clarke Moore's beloved 1828 poem "A Visit from St. Nicholas" by filling in a backstory for Santa Claus that recasts both him and the children he is visiting as specifically American. The first two shots, which show Santa shoveling hay for his reindeer's forage and toiling in his workshop to build toys for children, are instantly recognizable as outside the world of Moore's poem, whose point of view is limited to that of the father of the household Santa visits. So are the fifth shot, in which the children expecting Santa's visit, far from being "nestled all snug in their beds," as Moore describes them, arise and wage a boisterous pillow fight before they finally settle down (see Figure 2.4), and the sixth and seventh shots, in which Santa prepares to leave his workshop, checks a book that presumably contains children's addresses, gift ideas, and status as naughty or nice, makes some last-minute corrections, and then loads his sack onto his sleigh and leaves. The eighth shot, the film's showpiece attraction, is an exhilarating seventy-second tracking shot from right to left that follows the winding path of a miniature sleigh pulled by eight reindeer as it leaves the workshop, passing over hills and through valleys to a brightly lit town. All these are additions to Moore's poem, which is represented by five intertitles reproducing four lines each of the fifty-six-line poem, three shots of the family preparing for Santa's visit, and three more shots. The first of these shows Santa standing on the roof, dropping his sack down the chimney, and then letting himself down after it. The second, duplicating the interior space of the film's third shot, shows Santa emerging from the chimney and tugging his sack, which he has somehow managed to pass on the way down, behind him before he methodically fills the stockings hung from the mantelpiece, tosses some larger packages onto the floor, and then produces a fully trimmed Christmas tree and a room full of gifts by magically waving his hand. In the

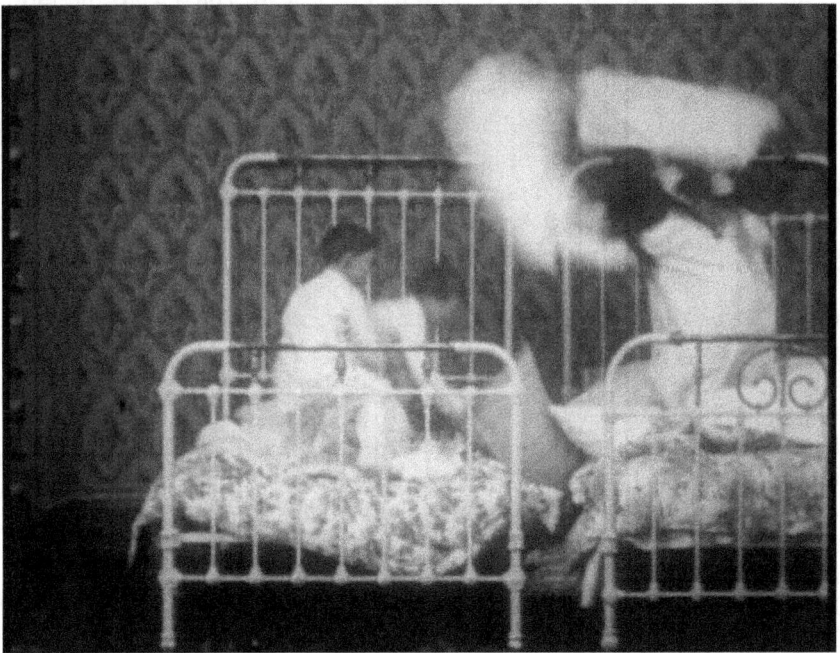

FIGURE 2.4 *Before they get nestled all snug in their beds, the children in* The Night before Christmas *(1905) occupy themselves quite differently.*

third, the children come downstairs the following morning, marvel at the gifts he has left, and play with them before a final mid-shot that echoes the famous last shot of *The Great Train Robbery* presents Santa looking directly into the camera and saying "Merry Christmas" as he lays his finger aside of his nose. Although much of the material in these shots also represents additions to the poem, the film omits the central event of the poem, the father's unexpected meeting with Santa, along with any suggestion that the events are presented as he sees or remembers them. Nor is it very punctilious in reproducing the spelling or punctuation of the poem, as in an intertitle that reads:

"NOW DASHER! NOW DANCER!
NOW PRANCER AND VIXEN!
ON! COMET; ON! CUPID;
ON! DUNDER AND BLITZEN"

The film's clear intention is not to reproduce the poem or to dramatize it completely but to select particularly attractive moments from it, supplement them with other moments likely to attract a Yuletide audience, and use strategically selected excerpts from the poem to monstrate them in an appealingly playful way.

Still more playful is Porter's *The Dream of a Rarebit Fiend*, the most popular film Edison released in 1906. The film is a surprisingly close adaptation of a single episode, published on January 28, 1905, of *Dream of the Rarebit Fiend*, a comic strip by Winsor McCay, using the pseudonym "Silas," originally titled *Dream of a Welsh Rabbit Fiend* that, running from 1904 through 1911 and returning in 1911–13 and 1923–5, presented self-contained, discontinuous fantasies united by the climactic revelation that they were dreams inspired by the late-night consumption of rarebit or other equally imprudent foods (see Figure 2.5).

Comparing the seven-minute film to the eight-panel strip shows how much Porter added to his source. The first shot shows the gluttonous hero polishing off a dish of welsh rarebit and washing it down with copious drink. The second shows him staggering out of the restaurant and down the street. The double-exposure third shot shows the whirling cityscape behind him as a lamppost mocks his efforts to cling to it by swinging like a pendulum. The fourth shows him back home, getting into bed, then watching in mounting alarm as his slippers, thanks to stop-motion photography, glide away from his bed, followed by all the other furniture in the room. The fifth literalizes his dream of three tiny demons emerging from a rarebit pot to poke and hammer his head. The sixth shows the bed leaping back and forth, then rapidly twirling around before it leaps out the window. It is not until the seventh of the film's eleven shots, in which the hapless glutton holds frantically to first the head rails, then the foot

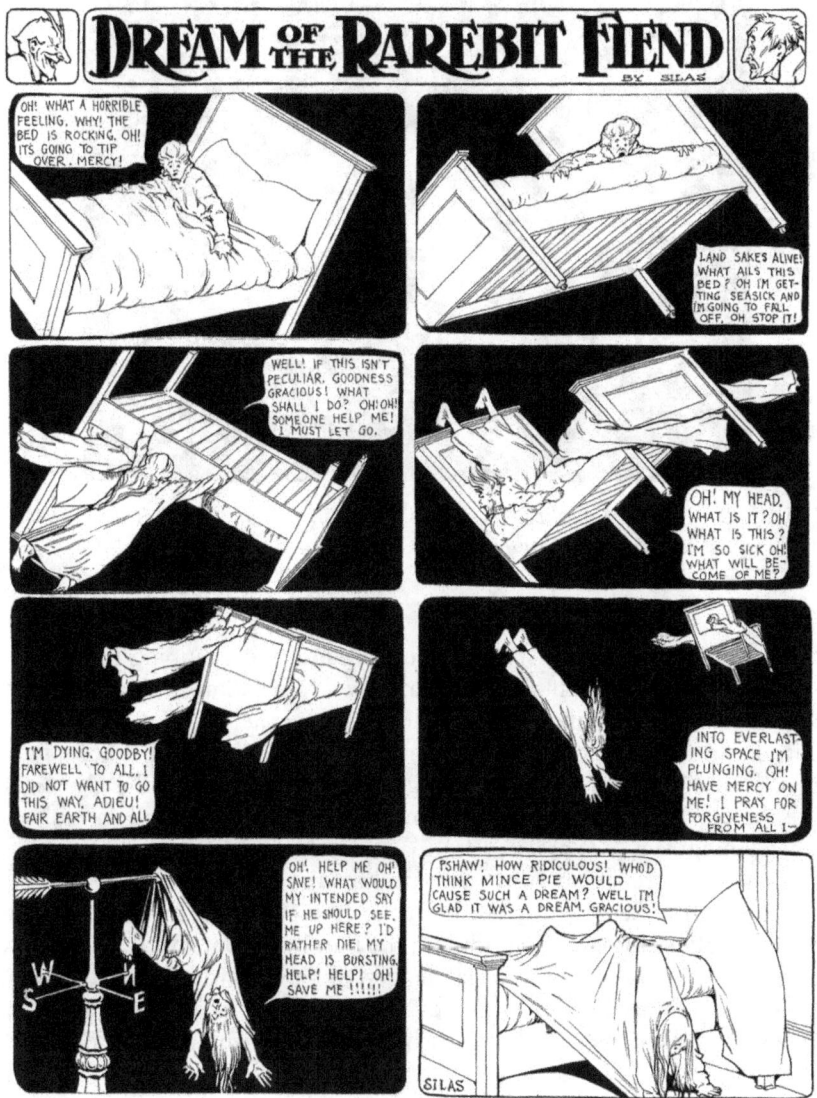

FIGURE 2.5 *A celebrated episode of Winsor McCay's* Dream of the Rarebit Fiend *provides a surprisingly detailed blueprint for Edwin S. Porter's 1906 adaptation.*

rails of his bed as it hurtling through the night sky, that its narrative time catches up with that of McCay's comic strip, which begins with the bed already flying through the air. In the eighth shot, the bed flies past a steeple surmounted by a weathervane and dumps off the glutton, who is shown in the ninth shot, the only one that attempts an exact reproduction of any of McCay's individual frames, hanging from the weathervane (see Figure 2.6),

FIGURE 2.6 *Porter's duplication of a single panel from McCay's strip in* The Dream of a Rarebit Fiend *(1906).*

which adds the effects of spinning him around and dropping him before the film cuts to its tenth shot, which shows him falling through the sky toward another building, and the eleventh, another interior shot of his bedroom in which he crashes through the ceiling, falls onto the floor, pulls himself onto the bed, and sits there growling in chagrin as the film ends. Like the comic strip, the film revels in its wildly unmotivated surrealism, transforming McCay's precise, deadpan visuals, which manage to suggest both stasis and frenetic motion, with the kinds of visual effects most closely associated with Georges Méliès. Both the comic and the film are displays of impossible attractions. In addition, the film both roots McCay's fantasy more firmly in the circumstantial reality of the glutton eating the meal that will give him nightmares and displays its adaptation of a comic-strip adventure audiences might have felt beyond the capabilities of the cinema in 1906.

Adaptation on trial

The pivotal film in the transition from displaying adaptations as attractions to presenting them as retellings of their stories was *Ben Hur*, which Frank Oakes Rose and Sidney Olcott directed for Kalem in 1907. The fifteen-minute film remains firmly in the mold of monstration, selecting eight scenes from Lew Wallace's 1880 novel *Ben-Hur: A Tale of the Christ,* introducing them with intertitles from "JERUSALEM REBELS AT ROMAN MIS-RULE" to "BEN HUR VICTOR" that emphasize their status as spectacle rather than their role in developing a sustained plot, and omitting most of the scenes that drove the novel's plot—the film leaps directly from "BEN HUR TO THE GALLEYS," which shows the captured hero brought into his friend-turned-enemy Messala's encampment, to "BEN HUR—RESCUER OF ARRIUS—ADOPTED AND FREED FROM SLAVERY," without presenting any shots showing Ben Hur rescuing the slaver Arrius, or indeed of Ben Hur as a galley slave aboard his ship. The film's intertitles decline to identify any characters: even in its climactic chariot race, it is impossible to identify either Messala or Ben Hur, and although the film's final intertitle tells which one of them won, it says nothing about what has been at stake in the race or what the victory means.

What has given *Ben Hur* its enduring historical importance is a lawsuit Wallace's son Henry filed together with his publisher, Harper and Brothers, and Broadway producers Marcus Klaw and A.L. Erlanger, who held the theatrical rights, filed against Kalem for copyright infringement on the ground the Kalem had not paid for the rights to film Wallace's novel. After two lower courts issued injunctions against further screenings of the film, the Supreme Court, in Oliver Wendell Holmes's landmark 1909 decision in *Kalem v. Harper Brothers*, rejected Kalem's claims that "by creating 'Roman Spectacles' inspired by the novel *Ben-Hur* [...] the filmmakers were simply building on Lew Wallace's ideas, not copying the expression—the words and narrative—used to clothe those ideas," and that "the Kalem Company had not staged a chariot race at all; it had merely filmed a real chariot race" by the Brooklyn Fire Department, one of many staged publically in the light of the success of Klaw & Erlanger's theatrical adaptation of Wallace's novel.[29] The Supreme Court's ruling that "film producers needed to obtain permission in order to adapt works for the screen" effectively "banned the business model on which the American film industry had been built."[30] Establishing the cinema as a storytelling medium with its own particular language of expression and communication decisively altered not only the legal status of film adaptation but filmmakers' own assumptions about what it meant to adapt a literary property.

Once the American cinema had begun the conversion from tableaux, *actualités,* and newsreels to fictional narratives around 1903, filmmakers naturally sought models for their films in novels, plays, and poems already familiar to their audience. *Kalem v. Harper Brothers,* combined with the shift from one-reel to two-reel subjects beginning a year or two later, paved the way for a shift from a cinema of narrative recognition that did not so much tell stories as allude to them, confident in the knowledge that audiences already familiar with the stories would fill in the blanks, to a cinema of narrative generation, which relied on filmgoers to use general narrative cues and conventions, whether or not they were specific to cinema, rather than their familiarity with particular earlier texts to figure out the story. Between 1907 and 1915, American cinema was largely defined by the shift from the first of these two models, which drew on American literature as a collection of stories in the public domain, to the second, which treated literary originals, particularly plays, as both a licensed inspiration and an established competitor. In her 1920 volume *Cinema Craftsmanship: A Book for Photoplaywrights,* Frances Taylor Patterson warned budding screenwriters: "As far as the photoplay market is concerned, adaptations of books upon which the copyrights have expired, are rarely, if ever, saleable. Such books are the property of everybody, and producers do not feel they ought to buy material which is already at their disposal."[31] Since "film companies did not even want to adapt the classics for the screen if they could not be assured of a monopoly on the story," it made sense that "the Bosworth Company [...] acquired the exclusive rights to Jack London's work. The Éclair Company [...] licensed all of O. Henry's short stories. By 1918 every publisher had established a film rights department with a cadre of agents."[32]

Just as filmmakers became legally obligated to purchase adaptation rights they had formerly assumed were theirs for the taking, literary cachet became an increasingly important defense against threats of censorship. Chicago's 1907 censorship ordinance reserved to its police department the decision whether any film could be exhibited on local screens. After Detroit enacted similar legislation the same year, several states followed suit: Pennsylvania in 1911, Ohio in 1914, Kansas in 1915, and Maryland in 1916. As individual American localities and states became more aggressive in preventing a wide range of films from opening in their jurisdiction, filmmakers sought within literature a bulwark against threats of censorship. The effect was to redefine the cinema's take on American literature as both a new kind of attraction, an exclusive display that could be witnessed nowhere else than in the work of licensed adapters, and a new kind of problem, a minefield for aspiring adapters schooled to fear competition for the adaptations of any works in the public domain and excessive costs for the right to adapt successful properties.

Cinema's approach to American literature did not change overnight. In 1910, the *Moving Picture World,* reviewing the first reel of Vitagraph's three-reel version of *Uncle Tom's Cabin,* summarized it in terms that emphasize the very same attractions, discontinuities, and self-congratulatory moments of historical hindsight that characterized Edison's 1903 version:

> The first of a series of three reels, each approximately 1,000 feet, and intended to adequately present this powerful and fascinating drama. This reel depicts the escape of Eliza and the removal of Uncle Tom from his old home in Kentucky. Most of the salient facts in the story up to that

point are graphically produced. It is scarcely necessary to go over the story. It is well known to practically every one. [...] While the story has lost most of its power with the removal of the reason for its existence, it still has a fascination which few are able to resist, and in this film that fascination is retained.[33]

Hiawatha: The Indian Passion Play, which Edgar Lewis directed for Colonial in 1913, looks to the future in one regard—it is the first American film to feature an entire cast of Native Americans—but to the past in its treatment of Longfellow's ambitious 1855 attempt to create an epic American poem. Only fifteen of the film's original forty minutes survive, and apart from a fragmentary final scene evidently based on "Pau-Puk-Keewis," Canto 16 of Longfellow's poem, the surviving footage ends with Hiawatha's wedding to Minnehaha, whom he has long loved from afar, halfway through the poem. Although it may be difficult to generalize about the larger structure of the film, the film's twenty-nine intertitles, all but two of which quote passages from Longfellow, make it clear that the visuals are presented as monstrations of particular passages from Longfellow's poem themselves keyed to Native American courtship and coming-of-age rituals presented almost entirely in long shots as both exotic and universally human, not pivotal moments in the story of a particular group of individual characters.

Franchising Oz

The easiest way to kindle and maintain the rooting interest absent from *Hiawatha,* the kind of interest that hooked audiences even before the film began and kept them coming back for more, was to establish a fictional franchise with continuing characters like Happy Hooligan, Mutt and Jeff, Buster Brown, or the Katzenjammer Kids. The most ambitious of these early franchises, and the one whose mixed fortunes best reveal the opportunities and problems a franchise offered, begins with L. Frank Baum's 1900 children's book *The Wonderful Wizard of Oz.* George M. Hill, the Chicago publisher to whom Baum, already an established poet, storyteller, and playwright, offered the volume, accepted it only when the Chicago Grand Opera House agreed to use it as the basis of a stage musical aimed at both children and adults. Although Hill's publishing house went bankrupt before the musical opened in 1902, it was a notable success in Chicago, in New York the following season, and on a nationwide tour. Baum, always restless to explore new fictional worlds, often under different pseudonyms, was in no hurry to continue the series: *The Marvelous Land of Oz* appeared only in 1904, and its successor, *Ozma of Oz,* in 1907. Like Conan Doyle, the author repeatedly expressed his desire to be done with his most popular creation, most emphatically in chapter 29 of *The Emerald City of Oz* (1910), in which the good witch Glinda makes Oz invisible to the rest of the world, and chapter 30, in which Baum's heroine, Dorothy Gale, sends the author a note telling him: "*You will never hear anything more about Oz, because we are now cut off forever from all the rest of the world. But Toto and I will always love you and all the other children who love us.*"[34] Despite all these resolutions, Baum returned to Oz three years later with *The Patchwork Girl of Oz*, a new adventure Dorothy allegedly conveyed to Baum by wireless telegraph,[35] and followed it up with a new installment every year, the last two appearing after his death in 1919.

The Oz books provided perfect material for a silent-film franchise. They took place in a fairyland that was under no pressure to look realistic and featured characters like the Scarecrow, the Tin Woodman, and the Cowardly Lion who could never be compared unfavorably to either real-life or animated prototypes. Most of the early installments were structurally road stories that brought Dorothy, Betsy Bobbin, or Trot and Cap'n Bill from America to Oz by different marvelous means for a series of adventures among variously grotesque creatures—Jack Pumpkinhead, the Wogglebug, the Gump, the Gnome King, the Mangaboos, the Gargoyles, and so on—that could be freely abridged, transformed, or expanded in film adaptations. And since marvelous occurrences were the order of the day, the films offered plentiful opportunities for the kinds of magical attractions driven by visual effects like stop-motion animation, overprinting, and double exposures.

The first surviving Oz film, *The Wonderful Wizard of Oz* (1910), traded on the popularity of the 1902 musical. The one-reel film, written and directed by Otis Turner for Selig Polyscope, was created to fulfill a contractual obligation arising from the bankruptcy into which Baum's investments in multimedia stage presentations had driven him. Its screenplay, based more directly on the musical than on the book, follows its source surprisingly closely even though its thirteen scenes almost all take the form of independent attractions (only three of them include more than one shot) designed to display dance ensembles and magical events whose presumed familiarity is indicated by intertitles like "THE CYCLONE," "THE RUSTY TIN WOODMAN AFTER BEING OILED PROVES GRATEFUL," and "DOROTHY LEARNS THAT WATER IS FATAL TO A WITCH"—the first references the film makes respectively to the cyclone that carries Dorothy to Oz, the Tin Woodman, and Dorothy's name. Like the musical, the film attempts to appeal to both children and adults by including such details as the Wizard's proclamation: "<u>On the level</u>—As a Wizard I'm a <u>humbug</u> and tired of this King business." Later, as a room full of seamstresses toil to make the balloon that will carry the Wizard back home, all work abruptly ceases as a prominently displayed clock strikes twelve and the seamstresses get up and dance in formation, one of them holding a sign that reads "UNION RULES/NO WORK AFTER 12." As the Wizard sits in the completed balloon, he pulls one dove after another from his top hat until the balloon is light enough to rise. The film does cut several events from the play. Although its Scarecrow is still in quest of a brain, the Tin Woodman expresses no desire for a heart or the Cowardly Lion for courage; the first time any of them meet the Wizard is after the death of the witch; and the Wizard's departure in a hot air balloon leaves Dorothy with no apparent way to return home. Even so, her anxiety is only momentary; moments later she is dancing with her friends, presumably because she knows that other sequels are on the way.

The first of these arrived later that same year, the Selig Polyscope productions *Dorothy and the Scarecrow in Oz* and *The Land of Oz*. Because neither of these one-reelers has survived, the next Oz film available to modern audiences is *The Patchwork Girl of Oz* (1914), which J. Farrell MacDonald directed and Baum wrote and produced for the Oz Film Company, which he had recently launched. Far from backing away from Oz, as he had been determined to do only four years earlier, Baum now moved in the opposite direction, adding to his most recent book's extensive cast Jinjur (Marie Wayne), a maid from *The Marvelous Land of Oz*, and stepping up the magic in the final scene, which followed the book in showing the Wizard restoring to life Unc Nunkie (Frank Moore) and Margolotte (Leontine Dranet), frozen into marble statues when the antics of the Patchwork Girl, whom Margolotte's husband, Dr. Pipt (Raymond Russell), had miraculously brought to life as a servant for his wife, upset a bottle of petrifying liquid from Dr. Pipt's shelf. Unlike the book, however, the film prepared for this climactic scene by suddenly and magically transporting the statues from Dr. Pipt's home to the Emerald City and having the Wizard restore a third petrified character added to the book, Danx (Richard Rosson), the sweetheart of Dr. Pipt's daughter Jesseva (Bobbie Gould), from the miniature size to which Dr. Pipt has shrunk him to allow Jesseva to take him with her as she and Unc Nunkie's nephew, Ojo the Lucky (Violet MacMillan), travel around Oz seeking the ingredients for the spell that will bring their loved ones back to life. These individual changes, however, are less important than a small but consistent visual feature in the film's intertitles, each of which is surmounted by a stylized Z inside a capital O. Baum, who had already created the worlds of Mo and Ix alongside Oz, was acutely sensitive to the possibilities of branding, and the repeated symbol that combines the two letters of his most famous creation into an even more economical and distinctive icon suggests that the brand *The Patchwork Girl of Oz* is most intent on promoting is not Baum or this particular novel but Oz itself. To the extent that the film is concerned with fidelity, it is fidelity to the larger trajectory of the book and the character of specific scenes and adventures—for example, the composition of its final shot, in which Ojo joyfully hugs

Unc Nunkie, closely follows that of John R. Neill's final illustration for the book—not the questions of who is having those adventures or of what their place is in the story's narrative.

Baum's inability to decide whether it was more important to present his film as displaying a familiar fantasyland or telling a new story, along with his continuing attempt to walk the fine line that would allow his film to appeal to both children and adults—it is one of the few Oz films with a romantic interest, something Baum thought children would find unappealing or boring— may have contributed to the film's failure at the box office. Whatever the reason, his next project, *The Magic Cloak of Oz* (1914), doubled down on his ambition to turn Oz into a durable franchise. A year earlier, Baum had finally brought to the stage his long-delayed adaptation of *Ozma of Oz*. When *The Tik-Tok Man of Oz* proved not successful enough to transfer from Los Angeles to Broadway, Baum thriftily repurposed some of its leading incidents in his book *Tik-Tok of Oz* (1914), although his introductory note warned young readers: "There is a play called 'The Tik-Tok Man of Oz,' but it is not like this story of 'Tik-Tok of Oz,' even though some of the adventures recorded in this book, as well as those in several other Oz books, are included in the play."[36] Baum would continue to struggle with the problem at the heart of all franchises, the need to retain enough older elements to hold the interest of established fans while introducing enough new elements to win new ones and keep up the enthusiasm of the old, in the two remaining films in which he returned to Oz before his death.

Despite its title, the source for *The Magic Cloak of Oz* is another Baum fairy tale, *Queen Zixi of Ix* (1905), which takes place in a completely different place (and not, for the most part, in Ix either). The five-reel film was split into two two-reelers, *The Magic Cloak* and *The Witch Queen*, for its first English release, and some ambiguity has remained ever since about its correct title. The only allusions surviving prints of the film make to Oz apart from its title are a reference to fairies of Burzee as "Fairies of Oz" in the film's third intertitle and the appearance of the Oz logo on a bell the fairies toll to summon the Fairy Messenger to take the cloak to the most unhappy person she can find. The film establishes its affinities to the franchise in other ways. It is once again written by Baum and directed by J. Farrell MacDonald. Violet MacMillan, who had played Ojo the Lucky in *The Patchwork Girl of Oz*, once again crosses gender lines to play Bud, the boy who is chosen as King of Noland because he is the forty-seventh person to enter the town after the old king dies. And Fred Woodward, who had played both the Woozy, an animal whose body seems to have been constructed almost entirely of boxes, and Mewel, a donkey who does not appear in Baum's book *The Patchwork Girl of Oz*, returns to play Bud's donkey, now given the name Nickodemus, a great deal of screen time, and a major role in developing the plot (see Figure 2.7).

FIGURE 2.7 *The Cowardly Lion greets the donkey Nickodemus in* The Magic Cloak of Oz *(1914).*

Following the sequence in which the fairies weave a magic cloak that will grant one wish to each person who wears it, Bud and his sister Fluff (Mildred Harris) pose separately in front of angled mirrors that display different views of them to the audience. A similar third shot introduces Nickodemus, shaking his head slowly back and forth as if he knows how much more important he will be in the film. And when Nickodemus is captured by robbers who play jacks, he takes the lead in organizing half a dozen other animals—an elephant, a tiger, an alligator, a kangaroo, an enormous crow, a Woozy, and a Zoop—to "lick the stuffing out of those robbers" and rescue Mary, a girl they have already kidnapped. The film is rich in individual attractions. Its opening scene presents the fairies dancing in spectral double-exposure against a woodland background. The prevision Bud and Fluff's Aunt Rivette has of their father's drowning, which will orphan them, is shown in a vividly immediate split screen. When Aunt Rivette offers to beat the Fairy Messenger who gives Fluff the magic cloak with a switch, the Messenger magically disappears. The trappings of the court to which Bud and Fluff are introduced are sumptuous.

When Queen Zixi, who at 683 years old looks ravishingly young to everyone but herself, is shown peering into a mirror, her aged self peers back at her, motivating her determination to steal the cloak so that she can be granted the wish of looking equally young and beautiful to herself. After a seamstress to whom Zixi has given the cloak when it will not grant her wish because she has stolen it cuts it into pieces, a stop-motion shot shows the pieces magically reassembled into a cloak that will allow its wearer to repel an invasion by the Rolly Rogues, balloon-shaped marauders who have rolled down the hill from their own home in search of "a new kind of soup." The Rolly Rogues' retreat is indicated by a shot run backwards that shows them all rolling back uphill. And Nickodemus adds acrobatics, resourcefulness, and good humor to every scene in which he appears. Although it includes only a few bits likely to have aimed at adults, the film seems to have every other ingredient that would make it a successful installment of the Oz franchise except for Oz.

The last Oz film Baum produced, *His Majesty, the Scarecrow of Oz* (1914), re-released a year later as *The New Wizard of Oz*, is in some ways the ultimate franchise installment. From its opening two shots, a disembodied close-up of Princess Ozma looking into the camera and smiling, just as she had done in introducing *The Patchwork Girl of Oz,* and a main title indicating that the film has been released by Oz Productions, to its last two shots, the first repeating this opening shot, the second announcing "The End" under the Oz logo—the only intertitle in surviving prints to display this logo—it proclaims its membership in the franchise. Yet the film is based on an original screenplay which Baum in turn used as the basis for his 1915 book *The Scarecrow of Oz,* which thus became one of the very first novelizations of an earlier film. Violet McMillan returns, this time playing Dorothy, along with Raymond Russell, Mildred Harris, and Fred Woodward, who is billed as playing the Cowardly Lion, the Kangaroo, the Crow, the Cow, and the Mule, although his presence must have been supplemented in group shots of these animals. Of these, the Cow is evidently borrowed from the 1902 musical and the 1910 film *The Wonderful Wizard of Oz,* and the Mule is readily recognizable as Nickodemus, though Bud and Fluff are nowhere to be seen.

On the one hand, Baum seems to revel in the opportunity to raid his earlier stories for novel elements, from Button-Bright (Mildred Harris), a young boy who had appeared in *The Road to Oz* (1909) and the non-Oz adventure *Sky Island* (1912), to the Zoop, who is shown battling the Cowardly Lion in the Lion's first appearance. On the other hand, it goes out of its way to introduce a new creation story for the Scarecrow, who is now fashioned by a farmer for the first time and brought to magical life by the Spirit of the Corn, and to show the Tin Woodman once again rusted into paralysis in his opening shot, ready to be oiled by the Scarecrow, Dorothy, and Button-Bright. The film's apparent uncertainty over whether its audience will regard the leading characteristics and relationships of its franchise attractions as new or familiar is echoed by its uncertain tone. Perhaps because it was conceived from the beginning as a film rather than a children's book, *His Majesty, the Scarecrow of Oz* promotes the romantic subplot that had been added to the film adaptation of *The Patchwork Girl of Oz* to center stage. Its story is organized around the travails of Princess Gloria (Vivian Reed), whose guardian King Krewl

(Raymond Russell) wants her to marry his courtier Googly-goo (Arthur Smollet), and Pon (Todd Wright), the gardener's son she loves instead. When the king engages the witch Mombi (Mai Wells) to separate the lovers, she responds by freezing Gloria's heart in a striking shot that presents the heart fading into the hand Mombi has outstretched in front of Gloria's breast, freezing over, and then fading out. As soon as he sees her, "the Scarecrow falls in love with Gloria and tries to melt her frozen heart," and later, "the Tin Woodman's heart is captured by the Princess." None of this super-cooled romance is resolved by the Scarecrow's proposal to conquer King Krewl and make Gloria queen because the film is more interested in dramatizing the adventures the would-be conquerors have on their way to the battle than in showing either the battle itself, which is remarkably perfunctory, the unfreezing of the Princess's heart, a striking visual inversion of the original freezing that now seems effortless, or the reunion of the weightless romantic leads, who are much less interesting than the franchise characters who have been shunted into supporting roles. Given the film's failure to appeal to adult audiences without diluting its appeal to children, to meld attractions and narrative, and to integrate new scripts into the established franchise it continues to monstrate, it is not surprising that there were no new Oz movies until Larry Semon's slapstick version of *The Wizard of Oz* in 1925.

Outside the franchise box

Filmmakers who sought projects outside established franchises courted even greater risks than Baum and his collaborators, for the need to purchase film rights to successful literary and theatrical properties made adaptation a much riskier gamble than it had been just a few years earlier. Although pioneering narrative filmmaker Alice Guy-Blaché's *Falling Leaves* (1912) borrowed its central conceit—a central figure intent on preventing the death of an ailing young woman who has decided that she will die when the last leaf falls from a tree outside her window takes unusual measures to prevent the last leaf from falling—from O. Henry's 1907 story "The Last Leaf," the film treated its story too freely to require either payment or a formal acknowledgment of its source. By contrast, Mack Sennett's decision to make *Tillie's Nightmare,* the 1910 Broadway comedy with music by A. Baldwin Sloane and a book and lyrics by Edgar Smith, was daring not only because the film would be the first feature-length comedy in Hollywood history, but because the rights themselves would push the budget over $200,000. Marie Dressler, who played the lead in *Tillie's Nightmare,* was an established Broadway star with scant respect for moving pictures who consented to make her film debut only when Sennett offered her a salary of $2,500 a week to join Mabel Normand and Charlie Chaplin, also making his feature-film debut, in the project that became *Tillie's Punctured Romance* (1914). Nor did Sennett's troubles end when he signed Dressler, for the film's unusual length made theater owners reluctant to book it, and after it languished for three months between its completion in June and its first booking in September, Dressler, fearing that she would never be paid, launched the first of two lawsuits against Sennett and Keystone Pictures, ultimately accepting a $50,000 settlement and a five-year ownership of the film's negative. Luckily for Keystone, *The Face on the Barroom Floor,* in which Chaplin had directed himself earlier that year, was a burlesque satire rather than a straightforward adaptation of Hugh Antoine d'Arcy's sentimental poem in which a once successful artist fallen into the gutter explains how his love for Madeline, a beautiful model who left him for another of his sitters, proved to be his undoing. The film quoted variously altered passages from d'Arcy's poem throughout its one-reel length, the most striking of which was the final word it added to the poem's last two lines, which accompany the ridiculously childish drawing of Madeline that Chaplin draws on the barroom floor (see Figure 2.8):

> Then, as he placed another lock
> Upon the shapely head,
> With a fearful shriek he fell across
> The picture dead ... drunk

FIGURE 2.8 *Charlie Chaplin's heartbroken artist displays his grief by executing a comically amateurish drawing of his lost love in* The Face on the Barroom Floor *(1914).*

Despite its extensive and explicit borrowings from the poem and its surprising lack of the consistently broad humor Chaplin's audience had already come to expect, the film's status as a parody saves it from both the obligation to purchase the adaptation rights from the poem's author and any possibility of literal monstration of his poem.

Although Sennett is best remembered for his comedies featuring the Keystone Cops and his extended chase finales, he was also fond of the self-reflexivity the movies licensed, and his films *A Movie Star* (1910), *Mabel's Dramatic Career* (1913), and *A Film Johnny* (1914) continue the tradition of self-reflexivity whose most celebrated example is *Those Awful Hats* (1909), a three-minute curtain-raiser D.W. Griffith made warning female moviegoers that if their headgear obstructed the view of other audience members, they might face surrealistic consequences. *Those Awful Hats* offers clear evidence of Griffith's increasingly double awareness of his films' status as both monstrations and narratives—an awareness at the heart of his most celebrated short adaptations. Griffith has frequently and justly been hailed for his mastery of technical innovations—close-ups, iris shots, crosscutting, accelerated editing, and parallel editing—and his cultivation, in collaboration with performers like Blanche Sweet, Lillian Gish, and Mary Pickford, of a new style of cinematic performance that tempered heightened expressiveness with understated naturalism. Without meaning to abate these encomiums, it could be argued that Griffith's success was as much an effect as a cause of the rapid evolution of film narrative because he came on the scene at exactly the moment the industry most needed these very specific gifts.

A Corner in Wheat (1909), Griffith's fourteen-minute adaptation of Frank Norris's novel *The Octopus* (1901), presents only a small number of scenes from Norris's novel, the first installment in the trilogy *The Epic of the Wheat*, whose focus on the economic problems involved in raising the wheat crop was to be supplemented by an equally remorseless anatomy of the commodities trading that manipulated the price of wheat in *The Pit* (1902) and an examination of the marketing and consumption of the wheat in the unwritten *The Wolf*. It borrows little of Norris's plot and presents only one memorable character, the Wheat King (Frank Powell), whose success at cornering the market in wheat, which leads to disaster for poor customers who can no longer afford a loaf of bread, is capped by a climactic sequence, modeled closely on the last chapter in *The Octopus,* in which the Wheat King, having accidentally fallen into a storage container, is gradually suffocated by the commodity he foolishly sought to control. Even so, *A Corner in Wheat* is indeed "an epic built on an epic."[37] The *New York Dramatic Mirror,* in its review of the film—the first review of any film by any New York newspaper—hailed it as "not a picture drama" but "an argument, an editorial, an essay on a subject of deep interest to us all."[38]

A Corner in Wheat integrates its most notable attractions—the Wheat King's frenzied celebration of his success in cornering the market, the before-and-after shots in a general store that show the disastrous effects of his monopoly on the poor, the paired shots echoing Jean-François Millet's 1850 painting *The Sower* that bookend the film by claiming a transcendental timelessness for the job of sowing the wheat even as the solitary sower in the final shot portends its historical decline—into a structure that depends less on narrative than on polemical argument. As a piece of entertainment, the film, as the *New York Dramatic Mirror* recognized, was an outlier on its first release and remains one now, less like *Places in the Heart* (1984) than like *An Inconvenient Truth* (2006) and *The Big Short* (2015). Griffith's equal mastery of more traditional ways of integrating monstration with narrative is displayed in *Ramona* (1910).

Ramona, which announces itself as "The Story of the White Man's Injustice to the Indian," echoes Helen Hunt Jackson's 1884 novel, still widely known in 1910, in showing the calamitous consequences of the Mexican-American community's resistance in mid-nineteenth-century California to the romance between Ramona (Mary Pickford) and Alessandro (Henry B. Walthall), the Native American who has been instantly smitten with her and whose love she comes to return, rejecting the more widely approved Mexican suitor Felipe (Francis J. Grandon). When she discovers that she herself is partly of Native American blood, Ramona agrees to elope with Alessandro, and the rest of the film traces the tragic outcome of a romance whose leitmotif, made explicit in intertitles given to two different characters in two different scenes, is "THIS LAND BELONGS TO US." After white settlers destroy Alessandro's village, the couple wander from place to place, never allowed to remain anywhere for long before they are dispossessed by incoming citizens of the United States. Eventually the death of their infant daughter drives Alessandro to madness, and he is casually shot to death by yet another settler who sees him as a possible threat. Like *A Corner in Wheat,* the film offers its story in evidence of the polemical claim advanced by its subtitle.

At the same time, the film is first and last a far more intimate story of two distinctive individuals than *A Corner in Wheat* ever is. Although neither Pickford nor Walthall is an obvious choice to represent the ethnicities of the characters they play, they are both capable of understated gestures—Alessandro's gently stoic guitar playing, Ramona's shy smiles when he is not looking at her—that establish a deeper emotional interest in their dilemma than any of Baum's Oz films seek to do even when they present lovers like Pon and Princess Gloria whose straits are equally dire. When the film announces, "RAMONA THROWS HER WORLD AWAY FOR THE NOW PENNILESS ALESSANDRO," it displays the following scene both thematically as an effect of unjust discrimination and emotionally as a soulful revelation of the depth of these particular characters' feelings.

To the union of sentimentally doomed romance and rearguard social polemic, an amalgam recycled countless times in later films, *Ramona* adds a third monstration announced by its opening intertitle: its production at

Camulos, a location in California's Ventura County where Jackson had set the opening scenes of her novel (see Figure 2.9). At first the exterior backgrounds that are featured in nearly every shot seem purely functional. As Ramona and Alessandro are driven further and further to the edge of civilization, however, the backgrounds assume a grandeur that compensates visually for the increasing scarcity of other characters even as they imply an elemental dimension to the couple's plight. Unlike the visual attractions in the Oz films, the backdrops in *Ramona,* however breathtaking, never threaten to overwhelm the characters but serve instead to amplify and ennoble their suffering. The film provides a blueprint for the integration of visual attractions, polemical arguments, and intimately focused narratives.

To this widely imitated formula Griffith added still another element in *The Avenging Conscience, or "Thou Shalt Not Kill"* (1914), a loose adaptation of Poe's story "The Tell-Tale Heart." Griffith had already tackled Poe in two earlier films. *The Sealed Room* (1909) was an even freer adaptation of "The Cask of Amontillado" whose historical period, cast of characters, and primary motivations were all changed, leaving only Poe's central situation, a man's decision to seek revenge on someone he feels has wronged him by

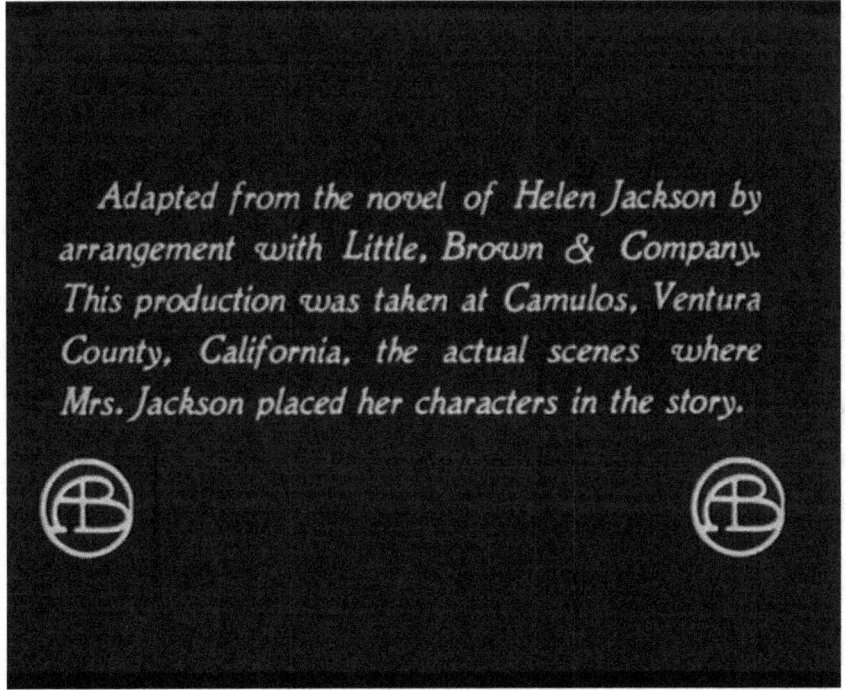

FIGURE 2.9 Ramona *(1910) directs attention to the scripts provided by both its literary source and its geographic locations.*

walling up his target (two targets, the adulterous lovers, in Griffith's film) alive in a sealed chamber. And *Edgar Allen Poe* (1909), which had misspelled its subject's middle name in its rush into release in time to commemorate the centennial of his birth, had freely mingled a pathetic account of Poe's composition and sale of "The Raven," his most famous work during his lifetime, with the decline and death of his wife Virginia. *The Avenging Conscience,* though no more faithful to Poe than these earlier films, charted new territory for Griffith and film adaptation generally.

From early on, Griffith establishes his film as both a monstration and an adaptation of Poe's story about a man who plots and executes the murder of an older man who shares lodgings with him and then suffers the consequences. Immediately after Griffith's antihero, the Nephew (Henry B. Walthall), is shown reading the opening page of Poe's story and looking at a photographic portrait of Poe, the film presents in an intertitle the first of four excerpts from Poe's poem "Annabel Lee," an obvious inspiration for the Nephew's attachment to the Sweetheart, "she whom you have chosen to call Annabel" (Blanche Sweet), which will be scattered through the film together with passages from "To One in Paradise," marking the film as both an adaptation and a meta-adaptation, the story of a fictional character consciously inspired by Poe's writings even when the course of his own crime departs from them.

In a signature passage, Poe's narrator emphasizes the absence of any rational motive for his crime: "Object there was none. Passion there was none. I loved the old man. He had never wronged me. He had never given me insult. For his gold I had no desire. I think it was his eye! yes, it was this!"[39] The Nephew, by contrast, has abundant motive for killing the Uncle (Spottiswoode Aitken), who disapproves so strongly of his romance with the Sweetheart that the two agree to part, setting the stage for the film's pivotal sequence, in which the Nephew sits alone reflecting on his grievance. After an intertitle announces, "THE BIRTH OF THE EVIL THOUGHT. Nature one long system of murder—the spider, the fly, the ants," the Nephew smiles as he watches a murderous spider and some despoiling ants, all shown in greatly magnified close-ups. The intertitle is both portentous and expository: audiences would probably have been hard-pressed to tease out the import of the visuals without it. As the Nephew enters the Uncle's office, another intertitle indicates his "REALIZATION THAT HIS UNCLE, ON WHOM HE IS DEPENDENT, STANDS BETWEEN HIM AND HAPPINESS." With this, the Nephew, recalling the spider feasting on a fly, sits in the Uncle's chair and falls asleep as the scene dissolves to a parallel shot of the Sweetheart weeping in her bed. Hatching a plan to kill the Uncle after he has returned unobserved to his home from a bogus rendezvous the Nephew has arranged, the Nephew, introduced by the now more purely metaphorical intertitle "THE SPIDER AND THE FLY," watches the Uncle dozing and finds that unlike Poe's narrator, he cannot kill him. It is not until the Uncle awakens and refuses his request for money that the two grapple and the Nephew strangles the Uncle, observed, though he does not yet realize this, by the Italian (George Siegmann), who watches the unfolding scene through a window. Agreeing after his initial resistance to submit to the Italian's blackmail, the Nephew sets about "CONCEALING THE BODY IN THE WALL OF THE OLD FIREPLACE," leaving "EACH BRICK SO CUNNINGLY REPLACED THAT NO HUMAN EYE CAN DETECT THE FRAUD," a pair of intertitles that combine the central situation of "The Cask of Amontillado" with echoes of the narrator's language in "The Black Cat."

What is most notable about the imagery of the spider and the fly is not its subtlety or originality but its single-minded determination to indicate in considerable detail the mental processes that drive the Nephew to murder the Uncle he loves. Nowhere in Griffith's earlier work is there such emphasis on the cinematic representation of mental states, particularly the psychopathology that infects the heretofore law-abiding and easily bullied Nephew. Griffith chooses this imagery not because it is necessary to explain the character's change of heart but because it displays his psychological development as an attraction quite apart from the murderous action to which it leads.

The film continues its revisionist departures from "The Tell-Tale Heart" with deepening engagement with what might called the spirit of Poe in its second signature sequence. The Nephew, returning from an open field in which, like Poe's narrator, "I saw all things on heaven and earth. I saw many things in hell," including in this case a vision of Moses unveiling the law, "Thou shalt not kill," returns to the Uncle's office, now his own, and a vision of the crucified Christ. Questioned by a detective (Ralph Lewis) suspicious of the Uncle's disappearance, he finds the detective's tapping pencil "LIKE THE BEATING OF THE DEAD MAN'S HEART," an abrupt analogy prepared only by repeated close-ups of the clock's pendulum and the Nephew twiddling his thumbs. The detective's tapping foot agitates him even more. So does an owl he hears outside, prompting two new intertitles: "CONSCIENCE OVERBURDENS THE TELL-TALE HEART" and a passage from Poe's poem "The Bells": "They are neither man nor woman;/ They are neither brute nor human;/They are ghouls!" (see Figure 2.10) Overwhelmed by guilt, the Nephew vainly attempts to escape and then, alerting the approaching Sweetheart to his danger, attempts to hang himself as she runs to a rocky seacoast and throws herself from a high cliff into the water. A sudden return to the Nephew sitting once more in the office chair reveals that he has dreamed the murder and its consequences. In a more agreeable postlude the nephew reads to the Sweetheart from "his successful book" a passage presumably inspired by Poe—"In your voice I hear Pan playing in the woods and all the world gives heed"—introducing an amusingly literal shot of Pan himself playing his pipes, summoning costumed children, jungle cats, and rabbits around him. The film ends with one last quotation from "Annabel Lee"—"And neither the angels in heaven

FIGURE 2.10 *Questioned by a detective (Ralph Lewis), the Nephew (Henry B. Walthall) involuntarily recalls his murder of his Uncle (Spottiswoode Aitken) in* The Avenging Conscience *(1914).*

above,/Nor the demons down under the sea,/Can ever dissever my soul from the soul/Of the beautiful Annabel Lee"—while reversing its force, since the lines now celebrate the union of the Nephew and the Sweetheart instead of providing an elegiac memorial of her death.

Instead of following Poe's story beat by beat, *The Avenging Conscience* creates a fantasia on a selection of images, narrative motifs, and the themes that it draws from the story only to withdraw from Poe's nightmare world by displaying it frankly as the basis for the Nephew's transformation into a latter-day Poe endowed with similar gifts but purged of the nightmares that gave them birth. The film is no model of performance: Henry B. Walthall is so consistently exaggerated in his torment that it is hard to see how he gets away with murder for so long, even in a dream. But it is an exemplary model of how stories were adapted to the cinema in the period after 1909. Instead of committing themselves to a single, sustained, coherent narrative, these films combined immersion and monstration, attractions and integration, narrative and meta-narrative in ways that could vary dramatically from one film to the next. The reason Griffith is not best remembered for films like *The Avenging Conscience* is because his most unforgettable adaptation lay ahead.

Notes

1. Tom Gunning, "The Cinema of Attraction: Early Film, Its Spectator, and the Avant-Garde," *Wide Angle* 8.3 (1986): 64.
2. Tom Gunning, "'Primitive' Cinema—A Frame-up? or The Trick's on Us," *Cinema Journal* 28.2 (Winter 1989): 8.
3. Raymond Chandler, "Introduction to *The Simple Art of Murder*," in Chandler, *Later Novels and Other Writings* (New York: Library of America, 1995), p. 1017.
4. Tom Gunning, "An Aesthetic of Astonishment: Early Film and the (In)credulous Spectator" (1989); rpt. in *Viewing Positions: Ways of Seeing Film*, ed. Linda Williams (New Brunswick, NJ: Rutgers University Press, 1995), p. 117.
5. Gunning, "An Aesthetic of Astonishment," p. 117.
6. Gunning, "The Cinema of Attraction," pp. 65–66.
7. Linda Hutcheon, with Siobhan O'Flynn, *A Theory of Adaptation*, 2nd ed. (New York: Routledge, 2013), pp. 120–21.
8. Victor Raskin, "Semantic Mechanisms of Humor," *Proceedings of the Fifth Annual Meeting of the Berkeley Linguistics Society* (1979): 325.
9. Kathleen Murray, "*To Have and Have Not*: An Adaptive System," in *True to the Spirit: Film Adaptation and the Question of Fidelity*, ed. Colin MacCabe, Kathleen Murray, and Rick Warner (New York: Oxford University Press, 2011), p. 111.
10. Jack Boozer, "Introduction: The Screenplay and Authorship in Adaptation," in *Authorship in Film Adaptation* (Austin: University of Texas Press, 2008), p. 4.
11. Kyle Meikle, "Phenomenal Adaptations," University of Delaware dissertation, 2015, p. 69.
12. I first used the word "display" in this sense in *What Stories Are: Narrative Theory and Interpretation* (University Park: Pennsylvania State University Press, 1986), pp. 26–41, and continue to use it because it is more idiomatic than "monstration," particularly when used as a verb ("to display" versus "to monstrate"). Throughout this book I will use the two terms more or less interchangeably, usually reserving "monstration" to emphasize either unexpected instances of display or instances that present what they display as something monstrous.
13. Gunning, "An Aesthetic of Astonishment," p. 120.
14. Anon, Review of *After Many Years*, *Moving Picture World* 3.19 (November 7, 1908): 364.
15. Anon, Review of *Puss in Boots*, *Moving Picture World* 3.20 (November 14, 1908): 408.
16. Anon, Review of *L'Arlesienne*, *Moving Picture World* 3.22 (November 28, 1908): 433.
17. Anon, "Dickens in Pictures," *Moving Picture World* 3.22 (November 28, 1908): 431.
18. Anon, Review of *The Face on the Barroom Floor*, *Moving Picture World* 3.4 (July 25, 1908): 67.

19 Anon, Review of *For the Love of Gold*, *Moving Picture World* 3.8 (August 22, 1908): 142.

20 Anon, Review of *The Lady or the Tiger*, *Moving Picture World* 3.22 (November 28, 1908): 430.

21 Judith A. Eldridge, *James Oliver Curwood: God's Country and the Man* (Bowling Green: Bowling Green State University Popular Press, 1993), p. 2.

22 These statistics, and those in the following two paragraphs, are drawn from Denis Gifford, *Books and Plays in Film 1896–1915: Literary, Theatrical and Artistic Sources of the First Twenty Years of Motion Pictures* (London: Mansell, 1991), and the Internet Movie Database (imdb.com).

23 Brian McFarlane, *Novel to Film: An Introduction to the Theory of Adaptation* (Oxford: Clarendon Press, 1996), p. 13.

24 Renata Kobetts Miller, "Nineteenth-Century Theatrical Adaptations of Novels: The Paradox of Ephemerality," in *The Oxford Handbook of Adaptation Studies*, ed. Thomas Leitch (New York: Oxford University Press, 2017), p. 60.

25 Sarah Meer, *Uncle Tom Mania: Slavery, Minstrelsy and Transatlantic Culture in the 1850s* (Athens: University of Georgia Press, 2005), p. 10.

26 Harriet Beecher Stowe, *Uncle Tom's Cabin; or, Life among the Lowly*, in Stowe, *Three Novels* (New York: Library of America, 1982), pp. 278–79.

27 Julie Grossman, *Literature, Film, and Their Hideous Progeny: Adaptation and ElasTEXTity* (Houndmills: Palgrave Macmillan, 2015), p. 2.

28 Charles Musser, commentary on *Life of an American Policeman* (1905), *Edison: The Invention of the Movies*, Kino DVD, 2005.

29 Peter Decherney, *Hollywood's Copyright Wars: From Edison to the Internet* (New York: Columbia University Press, 2012), pp. 48, 49.

30 Decherney, *Hollywood's Copyright Wars*, p. 54.

31 Frances Taylor Patterson, *Cinema Craftsmanship: A Book for Photoplaywrights* (New York: Harcourt, Brace and Howe, 1920), p. 81.

32 Decherney, *Hollywood's Copyright Wars*, pp. 56, 55.

33 Anon. "Review of *Uncle Tom's Cabin*." *Moving Picture World* 7.6 (August 6, 1910): 298.

34 L. Frank Baum, *The Emerald City of Oz* (Chicago, IL: Reilly & Lee, 1910), p. 295.

35 L. Frank Baum, *The Patchwork Girl of Oz* (Chicago, IL: Reilly & Lee, 1913), p. 15.

36 L. Frank Baum, *Tik-Tok of Oz* (Chicago, IL: Reilly & Lee, 1914), p. 9.

37 Thomas Leitch, *Film Adaptation and Its Discontents: From Gone with the Wind to The Passion of the Christ* (Baltimore, MD: Johns Hopkins University Press, 2007), p. 36.

38 Quoted in Tom Gunning, *D.W. Griffith and the Origins of American Narrative Film: The Early Years at Biograph* (Urbana: University of Illinois Press, 1991), p. 241.

39 Edgar Allan Poe, *Poetry and Tales* (New York: Library of America, 1984), p. 555.

3

1915–27: American Exotics

Familiar yet foreign

The Birth of a Nation changed the game for Hollywood. The costly production of D.W. Griffith's Civil War epic, the film's extraordinary length, its ambitious scope, its status as a road show blockbuster, and its ticket prices, which topped out at $2.00, were all unprecedented developments that signaled, even for audiences who rejected the millennialist implications of its title, a new day in the history of American film. Ever since the film's release on March 21, 1915, commentators have united in praising its masterful use of technical innovations like crosscutting, iris-ins, and chiaroscuro lighting and condemning its racist casting of white performers as either villainous Negroes or the Uncle Toms who were condescendingly set against them, its presentation of newly freed slaves as incompetent lawmakers and scheming rapists, and its horror of miscegenation in particular and of ceding power more generally in Reconstruction Piedmont, South Carolina, to carpetbaggers, African Americans, or the invading Union Army. Indeed the film's reputation has largely depended over the years on the status of debates weighing its technical achievements against its racism, and in particular against its historic role in reviving the moribund Ku Klux Klan through its idealistic portrayal of Ben Cameron (Henry B. Walthall) and his friends in the Klan as defenders of Southern womanhood and saviors of Southern identity.

What is largely overlooked in these debates is the film's status as an adaptation that seeks to monstrate two overlapping but quite distinct scripts: a specific literary text and an equally specific view of American culture. Everyone acknowledges that in *The Birth of a Nation* Griffith and Frank E. Woods adapt Thomas F. Dixon Jr.'s 1905 novel *The Clansman: An Historical Romance of the Ku Klux Klan*, but the identification of Griffith's epic with Dixon's novel typically ends the discussion instead of beginning it. *The Clansman* was the second novel of a trilogy that had begun with *The Leopard's Spots: A Romance of the White Man's Burden—1865-1900*

(1902) and concluded with *The Traitor: A Story of the Fall of the Invisible Empire* (1907). The other two novels, dealing with completely different characters than the two families—the Northern Stonemans and the Southern Camerons—who anchored *The Clansman,* have faded into obscurity; only *The Clansman,* fueled first by Dixon's own theatrical adaptation, which incorporated some characters and events from the other two novels, and Griffith's film have retained a place in the American consciousness.

That place is distinguished by Dixon's presentation of the Klan as vigilante dispensers of summary justice who violently and routinely avenged the rape of white women by newly freed slaves and cowed the freedmen into abjuring any power they might have wielded at the ballot box. Griffith, a native of Kentucky, was drawn to Dixon's portrayal of slavery as paternalistic and benign, the social order of the Old South as gracious and kindly, the Reconstruction imposed on the region after the "War between the States" as a disastrous threat to its racial purity and female-centered domestic values, and the Klan as a necessary force to reclaim rights former slaveowners were in danger of losing to Northern interlopers and their own former chattel. Griffith softens Dixon's anti-Negro presentation, invents "faithful souls" to counterbalance Dixon's villains, rejects Dixon's championing of Southern white-collar heroes, valorizes the myth of Southern cavaliers, and makes Dixon's Klan less bureaucratic and ritualistic: "Like the Confederate Army, Griffith's Ku Klux Klan is a folk organization, spontaneously organized and easily run."[1] In addition, Griffith rejects Dixon's view of millenialist conflict as a necessary prelude to the rebirth of the United States, instead suggesting in an opening intertitle: "If in this work we have conveyed to the mind the ravages of war to the end that war may be held in abhorrence, this effort will not have been in vain." In short, Griffith muddles, softens, and betrays Dixon's historical analysis and call to arms; what is notable is the dramatic ways in which he "illustrates"[2] it (see Figure 3.1). So it is particularly ironic that the film, originally scheduled for release as *The Clansman,* was retitled at Dixon's own suggestion,[3] since the birth it foretells of a nation that has forsworn civil war and its aftermath is both the same and different from the rebirth Dixon urged of a world of white purity and privilege.

The questions of what Griffith, who nowhere else in his films advocates racial purity but who often organizes those films around feminine ideals of domesticity, adapted from Dixon, what he modified, and what to make of the results continue to be hotly debated. But in fact the film, widely condemned at the time of its release by the National Association for the Advancement of Colored People, was no more racist than Cecil B. DeMille's *The Cheat,* released later that same year, which trades on exactly the same central paranoia: the fear of a society in which white women can be ravished by non-white men. Apart from the fact that DeMille's film is based on an original screenplay and set in the present day, the main differences between its sexual politics and those of *The Birth of a Nation* are that DeMille's heroine, Edith

FIGURE 3.1 *The Ku Klux Klan prepares to execute summary justice against the would-be rapist Gus (Walter Long) in* The Birth of a Nation *(1915).*

Hardy (Fannie Ward), deliberately, albeit reluctantly, puts herself in the power of Burmese trader Haka Arakau (Sessue Hayakawa) because of her desperate need to borrow $10,000 from him to replace the charitable funds she plundered for a speculative investment when her stockbroker husband Richard (Jack Dean) refused to pay for latest wardrobe bills; that Arakau, originally named Hishiru Tori until his name and nationality were changed for its 1918 re-release following the protests by the Japanese Association of Southern California, that greeted its initial release, was Asian American rather than African American; and that DeMille was much more interested than Griffith in exploring his villain's insinuating sexual appeal. Arakau's natty bowtie, brilliantined hair, and plaid cap make him every inch the ethnic American arriviste. When Edith learns that she has lost her borrowed stake, which a friend had promised to double for her by the next day, she goes into a faint, and Arakau fondles and kisses her unresisting body in a shocking violation of her virtue, which the film conflates with nativist white privilege over members of non-white races, even those as wealthy, polished, and socially successful as Arakau. Unlike the African American characters in *The Birth of a Nation,* who were played by white performers in blackface, Arakau was played by a Japanese-American performer. But *The Cheat* relies just as clearly on the tropes of minstrelsy through its insistence on monstrating its villain as first and foremost an Other, a powerfully threatening non-white character who makes an effective villain precisely because he is not white. The darkly atmospheric scenes in which Edith visits Arakau's home, first to agree to his unspoken conditions for covering her losses and then to pay the price he demands, are shot virtually without fill lights, giving both Arakau and his surroundings a look that is at once defamiliarized, stereotypical, monstrous, and alluring (see Figure 3.2).

The Birth of a Nation and *The Cheat* are both exemplary and revolutionary in their fascination with a new brand of exoticism. From its very beginnings, the cinema had sought different ways to balance the appeal of familiar places and people associated with the Lumière brothers against the appeal of novel stories and sensations most famously displayed in the films of Georges Méliès. The earliest adaptations, with their built-in promise of being both the same and different as their nominal sources, naturally focused and magnified that divided appeal. What is novel and distinctive about the feature films that followed *The Birth of a Nation* and *The Cheat* is their interest in a specifically *American* exotic. To its abiding interest in foreign lands, cultures, and stories, and in tales of the fantastic and exotic, the new cinema that flourishes in the wake of these films displays a keen eye for exotic Americana: hyphenate-Americans whose relationship with other Americans and whose status as Americans are up for debate, regional types that can be presented as both foreign and familiar, plots that reveal forbidden subcultures hiding beneath the surface of American public culture,

FIGURE 3.2 *Edith Hardy (Fannie Ward) seeks desperately to hide her submissive relationship with her creditor Haka Arakau (Sessue Hayakawa) from her socialite friends in* The Cheat *(1915).*

genres that configure their characters and incidents as both outlandish and predictable, and adaptations whose appeal depends both on the familiar elements they borrow from beloved American stories the audience has come to see and the exotic new elements they incorporate into those stories that offer distinctive attractions of their own that both reflect and redefine audiences' assumptions about those familiar stories.

It may seem odd to speak of adding new elements to familiar stories in an industry noted for paring down novels like *The Clansman* to a single evening's entertainment. But many of the feature films that followed *The Birth of a Nation* added material to the texts they adapted, even if they subtracted other material. *Manslaughter* (1922), the last of DeMille's important Jazz Age adaptations before he turned decisively to historical epics, displays this tendency in full flower. The film, based on polemical feminist Alice Duer Miller's 1921 novel, is in many ways a recapitulation of *The Cheat*. Lydia Thorne (Leatrice Joy), a high-living New York socialite who has already attempted to bribe Officer Drummond (Jack Mower), the motorcycle cop who pulled her over for speeding, with a jeweled bracelet, is out joyriding again when Drummond, whose wife has reproached him for accepting the bribe, sees and pursues her, intending to return the bracelet. Assuming that he is after her for speeding again, Lydia deliberately swerves into a tight corner she knows Drummond cannot make, and his motorcycle crashes into the side of her car, throwing him over the car and giving him injuries that lead to his death in the hospital. Lydia, like Edith Hardy, is horrified at the results of her heedless behavior. And her dilemma, like Edith's, is complicated further by the man in her life. Instead of attempting to rescue her from her infamy, as Richard Hardy had done in taking the blame when his wife shot and wounded Arakau, District Attorney Daniel J. O'Bannon (Thomas Meighan) announces his intention to save her from herself by prosecuting her and landing her in prison along with Evans (Lois Wilson), the maid who stole a valuable ring from Lydia when she refused to loan her the money to send her seriously ill son to California. Like *The Cheat, Manslaughter* plunges its heroine into a purgatory marked in this case by the loss of her social status, her groveling acceptance of prison routine, and her estrangement from the man who loves her, whom she angrily dismisses when he visits her in prison. Both films end by showing their heroines' redemption, *The Cheat* by allowing Edith to reveal herself as the person who shot Arakau and justifying her action by partly disrobing in court to show the brand he placed on her shoulder, *Manslaughter* by showing Lydia bonding with Evans, accepting her lot as a prisoner, joining Evans in opening a soup kitchen after her release, and ultimately inspiring O'Bannon, who has resigned his position and hit the bottle after earning plaudits for winning his case against her, to run for governor, a race he concedes at the last minute to avoid compromising his relationship with her. Although it may seem exhaustive, this summary excludes all of the most memorable scenes DeMille added to *Manslaughter*: a wild party at Lydia's home, complete with elaborate costumes, frenzied dancing, and an event for women on pogo sticks, which an intertitle compares to a Roman bacchanal; the even more decadent evocation of a Roman orgy O'Bannon evokes for Lydia's staid jurors during his summary of the case against her; and a later sequence in which O'Bannon imagines dragging Lydia up a flight of stairs during still another orgy. All of these scenes are formally gratuitous—in fact, the second of them is so extended that Lydia's attorney, former Governor Stephan Albee (John Miltern), objects on the grounds that contemporary America is not Imperial Rome (see Figure 3.3)—and it is no wonder that none of them appear in George Abbott's 1930 remake of *Manslaughter*. But they were essential to the film's appeal to its target audience. Even after he switched to biblical epics like *The Ten Commandments* (1923) and *The King of Kings* (1927), DeMille filmed stories of "rote degradation followed by rote moral uplift"[4] that allowed his audiences to wallow in the former before being cleansed by the latter.

Many other silent feature adaptations like *Young Romance,* William deMille's 1915 film adaptation of his own play for director George Melford, delighted in adding new attractions, especially those emphasizing the American exotic, to the familiar stories that provided their armature. *Young Romance*'s ultimate source material is O. Henry's 1904 short story "Transients in Arcadia," but neither it nor deMille's play is mentioned in the credits. O. Henry's story concerns the decorous romance between Madame Héloise D'Arcy Beaumont and Harold Farrington while they are both summer guests in Broadway's Lotus Hotel. The night before they are to leave, Madame Beaumont, thanking Farrington for treating her so

FIGURE 3.3 *The orgy that never happens in* Manslaughter *(1922).*

well, confesses that she is really Mamie Siviter, a shopgirl at the hosiery counter of Casey's Mammoth Store, who has put aside a portion of her wages for a whole year so that she could afford to vacation as an aristocrat, and Farrington responds by unmasking himself as Jimmy McManus, a bill collector for O'Dowd & Levinsky who has had the same idea. When he invites his newly renamed acquaintance, "Say, Mame, how about a trip to Coney Island Saturday night on the boat—what?,"[5] she delightedly accepts.

Following deMille's play, Melford converts O. Henry's characteristic setup of a surprise ending into an extended exercise in dramatic irony. Even before they arrive in Ocean Beach, Maine, the audience knows the plans both Nellie Nolan (Edith Taliaferro) and Tom Clancy (Tom Forman), two salespeople who work in different departments of the same store, have derived from reading the very same magazine serial about an American who, pretending that he is a Duke, has won the love of a Royal Princess: to masquerade as upper-crust guests, Nellie as Ethel Van Dusen of Fifth Avenue, Tom as Roderick de Vignier of Newport. Nellie checks into the Hotel Imperial; Tom, whose budget is tighter, makes do at neighboring no-frills Belleview Mansion. The main force that drives the film's narrative is a series of threats to unmask either or both of them after a meet-cute in which Nellie, lounging on a coastal boulder suddenly surrounded by the incoming tide, is rescued by Tom, who takes her in his arms and carries her to dry land. When wealthy Mr. and Mrs. Jenkins, arriving at the Imperial, recognize Ethel Van Dusen's name and call her on the house telephone to welcome her, she immediately packs her bags, planning to abandon her masquerade, but changes her mind when she realizes that the Jenkinses have not seen Ethel since she was ten years old. The news that Ethel has inherited half a million dollars leads Count Spagnoli (Al Garcia), another Imperial guest who turns out to be just as fraudulent, to kidnap her and strand her on a nearby island until the ransom check he has forced her to write clears the bank. Tom, learning of the plot by spying on Spagnoli, whose room at the Belleview adjoins his own, forces his accomplice to take him to Nellie, rescues her again, and parts from her still in character. It is not until Tom, on his return to work Monday morning, is suddenly promoted to drugs and perfumery and meets Nellie in her true identity that the lovers realize they have been fooled by each other and adjourn to lunch at a nearby tavern.

The film's early revelation of the short story's surprise, which so upends the story that it renders a close comparison of the two texts pointless, allows it to generate a new series of variously comic and melodramatic threats that could, in principle, be extended indefinitely. This series is demarcated not by a surprise ending but by a series of intertitles counting down the time toward the two guests' departure by indicating the days of the week: they arrive on Monday, meet for the first time on Tuesday, and advance inexorably to Friday, when Nellie is kidnapped, Saturday, when she is rescued, Sunday, when they bid each other sad adieux, and Monday, when they are unexpectedly reunited in propria persona. The strategic addition of Count Spagnoli both provides a surprising counterpoint to their masquerade and excuses it, since their aristocratic disguises are innocent of his criminal intent. As he and his accomplice leave a forlorn Nellie behind on the rocky island to which they have lured her, Spagnoli waves his cap to her in faux-gallant gesture that is a perfectly calculated revelation of American exoticism. The gesture, like the film's wholesale reworking of the story's plot, accurately indicates that this adaptation is less interested in American literature than in American national identity. Americans are entitled to take foreign models like Dukes and Royal Princesses as their inspiration, but pretending to be an ethnic non-American is a kind of minstrelsy that crosses a line.

Similar strategies are at work, and at play, in *Salomy Jane,* a 1914 film directed by Lucius Henderson and William Nigh based on Paul Armstrong's theatrical expansion of Bret Harte's short story "Salomy Jane's Kiss." The film's all-American mixture of homeliness and exoticism begins with its compound title, which implicitly compares its Western heroine to both the biblical Salome, who demanded the death of John the Baptist and then kissed the lips of his severed head, and Calamity Jane, the recent memoirist and putative widow of Wild Bill Hickok. Harte's 1898 story begins with a double reversal of the story of Salome. The leader of the vigilante posse who has just captured the horse thief Red Pete and his accomplice Jack Dart suggests that Salomy Jane Clay, who is looking on moments before the two are to be hanged, bid an appropriate farewell to the accomplice. Her kiss of the stranger, given before rather than after his death, brings him not condemnation but renewed vigor and purpose, and he loosens his bonds and escapes the posse on the horse he had stolen from Judge Boompointer. When Jack risks his life to return secretly to Salomy Jane to thank her by giving her the stolen horse, she reciprocates by giving him the coat and hat of her father, Madison Clay, and when he shoots Madison's mortal enemy Phil Larrabee, he is mistaken for Madison, who on the advice of his kinsman takes off on Boompointer's horse after leaving behind a letter disowning his daughter, who he thinks killed Larrabee herself. Hearing of the accusations against Madison, Jack offers to give himself up, but Harte supplies a fairy-tale ending that rescues him and his bride from "lifelong shame and misery."[6]

In his commentary to the DVD release of the film, Gary Scharnhorst notes that its producers, fearing a new version of the lawsuit Harte's estate had successfully filed against Armstrong's play, hired his daughter, Jessamy Harte Steele, as a technical consultant.[7] However much or little the film benefited from Steele's input, it is notable both for the amount of new material it follows Armstrong's play in adding to Harte's twenty-four-page story and for the ways the adaptation alters Harte's take on the American exotic. It adds many other characters, from stagecoach driver Yuba Bill and Baldwin, the seducer who drove the hero's sister to suicide, to pompous Colonel G.L.

Starbottle and the gambler Gentleman Jack Marbury, both recurring figures in Harte's other stories. It multiplies the case of mistaken identity central to Harte's story, in which Jack, wearing Madison's hat and coat, is mistaken for Madison when he kills Madison's sworn enemy, to a dizzying array of mistaken identities that embroil most of the characters and lead to countless accusations and counter-accusations. It gives Red Pete a wife and several children, one of whom becomes instrumental in bringing about one of these false accusations. It indicates that the heroine has been raped before the story begins and that Red Pete is hanged in the middle of the story, though without showing either event, for the film's exoticism is never *that* exotic.

More pointedly, the copious material the film adds to Harte's story, which would be readapted in 1923 and, as *Wild Girl*, in 1932, reframes both the events of the story and its attitude toward its heroine. The first two-thirds of the film, which begins with Madison and Salomy Jane's initial arrival in Hangtown, fills in the backstory for the scene in which Salomy Jane kisses the hero. In the process, it downplays its heroine's links to both her namesakes. Unlike Calamity Jane, the film's Salomy Jane is ultra-feminine rather than tomboyish. She spends much of the film either trying to get her suitors to act in her interests or fighting off their unwanted advances, for example by killing Baldwin after he forcibly kisses her in the woods. She accepts the proposal of Rufe Waters (William Nigh) because she believes his story that he has killed Baldwin but refuses to kiss him, adapting one of the only two lines of dialogue the film borrows from the story to tell him: "I'll kiss you when I know you're going to hang." Whenever she transgresses traditional female roles she is instantly punished. Her attendance at a vigilante meeting Starbottle (Clarence Arper) describes as no place for a woman and her possession of a bangle stolen from the stagecoach get her falsely accused of complicity in the robbery. And grabbing her father's rifle to fend off Rufe's persistent advances after she has rejected him leads the sheriff to accuse her of killing Larabee, whose name is spelled differently than in Harte's story.

The kiss she actually does confer is even less like Salome's monstrously transgressive kiss of John the Baptist than the kiss Harte's heroine gives Jack Dart. Unlike Harte's Salomy Jane, the film's heroine already knows the man she kisses in public two-thirds of the way through the film. He is innocent of the stagecoach robbery of which he is accused but guilty of killing Baldwin after an extended fight, in revenge for Baldwin's having seduced his sister and attacked Salomy Jane. Even though his longer, more intimate earlier relationship with the heroine reverses the transgressive force of her kiss, the hero Harte called Jack Dart remains nameless in the film, whether because calling him Jack Dart instead of simply The Man (House Peters) would indicate his sexuality too openly for the film or whether it would threaten the primacy of the film's star, Beatriz Michelena. So completely was the film intended as a vehicle for Michelena, who was starring in the first of three

Bret Harte adaptations she would headline, that her name appears in every intertitle throughout the film, even those accompanying scenes in which she is not present (see Figure 3.4).

Like many another Western, *Salomy Jane* finds pictorial exoticism in a series of long shots evoking the scenic splendors of Marin County, where it was filmed. Red Pete (William Pike) takes a breathtaking hundred-foot tumble from a mountain trail into the Russian River just before he is captured. The Man and Salomy Jane escape their own pursuers through a redwood forest shot from a majestically high angle. And the film's final long shot frames the lovers against Mount Tamalpais in the background. Even more important, however, is the film's determination to present its heroine and her not-so-transgressive kiss as both familiar and exotic, not the sort of thing audience members would ever do themselves but exactly the sort of thing they would leave the theater dreaming of doing. The film presents itself as a compound of exotica and Americana, defamiliarizing both of these apparently polar opposites by using each of them as a context or metric for the other. In the process, the film treats Harte's story less as a blueprint than as a point of departure, an attraction knowing audiences

FIGURE 3.4 *The name at the bottom of every intertitle in* Salomy Jane *(1914) leaves no doubt what the film considers its principal attraction to be.*

were invited to discover with a shock of pleasurable recognition in this dramatically expanded version that was both the same as the story in its location, leading characters, and central situation and different in almost every other way.

Plundering the archive

Audiences in the 1920s had a very different idea of what constituted American literature than contemporary audiences do. The absence of courses in American literature from college curricula, and indeed the absence of the college experience from most filmgoers, marginalized novelists from Herman Melville to Henry James. Storytellers like Frank Norris, Bret Harte, Mark Twain, and Jack London who have become widely recognized as regional classics had died too recently to be recognized as classics. Famous Players–Lasky filmed *The Great Gatsby* in 1926, only a year after F. Scott Fitzgerald's novel was published, but no prints of the film, as of most silent films, have survived. Most of the winners for the Pulitzer Prize in Drama, an award whose prestige grew only slowly over the first decade it was awarded, had to wait for the arrival of synchronized sound before they were picked up by Hollywood. Early Pulitzer winners the studios passed over included Jesse Lynch William's *Why Marry?*, which won the first award in 1917; Eugene O'Neill's *Beyond the Horizon* (1920), first adapted as a television film in 1959; Hatcher Hughes's *Hell-Bent fer Heaven* (1924); George Kelly's *Craig's Wife* (1926), first filmed ten years later; and Paul Green's *In Abraham's Bosom* (1927). The 1924 film adaptation of Owen Davis's *Icebound* has been lost. So has *The Secret Hour*, the 1928 adaptation of Sidney Howard's *They Knew What They Wanted* (1925), filmed again as *A Lady to Love* (1930) and once more under its original title in 1940—a property that came into its own only a generation later when it served as the basis for Frank Loesser's 1956 Broadway musical *The Most Happy Fella*. The only early Pulitzer Prize-winning plays whose silent film adaptations survive are Zona Gale's *Miss Lulu Bett* (1921) and O'Neill's *Anna Christie* (1921), filmed twice in 1923, once by Kenji Mizoguchi as *Kiri no minato*, and once by John Griffith Wray as a vehicle for Blanche Sweet said to be O'Neill's favorite among all the film adaptations of his work.

The American plays most likely to be adapted to the silent screen were not Pulitzer material but popular Broadway successes like Margaret Mayo's *Baby Mine* (1910, filmed 1917 and 1928, and with a synchronized soundtrack in Finland in 1954 and on French television in 1967) and *Polly of the Circus* (filmed 1917 as Samuel Goldwyn's first production and with synch-sound in 1932); Mayo and Salisbury Field's *Twin Beds* (1914, filmed 1920 and with synch-sound in 1929, 1934, and 1942); Winchell Smith and Frank

Bacon's 1918 *Lightnin'*, the first Broadway play to play for more than 1,000 performances (filmed 1925, and with synch-sound in 1930); Anne Nichols's *Abie's Irish Rose* (1922, filmed 1928 as a part-talkie, and with synch-sound in 1946); Maxwell Anderson and Laurence Stallings's Pulitzer contender *What Price Glory?* (1924, filmed 1926 and with synch-sound in 1952); Avery Hopwood's *Fair and Warmer* (1915, filmed 1919), *The Gold Diggers* (1919, filmed 1923, again in 1928 as *Gold Diggers of Broadway*, and further adapted in 1933, 1935, and 1937 as Warner Bros. sound pictures), *Ladies' Night* (1920, filmed 1926), *The Bat* (1920, filmed 1926 and 1930 as the synch-sound picture *The Bat Whispers*), *The Best People* (1924, filmed 1925 and 1930 as the synch-sound picture *Fast and Loose*), and *The Garden of Eden* (1927, filmed 1928); Wilson Collison and Avery Hopwood's naughty farce *Getting Gertie's Garter* (1921, filmed 1927); Collison and Otto Harbach's *Up in Mabel's Room* (1919, filmed 1926 and with synch-sound in 1944); and Owen Davis's *The Nervous Wreck* (1923, filmed 1924 and with synch-sound as *Up in Arms* in 1944, and adapted as the musical *Whoopee!*, 1928, filmed 1930) and *Lazybones* (1924, filmed 1925).

Many of the most successful theatrical productions on Broadway were musicals that resisted adaptation to the silent screen and therefore had to wait for synchronized sound. Among the most notable of these were Otto Harbach, Frank Mandel, and Vincent Youmans's *No, No, Nanette*, based on the 1919 Broadway play *My Lady Friends* and filmed in 1930 and 1940; Brian Hooker, William H. Post, and Rudolf Friml's *The Vagabond King* (1925, filmed 1930 and 1956); George S. Kaufman and Irving Berlin's Marx Brothers' vehicle *The Cocoanuts* (1925, filmed 1929); Guy Bolton, Fred Thompson, and Harry Tierney's *Rio Rita* (1927, filmed 1929 and 1942); Laurence Schwab, B.G. DeSylva, and Ray Henderson's *Good News* (1927, filmed 1930 and 1947); Herbert Fields and Vincent Youmans's *Hit the Deck* (1927, filmed 1930 and 1955); Fred Thompson, Paul Gerard Smith, and George and Ira Gershwin's *Funny Face* (1927, filmed 1957). The arrival of the synch-sound era in 1927 coincided with two pivotal Broadway productions. DuBose and Dorothy Heyward's *Porgy* (1927), based on DuBose's 1925 novel, provided Rouben Mamoulian with his stage directing debut before serving as the basis for the Gershwins' *Porgy and Bess* (1935, filmed 1959 as Samuel Goldwyn's last production). And Oscar Hammerstein II and Jerome Kern's celebrated *Show Boat* (1927, filmed 1936 and 1951), based on Edna Ferber's 1926 novel, offered a widely influential model of the integrated musical whose numbers advanced the plot, developed the characters, and marked dramatic turning points.

Adaptations like *No, No, Nanette* and *Porgy and Bess* exemplify a daisy-chain model of adaptation[8] in which successive adaptations were built on earlier adaptations instead of readapting a common source. This tendency, which offered many of the advantages of franchising without the necessity of purchasing a franchise vehicle, emerges in even purer form in the domestic comedies of Cecil B. DeMille. *Old Wives for New* (1918) was an adaptation of David Graham Phillips's novel. But *Don't Change Your Husband* (1919) and *Why Change Your Wife?* (1920) were based on original screenplays, even though, as their titles suggest, they clearly sought to piggyback on the reputation of the earlier adaptation.

Generally speaking, the Hollywood studios were no more eager to film great American novels than great American plays. There were of course notable exceptions. William Desmond Taylor directed *Tom Sawyer* in 1917 and Emmett J. Flynn a meta-adaptation of *A Connecticut Yankee in King Arthur's Court,* using Mark Twain's novel to supply the narrative framework and inspiration for the time-traveling hero's adventures. But the 1921 release of Flynn's Fox film was followed by a Twain blackout, with no new adaptations until 1930. Frank Norris's novels, which had already inspired *A Corner in Wheat* (1909), served as the basis for *The Pit* (1914), *Life's Whirlpool* (1916), and *Moran of the Lady Letty* (1922). But another Norris adaptation goes a long way toward explaining why the studios were so reluctant to take on notable American novels.

When he was fired by Universal for cost overruns on *Merry-Go-Round* (1923), director Erich von Stroheim came to MGM in the hope of making the studio's first feature film by fulfilling a long-standing dream: an uncompromisingly faithful adaptation of Norris's 1899 novel *McTeague*, which had already served as the basis for the short *Life's Whirlpool* in 1916. Stroheim had long cherished Norris's story of a San Francisco dentist's theft of a fragile woman from his best friend and the fallout from the ensuing marriage that left McTeague, Trina, and Marcus Schouler all dead as the acme of naturalistic fatalism. Assembling an unlikely cast—Danish émigré Jean Hersholt as Marcus, comedienne ZaSu Pitts as the pathetic and increasingly miserly Trina, and strong-featured Gibson Gowland in the title role—Stroheim insisted on shooting on location in San Francisco streets, storefronts, and houses that had survived the 1906 earthquake that had leveled many of the buildings Norris had described. After a period of two years, production moved for the brutal final sequence to Death Valley at the height of the summer, ultimately sending Hersholt to the hospital (see Figure 3.5). The forty-two reels of Stroheim's initial cut, which ran over nine hours, succeeded against all odds in adding a great deal of new material. "Stroheim expanded Norris's ten-sentence reference to McTeague's parents into a prologue that makes up twenty-five pages of the reconstituted script"[9] and added two new romantic pairs intended to serve as foils to McTeague's romance with Trina. Horrified by the film's inordinate length, studio executive Irving Thalberg demanded that it be cut to twenty-four reels. Stroheim prepared this shorter cut and accepted a still more abbreviated eighteen-reel version prepared by director Rex Ingram but then stonewalled, insisting that the four-hour film be screened in two installments on successive nights. Thalberg refused, took the film out of

FIGURE 3.5 *McTeague (Gibson Gowland, right) faces his nemesis Marcus Schouler (Jean Hersholt) in the Death Valley climax of* Greed *(1924).*

Stroheim's hands, gave it to editor June Mathis, and released a version in 1924 that ran just over two hours. The prologue showing McTeague as a miner remained in this release version, which "began like a documentary on gold mining,"[10] along with the harrowing finale in Death Valley and many other indelible moments. But the romantic subplots Stroheim had added were gone, along with so much of the story that new intertitles had to be added to bridge some of the more extended gaps, and the film failed to return more than a fraction of its enormous costs.

The story of *Greed* is often posed as a cautionary tale about autocratic directors like Stroheim who pay for their indifference to financial constraints and the box office by spending the rest of their lives mourning the destruction of their masterpieces. But it is equally a cautionary tale about the fate of adaptations that refuse to compromise. As it exists now in a two-plus-hour version and a four-hour version that incorporates a trove of still photos from the film's production discovered in 1979, long after most of Stroheim's full-length cut had been destroyed, the film is not only a magnificent torso, haunting in its central situation, overemphatic in many of the details that remain, moving at once too slowly and too quickly, but perhaps the single most fascinating road not taken in the history of the cinema. Had Stroheim prevailed in his fight with Thalberg and released anything like his first cut of the film, it would have launched the era of the dramatic miniseries seventy years early, changing the history of what cinema audiences think of as adaptations, of American literature, and of the experience of going to the movies as decisively as *The Birth of a Nation* had done against equally long odds only a few years earlier.

Instead of epics like *Greed,* Hollywood studios preferred to play it safe when they approached literary sources that might provide their projects cultural cachet and loyal audiences, but might also encourage invidious comparisons between the adaptations and their sources, invite impossible expectations of the films' fidelity to their sources, or court censorship for projects suitable for the page but not the screen. To take a representative sample of the adaptations released over the decade beginning in 1915: Edward Everett Hale's patriotic parable "The Man without a Country" was adapted in 1917, Jean Webster's romance "Daddy-Long-Legs" in 1919, William Hale's melodramatic novel *The Greatest Question* that same year, F. Scott Fitzgerald's novel *The Beautiful and Damned* in 1922, Bayard Veiller's play about a woman wrongly accused of theft's search for revenge *Within the Law* in 1923, Owen Wister's prototypical Western *The Virginian* that same year, Sinclair Lewis's satirical novel *Babbitt* in 1924, and Dorothy Donnelly's circus comedy *Poppy* as *Sally of the Sawdust* in 1925. *Alias Jimmy Valentine,* Paul Armstrong's stage adaptation of O. Henry's story "A Retrieved Reformation," was adapted twice, once in 1915 and again in 1920, before it served as the basis for MGM's first talkie in 1928. What most deeply unites all these films to *The Birth of a Nation, Manslaughter, Young Romance, Salomy Jane,* and each other is their focus on liminal figures, characters rendered exotic by their wealthy backgrounds, their questionable professions, or their buffoonish behavior, who struggle to find their places in different subcultures that both are and are not representative of America.

This pattern is perhaps clearest in *The Man without a Country,* the story of Philip Nolan (Holmes Herbert), a young naval officer accused of treason who expresses in court the fervent wish that he may never hear the name of the United States again and is granted his wish by a judge who arranges that he spend the rest of his life on a series of merchant ships aboard which the United States is never mentioned in his hearing. Nolan's estrangement from his motherland predictably brings about an acute and enduring sense of homesickness that establishes him ironically as more deeply American than he ever was before his sentence began. It is a pattern that returns more resonantly and profoundly in the two most distinguished adaptations of American literary classics to be released during the period: the first feature-length adaptation of *The Last of the Mohicans* begun by director Maurice Tourneur and completed by Clarence Brown in 1920, and Victor Sjöström's 1926 *The Scarlet Letter.*

The Last of the Mohicans is best remembered today for its visual splendor, and indeed its many outdoor scenes, filmed largely in Big Bear and Yosemite, remain among the most striking of its era. Tourneur and Brown display one memorable moment after another, especially monstrating solitary figures silhouetted on hilltops or as seen from the inside of caves whose dark interiors create compelling triangular frames for the scenic vistas outside. But the film is even more notable for its remarkable fidelity to James Fenimore Cooper's novel, which had already provided the basis for four short films, one of them German. Of all Cooper's Leatherstocking Tales, *The Last of the Mohicans* is the one that focuses most directly on the fear of sexual relations between white women and non-white men. Alone among all adaptations of the novel, Tourneur and Brown's film faithfully reproduces not only the villainous Huron Magua's lust for Cora Munro (Barbara Bedford, in her film debut), whose father commands Fort William Henry, but also Cora's pure and reciprocal love for Uncas (Alan Roscoe, here billed as Albert), the title character—even though "Uncas and Cora, the noble Indian and the white maiden, are doomed for their willingness to break the tabu against race mixing"[11] (see Figure 3.6). Unlike later adaptations beginning with B. Reeves Eason's 1932 serial, which move the scout Hawkeye to the center of

FIGURE 3.6 The Last of the Mohicans *(1920) balances its fear of miscegenation against the noble love between Cora Munro (Barbara Bedford) and Uncas (Alan Roscoe).*

the tale and anoint his character as the romantic lead, Tourneur and Brown keep Hawkeye, here played by stolid, middle-aged Harry Lorraine, on the margin, following the innovation of Cooper, who built his Leatherstocking Tales around a continuing figure who remained peripheral to the plots of most of them. Instead of organizing its view of the American colonies' relations to Native American culture around the glamorously liminal figure of Hawkeye, the film follows Cooper in dramatizing Americans' romantic attachment to the frontier and their primal fear of it by creating good and evil Native Americans who separately justify both attitudes. In fact, the film emphasizes Cooper's strategy of staging deep-seated dualities by assigning warring loyalties to different characters instead of internalizing them within a single figure by creating a new character, Captain Randolph (George Hackathorne), whose betrayal of the fort marks him as the evil white counterpart to Colonel Munro and Major Heyward's brave, unselfish, and compassionate white English officers. Although this adaptive procedure simplifies the characters into one-dimensional melodramatic types, it preserves the dark side of Cooper's exotic frontier romance far more successfully than its most notable successors, George B. Seitz's 1936 feature featuring Randolph Scott as Hawkeye and Michael Mann's 1992 vehicle for Daniel Day-Lewis, which remains virtually unique in including a credit identifying its screenplay as based on Philip Dunne's 1936 screenplay.

The kinds of divisions that Tourneur and Brown's film had exteriorized by parceling them out to different characters are harrowingly interiorized within both leading characters in *The Scarlet Letter*. Just as Stroheim had long wanted to film *McTeague*, Lillian Gish had wanted to star in an adaptation of Nathaniel Hawthorne's 1850 novel. Although she faced resistance from "the church and the women's clubs," they agreed to drop their opposition in response to her appeal "if I would be personally responsible for this film."[12] Given this background, it is hardly surprising that the film is not the paean to forbidden love and female empowerment that Roland Joffé's 1995 adaptation would be. Instead, the focus of the film, billed as directed by Victor Seastrom, focuses throughout on two elements it marks from the beginning as exotic outliers. One of these, announced in its opening intertitle ("A story of bigotry uncurbed and its train of sorrow, shame and tragedy"), is the seventeenth-century Puritan community that condemns Hester Prynne (Gish) for her adultery; the other is the heroic grace Hester maintains in accepting the condemnation that makes her and her daughter Pearl (Joyce Coad) pariahs and refusing to name her lover, Rev. Arthur Dimmesdale (Lars Hanson), the spiritual leader the community reveres. Repeated expository shots of the Governor (William H. Tooker) reading rules from the "Laws of Ye Colony" help both to explain the characters' behavior in the scenes that follow and to ridicule the rules meant to govern them as excessively restrictive and life-denying. The film's most notable departure from Hawthorne is its decision to devote its entire first half to the development of the forbidden romance between Hester and Dimmesdale, who, having overcome his scruples and confessed his love for her, recoils from her revelation that she has been given in loveless marriage to a husband she has not seen for many years. When Dimmesdale returns from a trip to England, where the colony has sent him with a suit to the King, he is even more horrified to discover that she has had a baby, the only sign the film gives to either the Puritans in the film or the audience outside it that Hester and Dimmesdale's love has been sexual.

In a sequence halfway through the film, Hester emerges from prison and, bidden by Dimmesdale in his capacity as spiritual leader, reveals the "A" she has been forced to wear as a badge of her adultery (see Figure 3.7). This scene has been preceded by one in which Dimmesdale, visiting Hester in prison, begs her to let him share her shame, and she suggests that he would better atone for his sin through a life of "devotion and service," since his confession would bring even greater suffering upon both her and the Puritans who rely on his guidance. The absolute clash of their wills, deepened perhaps by the fact that Gish filmed her shots speaking English and Hanson his shots speaking Swedish, sets the stage for the second half of the film, which charts Dimmesdale's gradual

FIGURE 3.7 *On her release from prison, Hester Prynne (Lillian Gish) is publicly shamed in* The Scarlet Letter *(1926).*

destruction by his overwhelming guilt and Hester's steadfast refusal either to name her lover or to give up her daughter to be "brought up by a Christian woman," an edict Dimmesdale is instrumental in thwarting. Although Hester's husband Roger (Henry B. Walthall), arriving unexpectedly at the colony and recognizing first Hester as his wife and then Dimmesdale as her lover, vows "infinite" revenge on them both, he enters the story much later than in Hawthorne, and Dimmesdale's tragedy grows more directly from his self-recriminations than from Roger's success in fanning their flames.

Gish's performance, which presents Hester as playfully naive and vulnerable before she confesses her love to Dimmesdale and stoically self-sacrificing afterwards, makes her a tragic outlier in a community whose iron morality, represented by images of tolling church bells, stocks and pillories, prison bars, and birds restored to the cages from which they have escaped, makes it equally exotic, as remote in temper as in time from its audience. At the same time, neither Hester nor the Puritan community is merely exotic: Gish's heart-rending performance gives her character a deeply moving appeal, and just as Master Giles (Karl Dane) repeatedly fails to live to his community's standards in a series of comically deflating moments, Hanson's performance poignantly internalizes the moral contradictions of his community. Without endorsing either Puritanism or adultery, the film compellingly creates a tragedy of forbidden love by dramatizing the unbearable collisions among the scripts generated by religious morality, guilt, and sexual responsibility.

The Scarlet Letter is exceptional in the intensity with which it presents its central couple as both exotic and empathetic. But there were many other ways contemporaneous films could show its characters as both fascinatingly exotic and empathetically American. The most obvious was by showing Americans abroad, as in *The Unbeliever* (1918), one of the last films the Edison Company made. Alan Crosland, later famed as the director of *The Jazz Singer* (1927), shows Philip Landicutt (Raymond McKee) encountering a Marine training unit, including his former chauffeur, Lefty (Darwin Kerr), while Landicutt is part of a golfing foursome. When a caddy suddenly refuses to carry the bag of another golfer who has ridiculed the ideal of military service, Phil, a son of privilege who has drifted through life without any strong beliefs, begins a process of conversion to the war effort, which Mary Raymond Shipman Andrews's source story had strongly endorsed. Once he enlists in the Marines, his second conversion begins in his struggle to overcome the class-consciousness that leads him to describe Lefty, a comrade-in-arms who still calls him "sir" despite their closeness, in a letter to his mother: "He isn't one of us. After all, he was born into the working class." It is not until Lefty dies in Phil's arms that Phil can tell him: "You've taught me to judge people as people, Lefty old pal—and class pride is junk!" Phil's third conversion, from unbelief to religious faith, must wait until he is lying seriously wounded on the battlefield and has an angelic vision that moves him to a sudden profession of faith in God, preparing him to respond with sympathy to the wounded Germans whom he will awaken beside in a church turned medical ward.

The film repeatedly parallels Phil's heroic experiences with the Marines to the equally heroic resistance of local civilians in the towns his company passes through. Marianne Marnholm (Gertrude Norman), an elderly woman about to be executed for concealing her anti-German daughter from an impromptu firing squad assembled by Lt. Kurt von Schniedizt (Erich von Stroheim), shouts, "*Vive la Belgique!*," and later young Virginie Harbrok (Marguerite Courtot), trapped in an attic with him, begs him to shoot her before the German soldiers below can take her alive, insisting, "I am not afraid to die—for Belgium!" (see Figure 3.8). But it does nothing to make Phil seem more European. Nor is the film's own outlook particularly cosmopolitan. Its war seems to be fought entirely between Germans and Americans, and the rabid hostility of its representation of the Germanic type represented by von Schniedizt is intensified rather than unrelieved when a German soldier who has repeatedly hesitated to follow his brutal orders finally shoots him, rips the Iron Cross from his own uniform, and cries: "Down with Militarism—long live Democracy!," completing a conversion

FIGURE 3.8 *Belgian Virginie Harbrok (Marguerite Courtot) begs American soldier Philip Landicutt (Raymond McKee), the hero of* The Unbeliever *(1918), to shoot her rather than allowing her to fall into the hands of the Germans.*

far more radical than Phil's. The value of exposing Phil to the World War, the film implies, is not that it makes him more cosmopolitan or pluralistic or European, but that it makes him a better American. It is thoroughly logical that the film ends not with Phil's acceptance of European values, but with his reunion with Virginie back in his family home, where she comes after he gives her a letter of introduction to his mother.

Defamiliarized Americans

The trajectory of *The Unbeliever* could be readily reversed in films that presented foreigners who exemplified American values as wholeheartedly as Americans. Among the most notable of these stories was John Ford's *Four Sons* (1928), based on Ida Alexa Ross Wylie's novel *Mother Bernle Learns Her Letters*. The film's opening movement establishes the Bavarian village of Burgendorf, where, according to the film's opening intertitle, "people are gentle and kind"—and quaintly exotic, from the mustachioed postman to the maidens in picturesque costumes to Mother Bernle (Margaret Mann) herself, whose birthday is celebrated by her four strapping sons and a bevy of beaming village dancers (see Figure 3.9). The mood darkens

FIGURE 3.9 *The calm before the storm: the Bernle family saying grace at dinner in the beginning of* Four Sons *(1928).*

with the arrival of Major von Stomm (Earle Foxe), a monocled Prussian who presumably shaves while looking at a photo of Erich von Stroheim. In short order the oldest Bernle son, farmer John (James Hall), responds to the urging of an émigré friend to go to America and two of the other sons, soldier Franz (Francis X. Bushman) and blacksmith Johann (Charles Morton), are dispatched to the Russian front, leaving only the fourth son, shepherd Andreas (George Meeker) behind to comfort his mother. As Joseph, whose friend Otto (Jack Pennick) calls him "Dutch," rises from employee to deli owner in New York, the postman brings Mother Bernle a letter notifying her that Franz and Johann have been killed in action, and she celebrates her next birthday in a far darker mood echoed by the rainy weather and worsened by the appearance of Major von Stomm, who calls Joseph a traitor and demands that Andreas immediately enlist in place of him. Predictably, Andreas is also killed at the front, discovered moments before he dies by Joseph, who has enlisted in the American service and offers him a last drink from his canteen before war and death separate them forever. After the Armistice, von Stomm, now a colonel, returns to Burgendorf, but his troops, rallying against him, demand that he commit suicide, and he shoots himself just as the postman enters with another letter announcing the death of Andreas. Although there is nothing left for Mother Bernle in the village, she is overjoyed to receive a letter from Joseph inviting her to America, and after several mishaps and adventures, she arrives in his home in the celebratory closing scene.

In an essay she wrote for the program booklet announcing the film's premiere, Miss I.A.R. Wylie, as she is billed, professes her surprise and delight that one of the movie studios she had heretofore considered charitable organizations because "they paid me large sums of money for titles they never used, stories they changed out of recognition and my name, if it had any value, was rarely mentioned,"[13] has adapted her story with such delicacy and fidelity, avoiding partisan politics in order to humanize characters on both sides of the war. In fact *Four Sons* is strongly partisan. Its primary division, however, is not between the United States and Germany but between good Germans, who are sweet, smiling, good-natured, neighborly, and fully worthy of emigrating to America despite the obstacles, and bad Germans, who are personified by Major von Stomm. As the 1920 *Last of the Mohicans* does with both its Native Americans and its British military officers, the film takes care to set von Stomm's cruelty against the charitable instincts of the soldier who winces when von Stomm slashes with his sword at a black cat that has crossed the path of his parade, the officer who returns briefly to kiss Mother Bernle's hand and salute her after von Stomm has demanded Andreas's enlistment, and the mutineers who demand his suicide. Good Germans, sentimentalized as denizens of a picture-postcard world, can readily cross the ocean to America, where Joseph, whose beautiful wife has made an even greater success of his business and borne him a son during his wartime absence, shows every sign of having been completely assimilated. The film's prefiguration of the postnationalist universalism that would blossom more fully in *All Quiet on the Western Front* (1930), which would also divide Germans into zealots and humanists, is compromised by the condescending minstrelsy with which it portrays good Germans as quaintly picturesque exotics uniquely capable of becoming real Americans.

The director Frank Borzage elaborated repeatedly on this pattern of portraying admirable foreign nationals as quintessential Americans. Having established in Steve Tuttle (Buck Jones) his trademark hero, the shy, sweet, decent, soft-spoken, ineffectual lead of *Lazybones* (1925), based on a play by Owen Davis, Borzage strategically modified the model and exported it to Europe. In *7th Heaven* (1927), based on Austin Strong's popular 1922 play, he pairs Diane (Janet Gaynor), an innocent regularly beaten by her sister, a prostitute and thief, with Chico (Charles Farrell), a Parisian sewerman whose fondest dream is to work on the surface as a street cleaner. When the police arrest Diane's sister and she sneeringly urges them to arrest Diane because she is no better than her, Chico comes to Diane's rescue by pretending that she is his wife. Warned that the police will check out his story, Chico accepts Diane's offer to stay at his home until the officer arrives. Despite Chico's assurance that she will have to leave immediately thereafter, love predictably blossoms between the two, and on the eve of his departure for the war, they conduct their own unofficial wedding service. *7th Heaven* thus defamiliarizes and exoticizes not only the couple's relationship but also the homely institutions of courtship and marriage themselves. *Street Angel* (1928), based on the play by the Englishman Monckton Hoffe, who also wrote the play on which Preston Sturges would base the archetypal remarriage comedy *The Lady Eve* (1941), transfers the two stars and much of the same story—the innocent heroine suspected of prostitution (this time because she has taken to the streets in the vain hope of raising money for her ailing mother's medicine before escaping the police and taking refuge in a circus), the aspiring hero (now a painter rather than a sewerman), the unlikely romance ultimately triumphing over separation (arising this time from the heroine's arrest and imprisonment)—to a version of Naples that is at once foreign, licentious, universal, and Hollywoodesque, as the film's opening intertitle suggests: "Everywhere—in every town, in every street we pass, unknowingly, human souls made great by love and adversity." The foreign settings of the two films provide both exotic, though understated, visuals and moral license that renders it more acceptable for Janet Gaynor to experiment with streetwalking in Borzage's Naples, where she is hopelessly out of her depth, than it would be in the United States. Although both films were shot in the Fox backlot, they both use the combination of all-American leading performers and mythical European settings to evoke a shimmering sense of romance that is neither European nor American but universal.

Charles Farrell and Janet Gaynor, who appeared in twelve films together, were only the most obvious examples of an aspirational universality that framed newly revealed stars as both exotic and American. This maneuver, which depended on the public's recognition of established stars, relied on surprising parallels between those stars and adapted screenplays. Like adaptations, the casting of stars supplied a series of scripts that implicitly promised that a given performer would be both the same and different than in previous films. The star system, depending as it did on the recognition of Hollywood stars, had begun in 1910, when Carl Laemmle, the head of Independent Motion Pictures, identified Florence Lawrence, hitherto known only as "the Biograph Girl," as the star of his own studio. Eileen Bowser notes that the same issue of *Moving Picture World* that carried Laemmle's announcement "featured an editorial stating that the public was now known to be 'unmistakably interested in the personalities of the chief performers. This interest is growing.' This comment came in response to the suggestion that authors ought to get credit for their scenarios, which the *World* thought was probably not worth doing because the public was not interested in who wrote the film."[14] The *World* editorial explicitly contrasted uncredited screenwriters with increasingly well-known performers: "The personal equation of the author has hardly yet manifested itself in the moving picture. [...] [A]t present, no outside reputation has been made by scenario writers."[15]

While screenwriters continued to work anonymously, any performer who established a star persona encouraged the audience to develop a relationship with the star that depended not simply on instantaneous recognition of the star, but often on a gradual recognition of an adaptive sameness-in-difference, a process in which the stars themselves might well collaborate by gradually revealing the recognizable personas they had hidden. Mary Pickford, widely recognized as "Little Mary," could play at being a Native American in *A Pueblo Romance* (1912), the Queen of Herzegovina in *Such a Little Queen* (1914), and Nell Gwyn in *Mistress Nell* (1915). Pickford's performances in the title role of *Cinderella* (1914) and Cho-Cho-San in *Madame Butterfly* (1915) show her masquerading in familiar roles that are more foreign to her than to the audience. Her ability simultaneously to inhabit and to undermine stock characters released and channeled by the star system enlivens her performances in the title roles of two adaptations of American originals. *Poor Little Rich Girl* (1917), based on Eleanor Gates's play, presents Gwendolyn (Pickford) as initially spoiled and unattractive, emerging only under pressure as America's Sweetheart. And *The Hoodlum* (1919), based on Julie Mathilde Lippmann's novel *Burkses' Amy*, sends Amy Burke (Pickford), another spoiled rich girl, into a lower-class ghetto as an enchantingly rough-and-tumble all-but-boy who succeeds through alliances, grit, and strategic bullying. Janet Gaynor, who told an interviewer, "I was the essence of first love," could try her hand as a prostitute and even serve a prison term in *Street Angel* without alienating the sympathies of an audience secure in their faith in the essential simplicity and innocence they had seen in Gaynor before. Rudolph Valentino, rocketing to fame as the seductive Arabian prince of *The Sheik* (1921), was cast the following year as Ramon Laredo, a San Francisco socialite shanghaied by smugglers in *Moran of the Lady Letty*, a performance intended specifically to extend his appeal to male audiences. Based on Frank Norris's 1898 novel, the film cast Valentino initially against type before allowing him to assume the active, exotically heroic role audiences expected. Even Clara Bow, "The It Girl" who was perhaps the most instantly recognizable Hollywood heroine of the 1920s, initially masked the bubbly flapper persona that eventually emerged in adaptations as different as *Mantrap* (1926) and *It* (1927), which reconfigured her persona as both exotic and all-American, a complement to Valentino as a wish-fulfillment figure of her audience's most wildly romantic dreams. Bow, playing an urban flapper who has just married a rugged outdoorsman, plays with her image by repeatedly checking her makeup in her compact mirror, primping her hair, and adjusting her waistband in order to get back into the Bow character in Victor Fleming's adaptation of Sinclair Lewis's 1926 novel *Mantrap*. In *It*, based on a novel whose author, Eleanor Glyn, makes a cameo appearance as herself, the story itself plays with Bow's image, casting her as a lowly shopgirl romanced by the store heir before she rises to claim the predictably happy ending.

Borzage's romances achieved their magical effects largely by defamiliarizing the rituals of courtship, romance, and marriage. In this they echoed F.W. Murnau's *Sunrise* (1927), a story "of no place and every place." *Sunrise*, the third film, along with *7th Heaven* and *Street Angel*, for which Janet Gaynor won the first Academy Award for Best Actress in 1928—the only time in Academy history when the award recognized a single star's performances in more than one film—showed a man (George O'Brien) falling deeply in love with the wife he had originally planned to kill at the behest of his mistress (Margaret Livingston). The couples in *7th Heaven* and *Street Angel*, brought together by happenstance and deception, enjoyed magically irregular unions in exotic lands while exuding American virtues like candor, self-reliance, and resourcefulness that won them lasting romance against formidable odds. Five years earlier, William deMille's adaptation of Zona Gale's novel and Pulitzer Prize-winning play *Miss Lulu Bett* had already adapted this model of defamiliarized romance to an American setting. The eponymous heroine (Lois Wilson), the "maltreated beast of burden" for the family of her sister Ina Deacon (Mabel Van Buren), is rescued by an inadvertent suitor: Ninian Deacon (Clarence Burton), the brother of Ina's husband Dwight (Theodore Roberts), who, returned from exotic South America after twenty years, playfully pretends to propose marriage to Lulu while they sit in a restaurant with Dwight and Ina. Only after Lulu, goaded by Dwight's ridicule, pretends to accept does Dwight realize that, as a Justice of the Peace, his presence has legalized the marriage vows, to the considerable dismay of both parties. Even so, Ninian says, "I'm a good sport—why can't we let it stand?," and Lulu agrees. Ensconced in her new home a week later, Lulu, appreciating Ninian's surprising sensitivity about what a woman wants, is crushed to hear his confession that fifteen years ago he married a woman who ran off two years later and may or may not still be alive. Returning to the Deacon home, Lulu resumes her domestic drudgery and becomes the target of merciless gossip. After discovering an abortive attempt by the Deacons' daughter Diana (Helen Ferguson) to elope with her spineless suitor Bobby Larkin (Taylor Graves), Lulu, persuading a station agent to hush the matter up, must face harsh questioning from Dwight, who is convinced that Lulu herself has been planning to elope. But now Lulu's brief experience of marriage to a man who treated her kindly even though he did not love her has stiffened her spine and revealed the Deacon home as a stifling prison rather than a locus of domestic values. Rebuffing Dwight's self-righteous attempt at an apology, she stomps around the kitchen breaking crockery, announcing, "My work's paid for these." An intertitle indicates that her new job in the village bakery assures Lulu, whose discovery that Ninian has returned to his first wife frees her to accept the marriage proposal of the local schoolteacher, of Life and Liberty and prepares her for the Pursuit of Happiness—quintessentially American ideals enabled by radically defamiliarized means.

Home-grown exotics

If *Miss Lulu Bett* defamiliarized the American domestic sphere in both senses of the word "domestic," other films exoticized American subjects without recourse to foreign settings by the simple expedient of multiplying Americas, dividing the nation into subcultures that found each other equally exotic. The most obvious vehicle for this brand of exoticism remained *Uncle Tom's Cabin,* a project on which Universal lavished a remarkable $2.6 million in the studio's 1927 adaptation. Director Harry Pollard followed Harriet Beecher Stowe's novel much more closely than earlier adaptations but still insisted on treating its black characters as exotic foreigners whose behavior had to be made palatable to white audiences. African American actor Charles Gilpin, originally cast as Uncle Tom, was replaced by James B. Lowe when Gilpin's portrayal was found too "aggressive."[16] Lowe, nominally playing the main character of the film, was onscreen for only nine minutes of its two-hour running time. Instead, the film focused on the slave Eliza, played in blackface by Pollard's wife, Margarita Fischer, for whom the film was "created as a star vehicle."[17] George, the husband whose marriage to Eliza opens the movie, is played by Turkish-born Arthur

Edmund Carewe and their son Harry by seven-year-old white actress Lassie Lou Ahern. Tom's original owners, the Shelbys (Jack Mower and Vivien Oakland), are presented as normative in their kindness and compassion; Haley (Adolphe Milar), the debtor to whom Shelby has to give both Tom and Harry, is the outlier in his ruthless greed. At the same time, Haley's incredulity that Tom, sent to Cincinnati to retrieve the money to service Shelby's debt, would actually return with the money seems to make Tom the outlier in his faithfulness.

The racial stereotypes in which the film traffics are gratingly reminiscent of minstrelsy. The adult slaves are constantly grinning, their children always bright and active. At one point, a dozen black children pursue a watermelon truck so that they can steal and eat a melon. Topsy (white actress Mona Gray) constantly rolls her eyes, plays tricks, and slows her reaction times to the death of Little Eva (Virginia Gray), haloed in light, who ascends from her deathbed in a double-exposure flight with an angel, a prefiguration of one of the film's two most significant additions to Stowe's novel: the climactic haunting of cruel slaveowner Simon Legree (George Siegmann) by Tom, who haunts him after death in multiple double exposures. The other most important addition is its extension of the timeline of Stowe's 1852 novel to 1861, showing the Civil War breaking out and Union soldiers riding into Legree's town just in time to rescue Eliza and Cassy (Eulalie Jensen). With this stroke, the film, whose focus on Eliza's romance with George rather than Tom's sacrificial suffering and death dramatically alters the import of Harriet Beecher Stowe's novel, which Pollard considered "little more than undisguised abolitionist propaganda,"[18] rewrites both fiction and history, apparently making blacks' survival depend on whites—even though Legree has been lured to his fatal fall out a window by Tom's last double exposure, and the Union army is on hand only to ratify, not to cause, Eliza and Cassy's liberation. The film's Uncle Tom is a prime example of the *movie-created* home-grown exotic, a home-grown figure who is at once non-American and quintessentially American, a figure meant, like the novel Pollard's film adapts, to be instantly recognized, nostalgically loved, and marked from beginning to end as a scandalous illustration of what America was not.

The figure of the home-grown American exotic does not depend on racial otherness; its exoticism can be purely social or cultural, as in Raoul Walsh's *Regeneration* (1915), whose director, adapting O.F. Kildare's memoir *My Mamie Rose,* called it "the first full-length gangster picture ever made." *Regeneration* evokes a realistically tawdry urban jungle hiding in plain sight beneath the veneer of the modern American cityscape. The film, whose director would go on from his debut feature to a fifty-year career directing action films of all kinds, shows its orphaned hero Owen growing up in a tenement to become a gangster who will be rehabilitated and redeemed by love and public service. Taken in after his mother dies by kindly neighbor Maggie Conway (Maggie Weston) but brutalized by her husband Jim (James

A. Marcus), a bullying drunkard, ten-year-old Owen soon learns that the Bowery is a place "where might makes right." The subculture that pointedly fails to nurture him, atavistic yet exotic, is marked by meticulously detailed exterior locations, interior sets that reek of the slums, and lower-class urban greeting, drinking, and competing rituals throughout, many of them enacted by extras recruited from tough New York City neighborhoods. Walsh's New York seems initially the very opposite of a melting pot. It is an arena that plays host to a series of elemental battles of all against all.

This turbulent city provides the backdrop to the film's story of moral regeneration. By the age of twenty-five, Owen, now played by sad-eyed Rockcliffe Fellowes, is already a leader of gangsters like Skinny (William Sheer), elevated to the top of the heap by the natural strength that caught a backer's eye when he was only seventeen. The film, which presents Owen as a hardened criminal, spends virtually no time showing him committing any crimes that do not originate in competitive games with his cohort or the self-defense necessary to ensure his survival. Instead, his life begins to take a turn away from crime as soon as he meets Marie Deering (Anna Q. Nilsson) at Grogan's, his neighborhood hangout, where her suitor, District Attorney Ames (Carl Harbaugh), has brought her because she has told him that she thinks gangsters "such interesting people" and would love to meet one. Ames and Marie stick out like sore thumbs in the honky-tonk, where the exotic hangers-on regard the interlopers as equally exotic (see Figure 3.10). But Owen gazes intently at Marie and earns her gratitude when he rescues the top-hatted Ames from the regulars who rough him up.

FIGURE 3.10 *Owen (Rockliffe Fellowes) casts an appraising eye on the offscreen interlopers in his criminal underworld in* Regeneration *(1915).*

Owen's conversion is preceded by Marie's. Her sense of duty awakened, she volunteers in the neighborhood's settlement house, where she breaks up a fight that breaks out in an adjoining room. Walsh stages the film's most memorable set piece during the settlement's annual outing, when Skinny's carelessly tossed match sets the boat on fire. Although the flames seem to consume the screen, an intertitle reports that "All the kiddies were saved," two of them by Owen himself. When the social worker Marie sends into a troubled home proves comically ineffectual, she asks a young man in her office to get Owen, since he is exactly the sort of man who can extricate a baby from this dangerous situation. And so he does, seeming genuinely smitten with the child himself.

Owen's social reformation as he is drawn into the orbit of Marie and the baby he rescued is treated as desertion by his gang, which has elected Skinny as its new leader. After Skinny, about to be arrested, stabs the police officer who has accosted him, his flight to Owen, who is still with Ames, poses a pivotal moral dilemma. Should Owen be true to the gangland principles of his youth or to his emerging love for Marie? The conflict is sharpened by a flashback that shows Skinny, arrested after an earlier pursuit in which Owen escaped, insisting that he was alone and allowing Owen to get away. Not until after Marie sends a detective who has come in search of Skinny away does she spot Skinny's cop and realizes he has indeed been there. Ames ironically commends Owen's loyalty to his old friend while pointing out that he has lost any chance he had with Marie, who begins weeping in the next room but stops when her eye alights on the bouquet Owen has brought her.

Having saved Skinny from the police, Owen tries to distance himself from his former friend. As he unburdens himself to an encouraging priest, Marie searches for him at Skinny's and ends up trapped by a leering Skinny in an upstairs room. Fleeing to an adjoining room, she struggles to hold the doorknob fast against Skinny, who fires one shot at the arriving Owen as he escapes out a window. The bullet strikes Marie, who dies after reminding Owen on her deathbed: "Vengeance is mine, saith the Lord." Resolving to hunt down the killer, Owen seizes a gun but then tosses it aside and runs off without it to find Skinny, whom he nearly strangles until a vision of Marie stops him, giving Skinny one last chance to escape before he is killed by another character, leaving Owen to deliver a heartbroken epitaph for Marie, "my Mamie Rose." The film's story thus establishes two New York worlds as equally foreign to each other, shows first the heroine's and then the hero's attempt to cross the boundaries between them, and ends up both celebrating the exotic yet all-American hero's conversion to the morality summarized by the motto "GOD IS LOVE" written on a school chalkboard and mourning the high price of his defection from the criminal underworld that has been his home.

Regeneration tells what would become the familiar story of a gangster, the consummate insider in his own world, struggling to win acceptance by the world that has made him a pariah. Both its hero and its heroine are attractive, ultimately well-meaning types whose deepest natures are kind, generous, and unselfish. The film, remade in 1924 as *Fool's Highway*, is a fairy tale that immerses its hero in a criminal environment in order to rescue him through his moral conversion. Although it differs from *The Cheat* and *Manslaughter* mainly in its steadfast refusal to glamorize the hero's underworld and its emphasis on the enduring cost of his conversion, it is like them essentially a parable of sin and forgiveness in an updated American setting. In all these respects it is the opposite of *Where Are My Children?*, one of the few surviving films directed by Lois Weber, Hollywood's highest-paid filmmaker at the time of its release in 1916. The film, based on a story by Lucy Payton and Franklin Hall, positions itself squarely as an adaptation of material considered taboo for movies, though not for books, from its very beginning, when two defensive full-screen intertitles make the case that movies should have all the freedom books do to deal with the issue of birth control. Unaccompanied children will not be admitted, these title cards announce, but the film will do them a world of good if you bring them along (see Figure 3.11).

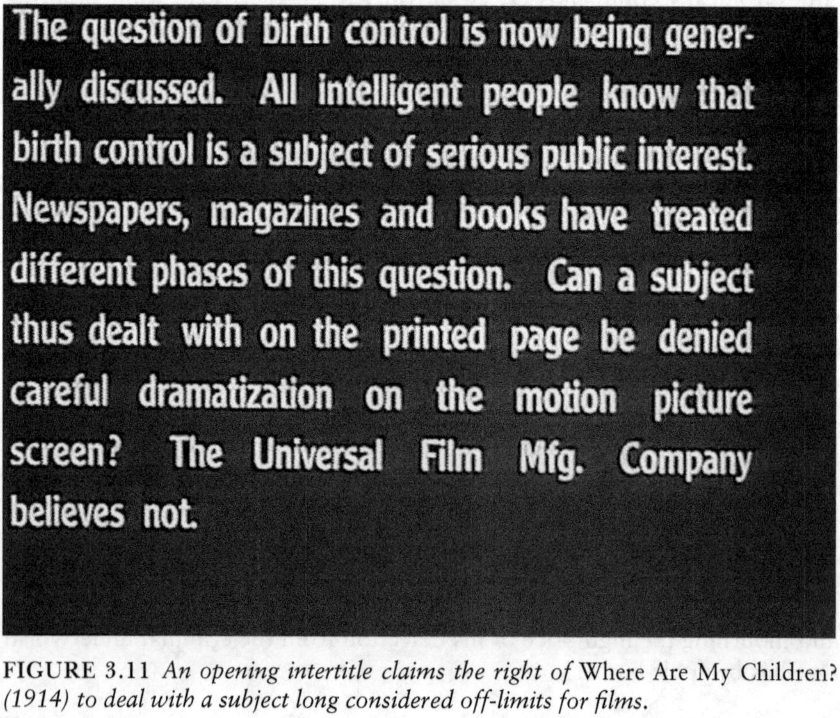

> The question of birth control is now being generally discussed. All intelligent people know that birth control is a subject of serious public interest. Newspapers, magazines and books have treated different phases of this question. Can a subject thus dealt with on the printed page be denied careful dramatization on the motion picture screen? The Universal Film Mfg. Company believes not.

FIGURE 3.11 *An opening intertitle claims the right of* Where Are My Children? *(1914) to deal with a subject long considered off-limits for films.*

The film, which follows pioneering birth-control advocate Margaret Sanger, whom Weber greatly admired, in framing eugenics and birth control as the only logical alternatives to the shattering horror of abortion, opens with a series of strikingly otherworldly opening shots that frame its story in quasi-religious terms, separating unwanted children who will never be born from those whom God will usher into the world. This sequence's repository of imagery—swirling winds and fires, angel babies, iron gates, shining crosses—will return at strategic points throughout the story. District Attorney Richard Walton (Tyrone Power [Sr.]) is envious of visits by his sister, who has "contracted a eugenic marriage and her first child was of great interest." Walton, unaware that his own wife (Helene Riaume) has ensured her childless status by repeated abortions, is prosecuting Dr. William Homer (C. Norman Hammond), a writer on birth control accused of "indecent literature" who, advocating the position of Weber and Phillips Smalley, her husband and collaborator, that "only children who are wanted are born," urges: "Let us stop the slaughter of the unborn and save the lives of unwilling mothers," arguing explicitly that the wider availability of birth control will be more humane to infants and improve the race. As the trial proceeds, Mrs. Walton's best friend, Mrs. William Carlo (Marie Walcamp) is tormented by an angel baby's whispered voice because she is "determined to evade motherhood." After her abortion is tacitly indicated, "One of the 'unwanted' ones returns, and a social butterfly is again ready for house parties."

When Mrs. Walton's brother Roger (A.D. Blake) gets Lillian (Rena Rogers), the daughter of her housekeeper, pregnant, she too is tormented by an angel baby whispering over her shoulder. Roger, telling Mrs. Walton, "A friend of mine is in trouble," gets her to put him in touch with her abortionist, but "this time the obliging Dr. Malfit bungled," and Lillian dies soon after leaving his office, accompanied by the minatory intertitle: "The dancing feet are stilled: 'dust to dust—ashes to ashes.'" When Walton gets an indictment against Dr. Malfit (Juan de la Cruz), the abortion provider threatens to implicate Mrs. Walton unless she calls off her husband. Forbidden from introducing his records of other patients in his defense, he erupts in court, telling Walton: "Before sitting in judgment on others, you should see to your own household." Stricken by doubts, Walton examines Malfit's ledger and finds two charges to his wife. Returning to a party at his house, he accuses her of manslaughter before her friends, and then, alone with her, asks plaintively: "Where are my children?" Calling her "a murderess," he spends the night "griev[ing] for his lost children and his lost faith in the woman who should have been their mother." Chastened by his accusations, Mrs. Walton seeks in vain to have a child of her own, but, "having perverted Nature so often, she found herself physically unable to wear the diadem of motherhood," and the fade-out finds the Waltons, now grown old, surrounded by children who are not their own.

Instead of following *Regeneration* in revealing a tempting, visually exotic underworld within the modern American cityscape in preparation for revealing an even more surprising core of unselfish kindness within its gangster hero, *Where Are My Children?*, which might have been called *Degeneration,* unmasks the normal world of social butterflies and decorous house parties as the real temptation to the hypernormal friends, neighbors, and relatives whose continued participation in that world depends on abortions that are presented as devastatingly routine when Mrs. Walton, having escorted Mrs. Carlo to Dr. Malfit's, yawns as she waits in his antechamber. Presenting its argument in favor of eugenic birth control in clearly racist and classist terms, the film implies in its opening scenes the disastrous results of unchecked births among the poor and nonwhite, arguing that white upper-class women have a moral obligation to reproduce and so release "the unwanted ones" from the locked gates of Heaven. District Attorney Walton's announcement to the women he finds his wife entertaining—"I should bring you all to trial for manslaughter"— presents upper-class white women who conceal their abortions as the true exotics, monsters far beyond the regeneration Walsh's film offers its gangster hero.

If *Regeneration* is marked in the end by the sentimentality that treats its hero as one of us rather than one of them, *Where Are My Children?* moves boldly in the opposite direction, demonizing an entire social class whose apparent normalcy is only the camouflage for a creeping moral rot that makes its members unworthy of love or forgiveness. Weber's keen awareness of the challenge in finding approaches to exotic characters and stories that combined sensitivity and sensationalism is revealed in both *The Hand That Rocks the Cradle,* a more direct but less sensationalistic fictionalizing of Margaret Sanger's career she made the year after *Where Are My Children?*, and in her ascription of the later film's commercial failure to the fact that it was "too tame [with] hardly a jolt in it."[19] Another film that notably failed to strike a commercially successful balance was *The Red Kimona* (1925), Walter Lang's adaptation of a newspaper story by Adela Rogers St. Johns about Gabrielle Darley (Priscilla Bonner), who, encountering in Los Angeles Harold (Carl Miller), the man who lured her into prostitution in New Orleans, just as he is buying an engagement ring for the woman he plans to marry, shoots him to death. Taken up as a pet cause but then abandoned by the socialite Mrs. Fontaine (Virginia Pearson), Gabrielle finally finds her true calling as a hospital nurse when war breaks out. The film, whose censor-baiting subject would have made it hard to market in any case, ran into further trouble when the real-life Gabrielle Darley, whose name and life story producer Dorothy Davenport had used in publicizing the film, sued Davenport for invasion of privacy, ruining her financially and establishing an important legal precedent for the same right to privacy in California that other states had already recognized.

Reports from the frontier

Hollywood was more successful in striking a balance between sensitivity and sensationalism in shaping an entire genre organized around American exotica, the Western, whose focus on negotiations over the border between what counted as American and what counted as exotic inevitably produced studies of American exotica and exotic Americans that confounded these borders. James Cruze's highly influential 1923 film *The Covered Wagon* set a conventional romantic triangle against the exotic scenery of the nineteenth-century American West. The film's historical setting turned out to pay unexpected dividends when Virginia K. Bridger Wachsman Hahn filed a libel suit against Famous Players-Lasky for the film's portrayal of her father, legendary mountaineer Jim Bridger (Tully Marshall), as a comical drunkard. A federal court ruled against her, finding that, in contrast to Gabrielle Darley's right to her own privacy, no one could recover damages for the defamation of an ancestor. The following year, Fox released John Ford's even more grandly scaled epic *The Iron Horse*, based on a story by Charles Kenyon and John Russell, which used the construction of the transcontinental railroad between 1863 and 1869 as the backdrop to another romantic triangle further complicated by the quest of one of its principals, Davy Brandon (George O'Brien), to avenge the death of his father at the hands of a white man disguised as a Native American.

A leading inspiration for many of the period's Westerns was Zane Grey, whose capacious novels, specializing in evocative physical descriptions and often covering many years and hundreds of pages, would seem to have resisted screen adaptation. Nonetheless, Grey's work was eventually adapted in over a hundred films, forty of them produced between 1915 and 1927. Three Grey adaptations released in 1925 revealed three different ways the Western staged the relationship between Americans and exotics. *Riders of the Purple Sage*, the second of four adaptations of Grey's most popular novel, shoehorns the twenty years of Grey's plot, in which Texas Ranger Jim Carson (Tom Mix) seeks first to find his missing sister, Millye Erne (Beatrice Burnham), who has been abducted with Bessie, her infant daughter, by crooked attorney Lew Walters (Warner Oland), and then to avenge her death and rescue Bessie (Sissyl Johnson), into fifty-six action-packed minutes. Like Grey's novel, the film uses its Western setting as an elemental backdrop for a story about love, legacy, identity, family ties, and conflicting loyalties. The main difference between Grey's contemplative novel and the film is the film's blistering pace. Despite its well-earned reputation for spectacular scenery, which grows both more spectacular and more instrumental as the film hurtles to its conclusion, its director, Lynn Reynolds, never lingers on the scenery or anything else. The film omits practically all of the events in between Jim's discovery of Millye's abduction and the events immediately leading up to his climactic revenge and rescue, accelerating closeups, two-shots, long shots, conversations, and intertitles to produce a scorching sense of non-reflective, nonstop action, distilling Grey's reflections about the inevitable collisions between equally authentic Western types—the man of action, the loyal helpmeet, the supportive townsfolk, the righteous vigilante—into an unreflective blur.

The Vanishing American might be called the anti–Riders of the Purple Sage. George B. Seitz's film, running twice as long as Riders of the Purple Sage, wastes no time in announcing its epic ambitions. Its opening sequence, showing the cave dwellers who inhabited the West in the mid-sixteenth century, employs hundreds of extras. Practically all the shots before the story's main action begins in 1915 are long shots; even shots of individuals in these early sequences are full shots rather than closeups. The majestically paced film tackles head-on the issues of racism that arise when Native Americans confront European settlers instead of following Riders of the Purple Sage in projecting the conflicts between these two groups onto all-white heroes and villains. From its title to its final shots, the film, reversing the customary condescension of minstrelsy while retaining its racial stereotypes, insists constantly on the metonymic valence of its noble title character, Nophaie (Richard Dix in redface) and his pathetic oppression at the hands of an ungrateful country, whose values are crystallized by the villainous, unstoppable clerk Booker (Noah Beery). The film treats Nophaie, who at one point reacts to a characterization of himself as American by saying, "American—me?," as both the quintessential American and the ultimate outsider in a country for which he is willing to refashion his most deeply held cultural attachments and volunteer for service in the First World War even if it takes his life. Nophaie's forbidden love, white schoolteacher Marian Warner (Lois Wilson), secretly loves him in return despite her courtship by Captain Earl Ramsdale (Malcolm McGregor). Since the audiences in 1925 would not have accepted her marriage to a Native American, however, it is clear that the price of her rejecting Ramsdale's own marriage proposal will be Nophaie's death. The plight of the laconic individual hero therefore becomes an example of a centuries-long story of cultural conquest and displacement that is more important than he is. The film confirms this identification most powerfully in its final intertitle, which affirms that the people pass away but the land endures (see Figure 3.12).

Another Seitz adaptation, Wild Horse Mesa, provides the most offbeat dramatization of the American exotic. The film traces the partnership of Benton Manerube (George Magrill), who scratches out a living by roping and selling wild horses, with even less successful Colorado shop owner Lige Melberne (George Irving), whom Bent persuades to use his stores of barbed wire to fence in the narrow exit from a natural canyon nearby so that large numbers of horses can be trapped, captured, and sold. After Lige agrees to sell his house and store to finance the enterprise, the scene shifts to another remote part of the mesa in which Chane Weymer (Jack Holt),

FIGURE 3.12 *The final image of* The Vanishing American *(1925) sets the universal endurance of the physical world against the transience of the exotic people who inhabit it.*

just as he is leaving with a herd of horses his Navajo friend Toddy Nokin (Bernard Siegel) has captured, is joined by sinister hand Bud McPherson (Noah Beery) and his two sidekicks, who steal Chane's weapon and plot to kill him. Escaping, Chane rides through the mesa toward a distant Mormon settlement but is rescued at the point of death by a party including Bent, Lige, and Lige's daughter Sue (Billie Dove). At the same time, Toddy's daughter Sosie (Margaret Norris), hopelessly in love with Chane, slips away from her father in the hope of meeting Chane alone. Instead, she falls into the clutches of Bud McPherson and his cronies, who make no secret of their intentions. Making her way back to Toddy, Sosie barely has time to point him toward "the three white men" before she dies. Back in the mesa, Chane tells Bent and Lige, who have completed their preparations for trapping the wild horses, that many of the horses will be injured or killed when they hurtle into the barbed wire. When he persuades Lige to pull out of the partnership, Bent joins forces with McPherson, who takes Lige's party prisoner until he and his accomplices are killed by Toddy, standing alone on a distant mountain peak, his eyes raised to heaven and a vision of his dead daughter. Chane's intervention saves Lige and Sue from the climactic stampede, and the film ends with Chane and Sue headed toward marriage.

This summary, accurate as far as it goes, omits what is most distinctive about *Wild Horse Mesa*: the systematic subordination of human conflicts and values to the care of the wild horses themselves, especially Penguitch, the white stallion described in an early intertitle as "the undisputed monarch of the herds." The horses in general and Penguitch in particular embody ideals of wildness and radical freedom even more atavistic than those of the Navajo that provide a benchmark for the morality of all the film's human characters, who are rated up or down in accordance with their respect and compassion for the horses. Chane proves himself worthy of Sue not only by preventing the herd from stampeding her and her father but also by accepting her love in exchange for letting Penguitch, who becomes vulnerable to capture when he is separated from his herd, escape to run free. Beneath the domestic union that secures the film's happy ending is an elemental and utterly opposed wildness Grey finds even more deeply American than the self-sacrifice of the vanishing American. The truest American exotic in the cast is not Lige or Chane or even Toddy but Penguitch.

Along with early Westerns that explored the frontier between Euro-American civilization and alternatives ranging from savagery to hallowed, ancient Native American civilizations, Hollywood was already generating anti-Westerns that anatomized American exotica on quite different terms. In *Womanhandled* (1925), his first feature for Paramount, Gregory La Cava, who had already directed 139 shorts but only two previous features, transfers the setting of Canadian writer Arthur Stringer's *Saturday Evening Post* story from Canada to the contemporary American West in order to satirize myths of the West and the unquenchable Eastern appetite for them. In the film, Molly Martin (Esther Ralston), romanced by Bill Dana (Richard Dix), who lives "south of 67th," is enamored of the West and suspicious of men who are "womanhandled." Pretending to share her taste for a manly outdoors life, Bill asks her to wait for him while he visits the dude ranch his Uncle Lester (Edmund Breese) owns. Once at the ranch, Bill finds that all the "real cowboys" have gone into the movies. His uncle's hands, natives of Brooklyn and the Bowery who scorn the colorful outfits he had imagined, use a flivver to round up cattle because they cannot ride horses and invite Bill to keep in shape by visiting the neighboring golf course. His plan to return east is complicated by Molly's plan to visit him, forcing him to pay, costume, and coach his uncle's employees to look and act like cowboys and make up the local African Americans as Indians whom he identifies to Molly as "Blackfeet." When Molly announces her intention of staying for two weeks, eliciting groans from Bill and his accomplices, Bill acts even tougher, picking a fight with one of them for spilling gravy on him and threatening to shoot him. Soon after Molly confesses that she liked him better as an Easterner and wants him to take her back home tomorrow, an accidental discovery reveals Bill's deception. Molly collapses in tears, but her aunt Clara (Cora Williams) explains that all men are womanhandled, and that Bill must truly have loved her to go to such lengths.

The film intensifies its central joke that the West as eager fans imagine it no longer exists by showing its hero, a dyed-in-the-wool Easterner, creating an alternative contemporary West even more stylized and preposterous than the one he expected in order to impress his inamorata, who at first accepts it unquestionably. This central joke, that the exotic American West is nothing more than a self-regarding figment of the American imagination, returns the following year in *Mantrap* when divorce lawyer Ralph Prescott (Percy Marmont), yearning for an escape from his citified lifestyle, agrees to join his rough-and-tumble friend Woodbury (Eugene Pallette) on a camping trip out West. The two are soon at each other's throats, and Ralph eagerly accepts an invitation from Joe (Ernest Torrence) to stay with him and his bride Alverna (Clara Bow). So far the film has followed Sinclair Lewis's novel, originally serialized in *Collier's Magazine*, fairly closely, but director Victor Fleming takes every opportunity to puncture Lewis's solemnly overheated tale of sexual temptation by ridiculing the masculine posturing the Western landscape would seem to encourage. When he fails to respond to Alverna's nonstop flirting, Ralph looks not so much virtuous as clueless, and when he accedes to Alverna's demand that he take her along after he finally leaves his host, he merely creates the circumstances under which she will unexpectedly blossom as a worthy partner in the physically demanding journey, even though she never abandons her propensity to flirt with every man who crosses her path. In Fleming's hands, the minatory parable indicated by Lewis's title becomes a sure-footed amalgam of romantic comedy and buddy movie whose two male leads, both constantly and comically falling short of their own ideals, are consistently put in their places by the radiant Alverna.

If Clara Bow was the most iconic Hollywood heroine of the later 1920s, her male counterpart was Douglas Fairbanks. Even more persistently and penetratingly than Bow, Fairbanks, whose partnership in United Artists gave him an exceptional degree of control over the roles he took, emerges as the ultimate non-American American, the quintessential American exotic. The name "United Artists" particularly suited the new company, which Fairbanks and his wife Mary Pickford had formed together with D.W. Griffith and Charlie Chaplin as a way of wresting control over their movies from Hollywood studios that a series of mergers were making evermore powerful. Of the four, Fairbanks was best-known to audiences in 1919 as Mr. Pickford, even though he had already appeared in thirty-one movies over the past four years. But his relative obscurity ended with United Artists' first release, *His Majesty the American*, in 1920. *His Majesty the American* is a title as well suited to Fairbanks as "United Artists" was to his company. Fairbanks stars as Bill Brooks, a New York volunteer firefighter and volunteer police officer who, learning that he is the heir to the throne of the little European country of Alaine, settles down there to run the country along strictly American lines, with lots of grins and clowning and acrobatics, along with all the good-natured directness contemporaneous audiences would expect from any American. *His Majesty the American* established Fairbanks as the quintessential American—or at least established his persona as the embodiment of the values Americans liked to think of as peculiarly American. Bill Brooks's identity as both non-American and super-American is his strongest link to a second superhero Douglas Fairbanks played the following year: Zorro, also known as Don Diego Vega, the scourge of the corrupt grandees of Spanish California. *The Mark of Zorro* was the first property selected for filming by Fairbanks and Pickford during their honeymoon in 1919, very shortly after Zorro made his first appearance in *The Curse of Capistrano*, a five-part magazine serial by Johnston McCulley.

The Mark of Zorro was a considerable risk for United Artists for two different reasons. Apart from Fairbanks, almost nobody had ever heard of Zorro. And *The Curse of Capistrano* was set in nineteenth-century California, when it was still under Mexican rule. Any film based on it would have to be a costume drama, a risky departure for both Fairbanks and United Artists. In addition, it might have seemed a dramatic departure for Fairbanks to shift from playing the all-American Bill Brooks to playing Don Diego Vega. But Fairbanks, who wrote the film's screenplay himself under the pseudonym Elton Thomas, had the inspired idea of retaining the qualities of his typical American persona—the brash extroversion, the acrobatics, the casual derring-do, the irrepressible grin—at least as Zorro; Don Diego, the alter ego who comes across as an effete fop, is distinctly un-American. The film makes three bold and novel moves with the exotic American. In backdating the setting from Mexican to Spanish rule over California, it attempts to avoid offending Mexico by reframing its conflict as the New World versus the Old. It recuperates a Latino action hero as American, as of course all Latin Americans are. And it implies that real Americans are heroic, playful vigilante outlaws, and that their effete doubles, like Don Diego, are fake Americans in every sense of the term.

In spite of the patronizing attitude the film's minstrelsy took toward Spanish Californians and the risks of putting Fairbanks into a costume drama, *The Mark of Zorro* was an enormous hit that spurred Fairbanks to spend much of the silent era playing non-American heroes—Robin Hood, the Thief of Baghdad, Judah Ben-Hur, the Black Pirate, and D'Artagnan of the Three Musketeers—even though "whatever garb he wore, or whatever exotic locale he found himself in, 'Doug' remained the smiling All-American optimist."[20] One particular reason *The Mark of Zorro* was such a hit was the enduring popularity of a hero split into two roles. Zorro was a fearless avenger and dashing champion of the people; Don Diego was a lily-livered milquetoast who courted a woman in love with his alter ego, a hero whose sidekick, the mute Bernardo (Tote Du Crow), faithfully kept his secret as he rallied the people, rescued his love from danger, and fought an unending battle for truth, justice, and the American way (see Figure 3.13). Small wonder that Zorro would be endlessly copied by later heroes from Superman to Spider-Man and prove an especially crucial influence on Batman, as creator Bob Kane has acknowledged.

Five years after *The Mark of Zorro*, Fairbanks returned in *Don Q, Son of Zorro* to play both the aging Zorro and his son, Don Cesar, who on a trip to Spain gets involved in a romantic triangle, is framed for murder, and has to escape and clear himself using his whip as a signature weapon. Already in 1925, *Don Q, Son of Zorro* follows the tried-and-true superhero formula of generating endless sequels that are hard to tell from remakes, since they recycle the same story over and over again. Even before the release of *Don Q, Son of Zorro*, Johnston McCulley, motivated by the first movie's success, had written a second Zorro novel. He would go on to write two more novels and a more extensive corpus of short stories, and Zorro returned in many later stories, novels, plays, movies, radio programs, comic books,

FIGURE 3.13 *The masked Zorro (Douglas Fairbanks) exults over his enemy and romantic rival Captain Juan Ramon (Robert McKim) in the climactic swordfight in* The Mark of Zorro *(1920).*

videogames, ballets, operas, and action figures. The proliferation of Zorro Halloween costumes and his appearance in at least one role-playing game are particularly appropriate for a hero who is most truly himself when he appears in disguise. In short, Zorro is one of the most enduringly popular of all franchise heroes, the Latino Batman—although it would be more accurate to call Batman the Anglo Zorro—and one who sets the pattern for the heroes who would follow once the movies had begun to talk.

Notes

1. Russell Merritt, "Dixon, Griffith, and the Southern Legend," *Cinema Journal* 12.1 (Autumn 1972): 26–45, at 39.
2. Merritt, "Dixon, Griffith, and the Southern Legend," p. 41.
3. See Arthur Lennig, "Myth and Fact: The Reception of Birth of a Nation," *Film History* 16.2 (2004): 119.
4. Scott Eyman, *Empire of Dreams: The Epic Life of Cecil B. DeMille* (New York: Simon and Schuster, 2010), p. 185.
5. O. Henry, "Transients in Arcadia," in *The Voice of the City: Further Stories of the Four Million* (Garden City, NY: Doubleday, Page, 1920), p. 178.
6. Bret Harte, "Salomy Jane's Kiss," in *The Writings of Bret Harte* (Boston: Houghton Mifflin, 1900), 15.260.
7. Gary Scharnhorst, commentary on *Salomy Jane, Treasures from American Film Archives 5: The West, 1898–1938*, Image DVD, 2011.
8. See Thomas Leitch, "Jekyll, Hyde, Jekyll, Hyde, Jekyll, Hyde, Jekyll, Hyde: Four Models of Intertextuality," in *Victorian Literature and Film Adaptation*, ed. Abigail Burnham Bloom and Mary Sanders Pollock (Amherst: Cambria, 2011), pp. 36–38.
9. George Wead, "Frank Norris: His Share of *Greed*," in *The Classic American Novel and the Movies*, ed. Gerald Peary and Roger Shatzkin (New York: Ungar, 1977), p. 150.
10. Herman G. Weinberg, "Foreword," in *The Complete Greed of Erich von Stroheim* (New York: Arno, 1972), n.p.
11. Jan-Christopher Horak, "Maurice Tourneur's Tragic Romance," in *The Classic American Novel and the Movies*, ed. Gerald Peary and Roger Shatzkin (New York: Ungar, 1977), p. 19.
12. Lillian Gish, with Ann Pinchot, *The Movies, Mr. Griffith, and Me* (Englewood Cliffs: Prentice-Hall, 1969), p. 285.
13. Miss I.A.R. Wylie, "An Impression of 'Four Sons' by Its Author," Souvenir Program for *Four Sons*, rpt. and included with the DVD release *Ford at Fox*, Twentieth Century Fox, 2007, unpaged [p. 4].

14 Eileen Bowser, *The Transformation of Cinema, 1907–1915 [History of the American Cinema, Volume 2]* (New York: Scribner's, 1990), p. 112. The quoted passage is from "Giving Credit Where Credit Is Due," *Moving Picture World* 6.10 (March 12, 1910): 369.
15 Anon. "Giving Credit Where Credit Is Due," pp. 369, 370.
16 John W. Frick, *Uncle Tom's Cabin on the American Stage and Screen* (Houndmills: Palgrave Macmillan, 2012), p. 211.
17 Frick, *Uncle Tom's Cabin on the American Stage and Screen*, p. 211.
18 Frick, *Uncle Tom's Cabin on the American Stage and Screen*, p. 215.
19 Florence Lawrence, "'The Hand That Rocks the Cradle' Says Laws React against Race Benefits," *Los Angeles Examiner*, June 24, 1917, quoted by Shelley Stamp, *Lois Weber in Early Hollywood* (Berkeley: University of California Press, 2015), p. 138.
20 Ronald Bergan, *The United Artists Story* (New York: Crown), p. 9.

4

1927–39: Novel Impressions

Garbo talks!

What was it like for Hollywood to make film adaptations in the first decade of the sound era? Samuel Marx, the head story editor at Metro-Goldwyn-Mayer (MGM), has left a brief but vivid account in "Looking for a Story." The challenge begins with "the task of finding a suitable screen story":

> The larger studios comb through twenty thousand stories a year to find fifty. The twenty thousand are the better magazine stories, foreign and American plays, novels published throughout the world, and stories created directly for the screen by authors of known reputation. From these sources the studios find twenty thousand pieces of material to consider. They do not always find the fifty stories to film.[1]

Many are called to this banquet but few are chosen, and they are chosen at second-hand. Because the story editor "is physically unable to read every submission in its entirety, a corps of readers reduces the basic material to synopsis form. [...] A competent reader reduces the elements of a story plot to a synopsis of from one to twenty pages, briefly adding his own opinion of its celluloid possibilities,"[2] as in this 1936 summary comment by Dorothy Robinson, of the Warner Bros. story department, on Edna Ferber's 1924 novel *So Big*: "This is a valuable piece of property. With skillful treatment, it can be made into a fine picture. The characters are real and interesting: the story is convincing. It offers an important role for an actress—Bette Davis perhaps."[3] Robinson's eye for the possibilities the novel held for a particular Warners contract star is no accident, for properties were acquired and tailored for specific stars: "The studio has expensive stars under contract, each possessing an individual talent and a comparatively short professional life. The story must not be too similar to the star's previous pictures, yet within the realm of the star's capabilities. [...] It is when a star appears in material perfectly suited to what the public wants, that a 'box office success' emerges."[4]

The size, the power, the remarkable capital-intensiveness, and the assembly-line approach to filmmaking of the five major Hollywood studios—MGM, Paramount, Warner Brothers, Twentieth Century Fox (formed by the merger of Fox Film Company with Twentieth Century Pictures in 1935), and Radio-Keith-Orpheum (RKO)—that functioned as fully integrated monopolies for film production, distribution, and exhibition, and the three minor studios that owned a much smaller number of theaters—Universal, Columbia, and United Artists—combined to produce a rapacious appetite for new material tailored to their stars. Seeking first to increase their profits in the early years of synchronized sound and then to recover from the financial losses all of them suffered in 1932–3, when only MGM turned a profit, the studios consistently sought to maximize their efficiency by keeping their fabled rosters of stars and their thousands of production personnel at full employment. Clark Gable made thirteen films in 1931; Shirley Temple made ten in 1934, the year she turned six; Will Rogers's string of five films in 1935 was ended only by his death in a deeply mourned aviation accident on August 15.

The key words in Marx's description of the process of selection and acquisition are "material" and "story." The Hollywood studios in the 1930s, most of them vertically integrated monopolies that controlled the production, distribution, and exhibition of their films, saw the novels and plays they adapted as so much raw material. Unless they were adapting a wildly successful novel whose readers would be outraged by any changes, they felt no more responsibility to be faithful to its leading characters and events than farmers or miners or manufacturers would feel to be faithful to their raw material. Noting that there was once "a hue and cry in the land if a well-known book or play reached the screen in form different from the original," Marx adds: "We rarely hear the complaint today," not because "the screen changes less," but because the screenwriters employed by a studio like Samuel Goldwyn are widely acknowledged to be "generally superior to the material available for them to work on, and any changes made by them are likely to be for the better."[5] The process of making decisions about acquiring specific properties on the basis of synopses prepared by story editors was designed to reduce novels and plays to their plot summaries, and unless there was a particular reason to go back to original properties, it was these summaries, these stories, that the studios sought to film, not the novels and plays that had presented them.

Throughout the 1930s the Hollywood studios, under the "unit-production system"[6] under which the studios delegated responsibility for their product to a galaxy of individual producers heading production teams that specialized in particular kinds of movies—melodramas, musicals, romances, thrillers, monster films—turned out an impressive number of movies that combined assembly-line efficiency with high production values. The unit-production model allowed all these genres to coexist without encroaching on each other. The leading development in Hollywood adaptation over the course of the decade was the gradual shift from theatrical to novelistic models. It was not simply the case that the studios turned from filming plays to filming novels. Instead, the shift was to filming different kinds of novels, to approaching the adaptation of novels on different terms, and ultimately to adopt and internalize a novelistic aesthetic.

The rise of the talkies was largely fueled by a theatrical aesthetic. At MGM, by far the dominant American studio throughout the 1930s, "for both [Louis B.] Mayer and [Irving] Thalberg, quality meant not the movies, but the theater."[7] In his review of the 1929–30 Hollywood season of "flirting with theater," however, Donald Crafton cautions that "the word *theatrical* as a formal description is vague and almost meaningless. Critics and writers seem to have been using it in two ways: attempting to mimic the structure of the Broadway source, and relying on dialogue to tell the story."[8] Instead of thinking of the plays they purchased for adaptation, or of the theater generally, as a branch of literature, studio heads emphasized the non-literary aspects of theater: its immediacy, the opportunities it offered for star-making performances, its dependence on dialogue, and its emphasis on story. They sought and promoted these aspects even in films like *Alibi Ike*, Warner Bros.' 1935 adaptation of Ring Lardner's 1915 short story. Lardner's story is essentially a character sketch whose first part sets up the figure of Francis X. Farrell, the baseball pitcher who cannot help making excuses for both his every failure and his every success, and whose second part shows how this habit embroils him in some forgettable domestic complications. William Wister Haines's screenplay complicates the romance of Farrell (Joe E. Brown) with Dolly (Olivia de Havilland) by an account of his kidnapping by gangsters bent on fixing games during the Chicago Cubs' pursuit of the pennant. Even so, it is Brown's portrayal of Farrell, not the plot, that provides the film's greatest pleasures.

According to Ruth Vasey, "The introduction of talkies encouraged the studios to derive their subjects from the stage, despite the fact that plays were the most expensive story sources of all."[9] "Plays have always cost the studios most money," Marx explains, because "of all types of material the playscript most approximates the scenario. In the past decade, dialogue has become the most valuable ingredient of the screen story. Plays contain relatively most dialogue; hence plays are more desirable than novels and originals."[10] Although MGM's readers perused classic novels like Jack London's *The Call of the Wild,* best-selling modern novels like Pearl S. Buck's *The Good Earth,* and short stories and serials in mass-market magazines like *Colliers* and the *Saturday Evening Post,* Marx makes it clear why their preferred material, at least at the beginning of the decade, was the theater. In addition to providing potentially filmable dialogue, plays were much easier to adapt to the cinema than short stories, which required expansion, or long novels, which required compression. Even more important, movies had been seeking cultural cachet for years by competing more aggressively for the theatrical audience, offering themselves explicitly as what Richard Koszarski calls "an evening's entertainment,"[11] a less expensive, more democratic alternative to an evening at the theater whose main disadvantage, their lack of spoken dialogue, was suddenly neutralized by the adoption of synchronized sound. Hollywood could bring film versions of long-running Broadway plays into every small town in America with a theater wired for sound reproduction.

The studios' assembly-line approach to filmmaking, already well established in the 1920s, became both more precise and more exigent with the rise of synchronized sound. During the year or so before the development of double-system recording technologies that made it possible to record and manipulate soundtracks independently of the visual tracks they accompanied, the demands of live sound recording, which required the simultaneous recording of images with whatever sounds would accompany them, made the moviemaking process more grueling and unforgiving even as audiences already attracted to sound by their increasingly universal acceptance of radio reveled in the new dimensions of setting and character that sound permitted. Gambling on the appeal of synchronized sound, Warner Bros. premiered *The Jazz Singer* (1927), an adaptation of the 1925 Broadway play Samson Raphaelson had based on his 1922 story "The Day of Atonement," on October 6, 1927, a date chosen to commemorate the ending of Yom Kippur, the solemn holiday celebrated at the end of the film. Although Al Jolson's first singing role had been eagerly anticipated, the moments to which the audience responded most intensely were not any of the six songs sung by Jolson as Jack Robin, the cantor's son who had left his family to make a living as a blackface performer, but the two minutes of spoken dialogue, from "Wait a minute, wait a minute, you ain't heard nothing yet!," the signature line Jolson cried out just after his first number, "Dirty Hands, Dirty Face," to his largely improvised dialogue with Eugénie Besserer, who played his mother, before the film reverted to the silent convention of intertitles to convey the dialogue (see Figure 4.1).[12] Audiences, it seemed, were entranced not so much by the possibility of *hearing* the film's characters in performances that had clearly been staged for the movie camera as to the possibility of *overhearing* "conversations purportedly addressed to others, by conversations that—in reality—are designed to communicate certain information to the audience."[13]

Although *The Jazz Singer* continued to circulate in both silent and synch-sound prints, most studios weaned themselves away from silent films altogether by mid-1929. The rapid triumph of synchronized sound presented film adapters with both new opportunities and new challenges. On the one hand, MGM could lure audiences into screenings of the studio's dour 1930 adaptation of Eugene O'Neill's 1921 play *Anna Christie* with

FIGURE 4.1 *His song finished, Jack Robin (Al Jolson) strikes up an impromptu conversation with his mother (Eugénie Besserer) in* The Jazz Singer *(1927)*.

the promise, "Garbo talks!" Everyone who had been faithfully following movie stars for years could now hear them break their silence, even if some of these stars were eventually sidelined by voices that were thickly accented (Lars Hanson, Lillian Gish's costar in the 1926 *The Scarlet Letter*), hard to understand (silent vamp Pola Negri), or incongruous with the stars' screen personas (John Gilbert, whose tenor voice was higher than his frequent costar Garbo's). Overnight a call for performers with stage-trained voices, along with writers and directors who had been successful in the theater, seemed to cross the country from Hollywood to Broadway. As far back as *The Avenging Conscience* (1914), movies had monstrated subjective states by exteriorizing them, a task made much easier by synchronized dialogue, sound effects, and music. At the same time, however, the potential ubiquity of auditory information raised new problems for filmmakers suddenly tempted to provide endless shots of talking heads that would minimize visual variety even as they provided audiences with all too easy and complete access to the thoughts of characters who could not afford to reveal themselves too quickly or completely. After the talkies' initial infatuation with spoken dialogue, movies set about exploring the expressive possibilities of music and sound effects, both of which could provide some information about characters and tone while keeping other information in reserve.

The studios' newly galvanized appetite for theatrical properties produced a wide range of marquee movies based on American plays. Joining war-themed adaptations like *All Quiet on the Western Front*, the top-grossing film of 1930, were top-grossing theatrical adaptations like *The Broadway Melody* (1929), *Frankenstein* (1931), and *The Merry Widow* (1934). The musical theater was uniquely poised to make the leap to Hollywood, as George Jessel realized when his starring role in the third season of a touring production of the stage play *The Jazz Singer* was abruptly ended along with the production: "A week or two after the Washington engagement the sound-and-picture version of *The Jazz Singer* was sweeping the country, and I was swept out of business."[14]

Early synch-sound adaptations of American plays often depended on the work of Pulitzer Prize-winning playwrights. Eugene O'Neill's plays were adapted to the screen as *Anna Christie, Strange Interlude* (1932), *The Constant Woman* (1933), *The Emperor Jones* (1933), *Ah, Wilderness!* (1935), and *The Long Voyage Home* (1940). Owen Davis, who had won the Pulitzer for his 1923 play *Icebound* after contributing material to seventeen earlier films, continued to supply material for some twenty sound films, some of them adaptations of his plays from *The Donovan Affair* (1929) to *Jezebel* (1938), others based on the work of other writers, from Homer Croy's *They Had to See Paris* (1926, filmed 1929) to F. Scott Fitzgerald's *The Great Gatsby* (1925, filmed 1949). Although his most original play, *The Adding Machine* (1923), had to wait twenty-five years for a television adaptation, Elmer Rice, who received his first movie credit in the 1917 adaptation of his 1914 play *On Trial*, continued to work intermittently in movies and television for over thirty years after winning the Pulitzer for *Street Scene* (1929), writing plays that served as the bases for *Oh, Sailor Behave!* (1930), *Street Scene* (1931), *Counsellor at Law* (1933), and *Dream Girl* (1948), and collaborating on the television movie *Who Killed Cock Robin?* (1938) and the feature film *Holiday Inn* (1942). Beginning ten years after these two writers, Maxwell Anderson, who won the 1933 Pulitzer for *Both Your Houses*, wrote plays that were adapted to the films *Mary of Scotland* (1936), *Winterset* (1936), *The Private Lives of Elizabeth and Essex* (1939), and later *Key Largo* (1948), *Joan of Arc* (1948), and *The Bad Seed* (1956), and in between collaborated in the adaptations of films like *All Quiet on the Western Front, Rain* (1932), *We Live Again* (1934), and *So Red the Rose* (1935). Sidney Howard, who won in 1925 for *They Knew What They Wanted*, contributed material to twenty films from *A Lady to Love*, a 1930 adaptation of *They Knew What They Wanted*, to *Arrowsmith* (1931), *Dodsworth* (1936), and *Gone with the Wind* (1939), on which he was the only writer besides Margaret Mitchell to receive screen credit. Three-time Pulitzer winner Robert E. Sherwood, who had won for *Idiot's Delight* (1936) and *Abe Lincoln in Illinois* (1939), both of whose screenplays he was credited with writing when the films were released in 1939 and 1940 respectively, supplied the dramatic basis for *Waterloo Bridge* (1931, remade in 1940), *Two Kinds of Women* (1932), *Reunion in Vienna* (1933), *The Petrified Forest* (1936), and *Tovarich* (1937), worked on adapting material by other hands in *The Age for Love* (1931) and *The Scarlet Pimpernel* (1934), and produced an original story for *Roman Scandals* (1933) and an original screenplay for *The Ghost Goes West* (1935). In addition, the studios adapted plays by Pulitzer winners George Kelly, Marc Connelly, and Thornton Wilder, all of whom went on to work on other film projects as well.

During this period Pulitzer Prize-winning novels also attracted the attention of Hollywood studios. But novels that won Pulitzer prizes between 1917 and 1936, the first two decades the prizes were awarded, were less likely than winners of the Pulitzer Prize for Drama to be filmed, and they took longer to reach the screen, even though the openings of dramatic adaptations from *Grand Hotel* (1932) to *Arsenic and Old Lace* (filmed in 1940 but not released until 1944) were delayed by contract until the plays' theatrical run had ended. Not until the second half of the decade did the studios begin to show as much interest in Pulitzer-winning novels as in Pulitzer-winning plays.[15]

Despite the advantages playwrights enjoyed over novelists in winning Hollywood contracts for their properties or their ongoing services, the transition from Broadway to Hollywood could be complicated for playwrights like Clifford Odets who feared accusations by others or themselves of selling out. Hailed as Eugene O'Neill's successor for his bold one-act agitprop piece *Waiting for Lefty* and the full-length *Awake and Sing!* (both 1935), Odets then turned from stories of social oppression and political resistance to the more conventional psychological realism of *Golden Boy* (1937, filmed 1939), *Clash by Night* (1941, filmed 1952), *The Big Knife* (1949, filmed 1955), and *The Country Girl* (1950, filmed 1954). From 1936 on, however, he spent most of his time in Hollywood, where he hoped to raise enough money to subsidize the Group Theatre's production of his adaptation of *Paradise Lost*. Although he was credited with writing the original screenplays for *The General Died at Dawn* (1936) and *None but the Lonely Heart* (1944), and collaborating on the adaptations *Deadline at Dawn* (1946), *Humoresque* (1946), and *Sweet Smell of Success* (1957), Odets chafed under the strictures of Hollywood's assembly-line approach to production, which he considered stifling. *The Big Knife* in particular is a lacerating portrait of the costs of compromising with Hollywood, and it is sadly fitting that Odets, who surely saw himself in the hard-used figure of actor Charles Castle (Jack Palance), driven to suicide by the morally bankrupt figures who have enabled his success, became the principal model for the disillusioned playwright-turned-screenwriter Barton Fink (John Turturro) in Joel and Ethan Coen's 1991 film.

Apart from their pursuit of cultural cachet in highbrow Broadway properties, the talkies drew inspiration from less culturally ambitious dramatic material as well. The studios' acceptance of synchronized sound coincided almost exactly with the first staging of *Show Boat,* the pioneering Broadway musical based on Edna Ferber's 1926 novel that opened on Broadway on December 27, 1927. The show was widely hailed for its skill at integrating musical numbers that might have stood alone in earlier musical revues into a coherent story that combined intimate romance and epic sweep. Songs like "Make Believe," "Can't Help Lovin' Dat Man," "You Are Love," and "Why Do I Love You?" traced the stages in Magnolia Hawks's love for the gambler Gaylord Ravenal, while "Old Man River" invoked an eternal, never-changing backdrop against which the vicissitudes of this love played out. After the success of MGM's first two musicals, *The Broadway Melody* (1929), which won the Academy Award for Best Picture, and *The Hollywood Revue of 1929,* an essentially plotless series of individual star turns, other studios sought ways to follow or combine these two models. Warner Bros. drew on its 1923 adaptation of *The Gold Diggers* for a series of backstage musicals choreographed by Busby Berkeley— *Gold Diggers of 1933, Gold Diggers of 1935, Gold Diggers of 1937,* and *Gold Diggers in Paris* (1938)—that complemented the studio's other Berkeley-choreographed musicals like *42nd Street* (1933), based on Bradford Ropes's 1932 novel, and *Footlight Parade* (1933), based on Manuel Seff and James Seymour's original screenplay. RKO integrated musical numbers more closely into the plot by using them to express the emotions of dancing stars Fred Astaire and Ginger Rogers as they fell in love to the music of Vincent Youmans in *Flying Down to Rio* (1933), Cole Porter and others in *The Gay Divorcee* (1934), Jerome Kern in *Roberta* (1935), and Irving Berlin in *Follow the Fleet* (1936). Having already produced *Show Boat,* Harry A. Pollard's mostly silent 1929 adaptation of Ferber's novel to which several songs were added at the last minute in response to the talkie craze, Universal released James Whale's more fully integrated adaptation of the show in 1936.

The two poles of the Hollywood musical of the era are aptly represented by composer Richard Rodgers's collaborations first with lyricist Lorenz Hart (1919–42), then with lyricist Oscar Hammerstein II (1943–60). Although the long series of successful Rodgers and Hart musicals were often adapted by Hollywood in films like *On Your Toes* (1939), *Babes in Arms* (1939), *The Boys from Syracuse* (1940), *Too Many Girls* (1940), *I Married an Angel* (1942), *Higher and Higher* (1943), and *Pal Joey* (1957), few of these adaptations preserved all of their often acrid or anti-romantic songs. The pair's greatest success in Hollywood came not through adaptations of their Broadway shows but through their own success in adapting to the movies in the original scores they wrote for *Love Me Tonight* (1932), *The Phantom President* (1932), *Hallelujah, I'm a Bum* (1933), and *Mississippi* (1935). Hart's failing health and eventual death led Rodgers to team with

Hammerstein in a series of very different musicals that presented themselves less as monstrating revues than as fully developed stories: *Oklahoma* (1943, filmed 1955), *Carousel* (1945, filmed 1956), *South Pacific* (1949, filmed 1958), *The King and I* (1951, filmed 1956), *Flower Drum Song* (1958, filmed 1961), and *The Sound of Music* (1959, filmed 1965), with interruptions for the original film musicals *State Fair* (1945) and *Cinderella* (1957). These shows could be much more faithfully adapted to the movies, partly because Hammerstein's lyrics were wholesome and uplifting rather than witty and prickly, but mostly because the shows themselves integrated their numbers much more closely into the narrative, following a model that by this time had become the dominant model for Hollywood musicals as well, a pattern that would eventually produce such blockbuster musical adaptations as Joseph L. Mankiewicz's *Guys and Dolls* (1955), Robert Wise and Jerome Robbins's *West Side Story* (1961), and Morton DaCosta's *The Music Man* (1962) before the fashion changed once more.

Out of all the playwrights whose work was adapted to the talkies, the one who found the greatest variety of ways to straddle the worlds of Broadway and Hollywood was George S. Kaufman. Kaufman, who had collaborated with Marc Connelly in *Merton of the Movies* (1923), which was filmed in 1924 and 1947, and on *Beggar on Horseback* (1924), which was filmed in 1925, then partnered with Edna Ferber on *The Royal Family* (1927), which was adapted as the sound film *The Royal Family of Broadway* (1930); *Dinner at Eight* (1932, filmed 1933); and *Stage Door* (1936, filmed 1937). In between, he wrote a solo play, *The Butter and Egg Man* (1925, filmed 1928); joined Morrie Ryskind in writing the books for two musicals starring the Marx Brothers, *The Cocoanuts* (1927) and *Animal Crackers* (1929), which provided the basis for the foursome's first two films in 1929 and 1930; and later collaborated on the original screenplays for two more Marx Brothers vehicles, *A Night at the Opera* (1935) and *A Day at the Races* (1937). Although Groucho Marx pronounced Kaufman his idol, one of the few writers he actually enjoyed working with, he is best remembered for his non-musical collaborations with Moss Hart: *Once in a Lifetime* (1930, filmed 1932), a broadly satirical look at the talkies; *Merrily We Roll Along* (1934), a tale revealing the gradual corruption of an aspiring playwright that began at the end of the story and then moved back through scene after scene to its beginning, whose dark moralism discouraged anyone from filming it until Stephen Sondheim's 2013 musical version; the Pulitzer Prize-winning *You Can't Take It with You* (1936), whose 1938 film adaptation won Oscars for Best Picture and Frank Capra as Best Director; *I'd Rather Be Right* (1937), a political satire starring George M. Cohan as President Franklin W. Roosevelt, which supplied the frame story for the flashbacks that told the story of Cohan's life in the 1942 film *Yankee Doodle Dandy*; *The Man Who Came to Dinner* (1939, filmed 1942); and *George Washington Slept Here* (1940, filmed 1942).

Franchise adaptations

Samuel Marx's portrait of Hollywood studios beating the bushes for promising theatrical properties is complicated by several other tendencies he passes over. Although novels were harder than plays to adapt and less obvious analogues for the cinema, Brian McFarlane has aptly noted, "As soon as the cinema began to see itself as narrative entertainment, the idea of ransacking the novel—that already established repository of narrative fiction—for source material got underway."[16] But even when producers of silent photoplays sought this cachet in bookstores, they typically framed their adaptations in theatrical terms.

Rick Altman resolves this apparent contradiction by suggesting that if you "take any list of silent films apparently derived from novels, [and] submit to a few hours of research in a serious library, [...] you will have little trouble discovering that a very high proportion of the novels were turned into extremely popular stage shows in the year preceding the film."[17] As Altman explains in a note: "Early editions of *Variety* and *Moving Picture World* regularly insist on a film's novelistic paternity, recognizing recent theatrical adaptations as a second parent only when the film borrows its title from the dramatic version rather than from the original version. [...] There is good reason for cinema to avoid mentioning its debt to the stage, especially through the teens, for the popular theater remained cinema's strongest competitor through the war years."[18]

This disavowal of its theatrical roots, which allowed silent cinema to draw on the cultural capital of the novel while borrowing its material more directly from the theater, continues with the rise of the talkies. Peter Lev has shown that according to the American Film Institute (AFI) catalog, American film adaptations throughout the 1930s more often credited novels than movies as their sources. But the AFI catalog lists films as different as *An American Tragedy* (1931), *A Farewell to Arms* (1932), *Dr. Jekyll and Mr. Hyde* (1932), *Stella Dallas* (1937), and *A Christmas Carol* (1938) as adaptations of novels, even though all these novels had already spawned stage adaptations the films followed more closely than the novels they identified as their sources.[19]

Given the problems of shoehorning a three-hundred-page novel into a two-hour film without making it sound intolerably talky, many producers of early sound films opted to pursue an alternative route pioneered by MGM's 1932 adaptation of *Grand Hotel* (see Figure 4.2). MGM purchased the rights not to Vicki Baum's 1929 novel *Menschen im Hotel* but to the unsuccessful German play based on the novel. In order the secure the adaptation rights from Harry Moses, the New York businessman who had purchased them, MGM agreed to share the cost of an American stage production with Moses on the condition that "Moses affiliate himself with some tried stage producer."[20] When Moses succeeded in interesting Herman

FIGURE 4.2 *A characteristically intimate moment between the ballerina Grusinskaya (Greta Garbo) and Baron Felix von Geigern (John Barrymore) in* Grand Hotel *(1932).*

Shumlin, producer of *The Last Mile,* in the venture, William Absalom Drake's "play became a world sensation and M-G-M owned the movie rights without cost."[21] The most immediate cue MGM took from the critical and financial success of *Grand Hotel* (1932) was not for more adaptations of best-selling contemporary novels but for non-novelistic vehicles that could accommodate the studio's impressive roster of stars, from *Rasputin and the Empress* (1932) to *Dinner at Eight* (1933). It was not until well after MGM's initial push toward star-laden showcases that studios took a more lasting lesson from MGM's adaptation of *Grand Hotel*: that filmmakers could adapt novels whose impact depended on characters or moods or ideas rather than pageantry or dramatic action, novels of contemporary life in which, it might be, nothing much happened.

For the moment, however, the terms on which movies were presented, marketed, and exhibited continued be framed in largely theatrical terms. Indeed, the first step in adapting a novel to the screen was to break it into dramatic scenes, a practice that is still recommended in the widely influential screenwriting manuals of Syd Field and Robert McKee.[22] Cinema drew on theatrical models not only for its sources but as a social and phenomenological framework for the experience it offered. Although early movie theaters more closely resembled burlesque houses than legitimate theaters, exhibitors consciously copied the look and feel of Broadway temples in movie palaces like Grauman's Chinese Theatre and Radio City Music Hall in order to underline movies' affinities with the theater. Unlike novels, which might be kept in print indefinitely, even the most popular stage plays enjoyed limited runs, offering an irresistible opportunity to film studios to meet the untapped demand for what in many cases amounted to a touring version of the play that could reach every small town with a movie theater. The rush to convert motion-picture theaters to exhibit talkies was soon matched by a rush to bring stage-trained performers, writers, and directors to Hollywood so that they could teach the movies to talk. Neither playwrights nor stage directors like Rouben Mamoulian and George Abbott had any obvious analogue among novelists because nobody wanted movies to sound like books. And as performers like Greta Garbo and Bette Davis gradually gained more power over the roles in which they were cast, they naturally competed to win well-known theatrical parts; nobody came to Hollywood hoping to play Madame Bovary or Mrs. Dalloway. Sergei Eisenstein may have venerated James Joyce, but few studio filmmakers were interested in exploring what George Bluestone has called the defining subject of the modern novel: "the inability to arrest a reality that is perpetually out of reach."[23]

When the talkies looked to American novels, they were less likely to seek distinguished literary properties than promising vehicles for their contract stars because these stars provided much stronger and more visible attractions than the stories in which they starred. Best-selling novels, like successful plays, "had the advantage of having been pretested in the public arena, and their existing reputations constituted advance publicity" and also enabled producers "trying to defend their choice of material against criticism from the Motion Picture Producers and Directors of America" to "argue that they were not responsible for the kinds of themes that reached the screen" if they presented novelists and playwrights as cultural gatekeepers.[24] But studio heads and producers still saw novels mostly as raw material for movies, or better yet for movie franchises featuring continuing characters.

Rick Altman contends that throughout the studio era, individual studios were less interested in identifying their products as members of industry-wide genres "that must be shared with their competitors" than as members of "cycles of films [...] identified with only a single studio."[25] It was only natural then that so many early sound adaptations of novels spawned franchises that could be licensed and controlled by a single studio—franchises which, as James Naremore has said, "functioned much like the comic strips in the daily newspapers, showing the continuing adventures of Roy Rogers, Boston Blackie, the Bowery Boys, Blondie and Dagwood, Charlie Chan, and so on."[26] MGM discovered the imperishable Andy Hardy (Mickey Rooney) in Aurania Rouverol's 1928 play *Skidding*. Paramount launched the long screen life of Dr. James Kildare by starring Joel McCrea in a 1937 adaptation of Max Brand's 1936 *Cosmopolitan* story "Internes Can't Take Money."

A pair of even more popular franchise heroes emerged around the same time as Fu Manchu. One of them had made his debut the year before, when

Edgar Rice Burroughs published *Tarzan of the Apes* (1912). Burroughs, who had originally considered calling his hero Zantar or Tublat Zan, was determined to create an iconic figure. Tarzan was born John Clayton, Viscount Greystoke, the son of British aristocrats marooned by mutineers on the Atlantic coast of Africa. Raised after Lady Clayton's death by the ape mother Kala, Tarzan teaches himself to read after finding books in his late parents' log cabin. He is literate in many languages, and he can master any new language in a few days, but he must be taught spoken English as an adult by a visiting Frenchman. Though unselfish and noble, the king of the jungle is quick to seek revenge when Kala is murdered, and again when he thinks Jane Porter, the Baltimore native who first meets him when her father's party is marooned in the same spot as his parents, has been killed in *Tarzan the Untamed* (1920). Burroughs's hero, who introduces himself to Jane as "Tarzan, the killer of beasts and many black men," follows her back to the United States when she leaves Africa, marries her in *The Return of Tarzan,* and lives for a time with her in England, his parents' homeland. Tarzan consistently acknowledges Jane as his equal in accomplishments and power. His most distinctive feature, however, is not his forward-looking gender politics but his racial identity, which is both completely Aryan and so deeply African that he struggles to accommodate himself to England or America. Tarzan is an apostle of the return to nature in a very specific sense. He is a white man for whom Africa, in a novel turn on blackface minstrelsy, becomes the ultimate vacation home, an exotic retreat from a civilization he can no longer endure.

Of all Tarzan's film appearances, the most faithful to Burroughs's books are the first two, both released in 1918: *Tarzan of the Apes* and its sequel *The Romance of Tarzan,* both starring Elmo Lincoln. The films that followed include *The Revenge of Tarzan* (1920), the fifteen-part serial *The Son of Tarzan* (1920), and a lost 1928 serial, *Tarzan the Mighty*. The Tarzan movies most audiences remember best, however, are the twelve films beginning with *Tarzan the Ape Man* (1932) starring German-Romanian swimmer Johnny Weissmuller, who had won five gold medals in the 1924 and 1928 Olympic Games. Although "any other studio would have churned out Tarzan movies like so many sausages" after the success of *Tarzan the Ape Man,* Irving Thalberg convinced Louis B. Mayer "to limit production to one Tarzan movie every two years, hoping to keep the premise fresh and to maximize profits."[27] This strategy produced *Tarzan and His Mate* (1934), *Tarzan Escapes* (1936), *Tarzan Finds a Son!* (1939), *Tarzan's Secret Treasure* (1941), and *Tarzan's New York Adventure* (1942). Since MGM's contract with Burroughs did not prevent the author from licensing other Tarzan films, the MGM franchise had to compete with two low-budget serials—*Tarzan the Fearless* (1933), starring Olympic swimmer Buster Crabbe, and *The New Adventures of Tarzan* (1935), which was in turn re-edited into two features, *The New Adventures of Tarzan* (1935) and *Tarzan and the Green Goddess* (1938)—

and with still another 1938 feature, *Tarzan's Revenge*, in which Twentieth Century Fox featured two more Olympic athletes, decathlon champion Glenn Morris as Tarzan and aquatic medalist Eleanor Holm as his mate Eleanor. MGM reacted to these competitors by seeking to identify Tarzan closely with their own star, who apart from two appearances as himself in the celebrity cowboy short *Rodeo Dough* (1936) and the revue *Stage Door Canteen* (1943) played no role but Tarzan throughout the MGM series. Maureen O'Sullivan, introduced as Jane Parker in *Tarzan the Ape Man*, was cast in a much wider range of roles—she appeared in seven other MGM films in 1932 alone—but returned to play Tarzan's mate in every other MGM entry (see Figure 4.3). When the franchise moved to RKO, Weismuller moved with it, playing Tarzan in six new entries produced and released much more rapidly between 1943 and 1947. The first two of these, *Tarzan Triumphs* and *Tarzan's Desert Mystery* (both 1943) eliminated the role of Jane, since MGM would not release O'Sullivan to play the role; it was not until *Tarzan and the Amazons* (1945) that Jane returned, played by Brenda Joyce, who remained for *Tarzan's Magic Fountain* (1949) even after Weismuller, feeling that he had aged out of the role, made way for Lex Barker.

If Tarzan's development showed its franchise hero gradually floating free of his source novels and striking out on his own, an even more prominent

FIGURE 4.3 *The dawn of a franchise romance: Tarzan (Johnny Weismuller) meets Jane (Maureen O'Sullivan) in* Tarzan the Ape Man *(1932).*

talkie franchise sought its all-American virtues not in a corpus of American novels but in an American hero personified by a single performer who could be grafted onto any number of literary sources. Will Rogers, who had made the transition from the Ziegfeld Follies to the movies in 1918, starred in thirty-two silent films before his first talkie, *They Had to See Paris*. On the face of it, Rogers, who turned forty in 1929, was the world's most unlikely franchise hero. His aw-shucks Midwestern persona, honed by years appearing in vaudeville and writing newspaper columns, was shy, homespun, grizzled, and utterly unromantic, and his satirical political commentary would have made him highly polarizing if it were not delivered so unassumingly. Rogers's unsuitability as a romantic lead made it thoroughly logical that in *Jubilo* (1919) and *Too Busy to Work* (1932), silent and sound adaptations of Ben Ames Williams's *Saturday Evening Post* story "Jubilo," Rogers would play a hobo who sets out to look for the wife who left him for another man when he went off to war but finds his daughter instead of his wife. But his enduring appeal in the role made Jubilo an ideal franchise character in *Jus' Passing Through* (1923) and *Jubilo, Jr.* (1924), two more films in which the character outlived the plot of Williams's story. Despite, or because of, his notorious preference for ad-libbing rather than learning his lines, the coming of synchronized sound identified Rogers as the definitive American common man, and at the time of his death in 1935 he was the second biggest box office star in America, having been dislodged from the top position he had held the year before by the irresistible rise of Shirley Temple.

Rogers's persona, relaxed, understated, matter-of-fact, unpretentious, yet shrewd and sharply observant, was the product of "a kind of dual consciousness he displayed all his life: the way he could be a hero to the forces of 'decency' and yet be a headliner in the all-but-pornographic *Ziegfeld Follies,* the way he could present himself as a mere comedian and yet be an extremely influential political voice in the country, the way he could take strong stands without, usually, offending those on the opposite side of the issue."[28] Rogers's persona could be readily transplanted to many different properties because his characters actively resisted plots and plotting, preferring to hover outside other people's plans and romances and comment on them or to repeat the same schemes himself over and over again. He played much the same character in different stories, often establishing him through a single line of dialogue. In *Mr. Skitch* (1933), his character Ira Skitch, whose house has been repossessed by the bank, tells his wife Maddie (ZaSu Pitts) as they pass with their four children through Yellowstone Park en route to California, "from now on I'm going to be mean and nasty," guaranteeing that he will be anything but. He enters *David Harum* (1934), a period adaptation of Edward Noyes Westcott's best-selling 1897 novel, with the opening line, "all I know is what I read in the papers," the signature line from Rogers's political commentary.

As horse-trading small-town banker Harum and young Ann Madison (Evelyn Venable), whose romance with John Lennox (Kent Taylor) Harum has done everything possible to encourage, talk about entering Cupid, a horse Ann has taught to overcome his tendency to balk by singing songs to him, in a climactic race that will end up winning John enough money to guarantee their future, she threatens to pull Cupid out of the race if he doesn't help her make John propose, and he protests: "You can't mix women and business, and racin' and horses, and love and singin', and 'Ta-ra-ra-boom-dee-ay,' and—well, I'll see what I can do about it anyhow" (see Figure 4.4). In fact it is exactly the ability of Rogers to adapt to stories mixing all these apparently irreconcilable scripts that makes him a successful franchise hero in such diverse adaptations as *Down to Earth* (1932), a sequel to *They Had to See Paris*; *State Fair* (1933), the first of many adaptations of Phil Stong's 1932 novel; *Doctor Bull* (1933), based on James Gould Cozzens's 1933 novel *The Last Adam*; *Mr. Skitch,* based on Anne Cameron's 1926 story "Green Dice"; *Judge Priest* (1934), whose hero was based on a repeating character created by Irvin S. Cobb in 1916; and *Life Begins at 40* (1935), which borrowed its title but nothing else from Walter B. Pitkin's 1932 self-help book. Rogers's comedies frequently touched on serious matters. The expatriate American

FIGURE 4.4 *David Harum (Will Rogers) protests that he can't possibly meet all the demands of Ann Madison (Evelyn Venable) in* David Harum *(1934)—even though it is clear that he will.*

couple in *They Had to See Paris* play like a warm-up for William Wyler's *Dodsworth* (1936), and the family heading to California after losing their house in the Midwest like a comical preview of John Ford's *The Grapes of Wrath* (1940). *Too Busy to Work,* which dramatizes Jubilo's awkward interactions with the daughter who has never known him and the stepfather who has taken his place, can scarcely be called a comedy at all. Even in movies like *Dr. Bull, Judge Priest, David Harum, Life Begins at* 40, and *Steamboat Round the Bend* (1935), which end with Rogers caught up in courtroom dramas or high-stakes races, his heroes are best remembered for the time they spend going through uneventful rounds of judging, healing the sick, steaming up and down the Mississippi River, or trekking through the American countryside in characteristic, inconsequential episodes that could be repeated indefinitely.

The most obvious source of franchises whose characters continued from one story to the next was the fictional detectives in novels whose adaptation rights studios hastened to acquire. First Paramount, then Warner Bros., purchased the rights to Philo Vance, whose film debut in *The Canary Murder Case* (1929) was based on S.S. Van Dine's 1927 novel. Fox purchased the rights to Charlie Chan, who had debuted in the ten-part Pathé serial *The House without a Key* (1926), based on Earl Derr Biggers's 1925 novel, and taken supporting roles in Universal's 1928 feature *The Chinese Parrot* and Fox's *Behind That Curtain* (1929), his first sound film, before the studio cast Warner Oland in *Charlie Chan Carries On* (1931), the first of sixteen films in which the iconic Oland would star. RKO released *The Penguin Pool Murder,* the first of six mysteries pairing schoolteacher Hildegarde Withers (Edna May Oliver) with NYPD Homicide Inspector Oscar Piper (James Gleason), in 1932, a year after the publication of Stuart Palmer's novel. Having rushed an adaptation of Dashiell Hammett's 1934 novel *The Thin Man* into production for a May 1934 release, MGM followed it with five other films starring William Powell and Myrna Loy as the sleuthing duo Nick and Nora Charles. Perry Mason, played by Warren William, made his film debut in Warner Bros.' *The Case of the Howling Dog* (1934) only a year after Erle Stanley Gardner's first novel about the durable attorney, *The Case of the Velvet Claws.* The cerebral Ellery Queen, whose novels characteristically featured a Challenge to the Reader to solve the mystery at hand before Queen did so in the final chapter, took longer to make his way to Hollywood, but when Queen produced the unbeatable hook of *The Spanish Cape Mystery* (1935)—a man naked under a long cape is found strangled on a beach—Republic purchased the rights and released its adaptation, starring Donald Cook as Ellery Queen, in October of the same year, following it with *The Mandarin Mystery* (1936), in which Cook was replaced by Eddie Quillan. The first two novels about corpulent, sedentary New York detective Nero Wolfe and his legman Archie Goodwin were filmed as *Meet Nero Wolfe* (1936), with Edward Arnold and Lionel Stander, and *The League of*

Frightened Men (1937), with Walter Connolly and Stander, before Wolfe's creator Rex Stout, who had "wanted Charles Laughton to play Wolfe" and "thought [Stander] had been miscast,"[29] refused to authorize any further movie adaptations. Mr. Moto, the Japanese detective John P. Marquand had created three years before he won the 1938 Pulitzer Prize for his novel *The Late George Apley* in response to the *Saturday Evening Post*'s request for another Asian detective after the death of Earl Derr Biggers two years earlier, was played by Peter Lorre in *Think Fast, Mr. Moto* (1937), the first of eight films released by Twentieth Century Fox. Kennedy, the wisecracking reporter who had appeared in the MacBride and Kennedy magazine stories by Frederick Nebel, appeared in *Smart Blonde* with a new name, Torchy Blane, and a new gender in 1937 in the first of nine Warner Bros. adaptations mostly starring Glenda Farrell. She was swiftly followed by Nancy Drew, played by Bonita Granville in four Warner Bros. films beginning with *Nancy Drew … Detective* (1938), whose adventures were based on those of the teenage sleuth who first appeared in *The Secret of the Old Clock*, written by Edward Stratemeyer under the pseudonym Carolyn Keene, in 1930. Poverty Row studio Monogram Pictures, which had already starred Bela Lugosi in *The Mysterious Mr. Wong* (1935) as James Lee Wong, still another Asian detective whose cases Hugh Wiley had chronicled in twelve stories that *Colliers* published between 1934 and 1938, signed Boris Karloff to play the returning hero in a low-budget franchise series of five films beginning with *Mr. Wong, Detective* (1938).

Several franchises involving American-bred detectives illustrate the range of strategies studios devised to build, protect, and adapt their franchises. In 1931, after five of Earl Derr Biggers's Charlie Chan novels had been filmed, Fox asked Biggers to write further adventures for Chan or, failing that, allow the studio to create original scripts for the character. When Biggers refused permission, Fox produced remakes of three earlier adaptations, *Behind That Curtain* as *Charlie Chan's Chance* (1932), *The House without a Key* as *Charlie Chan's Greatest Case* (1933), and *The Chinese Parrot* as *Charlie Chan's Courage* (1934). It is hard to judge the quality of these three films because all of them have been lost. But Chan's Hollywood career did not seriously take off until after Biggers died in 1933 and Fox, upon purchasing the rights to the character from his widow, created a series of eleven vehicles for Warner Oland that borrowed Biggers's character but not his plots. It was these films, from *Charlie Chan in London* (1934) through *Charlie Chan at Monte Carlo* (1937), that made Chan a household name before Oland's death in 1938 led to his replacement by Sidney Toler and Roland Winters for a total of twenty-eight further filmed adventures of Charlie Chan.

Even as Chan's fame spread—he appeared in two Spanish-language adaptations in 1931 and 1937, and five Chinese adaptations would follow between 1937 and 1950—Fox's franchise hit a snag. The stress of Oland's divorce and his fear of catching pneumonia at the studio at which *Charlie*

Chan at Ringside, his sixteenth outing as Chan, was being filmed led him to balk at the production. Fox first delayed production on the film, then recast it as a vehicle for Mr. Moto. What was most remarkable about this last development was how quickly and smoothly it went. Despite the differences between the placid, oracular Chan and the physically active Moto, who regularly donned elaborate disguises and foiled villains with judo moves, surprisingly little of the film had to be rewritten—even Keye Luke remained in his role as Number One Son to bring Chan's regards to Moto in the opening sequence and then serve as one of Moto's foils for the rest of the film (see Figure 4.5)—although the result was a Moto considerably more sedate than usual. Less than a month after production had been suspended on *Charlie Chan at Ringside* in January 1938, it resumed on *Mr. Moto's Gamble,* which was released in April 1938, four months before Oland, during a visit to his mother in Sweden, died of pneumonia.

As he had with Tarzan, Louis B. Mayer followed a distinctively conservative strategy in marketing and developing *The Thin Man*. A promotional video for the studio's 1934 film adaptation of Dashiell Hammett's 1934 novel shows William Powell, posing as Nick Charles inside a giant dust jacket

FIGURE 4.5 *Mr. Moto (Peter Lorre) accepts the greetings Charlie Chan's Number One Son (Keye Luke) brings from his father in* Mr. Moto's Gamble *(1938), a vehicle that began life as* Charlie Chan at Ringside.

for *The Thin Man* that managed to identify Powell with both the character and his author, whose name at the bottom of the jacket he stepped over to chat with Philo Vance—Powell again, in a double exposure on the left side of the screen (see Figure 4.6). At a stroke, MGM sought to stake its claim to possession of Vance, who had never appeared in an MGM film but would be played the following year by Paul Lukas in the MGM adaptation *The Casino Murder Case,* and to establish *The Thin Man* as another Philo Vance film—something it certainly was not, either legally or aesthetically—even as the rest of the promotional film showcased comical moments that would never have appeared in a Vance film. Like Tarzan, Nick and Nora Charles had to wait two years for their first sequel, the revealingly titled *After the Thin Man* (1936)—their subsequent adventures, which MGM parceled out as abstemiously as Tarzan's, appeared in 1939, 1941, 1945, and 1947—which the film's trailer announced as featuring "The <u>same</u> stars ... The <u>same</u> writers ... The <u>same</u> director," and described as "The Comedy-Drama that Hollywood Has Been Trying to Make ... But Only MGM Could Do It!" As late as 1947, the opening and closing credits for *Song of the Thin Man* carried a design that identified Powell as the enduring title character, even though Hammett's title actually referred to a murder victim who turned out

FIGURE 4.6 *William Powell as Nick Charles (right) greets William Powell as Philo Vance in MGM's trailer for* The Thin Man *(1934).*

to be "as thin as the paper in that check and in those letters people have been getting"[30] (see Figure 4.7).

The progress of Charlie Chan and Nick and Nora Charles underlines the ways in which studios sought to root their franchises in durable characters rather than distinctive plots; the ways they sought to link those characters to both their own contract stars and, in the audacious case of *The Thin Man*, based on a novel that had not been planned as part of a series, to a successful earlier franchise hero from another studio; and the ways franchises drifted further and further from their nominal source novels even as they proclaimed their links to those novels as a vital part of their branding and marketing strategy. Other franchise detectives followed similar trajectories. After starring Edna May Oliver three times as Hildegarde Withers, RKO replaced her with Helen Broderick in *Murder on a Bridle Path* (1936), which was based on an original screenplay, then with ZaSu Pitts in *The Plot Thickens* (1936) and *Forty Naughty Girls* (1937), neither of them based on any of Stuart Palmer's novels. Warner Bros. inverted this procedure, retaining leading elements of Erle Stanley Gardner's plots and in most cases his titles for its Perry Mason franchise but replacing Warren William with Ricardo

FIGURE 4.7 *The title credit for* Song of the Thin Man *(1947) implies that the title character is Nick Charles, not an altogether different character who died in* The Thin Man.

Cortez in *The Case of the Black Cat* (1936) and Donald Woods in *The Case of the Stuttering Bishop* (1937). Along the way, the studio, presumably inspired by the success of *The Thin Man,* adopted an increasingly antic tone, humanizing Mason by giving him an old flame as a client in *The Case of the Curious Bride* (1935), presenting him as comically tipsy in *The Case of the Lucky Legs* (1935), and introducing *The Case of the Velvet Claws* (1936) by showing Mason honeymooning with his longtime secretary Della Street (Claire Dodd). Mr. Moto floated free of John P. Marquand's plots after *Thank You, Mr. Moto* (1937), the second of Peter Lorre's eight film appearances as the Japanese detective. Only the first of the Torchy Blane movies followed any of Frederick Nebel's storylines. After *Nancy Drew ... Detective,* the following three Nancy Drew films broadened their comedy, and only one of them, *Nancy Drew and the Hidden Staircase* (1938), owed its story to the pseudonymous Carolyn Keene.

All this evidence makes it abundantly clear that, *pace* Samuel Marx, the studios were by no means always looking for a story. In the case of successful fictional franchises, they were looking for a continuing character as distinctive and resilient as Universal's resident monsters, Frankenstein, Dracula, and the Invisible Man, and, years later, as James Bond and the X-Men. Better still, studios took care to build their franchises around pairs of characters as imperishable as Hildegarde Withers and Oscar Piper, Nick and Nora Charles, or Perry Mason and Della Street. Individual studios tailored these characters to their contract stars in the hope that they would become identified with those stars as closely as Tarzan and Jane became identified with Johnny Weismuller and Maureen O'Sullivan while still allowing them to be played in a pinch by other performers instead.

The fate of Ellery Queen is particularly instructive. The most characteristic qualities of the novels pseudonymously written by the cousins Frederic Dannay and Manfred B. Lee, the formidable complexity of their whodunit plots and their scrupulous fairness in making all clues available to readers who wished to race the detective to the solution, constituted both their principal attraction for Hollywood and their principal obstacle, and it is no surprise that the first Queen film did not appear until six years after its hero's debut in the novel *The Roman Hat Mystery* (1929). Although the cousins, capitalizing on the fact that most readers could remember the names of fictional detectives much more easily than the names of their authors, had had the inspired idea of taking the same name as their deductive hero, the puzzles they devised were too cerebral to be readily adapted, and their Challenge to the Reader too metafictional. When Columbia acquired the rights to the Queen novels after Republic had released *The Spanish Cape Mystery* and *The Mandarin Mystery* (1936), the studio faced an unusual problem. What made the Queen novels most appealing to readers were their distinctively detailed mystery plots. Yet any film that closely replicated any of those plots risked both boring readers unfamiliar with the novel it was based on and disappointing fans of the novel who could no longer compete with the detective to solve the puzzle because they already knew the solution. After buying the rights to the character, the working title Columbia Pictures gave its first film was *John Braun's Body* before the studio, following the lead of the author, realized the branding power of embedding the name of the popular sleuth in the title and renamed it *Ellery Queen, Master Detective,* then followed the same strategy for the rest of its Ellery Queen films. *Ellery Queen, Master Detective,* starring Ralph Bellamy as the detective and Margaret Lindsay as Nikki Porter, the wannabe writer who becomes his secretary, takes its crucial clue from Queen's 1937 novel *The Door Between,* prominently displayed as the last in a row of Queen novels shown behind the opening credits, but changes so many details—the background, the setting, the names and functions of the characters, and the relationship between Ellery and Nikki, who does not appear in *The Door Between*—that the main challenge facing fans of the Queen novels is to identify which of them provides this pivotal contribution.

It has been widely observed that studios consistently sought to pair contract stars in order to attract different audiences and build fan loyalty. But there were more particular reasons why franchise detectives needed partners. The most obvious was to broaden the appeal of the whodunit plot by providing a romantic interest, as Nikki Porter had been created for the radio program *The Adventures of Ellery Queen* "to provide the mandatory 'love interest' that was supposed to attract the female audience."[31] The audience's putative appetite for this love interest is presumably the reason that Warner Bros. allowed romance to blossom between Perry Mason and Della Street and provided Rosalind Russell as a possible romantic interest for the courtly but utterly unromantic Paul Lukas when he played Philo Vance in *The Casino Murder Case*. The pairing of William Powell and Myrna Loy, whose six *Thin Man* films comprise less than half of the fourteen films in which they appeared together, suggests that the appeal of their sleuthing couple was broader than romance, even married romance: it included the whole range of witty, flirtatious, competitive byplay available to a married couple who were still in love with each other. Charlie Chan's many scenes with his Number One Son showed that romance was not a precondition for this sort of byplay. Indeed the first appearance of Keye Luke as the younger Chan in *Charlie Chan in Paris* (1935), Fox's eighth Chan film and the seventh to star Warner Oland, coincides with the omnipresent visibility of the star and the greater financial success of the franchise.

Chan's Number One Son reveals an even more foundational reason movie detectives need sidekicks: to give them someone to talk to. This requirement, first revealed in radio adaptations, illuminates a paradox at the heart of the fictional detective's appeal. If they are to establish themselves as heroes, they must solve a mystery that has baffled the authorities. Yet their solutions must be deferred until the end of each film, which in the meantime must give them something to do. The scenes between Chan and his son, Nick and Nora, Perry and Della, Ellery and Nikki all identify the fictional sleuths as both dominant and human and provide distractions that help explain why it has taken so long for the sleuths to solve the crimes at hand even as they fill the time before the climactic moment when the detective can finally announce the mystery's solution.

Giving fictional detectives amusing sidekicks, in other words, transformed the detective heroes from mental magicians whose own powers and abilities were shrouded in mystery to fully exteriorized characters who could freely enter into the world of the suspects while reserving to the detectives the right to ring down the final curtain. This transformation was not only strategic but necessary, since although the Hollywood studios were more interested in adapting the franchise detective heroes than in recreating the particular mysteries that had won them an audience, they were considerably less invested in those heroes' subjectivity. In fact, subjectivity was a positive liability for fictional detectives whose stories depended on concealing their thoughts about the mystery at hand from even their closest associates until the denouement.

The severe limits on their subjectivities, which were presented as impressively analytical but largely inscrutable, allowed audiences limited opportunities for Hollywood detectives' psychological development. Audiences rejected Warner Bros.' successive attempts to humanize Perry Mason by giving him a private life devoted to drinking and romancing; some of them even resisted the introduction of Nick Charles, Jr. in *Another Thin Man*. Fox's handling of Charlie Chan was far more typical. The franchise gave him a distinctive appearance and added to Biggers's novels an iconic sidekick and a memorable penchant for aphorisms like "Only foolish man waste words when argument is lost." Instead of developing him psychologically as a character, the franchise varied its menu by constantly introducing him to new cultures or subcultures. Between 1934 and 1937 Chan visited London, Paris, Egypt, Shanghai, the circus, the race track, the opera, the Olympics, Broadway, and Monte Carlo; his return to Honolulu in 1938 was prevented only by Warner Oland's death. Each of these films cast Chan in a distinctively appealing insider–outsider relationship to most of the mysteries he solved, an exotic hero confronted by even more exotic settings evoked not visually by the studio-bound sets but ideationally by the films' titles and references.

Hollywood discovers the novel

The flood of franchise adaptations in the early years of the talkies was followed by a gradual shift, not to more film adaptations of novels, but to adaptations of different kinds of novels and adaptations that took a different attitude toward the novels they adapted. The pivotal figure in this transition was David O. Selznick, who had left MGM upon his marriage to Louis B. Mayer's daughter Irene to work first at Paramount, then at RKO, before returning to MGM in 1933—a return that provoked the widespread reaction, "the son-in-law also rises." And the pivotal moment in this transition was a memo Selznick wrote to the MGM's sales and distribution executives in February 1934 that announced: "There is no question in my mind that the public has finally decided to accept the classics as motion picture fare."[32]

At Paramount Selznick worked as Associate Producer on two adaptations based on American properties, *Chinatown Nights* and *The Dance of Life*, both released in 1929. Moving to RKO, Selznick anointed himself Executive Producer of *The Lost Squadron* (1932), a title he was the first to use, and retained the credit on a string of American adaptations all released in 1932: *What Price Hollywood?*, *The Most Dangerous Game*, *A Bill of Divorcement*, *Little Orphan Annie*, *The Penguin Pool Murder*, and *The Half-Naked Truth*. In addition, he was billed as Producer on *The Animal Kingdom* (1932), based on Philip Barry's 1932 play; *Topaze* (1933), based on Marcel Pagnol's 1928 play; *Christopher Strong* (1933), based on Gilbert Frankau's 1932 novel; and *King Kong* (1933), "from an idea conceived by" English crime novelist Edgar Wallace. At MGM, Selznick, who would later maintain that "my function is to be responsible for everything,"[33] began by producing *Dinner at Eight*, a star-studded 1933 adaptation of the 1932 play by George S. Kaufman and Edna Ferber, and followed it with *Night Flight* (1933), based on Antoine de Saint-Exupéry's 1931 novel, and *Viva Villa!* (1934), based on Edgecumb Pinchon's 1933 biography of the Mexican bandit, warrior, and patriot. Beginning with *David Copperfield* (1935), Selznick turned decisively toward novels as his preferred source material. This was an unprecedented move, for even when ambitious or mainstream novels were adapted into box office successes, studios had been slow to interpret their success as an invitation to adapt more novels. Carl Laemmle's promise in *Film Daily* to follow the acclaim Universal received for releasing *All Quiet on the Western Front* by making "bigger, better and fewer pictures" was soon swallowed up by Universal's need for "steady returns on traditional fare like Hoot Gibson's Westerns"[34]—or for franchise films displaying the likes of Tarzan or Charlie Chan. Samuel Marx traces the rise of MGM's commitment to novels to Selznick's rivalry with producer Irving Thalberg. When Selznick, attempting to assert his power at his new home studio, "lined up films for the major stars [...] Garbo, Gable, Joan Crawford and Jean Harlow were hinting broadly they preferred Thalberg as their producer. To circumvent the future loss of those stars, Selznick asked us to bring him extensive analyses of literary classics. He wanted large scale canvases that might preclude the need for big stars."[35]

After producing *Vanessa, Her Love Story* (1935), *Anna Karenina* (1935), and *A Tale of Two Cities* (1935) at MGM, Selznick left to found his own company, Selznick International, where he further pursued his interest in adaptations like *Little Lord Fauntleroy* (1936); *The Garden of Allah* (1936); *A Star Is Born* (1937), loosely based on the same story by Adela Rogers St. Johns that had supplied the basis for *What Price Hollywood*; *The Prisoner of Zenda* (1937), which presented another quasi-American hero already memorably played by Lewis Stone in Rex Ingram's 1922 silent film; *The Adventures of Tom Sawyer* (1938); *The Young at Heart* (1938), *Intermezzo* (1939), and *Gone with the Wind* (1939). All of them were high-budgeted prestige productions, the kinds of large-scale canvases Marx describes. But out of them all, only *A Star Is Born*, which Selznick considered "an original," *The Adventures of Tom Sawyer*, and *Gone with the Wind* were based on American fiction. When Selznick thought of "the classics," he thought of England, France, Sweden, even Australia, but not the United States.

For the most part, Americans occupied the same place in Selznick adaptations that they had in Will Rogers's films, supplying not prestigious literary source material but cultural prototypes for heroes like Little Lord Fauntleroy, *The Prisoner of Zenda*'s Rudolf Rassendyl, and Tom Sawyer. When the success of *The Adventures of Tom Sawyer* led MGM to make *The Adventures of Huckleberry Finn* in 1939, the producer was Joseph L. Mankiewicz. Even though *Huckleberry Finn* is a far more probing, ambitious, and successful novel than *Tom Sawyer*, which the producer had appropriately treated as a slice of charming period Americana, Selznick avoided the sequel because he and Thalberg

> jealously guarded their autonomy and regarded each production as a distinct venture, differentiated not only from their competitors' high-class products, but from other MGM productions as well. They avoided rehashing their successes and rarely used the same above-the-line personnel from one project to the next. Thus neither really developed a production unit as such at MGM. That was particularly ironic in Selznick's case; he had been a proponent for years—since his stints at Paramount and RKO—of just the kind of unit production that [Hunt] Stromberg was doing.[36]

In addition to largely ignoring American literature for source material and declining to establish his own production unit, even for the sake of producing so potentially distinguished a sequel as *The Adventures of Huckleberry Finn*—a distinction MGM's routine adaptation, directed by Richard Thorpe, utterly lacked—Selznick offers a final complication to Samuel Marx's description: early and late, he maintained a keen interest in cultivating stars. He cast at least four actresses in the roles that made them stars: Katharine Hepburn in *A Bill of Divorcement* (1932), Vivien Leigh in *Gone with the Wind* (1939), Joan Fontaine in *Rebecca* (1940), and Jennifer Jones in *The Song of Bernadette* (1943). After he left MGM, he brought

Ingrid Bergman to America for *Intermezzo*, the remake that launched her international stardom, and signed Gene Kelly to his first Hollywood contract after seeing him in the Broadway production of *Pal Joey*, even though he sold the contract to MGM before he could find Kelly a suitable role. During the war years, when Selznick International's production slowed to a crawl, the studio served mainly as the ultimate talent agency, with Selznick assembling more filmmaking packages than he produced. After luring Alfred Hitchcock from England with a seven-year contract, Selznick loaned him to United Artists, RKO, Universal, and Fox, making only three films with Hitchcock himself. Having assembled screenplays and casts for *Claudia* (1943), *Jane Eyre* (1943), *The Keys of the Kingdom* (1944), and *Notorious* (1946), he sold the first three packages to Fox and the fourth to RKO. All these deals reveal the true nature of Selznick's interest in (largely non-American) literature: as one more attraction to be packaged with bankable stars and high production values in films designed to sweep audiences off their feet.

Despite his ultimately instrumental view of literature, Selznick's aesthetic moved away from the stage aesthetic of stars carrying movies. Under his supervision, the stars themselves were part of a bigger package. "Bigger" is indeed perhaps the single word most applicable to Selznick's aesthetic, which indicates that even though novels were more difficult than plays to adapt to the screen, they offered several advantages that loomed larger and larger as the 1930s wore on.

Filmmakers who followed Selznick's lead in turning to the novel found not simply raw material for individual products but a defining aesthetic for the talkies comparable to the aesthetic Dudley Andrew finds in the French poetic realism of the later 1930s, when "cinema's rapport with prose fiction [...] gained ascendancy, infecting even 'original scripts' with an aesthetic that avoids verbosity and that mixes description, narration, and dialogue," all under the rising influence of "a novelistic aesthetic that demanded the subtle participation of visual artists, composers, and directors in orchestrating and balancing all registers."[37] If, as Mikhail Bakhtin has ruled, the novel's distinctive "style is to be found in the combination of its styles,"[38] Hollywood gradually moved to adopt this novelistic style itself.

Despite the convenience of theatrical models for screenwriters and stars alike, novelistic alternatives offered enticing advantages of their own. As Selznick showed in his hugely successful adaptations of *David Copperfield*, *Anna Karenina*, and *A Tale of Two Cities*, novels could provide a large-scale canvas and historical sweep far beyond the reach of plays wedded to the Aristotelian unities of space, time, and action. They could be expansive rather than intensive, showcasing spectacles based on outsized sets and thousands of extras. They could provide the basis for "a number of pedagogical tools for high school film appreciation that would further shape the audience"[39] for films like *David Copperfield*. If the best plays traced the inexorable unfolding of a dramatic action, the best novels created compelling worlds that the studios could recreate in literal detail. Although a long series of more discursive plays from *Tamburlaine the Great* and *Hamlet* to *Peer Gynt* and *The Iceman Cometh* had challenged Aristotelian norms of selection and compression, few plays could challenge the novel's mastery of what Bakhtin called heteroglossia, its ability to incorporate many different voices within a given novel, sometimes even within an single narrative voice like the one Dostoevsky developed in *Notes from Underground*. And novels offered audiences unrivaled access to the subjectivity of their characters through first person confessional narrators like Huckleberry Finn, third person narrators who could enter at will the minds of heroes like Henry Fleming in *The Red Badge of Courage* or display a more virtuosic ability to enter different characters' minds at different points, in different ways, and to different degrees of intimacy, as Henry James had done in a series of novels from *Washington Square* to *The Golden Bowl*. Eugene O'Neill's 1923 play *Strange Interlude,* which sought to revive the device of the dramatic soliloquy, had won the Pulitzer Prize for Drama when it was finally staged in 1928. When MGM released an adaptation of the nine-act play, which shortened its running time to two hours while still preserving the conceit that its leading characters could take turns voicing the thoughts they dared not speak to each other while everyone else remained motionless in the frame, the film, despite the A-list pairing of Norma Shearer and Clark Gable, did only modest business and was widely dismissed as a curio, as Groucho Marx had already characterized O'Neill's play when he burlesqued the technique in *Animal Crackers* (1930) (see Figure 4.8). But contemporaneous films as different as *An American Tragedy* (1931), *Cimarron* (1931), and *The Age of Innocence* (1934), following the lead of silent films like *The Scarlet Letter* (1926), could powerfully reveal the thoughts of their leading characters, if they chose, through increasingly idiomatic combinations of expressive close-ups, reaction shots, and musical cues.

The path to a full-blown novelistic aesthetic, however, was strewn with difficulties. The length and complexity of most novels made them highly resistant to adaptation, and the ease which with they provided access to characters' thoughts posed a major obstacle for screenwriters like Aldous Huxley, who observed:

> In any picture or play, the story is essential and primary. In Jane Austen's books, it is a matter of secondary importance (every dramatic event in *Pride and Prejudice* is recorded in a couple of lines, generally in a letter) [...] and the insistence upon the story as opposed to the dilute irony which the story is designed to contain, is a major falsification of Miss Austen.[40]

Despite the audacity of Selznick's claim about what the public wanted, it was not at all obvious that Hollywood was equipped to present the leading qualities of the nineteenth- and early-twentieth-century novels that public would have regarded as classics.

FIGURE 4.8 *Captain Spalding (Groucho Marx) steps forward from his fellow cast members in* Animal Crackers *(1930) long enough to indulge a "strange interlude" in a burlesque of Eugene O'Neill.*

Movies excelled at the extensive world-building required by adaptations of Balzac and Dickens, especially if they required settings in earlier historical periods. But the talkies' capacity for the kind of psychological penetration found in Austen, Dostoevsky, and Henry James was largely unproven, and they showed little interest in the experiments of foregrounding narrative voices undertaken by Thackeray, Joyce, Woolf, and Faulkner. Describing the distinctive achievement of modernist novels like Woolf's *To the Lighthouse* (1928), Erich Auerbach concludes: "There is greater confidence in syntheses gained through full exploitation of an everyday occurrence than in a chronologically well-ordered total treatment which accompanies the subject from beginning to end, attempts not to omit anything externally important, and emphasizes the great turning points of destiny."[41] When the studios had undertaken historical projects like *Uncle Tom's Cabin*, by contrast, they did not share the modern novel's confidence that exploiting the full implications of everyday events could release illuminating information or even create characters like the heroes and heroines of *The Scarlet Letter, Madame Bovary*, and *The Red Badge of Courage* who were at once sharply individual, typical of their time, and likely to appeal to modern audiences;

instead they seized on social and racial stereotypes and exaggerated them even further. Instead of assimilating the most notable tendencies of modern or classic novels, Hollywood seemed more or less deliberately to turn its back on them. The programmatic obscurity, pessimism, and sometimes encyclopedic length of the Anglophone fiction contemporaneous with the early talkies was a particularly tough sell, and such pillars of modernist fiction as Virginia Woolf made no secret of their disdain for cinematic adaptations. In the middle of writing his monumental trilogy *U.S.A.*, John Dos Passos stopped long enough in Hollywood to work on Joseph von Sternberg's 1935 adaptation of Pierre Louys's novel *The Devil Is a Woman*. But no one showed any interest in adapting *U.S.A.* itself, even though it had been more deeply influenced by the cinema than any other novel of its time. Hollywood had rejected High Modernism's attempt to use ordinary events to reveal hidden subjective realities and fallen back instead on the older models of comedy and melodrama, whether they were derived from stage plays like *Stage Door* or novels like *The Last of the Mohicans*.

Some early experiments in adapting contemporaneous novels to sound cinema succeeded brilliantly; others either failed in ways that reminded studios of the spectacular disaster of *Greed* (1924) or, at very least, made them wary of novelistic adaptations. Paramount's ill-fated 1931 adaptation of Theodore Dreiser's 1925 novel *An American Tragedy,* which had already been theatrically staged in 1926, had originally been envisioned by Sergei M. Eisenstein as indicting American social culture for the murder of Roberta Alden (Sylvia Sidney) by Clyde Griffiths (Phillips Holmes), the coworker who has gotten her pregnant but now wishes to move on to the heiress Sondra Finchley (Frances Dee). But Josef von Sternberg's film, treating Clyde instead as an individual case of social-climbing cowardice, warned the studios of the dangers of psychological dramas that—as David O. Selznick wrote in a vain attempt to get B.P. Schulberg, his boss at Paramount, to abandon the project—"cannot possibly offer anything but a most miserable two hours to millions of happy-minded young Americans."[42] The studio's adaptation of *A Farewell to Arms* the following year was far more successful on its own terms as a delicately sensitive romance between the star-crossed lovers played by Gary Cooper and Helen Hayes, but Frank Borzage's soft-focus Hemingway, which relegated the First World War to the background, did nothing to encourage other filmmakers to consider Hemingway adaptations. James M. Cain's scandalous crime novels *The Postman Always Rings Twice* (1934), *Double Indemnity* (1936), *Serenade* (1937), which might well have been more successful, were ruled off-limits by the Hays Office.

Most telling of all was the fate of Sinclair Lewis's 1935 novel *It Can't Happen Here*. MGM promptly purchased the rights to Lewis's account of a small-town activist's reaction to the election of a native-born American fascist to the American Presidency for $50,000 and submitted a draft screenplay by Sidney Howard to the Production Code Administration. Joseph I. Breen, who expressed his concern in a letter to Will H. Hays about the likely reaction of "foreign governments" to "a story portraying a Hitlerization of the United States of America,"[43] did not forbid the project, but he expressed grave reservations to Louis B. Mayer, warning him: "The story is of such inflammatory a nature, and so filled with dangerous material that <u>only the greatest possible care</u> will save it from being rejected on all sides."[44] The day after Lewis gave a newspaper interview protesting that the Hays Office had banned the production,[45] Hays issued a statement maintaining that "no Association action was taken to prohibit this picture. The decision respecting the production of the picture was made by the company."[46] Producers David O. Selznick and Harry Rathner both expressed an interest in purchasing the rights from MGM over the following year,[47] and in March 1939 the studio submitted a revised script to Breen, who pronounced the material "acceptable under the provisions of the Production Code and [...] reasonably free from any serious danger at the hands of political censor boards in this country"[48] but still urged that "you will take counsel with your Foreign Department as to the likely reception of a picture of this kind outside the United States."[49] The outbreak of the Second World War dealt the project a death blow. Mayer was not about to push the envelope by releasing a film whose subtext might compromise the nation's political neutrality. Samuel Marx notes that despite its enormous box office potential, Lewis's novel "scared the daylights out of a lot of readers, which finally included the top executives of Metro-Goldwyn-Mayer. It scared Louis B. Mayer into shelving the property, at the urging of the timid Motion Picture Producers Association."[50] Although the project remained on the studio's books through 1941, *It Can't Happen Here* was never filmed. The moral Hollywood took from these false starts and dead ends—that all the literary prestige in the world doesn't guarantee box office success—may have been unduly broad, but it factored into the studios' wary approach to novels for years to come.

One surprising influence that helped the studios overcome their resistance to novel adaptations has been consistently overlooked or minimized by adaptation scholars and film historians alike: the rise of radio storytelling. In 1930, ten years after the first radio broadcast, 40 percent of American households owned a radio, a percentage that would double by 1940, and "surveys found that listeners in the 1930s spent an average of more than four hours a day listening to radio broadcasts."[51] Although early broadcasts were dominated by programs of live music, these were soon supplemented by social and political commentaries, news and sports broadcasts, and dramatizations of fictional stories, some written directly for radio, some adapted themselves from novels or plays.[52] Even more than the Hollywood studios, which depended on a constant stream of new projects and properties to keep their salaried staff busy and justify the expense of wiring their studios—and, much more expensively, the many movie theaters they owned—for synchronized sound, radio abhorred a vacuum. Once the pioneering Columbia Broadcasting System (CBS) and the National Broadcasting Company (NBC) had been launched in 1926 and 1927, they swiftly developed a need for programming material they could broadcast for all the hours they operated. Because radio was an exclusively auditory medium, each program had to provide a nonstop stream of auditory information and stimulation. Silence was the great enemy of radio aesthetics, because radio audiences would read any silence between songs or speeches not as a dramatic pause but as an indication that the transmission had been interrupted. So radio programming required not only a constant influx of material, but an unending series of auditory cues and a positive terror of extended silences, qualities that came to shape the emerging aesthetic of the talkies. In the meantime, dialogue in films from *Stella Dallas* (1937) to *The Philadelphia Story* (1940), increasingly influenced by radio, assimilated the anti-normative norms of contemporaneous fiction, whose "heteroglot dialogue was far more flexible and expressive of a much wider range of social classes and ethnic types" than the normative "transatlantic diction and elocution" modeled by Broadway's theatrical practice.[53] Once it established itself, an American version of this novelistic aesthetic, assimilationist, inclusive, and heteroglot rather than streamlined and unified, became and remained the dominant aesthetic of both Hollywood dialogue and Hollywood storytelling.

Somebody's impression

What might be called Hollywood's discovery of the novel in the 1930s is in important ways like Columbus's discovery of the New World. The novelistic world it discovered was not really new; earlier explorers, including several pioneer Hollywood filmmakers, had already staked out claims to its territory. Nor did this discovery lead to a dramatic shift in the proportions of novels versus plays in the course of the decade. Hollywood's discovery of the novel was accidental; no one was looking to claim the novel, or the modern novel, or the novelistic aesthetic for Tinseltown. The leading Hollywood studios, like Columbus, discovered their America in the process of looking for something else—the global cultural capital and cachet they had already found in the novel for at least twenty years, and melodramatic stories, rich in dramatic and visual spectacle, that just happened to offer tantalizing possibilities of framing their stories, as Henry James said of his own work, "not as my own impersonal account of the affair in hand, but as my account of somebody's impression of it."[54] As the decade wore on, the industry's experiments in using novelistic heteroglossia to evoke novelistic subjectivities were more and more firmly integrated into an emerging aesthetic that Michael Wood has identified with "*the movies*."[55]

These experiments took a surprisingly wide range of forms. By 1926, novelist Oscar Micheaux, whose father had been a slave, had already made seventeen films, several of them based on his own novels, for his own production company. Most of Micheaux's silent films have been lost, but *Within Our Gates* (1920), which survives in a reconstructed and incomplete print, gives some sense of what they were like. The film, a heartfelt polemic urging education for African American children and unimpeded access to the ballot box for their parents, follows schoolteacher Sylvia Landry (Evelyn Preer), whose visit to her cousin Alma (Flo Clements) up north ends abruptly when her fiancé, Conrad Drebert (James D. Ruffin) catches her in a compromising situation arranged by Alma, a divorcee in love with Conrad, and nearly strangles her. Back in her southern home of Piney Woods, Sylvia helps at a school for African American children that is about to close because it is woefully underfunded. Returning north in the hope of raising money, Sylvia is hit by a car driven by Geraldine Stratton (Bernice Ladd), a rich white southerner passing through Boston, who at length gives Sylvia $5000 and pledges a total of $50,000 toward the school even though Elena Warwick (Mrs. Evelyn), the friend she asks for advice, curtly dismisses the dreams of African Americans: "Their ambition is to belong to a dozen lodges, consume religion without restraints, and, when they die, go straight up to Heaven." Despite a murky past further detailed in a long flashback, Sylvia triumphs with the help of Dr. V. Vivian (Charles D. Lucas), a social activist who urges her to "be proud of our race" because "we were never immigrants."

Not surprisingly, the major conflicts in *Within Our Gates* are between progressive African Americans and bullying whites and African American collaborationists. By the time Micheaux begins to make synch-sound films, however, his focus has shifted in important ways. *The Exile* (1931), based on Micheaux's anonymously published first novel, *The Conquest* (1913), and his lost film adaptation *The Homesteader* (1919), turns on the question of what constitutes whiteness and blackness, narrativized by the question of who should marry whom. Despite the assurance Jean Baptiste (Stanley Morrell) voices that "part black is all black," he abandons his romance with white South Dakota girl Agnes Stewart (Nora Newsome) until her discovery that her mother was Abyssinian moves her to follow him to the menacing city, where she finds his name in the headlines as the leading suspect in the murder of Edith Duval (Eunice Brooks), the African American lover he left over her plans to open a speakeasy. True marriages, the film suggests, are rooted more firmly in shared values than shared race, although racial affinities are always welcome. *Veiled Aristocrats* (1932), a remake of Micheaux's lost film *The House behind the Cedars* (1927), which was based in turn on Charles W. Chesnutt's 1900 novel about a light-skinned African American brother and sister passing as white, raises questions about what makes a given person white or black (genetics? reputation? subjective feelings?), who gets to decide who is white or black, whether there are meaningful gradations between being really white and really black, whether African American narratives should take a progressive form, and if so, whether their progress should be measured in terms of attaining quasi-white cultural capital. The most dramatically intense episode in *The Girl from Chicago* (1932), an all-African American remake of *The Spider's Web* (1926), a silent film Micheaux had based on his story "Jeff Ballinger's Woman," involves neither the rescue of Mary Austin (Eunice Brooks) from gangster Jeff Ballinger (John Everett), her sinister suitor, nor her arrest, trial, or conviction for his murder, all of which are presented by a montage of newspaper headlines, but her agonized internal debate over whether she ought to play twenty dollars on the numbers she has dreamed of, chasing so many other bad bets that have defined her life by keeping her impoverished, or use the money instead to help pay for her ailing sister's medical care. *Birthright: A Story of the Negro—and the South* (1938), a remake of Micheaux's lost 1924 adaptation of T.S. Stribling's 1922 novel, returns to the subject of *Within Our Gates*. Upon his graduation from Harvard, Peter Siner (Carman Newsome) returns to his Tennessee hometown to build a school for African American children. Although he added a happy ending to Stribling's more downbeat novel, Micheaux complicates the racial conflicts of *Within Our Gates* by exploring the relationship Stribling had developed between Peter and Tump Pack (Alec Lovejoy), a First World War veteran who serves as Peter's romantic rival and his increasingly bitter enemy (see Figure 4.9). The conflict between Peter and Tump focuses not only on the ideological differences that had divided the characters in *Within Our Gates* but on social and class differences—Peter, for example, speaks a formal transatlantic English free of contractions, while Tump speaks African American vernacular—that cannot be resolved even by Tump's death. *Birthright* dramatizes more clearly than any other single film Micheaux's signature subject: not the relations between African American and white characters, but divisions within the African American community, and ultimately within the African American subjectivity, that repel facile generalizations about what black people are like.

Micheaux's sound films present this subject in still another way, through elaborate musical numbers that are both the most expertly staged and performed sequences in the films and the most incongruous with the films' tone and extraneous to their plots. Taking these numbers, which are indeed incongruous, as seriously as the musical interludes in John Ford's films from *The Grapes of Wrath* (1940) to *My Darling Clementine* (1946) to *The Quiet Man* (1952), which represent the familial and communal values threatened by upheaval, conflict, and hostile environments, shows that they provide one more way of understanding African American identity—through individual and collective performance, a mode that raises as many questions as defining it through genetics, reputation, or social status—and raises additional questions the films stage without resolving: Does presenting spectacles of

FIGURE 4.9 Birthright *(1938) establishes Tump Pack (Alec Lovejoy) and Peter Siner (Carman Newsome) as natural opposites.*

African Americans performing musical numbers automatically cast these performers and performances as exotic? If it does, does it objectify and dehumanize them like the blackface figures of minstrel shows, or reconfigure the exotic as an adaptive space that defines the characters as both like and unlike the audience, both us and them?

Micheaux's anatomies of a specifically raced subjectivity limited the commercial impact of his films, which were shown almost entirely to African American audiences. But these films offered a potentially important alternative to franchise adaptations that exteriorized or suppressed the subjectivity of heroes like Charlie Chan and Tarzan. The novelistic adaptations Selznick produced at MGM show the studio's gradual embrace of A-list literary sources that placed a new emphasis on novelistic heteroglossia and subjectivity, not merely as qualities that movies had developed the ability to reveal, but as those movies' true subjects. This was especially true in so-called women's movies that used melodramatic plots as vehicles to explore the divided loyalties of heroines like those played by Greta Garbo in *Susan Lenox (Her Fall and Rise)*, Robert Z. Leonard's 1932 adaptation of David Graham Phillips's posthumous 1931 novel, and Bette Davis in *All This, and Heaven Too,* Anatole Litvak's 1940 adaptation of Rachel Field's 1938 novel.

Like the long-suffering heroines of these films, the leads in romantic comedies, together with musicals and gangster films the most important Hollywood genre to emerge in the 1930s, were often burdened with conflicted thoughts and feelings that could not adequately be expressed in exteriorized action. Film adaptations like *It Happened One Night* (1934), based on Samuel Hopkins Adams's 1933 story "Night Bus," *The Awful Truth* (1937), based on Arthur Richman's 1924 play, and *The Philadelphia Story* (1940), based on Philip Barry's 1939 play, managed to develop seriously funny romantic plots without ever showing so much as a kiss between romantic leads whose inability to admit their love for each other, even if they had already been married, fueled both the comic and the romantic sides of their stories.

The work of Edna Ferber, whose unparalleled commercial success as both novelist and dramatist made her work especially attractive to Hollywood, shows her ability to create both characters who are essentially theatrical, like those in *Stage Door* (1926, filmed 1937), *The Royal Family* (1927, filmed 1930), and *Dinner at Eight* (1932, filmed 1933), all coauthored by George S. Kaufman, and characters driven by the unbridgeable gaps between their active interior lives and their suppressive exterior circumstances like Selina Peake De Jong, the artistically sensitive farm wife in the Pulitzer Prize-winning *So Big* (1924); Barney Glasgow, the lumberjack in *Come and Get It* (1935) who abandons his true love, Lotta Morgan, for the boss's daughter only to fall in love with Lotta's daughter a generation later; Clio Dulaine, the Creole banished from her aristocratic family who joins forces with Col. Clint Maroon to avenge herself in *Saratoga Trunk* (1941); and Leslie Lynnton Benedict, who must watch from the sidelines as her rancher husband Bick Benedict struggles to preserve his family's legacy in *Giant* (1952) even though their children, who have dreams of their own, refuse to take control of the ranch, on which oil has been discovered. Ferber specialized in creating heroines whose strong-willed personalities embodied the contradictions of large-scale historical events like the Oklahoma land rush in *Cimarron* (1929) and the debate over Alaskan statehood in *Ice Palace* (1959). The success of the 1931 film adaptation of *Cimarron,* which together with *The Best Years of Our Lives* (1946) was one of only two RKO films to win the Oscar for Best Picture, and the critical and commercial failure of both its 1960 remake and the 1962 film adaptation of *Ice Palace* marks Ferber as "the ultimate middlebrow"[56] novelist who spoke most directly to audiences of the 1920s and 1930s, and whose work encouraged Hollywood studios to develop a new formula for novelistic adaptations: embed a divided subjectivity within an epic historical subject that encouraged a treatment both spectacular and intimate.

This formula was taken up with various degrees of success by adaptations as different as *So Red the Rose* (1935), based on Stark Young's 1934 novel; *Anthony Adverse* (1936), based on Hervey Allen's 1933 novel; and especially

The Good Earth (1937), based on Pearl S. Buck's Pulitzer Prize-winning 1931 novel. *The Good Earth,* the last project Irving Thalberg completed, carries a rare credit identifying him by name and dedicating the film to his memory. An opening intertitle immediately following the credits announces that the film, based on both Buck's novel and Owen and Donald Davis's 1932 dramatization, promises that "this story of a humble farmer can illuminate the soul of a great nation." The story begins with the marriage of Wang Lung (Paul Muni) to O-Lan (Luise Rainer) and then shows his gradual neglect of her as he focuses first on the acquisition of larger and larger parcels of land from the Hwang family, using jewels O-Lan has looted from a rich man during a food riot to make the climactic purchase, and then on Lotus (Tilly Losch), the concubine he has taken. The hard work of the couple and their children maintains the farm through numerous vicissitudes, most notably a climactic locust invasion. Only on O-Lan's deathbed, however, does Wang Lung realize that he has been sustained throughout his adult life by his uncomplaining wife, not by the land he heretically took as his security. "O-Lan, you are the earth," he tells her longingly after she has died, putting the seal on a story that is both epic and intimate, exotic and universal, foreign and inferentially American, with Wang Lung standing in for every citizen struggling to survive the Great Depression[57] (see Figure 4.10).

FIGURE 4.10 *Wang Lung (Paul Muni) realizes at last that O-Lan (Luise Rainer), the wife he has neglected in his obsessive pursuit of land and wealth, has been the mainstay of his life in* The Good Earth *(1937).*

Hollywood story departments were especially interested in novels that would enable each studio "to identify its pictures with multiple genres, in order to benefit from the increased interest that this strategy inspires in diverse demographic groups."[58] Studios used period adaptations like *The Scarlet Pimpernel* (1934), *Mutiny on the Bounty* (1935), and *Anthony Adverse* to conflate history and literature in order to give popular fantasies cultural cachet. Pairing physically active heroes like Errol Flynn with actresses like Olivia de Havilland who could suggest untapped emotional and psychological depths allowed Warner Bros. to market its unlikely adaptations *The Charge of the Light Brigade* (1936), based on a poem, and *The Adventures of Robin Hood* (1938), based on an operetta, as "offering something for the men [...] something for the women [...] and an added something for that *tertium quid* audience that prefers travel to adventure or romance."[59] The same year that David Harum had pointed the way toward these portmanteau adaptations with his warning that you couldn't possibly mix women and business, or racing and horses, or love and singing "Ta-ra-ra-boom-dee-ay," *Murder at the Vanities* (1934) presented a murder plot devised by Rufus King that took place during a performance of Earl Carroll's Vanities, so that crime and detection played out against an ongoing background of elaborate musical numbers from the 1933 version of Carroll's revue. The strategy of seeking properties that combined action and romance, or adding romance to properties devoid of it, paid off for other studios with *The Good Earth* (1937), *Gunga Din* (1939), and *The Hunchback of Notre Dame* (1939). Studios increasingly combined scripts from strikingly different genres within such films to appeal to the widest possible audience.

By the end of the decade, the novelistic aesthetic that had overtaken the Hollywood studios began to appear more frequently on the Broadway stage as well. Important American plays increasingly domesticated the experiments of Elmer Rice and the agitprop of Clifford Odets by displaying the psychological dynamics of characters torn between pressing moral choices, and Hollywood adaptations responded by preserving those momentous moral dilemmas while placing them in a more realistic and extensive worldly context. Sidney Kingsley's *Dead End* (1935, filmed 1937) explored the obstacles facing slum dwellers intent on freeing themselves from their stifling criminal environment. Owen Davis's *Jezebel* (1933, filmed 1938) presents a strong-willed southern belle whose imperious attempts to exert control over the men in her life cost her any chance at love. Odets's *Golden Boy* (1937, filmed 1939) forced its sensitive, determined hero to choose between a career as a concert violinist and the shot at a championship boxing match. Any of these deeply heteroglot plays could easily have been conceived as a novel. Thornton Wilder's *Our Town* (1938, filmed 1940) combined Odets and Rice's metatheatricality with the social-problem strain of *Dead End* and *Golden Boy* to elevate three apparently inconsequential days in Grovers Corners, New Hampshire, separated from each other by years, to universal status by emphasizing the pathos of the distance between the dramatic perspectives of characters caught in the moment and the compassionate, Olympian, novelistic detachment of the Stage Manager, who alone sees the larger rhythms of lives comprising nothing but moments like these. The play is a tour de force of world-building that uses a single community, a mostly bare stage, and repeated devices that break the fourth wall normally insulating the performers from the audience by allowing some characters to take questions from the audience and the Stage Manager to comment on the significance of the action.

The growing impact of the novelistic aesthetic on both movies and the plays they adapted reached a climax in *Gone with the Wind,* at once a grandly scaled historical epic, an intimate love story, a chronicle of war, a woman's picture, and an adaptation of a best-selling contemporary novel, which represented both Hollywood's climactic embrace of the novelistic aesthetic and a template for the marketing of a single film adaptation as all things to all audiences. Selznick's adaptation of Margaret Mitchell's novel, which did its utmost to retain her dialogue even in the face of the wholesale abridgment required to bring its thousand-page length under four hours, was the logical successor to his own string of MGM adaptations, the blueprint Edna Ferber's intimate epics had established for commercial success, and the Depression-era allegory of *The Good Earth.* Although the film was the most expensive Hollywood production to date, "that single picture accounted for over one-half of Hollywood's net profits in 1940."[60] Passing unnoticed among the film's prodigious commercial and critical success—its eight competitive Oscars, with a ninth honorary award for production designer William Cameron Menzies, remained a record for any single film until it was surpassed twenty years later by *Ben-Hur*'s eleven— was the fact that its celebrated ending, in which Scarlett O'Hara (Vivien Leigh), desperately attempting to recover from her sudden abandonment by Rhett Butler, is surrounded by an all-encompassing montage of voices murmuring, "Tara," assuring her that her identity depends less deeply on her marriage to Rhett than to her ties to her family's plantation and its land (see Figure 4.11), precisely inverts the ending of *The Good Earth,* in which Wang Lung realizes that he has imprudently attached more value to his ties to the earth than to the sustaining love he has shared with O-Lan. It is hardly surprising that this contrast could have passed unnoticed, even among filmgoers who noticed the many similarities between the two films, because the two climactic sequences have very much the same sentimental force even though they advance logically opposite propositions. The cognitive content of both propositions is less important than their emotional conviction and epic sweep.

Much the same could be said of *The Wizard of Oz,* MGM's other best-remembered release of 1939. On the face of it, the studio's return to the

FIGURE 4.11 *Abandoned for good by Rhett Butler, Scarlett O'Hara (Vivien Leigh) is solaced by her still deeper ties to Tara in* Gone with the Wind *(1939).*

land of Oz would seem to have all the earmarks of a B-movie franchise. The talking animals, magical transformations, improbable adventures, and hyperstylized mise-en-scene of the Oz stories presented a perfect recipe for a distinctive franchise. But by revealing that all of Dorothy Gale's fantastic adventures had taken place in a dream, the film framed her story in terms of her imagination and desire—a desire expressed most poignantly in the song "Over the Rainbow," sung in the opening sequence by sixteen-year-old Judy Garland with a palpable yearning that gives audiences more direct and moving access to the young heroine's subjectivity than the earlier Oz novels and plays and comic strips had ever dreamed of—and ultimately implies that her imagined journey has truly been a once-in-a-lifetime adventure. Instead of merely releasing the heroine's subjectivity, the film discovers an entirely new subjectivity within a heroine whose leading features had long been accepted as settled.

Ironically, the device of the psychologically revealing solo song, taken directly from the musical theater, helped give MGM's film the anti-establishment stance, the expressive resonance, and the polyglot inclusiveness that Bakhtin reserves for the novel. The novelistic aesthetic that blossoms improbably in *The Wizard of Oz*, a combination of extroverted melodrama, suppressed emotion, and a *tertium quid* of fantasy, emerges as pervasive by the end of the 1930s. In biopics, musicals, monster films, and tearjerkers, Hollywood, which had long drawn on the novel's cultural capital while employing resolutely dramatic models of construction and exhibition, finally and wholeheartedly embraced the novel and, along with it, a novelistic aesthetic that would decisively set the course for its future.

Notes

1. Samuel Marx, "Looking for a Story," in *We Make the Movies*, ed. Nancy Naumberg (New York: Norton, 1937), p. 16.
2. Marx, "Looking for a Story," p. 17.
3. Dorothy Robinson, reader's report on *So Big*, May 23, 1936, Jean and Dusty Negulesco papers, Margaret Herrick Library, 65.f-1043.
4. Marx, "Looking for a Story," p. 18.
5. Marx, "Looking for a Story," pp. 19–20.
6. Thomas Schatz, *The Genius of the System: Hollywood Filmmaking in the Studio Era* (New York: Pantheon, 1988), p. 162.
7. Scott Eyman, *The Speed of Sound: Hollywood and the Talkie Revolution, 1926–1930* (New York: Simon and Schuster, 1997), p. 332.
8. Donald Crafton, *The Talkies: American Cinema's Transition to Sound, 1926–1931 [The History of American Cinema, Volume 4]* (New York: Scribner's, 1997), p. 352.
9. Ruth Vasey, *The World According to Hollywood, 1918–1939* (Madison: University of Wisconsin Press, 1996), p. 102.
10. Marx, "Looking for a Story," p. 27.
11. See Richard Koszarski, *An Evening's Entertainment: The Age of the Silent Feature Picture, 1915–1928 [History of the American Cinema, Volume 3]* (Berkeley: University of California Press, 1994).
12. Eyman, *The Speed of Sound*, p. 139.
13. Sarah Kozloff, *Overhearing Film Dialogue* (Berkeley: University of California Press, 2000), p. 14.
14. George Jessel, *So Help Me: The Autobiography of George Jessel* (Whitefish, MT: Kessinger, 1943), p. 91.
15. See Thomas Leitch, "The Pulitzers Go to Hollywood," in *Adaptation, Awards Culture, and the Value of Prestige*, ed. Colleen Kennedy-Karpat and Eric Sandberg (Houndmills: Palgrave Macmillan, 2017), pp. 23–39.
16. Brian McFarlane, *Novel to Film: An Introduction to the Theory of Adaptation* (Oxford: Clarendon Press, 1996), p. 6.
17. Rick Altman, "Dickens, Griffith, and Film-Theory Today," *South Atlantic Quarterly* 88.2 (1989): 325.

18 Altman, "Dickens, Griffith, and Film-Theory Today," p. 356.
19 Peter Lev, "How to Write Adaptation History," in *The Oxford Handbook of Adaptation Studies*, ed. Thomas Leitch (New York: Oxford University Press, 2017), p. 667.
20 Marx, "Looking for a Story," p. 22.
21 Marx, "Looking for a Story," p. 22.
22 See Syd Field, *Screenplay: The Foundations of Screenwriting*, revised and expanded edition (New York: Dell, 1984), and Robert McKee, *Story: Substance, Structure, Style, and the Principles of Screenwriting* (New York: Regan, 1997).
23 George Bluestone, *Novels into Film* (Baltimore, MD: Johns Hopkins University Press, 1957), p. 11.
24 Vasey, *The World According to Hollywood*, p. 102.
25 Rick Altman, *Film/Genre* (London: British Film Institute, 1999), p. 59.
26 James Naremore, *More Than Night: Film Noir in Its Contexts*, updated and expanded edition (Berkeley: University of California Press, 2008), p. 141.
27 Schatz, *The Genius of the System*, p. 170.
28 Ben Yagoda, *Will Rogers: A Biography* (New York: Knopf, 1993), pp. xii–xiii.
29 John McAleer, *Rex Stout: A Biography* (Boston, MA: Little, Brown, 1977), pp. 254, 255.
30 Dashiell Hammett, *The Thin Man*, in Hammett, *Complete Novels* (New York: Library of America, 1999), p. 937.
31 Francis M. Nevins and Martin Grams, Jr., "The Radio Adventures of Ellery Queen: The First Season," http://www.otrr.org/FILES/Articles/Martin_Grams_Jr_Articles/Adventures_Of_Ellery_Queen.htm.
32 Quoted by Schatz, *The Genius of the System*, p. 168.
33 David O. Selznick, Interview with Art Buchwald, 1957, quoted in Joanna E. Rapf, "Classical Hollywood, 1928–1946," in *Producing*, ed. John Lewis (New Brunswick, NJ: Rutgers University Press, 2016), p. 45.
34 Donald Crafton, *The Talkies*, p. 347.
35 Samuel Marx, *A Gaudy Spree: The Literary Life of Hollywood in the 1930s When the West Was Fun* (New York: Franklin Watts, 1987), p. 113.
36 Schatz, *The Genius of the System*, p. 169.
37 Dudley Andrew, *Mists of Regret: Culture and Sensibility in Classic French Film* (Princeton, NJ: Princeton University Press, 1995), p. 150.
38 M.M. Bakhtin, *The Dialogic Imagination: Four Essays*, ed. Michael Holquist, trans. Caryl Emerson and Michael Holquist (Austin: University of Texas Press, 1981), p. 262.
39 Guerric DeBona, *Film Adaptation in the Hollywood Studio Era* (Urbana: University of Illinois Press, 2010), p. 47.

40 Aldous Huxley, letter to Eugene F. Saxton, November 2, 1939, quoted in Ian Hamilton, *Writers in Hollywood, 1915–1951* (New York: Harper and Row, 1990), p. 138.

41 Erich Auerbach, *Mimesis: The Representation of Reality in Western Literature*, trans. Willard R. Trask (Princeton, NJ: Princeton University Press, 1953), pp. 547–48.

42 David O. Selznick, *Memo from David O. Selznick*, ed. Rudy Behlmer (New York: Viking, 1972), p. 28.

43 Joseph I. Breen, letter to Will Hays, December 18, 1935, Motion Picture Association of America, Production Code Administration records, Margaret Herrick Library.

44 Joseph I. Breen, letter to Louis B. Mayer, January 31, 1936, Motion Picture Association of America, Production Code Administration records, Margaret Herrick Library.

45 "Lewis Says Hays Bans Film of Book," *New York Times*, February 16, 1936, pp. 1, 35.

46 Will H. Hays, "Statement issued by Mr. Hays to newspapers in connection with IT CAN'T HAPPEN HERE," February 17, 1936, Production Code Administration records, Margaret Herrick Library.

47 See Val Lewton, letter to Joseph I. Breen, June 8, 1936; and Harry Rathner, letter to Joseph I. Breen, April 8, 1937, Production Code Administration records, Margaret Herrick Library.

48 Joseph I. Breen, letter to Louis B. Mayer, March 22, 1939, Production Code Administration records, Margaret Herrick Library.

49 Joseph I. Breen, letter to Louis B. Mayer, June 2, 1939, Production Code Administration records, Margaret Herrick Library.

50 Marx, *A Gaudy Spree*, pp. 193–94.

51 Stephen Smith, "Radio: The Internet of the 1930s," *American RadioWorks*, November 10, 2014, http://www.americanradioworks.org/segments/radio-the-internet-of-the-1930s/.

52 For a more extensive discussion of the aesthetics of radio adaptation, see Richard J. Hand, "Radio Adaptation," in *The Oxford Handbook of Adaptation Studies*, ed. Thomas Leitch (New York: Oxford University Press, 2017), pp. 340–55.

53 Thomas Leitch, "You Talk Like a Character in a Book: Film Dialogue and Adaptation," in *Film Dialogue*, ed. Jeff Jaeckle (London: Wallflower, 2013), pp. 97, 96.

54 Henry James, "Preface to *The Golden Bowl*," in Henry James, *Literary Criticism: French Writers, Other European Writers, The Prefaces to the New York Edition* (New York: Library of America, 1984), p. 1322.

55 Michael Wood, *America in the Movies, or "Santa Maria, It Had Slipped My Mind"* (New York: Basic, 1975), p. 8.

56 J.E. Smyth, *Edna Ferber's Hollywood: American Fictions of Gender, Race, and History* (Austin: University of Texas Press, 2010), p. 29.

57 Following the award of the Pulitzer to *The Bridge of San Luis Rey* in 1928, the Pulitzer Prize committee changed the wording of Pulitzer's charge from "the American novel published during the year which shall best present the whole atmosphere of American life, and the highest standard of American manners and manhood," to "the best novel of the year by an American author" so that they could give Buck the prize. See Leitch, "The Pulitzers Go to Hollywood," pp. 31–32.
58 Altman, *Film/Genre*, p. 57.
59 Altman, *Film/Genre*, p. 57.
60 Thomas Schatz, *Boom and Bust: American Cinema in the 1940s [History of the American Cinema, Volume 6]* (New York: Scribner's, 1987), p. 12.

5

1939–51: Invisible Adaptation

In with the wind

The runaway success of *Gone with the Wind* provided an invitation for a new era of novelistic adaptations that explored a leading character's subjectivity in the context of a large-scale exterior canvas set in the historical past or a foreign or exotic cultural present. This recipe inspired many Hollywood adaptations throughout the 1940s, a decade bracketed by *The Grapes of Wrath* (1940) and *All the King's Men* (1949) that might be called the Golden Age of Hollywood subjectivity. Although wartime Hollywood continued to seek literary and cultural cachet in adaptations of British novels like *Pride and Prejudice* (1940), *How Green Was My Valley* (1941), *Random Harvest* (1942), and *The Keys of the Kingdom* (1944), the number, range, and idiomatic assurance of notable adaptations of twentieth-century American fiction during the 1940s is remarkable. Some were based on novels acknowledged as modern classics like *The Maltese Falcon* (1941), *The Magnificent Ambersons* (1942), and *A Tree Grows in Brooklyn* (1945). Others were based on contemporaneous best sellers that have since faded into obscurity like *Daisy Kenyon* (1947), *The Egg and I* (1947), and *The Hucksters* (1947). Still others, like *Stagecoach* (1939), *Meet John Doe* (1941), *My Friend Flicka* (1943), and *It's a Wonderful Life* (1946), were based on short stories that have long been forgotten or pigeonholed as children's fiction. Adaptations from *Drums along the Mohawk* (1939) to *Mr. Blandings Builds His Dream House* (1948) have had more durable reputations than the novels on which they were based. The limiting case of a film eclipsing its literary source is *Casablanca* (1942), perhaps the most fondly remembered film of the decade, which was based on an unproduced play. Ernest Hemingway, who was routinely described as the most cinematic of all American novelists even though his only adaptation to date had been *A Farewell to Arms* (1932), was memorialized in adaptations of *For Whom the Bell Tolls* (1943), *To Have and Have Not* (1944), *The Killers* (1946), and *The Macomber Affair* (1947). James M. Cain, whose novels the Breen Office had long ruled off-limits despite their publication by the prestigious firm of Alfred A. Knopf, was finally brought to the screen in *Double Indemnity* (1944), *Mildred Pierce* (1945), and *The Postman Always Rings Twice* (1946). Suddenly, no novel, whatever its length, complexity, or licentiousness, seemed beyond Hollywood's reach.

A fundamental driver of the studios' move to adapt novels past and present was their appeal to contract stars hungry for meatier roles than their home studios afforded them. Bette Davis, whose early career had included roles in the adaptations *The Man Who Played God* (1932), *So Big!* (1932), *The Cabin in the Cotton* (1933), *20,000 Years in Sing Sing* (1933), and *Of Human Bondage* (1934), her breakthrough role, demanded more serious roles after winning an Oscar for *Dangerous* (1935) and appearing in the adaptations *The Petrified Forest* (1936) and *Satan Met a Lady* (1936), the second of three Warner Bros. adaptations of *The Maltese Falcon*. The studio responded by suspending her without pay in 1936. Although Davis lost a lawsuit against Warners, she was ultimately rewarded with a series of just the sort of complex roles she had sought in a remarkable series of adaptations: *Jezebel* (1938), *The Sisters* (1938), *Dark Victory* (1939), *The Old Maid* (1939), *The Private Lives of Elizabeth and Essex* (1939), *The Letter* (1940), *The Great Lie* (1941), *The Little Foxes* (1941), *The Man Who Came to Dinner* (1942), *In This Our Life* (1942), *Now, Voyager* (1942), *Watch on the Rhine* (1943), *Old Acquaintance* (1943), *The Corn Is Green* (1945), *A Stolen Life* (1946), *Deception* (1946), and *Beyond the Forest* (1949).

The kinds of roles Davis sought—strong-willed, magnetic heroines who were torn by conflicting loyalties whose interplay her performances could trace—were most consistently found in novels. So it was only natural that her demand for more challenging roles would lead her studio to commission more adaptations of novels. Several years later, Davis's legal challenge to Warner Bros. was echoed by Olivia de Havilland, who had appeared in many earlier adaptations—*Alibi Ike* (1935), *A Midsummer Night's Dream* (1935), *Captain Blood* (1935), *Anthony Adverse* (1936), *The Charge of the Light Brigade* (1936), *The Adventures of Robin Hood* (1938), *The Private Lives of Elizabeth and Essex* (1939), *Raffles* (1939), *Gone with the Wind* (1939), *The Strawberry Blonde* (1941), *Hold Back the Dawn* (1941), *The Male Animal* (1942), *In This Our Life* (1942)—often as a foil to physically dominant heroes played by Errol Flynn. Like Davis, de Havilland was suspended in 1941 after she demanded stronger, more complex, less dependent roles. When her contract with Warner Bros. ended in 1943 and the studio informed her that it was extending the contract by six months to make up for the time she had been under suspension, she sued in protest against what she argued was an arrangement that treated contract stars as chattel. Unlike Davis, she won, establishing in the process the De Havilland Law, which limited seven-year contracts to the seven years after their original signing. Coming just two years before the landmark Paramount decision that would order the studios to divest themselves of the theaters that established them as a vertically integrated monopoly, the 1944 decision already diminished the leverage of the studios in assignments and contract negotiations even as it freed de Havilland to sign a new contract with Paramount, which rewarded her with starring roles in three critically acclaimed adaptations—*To Each Her Own* (1946), *The Snake Pit* (1948), and *The Heiress* (1949)—the first and last of which won her Academy Awards, making her the most highly regarded actress in Hollywood by the end of the decade.

Most striking of all in her tropism for literary adaptations was Katharine Hepburn. Twenty-one of her twenty-six films through 1951, from *A Bill of Divorcement* (1932) to *The African Queen* (1951), were adaptations, including fifteen of her first sixteen films; the sixteenth, *Break of Hearts* (1936), was based on an original story written expressly for her. Hepburn's transatlantic diction and patrician bearing often led to her casting in adaptations of British plays and novels, but her adaptations of American material included *Morning Glory* (1933), an adaptation of Zoë Atkins's unproduced stage play for which she won her first Academy Award; *Little Women* (1933), the first of four high-profile film adaptations of Louisa May Alcott's 1869 novel and the most highly regarded of her early performances; *Alice Adams* (1935), based on Booth Tarkington's Pulitzer Prize-winning 1921 novel; *Stage Door* (1937), an unusually free adaptation of George S. Kaufman and Edna Ferber's 1936 play; *Bringing Up Baby* (1938), an expansion of Hagar Wilde's 1937 short story; and a pair of films based on plays by her friend Philip Barry, *Holiday* (1938) and *The Philadelphia Story* (1940). After a string of financially disappointing films like *Bringing up Baby* landed Hepburn on a list of Hollywood performers including Greta Garbo, Mae West, Marlene Dietrich, Joan Crawford, John Barrymore, and Fred Astaire labeled "box-office poison" in 1938, she asked Barry to write *The Philadelphia Story* as a stage vehicle for her, agreeing to work without salary in return for a percentage of its profits, and accepted the film rights to the play as a gift from the airplane magnate and sometime producer Howard Hughes. When MGM sought to buy the rights, Hepburn offered them for the bargain price of $250,000 on the condition that she star in the role of spoiled heiress Tracy Lord and retain veto control over the producer, director, screenwriter, and other members of the cast. The result was a triumphant comeback for Hepburn and a notable critical and commercial success for her new studio.

Interestingly, the most prominent movie stars to seek stronger, more complex and conflicted roles in adaptations of novels and plays were women. Perhaps the closest male analogue is Tyrone Power, whose casting in the historical demi-epic romances *The Mark of Zorro* (1940), *Blood and Sand* (1941), *This Above All* (1942), *The Black Swan* (1942), *Captain from Castille* (1947), *Prince of Foxes* (1949), and *The Black Rose* (1950) attest to the dramatic difference between Hollywood's notions of what constituted strong roles for women (internal conflict, expressive subtlety, emotional range) and men (a mastery of physical action in period costume dramas). But Power's roles as spiritual quester Larry Darrell in *The Razor's Edge* (1946), a role he was given when he asked Fox for a break from his swashbucklers, and the criminally ambitious carnival worker Stan Carlisle in *Nightmare Alley* (1947), adapted from William Lindsay Gresham's 1946 novel, gave him an opportunity to show a more dramatic side that would return to eclipse until his two final films, *Witness for the Prosecution* (1957) and *The Sun Also Rises* (1957).

Despite Hollywood's greater interest in Hemingway in the period beginning with the Second World War, which gave both his novels and his heroic ethos greater currency, and continuing through the aura surrounding his reception of the Nobel Prize for Literature in 1954, the American novelist who was best served by the movies during the 1940s, and perhaps the most consistently well filmed of all notable American novelists, was John Steinbeck. Long before his own Nobel Prize in 1962, most of Steinbeck's major works were adapted to film shortly after their publication; most of the adaptations were critically and financially successful; and most of them displayed Steinbeck's name prominently in both their screen credits and their publicity, achieving a cross-branding synergy of author and adaptations other American novelists could only envy.

The first Steinbeck adaptation, based on his 1937 novella and stage play *Of Mice and Men* (1939; another film adaptation would follow in 1992, along with adaptations to American television in 1968 and 1981, an 1972 Iranian adaptation, a 1975 Turkish adaptation, a 1992 Malayalam adaptation, a 2015 Danish adaptation, and a filmed version of the Broadway revival of Steinbeck's play in 2014), already announces itself in its main title as "'Of Mice and Men' by John Steinbeck." Whether because Steinbeck's novella had been chosen by the Book-of-the-Month Club or because Steinbeck had meanwhile published the prodigiously best-selling *The Grapes of Wrath* (1939), United Artists, which released the film, made his name the most prominent authorial brand in Hollywood, a status that was quickly confirmed by the success of Twentieth Century Fox's 1940 adaptation of *The Grapes of Wrath,* which was nominated for seven Academy Awards, won three, and has been hailed ever since as one of the most distinguished film adaptations of an American novel. MGM's trailer for *Tortilla Flat* (1942) sought to link the film to several earlier scripts in successive title screens: "Spectacularly filmed against the giant background of a California wonderland!/Brilliantly told by John Steinbeck, author of 'Grapes of Wrath'!/Directed by Victor Fleming, who gave you 'Gone with the Wind'!/Presented by Metro-Goldwyn-Mayer ... as its Outstanding attraction of the year!" Although *Tortilla Flat* never enjoyed anything like the success of *The Grapes of Wrath,* Steinbeck continued to be a hot property in Hollywood, sought by Alfred Hitchcock to write the original story for

Lifeboat (1944) and lending his name and reputation to the adaptations *The Pearl* (1947), *The Red Pony* (1949), and *Viva Zapata* (1952). Largely because of the success of *The Moon Is Down,* his 1942 parable, originally set in the United States, of a townspeople's resistance to the occupation of their village by an unidentified military force, and its 1943 film adaptation, which explicitly identified its setting as Norway and the occupying force as the Third Reich, Steinbeck became one of the first American novelists to maintain a substantial following abroad, especially in the USSR, and foreign filmmakers have frequently adapted his work.

Yet despite all these high-profile adaptations and many others, the 1940s saw a shift from the novelistic aesthetic and marketing strategy David O. Selznick had pioneered at MGM to a movement away from marking adaptations as adaptations. A surprising number of 1940s adaptations soft-pedal their status as adaptations, burying the titles of their source texts and the names of their authors deep in their credits, nominating more powerful alternative authors from actresses like Davis and de Havilland to star producers, directors, or genres, or presenting them as authorless, invisible adaptations that either decline to trade on their status as adaptations or emphasize that branding while changing the texts they were adapting virtually beyond recognition.

This sharp turn in adaptive strategies is reflected in the difference between Twentieth Century Fox's film adaptations of *The Grapes of Wrath* and of *Tobacco Road* the following year. RKO, Warner Bros., and Columbia had long coveted Erskine Caldwell's 1932 novel and its 1933 dramatization by Jack Kirkland, but they had all been discouraged by the Breen Office, which considered the novel unfilmable because of its unflinching emphasis on its Georgia tenant farmers' abject poverty, physical deformity, religious fundamentalism, marriages to underage spouses, and obsession with their own mortality. Eventually Caldwell and Kirkland sold the rights to Fox, the studio they felt offered the greatest promise that *Tobacco Road* "would be picturized honestly and fearlessly."[1] Nunnally Johnson, who had written the screenplay for *The Grapes of Wrath,* prepared the adaptation of the new property; John Ford, who had directed the earlier film, agreed to take on *Tobacco Road* as well; and Ford insisted that Charley Grapewin, who had played Pa Joad, be cast as Jeeter Lester, the ineffectual paterfamilias who heads the cast. Fox, keenly aware that merely trading on the links between the two films would not guarantee the success of *Tobacco Road,* decided to forego location shooting in Georgia, shoot the entire film on a closed set, and avoid any advance publicity that might have courted preemptive censorship. In response to Joseph I. Breen's warning that "many religious folk throughout the nation may be offended by the [film's] religious aspects,"[2] Ford gave an interview announcing "we have no dirt in the picture. We've eliminated the horrible details and what we've got left is a nice dramatic story. It's a tear-jerker, with some comedy relief. What we're aiming at is to have the customers sympathize with our people and not feel disgusted."³ In fact, the comic relief of which Ford speaks overruns the film, which treats Jeeter Lester and his wildly dysfunctional family as exotic American types invoking a marginalized subculture through elegiac farce.

Lacking the hard-won, we're-the-people dignity and universality of the Joads in *The Grapes of Wrath,* the Lesters come across as comically atavistic hillbilly halfwits. Audiences for the film did not feel the disgust they might have felt from reading Caldwell's novel, but neither were they invited to admire the attachment to their family or their land so dramatically displayed in *The Grapes of Wrath* by Tom Joad (Henry Fonda) and his mother (Jane Darwell). Instead, *Tobacco Road* was an all-white minstrel show that invited them to look down at the Lesters as shiftless, heedless, and contemptible (see Figure 5.1). A key difference between the two films lies in their use of traditional music. In *The Grapes of Wrath,* this music, especially the song "Red River Valley," is consistently used to link the Joads as a family, subordinating their individual problems and identities to the survival of the family unit, as opposed to their membership in the "family of man"⁴ and the link between the characters and the land that Vivian C. Sobchack finds paramount in Steinbeck's novel. *Tobacco Road,* by contrast,

FIGURE 5.1 *The incorrigibly shiftless Lesters of* Tobacco Road *(1941): Jeeter (Charley Grapewin), Dude (William Tracy), Ada (Elizabeth Patterson), and Ellie Mae (Gene Tierney).*

is a white-trash minstrel show that consistently burlesques both the family ties among the Lesters, each of them selfishly willing to betray the others for the sake of their individual survival, and between the family and the land, which Jeeter refuses to leave for a factory job even though he no longer has the money for the seeds and supplies that would allow him to farm it. Sister Bessie (Marjorie Rambeau), the evangelist who marries Jeeter's sixteen-year-old son Dude (William Tracy), repeatedly and strategically sings hymns like "Bringing in the Sheaves" to defang any official enemies who threaten her activities by inviting them to an evanescent circle of love and community that will make them forget their complaints. The non-diegetic music on the film's soundtrack has much the same function. Sentimental background music, largely based on the same hymns, brackets the film's opening and closing scenes. When this music plays behind the Lesters' brief gesture at packing up their belongings before the bank forces them to leave by foreclosing on their farm, it seems to promise a close parallel between the powerful scene in which Ma Joad packs her family's memorabilia in *The Grapes of Wrath* until the Lesters suddenly realize they own nothing worth packing. In other scenes, the sentimental force of this background music is undermined by its alternation with the rollicking music for banjo and orchestra that runs over the opening credits and returns to impart a comic edge to the scene in which the Lesters savagely beat their neighbor Lov Bensey (Ward Bond) and rob him of a sack of turnips and a later scene in which Dude recklessly drives the car his much older bride has bought down a country road, honking furiously, and running another car he is passing off the road and into a ditch—a scene that had ended in Caldwell's novel with the death of the other driver. If the music in *The Grapes of Wrath* seeks to merge the characters' individual subjectivities with the more general subjectivities of their family or their country, the music in *Tobacco Road* undermines any lasting claim Jeeter Lester and his clan might make to the dignity accorded both memorable individuals and representatives of respected groups. It is as if Fox, having created a distinctive crux between American literature and American cinema in *The Grapes of Wrath,* was now determined to satirize that alliance in ways that rendered it impossible to sustain.

Adaptation goes to war

Hollywood, which had largely avoided the First World War as a subject until it had ended, volunteered much more eagerly for service in the Second World War, which the studios saw as both a great subject for rousing cinema and an opportunity to demonstrate the industry's patriotism and indispensability through its support for the war. What is often lost in this story is the delicate balancing act of adaptations released before the United States entered the war that traded on images of battle without violating the nation's official neutrality. The safest way to achieve this balance was to make movies like *Sergeant York* (1941) that were ostensibly about earlier wars. But a pair of adaptations set in the apparently remote eighteenth century give some idea of how tricky this balancing act could be.

In November 1939, two months after England declared war on Germany, Twentieth Century Fox released John Ford's *Drums along the Mohawk*. An opening intertitle, which sets the scene in "1776: at the Borst home in Albany, New York," immediately identifies its period as that of the American Revolution, when the thirteen colonies were fighting to achieve independence from England. Yet Lamar Trotti and Sonya Levien's screenplay, unlike Walter D. Edmonds's 1936 novel, does everything it can to disguise, displace, and efface the conflict between the colonials and the British. Early on, Caldwell (John Carradine), a sinister eye-patched figure, arouses the suspicions of Gil Martin (Henry Fonda), who is bringing his bride Lana (Claudette Colbert) from her parents' well-appointed home in Albany to his isolated cabin in Deerfield, by asking if there are any Tories in the area and saying, "They say the Indians are going to line up with the British, but I suppose that's just talk." Apart from Caldwell, however, the British are represented entirely by proxies, the Indians who attack the cabin and other homes in Deerfield, and who are balanced in turn by Blue Back (Chief Big Tree), the Indian who remains fiercely loyal to the colonists. Only a single one of the former group wears a red coat of the sort audiences would have associated with British troops. For the most part, the film subordinates the conflict between the colonists and the British to a series of other dualities: the order of the formal wedding service with which the film begins versus the disorder represented by the awkwardness of the newlyweds, the determined future orientation of Lana ("It's going to be beautiful," she assures Gil of their farm) versus the grim present orientation of Gil ("Don't look back," he enjoins her as they leave the farm just ahead of an Indian attack); the relatively polished civilization of Albany versus the hardscrabble frontier on which Gil's cabin sits, a duality Ford would exploit in a distinguished series of Westerns that had already begun earlier that year with *Stagecoach*; and the tropism toward individual survival, which Gil's employer, Sarah McKlennar (Edna May Oliver) rejects when she refuses to leave her burning house to save her own life, versus the tropism toward communal identity Gil represents when he risks his life to leave the besieged Fort Schuyler to seek reinforcements from nearby Fort Dayton. The most powerful image of this triumph of community over individuality is the hoisting of the new American flag above Fort Schuyler in response to an announcement that Lord Cornwallis has surrendered to General Washington, ending the war. "So that's the flag we've been fighting for," says one of Gil's neighbors, and Lana adds, "It's a pretty flag, isn't it?"—establishing the film's all-American sympathies while minimizing any awkward anti-British sentiments. Edward Countryman has summarized the adaptation by observing:

> Edmonds wrote a novel that combined hard research into the dynamics of a social crisis with a form that opened that research to a mass public. Ford made of that novel a film which pictures two forces that must conflict because their nature demands it and which argues that the triumph of the American cause obliterates all divisions, whether of race, class, or sex.[5]

A year later, MGM's release of *Northwest Passage* required a similarly delicate balancing act that Kenneth Roberts's 1937 novel had been able to avoid. King Vidor's film, from a screenplay by Laurence Stallings and Talbot Jennings, is set during the French and Indian Wars, when the American colonies were still under British dominion. But its hero, Major Robert Rogers (Spencer Tracy), is a celebrated Indian fighter who has little use for the redcoats who give him his orders, and against whom his green-attired troops are repeatedly set. The film, shot, like *Drums along the Mohawk*, in Technicolor—it was MGM's most expensive release of 1940—presents Rogers's Rangers, a corps hardened more regularly by grueling physical deprivations than by battles against Indians, as initially looking a good deal like the outlaws of Sherwood Forest featured in Warner Bros.' *The Adventures of Robin Hood* (1938), though the longer they spend tramping through the wilderness, the more their faded uniforms resemble those of contemporaneous American servicemen. The war in *Northwest Passage*, like the war England was fighting in 1940, demands not heroic initiative but stoic endurance as Rogers leads his troops from one dry hole to the next without food or rest. "Keep moving" is his mantra to his followers. When they are wounded, he leaves them behind lest they slow the remaining troops—all but Langdon Towne (Robert Young), the mapmaker and aspiring artist he cheers on after he is gut-shot by telling him, "How do you know you can't walk unless you've tried it?" Although Rogers's Rangers are overjoyed to hear the pipes of the redcoats returning to deserted Fort Wentworth with sorely needed provisions, Rogers, commanded to read the Rangers' next orders aloud to them, stumbles over the phrase "my devoted liege," which King George II uses to describe Rogers, and the Rangers laugh at him. Instead of reading the orders, he ends up summarizing them in a stirring speech about the search the King bids them undertake for the fabled Northwest Passage, the river route through the colonies and their western territories that will allow the crown to expedite Oriental trade by allowing its ships to pass from the Atlantic to the Pacific.

The main title of the film describes it as *"Northwest Passage" (Book I ... Rogers' Rangers)*, broadly promising the sequel that would have covered the events in the second half of Roberts's novel (see Figure 5.2). But no sequel was ever produced because Roberts, who had wanted MGM to include the

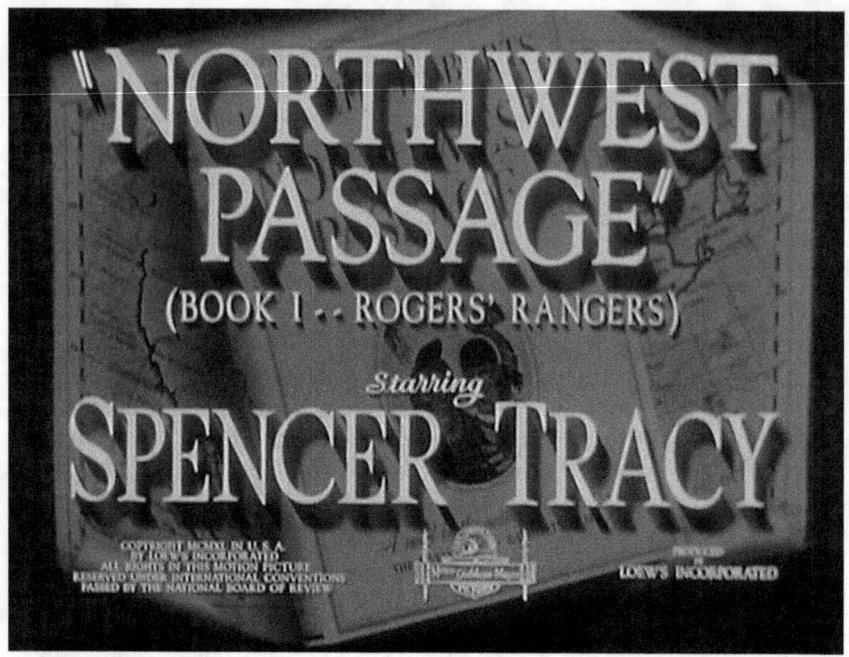

FIGURE 5.2 *The title credit of* Northwest Passage *(1940) seems to promise a sequel that never materialized.*

action of the entire novel, refused to cooperate on a sequel, because Tracy refused to work with Vidor again, and because any attempt to film a sequel that remained faithful to either the historical record or the second half of Roberts's well-known novel, which had been outsold in 1937 only by *Gone with the Wind*, would have opened old fissures between the United States and the United Kingdom at just the moment when the special relationship between the two nations was most urgently required. Instead, the film ends with Towne returning to his fiancée Elizabeth Browne (Ruth Hussey), who tells Rogers that they will leave the colonies for London because "I want him to be a great painter," blissfully unaware that in Roberts's novel, as in real life, Elizabeth left Towne to marry Rogers herself.

Once the war came to America, the portrayal of all wars, past and present, shifted accordingly. One of the most notable of these shifts was a trend away from adaptations. Just as individual volunteers and conscripts for military service trade their individual identities for more urgent roles as members of a coherent group, it is only natural for adaptations that announce themselves as such to be eclipsed during wartime. This was particularly so during the Second World War, which Hollywood supported so frequently and vigorously on so many fronts. In the authoritative filmography compiled by Jeanine Basinger and Jeremy Arnold,[6] the number of combat films set during the Second World War and the Korean War peaks in the years just after the Japanese attack on Pearl Harbor brought the United States into the war (fourteen in 1942, sixteen in 1943, thirteen in 1944, and sixteen in 1945), then again during the Korean War (thirteen in 1951, nine in 1952, and twelve in 1953) and the Vietnam War (seven in 1967, ten in 1968, eight in 1969, and ten in 1970). But most of these combat films were not adaptations. The number of Hollywood war films adapted from other sources does not peak until 1958, long after the war, when ten of eleven war films were based on previously published material. The only other years when more than half a dozen war adaptations were released were 1943 (eight of sixteen films), 1951 (seven of thirteen films), and 1968 (eight of ten films).

The reasons why adaptations lagged behind other combat films are obvious. Because large-scale military combat is difficult to stage, many of the most celebrated plays about the war, from Steinbeck's *The Moon Is Down* to Lillian Hellman's *Watch on the Rhine* (1941), are set well behind the battle lines. Novels about Americans at war did not begin to appear until months after Americans first saw combat. In the meantime, studios rushing to bring the war home to American audiences turned to documentaries (like five of the fourteen combat films released in 1942) or adaptations of British sources. Even before Pearl Harbor, the United States had embarked on an informal program in support of British cultural values by producing films like *Goodbye, Mr. Chips* (1939), *Waterloo Bridge* (1940), *Rage in Heaven* (1941), and *Mrs. Miniver* (1942). Since the British had entered the war two years before the Americans, Hollywood could draw immediately on British wartime fiction to make *Random Harvest* (1942), *Mrs. Miniver*, and *This Above All* (1942). American adaptations, which were initially less likely to focus on the combat experience than portraits of an England besieged and existentially threatened by the Reich, arrived later on both the battlefront— *I Wanted Wings* (1941), *Cry "Havoc"* (1943), *The Sea Chase* (1955), *The Enemy Below* (1957), *Run Silent Run Deep* (1958), *Torpedo Run* (1958), *The Young Lions* (1958), *Darby's Rangers* (1958), *Up Periscope* (1959), and, apart from the 1939 release *Idiot's Delight*, the home front—*Four Sons* (1940, a remake of John Ford's 1928 film), *One Night in Lisbon* (1941), *The Major and the Minor* (1942), *The Moon Is Down*, *Edge of Darkness* (1943), *Watch on the Rhine*, *Since You Went Away* (1944), *The Searching Wind* (1946), and *Bright Victory* (1951). The three most important American novels about the war, Norman Mailer's *The Naked and the Dead* (1948), James Jones's *From Here to Eternity* (1951), and Joseph Heller's *Catch-22* (1961), were not filmed, like the great majority of Hollywood movies about the First World War, until years after the war they chronicled—in 1958, 1953, and 1970, respectively—for the excellent reason that the war ended before they were written, and Irish-American journalist Cornelius Ryan did not publish his history *The Longest Day,* which served as the basis for Twentieth Century Fox's 1962 epic about the Normandy invasion, until 1959.

In the immediate absence of American novels, plays, and histories about the Second World War that could be quickly and successfully filmed, Hollywood turned to another kind of source material: diaries, memoirs, autobiographies, and journalistic accounts of people who had participated in one way or the other in the war. This new wave of films included *Confessions of a Nazi Spy* (1939), *Sergeant York,* a story about the conscientious objector who had become a hero of the First World War, *Gung Ho* (1943), *Guadalcanal Diary* (1943), *Thirty Seconds over Tokyo* (1944), *A Walk in the Sun* (1945), *The Story of G.I. Joe* (1945), *The House on 92nd Street* (1945), *Three Came Home* (1950), and *To Hell and Back* (1955). With the exception of *To Hell and Back,* which was based on the autobiographical account of Audie Murphy, the most decorated soldier in the war, played by Murphy himself, and perhaps *The Story of G.I. Joe,* which starred Burgess Meredith as Ernie Pyle, the American journalist killed in action before its release whose reportage provided the basis for the film, the most important claim of these adaptations is not that they are based on books or journals or diaries, but that they tell the truth about the war. In other words, the films position themselves not as adaptations of identifiable literary sources but as reports that use these sources as a window through which the films can reveal the ostensive, however arguable, arbitrary, or self-evident, truth about the war.[7]

The film that most clearly establishes Hollywood's redefinition of what it meant to adapt a literary source to the screen during the Second World War is *This Is the Army* (1943), Warner Bros.' first three-strip Technicolor musical. Its opening credits, which begin by listing the civilian members of its cast and crew, proceed next to list all active members of the military service, including their ranks, who have taken part in its production before ending with an unusual full-screen acknowledgment: "We wish to thank Mr. Irving Berlin for making this motion picture possible through his two soldier shows 'Yip, Yip, Yaphank'—1918 and 'This Is the Army'—1943." This credit accurately identifies Berlin's two wartime Broadway revues as inspirations for the film without explicitly identifying them as sources. The refusal to identify the film as an offspring of either *Yip, Yip, Yaphank,* the comic and patriotic military revue Berlin had composed and produced during his First World War service at the request of the commanding officer of Camp Upton, in Yaphank, New York, or *This Is the Army,* the equally comical Second World War musical in which Berlin toured with the troops performing it for three and a half years, is an apt prelude to the film's resourceful strategies for tagging, disavowing, and complicating the scripts that had inspired it. Like *Stage Door Canteen* (1943), *Thank Your Lucky Stars* (1943), and *Hollywood Canteen* (1944), the film is formally a backstage musical, but this time the backstage is the two world wars. A generation after song-and-dance man Jerry Jones (George Murphy) and his fellow soldiers mount the morale-boosting musical *Yip, Yip, Yaphank* during the First World War, his son Johnny (Ronald Reagan) and his friends follow suit in the Second World War. Although the film includes a brief sequence of combat footage in which Jerry's leg is injured, ending his career as a dancer and forcing him to become a producer, most of its running time is devoted to stagings of its many musical numbers. Apart from Jerry's wounding, the only narrative through line is Johnny's running quarrel with his fiancée Eileen Dibble (Joan Leslie) about whether they should get married before he is called to the front. The rest of the film presents itself as a service-oriented backstage story focusing on the spectacular display of Berlin's songs. So it would be more precise to describe the film as telling a story about the staging of a pair of live-action shows than as an adaptation of the shows.

The film's systematic preference for monstration over narrative is revealed in several ways in which it persistently breaks the fourth wall to announce its own fictionality and frame its performances as performances. These include not only musical numbers, most of them celebrating service in the armed forces, but stand-up routines, tumbling, acrobatics, cross-dressing, and impersonations of Lynn Fontanne, Alfred Lunt, Charles Boyer, and Herbert Marshall, all of them performed full-face toward the movie audience. Kate Smith, Frances Langford, and Joe Louis all appear as themselves. Smith sings "God Bless America," with which she had already become indelibly identified since introducing it in 1938, twenty years after Berlin had dropped it from the score of *Yip, Yip, Yaphank* (a decision the film transfers from Berlin to Jerry Jones). After delivering a single line of halting dialogue, Louis is shown methodically working out with a leather punching bag as a cadre of African American performers sing and dance "What the Well-Dressed Man in Harlem Will Wear" in another part of the stage; not until the end of the number does Louis break through the line to come forward and salute the audience. Berlin, introduced as himself, emerges from a tent pitched onstage at the center of a set in which other tents appear against a stylized monochrome red backdrop, dressed as a First World War doughboy. Brightly spotlighted for his performance of "Oh, How I Hate to Get up in the Morning," he is greeted by a thunderous round of diegetic applause and soon joined by other singers marching and dancing in formation.

The net effect of these self-reflexive moments, nods to history, conflations of actual and fictional performers and performances, and shout-outs to the armed services is to subordinate the normal economy of adaptations, in which the film would present itself as based on Berlin's two revues, to a radical new economy that proposes the First World War, which spawned *Yip, Yip, Yaphank,* as the logical progenitor of the Second World War. This may sound perverse. After all, why would a morale-building film invoke *any* non-literary, non-theatrical scripts, let alone the war to end all wars? But positioning the Second World War as an adaptation of the First World War makes perfect sense. After all, the first war is over, and it ended happily in victory for America and its allies apart from a few tears (the wounding of Jerry and the loss of his dancing career). Just as Jerry Jones begat Johnny Jones, his son and successor in producing the new show, the earlier war is the perfect aspirational model for a new war that is still raging uncompleted—a tendency emphatically confirmed in the film's final number, "This Time (Is the Last Time)," which embraces a frankly revisionist attitude toward adaptation by making it as clear as possible that this war will definitively finish the business the last war only started (see Figure 5.3). In the end, the film proved prophetic not only in this promise, but in its casting of George Murphy and Ronald Reagan as entertainers whose deepest energies were released by a commitment to public service. Murphy's election as a US Senator from California in 1965 and Reagan's election a year later as Governor of California, and ultimately as the American president, suggested that the adaptive interface between politics and entertainment might well continue to develop long past its embodiment in any single film.

FIGURE 5.3 *The massively produced climactic number of* This Is the Army *(1943) promises both the characters and the audience that "This Time (Is the Last Time)."*

Americans abroad

Hollywood studios had several reasons to produce adaptations from *I Wanted Wings* to *This Is the Army* designed to support the war effort. Even studio heads who had resented the trust-busting of Franklin Roosevelt's Supreme Court were largely converted to the cause by the attack on Pearl Harbor. Public sentiment might well have turned against young male stars who were physically fit for the armed services. Studio chiefs like Darryl F. Zanuck fancied the prospect of attaining an advanced military rank while continuing to work their regular jobs. And of course sentiment throughout most of the industry, as throughout most of the country, was overwhelmingly in favor of the war that the Japanese attack had suddenly brought uncomfortably close to home. An additional reason was more purely financial: the war in Europe had closed many of Hollywood's most lucrative foreign markets, and the studios actively sought alternative ways to make up the revenue their products could no longer earn in England, France, Italy, or Germany.

Foreign cinema's neglect of American literature, which might have seemed to stem from the rise of national sentiment in Europe during the war and the unofficial embargo on new books whose publishers were reluctant to send them across the Atlantic to an uncertain fate, was in fact nothing new. The European powers had considered the United States a provincial culture before the war. Even England, which shared a language and a number of state and social institutions with its former colony, had little appetite for adaptations of American fiction, which seemed thin, exotic, and unrewardingly foreign.

The years after the war ended in 1945 saw a dramatic resurgence in American export culture. Hollywood movies were especially popular in France, where they were greeted by critics and audiences whose enthusiasm had only been sharpened by the embargo. Even now, however, European cinemas remained notably uninterested in adapting American novels from *The Scarlet Letter* to *For Whom the Bell Tolls*. *Uncle Tom's Cabin,* which has been translated into seventy languages[8] and indigenized in local cultures around the world,[9] was adapted only four times by filmmakers outside the United States: in Antônio Serra's *A Cabana do Pai Tomás* (Brazil, 1909), Riccardo Tolentino's *La capanna della zio Tom* (Italy, 1918), Jean-Christophe Averty's television episode *La case de l'oncle Tom* (for *Le théâtre de la jeunesse,* France, 1963), and the television series *A Cabana do Pai Tomás* (Brazil, 1969–70). As far back as 1920, the German filmmaker Arthur Wellin had directed *Lederstrumpf,* a two-part adaptation of J. Fenimore Cooper's *The Last of the Mohicans* that cast Bela Lugosi as the noble Chingachgook. In general, however, Cooper's exotic Americanism was no more appealing to foreign filmmakers than James's reflective cosmopolitanism. The English, following the lead of F.R. Leavis, had "accorded [American writers] honorary status in the English pantheon," but the writers thus honored were not "allowed to remain American": their "social and historical context was ignored or simply sketched in as a series of stereotypes."[10] Across the channel, where "American literature in France became more widely known between the two world wars," intellectual mandarins like Emerson, Hawthorne, and James were deracinated and universalized, and anti-establishment writers like Melville, Twain, Hemingway, Steinbeck, and the authors of hard-boiled detective fiction were exoticized: "The taste of the French public, shaped by journalistic views, tend[ed] to be attracted by the anti-intellectual tradition in American literature while French criticism and academic life either [fed] more generally on authors that are closer to continental literary preoccupations or consider[ed] other American writers from an angle less sociological, cultural, or mythical than theoretical and aesthetic."[11] Michele Bottalico observes that the American novelists most popular in Italy before the rise of Benito Mussolini turned the tide against them—"Steinbeck, Caldwell, [William] Saroyan, [Sherwood] Anderson, James Cain, [John] Dos Passos, Sinclair Lewis"—were taken up by Italian intellectuals because they "stressed the importance of a social commitment that was lacking in Italian writers," not because of any specifically literary or American qualities they might have had.[12] Savas Patsalidis maintains that "it was not until the implementation of the Marshall Plan in 1947 that American literature and American culture in general started making their presence felt in the Greek market."[13] Writing in 1991, Rolf Lundén deplored the fact that the "unwillingness to fully acknowledge the United States as a producer of quality literature comparable to the best European literature is still noticeable in Sweden."[14] On the whole, even foreign audiences who were wildly enthusiastic about American movies but did not happen to be scholars or students showed little commensurate interest in American literature.

Although few early American sound films for foreign export were adaptations of American literature, literary originals would play an important role a generation later in the French New Wave. Their most obvious impact was on François Truffaut, whose landmark films included a number of adaptations of American genre novels—*Shoot the Piano Player* (1960), based on David Goodis's 1956 novel; *Fahrenheit 451* (1966), based on Ray Bradbury's 1953 novel; *The Bride Wore Black* (1968), based on Cornell Woolrich's 1940 novel; *Mississippi Mermaid* (1969), based on *Waltz into Darkness*, the 1947 novel Woolrich published under the pseudonym William Irish; *Such a Gorgeous Kid Like Me* (1972), based on Henry Farrell's 1967 novel—and, a few years before his death, *The Green Room* (1978), based on Henry James's 1895 story "The Altar of the Dead." In addition, Claude Chabrol directed *The Breach* (1970), based on Charlotte Armstrong's *The Balloon Man* (1968); *Ten Days Wonder* (1971), based on Ellery Queen's 1948 novel; *Dirty Hands* (1975), based on Richard Neely's *The Damned*

Innocents (1971); *Blood Relatives* (1978), based on Ed McBain's 1975 police procedural about the 87th Precinct; *The Cry of the Owl* (1987), based on Patricia Highsmith's 1962 novel; *Quiet Days in Clichy* (1990), based on Henry Miller's 1956 novel; and *Merci pour le chocolat* (2000), based on Charlotte Armstrong's *The Chocolate Cobweb* (1948).

Day for Night, which Truffaut directed from an original screenplay he wrote with Jean-Louis Richard and Suzanne Schiffman in 1973, is in some ways as American in its inspiration as any of his adaptations of American literary material. The film, dedicated to Lillian and Dorothy Gish, chronicles the adventures of a director attempting to complete *Je vous présente Pamela,* a romantic melodrama, amid the daily vicissitudes of filmmaking compounded by the soap-opera intrigues of his cast. *Day for Night* is less interested in American literature than American movies, which also played a vital role in inspiring Jean-Luc Godard's earlier New Wave films *Breathless* (1959), *Vivre sa vie* (1962), *Contempt* (1963), and *Masculin féminin* (1965), none of them based on American novels or stories, although Godard did base *Bande à part* (1964) and *Made in U.S.A.* (1966) on American novels by Dolores Hitchens and Richard Stark.

When they were not using American sources as occasions to play with notions of American culture refracted through Hollywood, New Wave filmmakers typically indigenized their sources, translating American characters and settings into French people and places. Although they did not conceal their sources, these adaptations were invisible in the sense that they did nothing to announce their Americanness, a development that would have to wait for a still later generation. In the meantime, Hollywood exerted perhaps its most profound and lasting effect on French cinema through the work of several influential French theorists. The term *film noir,* to take the most obvious example, was coined not by Hollywood publicists but by French journalists who "invented the American film noir [...] because local conditions predisposed them to view Hollywood in certain ways."[15] Nino Frank's essay "Un nouveau genre 'policier': L'aventure criminelle" and Jean-Pierre Chartier's "Les Américains aussi font des films 'noirs,'" both published in 1946,[16] grouped together a series of Hollywood films released in Paris the same week after the war embargo ended—*The Maltese Falcon* (1941), *Double Indemnity* (1944), *Laura* (1944), *Murder, My Sweet* (1944), and *The Lost Weekend* (1945)—because of their distinctively fatalistic flashback structure, their misogyny and moral pessimism, their fascination with criminal psychology, their stylistic decadence, and their anti-heroic worldview, but not because of their roots in any similar tendencies in American literature, which both Frank and Chartier ignored. Nine years later, Raymond Borde and Étienne Chaumeton[17] again bypassed American fiction in favor of French surrealism and existentialism as touchstones for a ritualistic, oneiric, erotic noir corpus, "an antigenre that reveals the dark side of savage capitalism,"[18] whose genealogy was retrospectively constructed "by two generations of Parisian intellectuals, most of whom declared the form extinct soon after they invented it."[19] Whatever impact American literature might have had on the film noir was buried in these accounts beneath the impact of French philosophy, anti-capitalist critique, and Hollywood movies.

Another way American literature made its way to foreign cinemas beneath the radar was through adaptations that failed to acknowledge their literary sources. This practice, which had been normal and widely accepted in Indian cinema through most of its history, was adopted by few European filmmakers because its most celebrated earlier instance, the 1922 vampire film *Nosferatu*, had ended in disaster for producer Albin Grau and his company, Prana Film Gesellschaft, both of them driven to bankruptcy by a copyright-infringement lawsuit by Bram Stoker's widow Florence. In addition, the court ordered all prints of the film destroyed. Only one copy escaped and made its way to the United States, whose failure to sign the Berne Convention kept the print from legal destruction so that it "managed to stay alive [even] with a stake through its heart."[20]

When Jean Renoir gave Luchino Visconti, who had worked as assistant director on *A Day in the Country* (1936), *The Lower Depths* (1937), and *La Tosca* (1940), a copy of James M. Cain's hardboiled 1934 novel *The Postman Always Rings Twice*, which had already been adapted as the French film *Le dernier tournant* (1939), Visconti was attracted to the idea of adapting the novel himself because the resulting film would be more likely than most to fly under the radar of fascist censorship. "Due to the war, Visconti never got the official rights to film Cain's novel"[21] but pressed on with the project anyway. On its 1942 release, *Ossessione*, the Italian cinema's first harbinger of neo-realism, was quickly denounced by Mussolini's government for its harshly critical depiction of contemporary Italian mores, and especially its emphasis on poverty and adultery, both subjects the government-controlled film industry was encouraged to ignore.

Forced to withdraw the film from circulation in his native land, Visconti faced an even greater challenge when Alfred A. Knopf, Cain's publisher, sued him for copyright infringement and prevented its distribution in America until 1976. But Visconti's invisible adaptation remained the single most influential filming of an American crime novel until the rise of the New Wave.

Dark adaptation

Ossessione's failure to identify Cain's novel as its source may have been an exceptional case, but it was a logical outgrowth of the tendency in films like *This Is the Army* to subordinate readily identifiable source texts to more amorphous, nonliterary, nontheatrical, non-textual source scripts, a tendency that became a hallmark of 1940s adaptations. This tendency was amplified by the disappearance of several kinds of adaptation that went missing in action during the war. The Japanese-American Mr. Moto was an immediate and predictable casualty of the war. But other detectives like Philo Vance, Hildegarde Withers, Perry Mason, Nero Wolfe, Torchy Blane, and Nancy Drew also disappeared because of their creators' deaths or refusals to license any more adventures, their stars left the studios that had produced the franchises, or the war had made those adventures seem irrelevant. Nick and Nora Charles soldiered on in *Son of the Thin Man* (1941), *The Thin Man Goes Home* (1944), and *Song of the Thin Man* (1947), but the survival of other fictional detectives from Sherlock Holmes to Ellery Queen depended on their ability to adapt to battling avatars of the Third Reich. The Hollywood musical went into a decline that sent Busby Berkeley, who had choreographed most of Warner Bros.' musicals from *42nd Street* (1933) to *Gold Diggers in Paris* (1938), to MGM, where he directed a less extravagant, more domesticated series of musicals from *Babes in Arms* (1939) to *Take Me out to the Ball Game* (1949), interspersed with occasional nonmusical adaptations like *Blonde Inspiration* (1941). The string of tightly integrated Broadway musicals beginning with *Oklahoma!* (1943) would wait years for a series of film adaptations that began with MGM's *On the Town* (1949). In the meantime, the Hollywood musical survived the war by downplaying the ritual romances that had driven RKO's nine films featuring Fred Astaire and Ginger Rogers and returning to its roots in the stage revue in films like *The Gang's All Here* (1943), *Stage Door Canteen,* and *This Is the Army.*

More surprisingly, the studios showed little interest throughout the war in the brand of Americana that crowded Broadway stages in shows like *Oklahoma!, On the Town* (1944), *Carousel* (1945), and *Annie Get Your Gun* (1946). *Cheers for Miss Bishop* (1941), United Artists' attempt to recapture the audience for *Goodbye, Mr. Chips* with an adaptation of Bess Streeter Aldrich's account of a female teacher in a Midwestern setting, failed to ignite the box office, and adaptations of classic American novels like *The Adventures of Huckleberry Finn* (1939), *The House of the Seven Gables* (1940), and *The Deerslayer* (1943) were few and far between and released with no special fanfare that highlighted their literary roots. In truth, such classics, presenting an America riven by racial, moral, and cultural divides, offered precious little sustenance to a nation at war.

A more surefire way to valorize American literature during the war was to film biographies of American authors. Fox entered the ring with the preposterous *The Loves of Edgar Allan Poe* (1942); United Artists' *Jack London* (1943) served double duty as a propaganda vehicle by showing its hero traveling at the dawn of the twentieth century as a correspondent to Japan, where his prophetic hosts reveal their country's plan for world domination through what London calls "a sucker punch"; and Warner Bros.

cast Fredric March in the title role of the more elaborately produced *The Adventures of Mark Twain* (1944).

Throughout the war, adaptations of American classics took a backseat not only to biographies of their authors, but to adaptations of English classics from *Pride and Prejudice* to *Henry V* (1944), Laurence Olivier's rousing Shakespearean adaptation, which cloaked its dramatization of an earlier British invasion of France in a heartfelt appeal to the kind of military heroism on which national identity depended.

Instead of turning to the American classics, wartime Hollywood favored other kinds of adaptations. Warner Bros. toiled mightily to tailor the curdled Americana of *Kings Row*, Harry Bellaman's best-selling 1942 novel, to the screen by eliminating the small-town soap opera's references to incest, nymphomania, homosexuality, nude bathing, and euthanasia, producing a tale of an idealistic doctor's triumph over small-town hypocrisies that looked forward to the adaptation fifteen years later of *Peyton Place*. In a more airbrushed version of home-front life, MGM produced *The Human Comedy* (1943) from an original screenplay by William Saroyan, who, dismissed by the studio, rushed to turn it into a novel that was published before the film's debut. Greer Garson, who had shot to stardom in *Goodbye, Mr. Chips* and *Pride and Prejudice*, two adaptations of celebrated English novels, returned to anchor the American adaptations *When Ladies Meet* (1941), *Mrs. Parkington* (1944), and *The Valley of Decision* (1945). The title role Garson played in *Madame Curie* (1943) fit neatly into a new pattern of wartime adaptations of inspirational best sellers celebrating universal values that just happened to correspond to American values set in exotic places like France (*The Song of Bernadette*, 1943) and Italy (*A Bell for Adono*, 1945). Filmmakers hoping to capitalize on wartime sentiment without immersing themselves in wartime battlefields or politics could engage audiences more safely by changing their wartime settings to another time (as in *Sergeant York*) or another place (*Four Sons*, which updated the setting of I.A.R. Wylie's Bavarian family to 1939 Czechoslovakia). *A Tree Grows in Brooklyn* (1945), Elia Kazan's debut as a film director, avoided the war by sticking to the early-twentieth-century setting of Betty Smith's novel even as it replicated the battle between idealism and circumstantial necessity common to many war stories. Vincente Minnelli's directorial debut, his adaptation of Lynn Root's musical *Cabin in the Sky* (1943), universalized its African American allegory of devilish temptation and angelic redemption by excluding all but a single glancing reference to the war. John M. Stahl's glossy Technicolor noir romance *Leave Her to Heaven* (1945), an adaptation of Ben Ames Williams's 1944 novel that became Fox's top-grossing film of the decade, more resolutely ignored the war from beginning to end.

Leave Her to Heaven was an atypical representative of a highly influential genre that blossomed after the war: the film noir, typically a story of a tormented amateur criminal caught in a claustrophobic web of forbidden love, deception, betrayal, and self-alienation. Like *Public Enemy* (1931), *Little Caesar* (1931), *Scarface* (1932), and the gangster films that followed them through the 1930s, many films noirs were adaptations of American crime novels. But the novels themselves were different, and so were the films' attitudes toward those source novels in particular and literary aesthetics in general. James Naremore has noted that "virtually all of the initial cycle of American films noirs were adapted from critically admired novels."[22] The five films the French journalist Nino Frank first identified as films noirs—*The Maltese Falcon, Double Indemnity, Laura, Murder, My Sweet,* and *The Lost Weekend*—were all based on American novels. Fifty years later, when Robert Polito edited a two-volume collection of crime novels for the Library of America that included James M. Cain's *The Postman Always Rings Twice* (1934), Horace McCoy's *They Shoot Horses, Don't They?* (1937), Edward Anderson's *Thieves Like Us* (1937), Kenneth Fearing's *The Big Clock* (1946), William Lindsay Gresham's *Nightmare Alley* (1946), Cornell Woolrich's *I Married a Dead Man* (1948), Jim Thompson's *The Killer Inside Me* (1952), Patricia Highsmith's *The Talented Mr. Ripley* (1955), Charles Willeford's *Pick-Up* (1955), David Goodis's *Down There* (1957), and Chester Himes's *The Real Cool Killers* (1959), nine of the eleven novels he chose—all of them except for *Pick-Up* and *The Real Cool Killers*—had served as the basis for movies. Even the term "film noir" adapted its name from the Série noire literary imprint Marcel Duhamel developed for the French publisher Gallimard.

Naremore's formulation, which roots film noir in a "modernist concern with subjectivity and depth psychology,"[23] is complicated by several factors concerning the genre's attitude toward its literary antecedents. Because the doomed heroes of noir, almost by definition, had little likelihood of surviving any given story to root a durable franchise, there was no noir equivalent of Charlie Chan or Ellery Queen. What made noirs most memorable was not continuing characters but the equally compelling scripts provided by enduring character types—the reluctant criminal antihero, the femme fatale, the virtuous woman who served as her counterpart, the brutal crime boss, the corrupt or implacable police detective—who could be played by any number of different performers in distinctive but non-proprietary worlds different studios could readily recreate.

The hallmarks of these worlds were both thematic and visual. A founding convention of film noir was a philosophical fatalism that both underlined and undermined the heroes' efforts to work their will upon a hostile world. Like the gangster film, the film noir was characterized by a particular way of talking, in this case a world-weary, disillusioned cynicism leavened with knowing wit. The apotheosis of this dialogue is found in *Out of the Past* (1947), in which alluring fugitive Kathie Moffat (Jane Greer) confesses to private eye Jeff Markham (Robert Mitchum), who has tracked her to Mexico at the behest of gangster Whit Sterling (Kirk Douglas) and then betrayed his employer by falling in love with her, that she did indeed shoot and wound Whit, "but I didn't take anything. I didn't, Jeff. Won't you believe me?" and Markham, reaching toward her, replies, "Baby, I don't care." The film's dialogue, which is as stylized as the early exchanges between Phyllis Dietrichson (Barbara Stanwyck) and Walter Neff (Fred MacMurray) in *Double Indemnity*, sounds so patently literary that it is a shock to find no trace of it in its source novel, Daniel Mainwaring's *Build My Gallows High* (1946), or indeed of Phyllis and Walter's banter in Cain's novel. In both cases, as in many other films noirs, the dialogue has been deliberately punched up, in the first case by uncredited screenwriter Frank Fenton, in the second by prominently credited screenwriter Raymond Chandler, to sound more stylized, more artificial, more literary, than that of the novel from which it is adapted.[24]

In addition to sounding more like characters in books than the characters in the books on which they were based, the leading characters in films noirs were frequently trapped in worlds fatalistically defined in narrative terms borrowed from *Citizen Kane* (1941). An extended series of flashbacks showing how the heroes reached their most desperate point encouraged their audiences to savor the contrast between the characters' contingent, incomplete, and often hopelessly limited understanding of the situations which called on them to make consequential moral decisions and the more Olympian view the flashback structure allowed the audience, and sometimes the heroes themselves, who described their ill-judged decisions in retrospective voiceovers like Walter's sadly ironic introduction to his first meeting with Phyllis: "How could I have known that murder can sometimes smell like honeysuckle?" Finally, the heroes who used mordantly witty dialogue to express or battle their claustrophobic sense of entrapment took their identities from a strikingly evoked visual world whose leading features—night-for-night exterior shots; low-key, high-contrast, often highly directional lighting for both exteriors and interiors; visual compositions that doubled characters by setting characters against each other, against the physical objects to which they are reductively compared, or, in the most unbalanced examples, against blank spaces; hyper-expressive groups of objects and settings borrowed from Weimar expressionist cinema and French poetic realism of the 1930s—all support Paul Schrader's dictum that "compositional tension is preferred to physical action."[25] "Took their identities" is none too strong a formulation for a genre whose mise-en-scene was consistently more expressive of the characters' innermost thoughts, fears, emotions, or philosophical worldviews than either their dialogue, which was typically either deceptive or obtuse, or their overt actions, which as often contradicted as fulfilled their desires.

Although most noir novels depended on creating a doomy, fatalistic atmosphere, most of them achieved this atmosphere through purely linear stories; only a handful of them followed *They Shoot Horses, Don't They?*

in casting their narratives as a series of flashbacks. Nor were most of the defining visual devices of films noirs available to their source novels. So noir adaptations are characterized by four central ironies. Unlike the detective adaptations of the 1930s, they recount the adventures of heroes and heroines virtually guaranteed to have no enduring life outside the confines of their particular once-in-a-lifetime stories. Their highly stylized dialogue is more literary than anything in the novels they are adapting. Their defining narrative convention is largely an invention of the movies themselves, not their source novels. And more than any other Hollywood genre, they depend on a bleakly expressive visual style that has been borrowed not from literature but from other visual arts.

Film noir thus trades on its literary foundations in a way marked by a combination of citation, selective imitation, and disavowal illustrated by Hollywood's treatment of the prolific novelist and storyteller Cornell Woolrich, whose dark-hued fiction, often adapted to the movies, gives him some claim to be the American godfather of film noir. Woolrich's very productivity, which encouraged him to publish his books and stories under three different bylines, made it difficult from the beginning to construct a brand based on his authorship. After publishing several high-society novels in the early 1930s, he settled into a darker groove. Under his own name, he published *The Bride Wore Black* (1940), *The Black Curtain* (1941), *Black Alibi* (1942), *The Black Angel* (1943), *The Black Path of Fear* (1944), *Rendezvous in Black* (1948), *Savage Bride* (1950), and *You'll Never See Me Again* (1951). Under the pseudonym William Irish, he published *Phantom Lady* (1942), *Deadline at Dawn* (1944), *Waltz into Darkness* (1947), *Dead Man Blues* (1948), *I Married a Dead Man* (1948), *Six Nights of Mystery* (1950), and the short stories collected in *I Wouldn't Be in Your Shoes* (1943), *After-Dinner Story* (1944), *If I Should Die before I Wake* (1946), *Borrowed Crime* (1946), *The Dancing Detective* (1946), *The Blue Ribbon* (1949), and *Somebody on the Phone* (1950). *Night Has a Thousand Eyes* (1945) and *Fright* (1950) appeared under the George Hopley byline. More of Woolrich's novels and stories served as the basis for films noirs than those of any other author. His adaptations include *Street of Chance* (based on *The Black Curtain*, 1942), *The Leopard Man* (based on *Black Alibi*, 1943), *Phantom Lady* (1944), *The Mark of the Whistler* (based on his short story of the same name, 1944), *Deadline at Dawn* (1946), *Black Angel* (1946), *The Chase* (based on *The Black Path of Fear*, 1946), *Fall Guy* (based on his short story "Cocaine," 1947), *The Guilty* (based on his short story "He Looked Like Murder," 1947), *Fear in the Night* (based on his story "Nightmare," 1947), *I Wouldn't Be in Your Shoes* (1948), *Night Has a Thousand Eyes* (1948), *The Window* (based on his story "The Boy Cried Murder," 1949), *No Man of Her Own* (based on *I Married a Dead Man*, 1950), *Rear Window* (based on his short story "It Had to Be Murder," 1954), and *Nightmare* (a remake of *Fear in the Night*, 1956). Long after the heyday of noir had passed, Woolrich's fiction continued to provide the basis for films produced in Argentina—*The Earring* (based on his short story of the same name, 1951), *The Imprint of Lips* (based on his short story "The Shirt Collar," 1952), and *Don't Ever Open That Door* (based on his short stories "Somebody on the Phone" and "Hummingbird Comes Back," 1952)—in France—*Obsession* (based on his short story "Silent as the Grave," 1954), *Escapade* (based on his story "Cinderella and the Mob," 1957), *The Bride Wore Black* (1968), and *Mississippi Mermaid* (based on *Waltz into Darkness,* 1969)—in the Soviet Union—*Dro itsureb gantiadisas* (1965)—in England—*The Boy Cried Murder* (based on his short story of the same name, 1966)—in Italy—*Seven Blood-Stained Orchids* (based on *Rendezvous in Black,* 1972)—in Germany—*Martha* (a television segment that Rainer Werner Fassbinder based on his story "For the Rest of Her Life," 1974)—and in India— *Kati Patang* (based on *I Married a Dead Man,* 1970) and its Telugu remake *Punnami Chandrudu* (1987).

However eager these films may have been to claim Woolrich as a literary source, most of them took serious liberties with the works they chose to adapt. *Street of Chance,* the earliest of them and the most faithful in reproducing the main sequence of events in Woolrich's plot and even much of his dialogue, changes the identity of the killer the amnesiac hero suspected of murder must find to vindicate himself. *Phantom Lady,* which focuses on a Girl Friday's search for the unknown woman who could give her boss an alibi in the murder of his wife, reveals the identity of the murderer much earlier, changing in the process from a mystery to a suspense thriller. The film adaptation of *Black Angel,* a novel whose plot revisits *Phantom Lady* by arming its heroine with a brief directory of telephone numbers belonging to alternative suspects who might have committed the murder for which her husband is imprisoned, eliminates most of these suspects and turns its hero into an amnesiac like the hero of *Street of Chance.* Clifford Odets's screenplay for *Deadline at Dawn,* the only film directed by Broadway producer Harold Clurman, retains Woolrich's leading premise, which might be described as *Phantom Lady* with a much tighter deadline, but changes the hero to a young serviceman on shore leave, the murder victim from his male ex-client to a blackmailing prostitute, and the killer to the fatherly cabdriver who has been helping the hero solve the murder of which he is bound to be suspected before he must return from New York to Norfolk in the morning. Virtually alone of these films, *No Man of Her Own* is unusually faithful to Woolrich in developing its story of a woman unlucky in love drawn into masquerading as another woman who is killed along with her bridegroom when the train they are all taking crashes, then immersed in a web of blackmail and murder when she is recognized as an imposter before she finally succeeds in plucking a new murderer out of nowhere to deliver an improbably happy ending for Woolrich's most nightmarish story, and his most often adapted. Much as the studios valued Woolrich's ability to create arresting hooks and evoke criminal nightmares, they were always ready to tailor these hooks and nightmares to their own measure.

The studios were equally selective and equally variable in their presentation of Woolrich as a literary property. The 1944 trailer for *Phantom Lady* gives the author the full literary treatment. Its opening shot, in which a hand plucks William Irish's novel from a crowded bookshelf, treats him like a canonical author, and the text over its following four screens—"From the pages of the famous mystery novel ... Unique as 'The Thin Man,' Gripping as 'The Maltese Falcon' [...] Step the Strange and Unforgettable Characters ... Who thrilled millions of readers"—trade on the literary cachet of both Woolrich and Dashiell Hammett, though they emphasize their credentials as best sellers rather than literary landmarks. Never again would Hollywood accord Woolrich such respect as an author. The films based on his fiction were released by several different studios: *Street of Chance* by Paramount, *The Leopard Man* and *Deadline at Dawn* by RKO, *Phantom Lady* and *Black Angel* by Universal, *The Mark of the Whistler* by Columbia, *The Chase* by United Artists. None of these studios had any reason to promote an authorial brand just as likely to serve a competing studio's interests as its own, and none of them made any attempt to capitalize on Woolrich's one attempt at self-branding through the parallel titles he published under his own name: *The Bride Wore Black, The Black Curtain, Black Alibi, The Black Angel, The Black Path of Fear,* and *Rendezvous in Black,* most of which were filmed under different titles that obscured their common authorship. Nor did Woolrich, a reclusive alcoholic who rarely left the New York hotel where he lived with his mother, succeed in leveraging any more control over these adaptations as his reputation grew. Instead, the films based on his novels and stories became ever more anonymous until the two posthumous Indian adaptations, neither of which identified him in its credits.

Hollywood's interest in trading on Woolrich's literary status only intermittently and inconsistently finds an echo in its handling of James M. Cain, who had been notorious ever since the publication of *The Postman Always Rings Twice*. Although several studios had expressed an interest in filming both this novel and *Double Indemnity* as soon as it was first serialized in *Liberty* in 1936, they were kept at bay by the Breen Office until Paramount purchased the rights to *Double Indemnity* and, undeterred by Breen's rote response, worked with screenwriter Billy Wilder, who had begun to direct with *The Major and Minor* and *Five Graves to Cairo* (1943), on a treatment that won Breen's qualified approval. The principal benefit to Cain, who had to accept $15,000 for adaptation rights for which he had been offered $25,000 eight years earlier before Breen vetoed the project, was to lift Hollywood's taboo against his work. When Warner Bros. produced an adaptation of his 1941 novel *Mildred Pierce* the following year, Ranald MacDougall's screenplay for Cain's Depression-era parable of an abandoned wife's sexual affairs, business rise, and hopeless love for her unworthy daughter, which would be more faithfully retold in Todd Haynes's 2011 period miniseries for HBO, opened by adding the murder of one of the novel's lead characters to Cain's unusually crime-free story, casting most of the film as a flashback leading up to the murder, and in the process bringing Cain's hard-boiled story into the more predictably felonious orbit of the film noir.

When *The Postman Always Rings Twice* was filmed in 1946, the studio responsible was MGM, the most unlikely home imaginable for a Cain adaptation. Although this film is by any measure the least successful of the three, its repeated attempts to homogenize Cain's casually brutal view of American mores by passing it through the two sieves of the Breen Office and the resolutely middlebrow MGM house style make it in many ways the most interesting. The main title in its opening credits was a shot of Cain's novel in its original dust jacket (see Figure 5.4). This shot could be read as treating the novel as either a contemporary best seller, even though it was already twelve years old, or a canonical classic, despite the censors' frequent protests against its lurid sex and violence (in its most celebrated scene, its two leads make love on an isolated hill alongside the wrecked car containing the corpse of her husband, whom they killed just before running his car off the road). MGM won the approval of the Breen Office by removing any overt scenes of sex or violence, many of which the 1981 remake scripted by David Mamet and directed by Bob Rafelson duly restored, and by recasting the film's sordid tale of adultery and murder as a fatal *folie à deux* considerably more romantic in the lovers' forbidden yearning for each other.

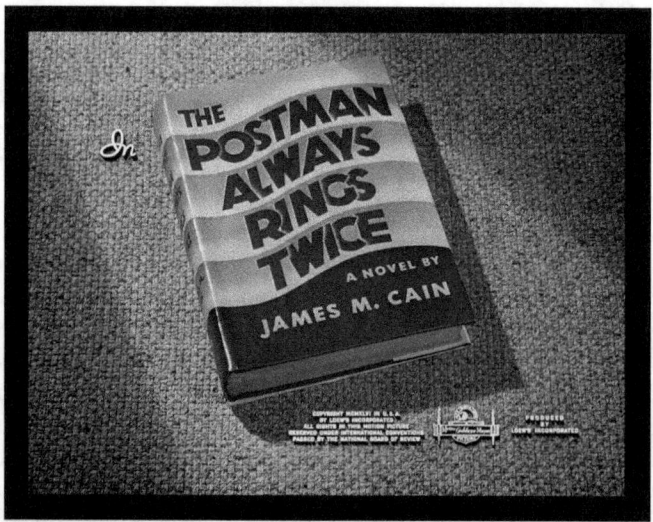

FIGURE 5.4 *James M. Cain's novel gets the star treatment in the title credit for* The Postman Always Rings Twice *(1946).*

Although the film enjoyed substantial success at the box office, it did nothing to make Cain, who had left his journalistic career to toil for years as a mostly uncredited writer in Hollywood, any more marketable. Perhaps because his outspoken advocacy in 1946 of the creation of an American Authors' Authority that would represent writers in contract negotiations and legal proceedings led the novelist James T. Farrell to brand him a Communist, Cain, like Woolrich, never again enjoyed the same currency as in the previous two years.

Hollywood expressionism

Forties adaptations that subordinated their literary sources and the authors of these sources to other scripts like an evocative atmosphere, a striking visual style, or a wholesale rewriting of the nominal source to satisfy industry censors, generic imperatives, or guesses about what was most likely to appeal to audiences often buried their authorship beneath still another script: the revelation of a compelling subjective consciousness. Beginning with *The Maltese Falcon,* adaptations of detective stories, for example, make an issue of the detective's consciousness in ways no earlier film adaptations had done. Audiences never knew what Philo Vance or Ellery Queen was thinking, for to learn those thoughts too quickly would have revealed the mystery's solution prematurely. The fortune-cookie wisdom of Charlie Chan established an ongoing, comically impersonal subjectivity that reassured audiences that there was no need to worry about how close Chan was to solving the mystery. And Nick and Nora Charles, like Hildegarde Withers and Oscar Piper, kept up a running stream of comically hostile badinage that displaced the mystery as the true center of their stories.

Warner Bros. had already filmed Dashiell Hammett's earlier novel *The Maltese Falcon* in 1931 as a cynically efficient pre-Code whodunit and, as *Satan Met a Lady,* in 1936, in a seriocomic version whose change in Hammett's title and tone, the names of all his characters, the gender of Casper Gutman the Fat Man, and the MacGuffin the characters were seeking (the Maltese falcon is replaced by the jewel-filled Horn of Roland) seemed governed by the twin desires of sharing MGM's success with *The Thin Man* and making the new adaptation resemble the earlier adaptation of *The Maltese Falcon* as little as possible. When John Huston, the screenwriter son of Hollywood star Walter Huston who had already made a name for himself in such adaptations as *Law and Order* (1932), *It Happened in Paris* (1935), *Jezebel* (1938), *Juarez* (1939), and *High Sierra* (1941), asked to direct his first film, the studio considered *The Maltese Falcon* a low-risk project. Huston's film, performed by what turned out to be a legendary cast headed by Humphrey Bogart, Mary Astor, Sydney Greenstreet, Peter Lorre, and Elisha Cook, Jr., departed from the two earlier adaptations in following Hammett's novel virtually scene by scene, often lifting long stretches of his dialogue almost verbatim. The most interesting consequence of Huston's literal approach was to foreground once again a question that both earlier adaptations had glossed over: when exactly does private detective Sam Spade (Humphrey Bogart) decide that his partner, Miles Archer (Jerome Cowan), was killed by Brigid O'Shaughnessy (Mary Astor), the client Spade has fallen in love with (see Figure 5.5)? Spade's explanation of his reasoning in Hammett's closing scene, which makes it clear that he has known almost from the beginning that Brigid is the killer, casts his whole relationship with her in a retrospectively troubling new light. In retaining the same explanation in much the same words, Huston's film suddenly casts in doubt all the clues it has given to the mental processes of Spade, who has appeared in every scene without the film ever directly indicating what he thinks about anything, from his disarmingly frank dialogue to his trademark stroking of his earlobe, making the film as disturbing in its way as Roy Del Ruth's more sexually explicit 1931 adaptation.

If *The Maltese Falcon* makes the hero's consciousness a riddle it pointedly declines to answer, other adaptations make more forthright attempts to exteriorize their detective heroes' consciousness, especially when those detectives are incarnations of Philip Marlowe, Raymond Chandler's soiled contemporary knight errant. *Murder, My Sweet* casts its story as an extended

FIGURE 5.5 *As he interrogates Brigid O'Shaughnessy (Mary Astor) in* The Maltese Falcon *(1941), does Sam Spade (Humphrey Bogart) already know that she has killed his partner?*

flashback with intermittent narration by Marlowe (Dick Powell), uses its stylized noir mise-en-scene to represent Marlowe's increasing immersion in the lurid crimes and betrayals that lie beneath the moneyed veneer of the Grayle family, and presents Marlowe's drugging by the villainous Dr. Sonderborg (Ralf Harolde) through a series of subjectively distorted visuals. *The Big Sleep* (1946), following director Howard Hawks's informal rule of never burdening the characters with any thoughts that could not be translated into immediate action, places even greater emphasis than *The Maltese Falcon* on the question of how far Marlowe (Humphrey Bogart) can trust Vivian Rutledge (Lauren Bacall), with whom he has a relationship by turns playful, flirtatious, adversarial, and fraught with questions. Most literal and extreme in its dramatization of Marlowe's consciousness is *Lady in the Lake* (1946), which Steve Fisher's screenplay recasts as a narrative whose frame shows Marlowe (Robert Montgomery, who also directed) talking directly to the camera, promising a baffling mystery that unfolds in a series of long takes purporting to represent Marlowe's point of view as he questions the suspects, walks down the street, and gets kissed or socked in the jaw. The premise of the exercise—that locking the audience into Marlowe's optical viewpoint would make their presumed race with Marlowe to identify the killer more disciplined, fair, and urgent—is farfetched, and its rigorous execution prevents cuts within scenes, restricts shots of Marlowe's face to moments when he looks into fortuitously placed mirrors, and creates so many barriers to the kinds of identification to which Hollywood audiences had become accustomed that it has earned a perverse reputation as a textbook example of how to occlude a character's subjectivity through the indiscriminate overuse of a device intended to display it.

The subjectivities that noir adaptations explore displace both the rational but hidden consciousness of detectives from Charlie Chan to Nick and Nora Charles, whose subjectivity had never been an issue until the 1941 adaptation of *The Maltese Falcon*, and the figure of the author—a shift further emphasized by the turn from active gangsters and rational detectives to doomed noir heroes who could not possibly be recycled. It is thoroughly logical for the mise-en-scene to reveal more about the characters than the dialogue of adaptations like *Double Indemnity, The Killers* (1946), *Out of the Past, The Lady from Shanghai* (1948), *Criss Cross* (1949), *The Set-Up* (1949), and *In a Lonely Place* (1950) because the leading characters in these films are not given to self-analysis, not very perceptive when they try it, and frequently deceptive in what they say to each other. The exploration of Walter Neff's subjectivity in *Double Indemnity* draws only incidentally on the fact that the novel it adapts is written in the first person: it depends much more directly on the contrast between the character's blindness in the moment to the consequences of his actions and his ironic awareness of those consequences afterwards, an awareness Cain's novel is at pains to avoid. More generally, *Double Indemnity*'s most important aesthetic models for evoking subjectivity are drawn from Expressionist painting and German and French cinema rather than from literature. The subjective distortion of mise-en-scene to represent the consciousness of fictional characters, a staple of German cinema since *The Cabinet of Dr. Caligari* (1920), had been freely available to filmmakers around the world for twenty years, but it was not widely adopted as a Hollywood practice until the arrival of the filmmakers in question, from Fritz Lang to Billy Wilder, who left Austria and Germany behind but brought with them some of the most precious cultural treasures of their regional heritage.

At the same time, Hollywood consistently sought to naturalize or domesticate the disorienting visual distortions of Weimar cinema. Instead of flaunting the painted shadows and skewed architectural angles of *The Cabinet of Dr. Caligari*, films noirs like *The Killers* motivated their shadows and diagonals more conventionally, producing an atmosphere at once stylized and realistic (see Figure 5.6). Many noir adaptations sought to exteriorize consciousness through visualizations like the literal projections of the hero's fears and fragmentary memories in *Street of Chance*, the detective's nightmarish descent into a drugged stupor in *Murder, My*

FIGURE 5.6 *The title characters of* The Killers *(1946) approach Henry's Diner in an opening scene whose blocking and lighting are both realistic and nightmarishly expressionistic.*

Sweet, and the climactic revelation that the plots occupying virtually the entire running time of *The Woman in the Window, The Strange Affair of Uncle Harry* (1945), and *The Chase* were no more than paranoid dreams. More original and successful was the use of multichannel soundtracks to supply voiceovers and background music that could play against both the images and other diegetic sounds like dialogue and live sound effects. The hero of *Street of Chance* and the heroine of *No Man of Her Own* both talk to themselves in voiceover. *Kitty Foyle* (1940), which repeatedly associates the memories of the eponymous heroine (Ginger Rogers) with a snow globe right out of *Citizen Kane,* a gift from her father that marks transitions between the narrative present and the past she is recalling, stages her indecision about which of her suitors she should go off with as an argument between herself and her mirrored reflection, each of them urging her to pledge herself to one of the two candidates. The "Alter-Ego" dance in MGM's *Cover Girl* (1944), goes even further, showing Danny McGuire (Gene Kelly) acting out his romantic ambivalence toward the title character (Rita Hayworth) by dancing with his own imagined double. The apparently authoritative voiceover commentary producer Mark Hellinger supplies for *Naked City* (1948) both engages and abstracts the audience from the onscreen action it frames. Apart from indicating thoughts the characters could not express through action, these subjective sounds made movies more novelistic by expanding the heteroglot range of voices they followed the model of the novel in incorporating. At length "the heteroglossia of the novel, especially when it was complicated by radio's demand for distinctive vocal characterisations, opened the movies to a mode of dialogue, at once stylized and realistic, that was far more comprehensive in expressive range and sensitive to subtle distinctions in class"[26] until the ethnic gangsters painted with such broad and indiscriminate strokes in the soundtracks of *The Public Enemy* and *Scarface* were replaced by the symphony of diverse voices of the gang members in *The Asphalt Jungle* (1950).

A particularly obvious way to invoke psychological depth was to explain away characters' contradictory emotions and deviant behavior as motivated by their unseen past, often by placing them on psychiatrists' couches. Although Hollywood had already flirted with psychiatry in earlier films as different as *Carefree* (1938) and *Blind Alley* (1939), the studios began to take psychiatrists more seriously as authority figures in adaptations like *Kings Row, Now, Voyager, Random Harvest,* and *Crime Doctor* (1943), which supplied a backstory for the eponymous radio hero, now revealed as an amnesiac former gangster. MGM spun off a series of films about the mystery-solving Dr. Gillespie—*Calling Dr. Gillespie* (1942), *Dr. Gillespie's New Assistant* (1942), and *Dr. Gillespie's Criminal Case* (1943)—from its long-running Dr. Kildare franchise. The presentation of psychiatrists as moral authorities who just happened to be medical professionals capable of diagnosing the maladies of their conflicted patients blossomed in *Lady in the*

Dark (1944) and *Dishonored Lady* (1947). By the time Paramount released *Detective Story* (1951), based on Sidney Kingsley's 1949 play, hard-charging, uncompromising Det. James McLeod (Kirk Douglas) did not even need a psychiatrist to diagnose him. Mary (Eleanor Parker), the loving wife he has just condemned upon learning that she had an abortion years ago, tells him as she walks out of the precinct house that has been the unforgivingly public backdrop to their private revelations, "You're everything you always said you hated in your own father." McLeod, instantly picking up this insight, muses, "I built my whole life on hating my father. All that time he was inside me, laughing," just before he confronts a career criminal under arrest who has grabbed another officer's gun and provokes the criminal to shoot him to death.

The vanishing author

Dissenting from Catherine Grant's assertion that "there is no such thing as a 'secret' adaptation,"[27] Patrick Cattrysse, noting the high number of largely unacknowledged adaptations of fictional Westerns, monster stories, gangster stories, and noir fiction, has concluded that "pseudo-originals or hidden/secret adaptations greatly outnumber overt adaptations"[28]—that the explicitly identified examples to which Linda Hutcheon limits the term in her definition of adaptation as "an announced and extensive transposition of a particular work or works"[29] are actually the exception rather than the rule. This corpus of unacknowledged adaptations would be even larger if it included remakes whose credits mention their novelistic or dramatic sources but not the earlier movies they are more explicitly adapting. When Howard Hawks directed *His Girl Friday* in 1940, the credits for his film included Ben Hecht and Charles MacArthur, the authors of the 1928 play, but made no reference to Lewis Milestone's 1931 film adaptation of the play. Neither did the credits for Billy Wilder's 1974 period remake *The Front Page,* or the credits for Ted Kotcheff's even freer 1988 remake *Switching Channels.* William Keighley's *Torrid Zone,* a 1940 film Warner Bros. released only four months after *His Girl Friday*, mentions neither the earlier film nor its dramatic source, even though *Torrid Zone* is widely regarded as an informal remake that shifts the story's central situation—a hard-charging boss tricks an employee whose professionalism he badly needs into staying in a job that will entangle the employee with both romance and an escaped convict—to a Central American banana republic. Throughout the studio era, in fact, Warner Bros. enjoyed a reputation as a model of efficiency in recycling its own and other studios' products, often without acknowledgment. Along with *Torrid Zone,* Warners released not only the three versions of *The Maltese Falcon,* all of which explicitly credited Dashiell Hammett's novel as their source, but also Raoul Walsh's *Colorado Territory* (1949) and Stuart Heisler's *I Died a Thousand Times* (1955), two unacknowledged remakes of Walsh's own *High Sierra* (1941). A generation later Lawrence Kasdan's *Body Heat* (1981) paid homage to the films noirs of the 1940s by elaborating the plot of *Double Indemnity* (1944), again without acknowledgment, and *Miller's Crossing* (1990), whose credits listed Joel and Ethan Coen as its writers, was an obvious, though uncredited, homage to Dashiell Hammett's 1931 novel *The Glass Key* and its two earlier film versions.

Even when the authors of literary properties were duly credited, studio executives and publicists had a battery of techniques for suppressing their impact by subordinating them to other, more powerful or appealing scripts. Although *This Is the Army*'s nomination of the First World War as the author of the Second World War might have seemed strained or tendentious, it faithfully reflected a tendency Warner Bros. adaptations had shown as early as *I Am a Fugitive from a Chain Gang* (1932), *Black Fury* (1935), and *Bullets or Ballots* (1937): to emphasize the movie's status as a monstration of history or present-day social reality over its status as an adaptation.

The main title of Twentieth Century Fox's inspirational 1943 film adaptation of the story of French peasant Bernadette Soubirous's vision of a beautiful lady who may or may not have been the Virgin Mary identified it as "Franz Werfel's *The Song of Bernadette*," a locution faithfully reproduced in its publicity materials. But the taglines used to market the film—"Here is greatness ... wonder ... and majesty ... no human words can describe!" and "A miracle of motion picture achievement!"—sought to link the film more closely to its heroine's miraculous vision than to Werfel's best-selling novel. By the time RKO released *Joan of Arc* in 1948, its description of the film as "based on the stage play 'Joan of Lorraine' by Maxwell Anderson" was buried deep in the credits, and the typeface for Anderson's name on the advertising posters was smaller than the typeface for "TECHNICOLOR" and "A CAST OF THOUSANDS," emphasizing the film's status as historical spectacle over its status as an adaptation of the 1946 play-within-a-play, whose frame it jettisoned and whose story it expanded by adding new historical characters and incidents, by one of America's most distinguished playwrights.

If these movies were windows designed to be looked through, as contemporaneous film theorists like André Bazin argued, what audiences were encouraged to see through them was not the novels or plays or stories or memoirs or poems they adapted, which the films treated as a further set of transparent, non-distorting windows, but the ostensive social or spiritual realities behind those source scripts. This tendency flowered in the cycle of social-problem adaptations that became one of Hollywood's most prestigious undertakings after the war. *The Lost Weekend, The Best Years of Our Lives* (1946), *Crossfire* (1947), *Gentleman's Agreement* (1947), *Intruder in the Dust* (1948), *Pinky* (1949), and *Home of the Brave* (1949) were all adaptations, but they were marketed mainly as fearless exposés of exigent social realities like alcoholism (*The Lost Weekend*), anti-Semitism (*Gentleman's Agreement*), racism (*Intruder in the Dust* and *Pinky*), and the difficulties combat veterans faced in adjusting to life back home (*The Best Years of Our Lives, Home of the Brave*), not adaptations of literary treatments of these realities. *Crossfire* showed how easily one social malady (homophobia, the motive for the murder in Richard Brooks's 1945 source novel *The Brick Foxhole*) the Breen Office would not allow to be represented onscreen could be replaced by another (anti-Semitism, the motive for the murder in the film) with minimal adjustments to the story, suggesting that the real point of these films was neither to adapt the literary sources they credited nor to expose the specific social problems they identified, but rather to give urgency to their stories by trumpeting their exposure of something—anything—real, unpleasant, and dangerous in postwar America.

Books continued to play an iconic role in identifying and publicizing the film adaptations based on them. But the resourceful studios found a surprising range of subtly different ways to signal their adaptations' relation to their source books. The images in the advertising poster for RKO's *Kitty Foyle* (1940), whose main title featured a photograph of Christopher Morley's novel, complete with the superscription, "A Novel by Christopher Morley" dissolving into Morley's subtitle, "The Natural History of a Woman," more circumspectly emphasized the importance of writing—or, more accurately, of the heroine's typing and shorthand transcriptions—without mentioning the best-selling, censor-baiting novel on which it is based. *Nation Wide,* the working title Morley had originally chosen for this novel of the working-class heroine's professional life and her affair, pregnancy, and abortion, adumbrates another strategy MGM used with an utterly different force in its opening and closing credits for *Northwest Passage* (1940): to suggest that Kenneth Roberts's historical novel, shown against the background of an eighteenth-century map, was every bit as big as America. The posters Fox used to advertise *Tobacco Road,* whose credits had emphasized the success of its record-breaking run as a Broadway play over any feature of the Erskine Caldwell novel from which the play was drawn, announced, "At Last ... It's on the screen!," without indicating just what "it" was.

Warner Bros.' posters for *Kings Row*, which showed the characters in the film floating above the novel that gave them birth, used such an aggressively sized typeface for the best-selling novel's title on the new book cover the studio's publicists devised for the posters that it left no room for the author's name, which appeared in microscopic print to the right. The title credit for Fox's *Leave Her to Heaven* faithfully reproduced the dust jacket of Ben Ames Williams's novel while adding a new author, producer Darryl F. Zanuck, whose name at the top of the screen dominated Williams's at the bottom (see Figure 5.7). The title credit for Universal's *Black Angel* pushed this tendency to bury the author to its logical conclusion by inventing a

FIGURES 5.7 AND 5.8 *Authors' names get upstaged by producers' names or disappear entirely in the main titles of* Leave Her to Heaven *(1945) and* Black Angel *(1946).*

new book jacket that omitted the author's name, invoking the cachet of the printed book without qualifying it by limiting the credit to any single author (see Figure 5.8). The ascendancy of producer over author was completed in the credits for *Duel in the Sun,* David Selznick's 1946 adaptation of screenwriter and story editor Niven Busch's novel. Although the novel had been a best seller upon its publication in 1944, the advertising posters made no mention of it, emphasizing the stars and the larger-than-life characters they played instead, and the opening credits identified the film as based on a "Screen Play by the Producer David O. Selznick, suggested by a novel by Niven Busch, adapted by Oliver H.P. Garrett," forcing Busch to share authorship with the two names he was sandwiched between, one of them belonging to the producer who had presented *Gone with the Wind.* The title credit for *The Postman Always Rings Twice* again ignored Busch, this time in his capacity as one of the two screenwriters the later credits listed, by replacing the customary superimposed title with a photograph of the novel introduced by the word "In." The implication was that leading performers John Garfield and Lana Turner were not only in the movie but in the book, which had served as forbidden fruit to the studios for twelve years before MGM created a movie that was presumably identical to the book, with the additional promise of showing its leading characters played by two of the top box office stars in America. The posters for *All the King's Men,* Columbia's 1949 adaptation of Robert Penn Warren's 1946 novel, and *Harvey,* Universal's 1950 adaptation of Mary Chase's 1944 play, subordinated Warren's and Harvey's names to the Pulitzer Prizes they had won, signaling the studio's greater faith in the prize than in any novelist or playwright as a sign of literary and cultural prestige—a tactic Hollywood had already been using for years.

The persistence of literary adaptation

Several best-selling novels of the period took years to make it to the screen, delayed by controversy, censorship, or the studios' timidity. Properties that were not filmed until the 1950s or even later ranged from *Mister Roberts* (1946), Thomas Heggen's novel set aboard a Second World War supply ship, which was adapted to the theater in 1948 and to the movies in 1955, to *Raintree County* (1947), Ross Lockridge's nineteenth-century Midwestern epic, which was adapted in 1957, to Henry Morton Robinson's *The Cardinal* (1950), which was adapted in 1963. By the time that John O'Hara published his epistolary novel *Pal Joey* in 1940, it was already headed for Broadway, where it became the basis for Rodgers and Hart's musical, with Gene Kelly in the title role. But O'Hara's memorable antihero would not make his movie debut until 1957, when Frank Sinatra proved he could be just as big a heel as Kelly. Perhaps the most notable delay in adapting a novel of the 1940s was that of Lillian Smith's *Strange Fruit,* the best-selling novel of 1944, whose emphasis on interracial romance, pregnancy, murder, and lynching led it to be banned in Boston. Although Smith turned the novel into a play in 1945, Hollywood ignored it until 1979, when it was made into a short film that was nominated for an Academy Award.

Although novels like these remained invisible to the movies until years after their publication, the decade ended with half a dozen high-profile films that illustrated the increasingly wide range of attitudes Hollywood cultivated toward American literature. The unofficial model audiences expected from the studios at the time—purchase the rights to a prestigious literary property that tapped into hot-button issues and emotions in contemporary American culture, pump up the leading roles, simplify the issues, toss out the circumstantial details and the highly wrought prose that had earned the property its prestige in the first place—are best exemplified by *All the King's Men* (1949). In the hands of Robert Rossen, Robert Penn Warren's Pulitzer Prize-winning 1946 novel inspired by the meteoric rise and assassination of Louisiana governor Huey Long, became a compelling parable of the corruption that threatened American political populism. Rossen's screenplay dropped both Warren's often lyrical descriptions of the hardscrabble landscape of the rural South and its people and his emphasis on Jack Burden, a political reporter through whose first person narrative Willie Stark is revealed. In its melodramatic view of dog-eat-dog politics, Rossen's film is more simplified and one-dimensional than Warren's highly subjective novel; in other ways, like its deliberately flat visuals and its casting of the thuggish Broderick Crawford as the ingratiating, brutal demagogue Willie Stark and newcomer Mercedes McCambridge as his take-no-prisoners campaign aide Sadie Burke, it was less slick and more daring than most Hollywood adaptations. Both Crawford and McCambridge won Academy Awards for their roles, and the film itself, with its clear echoes of *Citizen Kane,* won the Oscar for Best Picture. At the same time, its studiously unaligned politics—Willie Stark was never identified as conservative or liberal, Democrat or Republican—served as still another reminder, after the abortive adaptation of Sinclair Lewis's *It Can't Happen Here,* why so few studios were willing to make movies about American politics.

The Heiress (1949) was an altogether safer undertaking. Its director, William Wyler, had an unexcelled pedigree as a craftsman who specialized in literary adaptations. No other filmmaker of his time was more successful with such a distinguished record of adaptations, including several based on American plays and novels. In addition to completing *Come and Get It* (1936) when producer Samuel Goldwyn fired Howard Hawks from the filming of Edna Ferber's 1935 novel, Wyler had directed *Counsellor at Law* (1933), based on Elmer Rice's 1931 play; *These Three* (1936), based on Lillian Hellman's 1934 play *The Children's Hour; Dodsworth* (1936), based on Sinclair Lewis's 1929 novel; *Dead End* (1937), based on Sidney Kingsley's 1935 play; *Jezebel* (1938), based on Owen Davis's 1933 play; *The Little Foxes* (1941), based on Lillian Hellman's 1939 play; and *The Best Years of Our Lives* (1946), based on MacKinlay Kantor's verse novel *Glory for Me* (1945). More than anyone in America, Wyler would have seemed the obvious choice to direct a period adaptation of Henry James's 1881 story of a calmly determined young woman torn between a tyrannical father and a fortune-hunting suitor. Yet the film, whose main title identified it as "William Wyler's THE HEIRESS," was not directly based on James's play. As its credits accurately stated, it was "Written for the Screen by RUTH AND AUGUSTUS GOETZ From their [1947] play 'The HEIRESS' Suggested by the Henry James novel 'WASHINGTON SQUARE.'" In addition to compressing and streamlining James's novel, the Goetzes completely reversed its ending. James's heroine, Catherine Sloper, who has been bullied since birth by the overbearing father, a society physician whose wife died in childbirth, first quietly refuses to bow to his threat to disinherit her if she does not refuse to see the unsuitable Morris Townsend, and then, after her father's death has left her wealthy after all, admits Morris to see her one last time but refuses his suit as well and returns to working the needlepoint that has come to define her deceptively tranquil refusal of both men's demands. The Goetzes's play unleashed Catherine's suppressed emotions by giving her two climactic scenes in which she first told off her dying father and then arranged to elope with the returning Morris, only to bar the door to him on his return as she watched him through a window with steely disdain. The film, favoring the Goetzes' highly satisfying melodrama over James's understated pathos, provided the perfect vehicle for Olivia de Havilland, who won her second Academy Award for playing Catherine as a mousy spinster whose final scenes allowed a shockingly withering scorn to emerge from the film's decorous period trappings.

If *The Heiress* was an adaptation with many parent scripts, *A Letter to Three Wives* (1949) and *All about Eve* (1950) approached ever more closely the ideal of invisible adaptation. Although the trailer for *A Letter to Three Wives* highlighted the film's literary source, a story John Klempner had published in *Cosmopolitan* in 1946, its visuals showed a partial cover of the magazine featuring the legend "In this Issue ... A LETTER TO THREE WIVES" without Klempner's name. This subtle alteration of the actual cover was hardly surprising, since Klempner was largely unknown in New York or Hollywood, where his sole movie credit was as author of the story that had served as the basis for the 1948 musical *Give My Regards to Broadway*, and when it first ran in *Cosmopolitan*, his story was titled "A Letter to Five Wives" (Fox dropped first one, then a second, wife in the course of the project). Instead, the film's own credits announced that it had been "Adapted by Vera Caspary/From a Cosmopolitan Magazine Novel by John Klempner," with a "Screenplay and Direction by Joseph L. Mankiewicz." Mankiewicz, a veteran Hollywood screenwriter and producer whose brother Herman had collaborated with Orson Welles in the screenplay for *Citizen Kane*, had turned to directing in 1946 with *Dragonwyck*, an adaptation of Anya Seton's 1944 gothic romance, and followed it with *The Late George Apley* (1947), an adaptation of John P. Marquand's Pulitzer Prize-winning 1937 novel. The hallmark of Mankiewicz's films, whether or not they were adaptations, was a civilized, urbane literacy the publicity sought to attach to the characters, the performers, and the director rather than any particular literary sources. It is telling that the credits for *A Letter to Three Wives*, whose irresistible hook was a letter from a quietly duplicitous small-town woman to three of her friends informing them that she had run off with one of their husbands without telling them which one, referred to "a Cosmopolitan Magazine Novel," informing them rather than reminding them of Klempner's work, as the alternate phrase "the Cosmopolitan Magazine Novel" would have done.

Invisible adaptation reached a high water mark with *All about Eve*, the deliciously gossipy story of an even more scheming young woman who uses her friendship with the friend of a Broadway star to worm her way into the star's entourage, first becoming her understudy, then taking her place when the star is prevented from going onstage one night, and finally making a play for first the star's husband, then the friend's. The film, whose credits described it as "Written for the Screen and Directed by Joseph L. Mankiewicz," was based on another *Cosmopolitan* piece, Mary Orr's 1946 short story "The Wisdom of Eve," which Orr had adapted for radio in 1949. When this broadcast caught the attention of Twentieth Century Fox, Orr sold the studio the adaptation rights for $5000 but received no writing credit for her story, which contains none of Mankiewicz's sparking dialogue—most of Orr's story takes the form of a narrative monologue delivered by the actress Margola Cranston to her friend Karen Richards about the treachery of Eve Harrington—even though it contains most of the film's major characters and plot elements.

Unlike Mary Orr, Tennessee Williams was in no danger of being erased from the credits of *A Streetcar Named Desire* (1951). The first credit to follow the Warner Bros. logo announced "THE PULITZER PRIZE AND NEW YORK CRITICS AWARD PLAY," an unprecedented prelude to the second, "'A STREETCAR NAMED DESIRE'/AN ELIA KAZAN PRODUCTION." But this opening credit emphasized not the name of the play or its author but the awards it had won. (Although only two other plays, *The Time of Your Life* and *Death of a Salesman*, had won both of these awards at the time the film was released, every single play that won either of them between 1952 and 1958 won the other as well.) It was not until the fifth credit, following the names of the principal performers, that Williams's name appeared—"Screen Play by TENNESSEE WILLIAMS/Adaptation by OSCAR SAUL," and not until the sixth that the film was explicitly identified as "Based upon the Original Play 'A STREETCAR NAMED DESIRE' by

TENNESSEE WILLIAMS/As presented on the stage by IRENE MAYER SELZNICK." Williams's 1947 play was both so renowned and so notorious by the time Warner Bros.' adaptation appeared that the studio was willing to go to unusual lengths to remain faithful to it.

When the Breen Office forbade any representation of the climactic rape of faded Southern belle Blanche DuBois (Vivien Leigh) by brutish Stanley Kowalski (Marlon Brando), Kazan threatened to quit the film. The resulting compromises—cutting several lines of Williams's dialogue, indicating the rape briefly and impressionistically enough to allow audience members who did not want to see it to believe that it had never happened (see Figure 5.9), and providing a new ending in which Stanley's long-suffering wife Stella (Kim Hunter), the sister Blanche had come to visit, refuses to forgive him but announces that she and her child will "never, never" return to him—paid the double dividend of remaining relatively faithful to Williams's play and preserving, in however attenuated a form, its single most sensationalistic moment. The resulting adaptation, still widely hailed as the single most powerful film version of an American play, won the Academy Award for Best Picture and Oscars for three of its four leading performers—Leigh, Hunter, and Karl Malden. Only Brando, who had shot to Broadway stardom when he originated the role of Stanley onstage, was passed over.

FIGURE 5.9 *The shattered mirror in* A Streetcar Named Desire *(1951) provides an elliptical representation of the rape of Blanche DuBois (Vivien Leigh).*

Both the industry and the popular audience have long considered *A Streetcar Named Desire* to be the ultimate Hollywood theatrical adaptation, the product of an ideal alliance between the movie industry and the culture industry. The flip side of this cozy-seeming but fraught relationship is revealed by another adaptation released the same year: *The Red Badge of Courage*. In *Picture,* her acerbic 1952 account of the making of the film, *New Yorker* staff writer Lillian Ross detailed the comically painful process by which MGM took the film from director John Huston, fresh from *The Asphalt Jungle,* who had thought it represented his best work yet, after he had wrapped up principal photography, assembled a rough cut, and left the country to film *The African Queen* (1951). Huston, who had confronted the experience of the Second World War in the documentaries *Report from the Aleutians* (1943), *The Battle of San Pietro* (1945), and *Let There Be Light* (1946) before retreating from the war in *Key Largo* (1948), his adaptation of Maxwell Anderson's 1939 melodrama about a powerful gangster installing himself on the Florida island, and *We Were Strangers* (1949), his adaptation of *Rough Sketch,* Robert Sylvester's 1948 novel of anti-government intrigue in Cuba, had wanted to engage the Civil War through an adaptation of Stephen Crane's 1895 novel. Albert Band's adaptation and Huston's screenplay emphasized the episodic nature of Crane's story of a Union recruit who runs from his first battle and then struggles to redeem himself, his intimate, apparently unrelated encounters with several other soldiers, and his ultimate growth into the courageous man he had once fancied himself. Basing the film's visual style on Matthew Brady's photographs and the compositional conventions of film noir, Huston deliberately avoided casting it with Hollywood stars, instead choosing a pair of veterans—Audie Murphy, who had not yet become a professional actor, and war cartoonist Bill Mauldin—for the two leading rules. In the face of negative preview screenings, executive producer Dore Schary, immersed in a power struggle with New York studio executive Joseph M. Schenck, ordered the film drastically recut, reducing its length from two hours to seventy minutes, added voiceover narration by another veteran, James Whitmore, to bridge its narrative gaps and provide a fulsome introduction, and released it as a B-picture. The new cut largely accepted the post-preview suggestions of producer Gottfried Reinhardt, who "wanted to put narration—passages from the Crane novel—into the picture and to add a scene at the beginning that would show the Stephen Crane novel being opened and its pages being turned, so that the audience would know the picture was based on a great book."[30]

MGM's release version pulled out all the stops in emphasizing the film's literary pedigree, singing Crane's praises in the opening credits and identifying him by name on the advertising posters, a status that had eluded Christopher Morley, Erskine Caldwell, Harry Bellaman, Cornell Woolrich, Niven Busch, Mary Chase, and Robert Penn Warren (see Figure 5.10). Even

FIGURE 5.10 *The opening frame of* The Red Badge of Courage *(1951) introduces Stephen Crane's name and status even before those of director John Huston fade in beneath.*

so, the publicity campaign failed along with the movie because although Crane's novel was undeniably a classic, the studio made no attempt to mount a successor to its campaign seventeen years earlier to establish *David Copperfield* as an indispensable school text, and on its own it was not widely enough read or fondly enough remembered to anchor such an austere and unspectacular film. Thanks in part to Ross's tell-all book, *The Red Badge of Courage* is most often remembered as a textbook example of lost opportunities, Hollywood butchery, and the fate of indiscriminate attempts to fetishize literary adaptation. It was in this last capacity that it looked forward most prophetically to new developments that were just around the corner.

Notes

1 "Sensational Screen Play Comes Thurs. to Fox California," *San Jose Evening News*, March 12, 1941, p. 13.
2 Quoted in "*Notes for Tobacco Road (1941),*" *Turner Classic Movies*, http://www.tcm.com/tcmdb/title/93489/Tobacco-Road/notes.html.

3   Frederick C. Othman, "'Tobacco Road' Cleaned Up for Production as Movie," *St. Petersburg Times*, December 15, 1940, Section B, p. 9.
4   Vivian C. Sobchack, "*The Grapes of Wrath*: Thematic Emphasis through Visual Style," *American Quarterly* 31.5 (Winter 1979): 596–615; rpt. in *Literature and Film: A Guide to the Theory and Practice of Film Adaptation*, ed. Robert Stam and Alessandra Raengo (Malden, MA: Blackwell, 2005), p. 124.
5   Edward Countryman, "John Ford's Drums along the Mohawk: The Making of an American Myth," *Radical History Review* 24 (1980): 111.
6   See Jeanine Basinger, *The World War II Combat Film: Anatomy of a Genre*, with an updated Filmography by Jeremy Arnold (Middletown: Wesleyan University Press, 2003), pp. 263–341.
7   For more on "ostensiveness," see Hans W. Frei, *The Eclipse of Biblical Narrative: A Story in Eighteenth and Nineteenth Century Hermeneutics* (New Haven, CT: Yale University Press, 1974), p. 310.
8   See "Stowe's Global Impact: Her Words Changed the World," *Harriet Beecher Stowe Center*, https://www.harrietbeecherstowecenter.org/harriet-beecher-stowe/her-global-impact/.
9   See *Uncle Tom's Cabins: The Transnational History of America's Most Mutable Book*, ed. Tracy C. Davis and Stefka Mihaylova (Ann Arbor: University of Michigan Press, 2018).
10 Robert Lawson, "Dean Acheson and the Potato Head Blues; or, British Academic Attitudes to America and Its Literature," in *As Others Read Us: International Perspectives on American Literature*, ed. Huck Gutman (Amherst: University of Massachusetts Press, 1991), p. 27.
11 Marc Chénetier, "American Literature in France: Pleasures in Perspective," in *As Others Read Us: International Perspectives on American Literature*, ed. Huck Gutman (Amherst: University of Massachusetts Press, 1991), pp. 82, 80, 83.
12 Michele Bottalico, "A Place for All: Old and New Myths in the Italian Appreciation of American Literature," in *As Others Read Us: International Perspectives on American Literature*, ed. Huck Gutman (Amherst: University of Massachusetts Press, 1991), p. 150.
13 Savas Patsalidis, "(Mis)understanding America's Literary Canon: The Greek Paradigm," in *As Others Read Us: International Perspectives on American Literature*, ed. Huck Gutman (Amherst: University of Massachusetts Press, 1991), p. 114.
14 Rolf Lundén, "The Dual Canon: A Swedish Example," in *As Others Read Us: International Perspectives on American Literature*, ed. Huck Gutman (Amherst: University of Massachusetts Press, 1991), p. 237.
15 James Naremore, *More Than Night: Film Noir in Its Contexts*, updated and expanded edition (Berkeley: University of California Press, 2008), p. 13.
16 See Nino Frank, "Un nouveau genre 'policier': L'aventure criminelle," *L'écran français* 61 (August 28, 1946), pp. 14–16, and Jean-Pierre Chartier, "Les Américains aussi font des films 'noirs,'" *Revue du cinéma* 2 (1946): 67–70.

17 See Raymond Borde and Étienne Chaumeton, *Panorama du film noir américain, 1941–1953* (Paris: Éditions de minuit, 1955), translated as *A Panorama of American Film Noir, 1941–1953* (San Francisco, CA: City Lights, 2002).
18 Naremore, *More Than Night*, p. 22.
19 Naremore, *More Than Night*, p. 27.
20 Jonathan Bailey, "Dracula vs. Nosferatu: A True Copyright Horror Story," *Plagiarism Today*, October 17, 2011, http://www.plagiarismtoday.com/2011/10/17/dracula-vs-nosferatu-a-true-copyright-horror-story/.
21 John Greco, "*Ossessione* (1943)/Luchino Visconti," *Twenty Four Frames: Notes on Film*, July 11, 2012, http://twentyfourframes.wordpress.com/2009/07/11/ossessione-1943-visconti/.
22 Naremore, *More Than Night*, p. 40.
23 Naremore, *More Than Night*, p. 43.
24 See Jeff Schwager, "*The Past* Rewritten," *Film Comment* 27.1 (January–February 1991): 12–17.
25 Paul Schrader, "Notes on Film Noir," *Film Comment* 10.1 (January–February 1974): 30–35; rpt. in *Film Noir Reader*, ed. Alain Silver and James Ursini, p. 57.
26 Thomas Leitch, "You Talk Like a Character in a Book: Dialogue and Film Adaptation," in *Film Dialogue*, ed. Jeff Jaeckle (London: Wallflower, 2013), p. 94.
27 Catherine Grant, "Recognizing Billy Budd in Beau Travail: Epistemology and Hermeneutics of an Auteurist 'Free' Adaptation," *Screen* 43.1 (2002): 57.
28 Patrick Cattrysse, *Descriptive Adaptation Studies: Epistemological and Methodological Issues* (Antwerp: Garant, 2014), p. 123.
29 Linda Hutcheon, with Siobhan O'Flynn, *A Theory of Adaptation*, 2nd ed. (New York: Routledge, 2013), p. 7.
30 Lillian Ross, *Picture: A Story about Hollywood* (New York: Rinehart, 1952), p. 167.

6

1951–67: Weaponized Best Sellers

A fork in the road

1952 was a banner year for John Steinbeck. He published his longest novel, *East of Eden*, and enjoyed the enthusiastic critical reception that greeted Elia Kazan's biopic *Viva Zapata!*, for which he had written the original screenplay, and for which he would be nominated for an Academy Award the following year. In addition, he took on a less accustomed role, one he admitted made him uncomfortable: appearing on camera as himself introducing the five short films—"The Cop and the Anthem," "The Clarion Call," "The Last Leaf," "The Ransom of Red Chief," and "The Gift of the Magi"—in Twentieth Century Fox's feature anthology *O. Henry's Full House* (see Figure 6.1).

For all his proficiency in introducing each of O. Henry's five stories, Steinbeck's discomfort in appearing before the cameras for which he supplied so much material—he was already credited as novelist or screenwriter on eleven films and would go on to amass a total of twenty-eight film writing credits during his lifetime and twenty-four more after his death in 1968—raises a question he must have pondered himself: What was he doing there? There was no question of asking William Sidney Porter to introduce the stories he had written as O. Henry, since he had died in 1910. But why did Fox collect five of his stories into a single film, and why did they feel the need to supply any introduction to them at all? The script for anthology adaptations, which enjoyed a short but significant vogue in the late 1940s and early 1950s, had its roots in films as different as Paul Leni's *Waxworks* (1924), Walt Disney's *Fantasia* (1940), and Ealing Studios' *Dead of Night* (1945), but reached its most conventionally literary form in *Quartet* (1948) and *Trio* (1949), two feature-length collections of stories by W. Somerset Maugham, individually introduced by the author. These two Gainsborough

FIGURE 6.1 *Standing in for the author of* O. Henry's Full House *(1952), John Steinbeck reaches for the obligatory volume of O. Henry's stories.*

films, which marked a high water mark of English cinema's infatuation with living authors, spawned an American television series, *Somerset Maugham TV Theatre* (1951–2), some of whose episodes were again introduced by Maugham.

What is striking about Steinbeck's role in *O. Henry's Full House* is what it reveals about Hollywood's lack of interest in American Maughams—living American short story writers like Ernest Hemingway, William Faulkner, Irwin Shaw, John O'Hara, or Steinbeck himself whose work it might have selected instead. Of the prominent short-story writers active in 1952, Flannery O'Connor and John Cheever were just beginning their distinguished careers, and magazine writers like Faith Baldwin and Cornell Woolrich enjoyed nothing like Maugham's literary cachet. It might indeed be argued that the United States had no Somerset Maugham of its own because so few American writers achieved either classic status or even literary respectability before they were dead.

Steinbeck is a reasonable stand-in for O. Henry because of his proletarian background, his extensive travels, his regionalist credentials, his success with both critics and the general public, his cultivation of a persona that represents a specifically American directness and lack of pretension, and his consequent ability to represent America as such, which provides a script for *O. Henry's Full House* nearly as important as the anthology film and the stories of O. Henry, whose literary status ends up being elevated by his association, however brief, with Steinbeck. The film and Steinbeck's introduction in particular are important because they are echoed not by later anthology feature films but by so many television anthology series that both precede and follow them. *O. Henry's Full House* marks a crucial fork in the road between Hollywood cinema, which largely rejected its model of the anthology of adaptations whose literary credentials it emphasizes, and contemporaneous American television, an emerging medium particularly eager to seize and exploit that model. This period has come to be remembered as the Golden Age of Television, at least until new subscription networks like Home Box Office and Showtime and streaming services like Netflix, Hulu, and Amazon Prime produced critically acclaimed series like *The Sopranos* (1999–2007), *Six Feet Under* (2001–05), *The Wire* (2002–08), *Lost* (2004–10), *Mad Men* (2007–15), and *Breaking Bad* (2008–13).

Unlike these continuing series, whose principal innovation was stories that developed long narrative arcs and correspondingly complex characters over a period of several seasons, the first Golden Age of Television was marked by anthology series that presented a single story, often an adaptation of a particular story, play, or novel, on every episode. Encouraged by the success of radio anthology programs that had presented a new story in each episode, early television producers and their sponsors launched an analogous series of television programs, many of them introduced, like *O. Henry's Full House,* by well-known figures addressing the audience directly. The pioneering example, *Kraft Television Theatre* (1947–58), presented not only original teleplays like Rod Serling's *Patterns* (1955), its best-remembered episode, but adaptations of Harry Leon Wilson's *Merton of the Movies* (1947), George Kelly's *Craig's Wife* (1947), Washington Irving's *Rip Van Winkle* (1950), Mark Twain's *The Adventures of Tom Sawyer* (1951), and Tennessee Williams's *This Property Is Condemned* (1958), its final show, over its eleven-year run. Of the many anthology series that followed in its path, a few are especially notable for their distinctive approaches to adaptation. Although *The Chevrolet Tele-Theatre* (1948–50) specialized in original one-act teleplays, *The Philco Television Playhouse* began its seven-year run (1948–55) by focusing on adaptations of Broadway plays and musicals, from *Dinner at Eight,* its first episode, to *What Makes Sammy Run?* (1949), then adaptations of well-known novels, plays, and stories from Nathaniel Hawthorne's *The House of the Seven Gables* (1949) to F. Scott Fitzgerald's *The Last Tycoon* (1949). The program that began as *Studio One,* a 1947–8 radio show whose initial episode was an adaptation of Malcolm Lowry's *Under the Volcano,* was repurposed for television in 1948 and known over its ten-year run as *Westinghouse Studio One, Studio*

One Summer Theatre, Studio One in Hollywood, Summer Theatre, and *Westinghouse Summer Theatre.* Its most notable offerings ranged from a 1950 adaptation of Hawthorne's *The Scarlet Letter* to Reginald Rose's original teleplay *Twelve Angry Men* (1954), which Sidney Lumet remade as a feature film in 1957. Unlike the short-lived *Your Show Time* (1949), which began with three adaptations of French short stories, *Pulitzer Prize Playhouse* (1950–2) restricted itself to adaptations of American material. Its productions in its first season included George S. Kaufman and Moss Hart's *You Can't Take It with You* (its initial episode), Robert E. Sherwood's *Abe Lincoln in Illinois* (1950), Booth Tarkington's *The Magnificent Ambersons* (1950), Thornton Wilder's *Our Town* (1950), Susan Glaspell's *Alison's House* (1951), and Owen Davis's *Icebound* (1951). By the second season, the limited range of Pulitzer Prize-winning plays whose copyright holders were willing to license them to a new medium still struggling for respectability led the series to complement Pulitzer winners like Wilder's *The Skin of Our Teeth* (1951) with adaptations of other work by Pulitzer winners: Maxwell Anderson's *Mary of Scotland* (1951), James Gould Cozzens's *The Just and the Unjust* (1951), George S. Kaufman and Edna Ferber's *The Royal Family* (1951), Tarkington's *Monsieur Beaucaire* (1952), and, most amusingly, John P. Marquand's *The Return of Mr. Moto* (1952).

If the field of Pulitzer material was thin, however, *Playhouse 90* (1956–60) demonstrated that the range of American novels, stories, and plays that could attract sponsors and audiences was much broader, especially if it could develop the material in the ninety-minute segments indicated by its title. Along with original teleplays later made into feature films—Rod Serling's *Requiem for a Heavyweight* (its second episode), William Gibson's *The Miracle Worker* (1957), J.P. Miller's *Days of Wine and Roses* (1958), and Abby Mann's *The Judgment at Nuremberg* (1959)—the program offered dozens of adaptations of American originals old and new: Cornell Woolrich's *Rendezvous in Black* (1956), John Cheever's *The Country Husband* (1956), Kay Thompson and Hilary Knight's *Eloise* (1956), F. Scott Fitzgerald's *The Last Tycoon* (1957), *Winter Dreams* (1957), and *The Great Gatsby* (1958), Clifford Odets's *Clash by Night* (1957), John P. Marquand's *Sincerely, Willis Wade* (1956) and *Point of No Return* (1958), James Thurber and Elliott Nugent's *The Male Animal* (1958), William Saroyan's *The Time of Your Life* (1958), Henry James's *The Wings of the Dove* (1959), William Faulkner's *Old Man* (1958) and *Tomorrow* (1960), and Ernest Hemingway's *For Whom the Bell Tolls* (presented in two episodes, 1959), *The Snows of Kilimanjaro* (1960), and *The Gambler, the Nun and the Radio* (1960).

There were several reasons why adaptations of American literature should have loomed so large in the Golden Age of Television. Like the Hollywood of an earlier generation, the infant medium sought respectability and cultural cachet. Broadway plays offered a steady stream of material readily suited for adaptation, especially if the episodes were broadcast live, as many of them were, rather than filmed by television cameras for rebroadcast. American novels like *The House of the Seven Gables, The Adventures of Tom Sawyer,* and *The Wings of the Dove* offered greater challenges to both adapters and performers but the compensating advantage of being in the public domain and so requiring no royalty payments. Even so, television's first Golden Age ended with the final broadcast of *Playhouse 90.* Despite the persistence of stand-alone programs like *Alfred Hitchcock Presents* (1955–62), *The Alfred Hitchcock Hour* (1962–5), and *The Twilight Zone* (1959–64), each of them an anthology series whose episodes were introduced by presenters Alfred Hitchcock and Rod Serling, the networks' schedules were already dominated by sitcoms like *I Love Lucy* (1951–7) and its sequels and genre series from *Gunsmoke* (1952–61) to *Perry Mason* (1957–66), which presented individual episodes featuring the same continuing cast.

On the whole, Hollywood took a completely different attitude toward adaptation. If the first wave of television programs rushed to advertise their literary roots, the film studios seemed to go out of their way to disavow their own. Practically all the films John Ford directed after 1950 were adaptations: *Rio Grande* (1950), *The Quiet Man* (1952), *The Sun Shines Bright* (1953), *Mogambo* (1953), *The Long Gray Line* (1955), *Mister Roberts* (1955), *The Searchers* (1956), *The Wings of Eagles* (1957), *The Rising of the Moon* (1957), *Gideon of Scotland Yard* (1958), *The Last Hurrah* (1958), *The Horse Soldiers* (1959), *Sergeant Rutledge* (1960), *Two Rode Together* (1961), *The Man Who Shot Liberty Valence* (1962), and *7 Women* (1966). Yet Ford continued to be identified more closely with a single popular genre, the American Western, than with American literature—an identification he accepted himself in beginning his famous 1950 rebuke to Cecil B. DeMille, who wanted to remove Joseph L. Mankiewicz as president of the Directors Guild of America for his alleged Communist sympathies: "I am a director of Westerns."[1] The contemporaneous output of John Huston includes an even higher proportion of adaptations, many of American novels and plays: *The Asphalt Jungle* (1950), *The Red Badge of Courage* (1951), *Moby-Dick* (1956), *Heaven Knows, Mr. Allison* (1957), *The Barbarian and the Geisha* (1958), *The Unforgiven* (1960), *The Night of the Iguana* (1964), *Reflections in a Golden Eye* (1967), *The Kremlin Letter* (1970), *Fat City* (1972), *Wise Blood* (1979), *Annie* (1982), and *Prizzi's Honor* (1985). But Huston, who lived for extended periods in Mexico and Ireland and renounced his American citizenship in 1964 to become an Irish citizen, resisted any identification with American literature, branding himself instead as an globe-trotting adventurer motivated to direct films "to express my pleasure at having read something."[2]

Hollywood's obligatory big-budget adaptations of Hemingway during the 1950s—*The Snows of Kilimanjaro* (1952), *The Sun Also Rises* (1957), and *The Old Man and the Sea* (1958)—were largely overshadowed by adaptations of best sellers that attracted studio heads precisely because they were deemed too controversial for television, whose need to appeal to the widest possible audience had suddenly and paradoxically cast the movies, quite against their will, as a niche medium. Otto Preminger's 1955 adaptation of Nelson Algren's *The Man with the Golden Arm* marked a notable, though hardly a complete, advance in Hollywood's willingness to show the ravages drug addiction took on drug users. *The Wayward Bus,* Victor Vicas's 1957 film adaptation of Steinbeck's 1947 novel, his best-selling novel to date, offered the chance to see three different actresses—Jayne Mansfield, Joan Collins, and newcomer Dolores Michaels—in frankly seductive roles. *To Kill a Mockingbird,* Robert Mulligan's 1962 adaptation of Harper Lee's Pulitzer Prize-winning 1960 novel, is best remembered now as a primer against racism as smugly self-satisfied in its way, though that way was clearly less racist, as earlier film adaptations of *Uncle Tom's Cabin.* At the time of its first release, however, the film, whose advertising posters clearly marked it as "NOT SUITABLE FOR CHILDREN," was widely regarded as controversial in its frank presentation of culturally entrenched racism as seen by Scout, the daughter of Atticus Finch, the attorney who is appointed to defend Tom Robinson (Brock Peters) against the charge of raping Mayella Ewell (Collin Wilcox), whom the film broadly hints was actually beaten and raped by her father, Robert E. Lee Ewell (James Anderson). The film was unusually explicit in following Lee's novel in its exploration of racism, incest, and mental illness, its purity (though not its suitability for children) warranted by the presence of Gregory Peck, who won an Academy Award for playing Finch, and the unblinking innocence of Mary Badham, who played the precocious Scout (see Figure 6.2).

Although *To Kill a Mockingbird* may be the most beloved American adaptation of the period, it was overshadowed at the time by a more long-standing phenomenon, the career of Lana Turner. Discovered, according to legend, at a drug store soda fountain, Turner shot to stardom in several Warner Bros. pictures before signing a long-term contract with MGM, where she headlined a surprising number of literary adaptations. In Victor Fleming's *Dr. Jekyll and Mr. Hyde* (1941), she was originally cast as barmaid Ivy Pearson until her costar, Ingrid Bergman, announced her interest in that role, leaving Turner to play the aristocratic Bea Emery. Following *Week-End at the Waldorf,* Robert Z. Leonard's Americanized 1945 remake of *Grand Hotel,* and Tay Garnett's 1946 *The Postman Always Rings Twice,* in which she was memorably cast as truck-stop siren Cora Smith, Turner settled into a series of costume roles in adaptations set in exotic locations or distant historical periods: *Green Dolphin Street* (1947), *Cass Timberlaine* (1947), *The Three Musketeers* (1948), *The Merry Widow* (1952), *Flame and the Flesh* (1954).

After starring in Richard Thorpe's *The Prodigal* (1955), another film for Warners, Turner moved to Twentieth Century Fox for Jean Negulesco's *The Rains of Ranchipur* (1955) and Mark Robson's *Peyton Place* (1957).

FIGURE 6.2 *In* To Kill a Mockingbird *(1962), Atticus Finch (Gregory Peck) turns the defense of accused rapist Tom Robinson (Brock Peters) into an unforgettable film Universal advertised as not suitable for children as young as Finch's daughter Scout (Mary Badham), the film's principal identification figure.*

Although her appearances in *Another Time, Another Place* (1958), *Imitation of Life* (1959), *Portrait in Black* (1960), *By Love Possessed* (1961), and *Madame X* (1966) took her to Universal, it is Turner's move from MGM to Fox that reveals a more general shift from what might be called the MGM conception of literature to the Fox conception of literature that is the most distinctive feature of the period's adaptations.

Hollywood fights back

After an initial period of what Virginia Wright Wexman calls their "ostrichlike" determination to ignore television—"at one studio it was even reported to be forbidden to use the word *television* in executive conversation"[3]—Hollywood fought its rise and spread with every weapon at the studios' disposal. All of the celebrated technical advances they embraced in the 1950s—Eastmancolor, widescreen, four-track magnetic sound (the features Fred Astaire and Janis Paige in *Silk Stockings* would lampoon as "Glorious Technicolor, Breathtaking CinemaScope, and Stereophonic Sound"), 3-D projection—were designed specifically to provide products that television could neither match nor adapt. Until the advent of color television some ten years later, they were largely successful, not in suppressing the rise of television, but in TV-proofing their own product.

Another important strategic weapon in the studio's anti-television arsenal was literary adaptations.

As Leonard J. Leff, Jerold L. Simmons, and Thomas Doherty have observed, the establishment of the Hays Office and the crackdown on movies by enforcing the 1930 Production Code beginning in 1934 marked both a defeat and a victory for Hollywood. The empowerment of the Hays Office marked a defeat, because for the next thirty-four years all Hollywood productions would be subject to a censorship code that was often absurdly strict and whimsical. But the Hays Office also marked a victory, or at least an accommodation, because it allowed the industry to police itself in anticipation of any of the government censorship studio executives feared much more.[4] An enduring legacy of the Hays Office, later the Breen Office (1934–54) and the Shurlock Office (1954–68), was another anticipatory strategy: preemptively preventing many adaptations from ever getting made. MGM had to cancel plans in 1940 and again in 1946, for example, to remake *Anna Christie,* the 1930 Eugene O'Neill adaptation in which Greta Garbo had first talked, because the Breen Office would not allow the presentation of Anna as a prostitute until 1962. But studios continued to be drawn to the power of this forbidden fruit even as they bowed to the yoke of the censors they had appointed themselves as a potential source of material forbidden from network television, which was even more tightly censored by the 1951 Code of Practice for Television Broadcasters, because "for studio accountants, the numbers in the ledger books were more worrisome than the text of the Code. So lately ascendant and unchallenged, the dominant, not to say only, moving image game in town, Hollywood was reeling from a humbling demotion in status and solvency. Television had supplanted its centrality, stolen its audience, and depleted its coffers."[5]

Despite the studios' investment in glorious Technicolor, breathtaking CinemaScope, and stereophonic sound, box office revenues continued to drop every year from their high water mark in 1946. In addition to the industry's embrace of Eastmancolor, widescreen, and four-track sound, and more short-lived experiments with 3-D and Cinerama, Hollywood's weapons included adaptation, which provided one of the industry's main lines of defense against its upstart competitor. In a memo to Fox staffers Julian Johnson, David Brown, and Joseph Moskowitz, Darryl F. Zanuck, the Fox vice president in charge of production, noted: "Today, when business has boiled down to weekend business at the theatres, the value of a pre-sold property has doubled." Speaking of MGM's recent release of *Ivanhoe,* Zanuck added: "They took broad liberties in adaptation. As a matter of fact they told half the book offstage. But I am sure no one will mind because the picture is good entertainment. I am afraid we passed up material of this nature because we are frightened by the production cost or frightened to take dramatic liberties with established material." He particularly encouraged the studio to be alert to possible remakes: "I would like to see each producer with at least one subject in work that has the obvious possibilities of entering this profitable realm. It is equally even more important than keeping a constant search for new material and watching the best sellers."⁶

Always keenly alert to shifts in the market, Zanuck sent a 1953 memo to Henry King, who had based the successful Fox picture *The Snows of Kilimanjaro,* released a year earlier, on Ernest Hemingway's fifteen-year-old story, analyzing the leading reasons for the success of recent box office champs: "In addition to sex KILIMANJARO also combines elements of spectacle and adventure, but the boxoffice sock of the picture remains the sex scenes between Peck and Ava Gardner. [...] Apparently sex is the only thing that can overcome a so-called downbeat or depressing story. [...] [E]ven a heavy, downbeat, depressing story can be lifted if it contains a really strong, violent sex situation. [...] If you feel the urge to make a 'message picture' or if you feel the urge to take an 'intellectual splurge,' be sure that it can be told in terms of adventure, showmanship, and certainly in terms of sex."⁷

Two cautions are in order here. *The Snows of Kilimanjaro* is a remarkably free adaptation of Hemingway that expands his 26-page story to 114 minutes by adding quite a number of new elements, from Cynthia Green, the character Ava Gardner plays, to a happy ending that completely reverses the trajectory of Hemingway's story. More specifically, the sex of which Zanuck speaks so glowingly between Gardner and Peck is a far cry from the really strong, violent sex situations Hollywood would serve up over the following decade (see Figure 6.3).

Historians who have noted the growing sexual explicitness of American movies between 1946 and 1968, the year the Production Code was officially replaced by a ratings system that allowed different films to be marketed to specific demographics, have settled on a list of landmark films that mounted successive challenges to the Code—*The Miracle* (1948), *The Moon Is Blue* (1953), *The Man with the Golden Arm* (1955), *Anatomy of a Murder* (1959)—sometimes adding *A Streetcar Named Desire* (1951), *The Man in the Gray Flannel Suit* (1956), *Baby Doll* (1956), *Tea and Sympathy* (1956), *Pal Joey* (1957), *The Chapman Report* (1962), *The Pawnbroker* (1964), and *Who's Afraid of Virginia Woolf?* (1966). Apart from *Baby Doll,* based on an original screenplay written by the foremost American playwright of his time, all these films were adaptations. And in every case, their status as adaptations worked both to tap into the market Zanuck had identified with presold properties and to strengthen their case against preemptive censorship. If audiences could hear words like *virgin* and *mistress* spoken in the stage production of *The Moon Is Blue,* why couldn't they hear them in the movie? And if they could read the words *rape* and *panties* in *Anatomy of a Murder,* why couldn't they hear them onscreen?

Otto Preminger, taking on board the lesson of Roberto Rossellini's *The Miracle,* had pioneered an influential strategy for dealing with the Breen

FIGURE 6.3 *Cynthia Green (Ava Gardner) and Harry Street (Gregory Peck) enjoy one of the torrid sex scenes Darryl F. Zanuck was convinced were behind the success of* The Snows of Kilimanjaro *(1952).*

Office's refusal to issue a seal of approval for controversial films: persuade his studio to release them without a Production Code seal of approval, counting on the ensuing publicity to stoke a popular interest that would outweigh any suppression of the audience by the Legion of Decency's moral threats against Catholic audiences who saw the offending films and some exhibitors' refusal to show them. This strategy worked so brilliantly for *The Moon Is Blue* and *The Man with the Golden Arm* that Howard Hughes adopted it for his 1953 *The French Line,* which was advertised as "Jane Russell in 3 Dimension[s]—and What Dimensions!,"[8] and *Baby Doll* and *Some Like It Hot* (1959) were also released without a seal. Twentieth Century Fox, however, took a different tack. Having purchased the rights to the 1955 Broadway hit *A Hatful of Rain,* which focused on the calamitous effects of a Korean War veteran's morphine addiction, the studio issued a public statement, "We will never make a picture at Twentieth that does not meet with Code approval,"[9] while lobbying feverishly behind the scenes for revisions to the Code that would allow a more graphic treatment of controversial material.

The result was a series of high-profile adaptations whose attitude to both their nominal sources and their potentially explosive themes was marked by radical disavowal. These adaptations, based on novels whose controversial treatments of race, crime, and especially sex had made them best sellers, embraced what Walter Benjamin might have called the aura[10] of the allegedly steamy books on which they were based while doing whatever was necessary to placate the Breen Office, which had now become the Shurlock Office. For the most part, these adaptations could be no more explicit than television in presenting taboo subjects. But they could be more suggestive, even as they strenuously disavowed that very suggestiveness.

The formula for weaponizing best sellers had been provided by a still earlier Preminger film. *Forever Amber* was based on Kathleen Winsor's 1944 historical novel, the best-selling American novel of the 1940s despite its daunting length of 972 pages and its banning by fourteen states. An assistant attorney general of Massachusetts who led the charge cited "seventy references to sexual intercourse, thirty-nine illegitimate pregnancies, seven abortions, and ten descriptions of women undressing in front of men"[11] as reasons for the ban, which played a pivotal role in refiguring the phrase "Banned in Boston" from a moral admonition to an unintentional imprimatur that drove sales. Not surprisingly, Joseph Breen celebrated the novel's publication by calling the thrice-married courtesan's sexual odyssey "'utterly and completely unacceptable,' little more than a 'saga of illicit sex [...] bastardy, perversion, impotency, pregnancy, abortion, murder and marriage without even the slightest suggestion of compensating moral values.'"[12]

Macmillan, the publishing house that had been so successful with *Gone with the Wind* (1936), promoted *Forever Amber* as the same kind of story, a triple-decker period saga pitting a strong-willed heroine against the vicissitudes of a distant historical era, and Fox pitched the film along similar lines, signing John M. Stahl, the director of *Imitation of Life* (1934) and *Leave Her to Heaven* (1945), to direct and Erich Wolfgang Korngold, who had written the scores for *Anthony Adverse* (1936), *The Prince and the Pauper* (1937), *The Adventures of Robin Hood* (1938), and *The Private Lives of Elizabeth and Essex* (1939) to compose the music. Echoing David O. Selznick's widely publicized search for the ideal star to play Scarlett O'Hara, Zanuck had some two hundred actresses tested for the role of Amber St. Clare before settling on newcomer Peggy Cummins. Within six weeks, however, all these principals were gone, the inexperienced Cummins replaced by Linda Darnell, the ailing Korngold by David Raksin, and the unenthusiastic Stahl by Preminger, who also made no secret of his distaste for the assignment.

Forever Amber's story, like that of *Gone with the Wind,* is driven by repeated deferrals of the obvious match between the beautiful heroine and the dashing hero, Bruce Carlton (Cornel Wilde), the father of her illegitimate son. This time, though, the obstacles to the lovers' union are generated not by historical circumstance but by Amber's relationships with other men: her engagement to Black Jack Mallard (John Russell), whom Bruce reluctantly kills in the duel to which Jack challenges him; her marriage to the wealthy, possessive Earl of Radcliffe (Richard Haydn); and her preferment by the dyspeptic Charles II (George Sanders). The film carries constant reminders of Amber's licentiousness, from the bangles an admirer notices on her wrist that hint at many admirers to the low-cut gowns she consistently wears, even when a brief domestic interlude requires her to wear an apron as well (see Figure 6.4). Despite establishing its heroine from beginning to end as a woman on the make, however, release prints of the film include no sex scenes nor any direct references to sex in the dialogue. What evidently infuriated the censors was not the film's fidelity to Winsor's notorious novel, but the possibility that watching it would stimulate lustful thoughts by simply reminding viewers of the novel.

If *Forever Amber,* altogether less explicit in its sexual representations and more explicit in its moralizing, departed from Winsor's novel in fundamental ways, it took exceptional pains to establish its literary credentials. It begins with a shot showing the image of a leather-bound book opening to reveal its

FIGURE 6.4 *Even during a rare domestic scene, Amber St. Clair (Linda Darnell) shows off to Bruce Carlton (Cornel Wilde) another of the plunging necklines she favors throughout* Forever Amber *(1947).*

credits presented in elaborate script lettering, illuminated in red—a cliché of Hollywood adaptations that is echoed this time by a closing shot in which the Fox credit appears on the final page of a similar book, then its back cover. Frequent script intertitle cards, the first jumping from 1644 to 1660, emphasize the historical background of the English Restoration.

Leon Shamroy shot the film in tastefully dark-hued Technicolor. Everything about *Forever Amber*'s presentation from its budget (it was the most expensive Fox film to date) to its running time (two hours and eighteen minutes) to its grosses (it was Fox's highest-grossing film of 1947, and Hollywood's fourth-highest-grossing film that year) marks it as an important project. Even though the studio had purchased the 25-year-old Winsor's first novel specifically because of its promise of overheated entertainment, all the textual features of the film were designed to establish its status as a literary adaptation, a period piece as respectable as it was sumptuous.

Released during the heyday of the film noir, *Forever Amber* looks nothing like a noir, but its ostensible moral, that men should beware of alluring women willing to trade on their sexuality in pursuit of power, marks it as both a Technicolor noir costume drama and a predecessor to the literary adaptations the studios would release ten years later, driven by sexually desirable, and often sexually voracious, women who sought power not through criminal enterprises but through American capitalism. An important transitional film between *Forever Amber* and this later generation of adaptations is Michael Gordon's *I Can Get It for You Wholesale* (1951), a Fox film based on the best-selling 1937 novel that launched Jerome Weidman's career. Weidman's roman à clef used the figure of Harry Bogen, whose meteoric rise in the New York garment industry is fueled by an unsavory blend of scheming, backstabbing, and betrayals, to expose the corruption that permeated New Seventh Avenue. Vera Caspary's adaptation and Abraham Polonsky's screenplay wrought many changes in Weidman's novel, but three of them stand out: the excising of any criminal activity, the addition of a happy ending, and the recasting of Harry Bogen as a woman.

The film follows the career of Harriet Boyd from her days as a model for the low-budget dresses in which the Seventh Avenue dressmakers specialized to her climactic apotheosis. It wastes no time in sexualizing Harriet Boyd (Susan Hayward), who along with another model is obliged to strip down to her slip in the opening sequence, which reveals the frantic pace of the models' work and their unending need to curry favor with buyers like the lecherous Savage (Harry von Zell) for whom they pose and parade, and who repay them with leering harassment. When Harriet, an aspiring designer as well as a model, caps an evening out with top salesman Teddy Sherman (Dan Dailey) by proposing that they leave their company and strike out on their own with their business colleague Sam Cooper (Sam Jaffe) and office boy Arnold Fisher (Marvin Kaplan), he listens to her pitch, asks whether she really knows this business, and greets her response—that she knows the business inside and out because of the way she's been treated as a model—with the memorable line: "Miss Boyd, you have the simple and astonishing beauty of an old-fashioned straight razor." The image crystallizes her status as a castrating beauty equally capable, like her noir forebears, of successfully competing with men and emasculating them in the bargain.

The film sets Harriet against her sister Marge (Randy Stuart), who is equally but more decorously sexualized by an introduction that presents her necking with her fiancé in the doorway of the apartment she shares with her sister and their mother. Once Harriet succeeds in launching Sherboyco Dresses with the shared legacy of $5000 from their late father that she has manipulated Marge into giving her control of, she never looks back. Instead of forcing herself to endure Savage's come-ons, she actively courts them in order to expand the business. When Teddy, finding the two of them drinking at a swanky restaurant, urges her to leave, she asks him, "Don't you wine and dine clients?," and refuses to leave until Teddy punches Savage, losing both his account and Harriet's good will. Soon enough she has set her sights even higher, on a relationship with upscale retailer J.F. Noble (George Sanders) that will free her to design more costly, more profitable fashions that the $10.95 items that throng Sherboyco and Seventh Avenue. After their first meeting at a formal industry dinner at which they dance and then enjoy a nightcap alone, Harriet's slow, teasing departure is accompanied by the *Liebestod* from Richard Wagner's *Tristan and Isolde*, a musical cue suggesting high-toned doomed romance. Enticed by Noble's offer to make her his sole designer, "Harriet of Noble's," if she will break her five-year contract with Sherboyco, she picks a fight with Sam and Teddy, who tells her: "You lied, cheated, and double-crossed your way out of a model's room into being a partner," and later, when she maintains that she's always delivered on her promises—an assertion Harry Bogen never could have made—Teddy retorts: "If there's one thing about Harriet Boyd, she's a girl who delivers—anywhere, anytime, any price." In light of his remarks, it comes as something of a surprise when Harriet's last-minute unwillingness to bankrupt her friends allows the film to end with her return to them.

Like Weidman's novel, which was highly characteristic of 1930s activist-muckraking fiction, the film is a creature of its time, riddled with postwar disillusionment that focuses, like that of film noir, on men's continued need to idealize and sexually fetishize females despite their often disillusioning and sometimes treacherous behavior. The film, produced nearly fifteen years after the novel, casts WASP performers in its lead roles while suggesting though the casting of Sam Jaffe and Marvin Kaplan that New York's fashion industry is dominated by ethnic Jewish characters. More specifically, it depends on exploiting the screen personas of two of its three stars. George Sanders plays a role remarkably similar to the suavely venomous critic Addison DeWitt in *All about Eve* (1950), for which he won a Best Supporting Actor Oscar. Even the production design of the formal banquet at which Harriet meets Noble suggests a greatly enlarged and socially more stratified version of the theatrical award ceremony of the elitist Sarah Siddons Society that opens *All about Eve*. Susan Hayward, whose roles in *The Hairy Ape* (1944), *Deadline at Dawn* (1946), *Smash-Up: The Story of a Woman* (1947), and *House of Strangers* (1949), an adaptation of Weidman's 1941 novel *I'll Never Go There Any More,* had established her as alluring, weary, hard-bitten, and shop-soiled, prepares the way for a series of hard-used temptresses she will play in *David and Bathsheba* (1951), *Garden of Evil* (1954), *Untamed* (1955), *I'll Cry Tomorrow* (1955), and *I Want to Live!* (1958), for which she won her own Oscar. Ultimately, Hayward found a home in a late-blooming series of literary adaptations that grew out of *Forever Amber* and *I Can Get It for You Wholesale,* a series that like *Forever Amber* were marketed as both more and less risqué than the best-selling novels on which they were based.

Hollywood's long relationship with the literary marketplace had often been fraught with danger and defiance, as its adaptations of *Leave Her to Heaven, Double Indemnity, Gone with the Wind,* and *Uncle Tom's Cabin* attest. The new wrinkle in Fox's counterattack against television was that instead of choosing safe properties like *A Christmas Carol* that could be adapted just as easily by television or domesticating equivocal best sellers like *Forever Amber* by stripping out the provocative elements that had made them best sellers in the first place, Fox sought at once to produce adaptations approved by the Production Code, to challenge the Code at every turn, and to trumpet the films' own controversial elements as a selling point television could not match while at the same time fetishizing the films' production values to establish their cultural cachet. The result was a new kind of adaptation, one that systematically suppressed certain values associated with literary culture while inflating other culturally upscale motifs to the bursting point with the goal of simultaneously invoking and disavowing both the taboo elements designed to lure audiences away from television and the cultural cachet that would keep the censors at bay. Like Just Jaeckin's soft-core feature *Emmanuelle* (1974), the strategy of these films was to make the audience feel good without making them feel bad.

Literary mischief

The pivotal film to exemplify this new strategy was Mark Robson's *Peyton Place,* produced for Fox by Jerry Wald. At 157 minutes, it ran even longer than *Forever Amber.* It was expensively mounted, with strikingly picturesque exteriors that began behind its opening credits, shot in Camden, Maine, complemented by equally sumptuous wood-paneled interiors for all but the most socially marginal characters' living and working spaces, all beautifully photographed in color by William Mellor. Franz Waxman provided a sweeping, romantic musical score. And the story was framed, like the novel, in specifically historical terms, unfolding from the season immediately preceding Pearl Harbor through the war years.

The keynote of Grace Metalious's best-selling 1956 novel had been the contrast between the placid surface of Peyton Place, Connecticut, and the widespread corruption beneath. Leslie Harrington schemed to keep his playboy son Rodney from being drafted after he got mill worker's daughter Betty Anderson pregnant. Rodney was hit by a truck while groping another woman's breasts. Norman Page affected a false limp when he pretended to be a war hero. Kindly Dr. Matthew Swain performed an abortion on Selena Cross after she was raped by her stepfather Lucas. Selena was abandoned by her childhood sweetheart Ted Carter. Aspiring writer Allison MacKenzie had an affair with a New York literary agent. Her mother Constance hid the secret of her own affair, which had led to Allison's birth. In the film, by contrast, Rodney gets drafted, marries Betty, and is killed overseas, expiating his sins. Norman enlists in the paratroopers, paving the way to become a real war hero. Selena suffers a miscarriage after falling down a hill while she is running from another assault by Lucas, although Dr. Swain still orders his nurse to record the procedure as an appendectomy. Ted Carter stands by Selena during her trial for murdering Lucas and ends up about to marry her. And Allison apparently remains virginal even after she moves to New York. By eliminating virtually all the novel's revelations of misbehavior, the film shifts the focus of the novel from the pervasive small-town hypocrisy of a community in which the deepest fear of the citizens is to be seen and judged for what they really are to their common need to accept life-giving love, as opposed to either corrosive lust or unhealthy repression, in all its forms.

Even in the film, these acceptable forms of love include the physical love Allison MacKenzie (Diane Varsi) discusses frankly with her friend Norman Page (Russ Tamblyn), the love schoolteacher Michael Rossi (Lee Phillips) urges Constance MacKenzie (Lana Turner) to accept after their initial argument about whether sex education should be taught in school, as Mike contends, or reserved for marriage, as Constance believes. Now, however, true love, which ennobles its participants and builds communities between them, is as easy to tell from false love as Mike and Constance's slowly blossoming relationship is from the liaison Rodney Harrington (Barry Coe) pursues with Betty Anderson (Terry Moore) or the assault of Lucas Cross (Arthur Kennedy) against his stepdaughter Selena (Hope Lange). Allison offers to let Norman kiss her in the name of rescuing him from sexual repression, reassuring him, "It's time you learned that girls want to do the same things as boys. [...] Everyone in this town hides behind plain wrappers." Mike lectures Constance after she resists his kiss: "That's affection, not carnality. [...] I'm not going to let you make something dirty about this. [...] It's not sex you're afraid of. It's love." And after Rodney tells

Betty, necking with him in his car, that yes, he *would* like to make love to her, she slugs him with her handbag and jumps out of the car (see Figure 6.5)—a dramatic change from the corresponding scene in the novel, in which Betty spitefully says, "Is it up, Rod? Is it up good and hard? [...] Now go shove it into Allison MacKenzie."[13]

In his review of the film, Bosley Crowther of the *New York Times* charged it with abandoning the novel's focus on "the quality of hypocrisy that corrupts a New England community. There is no sense of massive corruption here,"[14] and *Newsweek* observed, "John Michael Hayes's screenplay has no trace of bad taste."[15] But this latter characterization is untrue in revealing ways. The film does not so much seek to avoid as to contain and neutralize bad taste by overlaying it with suffocatingly fetishized good taste. Betty Anderson tempts Rodney Harrington but ends up marrying him and, after his death, is reconciled with his disapproving father. Alone among the residents of Peyton Place, the Cross family live in substandard housing and speak with southern accents that identify them as social outsiders. Constance MacKenzie, obviously mindful of her troubled relationship with her own daughter, achieves redemption by

FIGURE 6.5 *The petting party between Betty Anderson (Terry Moore) and Rodney Harrington (Barry Coe) in* Peyton Place *(1957) is about to turn out quite differently than it did in Grace Metalious's novel.*

testifying in court on behalf of Selena and her late mother Nellie (Betty Field), a maid who hanged herself in Constance's house. Dr. Swain (Lloyd Nolan), inspired by Constance's testimony, breaks his vow of silence to Selena, testifies that she killed her stepfather in order to protect herself from being raped again, and admonishes his fellow citizens: "It's time that someone spoke up. [...] She couldn't trust us with the truth. [...] We're all prisoners of each other's gossip. [...] It's time you people woke up." The film deliberately reveals just enough hints of bad taste to make its audience yearn for the moments when the town will be disinfected by the sunlight of openness and honesty.

Grace Metalious's Allison, returning to the town from New York when she hears that Selena has killed Lucas and that her agent and lover considers her first novel unpublishable, reflects as "she look[s] down at the toy village that was Peyton Place": "Oh, I love you, she cried silently, I love every part of you. Your beauty and your cruelty, your kindness and ugliness. But now I know you, and you no longer frighten me. Perhaps you will again, tomorrow or the next day, but right now I love you and I am not afraid of you. Today you are just a place."[16] The film ends, not with Allison's acceptance of Peyton Place, warts and all, but with her forgiveness of the mother who hid her paternity from her in a voiceover announcement, leading her to address the audience in one last voiceover: "We'd finally discovered that season of love. It is only found in someone else's heart. Right now, someone you know is looking everywhere for it. And it's in you." Peyton Place's variously titillating sins have been selectively displayed onscreen specifically so that they can be set in a tasteful and visually appealing little town, incarnated by attractive stars, developed at a stately, even stodgy, pace, festooned with top production values and upscale cultural tags (a Sunday morning scene is introduced by a tasteful montage of different churches, firmly establishing the film's non-affiliated pietism, and Allison describes Robert Schumann's Piano Concerto, playing discreetly in the background during her first scene with her mother, as "good breakfast music"), and so completely exorcised by true love and forgiveness that the film was nominated for nine Academy Awards, the most of any 1957 film, though it failed to win a single one.

In her study of *Peyton Place,* Emily Toth notes, "Despite their obvious opposition, the book and movie were both spectacular successes—perhaps because they met different needs. [...] Interested readers [...] could devour the book behind closed doors, in the privacy of their own homes, and enjoy the 'good parts' denied them in films. At the same time, they could see the *Peyton Place* movie publicly, without moral qualms, because the film had an A rating from the National Legion of Decency."[17] Toth points out that the strategy Fox followed in adapting Metalious's censor-baiting novel had been laid down twenty years earlier by the studios' response to the Production Code: "In the Hays Office theory of 'compensating values,' evil could in fact be shown on the screen—as long as vice eventually was punished, and virtue eventually rewarded. The result was inevitable: reel after reel of sin, vice, shame, and decadence, but good characters rewarded in the last reel, and evil ones either punished or, best of all, converted. 'Regeneration' was a Hollywood specialty—especially in films produced by Jerry Wald."[18]

The structure Toth describes—seven reels of spectacular sinning followed by an eighth reel of condign punishment or conversion—had been exploited even before the Code in Cecil B. DeMille's aptly titled *Regeneration* (1922). But if the Hays Office had made this structure a practical necessity for adaptations of risqué novels like *Forever Amber*, it took Jerry Wald, the producer of *Peyton Place*, to raise it to an aesthetic principle. For at the same time *Peyton Place* accepted a position as less than Metalious's novel—less shocking, less explicit, less probing and remorseless in its anatomy of small-town Americana—it also positioned itself as more than the novel—more glamorous, better looking, with more attractive characters leading lives far richer in cultural attainments, a more romantic soundtrack, more intimations of redemption, a happier ending, and more uplift throughout. Although it presented itself as more explicit than the novel, which could only describe what the film could show directly, the studio's determination to secure a Production Code Seal made it altogether less explicit. The film's visuals were sumptuous rather than shocking; even at its most outspoken—in the frank but decorous way its characters discussed sex—it paled beside the novel it adapted. By departing from certain qualities long associated with literary adaptations—fidelity to the source novel and its characters and milieu, serious thematic import, an unblinking eye for cultural contradictions and hypocrisies—Wald could present an adaptation that was more culturally upscale, more high-mindedly literary, than the original, with more cultivated characters who spoke better English, wore better clothes, and indulged in more extended speeches about themselves and their problems, all wrapped up in a deluxe production that placed them on an altogether higher plane than their audience. If Metalious's novel had provided an unsparing anatomy of Peyton Place, Wald's film succeeded in rescuing the characters, their town, and by implication American culture from the potentially baneful critique of American literature—and incidentally from the homogenous gloss of television, whose most enduring view of American domestic life was incarnated in millions of American homes in the homogenizing platitudes of *Father Knows Best* (1954–60).

Wald had already auditioned important parts of this formula in *No Down Payment*, released just two months earlier, which Fox advertised as an adaptation of "John McPartland's Explosive Novel that Tell-Tales on Young Married America!" Reviewers were quick to pick up the implication that Fox was showing them something they never could have seen on television. Writing for the *Los Angeles Times,* Philip K. Scheuer announced, "The simultaneous arrival of a sure best seller and the motion picture made from it is a rarity, but this is what is happening with 'No Down Payment.' John McPartland's scorching novel, bought in original manuscript by 20th's Jerry Wald, will reach local screens this week. It is sure to cause a comparable sensation."[19]

Unlike *Peyton Place,* the film was shot in black-and-white, though it was also presented in expansive CinemaScope. And, as its title suggests, it was set not even in the recent historical past but in the most up-to-the-minute present imaginable, in Sunrise Hills, California, a new housing development that played home to four couples: the Second World War veteran Troy Boone (Cameron Mitchell) and his wife Leola (Joanne Woodward), appliance store owner Herman Kreitzer (Pat Hingle) and his wife Betty (Barbara Rush), used-car salesman Jerry Flagg (Tony Randall) and his wife Isabelle (Sheree North), and a pair of newcomers, engineer David Martin (Jeffrey Hunter) and his wife Jean (Patricia Owens). *No Down Payment* remains novel among American movies for presenting its eight leading characters, at least at first, as being exactly like their target audience, working similar jobs—all four women are housewives—getting together for neighborhood barbecues, and confident of their upward mobility. Soon, however, the film, like McPartland's novel, reveals fault lines that break taboos established by both Sunrise Hills and the Production Code. Leola, who yearns to be a mother, reveals that she gave away Herman's child years ago after he temporarily abandoned her. Iko (Aki Aleong), an employee of Herman's looking to move into Sunrise Hills, is blackballed, and when Herman asks Betty, a devout churchgoer, to talk to Troy and Jerry about welcoming a Japanese-American family into the neighborhood, she replies, "Don't bring the church into it!" Jerry, a problem drinker who spins grandiose dreams of wealth to his wife and comes on to other women, gets called on the carpet after he presses a young couple buying a car into a usurious loan. Herman, who sits on the city council, has to tell Troy that he does not have the educational credentials to become chief of police, further frustrating Leola's dreams of motherhood. After an especially bitter quarrel with Leola, Troy wanders into Jean's house while David is off on business in San Francisco and approaches her menacingly in a close echo of *A Streetcar Named Desire*'s climactic sequence.

Having ripped the lid off the suburban paradise of Sunrise Hills, the film spends its final scenes healing the rifts. David, confronting Troy the morning after his assault, gets soundly beaten for his pains (departing from the novel, in which Troy absorbs David's beating) as Troy spews out his resentment of "college" types, but reassures Jean that "whatever's gonna hit us is gonna hit us together." Herman denounces "whatever it is that makes us afraid" and resignedly tells Betty, "You and I are what the insurance company calls average." He agrees to give Jerry a job in his store, though they both know the position will last only until Jerry gets his next big idea. And Leola, refusing to join Troy's plan to leave Sunrise Hills, accidentally knocks him under the car he is repairing, which providentially falls from its jack and kills him. Having spent ninety minutes attacking the shallow hypocrisy of Sunrise Hills's promise of an unlimited future for American couples that requires no down payment, the film, framing itself as both less and more powerful than literature, spends its final ten minutes regenerating the community by casting out its most hopeless cases (Troy is dead and Leola leaving) and showing the rest of the cast filing down the church sidewalk, presumably so that they can enjoy precisely that future.

Wald's script for adapting provocative best sellers—hint furiously at their most scandalous parts, challenge the Code on language but not on actions or imagery, raise hot-button social taboos that can be healed by the final fadeout, and wrap the whole story in fetishized production values that suggested either high-minded economic aspirations or a moneyed environment that shouted cultural prestige—was so successful that two years after *Peyton Place* he engineered an impressive back-formation for Fox. Instead of purchasing *Peyton Place* after it hit the best-seller lists or *No Down Payment* before it was published, Wald "essentially commissioned" Rona Jaffe to write *The Best of Everything,* a tell-all novel about a New York publishing firm based on Fawcett Books, where Jaffe herself had worked, and purchased the adaptation rights while the novel was still in manuscript.[20] Once Martin Ritt, originally scheduled to direct, withdrew over its casting and was replaced by CinemaScope specialist Jean Negulesco, the shape of the film was set. Negulesco, who had already directed high-profile trios of actresses in *How to Marry a Millionaire* (1953), *Three Coins in the Fountain* (1954), and *Women's World* (1954), could be counted on to emphasize the most spectacular elements of the multi-plot story, filling the widescreen with three-shots of Fabian Publishing stenographers Caroline Bender (Hope Lange), Gregg Adams (Suzy Parker), and April Morrison (Diane Baker), although even after Caroline, a newcomer to New York City, moves in with Gregg and April midway through the film, there are surprisingly few sequences set in the apartment they share. Instead, the film takes their office in the newly completed Seagram Building as its center, surrounding it with low-angle shots of modernist Manhattan buildings, several of them iconic skyscrapers, in an urban echo of *Peyton Place*'s bucolic New England exteriors (see Figure 6.6).

This echo was anything but accidental, for Fox did everything it could to align the film with *Peyton Place*. The opening scroll of its trailer announces: "In the outspoken tradition of 'Peyton Place,' Twentieth Century Fox brings another a great new best-seller to the screen .... It undresses the ambitions and emotions of the girls who invade the glamour world of the big city, seeking success, love, marriage, and the best of everything ... and who often settle for much less!" A female voiceover in the trailer confides: "This is the story of the female of the jungle—of the women who didn't marry at twenty—and of the men who wanted them—but not as wives." A closing

FIGURE 6.6 The Best of Everything *(1959) repeatedly frames newcomer Caroline Bender (Hope Lange) against the Seagram Building, her true home in New York.*

scroll describes the film as "The great best-selling story of … the girls who would do anything to get … The Best of Everything."

After this overheated come-on, the film itself is as decorously well mounted as *Peyton Place*. Its daring is confined mostly to language—for instance, the use of the words "pregnant" and "mistress," both of which are heard in the trailer—and irregular liaisons that are kept tastefully offscreen. As in *How to Marry a Millionaire* and *Three Coins in the Fountain*, its heroines follow schematically divergent paths. Demure Caroline fights off wolves, her caddish ex-fiancé, and the kind of careerism personified by her boss Amanda Farrow (Joan Crawford, taking her first supporting role in years to blaze a trail for Meryl Streep in *The Devil Wears Prada* [2006]) to find true love in the final two shots with her patient coworker Mike Rice (Stephen Boyd). After falling too hard for playwright David Savage (Louis Jourdain), hot-blooded Gregg dies in a flustered fall from the fire escape outside his corridor, where she has been lurking and pining.

Calculating April, successfully resisting predatory Fabian publisher Fred Shalimar (Brian Ahearne) but pregnant by smooth-talking Dexter Key (Robert Evans), leaps from Dexter's car en route to the doctor whom he has clearly arranged to perform an abortion and conveniently loses the unborn child she calls "her," but eventually finds love with Dr. Ronnie Wood (Ted Otis). And a fourth colleague, Barbara Lamont (Martha Hyer), rejects the married lover who wants to return to her but ends up with nobody. The film's plot, its visual design, and some of its characters turn up variously inflected half a century later in *Mad Men* (2007–15), whose creator Matthew Weiner acknowledged it as one of his series' primary inspirations, with the obvious difference that the film makes every attempt to resolve the unsavory complications that *Mad Men*, a stellar example of long-form television for a later generation, just keeps on complicating.

A certain kind of story

Since no elements of Wald's formula depended on resources specific to Fox, it could readily be copied by other studios. Four years after *Peyton Place*, United Artists released *By Love Possessed*, based on James Gould Cozzens's best-selling novel. Universal, which had already enjoyed a decade-long association with Douglas Sirk, produced remakes of the chestnuts *Back Street* (1932, 1941, and 1961) and *Madame X* (1910, 1916, 1929, 1937, and 1966) that were notably racier than their predecessors, and MGM released Stanley Kubrick's 1962 adaptation of *Lolita* before the circle closed in 1967 with *Valley of the Dolls*, which has some claim to be the ultimate example of the subgenre, the literary adaptation whose paratexts—publicity, trailers, reviews—promised explicit attacks on the representational limitations that hobbled novels and the taboos too hot for television, even as their texts provided ponderously literary adaptations that were, apart from a few inflammatory words of dialogue unfailingly cherry-picked for their trailers, largely decorous, well-mounted, elaborately expository stories peopled by characters who talked earnestly and often passionately about things other characters were doing, or things they would like to do themselves once they were offscreen.

Inevitably, these films' repeated tangos with the Production Code, which they continued to challenge ever more boldly even as they solicited its approval, made them increasingly explicit in deploying the credentials of the risqué best seller. The single most striking implication of this development for the history of American adaptation is its disdain for, and in some cases, its reversal of, traditional canons of literary quality. Rock Hudson's starring roles in adaptations as diverse as George Stevens's *Giant* (1956), Richard Brooks's *Something of Value* (1957), and Charles Vidor's *A Farewell to Arms* (1957) included star turns in Sirk's increasingly fevered, self-deconstructing melodramas *Magnificent Obsession* (1954), *All That Heaven Allows* (1955), *Written on the Wind* (1956), and *The Tarnished Angels* (1958). But Hudson felt the need, according to veteran *New Yorker* reviewer Pauline Kael, to apologize for this last film, which he said "was not like his others—that he disapproved of it, and that such nasty stories shouldn't be presented to the American public." As Kael noted, "The nasty material is William Faulkner's *Pylon*,"[21] a lesser 1935 work about daredevil stunt fliers by the greatest living American novelist, whose canonical stature was insufficient to protect the story from a charge the star did not choose to level against the novels of Ernest Hemingway, Robert C. Ruark, Edna Ferber, Robert Wilder, or Lloyd C. Douglas.

One way to chart the development of Hollywood's latest take on American literature is to consider four adaptations of John O'Hara novels, Philip Dunne's *Ten North Frederick* (1958), Mark Robson's *From the Terrace* (1960), Daniel Mann's *BUtterfield 8* (1960), and Walter

Grauman's *A Rage to Live* (1965). *Ten North Frederick,* which revolved around the discovery by Ann Chapin (Diane Varsi) that the unhappy last years of her alcoholic father Joe (Gary Cooper) were eased by his forbidden romance with Ann's friend Kate Drummond (Suzy Parker), was unfailingly decorous but not particularly opulent; its troubles with the censors focused on the question of whether it condoned the affair. When producer Charles Brackett wrote to John O'Hara, "At present we're hassling with the censors. It seems you glorify adultery. I've just finished producing THE WAYWARD BUS. It also glorifies adultery. Here at Twentieth we have a motto: Adultery is a Many Splendored Thing,"[22] O'Hara replied, "No careful reader of my novel can say adultery is glorified in it, if he considers that as a result of a romance in which both principals are kept apart by conventions, the male member gives up on life and proceeds to drink himself out of it."[23] The imagery and soundtrack of *From the Terrace,* in which the adulterous but pure love of David Eaton (Paul Newman) for Natalie Benziger (Ina Balin) provides a spiritual refuge and an eventual escape from the loveless marriage he has chosen to advance his career, are far more resplendent than those of *Ten North Frederick,* just as the adaptation of *From the Terrace* is far less censorious about David's affairs and more selectively uplifting.

Although MGM released *BUtterfield 8* the same year as *From the Terrace,* it departs from Wald's formula in obvious ways. Its setting is updated from 1935 to the present; it is much less interested in exploring class distinctions; its milieu looks much less posh; the language by and about its heroine, Gloria Wandrous, is considerably franker; Bronislau Kaper's austere score is less lush or even melodic; and as Gloria, a disaffected call girl the film changes into a model who just happens to have a lot of casual sex, Elizabeth Taylor—presumably inspired by her well-publicized resistance to making the film after the studio failed to honor the handshake deal freeing her from her contract it had made with her late husband, Michael Todd—gives a what-the-hell performance that plumbs raw depths of despair and self-loathing Wald's films had shied away from. The MGM publicity department struggled to find the right advertising campaign for the story. James Raker wrote to Eddie Lawrence in a 1960 memo: "APPROACH: We are in a little bit of trouble here. We can't come right out and make the story line clear—it not only sounds too sordid, but we'd never get away with it. Any euphemisms we employed would probably be equally offensive." Raker's suggestion, which would have warmed the heart of Jerry Wald, was to push the envelope while emphasizing the film's literary roots: "Instead of just JOHN O'HARA'S Butterfield 8 it could be JOHN O'HARA'S/FRANK AND SHOCKING NOVEL/Butterfield 8. […] We have a sensational kind of subject matter here and we must somehow get this across to the patron. Unfortunately the last few O'Hara books that have been filmed have made no great shakes as pictures, but still his name is linked with a certain kind of story and should be prominent in the ads."[24]

By the time United Artists released *A Rage to Live* in 1965, the production values had been dialed down still further. The film, shot in widescreen but in black and white, runs only 101 minutes, and its cast members, from Suzanne Pleshette on down, are largely drawn from the ranks of television performers. By now the heroine Grace Caldwell's nymphomania, though never identified as such, could be portrayed in far more clinical terms, from the opening scene in which Charlie Jay (Mark Goddard), a friend of her brother Brock (Linden Chiles), watches the shadow of the schoolgirl undressing, then rapes her (see Figure 6.7)—responding to her protest, "I hate you," by assuring her, "you don't hate this"—to her confession to Brock, "When I feel that way, I can't think of anything else," to other characters' frequent descriptions of her as a "slut," to her climactic showdown with the furiously jealous wife of one of the few men whose advances she has actually refused. Even so, the film closed with an incongruous reminder of its literary roots, quoting the lines O'Hara had taken from Alexander Pope's "Epistle to a Lady" for his title, though without identifying their source.

The later stages of Hollywood's strategy for weaponizing adaptations are best revealed by adaptations of Harold Robbins. Although Robbins's best-selling novels had provided the basis for both the period crime drama *Never Love a Stranger* and the Elvis Presley vehicle *King Creole* in 1958, Paramount chose his most successful novel, *The Carpetbaggers* (1961), for his most distinctive, lucrative, and influential film adaptation. Both the film and the novel, based loosely on the life and career of Howard Hughes,

FIGURE 6.7 *Transfixed by the shadow of Grace Caldwell (Suzanne Pleshette) as she undresses, Charlie Jay (Mark Goddard) will soon force himself on her in* A Rage to Live *(1965).*

follow Jonas Cord (George Peppard) as he moves from heading the gas works his father founded to becoming a power in the field of commercial aviation and finally a Hollywood producer and sometime director. Jonas systematically defines himself as a workaholic whose personal relationships with friends, lovers, and wives must always be subordinated to his career. Even so, the film's most widely remarked scenes invariably involve sex or nudity rather than Jonas Cord's work life.

The Carpetbaggers retains many characteristics of the risqué best-seller adaptation. Shot in Panavision and Technicolor, it boasts a period setting, a star-filled cast, a long running time, a full-throated musical score by Elmer Bernstein, and an opulent series of costumes and interiors especially remarkable given the hero's self-avowed fondness for hotel rooms. Like *The Best of Everything* and *From the Terrace*, the film systematically opposes work to domestic life; like *Peyton Place* and *A Rage to Live*, it sets sex against true love, with sensuous women marking the conflict by their unwilling surrender to the former despite their dreams of the latter.

More schematically even than *No Down Payment* or *BUtterfield 8*, the film shows a series of glamorous, beautiful characters behaving as badly as the battered Production Code allowed. Now, however, there is no longer any veneer of high-cultural aspiration or social respectability, simply a thick overlay of wealth and its trappings. The film's most important departure from *Peyton Place* and its ilk is in its lack of interest in packaging its story in literary, or even quasi-literary, terms. Although there is no onscreen coupling, the many double-entendres in the dialogue are unusually single-minded (the most famous: when Jonas asks his bride-to-be Monica Winthrop [Elizabeth Ashley] what she'd like to see on their honeymoon, she says, "Lots of lovely ceilings"). The film consistently aims for sexual shocks, even when it later qualifies them. The audience does not learn that Rina Marlowe Cord (Carroll Baker), the widow of Jonas Cord, Sr. (Leif Erickson), is Jonas's own ex-girlfriend until after he has invaded her bathroom and groped her offscreen shortly after his father's death. The next time Rina appears, she lifts her arms wide to reveal the black-trimmed merry widow under her negligee and asks Jonas, "How do you like my widow's weeds?" Arriving at the office of a film studio he's just purchased, Jonas announces, "If you want to work for me, stop looking like small-town librarians. Higher heels, shorter skirts," and the film does its best to make all its females look consistently alluring and Rina consistently whorish, whether or not she is doing a striptease astride a Paris chandelier (see Figure 6.8). Unlike the flaws of the characters in *No Down Payment*, *Peyton Place*, or *By Love Possessed*, Jonas's cold-blooded opportunism, which gives the story its name, does not gradually emerge from beneath a normal-seeming exterior; it is made explicit in his reaction to his father's sudden death as early as the second scene. Instead of pretending to link his problems to an American subculture it is probing, the film provides an elaborately Freudian explanation for his hatred of his

FIGURE 6.8 *Trading in cultural cachet for materialistic excess: the chandelier striptease of Rina Marlowe Cord (Carroll Baker) in* The Carpetbaggers *(1961)*.

father and his calamitous over-investment in his work. The film's relation to the novel it adapted, and to literary ideals in general, is best summarized by a remark *Newsweek* used to open its review of the film: "The book," said Joseph E. Levine, producer of *The Carpetbaggers*, "was filth. Filth and dirt. We don't have any of that in the picture, but the wonderful thing about the film is that you have the feeling you're reading the book."[25]

Conveying the experience of wallowing in filth while maintaining the protocols of the Production Code might seem a far cry from literary culture. But the next logical step in the weaponization of naughty best sellers was to adapt classics of American literature as if they were risqué best sellers. Here again Jerry Wald was preeminent, toning down the sexual irregularities in William Faulkner's novels for the adaptations of *The Hamlet* (*The Long, Hot Summer*, 1958) and *The Sound and the Fury* (1959) Martin Ritt directed for Fox, replacing the incestuous or bestial liaisons that initially raised Geoffrey Shurlock's eyebrows with merely suggestive relationships, allowing both stories to end with the promise of happiness and romantic fulfillment, and so paving the way for two further Fox adaptations, *Sanctuary* (1961) and *Tender Is the Night* (1962), that took remarkably similar approaches to Faulkner and Fitzgerald, at once juicing their material in the name of titillation and sanitizing it in the name of uplift. Walter Metz describes *The Sound and the Fury* as "a deconstructive adaptation" that "refuses both [the novel's] stylistically aggressive technique and its misogynist content."[26] It would be equally accurate to call Ritt's film a reconstructive adaptation that valorized a hypothetical ostensive narrative beneath Faulkner's fractured dramatization of the decline of the Compson family through the interior narratives the absent Caddy Compson provokes in her three brothers and a fourth section that shows her daughter reenacting her own version of her mother's break with the family. Ritt's adaptation manages to be both more progressive than Faulkner in its gender politics and more conservative in its representational strategies. It is both less and more literary than the novel it identifies as its source.

The publicity for these films emphasizes the name recognition rather than the cultural prestige of the novels and novelists they adapt and the literary aura of the adaptations rather than their fidelity, since marketing them as just as explicit as the novels consistently implies that they are even more explicit. The films are linked to each other as a subgenre and to a very particular idea of American literature by several other quasi-literary scripts. In addition to sharing the high production values associated with A-list productions, they are marked by a veneer of culture represented by the leading characters and their worlds: the anachronistically cultivated voices of Laurence Harvey in *BUtterfield 8* and Efrem Zimbalist, Jr. in *By Love Possessed*; the considerable wealth that insulates most of the characters from moneygrubbing; the aspirations of both the historical frameworks of *Peyton Place* and *Ten North Frederick* and the contemporary settings of *No Down Payment* and *The Best of Everything* to provide a sociological analysis of an American subculture; the cultural cachet signaled, for instance, by the horseback riding of *By Love Possessed* and the statuary behind the opening credits of *From the Terrace* (see Figure 6.9)—a motif picked up by *Where Love Has Gone*, generally the most lurid of all these films, which makes Valerie Hayden Miller (Susan Hayward) a sculptor who stabs herself to death with one of her chisels after she is forced to confront the sensational

FIGURE 6.9 *The classical sculpture behind the main title of* From the Terrace *(1960) assures the audience drawn by the promise of a scandalous adaptation that they will also enjoy some cultural uplift.*

truth about the alleged murder of her latest lover by her daughter Danny (Joey Heatherton), a framing episode clearly based on the fatal stabbing of Lana Turner's real-life gangster lover Johnny Stompanato by her daughter Cheryl Crane. The worlds of these films, in fact, so clearly represent or aspire to the trappings of high culture that the characters' florid peccadilloes become all the more striking by contrast in their violations of this culture's implicit norms. Since the world they inhabit feels considerably more literary than the soap-opera plots their films inflict on them, it is not surprising that when individual characters like Troy Boone or Gloria Wandrous are chastened or destroyed, their world is left intact, even, or especially, when they reject it, as they do in *Ten North Frederick, From the Terrace,* and *BUtterfield 8*.

Unlike contemporaneous television families who can seamlessly integrate their work lives with their domestic lives, the characters in these films, whether or not they have the family obligations so many television characters take for granted, are frequently confronted by situations that set work against love. *The Man in the Gray Flannel Suit, From the Terrace,* and *Imitation of Life* all revolve around such conflicts, and all of them share the promise that the true love that offers the only hope of rescuing John O'Hara's fallen heroines from their sins is more powerful than the allure of either sinful seduction or professional fulfillment. The multi-plot structure of *The Best of Everything, By Love Possessed,* and *Valley of the Dolls* allows these films, like *Hamlet* and *King Lear*, to explore divergent implications of parallel problems, suggesting that although life may be complicated for the group as a whole, the solution for any given character or couple is simple.

These contra-television adaptations establish their literary credentials by fetishizing carefully chosen scripts derived from the novels they adapt—their fame, their suggestiveness, their period settings and fashions—while rejecting scripts derived from those novels' style, texture, or themes. The films pose paratextually not as faithful transcriptions of their source novels but as improvements over the novels, which can only talk about the racy scenes the films will actually show. Yet the films end up showing precious little of this forbidden material; thanks to the Production Code and their own internalized aesthetics, they pose textually as portals to a deliciously forbidden world to which their source novels end up providing the key. Positioning themselves in between their two powerful competitors, the steamy novels they adapt and the bland programming found on television, they are less interested in evoking those specific novels, as an earlier generation of Hollywood adaptations like *The Postman Always Rings Twice* and *Forever Amber* had done by presenting images of books in their opening credits, than in evoking a more generalized image of American literature: a self-contained fantasyland, ostensive rather than literary, in which characters either live or strive for lifestyles marked by the kind of conspicuous consumption that shields them from all but the most baroque and taboo-busting complications—an image that smacks less of Edith Wharton than of Henry James.

Hollywood gradually pulled out of the economic tailspin to which television had seemed to condemn it. The 1960s saw the death of the long-term contracts that bound stars to particular studios, a fundamental change in the ways movies were financed, with the studios now appearing less like major-league baseball teams than like captains in an endless series of pickup ball games, the replacement of the Production Code with the ratings system, a new cultivation of the youth audience that eventually became Hollywood's core audience, and the beginning of the studios' rapprochement with television, to which they sold their libraries of old features and for whom they made new ones beginning in 1964. The strategy of weaponizing best sellers by trashing some of their literary associations while fetishizing others ended up playing a relatively minor role in the industry's economic history, but a much more important role in the history of Hollywood adaptation because of the enduring questions these films raise about what it means to be a literary adaptation and, by implication, what it means to be literature.

Notes

1 Scott Eyman, *Print the Legend: The Life and Times of John Ford* (New York: Simon and Schuster, 1999), p. 384.
2 Michael Ciment, "Two Encounters with John Huston," in *John Huston Interviews*, ed. Robert Emmet Long (Jackson: University Press of Mississippi, 2001), p. 143.
3 Virginia Wright Wexman, *A History of Film*, 7th ed. (Boston: Allyn & Bacon, 2010), p. 150.
4 See Leonard J. Leff and Jerold L. Simmons, *The Dame in the Kimono: Hollywood, Censorship, and the Production Code*, rev. ed. (Lexington: University Press of Kentucky, 2001), and Thomas Doherty, *Hollywood's Censor: Joseph I. Breen and the Production Code Administration* (New York: Columbia University Press, 2007).
5 Doherty, *Hollywood's Censor*, p. 313.
6 Darryl F. Zanuck, Memo to Julian Johnson, David Brown, and Joseph Moskowitz, July 5, 1952, Henry King papers, Folder 8.f-138, Margaret Herrick Library, Academy of Motion Pictures Arts and Sciences.
7 Darryl F. Zanuck, Memo to Henry King, May 7, 1953, Henry King papers, Folder 8.f-138, Margaret Herrick Library, Academy of Motion Pictures Arts and Sciences.
8 Leff and Simmons, *The Dame in the Kimono*, p. 211.
9 Doherty, *Hollywood's Censor*, p. 324.

10 Walter Benjamin, "The Work of Art in the Age of Mechanical Reproduction," in Benjamin, *Illuminations*, ed. Hannah Arendt, trans. Harry Zohn (1968; rpt. New York: Schocken, 1969), p. 221.
11 Neil Miller, *Banned in Boston: The Watch and Ward Society's Crusade against Books, Burlesque, and the Social Evil* (Boston, MA: Beacon, 2010), p. 169.
12 Joseph I. Breen, letter to Jason Joy, October 4, 1944, *Forever Amber*, Production Code Administration files, Margaret Herrick Library, Academy of Motion Picture Arts and Sciences; quoted in Gregory D. Black, *The Catholic Crusade against the Movies, 1940–75* (New York: Cambridge University Press, 1997), p. 56.
13 Grace Metalious, *Peyton Place* (1956; rpt. Boston, MA: Northeastern University Press, 1999), p. 124.
14 Bosley Crowther, "The Screen: Drama in 'Peyton Place,'" *New York Times*, December 13, 1957, p. 35.
15 "Best Seller on Film," *Newsweek*, December 23, 1957, p. 76.
16 Metalious, *Peyton Place*, p. 371.
17 Emily Toth, *Inside Peyton Place: The Life of Grace Metalious* (Garden City: Doubleday, 1981), p. 195.
18 Toth, *Inside Peyton Place*, p. 189.
19 Philip K. Scheuer, "'No Down Payment' Certain to Cause a Sensation/'No Down Payment' Filled with Disturbing Drama," *Los Angeles Times*, October 6, 1957, p. E1.
20 Mitchell Owens, "Rona Jaffe—Popular Novelist," *New York Times*, January 1, 2006, SFGate, http://sfgate.com/cgi-bin/article.cgi?file=/c/a/2006/01/01/BAGDCGG18V1.DTL.
21 Pauline Kael, *5001 Nights at the Movies* (New York: Holt, Rinehart and Winston, 1982), p. 743.
22 Charles Brackett, Letter to John O'Hara, March 11, 1957, Charles Brackett papers, Folder 5.f-[53], Margaret Herrick Library, Academy of Motion Picture Arts and Sciences.
23 John O'Hara, Letter to Charles Brackett, March 13, 1957. Charles Brackett papers, Folder 5.f-[53], Margaret Herrick Library, Academy of Motion Picture Arts and Sciences.
24 James Raker, Memo to Eddie Lawrence, MGM. James Raker papers, Folder 1.f-64, Margaret Herrick Library, Academy of Motion Picture Arts and Sciences.
25 "Robbins'-Egg Blue," *Newsweek*, July 6, 1964, p. 76.
26 Walter Metz, "'Signifying Nothing?': Martin Ritt's *The Sound and the Fury* (1959) as Deconstructive Adaptation," *Literature/Film Quarterly* 27.1 (1999): 22.

7

1967–75: Counterculture Classics

The old guard and the new

Like 1915, 1927, and 1939, 1967 marked a pivotal year in Hollywood history whose particular valence is indicated by the five films released that year that were nominated for the Academy Award for Best Picture: *Bonnie and Clyde*, *Doctor Doolittle*, *The Graduate*, *Guess Who's Coming to Dinner*, and *In the Heat of the Night*. Dismissing the notion that these five films presented "a collective statement—a five-snapshot collage of the American psyche as reflected in its popular culture," Mark Harris, writing forty years later, concluded that "all that was illuminated by the list of contenders was the movie industry's anxiety and bewilderment at a paroxysmal point in its own history."[1] At this crucial moment,

> the question of who was going to win had taken on more urgency than usual. Not who was going to win the Oscars, which would shortly be decided by the usual blend of caprice and conviction, but who was going to win ownership of the whole enterprise of contemporary moviemaking. The Best Picture lineup was more than diverse; it was almost self-contradictory. Half of the nominees seemed to be sneering at the other half: The father-knows-best values of *Guess Who's Coming to Dinner* were wittily trashed by *The Graduate*; the hands-joined-in-brotherhood hopes expressed by *In the Heat of the Night* had little in common with the middle finger of insurrection extended by *Bonnie and Clyde* [see Figure 7.1].
>
> What was an American film supposed to be? The men running the movie business used to have the answer; now, it had slipped just beyond their reach, and they couldn't understand how they had lost sight of it.[2]

FIGURE 7.1 *The drama of the uneasy professional alliance between visiting Detective Virgil Tibbs (Sidney Poitier) and Sparta, Mississippi police chief Gillespie (Rod Steiger) propelled* In the Heat of the Night *(1967) past its Oscar competitors* Bonnie and Clyde *and* The Graduate.

Doctor Doolittle, Harris argues, was a dinosaur, an overproduced, intermittently entertaining musical whose moment had long since passed. The old guard in American popular entertainment is better represented by Neil Simon, the most successful playwright of his generation. If Eugene O'Neill and Tennessee Williams had sought to plumb the depths of the American psyche, Simon mined "the frictions of urban living and the agonizing conflicts of family intimacy"[3] for laughs in a torrent of Broadway comedies—at one point in 1966, *Barefoot in the Park* (1963), *The Odd Couple* (1965), *Sweet Charity* (1966), and *The Star-Spangled Girl* (1966) were all running at once—most of which achieved further success in film adaptations, many of them also written by Simon: *Barefoot in the Park* (1967), *The Odd Couple* (1968), *Sweet Charity* (1969), *Plaza Suite* (1971), *Last of the Red Hot Lovers* (1972), *The Prisoner of Second Avenue* (1975), *The Sunshine Boys* (1975), *California Suite* (1978), and *Chapter Two* (1979). In between, Simon, following earlier playwrights from Owen Davis and Maxwell Anderson to Clifford Odets and Robert E. Sherwood, wrote original screenplays for *The Out-of-Towners* (1970), *The Heartbreak Kid* (1972), *Murder by Death* (1976), *The Goodbye Girl* (1977), and *The Cheap Detective* (1978). When the fashion for Simon's brand of sitcom writing passed largely from Broadway to television, he gradually deepened his explorations of neurotic characters in a series of dramedies beginning with *The Gingerbread Lady* (1970) and autobiographical plays beginning with *Brighton Beach Memoirs* (1983, filmed 1986). Hollywood's diminished interested in this later material reflects the ways in which Simon, who continued to work into the twenty-first century, "didn't know he was standing directly over a fault in American culture, one that even as he hit his stride started gapping and would eventually pull him down" because "independent films were diversifying their outlook and shaking off the formulas of Hollywood storytelling."[4]

"Diversifying" only hints at the tumultuous changes in American culture during the years of Simon's early success. Student protestors clashed with police forces across the country, peaceniks with anti-Communists, advocates of free love and drug use with authority figures of every stripe. The popular music beloved of a mass youth audience, always implicitly in competition with the classical music associated with their elders, effectively dethroned its competitor as a culture largely created by and for young people became the dominant culture in America, Britain, and France. Successive generations may have been in conflict as far back as *Romeo and Juliet*, and Hollywood may have codified these conflicts in romantic comedies like *It Happened One Night*, but the youth culture of the 1960s sharpened and broadened these relatively self-contained conflicts to a no-holds-barred, winner-take-all war in which New Left activist Jack Weinberg could say of the Free Speech movement: "You can't trust anyone over thirty."[5] As a result, literary canons began to inch toward more immediate political and social relevance, influenced for perhaps the first time in American history by the opinions and preferences of the very people who had previously been invited only to consume them.

The film industry was undergoing its own sweeping changes. The declining power of the Shurlock Office throughout the 1950s and 1960s had led to the loosening of the Production Code and emboldened the studios to release more films without the office's Seal of Approval, still confident that they could find a large enough audience to turn a profit. In 1968 the Code was formally retired and replaced by a voluntary ratings system that labeled films submitted to the Motion Picture Association of America G (general audiences), M (mature audiences), R (restricted audiences, allowing patrons under 16 only if they were accompanied by adults), or X (limited to audiences over 16). The ratings system would be tweaked several times in the coming years. The ages for admission to R- and X-rated films were raised from 16 to 17 in 1970; the M rating was replaced by GP in 1970 and then PG (parental guidance suggested) in 1972; a fifth category, PG-13 (recommended for audiences over 13), was added, largely in response to *Indiana Jones and the Temple of Doom*, which had originally been rated PG, in 1984; and the X rating was changed to NC-17 (no children under 17 admitted) in 1990 to avoid the confusion of studio-produced films like *Henry and June* with pornographic features whose producers eagerly embraced the rating. But these changes were relatively modest in their impact; it was the initial break with the Production Code that proved decisive. From this point forward, films could be made and marketed for specific audiences instead of having to pass muster for grandparents, parents, and children, sophisticates and bluenoses alike, before they could be approved.

The rejection of an industrywide self-censoring board in favor of a voluntary ratings system corresponded with several other crucial developments in Hollywood history. The most obvious of these was the slow-motion collapse of the studio system in the wake of the 1948 Supreme Court decision against Paramount for monopolistic practices stemming from its control of every stage of filmmaking: production, distribution, and exhibition. The Paramount decree "directed the eight Hollywood firms to end block booking and other practices which hampered independent exhibitors" and "ordered the Majors to divest themselves of their theater chains."[6] But the industry's crisis ran even deeper. As David A. Cook observes: "The old studio production system remained in place throughout the 1950s, but continued to crumble under the combined threats of political pressure, television, rising independent production, and, perhaps most serious, loss of the exhibition chains."[7] At the same time they became financially more vulnerable, the studios felt more dramatic intimations of mortality. By the time incoming Motion Picture Association of America (MPAA) president Jack Valenti condemned the Code in 1966, virtually all the first generation of Hollywood moguls had retired or died. Universal chief Carl Laemmle was the first to die in 1939. Louis B. Mayer, who had made MGM the most consistently profitable studio, was forced out in 1951 and died six years later. Harry Cohn, the head of Columbia, suffered a fatal heart attack in 1958. David O. Selznick, whose last film, *A Farewell to Arms*, was released in 1957, died in 1965. Samuel Goldwyn, who had been cut out of MGM, the studio whose middle initial he had contributed, as far back as 1922, retired as an independent producer in 1959, fifteen years before his death. Paramount head Adolph Zukor retired in 1959, though he would live until 1976, dying at the age of 103. After outmaneuvering his brothers for control of Warner Bros. in 1957, Jack L. Warner retired in 1973 and died in 1978. Darryl F. Zanuck, who had retired as head of Twentieth Century Fox but returned to take control of the studio after the success of *The Longest Day* in 1962, presided over a series of financially disastrous productions from *Cleopatra* (1963) to *Doctor Doolittle* (1967) before he was forced out of the company for good in 1971, eight years before his death.

This wave of deaths and retirements created a power vacuum in which, as the screenwriter William Goldman imperishably put it at the time, "NOBODY KNOWS ANYTHING."[8] The single most influential film of the period, *Easy Rider* (1969), a road movie based on an original screenplay credited to Terry Southern and its two stars, Peter Fonda and Dennis Hopper, produced by Fonda, and directed by Hopper, represents forces Hollywood studios had been repressing for years: sympathetic portrayals of a pair of motorcycle riders and a hippie commune, contempt for the law and kindred authorities, an extended sequence in a New Orleans brothel, and a matter-of-fact acceptance of the drug culture as both a gateway to higher consciousness and a profit center. The target audience for the film was clearly young people, a demographic whose importance had been identified, as Douglas Gomery points out, as early as 1947 and crystallized by its sympathetic response to movies like *The Blackboard Jungle* (1955) and *Rebel without a Cause* (1955) that presented themselves as "adult films examining juvenile delinquency problems."[9] The runaway success of *Bonnie and Clyde* and *The Graduate* among young people in 1967 persuaded any holdouts in the industry that teenagers, especially dating couples, were more than happy to seize the opportunity to enjoy entertainment outside the homes of their watchful parents and had the disposable income to pay for the privilege. The result was a new era in filmmaking in which Hollywood, having lost the guidance of first-generation studio heads who had been remarkably successful in predicting the success of filmmaking projects largely on the basis of their own personal tastes, struggled to attract a new audience.

The wooing of a hitherto ignored youth market whose economic power was revealed by the response to *Bonnie and Clyde* and *The Graduate* established a pattern for Hollywood's quest to identify and exploit other niche cultures and markets: "Rather than attempting to make all of the films for all of the people, producers and exhibitors realized they must appeal to very special tastes."[10] When the studios went looking for the forces that united the youth market after the success of these two films, what they discovered was the counterculture—a term coined by Theodore Roszak to describe "a cultural constellation that radically diverges from values and assumptions that have been in the mainstream of our society since at least the Scientific Revolution of the seventeenth century"[11]—whose treatment by the movies set the terms and the agenda for all the others.

As its name suggests, the counterculture combines several negative tropisms—against the Vietnam War, against the civil authority represented by the government and the police, against traditional religion and traditions generally associated with an older generation, against what it labeled the Establishment—with some equally positive, though less often noted, tropisms. The counterculture's frequent calls for political change expressed not only anti-Establishment defiance, but a call to social bonding among like-minded participants, especially on college campuses. A vital feature of the counterculture was a ubiquitous soundtrack of pop songs supplied by rockers like the Beatles and the Rolling Stones and protest folk singers like Woody Guthrie, Pete Seeger, Joan Baez, and Bob Dylan—

all marked by an ever-closer community between songwriters, performers, and listeners. Although the counterculture embraced the causes of civil rights and second-wave feminism, it was perhaps best known for several tropisms its elders considered negative but its participants positive: the bohemian or hedonistic embrace of recreational drugs, especially marijuana and psychedelics like LSD, the sexual license enabled by the widespread availability for the first time in human history of methods of birth control nearly as reliable as abstinence, and its calls for political, social, and economic revolution.

The worldwide resurgence of political liberalism during this period suggested a swinging pendulum bound to return eventually to a more conservative position. But this particular counterculture was fueled by several distinctive features that earned its designation as *the* counterculture, distinguishing it from both the majoritarian official culture of its time and the many countercultural movements that preceded and followed it. The explosive growth in the number of American births following the Second World War produced a record number of baby boomers available to participate in the counterculture. The assassinations of John and Robert Kennedy, Malcolm X, and Martin Luther King, the 1968 Russian crackdown on Czechoslovakia's Prague Spring, a series of inner-city riots in Watts, Detroit, and Newark, and the large-scale protests against the Democratic National Convention in Chicago and on college campuses from coast to coast were only the most traumatic signs of a moment charged with unusually rapid social and political change. Ironically, the more radical demands of the counterculture on mainstream culture in the period bookended by the Summer of Love and the Watergate hearings and punctuated throughout by protests against the Vietnam War were largely effaced by the dominant culture's remarkably quick embrace of many elements of the counterculture that went mainstream, from music and clothing to sexual freedom and the widespread use of recreational drugs. This embrace, which marked both the failure of the counterculture as a distinctive subculture and its success at infiltrating and changing the course of majoritarian culture, made its twilight almost as distinctive as its rise.

The counterculture and the culture

Looking more deeply into this generally accepted account of the counterculture reveals foundational conflicts at the heart of both the counterculture and the official culture it defines itself against. The United States has always been marked by cultures that have positioned themselves as oppositional or insurgent. The English colonies contended both with French, Spanish, and Dutch colonies and, more enduringly, with Native

American inhabitants of the lands they claimed. Once the states had declared their independence from England and banded together under the Constitution, a new fissure opened between the industrial North and the agrarian South. The conflict between an increasingly urban, individualistic, liberal culture with both eyes on the future and an enduringly rural, communal, conservative culture that took its values from its past history was sharpened by the issue of slavery—that "peculiar institution," as South Carolina senator John C. Calhoun called it[12]—that was both the lifeblood of Southern plantation economies and anathema to Northern abolitionists. Even before the Emancipation Proclamation and the War Between the States ended slavery without resolving the conflicts between North and South, a new competitive dynamic emerged between East and West. An established, continuous Eastern culture seeking to sustain itself by drawing on English and European cultural traditions was increasingly challenged by Huckleberry Finn's call to "light out for the Territory,"[13] rejecting this suffocating culture to live on a frontier that amounted to a fragmented, developing culture specifically marked by its competition with effete Easterners and its more overtly physical battles with the Native American cultures it sought to uproot, supplant, and destroy. Philip Rahv's 1939 essay "Paleface and Redskin" read this last conflict into American literature, opposing "patrician" palefaces like Nathaniel Hawthorne and Henry James, whose fiction anatomized Eastern culture, to "plebian" redskins like Walt Whitman and Mark Twain, whose work celebrated an American identity palefaces found "a source of endless ambiguities."[14] Rahv's essay portrays a radically bifurcated American literary culture split at its very foundation, an uneasy marriage of convenience between paleface and redskin.

Before the rise of the counterculture, Hollywood had never taken the measure of the cultural contradictions implicit in American literature. Consciously or not, however, it had often examined broader contradictions in American culture—in particular, conflicts between high-cultural institutions that were assumed to set the national tone and low-cultural habits that many Americans privately embraced while publicly deploring. A particularly striking prefiguration of Hollywood's presentation of hippies and their rejection of the Protestant work ethic in favor of recreational drugs and free love is the industry's portrayal a generation earlier of the professional gangsters whose gangs were financed by the illegal distribution of alcohol. The Eighteenth Amendment, which criminalized the sale of alcoholic beverages in 1920, fueled the rise of gangsters like Al Capone at the same time it forced otherwise law-abiding citizens who wanted a drink to break the law themselves. Prohibition's culture of disavowal, which was instrumental in intensifying calls for an enforcement of the 1930 Production Code, emerged in a different way in films like *Easy Rider*, which treated Wyatt (Peter Fonda) and Billy (Dennis Hopper) as latter-day American exotics. Wyatt and Billy's cross-country tour invited audiences on their own round of cultural tourism, looking in from the outside on a forbidden subculture Hollywood assured them only the movies could reveal.

Not only has the culture of the United States been riven by cultural conflicts since the days before the states united; in some ways, American culture has always set itself as a counterculture to the more established cultures of Europe in a conflict that provided a signature subject to Henry James in a series of novels and stories from "Daisy Miller" to *The Golden Bowl*, most of which would have to wait for nearly a century to be adapted to the screen. American novelists from Charles Brockden Brown to William Faulkner were much more likely to celebrate countercultures than majoritarian culture, social arrangements and philosophical verities American novelists, unlike their English counterparts, took it upon themselves to challenge as a defining condition of their vocation.

The foundational importance of countercultures in defining American culture from both without and within raises a series of questions about attempts to film the counterculture of the 1960s and 1970s. Is the counterculture to be presented as a *counter*culture, emphasizing its oppositional status, or a counter*culture*, emphasizing its status as a distinct and coherent subculture of its own? This question, so central to countercultural representations of any sort, takes on new urgency in countercultural adaptations, since both the legal history of adaptation and its more recent theorization by scholars have emphasized the ways in which the privileged status of original works of art is both challenged and reinforced by their copies and adaptations. Are counterculture adaptations to be viewed mainly as *countercultural* adaptations, adaptations that faithfully preserve the counterculture, or as countercultural *adaptations*, adaptations that seek to change the counterculture through the act of adapting it? What does it mean to be a counterculture adaptation? Although counterculture adaptations might seem intended to pronounce majoritarian culture unadaptable, they work to a surprising extent in the opposite way, by adapting the themes and strategies of majoritarian culture, as American novels from *The Scarlet Letter* to *Portnoy's Complaint* draw on the tropes of English and continental fiction to engage readers accustomed to the very models they will ultimately reject. Is the counterculture naturally adaptive or anti-adaptive? At least in the movies, the counterculture turns out to be surprisingly resistant to adaptation, unable either through principle or jerry-rigged social structures or ideological rigidity to adapt; indeed the unadaptability of the counterculture is one of its most appealing features for filmmakers planning their own adaptations. And although a wide range of countercultural currents has animated American cultural history from the arrival of the European colonists, counterculture adaptations typically treat the counterculture as *the* counterculture, focusing on a single unitary cultural phenomenon—Beats, hippies, bikers, drug users, college protesters, disengaged teenagers, even the police—that is either examined as a separate cage in the zoo or pressed into service as a vehicle for a critique of an official culture defined even more monolithically as *the* culture.

On the whole, the counterculture, whether or not it is defined as *the* counterculture, is less inclined to reject American literature than American social and political arrangements both because American literature from J. Fenimore Cooper and Edgar Allan Poe to *The Adventures of Huckleberry Finn* and *A Farewell to Arms* already defines itself in opposition to official American culture and because American literature has historically been more various, more flexible, and more constantly evolving than English literature. Instead of a steady diet of Shakespeare, Austen, and Dickens, American students are fed a diet whose components change at a pace that is both exhilarating and disconcerting. The American literary canon has never been as stable as its English counterpart, and its diverse offerings amount less to a prix fixe menu than a cafeteria buffet in which students are free to choose from among New England graybeards, slave narratives, political pamphlets, genre landmarks, proto-feminist polemics, children's classics, and *Moby-Dick*. American literature, with its strong libertarian streak, has generally sought cachet without coercion, and sometimes forgone cachet as well. Yet this model of American literature as a buffet raises questions of its own. What new dimensions of American literature and American culture do counterculture adaptations seek to reveal? In what ways do countercultural adaptations seek to challenge the cultural capital of American literature, and in what ways do they seek to claim that capital for themselves? What does it mean to seek or secure the status of counterculture classic, and how are the forces that have produced American literary classics related to the forces that produce counterculture classics? Does the emergence of an essentially countercultural American literature provide either example or guidance for the emergence of counterculture adaptations? Is there such a thing as a classic buffet, as courses in American literature implicitly assume, or are there merely classic individual dishes?

Although it never embraced the counterculture as fully as French cinema did in presenting outside heroes like Antoine Doinel (Jean-Pierre Leaud) in *The 400 Blows* (1959) or mounting critiques of the official cultural as annihilating as *Weekend* (1967), Hollywood took a leading role, if not in resolving these questions, then certainly in framing them. Popular music, it is true, provided an indispensable accompaniment for the counterculture. But the movies played a decisive role in shaping, refracting, marketing, and memorializing both the counterculture and its lessons for the dominant culture. In the United States, movies were driven by contradictions that echoed those of the counterculture it sought to adapt. By the later 1960s, Hollywood had outlived the founding generation of studio heads and lost much of its economic clout to television. At the same time, it was precisely at this moment, with ticket sales at historic lows, the studios floundering, and its self-censoring board in full retreat, that cinema began its ascent to what

Susan Sontag would call "the art of the 20th century."[15] Movies, cheaper than the weaponized best sellers of the 1950s but still comparatively very expensive to make, were at once the perfectly adaptable, perfectly accessible medium for countercultural art and the most unlikely, corporatized, capital-intensive medium imaginable. It is no wonder, then, that even though Hollywood, "because movies are expensive and time-consuming to make, [...] is always the last to know, the slowest to respond, and in those years it was at least half a decade behind the other popular arts," especially music, "this was a time when film culture permeated American life in a way that it never had before and never has since."[16]

The rise of Hollywood counterculture marks a high point of American literary adaptation, not because of the quality or consistency of individual films it produces but because the process of adaptation is so central to its mission. A remarkable number of American novels and plays and stories, most of them contemporary best sellers or underground classics rather than canonical texts, were adapted to the cinema between 1967 and 1975. The success of many of these adaptations fundamentally changed, or at least reflected fundamental changes, in the ways Hollywood approached adaptation in particular and did business in general. More importantly, since the foundational purpose of Hollywood adaptations was to market the counterculture, whether as dream or nightmare, to larger and more diverse audiences, the adaptations that had this decisive impact did not just happen to be adaptations; they had it because they were adaptations, making their impact through the process of adaptation itself.

Given the number and range of questions counterculture adaptations raise, it is not surprising to see the films themselves ranging over a wide spectrum of attitudes toward the dominant culture, alternative cultures that set themselves in opposition to it, representations of both cultures, and the fears, desires, and wishes of the audiences they aim to attract. For this reason, the most important counterculture adaptations can be categorized through a series of dualities.

The most obvious of these dualities concerns the films' sympathy or antipathy toward the counterculture they represent. Feature films like *Last Summer*, a 1969 adaptation of Evan Hunter's 1968 novel that showed the suddenly dire consequences for a not-quite-explicit ménage à trois among three self-consciously cool teenagers whose families were summering on Fire Island when a distinctly less cool outsider tried to join their club, and TV movies like *Helter Skelter* (1976), a horrified and horrifying account, based on the nonfiction book Curt Gentry had coauthored with prosecutor Vincent Bugliosi in 1974, of the murders carried out by the group of hippies Charles Manson had gathered around him in 1969, recoiled from the anti-social and ultimately violent and anarchistic threats to the Establishment from self-styled counterculture gurus like Manson and do-it-yourself dabblers like the teenaged trio in *Last Summer*. These films took their cue from a long line of earlier anti-teen, anti-authority adaptations like *The Wild One* (1954), *The Blackboard Jungle* (1955, also based on a novel by Hunter), and *Rebel without a Cause*. The exposés of juvenile delinquency typified by these 1950s films reached an apogee in *West Side Story*, Robert Wise and Jerome Robbins's 1961 adaptation of the 1957 Broadway musical written by Arthur Laurents, with songs by Stephen Sondheim and music by Leonard Bernstein. This inner-city spin on *Romeo and Juliet*, transforming the Montagues and Capulets into rival Italian American and Puerto Rican gangs in contemporaneous New York and portraying its leading couple sympathetically as star-crossed lovers while condemning the youth-gang culture that doomed their romance, recast Shakespeare's romance as quintessentially modern, urban, and cross-culturally American.

This ambivalence toward a youth culture in which sympathy for individual characters was set against a monitory social or anthropological climax made it tricky to adapt explicitly countercultural literary properties. *The Subterraneans* (1960), the first film adaptation of a Beat novel, first softened, then neutered, then reversed the force of Jack Kerouac's largely autobiographical 1958 account of his 1953 affair with African American Mardou Fox, which itself changed the setting of the love story from Greenwich Village to San Francisco. The film, which MGM marketed with the tagline, "Love among the new Bohemians!," retains the novel's emphasis on the jazz scene but changes Fox to a Frenchwoman played by Leslie Caron. Successive versions of the original cut increasingly rejected the Beat culture Kerouac had written his novel specifically to celebrate, until, following a disastrous preview screening, the studio handed the film over to veteran editorial supervisor Margaret Booth, who "proceeded to mutilate the movie beyond recognition, in an effort to protect the healthy roar of Leo the Lion and to uphold the 'American image.'"[17] The result was "a film adaptation resoundingly rejected by the mainstream public and utterly repudiated by the author and his milieu" (see Figure 7.2).[18]

If MGM had judged 1960 audiences not yet ready for a wholly sympathetic portrayal of the counterculture, studios were much more receptive to such portrayals a decade later. Although Warner Bros. announced its forthcoming adaptation of John Updike's 1960 novel *Rabbit, Run*, as early as 1963, its account of former high school basketball star Harry (Rabbit) Angstrom's inability to commit to either the wife or the part-time prostitute who bears his children was not released until 1970, when the passage of time had already dated the story. *Hair: The American Tribal Love-Rock Musical* first staged off-Broadway in 1967 as the opening attraction in Joseph Papp's newly constructed Public Theater—the first non-Shakespearean play Papp had produced—and then revised for a Broadway production that ran from 1968 to 1972 had to wait until 1979 for Milos Forman's film adaptation, an adaptation criticized by James Rado and Jerome Ragni as denaturing the

FIGURE 7.2 *The temptress Roxanne (Janice Rule) lets it all hang out in a timidly transgressive musical sequence in* The Subterraneans *(1960).*

rebellious energy of the stage play they had written, which frankly celebrated its tribe's embrace of free love and recreational drugs, largely dispensed with a linear plot, and featured a brief nude scene onstage and an open invitation to the audience to join the final reprise of "Let the Sun Shine In." If audiences had to travel to New York or one of *Hair*'s many regional productions to experience its energy for the ten years after its premiere, Hollywood kept its spirit alive in Arthur Penn's *Alice's Restaurant* (1969) and George Roy Hill's *Slaughterhouse-Five* (1972), which, though hardly uncritical of their counterculture heroes, were far more critical of the official culture against which these heroes set themselves. The most surprising feature of *Alice's Restaurant*, based nominally on Arlo Guthrie's hit single, was the elegiac tone it adopted toward the culture its hero, played by Guthrie, represented. Like *Slaughterhouse-Five*, *Alice's Restaurant* presents its hero as doomed, a brave, rumpled rebel whose time has already passed. In *Alice's Restaurant*, this passing is represented by the sale of the church in which Alice (Patricia Quinn) has operated a restaurant by Ray (James Broderick), her longtime lover and new husband, who concludes their climactic wedding celebration by announcing to the dismayed Alice and the few guests still present that the sale could raise enough money for the newlyweds to purchase a hundred acres in Vermont. *Slaughterhouse-Five* frames Kurt Vonnegut, Jr.'s protest against the tragic absurdity of the Vietnam War by the traumatic memories that haunt its hero, Billy Pilgrim (Michael Sacks), of the Allied bombing of Dresden while he was a prisoner of war there during the Second World War. Dancing playfully among different times and places, the film ends by criticizing not only the mindless imperialism of American politics and the emptiness of its social culture, but the constraints of linear time itself, from which Billy is ultimately rescued by his two abductions to the distant planet of Trafalmadore, whose inhabitants, as advanced in their attitudes as in their technology, assure him, "You are here, you have always been here, and you will always be here." Enlightened by the lessons he has learned about the arbitrary restrictions of Cartesian space and time, Billy tells the audience as he is shot to death by his old enemy Paul Lazzaro (Ron Leibman): "It's time for me to be dead for a little while and then live again. […] It's time for me to give you the Trafalmadorean greeting: Hello, farewell." What sets films like *Alice's Restaurant* and *Slaughterhouse-Five* most poignantly apart from earlier films about teenagers from *The Wild One* to *Rebel without a Cause* is their rejection of the earlier film generation's imperative to grow up. In *Rebel without a Cause*, Jim Stark (James Dean) never questioned his own need to grow out of adolescence and into manhood despite the flawed and ineffectual role model his own father (Jim Backus) offered. But counterculture films that proclaim the bankruptcy of mainstream adult culture reject any possibility of assimilating to that culture by internalizing its norms.

When the Production Code was replaced by the ratings system in 1968, transitional adaptations like *Lolita* (1962) and *The Graduate*, produced and marketed for the widest possible audience, gave way to adaptations that were made specifically with the goal of attracting a young audience. The audience for John Schlesinger's *Midnight Cowboy* (1969), one of the first adaptations released under the new dispensation, was sharply limited by its X rating, but the film still won three Oscars, including the Academy Award for Best Picture, the only X- or NC-17-rated film ever to be so honored. A 1971 reissue of *Midnight Cowboy* was able to reach a larger audience because the MPAA, raising the age limitation on X-rated films from 16 to 17 and allowing more disturbing content in R-rated films, enabled United Artists to secure the more inclusive R rating without recutting the film, which is still honored for its gritty portrayal of the seedy New York underculture against which an unlikely friendship springs up between streetwise con man Ratso Rizzo (Dustin Hoffman) and naive would-be stud Joe Buck (John Voight). New Hollywood, as the press dubbed it, concentrated ever more narrowly on films that targeted youth audiences.

Celebration, critique, ambivalence

New Hollywood adaptations followed two different paths in establishing their counterculture status. Some filmmakers chose to make relatively straightforward adaptations of counterculture plays like *Hair* or counterculture novels like *Cool Hand Luke* (1967), *Candy* (1968), *Catch-22* (1970), and Milos Forman's *One Flew over the Cuckoo's Nest* (1975). *Cool Hand Luke*, Donn Pierce's autobiographical 1965 novel about his years in a Florida prison work camp, was virtually unknown before it was filmed, but Stuart Rosenberg's film, remembered today mostly for Paul Newman's unflappable performance in the title role and for Strother Martin's immortal address to the convicts in his charge, "what we have here is a failure to communicate," effortlessly managed the tricky feat of channeling countercultural energies through the power struggles on a chain gang. *Catch-22*, like *The Graduate* written principally by Buck Henry and directed by Mike Nichols, explores several comical but ultimately murderous contradictions in the American military mentality during the Second World War, when Joseph Heller, who published the novel in 1961, served as a bombardier in Italy. In Nichols's theater of war, like Heller's, the Americans' nominal enemies, the military forces of the Third Reich, are nowhere to be found; instead, the crews' real enemies, the people most likely to get them killed, are their own commanders. Military thinking in *Catch-22* is so riven by contradictions and absurdities that Yossarian (Alan Arkin) and other members and commanders of the B-25 crews frantically seek their separate peace in a wide range of unofficial arrangements, corrupt deals, forbidden seductions, and private refuges. The military, for its part, offers an incentive for the bombers to keep flying, whether or not their bombs hit their targets, by promising rotations back home after a certain number of missions but raising that number as soon as anyone approaches it. Both novel and film take their name from the decree that any bombardier who could demonstrate that he was insane could get out of flying further missions, but, according to the mythical Catch-22, a term Yossarian ends up applying to any unwritten law that sanctions the madness of the military bureaucracy, anyone who sought to prove his insanity must in fact be sane enough to recognize the lunacy of the missions he was therefore required to keep flying.

Candy was an adaptation of Terry Southern and Mason Hoffenberg's 1958 counterculture novel of the same title, itself assumed to be a sexed-up satire of Voltaire's *Candide*, a counterculture satire that had long been tenured in as a landmark of high culture, even though Hoffenberg maintained that he had never read Voltaire until after the novel's publication.[19] Milos Forman's *One Flew over the Cuckoo's Nest* adapted Ken Kesey's 1962 novel setting the patients in a hospital's psychiatric ward, led by free-spirited Randle McMurphy (Jack Nicholson), against Nurse Ratched (Louise Fletcher). The film followed Kesey's novel in aligning the patients with the values of the counterculture and Big Nurse, as Chief Bromden (Will Sampson) calls her, with the repressive impulses of institutional authority. McMurphy, who is pretending to be mentally ill in order to avoid serving time for statutory rape, succeeds in creating an increasingly vocal and rebellious community out of the motley crew of patients in his ward but pays a high price in the end. Given a lobotomy that leaves him mentally incapacitated after he attacks Big Nurse and nearly kills her in revenge for her cold condemnation that leads stuttering Billy Bibbit (Brad Dourif) to kill himself after a night of sex with a woman McMurphy had smuggled in, he is smothered to death by the sympathetic Chief, diagnosed as a deaf–mute even though he can both hear and speak, whose escape from the ward ends the film. The film, which swept the major Academy Awards in 1977, the first time for such a sweep since *It Happened One Night* had done so in 1935, was widely regarded as a faithfully countercultural adaptation of a major counterculture text.

Even before they were filmed, both *Catch-22* and *One Flew over the Cuckoo's Nest* were widely recognized to be using Heller's military bureaucracy and the rules and administration of Kesey's mental hospital as metaphors for the more general madness of contemporary majoritarian culture. Adaptations like *Catch-22*, *One Flew over the Cuckoo's Nest*, and even *West Side Story* could be marketed as insinuating exotica, films that gave their audiences an even more compelling and immediate-seeming peek inside a world most of them had never experienced, or wished to experience, firsthand. *Midnight Cowboy* introduced audiences to a dark urban subculture remote from their own experience; Norman Jewison's *In the Heat of the Night*, which beat *Bonnie and Clyde* and *The Graduate* to win the Best Picture Oscar in 1968, revealed surprisingly deep-seated racial conflicts between Philadelphia homicide detective Virgil Tibbs (Sidney Poitier) and the white counterpart, Police Chief Gillespie (Rod Steiger) of Sparta, Mississippi, who calls on him for professional help while maintaining a dismissively racist attitude toward him. The films that took the greatest pains to deplore the horrors or injustices of the exotic settings they presented, like *Catch-22* and *One Flew over the Cuckoo's Nest*, were set against those like *Midnight Cowboy* that found something to celebrate in the human zoos they presented. But any number of films sought more or less deliberately to balance celebration and critique. A surprising number of these adaptations concerned the police: not only *In the Heat of the Night*, in which Gillespie and Tibbs eventually worked through their differences to an accommodation of sorts, but Peter Yates's *Bullitt* (1968), William Friedkin's *The French Connection* (1971), and Sidney Lumet's *Serpico* (1973), all of which followed adaptations of an earlier generation like Fritz Lang's *The Big Heat* (1953) in setting their maverick cops against both the criminals they were pursuing and their own lumbering, corrupt, or inefficient departments. The ambivalence toward the police, stoked by official reactions to urban riots across America and protests against the 1968 Democratic convention in Chicago, came to a boil in *Fuzz* (1972), Richard A. Colla's adaptation of Ed McBain's 1968 franchise novel about the 87th Precinct in the mythical city of Isola. Like the novel, but in a sharp departure from most of the 87th Precinct novels of McBain—the pen name of Evan Hunter, who had written the novels *Blackboard Jungle* and *Last Summer* and the screenplay for *The Birds* (1963)—*Fuzz* reimagined the precinct as a human zoo full of comical misfits united against a bewildering array of criminal enemies from the teenagers setting homeless men on fire to the thieves pulling off a series of robberies to the Deaf Man, a recurring figure in the novels, who threatens to kill various public officials if his extortion demands are not met. Instead of winnowing McBain's multiple plots, which was standard procedure in film adaptations of novels, Hunter's screenplay emphasizes their Rube Goldberg complexity, recasting the Boston Police Department, like the military in *Catch-22*, as violent, chaotic, funny, and disturbing.

As early as *The Subterraneans*, Hollywood had shown its willingness to compromise celebrations of the counterculture through adaptations that amounted to reversals or betrayals of their source texts' implicit critiques of mainstream culture. Hence John Belton, observing that "the majority of films that tried to deal with the 1960s youth culture, the civil rights movement, the student protest movement, or the women's movement depoliticized their agenda or disguised it in such a way that it no longer possessed any confrontational power," concludes: "As the films became more and more expensive and less and less exploitational, they lost their dissident status as attacks on the mainstream from the fringe and became mainstream themselves."[20] In this light, what is most surprising about most later counterculture adaptations is the more frankly ambivalent approach they took toward the counterculture. The first ninety minutes of Stuart Hagmann's 1970 film adaptation of *The Strawberry Statement*, James Simon Kunen's autobiographical 1968 portrait of the existential absurdity of the administration against which Columbia University students were revolting, mostly ridicules the naiveté of the self-styled revolutionaries like the hero, Simon (Bruce Davison), who joins the movement to meet girls. This portrait darkens suddenly, however, in the last twenty minutes of the film, which presents the student protestors as doomed martyrs to a tyrannical system willing to resort to violence against them. *Serpico* condemned the system as unjust or corrupt while withholding any positive suggestions more sweeping than civil disobedience or a maverick indifference to rules about how to change that system or make it more responsive to the social needs it frustrated. New Hollywood, no matter how expert it became in critique of either dominant or insurgent cultures, was much less invested in fomenting social change.

The result of the industry's ambivalence between celebration and critique was to recast critiques of either the dominant culture or the counterculture as high-wire balancing acts in which both sides came in for ridicule. *Getting*

Straight, Richard Rush's 1970 adaptation of Ken Kolb's 1967 novel, is exemplary in its strategies for balancing its portrayal of revolutionaries and establishmentarians at an unnamed university. Its hero, Harry Bailey (Elliott Gould), a Vietnam War veteran returning to school among a cadre of generally younger and more naive fellow students, is desperate to earn his MA so that he can get a job teaching in a public school, a vocation for which he clearly has both the motivation and the gifts. But his mentors, Dr. Willhunt (Jeff Corey) and Dr. Kasper (Cecil Kellaway), consistently encourage him to remain in the academy instead. Eventually Harry's loose habits—his constant quarrels, his inability to commit himself to his harried girlfriend Jan (Candice Bergen), his cheating on an assignment—enable Willhunt to bar Harry from ever teaching in the city's schools. Harry shows up at his MA exam determined to behave himself, but a series of hectoring questions by an examiner who insists that *Tender Is the Night* is F. Scott Fitzgerald's greatest novel, that Jordan Baker, in *The Great Gatsby*, is really a boy, and that Fitzgerald himself was gay, provoke Harry to reply: "That must have been quite a shock to Sheilah Graham!" and then answering the next question by announcing that the great American verse form is the limerick, a point he clinches by exuberantly reciting several off-color examples about Shakespeare and Milton as he leaps onto the conference table, insuring his banishment from the academic establishment. Yet the film heaps as much scorn on the students demonstrating outside the examination room, all of whom look up to Harry as a leader even though they are callow, vacuous, corrupt, and intellectually bankrupt themselves. For his part, Harry is consistently hampered rather than enlightened by his fatal ability to see the flaws of both high culture and counterculture. Although his passionate nature makes him the opposite of a fence-straddler, the curse of his probing insight prevents him from committing to anything until the film's final scene, when against the backdrop of a violent protest, he shouts exultantly to Jan, who had told him she was breaking off their relationship to marry her old suitor Dr. Greengrass (Paul Anders): "I got it back! I failed! I failed the Master's! [...] I didn't like it! I didn't belong there!" only to hear her reply that she has sent Greengrass packing: "I don't like him! I don't belong there!" (see Figure 7.3). The couple embrace as the protest around them grows more violently ritualistic until they seem to be choreographed to the film's gentle closing song in a moment that presumably brings everything into an impossible harmony.

Candy strikes a similar balance between satire of the establishment and of a more sympathetic anti-establishment figure. Christian Marquand's film traces the sexual odyssey of Candy Christian (Ewa Aulin), a nubile innocent whose search for love takes her from one exploitative sex partner to the next. Although she expresses no interest and takes no initiative in pursuing any of these liaisons, a series of male authority figures—a teacher, a famous poet, an Army brigadier general, a brain surgeon, a guru—find

FIGURE 7.3 *As a student demonstration boils around him, Harry Bailey (Elliott Gould) exultantly announces his final break with the academy he has long sought to fit into in* Getting Straight *(1970).*

Candy's combination of provocative attire and blank naiveté irresistible, and she is too clueless to resist their advances. When she briefly resists his demand to remove "your things" for a comprehensive physical examination, Dr. Krankheit (James Coburn), tells her, "You're a little girl who's not out of high school yet," whereas "I'm a medical professional who's attended eight schools and has more degrees than a thermometer." Pouting, helium-voiced Candy remains more sympathetic than any of her exploiters partly because the men around her are all so much more selfish and vicious than she is, partly because her innocence is so profoundly invincible (she greets each disorienting new encounter with the mantra "I don't understand").

An even more unlikely version of this balance of sympathies, which turns out to be a balance of antipathies, is *Fritz the Cat,* Ralph Bakshi's 1972 adaptation of Robert Crumb's X-rated underground comics. The film is best remembered today as the first X-rated cartoon, a rating it earned through its determined trashing of the taboos against urination on camera (broken as early as the credits, which ran over the stream produced by a construction worker on a New York skyscraper), blue language, drug use, incitements to violence against the establishment, and of course sex between cartoon animals. The film, notable for the virtually complete absence of any avatars of mainstream culture, presents New York as a reeking urban jungle whose psychedelically garish sets are policed by literal pigs. Yet the film's attack on the establishment is balanced by its critique of its hero (voiced by Skip Hinnant, who at the time was also playing Fargo North, Decoder, on the PBS children's series *The Electric Company*), a no-account college student who treats female cats as sex objects, constantly pursues his next drug high, and succumbs to the sexual advances of Big Bertha (Rosetta LeNoire) when she stuffs a series of joints into his mouth. Unlike Candy, whose blank disconnectedness raises her by default above the men who violate her, Fritz seems like an overgrown teenager, selfish, sloppy, hedonistic, and irresponsible; the African American characters are presented as crows, cool, self-contained, and altogether smarter but thoroughly stereotyped; the heavy-duty political activists toward whom the hero witlessly drifts are one-note, glum, and treacherous. The film comes across less as a journey of development or self-discovery than as a bad acid trip determined to poke every eye it can find—pretty much what the audience would expect structurally from an adaptation of a series of discontinuous comic books.

Films from *Alice's Restaurant* to *Getting Straight* work by maintaining a consistent conflict between the counterculture and the dominant culture it challenges, whether that culture is represented by academics or cops. *Little Murders* (1971), which marked the directorial debut of Alan Arkin, who had played Yossarian in *Catch-22* the year before, works instead by successively blurring the lines between these two cultures until they collapse into one another. The film, whose screenwriter, cartoonist Jules Feiffer, based on his own play, begins by setting the random violence rampant in New York against the promise of emotional fulfillment and safety represented by romance and the family. Street photographer Alfred Chamberlain (Elliott Gould), a self-styled "apathist" apparently incapable of emotional connections, is roused from his self-absorption by interior decorator Patsy Newquist (Marcia Rodd), who takes an unaccountable interest in courting him and making him over. At first Patsy's close-knit family seems to offer a refuge from the dog-eat-dog world of New York, but closer glimpses of the nonstop battles among Patsy's ranting father (Vincent Gardenia), brightly controlling mother (Elizabeth Wilson), and kid brother (Jon Korkes) and the family's spiral into a surrealistic incoherence after Patsy herself is shot identify the dysfunctional nuclear family as the true source of the apparently random urban violence amid which Harry has lived. The plague-on-both-your-houses attitude *Little Murders* shares with *Fritz the Cat* rules out even the valorization of Candy Christian's innocent sexuality or the last-minute resolution of *Getting Straight*. Instead, both films strongly imply that the middle-class culture, the scathingly labeled "midcult" Dwight Macdonald had located between elite and mass culture as an idealized site of marketing strategies for cultural institutions from Hollywood to the Book-of-the-Month Club, was even more bankrupt than the cultures it sought to position at the extremes.[21]

One last distinction that defined counterculture adaptations is that between those like *Alice's Restaurant, Little Murders,* and *Hair* that focused specifically on countercultural fads and phenomena that had increasingly grabbed the headlines in the 1960s and 1970s and those that sought the counterculture's roots, traces, or reflections in more remote cultures. William Friedkin's 1973 adaptation of William Peter Blatty's 1971 novel *The Exorcist* follows *Rosemary's Baby*, Roman Polanski's seminal 1968 adaptation of Ira Levin's influential best seller, in cloaking the horrors of demonic possession in an unusually decorous, subdued audiovisual style. Both films, handsomely mounted and deliberately paced, establish worlds that seem initially far removed from the diabolical forces that could impregnate Rosemary Woodhouse (Mia Farrow) or take possession of Regan MacNeil (Linda Blair). Both proceed from the gradual accumulation of almost imperceptible hints that something is not quite right in the posh, well-decorated worlds of their principals to more and more horrifyingly explicit signs of a demonic presence. But *The Exorcist* goes further than *Rosemary's Baby* in associating its demons with tokens of the counterculture. The only professional role it shows Chris MacNeil (Ellen Burstyn), Regan's actress mother, playing is that of a college student who seizes a bullhorn at a rally and entreats her fellow students, "If we want change, we have to work within the system." Later, the most frequent signs of Regan's possession—her scowling, her incongruously deep voice (courtesy of the actress Mercedes McCambridge), her green projectile vomiting, her rotating head, and the vicious, X-rated name-calling she directs toward anyone who tries to speak to her—echo exactly the sorts of wild behavior movie audiences would expect from drug-taking hippies, student revolutionaries, or other late-adolescent counterculture figures before a timely exorcism returns Regan to her winsome pre-adolescent innocence (see Figure 7.4).

Sidney Pollack's 1969 adaptation of Horace McCoy's 1935 novel *They Shoot Horses, Don't They?* softens the pulp contours of McCoy's first novel, which intersperses its presentation of a competitive dance marathon as a metaphor for existential despair, by adopting a generally reverential attitude toward its period setting and substituting a series of brief flashforwards hinting at the dark fate its hero, Robert Syverton (Michael Sarrazin), will suffer after acceding to the request of his exhausted partner Gloria Beatty (Jane Fonda) to shoot her to death for the ever more shocking single-page fragments of a judge's monologue set in capital letters which McCoy had used to separate his thirteen chapters. The film cuts the opposition to the marathon by the Mother's League for Good Morals that the novel had emphasized (185) and emphasizes instead the Hollywood dreams of Alice LeBlanc (Susannah York) and her grudgingly obliging partner Joel (Robert

FIGURE 7.4 *The demonic possession of Regan MacNeil (Linda Blair) in* The Exorcist *(1973) is consistently associated with the counterculture.*

Fields), a subplot that draws more attention to the characters' costumes than McCoy's novel; its playlist of 1930s tunes is more nostalgic than oppressive; its portrait of disintegration as the marathon forces its hapless participants to break one social convention after another is far more measured, even stately, than that of the feverish novel's hectic pace; and its muted colors and beautifully lit sepia interiors look forward to the cinematography and production design of *The Godfather* the following year (see Figure 7.5). Instead of ending with the judge's final words to Robert, whom he has just condemned to death—"MAY GOD HAVE MERCY ON YOUR SOUL"[22]— the film ends with a high-angle long shot of the mostly deserted dance floor as its soulless organizer, Rocky (Gig Young), urges the remaining couples on: "Yowzah, yowzah, yowzah! Here they are again, those wonderful, wonderful kids—still struggling, still hoping! As the clock of fate ticks away, the dance of destiny continues! The marathon goes on and on and on! How long can they last? Let's hear it! Let's hear it! Let's hear it!" Like *Bonnie and Clyde*, the film uses a Depression-era parable to speak to a later generation convinced that the institutions of modern culture have left them behind.

If the critically acclaimed *They Shoot Horses, Don't They?*, whose nine Oscar nominations still stands as a record number for a film not nominated for Best Picture, channeled its cultural critique through period drama, *Love Story* (1970) achieved an even greater popular success by projecting its critique onto a contemporary setting that never even mentioned the counterculture. Beginning with a plangent voiceover by Oliver Barrett IV (Ryan O'Neal)—"What can you say about a 25-year-old girl who died? That she was beautiful and brilliant? That she loved Mozart and Bach, the Beatles,

FIGURE 7.5 *Surrounded by competitors, Gloria Beatty (Jane Fonda) and Robert Syverton (Michael Sarrazin) drag themselves through the grueling dance marathon in* They Shoot Horses, Don't They? *(1969).*

and me?"—Arthur Hiller's film traced the doomed love story between Oliver and Jenny Cavilleri (Ali MacGraw), initially undergraduates at Harvard and Radcliffe whom the film positioned as both anti-establishment and ultra-establishment.

Oliver is defined early on by his position on the (establishment) hockey team, his (anti-establishment) two-minute penalty for holding, and his explanation to Jenny that he was "trying too hard" (a recuperation of anti-establishment behavior under establishment values). More enduringly, he is defined by his battles with both Jenny, a scholarship student whose lower-class origins do not prevent her from mocking him mercilessly, and his wealthy, stuffy father (Ray Milland). Jenny ingratiates herself with Oliver by telling him, "You look stupid and rich." Their romance, which plays out like a more foul-mouthed Henry James story of love among the privileged, is marked by ceaseless conflict, even when it is more gently modulated, as in their first scene with Jenny's father Phil (John Marley), a devout Catholic who wants them to have a church wedding. "We're a little negative on the church thing," Jenny tells him, and then, "We're a little negative on the God thing." Yet during the central sequence showing the couple's wedding, Phil amusingly insists on thinking of the officiant as a priest (see Figure 7.6).

The sudden news that Jenny cannot get pregnant because she has an unidentified illness that will soon kill her recalls a generation of earlier weepies from *Camille* (1936) to *Dark Victory* (1939). Yet the film continues to frame Oliver's loss within his improbably countercultural stance

FIGURE 7.6 *Jennie Cavilleri (Ali MacGraw) and Oliver Barrett IV (Ryan O'Neal) exchange vows in* Love Story *(1970)*.

toward the establishment values represented in such different ways by his sympathetically religious father-in-law, with whom he can share so little comfort, and his icy father, whom he encounters in a revolving door as he leaves the hospital for the last time. Oliver's reprise of Jenny's earlier speech to him—"Love means never having to say you're sorry"—is not an olive branch but a rebuke to his suddenly stricken father, to whom he refuses to be reconciled until the sequel *Oliver's Story* (1978).

Like *The Graduate, Love Story* infused its story of young love and generational conflict with countercultural tropes without ever leaving its enclave of wealth and social privilege—despite his plea of poverty to the Dean of Harvard Law, Oliver and Jenny are never shown wanting for any material goods—to show the counterculture itself. The film, often remembered as an adaptation, was in fact based on an original screenplay by Erich Segal, a former classics professor at Harvard and Yale with long experience of elite culture, who produced a novelization timed to coincide with the film's release that became the best-selling American novel of 1970—still another example of "American literature on film" in which, as in Tod Browning's *London after Midnight* (1927), Clarence Brown's *The Human Comedy* (1943), and George Seaton's *Miracle on 34th Street* (1947), the film preceded the literature.

Hollywood, in sum, could take a wide variety of approaches to adapting the counterculture. Movies could celebrate or condemn the counterculture; they could be made and marketed for all audiences or specifically for the newly identified youth audience; they could take the form of straightforward adaptations of counterculture classics or put countercultural spin on traditional sources; they could present the counterculture as an exotic destination for cinematic tourism or use it to expose the shortcomings of the dominant culture; they could compromise or emphasize the countercultural force of their source material; they could use the opposition between the dominant culture and the counterculture to subject both cultures to even-handed critique; they could maintain or blur the lines between elite and mass culture; they could embed countercultural tropes in costume dramas or upper-class parables in which the contemporary counterculture never appeared.

Beneath all these differences, however, counterculture adaptations share several crucial features. By presenting cultures or perspectives that had never before been filmed, they open American audiences to new ways of thinking about unfamiliar and familiar cultures alike. The interest films from *Midnight Cowboy* to *In the Heat of the Night* take in sociological or anthropological exotica, an interest that persisted even in films like *The Graduate* and *Love Story* that treated bastions of privilege as another series of cages in the human zoo, open new horizons to audiences the first-generation moguls had envisioned as monolithic in their tastes and desires. Whether they soft-pedal or trumpet it, countercultural adaptations from *Alice's Restaurant* to *The Strawberry Statement* to *Hair* are united by a revolutionary impulse, even if that impulse, once it is filtered by the movie industry, is less likely to urge audiences to overthrow the system than to find some more congenial alternative in Greenwich Village or San Francisco. *Catch-22* is anti-military, *Cool Hand Luke* and *One Flew over the Cuckoo's Nest* anti-authoritarian, *Slaughterhouse-Five* anti-government, *Little Murders* anti-family, *Love Story* anti-religion, and *Serpico* anti-police, even though its hero is a New York cop.

An even deeper affinity than these films' choice of institutional targets is that they have targets at all because they all pose as more or less defiantly anti-, more interested finally in the *counter*culture than in the counter*culture*. Counterculture films all adopt a satirical mode. Whether or not they are laugh-out-loud funny, many of them take the form of black comedies—so that *Newsweek*, for example, called *Little Murders*, released only four years after the debut of the Jules Feiffer play on which is was based, "funny in a new and frightening way"[23] because of the rapid changes in American urban culture since then. And most of them revolve around antiheroes like Fritz the Cat. The police heroes Frank Bullitt (Steve McQueen), Popeye Doyle (Gene Hackman), and Frank Serpico (Al Pacino) are cast as traditional maverick lawmen hamstrung by the hidebound policies of the police departments they work for. The oppositional behavior of Cool Hand Luke, Yossarian, and Randle McMurphy challenges the systems that reveal their moral bankruptcy through their increasingly tyrannical attempts to regulate it. The initially sympathetic teenagers in *Last Summer* suddenly, shockingly, and irreversibly affront their audience's moral code in their film's final sequence; *Rabbit, Run* is more successful in attacking middle-class verities than in championing the unappealing Rabbit Angstrom's refusal to accept them; and *Candy* alienated many contemporaneous reviewers by wallowing in the sexual carnival it sought to satirize instead of offering any alternatives to it. Typically, however, the antiheroes of counterculture adaptations like *The Graduate*, *Alice's Restaurant*, *Getting Straight*, and *Slaughterhouse-Five*, however flawed, ineffectual, or doomed they are, appeal to audiences precisely because of their ability to adapt to new challenges and perspectives that swamped more established codes and systems.

The most important result of organizing films around such adaptive antiheroes is to increase the likelihood of conflicts that cannot possibly be resolved by heroic action, either physical or moral. The most physically active characters in *Cool Hand Luke*, *Catch-22*, *Little Murders*, *Getting Straight*, *Slaughterhouse-Five*, and *One Flew over the Cuckoo's Nest* are the most ridiculous. Arlo Guthrie and Billy Pilgrim end up embodying a kind of Zen wisdom that rests comfortably in unanswerable questions instead of attempting to resolve them. Even less deeply centered counterculture antiheroes shun the traditional Hollywood path of the action hero.

These distinctively countercultural themes and characters are complemented by equally distinctive production habits. New Hollywood filmmakers, variously influenced by the run-and-gun habits of the French New Wave, reject the painterly, quasi-literary style of *Peyton Place*, *From the Terrace*, and *By Love Possessed* for a scruffier, scrappier look. Adaptations like *Fritz the Cat* are defiantly episodic, in the manner of sketch comedy, a tendency exaggerated still further in *Little Murders* by the characters' habit of breaking into long, diffuse rants that seem aimed at targets outside the frame rather than directed at other characters inside. *Catch-22* and *Slaughterhouse-Five*, whose hero is famously described as "unstuck in time," freely mingle past, present, and future, cutting between subplots and time frames and in the process leaving many audiences behind. Counterculture directors go outside the studio to film on location, whether the location is New York or California, Reading, Pennsylvania (for *Rabbit, Run*), or Stockbridge, Massachusetts (for *Alice's Restaurant*).

The distinctive look of counterculture adaptations is heralded by their plain-Jane credit sequences. Departing again from the self-consciously artsy credit sequences of films like *From the Terrace*, the unadorned opening credits of *Little Murders* and *Getting Straight* could have been plastered on billboards, and audiences have to wait till the very end of *West Side Story*, *Love Story*, and *The Exorcist* to see any credits beyond the main title. Except in period adaptations like *They Shoot Horses, Don't They?*, the camerawork that follows is unconventional in its obtrusive setups and movements like the disorienting zooms in *The Strawberry Statement*, choppy editing like the frequent crosscutting and cutting within crowd scenes in *Getting Straight*, and self-reflexive effects designed to challenge rather than reassure audiences in *Little Murders*. Like New Wave films, New Hollywood films often seem to revel in their low production values, counterbalancing their minimalist or non-insinuating visual style with pop musical soundtracks displayed far more prominently than the "unheard melodies"[24] Claudia Gorbman finds characteristic of most background music in the movies. *The Strawberry Statement* goes so far as to list all the pop songs on its soundtrack, most of which were not composed for the movie, in its opening credits, along with their composers and performers. Together with the newly emphasized musical tracks, overamplified sound effects often push the expository dialogue of these films into the background. Although all these devices might seem calculated to achieve the greatest possible realism, the results are more often surrealistic, making *Alice's Restaurant*, *Getting Straight*, and *Little Murders* feel just as cartoonish as *Fritz the Cat*, and shifting the balance of interest in all these movies from their narratives to the attractions—musical interludes, signature scenes, even distinctively edited montage sequences—the narratives seem designed to display rather than the other way around.

From counterculture to dominant culture

In their stories, their heroes, and their audiovisual style, counterculture adaptations embody rather than resolve an unusually wide range of contradictions. Despite their boldness in adapting the counterculture, films from *The Subterraneans* to *Rabbit, Run* are constantly compromising the very cultures they adapt as they strive to turn them into material that will entertain the largest possible audience, most of them outsiders to the counterculture. After the unexpected success of *Easy Rider*, studios scrambled to figure out how many markers to put down on the merging counterculture and how far to scurry back to the cover of a culture Hollywood had anointed as mainstream. Establishment filmmakers like Arthur Penn and Mike Nichols who used the counterculture to mount a critique of the dominant culture had to decide whether to exploit the counterculture for shock or entertainment value and how seriously to pursue its critique of the mainstream culture on which Hollywood continued to depend. No matter how bold their cultural critique was, very few counterculture adaptations of American properties were willing to follow their New Wave counterparts in extending it from targets like the police, the political establishment, the government, and the academy to Hollywood itself.

These conflicts, and the ambivalence they increasingly provoke from Hollywood, are most consistently and productively explored in the adaptations of Robert Altman, the most important American adapter to emerge in the 1970s. After a long apprenticeship in television and two indifferently received features, *Countdown* (1968) and *That Cold Day in the Park* (1969), Altman scored a major success with *M*A*S*H* (1970), his adaptation of Richard Hooker's 1968 novel. The film both launched Altman, already forty-five years old, on a major career and established the hallmarks of his style, which has been variously described as maverick, improvisatory, and anti-generic. A more accurate description would be antitelevision or even anti-early-Altman, for Altman's constantly moving camera, frequent and unpredictable zoom-outs and zoom-ins, encouragement to his performers to explore their own characters, delight in filling his widescreen compositions with large groups of characters, and trademark overlapping dialogue—the logical extension of New Hollywood's practice of burying dialogue beneath sound effects and pop music—are stellar instances of breaking the rules for television production, under whose highly regimented protocols Altman had worked for so long.

Altman's first decade in Hollywood is marked by a string of films based on original screenplays: *Brewster McCloud* (1970), *Images* (1972, released in tandem with a novelization of its screenplay by its star Susannah York), *California Split* (1974), *Nashville* (1975), and *3 Women* (1977). Yet the adaptations with which Altman interspersed them—*M*A*S*H*, *McCabe and Mrs. Miller* (1971), *The Long Goodbye* (1973), *Thieves Like Us* (1974), and *Buffalo Bill and the Indians* (1976)—are every bit as characteristic, and it is easy to see why. As Altman said in a recorded message played for the Academy audience over a montage of clips from his films when he was awarded an honorary Oscar shortly before his death in 2006: "I equate this work more with painting than with theater or literature. Stories don't interest me. Basically, I'm more interested in behavior. I don't direct, I watch."[25] Whether he is adapting a novel or play or filming an original screenplay, Altman treats the script as a starting point for creating interesting behavior rather than a collection of recipes that guarantees results to cooks who follow its every directive. In a broad sense, all of Altman's films in the 1970s and beyond are adaptations, even when they do not identify specific progenitor texts. *Images*, for example, was clearly inspired by two earlier films about the mental breakdown of their heroines, Roman Polanski's *Repulsion* (1965) and Ingmar Bergman's *Persona* (1966), whose influence returns even more pointedly in *3 Women*. Although *M*A*S*H* follows both the tone and the major incidents in Hooker's novel surprisingly faithfully, Altman's later adaptations, from *McCabe and Mrs. Miller* to *Buffalo Bill and the Indians*, are better described as deconstructions than recreations of their sources. In fact, Altman's restless attraction to one Hollywood genre after another makes him both an exemplary genre director and the most notable anti-genre director in Hollywood history, just as every one of his 1970s films, whether or not it identifies a specific source text in its credits, can fairly be described as both an adaptation and an anti-adaptation.

Altman's fraught relation to genre and adaptation is most fully on display in *The Long Goodbye*. Although the film is nominally based on Raymond Chandler's 1953 novel, the casting of Elliott Gould as Philip Marlowe and the updating of the film to the 1970s show how far the world and the hero are removed from the matrix of the 1946 adaptation of *The Big Sleep* in which Howard Hawks directed Humphrey Bogart. Altman's allegiance to Chandler's novel was even more attenuated than that of Hawks, who at one point reportedly telephoned Chandler to ask which character had killed Owen Taylor, the Sternwood chauffeur. Instead of reading the entire novel, Altman drew more freely from the essays and letters in *Raymond Chandler Speaking*, copies of which he distributed to his leading performers.[26] Gould's Marlowe is just as cool as Bogart's, but his cool is expressed not through his ingratiating energy, fearlessness, or irresistible sexual attractiveness—qualities James Garner had exemplified with a minimum of self-conscious irony when he played the role in Paul Bogart's *Marlowe* (1969)—but rather through his detachment from the vicissitudes of the world around him. Whether he is tracking down his old friend Terry Lennox (Jim Bouton), waving casually to his scantily clad female neighbors, feeding his finicky cat, getting beaten up by the police, or muttering to himself in a language that seems to mark him more as a beatnik of the 1950s than as a southern California private eye of the 1970s, Marlowe's attitude boils down to "whatever." His wisecracking expresses not Bogart's easy command of his world but his profound alienation from it. Like Altman himself, he is too cool for both his story and his world and consequently appears as an endearingly scruffy anachronism, less like Chandler's knight-errant than like a hipster beachcomber with a private investigator's license. The film, for its part, is less an adaptation of Chandler's novel than an updated return to its leading thematic question—how is it possible to act honorably in a world defined by incessant corruption?—that concludes that the only possible way for Marlowe to survive, let alone succeed, is to turn on, tune in, and drop out.

The film suffered a predictably dire fate at the box office when United Artists advertised it as a genre mystery, provoking genre expectations the film delighted in turning on their head. As Altman later recalled to David Thompson:

> I went to [United Artists executive] David Picker and said, "You can't do this. No wonder the fucking picture is failing. It's giving the wrong impression. You make it look like a thriller and it's not, it's a satire." So they pulled the film, and we got Jack Davis from *Mad* magazine to do a new poster with all the characters, and we opened it in New York and it was a smash hit.[27]

More perhaps than any of Altman's other films, *The Long Goodbye*, informed by an encyclopedic knowledge of film history and film technique, deeply immersed in the genre conventions it was sending up, and wholeheartedly invested in Hollywood and America rather than American literature as a double nexus of cultural capital to be adapted through satire, parody, pastiche, hybridization, and deconstruction, paves the way for the generation of film-school directors, the historic blockbusters they created, and the counter-generation of niche filmmaking that would follow in an irreducible dialectic in their allegiance to Hollywood rather than the New York of publishers and Broadway theaters as the newly anointed center of American culture.

The presiding spirit of the film-school generation was Francis Coppola, who had directed his first feature film, *Dementia 13* (1963) when he was only twenty-four. The critical and commercial success of *You're a Big Boy Now* (1966), an adaptation of David Benedictus's 1963 novel that served as Coppola's thesis project for his MFA at UCLA, encouraged Warner Bros. to offer Coppola the job of directing *Finian's Rainbow*, a 1968 fantasy based on E.Y. Harburg and Fred Saidy's 1947 Broadway musical. When Coppola arrived on the Warners lot, Jack L. Warner was taken aback to see that his bearded, long-haired new hire looked like a hippie. But although Coppola's looks were indeed comically at odds with his material, an Irish-American fairy tale starring Petula Clark and Fred Astaire, the film was another success. Heartened perhaps by Andrew Sarris's identification of him as "probably the first reasonably talented and sensibly adaptable directorial talent to emerge from a university curriculum in film-making," someone who "may be heard from more decisively in the future,"[28] Coppola founded his own organization, Zoetrope Studio, in the hope of giving opportunities to untried filmmakers and funding a wider array of low-budget projects the Hollywood studios would not touch. Ironically, Coppola's own work after the launch of Zoetrope immersed him ever more deeply in studio projects. After winning his first Academy Award for his original screenplay for *Patton* (1970), he agreed to direct Paramount's adaptation of Mario Puzo's 1969 novel *The Godfather*, the best-selling novel in the history of American publishing, when Sergio Leone, Peter Bogdanovich, and ten other directors declined.

Paramount producer Robert Evans, struck by the failure of Paramount's 1968 film *The Brotherhood*, which had been directed by the non-Italian Martin Ritt, insisted that this one "must be realistic to the core—you must smell the spaghetti."[29] The Italian-American Civil Rights League insisted that all references to the Mafia and the Cosa Nostra be expunged from the dialogue. Coppola, determined to cast the iconic Marlon Brando as Don Vito Corleone and the unknown Al Pacino as his son Michael, seized the League's challenge as an opportunity. Instead of the Mafia, his screenplay consistently referred to the Corleones and their New York counterparts as families and exploited the sinister power of this euphemism to pose the fortunes of the Corleone "family business" as a figure for the corruption of American capitalism (see Figure 7.7). The result was a potent blend of identity politics emphasizing the specifically Italian-American nature of the story, a figurative power aimed at identifying the Corleones with all of America, Coppola's furious anti-Hollywood energy, and Paramount's studio gloss. In becoming not only the top-grossing film of 1972 but for several years the highest-grossing film ever released, *The Godfather* stood as a symbol of the deeply contradictory impulses toward independence and community affiliation that drove New Hollywood.

Despite the historic success of *The Godfather*, the film-school generation, who naturally located themselves more decisively within the history of cinema than within literary history, were not generally drawn to literary adaptation. After drawing on his 1967 USC student short *Electronic Labyrinth THX 1138 4EB* for his feature debut *THX 1138* (1971) and directing *American Graffiti* (1973) from an original screenplay he co-wrote with Gloria Katz and Willard Huyck, Coppola's friend George Lucas drew on such diverse sources as Joseph Campbell's myth study *The Hero with a Thousand Faces* (1949) and Akira Kurosawa's samurai film *The Hidden Fortress* (1958) for *Star Wars: Episode 4—A New Hope* (1977). Brian De Palma, who reveled in the technical experimentalism of anarchic counterculture films like *Greetings* (1968) and *Hi, Mom!* (1970), first employed his signature split-screen shots in *Dionysius in '69* (1970), a film recording of The Performance Group's staging of Richard Schechner's adaptation of Euripides' play *The Bacchae*. But De Palma did not direct

FIGURE 7.7 The Godfather *(1972) uses the Corleone family—Sonny (James Caan), Vito (Marlon Brando), Michael (Al Pacino), and Fredo (John Cazale)—to redefine both the crime family and the role of the family in shaping American culture.*

another adaptation until *Carrie* (1976), based on Stephen King's 1974 debut novel; before and after its success put him on the map for good, the frankly commercial films De Palma wrote and directed—*Sisters* (1973), *Dressed to Kill* (1980), *Blow Out* (1981), *Body Double* (1984)—more often adapted tropes from Alfred Hitchcock's thrillers than literary properties. Terrence Malick, who graduated from the American Film Institute Conservatory in 1969, wrote his own original screenplays for *Badlands* (1973) and *Days of Heaven* (1978); it was not until *The Thin Red Line* (1998), his adaptation of the 1962 James Jones novel that Andrew Marton had already adapted in 1964, that Malick returned to filmmaking after a long break that included work on unproduced adaptations of Walker Percy's novel *The Moviegoer* (1961) and Larry McMurtry's *The Desert Rose* (1983). Paul Schrader, who survived a childhood with parents who forbade him to watch movies until he was seventeen, established his academic credentials in the more literary realms of film theory and criticism rather than production and wrote original screenplays for De Palma's *Obsession* (1975) and Martin Scorsese's *Taxi Driver* (1976) before directing his first feature, *Blue Collar*, in 1978, based on material by Sydney A. Glass, and followed it by directing his own original screenplays for *Hardcore* (1979), *Old Boyfriends* (1979), and *American Gigolo* (1980) before turning again to adaptation in *Cat People* (1982), a re-adaptation of the DeWitt Bodeen story that had already provided the basis for Jacques Tourneur's 1942 film; *Mishima: A Life in Four Chapters* (1985), which fictionalized the life and death of celebrated Japanese author Yukio Mishima; and *Patty Hearst* (1988), which drew on nonfictional books by Alvin Moscow and Hearst herself. The most adaptation-minded of the film-school generation was Scorsese, whose obvious love for literature took a surprisingly long time to bloom in his films. Of Scorsese's first nine films, only *Boxcar Bertha* (1972) and *Raging Bull* (1980) are adaptations; it was not until the 1980s that he would begin to turn more regularly to literary sources. Indeed, beginning with *The Color of Money* (1986), every feature Scorsese directed over the next thirty years—*The Last Temptation of Christ* (1988), *Goodfellas* (1990), *Cape Fear* (1991), *The Age of Innocence* (1993), *Casino* (1995), *Bringing out the Dead* (1999), *Gangs of New York* (2002), *The Aviator* (2004), *The Departed* (2006), *Shutter Island* (2010), *Hugo* (2011), *The Wolf of Wall Street* (2013), *Silence* (2016), and *The Irishman* (2019)—was an adaptation.

Of all the film-school graduates of this generation, the one whose sometime romance with adaptation was the most varied and expressive was Steven Spielberg. A dropout from California State University, Long Beach who would not complete his BA in Film and Electronic Arts until he returned to his alma mater in 2002, Spielberg won a seven-year contract with Universal on the strength of his short film *Amblin'* (1968). After directing several episodes of established television programs, he was assigned to direct several television films—*Duel* (1971), a highway nightmare based on a story by Richard Matheson; *Something Evil* (1972), an *Exorcist* knockoff; the pilot for the new series *Savage* (1973)—and his first feature, *The Sugarland Express* (1974), based on an original screenplay on which he collaborated. His breakthrough came with *Jaws* (1975), an adaptation of Peter Benchley's 1974 novel which was marketed not as an adaptation but as the latest arrival in what might be called Hollywood's disaster cycle whose most important entries to date—*Airport* (1970), *The Poseidon Adventure* (1972), *The Towering Inferno* (1974)—had all been adaptations of novels. Despite grueling production difficulties and the obligatory cost overruns, *Jaws*, its box office receipts juiced by an innovative television advertising campaign and its wide release in an unusually large number of theaters,[30] shot to the top of nationwide box office lists and remained there for long enough to replace *The Godfather* as the top-grossing movie in history (see Figure 7.8). In the process, it inaugurated a new genre, the blockbuster, characterized not by formal or thematic elements but by economic imperatives. Instead of planning a large and varied slate of family-friendly entertainments that would keep the members of filmmaking teams employed all year, studio executives reasoned, why not pin their hopes to a single release that would make so much money it could guarantee profits for the whole year irrespective of lesser projects' performance?

FIGURE 7.8 *Adventurer Quint (Robert Shaw), Police Chief Martin Brody (Roy Scheider), and oceanographer Matt Hooper (Richard Dreyfuss) join forces to kill the shark that has terrorized visitors to Amity Island in* Jaws *(1975).*

The runaway success of *The Godfather*, *Jaws*, and *Star Wars* firmly ensconced this new, winner-take-all approach to film production, decisively ending the period during which nobody knew anything. From now on studios would choose properties for the blockbusters they hoped to produce based on market research rather than any studio executive's gut instinct, and heads of production throughout the industry, no longer tenured in as members of the founding generation, would be summarily dismissed if they failed to perform. For his part, Spielberg, more frequently and consistently than any other director, continued to supply the blockbusters Hollywood dreamed of. The success of *Jaws* was followed by that of *Close Encounters of the Third Kind* (1977); *Raiders of the Lost Ark*, the biggest box office hit of 1981; and *E.T. The Extra-Terrestrial* (1982), which toppled *Jaws* as the all-time box office champ. None of these films was an adaptation, although Indian writer-director Satyajit Ray, claiming that *E.T.* drew without acknowledgment from his 1967 screenplay *The Alien*, threatened a lawsuit against Spielberg. Not until he had cemented his reputation as the most commercially successful director in Hollywood history did Spielberg begin irregularly interspersing original-screenplay blockbusters like *Saving Private Ryan* (1998) and the Indiana Jones films with other blockbusters based on literary originals—*Hook* (1991), *Jurassic Park* (1993), *Jurassic Park 2: The Lost World* (1997), *Minority Report* (2002), *War of the Worlds* (2005), and *The BFG* (2016)—and such prestige adaptations as *The Color Purple*, *Empire of the Sun* (1987), *Schindler's List* (1993), and *Lincoln* (2012), their own financial success driven by Spielberg's formidable reputation as one of the rare filmmakers like Walt Disney, Alfred Hitchcock, and Quentin Tarantino whose brand is more powerful than that of any property they might seek to adapt.

Spielberg's critical and popular success might seem to define him as a trans-adapter, a filmmaker so ambitious and accomplished that critics and audiences identified films like *The Color Purple* and *Schindler's List* not as adaptations of Alice Walker and Thomas Keneally but as ostensive adaptations of the African American experience and the Holocaust. Certainly much of the critical reception of both films, which sidestepped the books Spielberg had adapted to ask whether he was qualified to make films about the lives of slaves in America or Jews in the Third Reich, seemed to grant the premise of the film-school generation that movies had supplanted books as the nexus of American culture. But Spielberg's oeuvre offers another lesson as well: that minority adaptations like *The Color Purple* and *Schindler's List* and blockbuster adaptations like *Jaws* and *Jurassic Park* were all parts of a single new dialectic, each defining itself by acknowledging the pleasures audiences associated with the Other but subordinating those pleasures to the distinctive pleasures it provided itself, which may not be so different in the end.

This dialectic, which came to define Spielberg's career, played out in executive offices all over Hollywood whenever studio executives asked whether they should restrict themselves to make fewer, more expensive movies like *Jaws* with the potential to become breakout hits that would keep the studio in the black and satisfy its largely outside investors for another year, or finance minority adaptations, niche movies that could lure new audiences who would otherwise shun the movies. Even as film adaptations like *Alice's Restaurant* and *Slaughterhouse-Five* sought to give expression to the counterculture as a grassroots phenomenon, these very same adaptations recuperated the counterculture as the dominant culture for the same reason Joseph Heath and Andrew Potter give that "the hippies became yuppies":

> There simply never was any tension between the countercultural ideas that informed the '60s rebellion and the ideological requirements of the capitalist system. While there is no doubt that a *cultural* conflict developed between the members of the counterculture and the defenders of the establishment, there never was any tension between the *values* of the counterculture and the functional requirements of the capitalist economic system. The counterculture was, from its very inception, intensely entrepreneurial. It reflected […] the most authentic spirit of capitalism.[31]

The resulting recuperation became even more pronounced when Hollywood turned from screening the counterculture as such to targeting individual niche cultures it had historically marginalized or ignored.

Notes

1 Mark Harris, *Pictures at a Revolution: Five Movies and the Birth of the New Hollywood* (New York: Penguin, 2008), p. 1.
2 Harris, *Pictures at a Revolution*, p. 2.
3 Charles Isherwood, "A Broadway Master Who Paved the Way for a Sitcom Explosion," *New York Times*, August 27, 2018, p. A1.
4 Jesse Green, "Big Laughs and Then a Shift in Culture," *New York Times*, August 27, 2018, pp. C1, C4.
5 Ralph J. Gleason, "Joan's Conscience Honors Us All," "On the Town," *San Francisco Chronicle*, November 18, 1964, p. 43.
6 Kristin Thompson and David Bordwell, *Film History: An Introduction* (New York: McGraw–Hill, 1994), p. 375.
7 David A. Cook, *A History of Narrative Film*, 4th ed. (New York: Norton, 2004), p. 427.

8   William Goldman, *Adventures in the Screen Trade: A Personal View of Hollywood and Screenwriting* (New York: Warner, 1983), p. 39.
9   Douglas Gomery, *Movie History: A Survey* (Belmont, CA: Wadsworth, 1991), p. 306.
10 Gerald Mast and Bruce F. Kawin, *A Short History of the Movies*, 9th ed. (New York: Pearson, 2006), p. 517.
11 Theodore Roszak, *The Making of a Counter Culture: Reflections on the Technocratic Society and Its Youthful Opposition* (Garden City, NY: Doubleday, 1969), p. xii.
12 John C. Calhoun, "Speech on the Reception of Abolition Petitions, Delivered in the Senate, February 6th, 1837," in *Speeches of John C. Calhoun, Delivered in the House of Representatives and in the Senate of the United States [The Works of John C. Calhoun, Volume II]*, ed. Richard K. Crallé (New York: Appleton, 1853), p. 626.
13 Mark Twain, "*The Adventures of Huckleberry Finn*," in Mark Twain, *Mississippi Writings* (New York: Library of America, 1982), p. 912.
14 Philip Rahv, "Paleface and Redskin," *Kenyon Review* 1.3 (Summer 1939): 251.
15 Susan Sontag, "The Decay of Cinema," *New York Times*, February 25, 1996, http://www.nytimes.com/books/00/03/12/specials/sontag-cinema.html.
16 Peter Biskind, *Easy Riders, Raging Bulls: How the Sex-Drugs-and-Rock'n'Roll Generation Saved Hollywood* (New York: Simon and Schuster, 1998), pp. 14, 17.
17 Hugh Fordin, *MGM's Greatest Musicals: The Freed Unit* (New York: Da Capo, 1996), p. 503.
18 Michael J. Prince, *Adapting the Beat Poets: Burroughs, Ginsberg, and Kerouac on Screen* (Lanham, MD: Rowman and Littlefield, 2016), p. 12.
19 See Sam Merrill, "Mason Hoffenberg Gets in a Few Licks," *Playboy*, November 1973, http://theband.hiof.no/articles/mason_hoffenberg_gets_in_a_few_licks.html.
20 John Belton, *American Cinema/American Culture* (Englewood Cliffs, NJ: McGraw-Hill, 1994), pp. 290–91.
21 See Dwight Macdonald, "Masscult and Midcult," in *Against the American Grain: Essays on the Effects of Mass Culture* (New York: Random House, 1962), pp. 3–78.
22 Horace McCoy, "They Shoot Horses, Don't They?," in *Crime Novels: American Noir of the 1930s and 1940s*, ed. Robert Polito (New York: Library of America, 1997), p. 213.
23 Paul D. Zimmerman, "The City Game," *Newsweek*, February 15, 1971, p. 82.
24 See Claudia Gorbman, *Unheard Melodies: Narrative Film Music* (Bloomington: Indiana University Press, 1987).
25 Mitchell Zuckoff, *Robert Altman: The Oral Biography* (New York: Knopf, 2009), p. 7.

26 *Altman on Altman*, ed. David Thompson (London: Faber and Faber, 2006), p. 78. See Raymond Chandler, *Raymond Chandler Speaking*, ed. Dorothy Gardiner and Kathrine Sorley (London: Hamish Hamilton, 1962).
27 *Altman on Altman*, p. 81.
28 Andrew Sarris, *The American Cinema: Directors and Directions, 1929–1968* (New York: Dutton, 1969), p. 210.
29 Robert Evans, *The Kid Stays in the Picture* (New York: Hachette, 1994), p. 219.
30 See Biskind, *Easy Riders, Raging Bulls*, pp. 277–78.
31 Joseph Heath and Andrew Potter, *The Rebel Sell: How the Counterculture Became Consumer Culture* (Chichester: Capstone, 2005), p. 5.

8
1975–89: Screening the Silenced

Minority reports

The mid-1970s found the American film industry in a paradoxical place. It was buoyed by its commitment to the youth market even as it remained highly ambivalent about the counterculture associated with that market. Hollywood had made its peace with television: The studios had licensed many of the films on their backlists to the three national networks, which in turn had begun to produce their own feature-length products with Don Siegel's remake of *The Killers* in 1964. And the success of *Jaws* (1975) and *Star Wars* (1977) had suggested a new business model that focused on a limited number of potential blockbusters that could ensure a given studio's profitability for the whole year, a business model increasingly driven by market research, franchise sequels, and tie-in merchandise. At the same time, the studios found themselves unable to ensure their products' success by exploiting traditional channels—familiar genres, stars under binding contracts to parent studios, gossip items planted in newspaper columns and fan magazines—which held less and less interest for the new generation of filmgoers. Given this combination of successes, opportunities, and pressures, the industry complemented its pursuit of blockbusters like *Close Encounters of the Third Kind* (1977), *The Empire Strikes Back* (1980), *Raiders of the Lost Ark* (1981), *E.T. The Extra-Terrestrial* (1982), *Back to the Future* (1985), *Top Gun* (1986), and *Who Framed Roger Rabbit* (1988), only the last of these an acknowledged adaptation, by turning to a series of niche markets and subjects it had largely avoided for seventy years: movies exploring the experiences of racial minorities, especially African Americans; movies designed to appeal to the second-wave feminists newly empowered by the widespread availability of the Pill; movies whose leading characters had disabilities that would have prevented them from anchoring films in an earlier era; and the gay subculture galvanized by the riots that followed a 1969 police raid on Greenwich Village's Stonewall Inn.

Hollywood's new interest in identity politics, its willingness to give voice to distinctive minority subcultures it had long silenced, gave a new cachet to novels and plays and stories portraying these subcultures. These scripts served as the basis for a stream of movies from *The Miracle Worker* (1962) to *The Color Purple* (1985) and *The Joy Luck Club* (1993) and indirectly inspired many more. Equally revealing and even more influential were the industry's attempts to adapt what amounted to entire subcultures to what remained the conventions of cinematic entertainment. Just as the movies inevitably changed the material they adapted, the material changed the movies in decisive ways as the studios struggled to attract new audiences while maintaining their own identities. This attempt ultimately ended in defeat: all the leading Hollywood studios, continuing the downward spiral that had begun in 1946 with the Paramount decree, either went out of business or were purchased by corporate conglomerates between 1960 and 1980. The studios' failure to adapt to new social realities while maintaining their own independence stands in ironic contrast to their remarkable success in screening a wide variety of subcultures, populations, and genres earlier adaptations had silenced.

Hollywood's quest to package identity politics as mass entertainment reveals new dimensions to the ambivalence at the heart of the cinema of attractions. The most obvious tactic for movies to adopt was to create narratives in which individual representatives of oppressed or marginalized subcultures ascended to the power their people had been denied through heroic individual agency, adapting the time-honored formula in which underdogs defied their oppressors and either effected social revolution or, failing that, established their individual heroic credentials—a pattern displayed by Stanley Kubrick's 1960 adaptation of Howard Fast's 1951 novel *Spartacus* and readily available for repackaging in Blaxploitation films. A related narrative formula associated with both the many adaptations of *Uncle Tom's Cabin* and the so-called women's films of the 1930s and 1940s ennobled their heroes and heroines by showing them transcending the inevitable suffering decreed by their subordinate position instead of taking heroic action against their oppressors. This pattern was repurposed for second-wave feminist adaptations of the 1970s. As the traditional valence of the term "cinema of attractions" indicates, however, minority populations could be pressed into the service of mass entertainment by being displayed as remarkable or monstrous spectacles, in the manner of Tod Browning's exploitation film *Freaks* (1932), whether or not they were fully embedded in narratives. Other films might emphasize metatextual over textual narratives, more or less explicitly setting their portrayals against those of an earlier generation by displaying members of minority populations with a new sensitivity or lack of condescension or moving from exteriorized to interiorized presentations by exploring their distinctive subjectivities in more sympathetic detail. These two patterns, combined in different ways, produced the defining trope of what came to be called disability cinema. Whichever path these new adaptations took, they revealed a paradox at the heart of identity politics cinema: the combination of a focus on the strong, decisive individuals whom audiences expected to anchor their heroically inspirational stories with the abiding sense that these heroic individuals were above all representatives of larger communities that might well be defined as much by differences among themselves as by the commonalities that made representative figures representative. Beneath this paradox lay another still deeper: bringing silenced voices to the screen typically involved screening out many of the qualities that had defined them and provoked their silencing.

By far the most distinctive of the newly empowered subcultures Hollywood embraced, and the one that has been most often and illuminatingly studied, is the African American community. The African American characters played by Sidney Poitier had become increasingly prominent and admirable in film adaptations like *Lilies of the Field* (1963), which won Poitier a Best Actor Oscar, and *In the Heat of the Night* (1967). In these films, however, as in earlier adaptations like *Something of Value* (1957), Poitier played a white audience's idea of a black man, menacing and tormented in *Something of Value*, gruff and inspiring in *Lilies of the Field*, prickly but more professional than his white counterpart (Rod Steiger) in *In the Heat of the Night*. What made the new cycle of films distinctive was not simply the prominence of African American performers and filmmakers, but also the implicit or explicit celebration of black power established by three seminal films: *Cotton Comes to Harlem* (1970), *Sweet Sweetback's Baadasssss Song* (1971), and *Shaft* (1971). All of these films traded in racial stereotypes as florid as those of *Uncle Tom's Cabin* or the minstrel shows that had first held African Americans up as a subject to be perceived, and often performed, by white people. But "the essence of black film history is not found in the stereotyped role but in what certain talented actors have done with the stereotype"[1]—and what new ways shifting historical contexts allow different audiences to perceive the relations among performers, stereotypes, audiences, and lived experience.

Cotton Comes to Harlem is a raucous adaptation of Chester Himes's 1965 novel, the sixth of his tales of black NYPD detectives Grave Digger Jones and Coffin Ed Johnson. The film preserves most of Himes's antic plot about the detectives' search for the $87,000 stolen from a "Back to Africa" rally staged by the fraudulent Reverend Deke O'Malley (Calvin Lockhart), money that unbeknownst to the searchers has been hidden in a bale of cotton the exotic dancer Billie (Mabel Robinson) is using in her act. But the screenplay by Arnold Perl and Ossie Davis, an African American writer and actor directing his first film, places greater emphasis on detectives Grave

Digger Jones (Godfrey Cambridge) and Coffin Ed Johnson (Raymond St. Jacques) and makes them more comical figures in order to pave the way for a possible franchise adapting Himes's other novels. Even more than the novel, the film depends on comic reversals and inversions. Jones and Johnson clearly think of themselves as representatives of their people whose primary responsibility is not only to the law-abiding citizens of their precinct but to every African American in Harlem. For them, the gravest crime is not O'Malley's theft but O'Malley's betrayal of his own people by exploiting their dreams of black nationalism for his personal gain. Yet they are costumed as enforcers of a white establishment justice, and their policing tactics, from pursuing the thieves in a comically violent car chase that turns fatal for one pedestrian to using underworld contacts who are little better than the thieves they are pursuing, consistently characterize them as counterultural antiheroes rather than role models (see Figure 8.1). Characters like Uncle Budd (Redd Foxx), the homeless junkman who finds the $87,000 and uses it to finance his own private trip to Africa, at once exemplify and ridicule African American stereotypes long promulgated by white audiences. The passing reference to "a honky in the woodpile" both inverts and reinforces verbal stereotypes. *Black Beauty*, the ship O'Malley has reportedly hired to carry the faithful back to Africa, gets its name from the empowering slogan "Black is beautiful" but inevitably evokes memories of Anna Sewell's children's book about a horse.

FIGURE 8.1 *Detectives Grave Digger Jones (Godfrey Cambridge) and Coffin Ed Johnson (Raymond St. Jacques) take a break from the carnival of* Cotton Comes to Harlem *(1970) to question Iris (Judy Pace)*.

Vincent Canby, reviewing the film for the *New York Times*, called it "a conventional white movie that employs some terrible white stereotypes of black life" and announced: "It's strictly for people who don't care much about movies—or who persist in regarding movies as sociology."[2] Yet the failure Canby emphasizes stemmed perhaps inevitably from the sociological dimension he dismisses so casually. The achievement of both Himes's novel and Davis's film is to recast the epidemic violence associated with Harlem as a furiously entertaining carnival that is still disturbing and outrageous but now genuinely funny, driven by the same chaotic tendencies that make the story's labyrinthine plot, which remains as resistant to comprehension or cure as the real-life neighborhood itself, not only the movie's engine but also its broadest throwaway joke. Davis, impatient over his many clashes with MGM over the film, lost his enthusiasm for any sequels, and *Come Back Charleston Blue* (1972), the Harlem detectives' only other film appearance, was directed by Mark Warren.

Sweet Sweetback's Baadasssss Song was written, directed, edited, and coproduced by its star, Melvin Van Peebles, whose first film, *Watermelon Man* (1970), had used a racial spin on Franz Kafka's story "The Metamorphosis" to burlesque whites who considered themselves liberals despite their enduringly racist assumptions by turning one of them, Jeff Gerber (Godfrey Cambridge), into an African American overnight. *Sweet Sweetback* was not an adaptation but a veritable one-man show whose minimal story was merely a scaffold for a signature blend of images, songs, poses, attitudes, and montage sequences exemplifying the hero's militant code: "You bled my momma—you bled my poppa—but you won't bleed me." In fact, the film, produced on a shoestring, might be seen as primarily a promotional tool for its Earth, Wind & Fire soundtrack, which was released before the film to raise more money, and its advertising posters, which featured the slogan, "Rated X by an all-white jury."

The greatest innovation of MGM's screen adaptation of Ernest Tidyman's 1970 novel *Shaft* was changing the race of its hero. Tidyman's John Shaft was white, and the film was originally written for a white lead actor. Director Gordon Parks's casting of Richard Roundtree as the private detective dramatically changes the racial politics of the film (see Figure 8.2). It would be a mistake, however, to assume that this change is radical or complete. Like Sweet Sweetback, who wears velour outfits through most of his film until a helpful white man offers to change clothing with him to throw off the dogs on his trail, Roundtree's Shaft dresses in costumes stereotypically associated with black characters. Shaft has a deep, commanding voice, a willingness to risk violence in fighting crime and hiring a crew of mercenaries to rescue Marcy Jonas (Sherri Brewer), the daughter of Harlem gang lord Bumpy Jonas (Moses Gunn) who has been kidnapped by the Mafia, no compunction about killing one of the gangsters who has come to his office and lying to the police about it, and a decidedly equivocal relationship with

FIGURE 8.2 *John Shaft (Richard Roundtree), aglow with racial charisma, doing what he does best in* Shaft *(1971).*

Lt. Vic Androzzi (Charles Cioffi), the NYPD detective with whom he works to rescue Marcy and stave off a threatened race war. The film ends with a telephone call in which Androzzi tells Shaft that he expects him to mend fences between the Mafia and the Black nationalist mercenaries Shaft has hired and Shaft replies, "You're gonna have to close it yourself, shitty," hangs up on him, and walks away laughing. At the same time, the film goes out of its way to explain that although Shaft grew up in Harlem, he moved to Greenwich Village, whose geographic and cultural distance from his old neighborhood is a marker of both his success and his estrangement from his roots. Neither do the mercenaries Shaft hires evince loyalty to the larger black community, nor indeed to any cause larger than their own payday. The appeal of the film—it was a remarkable box office success, one of only three films MGM released in 1971 that returned a substantial amount of money—was rooted not in Shaft's racial ideology but in his racial charisma, a swaggering, unapologetically can-do, hypersexualized masculinity that was eagerly embraced by black and white audiences alike. Like *Sweet Sweetback's Baadasssss Song*, the film's musical score, this time including an Oscar-winning title song by Isaac Hayes, was so prominent and influential that it became a major selling point for both the film and its ideological charge.

Despite the success of *Cotton Comes to Harlem*, *Shaft*, and a handful of adaptations that followed (*Across 110th Street*, 1972; *Trick Baby*, 1973; *Black Samurai*, 1977), literary adaptation understandably played a limited role in what came to be called Blaxploitation cinema. The Blaxploitation films designed specifically to appeal to African American audiences, a cycle that crested in 1973–74, were mostly based on original screenplays that featured stylishly inflated black criminals (*Super Fly*, 1972; *The Mack*, 1973; *Black Caesar*, 1973); black law enforcers (*Black Belt Jones*, 1974) or freelance avengers (*Hit Man*, 1972; *Slaughter*, 1972); runaway slaves (*The Legend of Nigger Charley*, 1972); and contemporary black heroes fighting white nationalist plots against African Americans (*Three the Hard Way*, 1974; *Darktown Strutters*, 1975). It would be a mistake to think that adaptation played no significant role in the cycle. In her magisterial study *Literary Adaptations in Black American Cinema*, Barbara Tepa Lupack has identified three other adaptations of Chester Himes, *If He Hollers Let Him Go* (1968), *Come Back Charleston Blue* (1972), and *A Rage in Harlem* (1991) as, respectively, a prologue, an exemplar, and a long-delayed echo of the cycle.[3] And many Blaxploitation films were unacknowledged adaptations of earlier Hollywood movies. *Black Mama White Mama* (1972) recast Pam Grier and Margaret Markov in the roles Sidney Poitier and Tony Curtis had taken in *The Defiant Ones* (1958). *Abby* (1974) put an African American spin on *The Exorcist* (1973). The titles of *The Black Godfather* (1974) and *Black Shampoo* (1975) are self-explanatory. Like the output of the contemporaneous film-school directors, Blaxploitation films took their cultural cues from Hollywood cinema, to which they added not literature but popular music. When they did turn to classic novels for their inspiration, films like *Blacula* (1972), *Blackenstein* (1973), and *Dr. Black, Mr. Hyde* (1975) chose British, not American, novels. There is no Blaxploitation version of *The Scarlet Letter*, *Moby-Dick*, *The Great Gatsby*, *A Farewell to Arms*, or even *The Adventures of Huckleberry Finn*. At a time when Broadway casting began to be increasingly race-blind, there are no film versions of *Anna Christie* or *The Glass Menagerie* that cast African American performers in the roles written by Eugene O'Neill or Tennessee Williams. Despite the prominent role race plays in novels like *The Sound and the Fury*, *Absalom, Absalom!*, and *Go Down, Moses*, there has been no attempt to film William Faulkner's novels from an African American point of view. Even *The Wind Done Gone* (2001), Alice Randall's best-selling mulatto retake on *Gone with the Wind*, has never been filmed.

The reasons for the relative neglect of American literary material are illuminated by a brief consideration of *Blacula*. William Crain's film, released by American International, marries Blaxploitation tropes to the AI/Hammer formula of classic literary monsters juiced by sex and violence. Even after Mamuwalde (William Marshall), an African prince who comes to Europe to advocate to an end to the slave trade, is turned into a vampire by the aristocrat who covets his wife Luva (Vonetta McGee), he retains the courteous gestures and cultivated diction of the stage-trained Shakespearean William Marshall, who plays him so appealingly that Lisa, the apparent reincarnation of Luva originally so frightened that she runs from him, finds herself responding to him sexually. Mamuwalde's murderous hostility to his enemies prevents him from being entirely sympathetic, but he is far more charismatic than the authorities charged with his destruction. Throughout the film, the black characters, good or evil, are better-dressed and better-spoken than their less-important white counterparts. Although the film shows both black and white characters being bitten, only the black characters are shown being turned into vampires in a parable of the nightmarish allure of the Black Power that is Blacula's—that is, Mamuwalde's—deepest motivation. And the film, shunning stereotypical representations of black characters notable for their divided motives and complicated mix of emotions, reserves its stereotyping for the two "faggot" interior decorators Mamuwalde summarily kills after they unwittingly open his coffin and turn him loose on modern Los Angeles and the white cops who are on the right side but somehow never manage to do anything right. In *Blacula*, as Greg M. Colón Semenza and Bob Hasenfratz put it, "Crain brilliantly exploit[s] and interrogate[s] both the literal whiteness of [Bram] Stoker's pasty vampires and the cultural whiteness of traditional Brit-Lit."[4] The film's African American appropriation of specifically British literary models—especially the reworking of Dracula as a heroic villain who is fueled not by lust or blood-lust but by righteous rage—thus carries greater iconic power than any corresponding appropriation of an American novel. After all, American novels, which typically draw their heroes from the ranks of outsiders rather than a social order threatened by outsiders, already provide a model Blaxploitation cinema would be seen as emulating rather than upending.

The Blaxploitation phenomenon overshadowed a longer history of adaptations of novels and plays about the African American experience. *The Learning Tree* (1969), Gordon Parks's adaptation of his own 1963 autobiographical novel, was the first major studio release to be helmed by an African American director; its critical success helped Parks land the assignment of directing *Shaft*. Even though both its director, Martin Ritt, and the author of its source novel, William H. Armstrong, were white, *Sounder* (1972) is "nevertheless very much a black story."[5] The following years brought new adaptations of James Baldwin (Stan Lathan's 1985 adaptation of Baldwin's 1963 novel *Go Tell It on the Mountain* for the television series *American Playhouse*) and Richard Wright (Jerrold Freeman's 1986 remake of *Native Son*, the 1940 novel whose 1951 adaptation by Pierre Chenal had starred Wright himself as Bigger Thomas). But none of these attracted anything like the attention accorded the all-black musical *The Wiz* (1978), based on Charlie Smalls and William F. Brown's 1974 stage musical. *The Wiz*, a textbook case of adaptive repurposing for a new audience and its culture, inventively transposes the major incidents of L. Frank Baum's 1900 novel *The Wonderful Wizard of Oz* and the 1939 MGM adaptation directed by Victor Fleming to reflect the experiences of contemporary African Americans. Dorothy (Diana Ross) is now an inner-city kindergarten teacher who has never been south of 125th Street. Carried on a snowstorm to the land of Oz, she meets the Scarecrow (Michael Jackson) just as he is being forced to sing "I Was Born on the Day before Yesterday," the gloating song of the crows that oppress him in a pointed echo of Jim Crow: "You can't win, you can't break even, and you can't get out of the game." Later, her attempt to cheer up the Lion (Ted Ross) after he has cowered in the face of a battle takes the form of another song, "Be a Lion," an anthem of personal empowerment in the face of challenging circumstances (see Figure 8.3).

Each episode in which Dorothy meets a new traveling companion ends with the appearance of a series of taxicabs that put up "Off Duty" signs whenever they approach, obliging them to walk instead, as they do with increasing enthusiasm. When they arrive in the Emerald City, the exuberant song "You've Got to Be Seen Green," which expresses the joys of wealth and the need to put on your most prosperous-seeming public face even when you cannot afford to do so, is swiftly replaced at the broadcast edict of the Wiz (Richard Pryor) by "You've Got to Be Dead Red" and "You've Got to Be Seen Gold," illustrating the foolish dependence of the community on the whims of charismatic leaders. Evillene, the Wicked Witch of the West (Mabel King), runs a sweat shop whose oppressive character is lightened but not softened by the sign "EVILLENE'S SWEAT SHOP/PRODUCERS

FIGURE 8.3 *Dorothy (Diana Ross) is surrounded by the friends she has met in* The Wiz *(1978): the Scarecrow (Michael Jackson), the Lion (Ted Ross), and the Tinman (Nipsey Russell).*

AND IMPORTERS OF SWEAT." When Dorothy, alerted by the Scarecrow, triggers a fire alarm that sets off the jets of water that destroy Evillene, the Winkies she has enslaved sing "A Brand New Day," a celebration of freedom from oppression. Upon learning that the Wiz is a fraud, Dorothy bucks up her discouraged companions by singing "If You Believe," exhorting them to believe in themselves rather than seeking validation from outside. As she is about to return home, she deflects the Wiz's plaintive request for a favor, admonishing him that he'll never discover what's inside himself until he leaves the safety of the room where he's cowered in secret: "You have to begin by letting people see who you are."

Despite *The Wiz*'s box office failure, "the industry found no problem with continuing to appropriate black culture and music" in films like John Landis's *The Blues Brothers* (1980), in which the costumes and performances of the title characters, played by Dan Ackroyd and John Belushi, work to create "an updated symbolic blackface of the 1980s, neominstrelsy."[6] Whether or not they reversed *The Wiz* by adapting African American tropes to vehicles aimed at white audiences, most African American adaptations that were produced took care to neuter whatever calls they might be making to black empowerment in one of several ways. They could use the rise-and-fall arc of the gangster film to predict the ultimate demise of Black Caesar or the Black Godfather. They could rely on the self-containing conventions of Hollywood genres like the cop film or the vampire film. Or they could play interracial tensions for laughs, as *Cotton Comes to Harlem* had done. But one film took a markedly different road. *The Spook Who Sat by the Door*, Ivan Dixon's 1973 adaptation of Ben Greenlee's 1969 novel, tells the story of Dan Freeman (Lawrence Cook), the sole beneficiary of the CIA's new mission to recruit African American agents. Shunted to a subbasement as Top Secret Reproduction Center Section Chief, from which he is trotted out from his job operating the photocopy machine as window dressing for visiting dignitaries, Freeman quits the CIA to put his newly acquired tradecraft to work in organizing and training young men as guerrilla warriors in innercity Chicago. The soft-spoken Freeman, who openly advocates armed rebellion against the white authorities, urges his followers to replicate their tactics on a national scale: "What we got now is a colony; what we want is a new nation." The film, with its more serious and politically committed echoes of Robert Downey's controversial comedy *Putney Swope* (1969), attracted the attention of J. Edgar Hoover, the director of the FBI, and United Artists, its distributor, was pressured to withdraw it from theaters. Greenlee and Dixon, who had collaborated on its screenplay, were able to repurchase the film on the condition that they would not file suit against United Artists, but although half a dozen prints survived, the negative disappeared until 2004, when it was rediscovered, released on video, and hailed as the most politically revolutionary film of its era.

Marginalized cultures

Just as the Black Power movement fueled Blaxploitation cinema, it would be reasonable to expect second-wave feminism to produce a cinema of its own. First-wave feminism, the battle for women's suffrage and property rights that climaxed with the passage of the Nineteenth Amendment in 1920, had had little impact on films made during that time or later—the most notable example before the 1970s was the Will Rogers vehicle *The County Chairman* (1935), based on a 1903 play by George Ade, which had already provided the basis for a lost film directed by Allan Dwan in 1914. And second-wave feminism, which focused on women's sexual liberation, reproductive rights, equal pay, and freedom from harassment in the workplace and elsewhere, found surprisingly little more welcome in the movies. For many years, Hollywood had been friendlier to male than female employees, and women who lacked the attributes that could make them movie stars were welcomed mainly in such subordinate and behind-the-scenes roles as screenwriters, editors, secretaries, and continuity editors (tellingly called "script girls"). Pioneer female directors like Mabel Normand, Dorothy Arzner, and Ida Lupino and producers like Virginia Van Upp, Joan Harrison, and Harriet Parsons remained outliers among a flood of women's films "implying a generically shared world of misery and masochism the individual work [was] designed to indulge."[7] The women's revolution that inspired such explosive European films as Chantal Akerman's *Jeanne Diehlmann, 23 quai de Commerce, 1080 Bruxelles* (1975) had little immediate impact on Hollywood in large part because *Roe v. Wade*, the landmark 1973 Supreme Court case that struck down all state limitations on first-term abortions, was so deeply divisive and potentially alienating. *Alice Doesn't Live Here Anymore* (1974) and *Places in the Heart* (1984) were based on original screenplays that updated the old model by dramatizing the struggles of prematurely widowed women to survive and forge new lives. *Diary of a Mad Housewife*, the 1970 film adaptation of Sue Kaufman's 1967 novel written by Eleanor Perry and directed by her husband, Frank Perry, showed mainly that sexual liberation offered no genuinely new avenues to women who could be oppressed by both their condescendingly careerist husbands and their emotionally remote lovers. The new power female audiences sought could more often be found in Blaxploitation films like *Cleopatra Jones* (1973), *Coffy* (1973), *Foxy Brown* (1974), *The Arena* (1974), *Sugar Hill* (1974), and *Get Christie Love!* (1974), which conferred extraordinary powers on heroines fighting men even as they took care to present them as sexual objects. *9 to 5* (1980) was a fairy tale based on an original screenplay about three office workers drawn into a revenge plot against their laughably chauvinist boss. Even William Wyler's *The Children's Hour* (1961), which restored the lesbianism the Hays Office had excised from *These Three*, Wyler's 1936 adaptation of

Lillian Hellman's 1934 play, was widely viewed as less powerful than the sexually censored earlier film.

The dominant figure in the cycle of second-wave feminist cinema was Barbra Streisand. The iconic Sixties singer's film debut in *Funny Girl*, William Wyler's 1968 adaptation of Isobel Lennart's 1963 Broadway play about stage actress and comedian Fannie Brice, won her an Academy Award, which she shared with Katharine Hepburn, who had been nominated for her role in *The Lion in Winter* (1968), Anthony Harvey's film adaptation of James Goldman's 1966 play about Henry II's spectacularly troubled marriage to Eleanor of Aquitaine. Brice's persona—not conventionally attractive or initially outgoing but increasingly brash and assertive and ultimately irresistible—quickly became fused with Streisand's own screen image, and she went on to star in a long series of films about women overcoming formidable obstacles to their self-actualization. Many of these projects were adaptations: *Hello, Dolly!*, Gene Kelly's 1969 adaptation of Jerry Herman and Michael Stewart's 1964 Broadway musical; *On a Clear Day You Can See Forever*, Vincente Minnelli's 1970 adaptation of Burton Lane and Alan Jay Lerner's 1965 musical; *Up the Sandbox*, Irvin Kershner's 1972 adaptation of Anne Richardson Roiphe's 1970 novel; *A Star Is Born*, in which husband-and-wife screenwriters Joan Didion and John Gregory Dunne and director Frank Pierson transposed the Hollywood setting of the 1937 and 1954 films of the same name to the 1976 music scene; and *Nuts*, Martin Ritt's 1987 adaptation of Tom Topor's 1979 play.

Along the way, Streisand, who had become increasingly outspoken as a critic of the limits Hollywood placed on women's roles both onscreen and off, directed herself in *Yentl*, the 1983 adaptation of Leah Napolin's 1975 play based in turn on Isaac Bashevis Singer's 1963 story "Yentl the Yeshiva Boy" about a young woman who masquerades as a man in order to enter the yeshiva, which would otherwise bar her from receiving a Jewish education (see Figure 8.4). Streisand went on to direct and star in two more notable adaptations that continued her focus on female empowerment, *The Prince of Tides* (1991), based on Pat Conroy's best-selling 1986 novel, and *The Mirror Has Two Faces* (1996), a loose remake of André Cayatte's film *Le miroir a deux faces* (1958), before returning to a singing career punctuated by sporadic film appearances. More than any other figure of her time, she blazed a trail for female filmmakers and illustrated the criticisms female actor-directors were likely to face as imperious, uncompromising, and vain.

Hollywood showed no more concerted interest in ethnic Americans who did not happen to be African Americans than it did in second-generation feminists. After garnering universally enthusiastic reviews as the great American epic of its time and achieving historic box office success, *The Godfather* generated a 1974 sequel that generated even more rapturous reviews and even greater success at the Oscars—it won six Academy Awards and was the first sequel ever to win Best Picture. But apart from encouraging

FIGURE 8.4 Yentl *(1983) constantly trades on the discomfort of its eponymous heroine (Barbra Streisand) in her cross-dressing role as a yeshiva student smitten by her mentor Avigdor (Mandy Patinkin).*

Martin Scorsese to continue to explore his ethnic heritage in fictional films like *Mean Streets* (1973) and documentaries like *Italianamerican* (1974), it did nothing to rekindle the studios' interest in Italian Americans, who were widely held to be metaphorical representatives of Americans in general, or in other hyphenate-American subjects who could promise to attract sizeable new audiences. The new sensitivity the nation professed about ethnic issues and identities left few traces on the movie screen. *Hester Street*, Joan Micklin Silver's 1975 adaptation of Abraham Cahan's 1896 novel *Yekl: A Tale of the New York Ghetto*, dramatized the tribulations of Russian Jews seeking both to assimilate and to maintain their own cultural heritage in 1896 New York. The contemporaneous filmmaker most closely identified with the unique challenges of ethnic Americans was Wayne Wang. Beginning with *Dim Sum* (1985), which examined the deeply mixed emotions of a Chinese American immigrant in San Francisco contemplating a return trip to her homeland to pay her last respects to her ancestors, Wang interspersed a wide range of other projects with repeated explorations of similar tensions with Chinese American families and communities in *Eat a Bowl of Tea*, his 1989 adaptation of Louis Chu's 1961 novel about the immigration of Chinese families to America after the Second World War, and *The Joy Luck Club*, his 1993 adaptation of Amy Tan's best-selling 1989 novel.

Although the industry showed scant interest in any American ethnicities other than African Americans, the period was marked by a notable upsurge in disability cinema. Hollywood's long history of representing characters who were blind, deaf, mute, or crippled by physical or mental disabilities had rarely displayed these characters as anything but caricatures or freaks. The first films to take psychoanalysis seriously were *Lady in the Dark* (1944) and *Spellbound* (1945), adaptations in which psychoanalytic sessions were central to plots that focused on romantic or criminal problems. The postwar years produced a series of adaptations of nonfictional or autobiographical case studies from *The Snake Pit* (1948) to *The Three Faces of Eve* (1957) to *David and Lisa* (1962) in which psychotherapy itself became the central narrative. By the Seventies, characters whose psychological problems had risen to a clinical level dominated films like *The Haunting*, Robert Wise's 1963 adaptation of Shirley Jackson's 1959 novel *The Haunting of Hill House*; *Charly*, Ralph Nelson's 1968 adaptation of Daniel Keyes's 1959 short story and 1966 novel *Flowers for Algernon*; *Play It as It Lays*, Frank Perry's 1972 adaptation of Joan Didion's 1970 novel; *I Never Promised You a Rose Garden*, Anthony Page's 1977 adaptation of the 1964 novel Joanne Greenberg published as Hannah Green; *Looking for Mr. Goodbar*, Richard Brooks's 1977 adaptation of Judith Rossner's best-selling 1975 novel; and *One Flew over the Cuckoo's Nest* (1975).

Unlike the Blaxploitation cycle, none of these films was created or marketed for a target audience of the leading characters' blind, deaf, alcoholic, or mentally challenged peers. (Indeed, MGM's DVD release of *The Miracle Worker*, which offers a choice of French or Spanish subtitles and dialogue tracks, does not offer the option of English subtitles for hearing-impaired viewers.) So in addition to having to present other-abled characters whom audiences could take to their hearts, Hollywood had to market them to appeal to audiences whose own experiences were quite different, audiences who might have dreamed of being the strong characters played by Katharine Hepburn and John Wayne but who never dreamed of being Helen Keller or Charly Gordon. As Sharon L. Snyder and David T. Mitchell point out, "film promotes its status as a desirable cultural product largely through its willingness to recirculate bodies typically concealed from view. In this way the closeting of disabled people from public observation exacts a double marginality: *disability extracts one from participation while also turning that palpable absence into the terms of one's exoticism*."[8] Even under the most sympathetic presentation, these films traded on the sort of monstration that viewed disabled people as literally monstrous and, by casting nondisabled performers in these roles, engaged in still another form of minstrelsy. Not surprisingly, they were framed as case studies in humanistic compassion. Don Birnam suffered from alcoholism and Eve White from multiple personality disorder, but their films valorized the humanity they located beneath their disabilities. Audiences were moved to pity the deaf Belinda McDonald and the mentally ill Virginia Cunningham even as, and because, they sought to rise above their limitations.

This pattern, which "suggest[s] that disability is a product of psychological self-acceptance, of emotional adjustment," that can be resolved with the help of "nondisabled main characters [who] have no trouble accepting the individuals with disabilities" and indeed "understand better than the handicapped characters the true nature of the problem,"[9] reached a climax in *Charly*, whose hero is given treatments that briefly raise his IQ from a subnormal to a genius level before they stop working and he suffers the double torment of a mental relapse and his new status as an unbearably pitiable figure for everyone who knows his story. But the pattern was decisively broken by *Children of a Lesser God*, Randa Haines's 1986 film adaptation of Mark Medoff's 1979 play about the relationship between custodian Sarah Norman, whose deafness has led her to withdraw from the larger world, and James Leeds, the new teacher at the school for the deaf where she works, who encourages her to learn to speak aloud. Since Sarah is already fluent in sign language, she does not have to be taught to sign, as Belinda McDonald (Jane Wyman) is by Dr. Robert Richardson (Lew Ayres) in *Johnny Belinda*. Instead, the conflict between the pair involves not greater and lesser abilities to communicate but different ways of communicating and different views of the world that stem from those ways (see Figure 8.5). Leeds wants the pupil to enter the wider community by learning to read lips and speak aloud; Sarah, identifying the hearing-impaired community as her true cohort, resists. What might have seemed a particularly striking sequence featuring a group of hearing-impaired activists who argue vigorously that learning to speak aloud does not add to their perceptual

FIGURE 8.5 *James Leeds (William Hurt), who teaches at a school for the deaf, and custodian Sarah Norman (Marlee Matlin) struggle to overcome the obstacles* Children of a Lesser God *(1986) has placed between them.*

and communicative abilities but compromises and undermines them was in fact all that remained of "the activism at the play's core. [...] Instead of confronting issues of discrimination, the makers of *Lesser God* were content to turn it into a love story—a highly charged one, but nevertheless a basic love story—complete with a traditional conclusion quite different from the play's ambiguous one."[10] In a sign of the times, *Children of a Lesser God* was criticized by Roger Ebert and members of the hearing-impaired community for being presented entirely for audiences who could hear because, as Ebert pointed out, Sarah's signed dialogue is not accompanied by subtitles but translated by James Leeds, who repeated it "as if to himself."[11] Even so, the film was a notable critical and popular success. Three members of its cast—Marlee Matlin, who played Sarah; Piper Laurie, who played her mother; and William Hurt, who played Leeds—were nominated for Academy Awards, and Matlin won, making her, at 29, the youngest performer ever to win the Best Actress Oscar, and the first hearing-impaired performer to do so.

Out of the closet

The shift from presenting disabled characters sensitively enough to provoke compassion for their disabilities to presenting them as other-abled rather than disabled changes these characters from attractions whose stories sought to rescue them from their disabilities to variously strong and admirable characters with abilities and voices and stories of their own. This shift turns up, interestingly enough, in two Stanley Kubrick films that are rarely seen this way because the characters in question represent such dramatically marginalized groups: *Lolita* (1962), which gives a voice to the hitherto silenced pedophile community by carefully declining to specify the age of the title character, casting the fifteen-year-old Sue Lyon in the role, and soft-pedaling the explicit sex scenes over which Vladimir Nabokov's novel had poetically and perversely lingered; and *2001: A Space Odyssey* (1968), which gives a voice, the most unforgettable in the film, to HAL 9000, the onboard computer nicknamed Hal that reacts to the threat of being disabled by attempting to kill all the humans aboard the spacecraft and succeeding in every case but one. The sequence during which surviving astronaut Frank Bowman (Keir Dullea) slowly disconnects Hal's circuits, reducing its hitherto inhuman voice to a series of increasingly impassioned pleas before it finally reverts to its earliest programmed memory, singing "A Bicycle Built for Two" as Bowman pulls the last plug, is by far the most touching moment in a film whose general tone, not unusually for Kubrick, is remarkably chilly (see Figure 8.6).

Since neither *Lolita* nor *2001: A Space Odyssey* was marketed to appeal to pedophiles or computers, the problems that faced adaptations

FIGURE 8.6 *The disabling of the renegade computer HAL 9000 by Dave Bowman (Keir Dullea) provides a surprisingly touching moment in the generally chilly* 2001: A Space Odyssey *(1968).*

focusing on identity politics are best illustrated by another subgenre that emerges in the 1970s: gay cinema. There had of course been many earlier representations of characters who were marked more or less explicitly as gay in earlier films. Although the murderous homophobia that drove the plot in Richard Brooks's 1945 novel *The Brick Foxhole* was changed to anti-Semitism in Edward Dmytryk's 1947 film adaptation *Crossfire*, important characters were clearly marked as gay in adaptations like *Rope* (1948), *Tea and Sympathy* (1956), *Compulsion* (1959), *Victim* (1961), *Advise and Consent* (1962), *The Servant* (1963), *Reflections in a Golden Eye* (1967), and *The Sergeant* (1968). Lesbian characters, although far less prevalent, appeared in *Dracula's Daughter* (1936), *The Children's Hour* (1961), *The Fox* (1967), and *The Killing of Sister George* (1968). Lead characters were coded as gay or lesbian only when their sexual identity was essential to plots that required motives or correlatives for their criminal behavior, evidence of character flaws, or opportunities for them to be blackmailed; character performers like Franklin Pangborn and Mercedes McCambridge could be coded as gay for no particular reason. The turning point in Hollywood's presentation of gay characters was another William Hurt vehicle, *Kiss of the Spider Woman*, Héctor Babenco's 1985 adaptation of Manuel Puig's 1976 novel. Hurt played Luis Molina, a gay hairdresser imprisoned for a sexual relationship with an underage boy, whose cellmate, Valentin Arregui (Raúl Julia), is a revolutionary whose jailers have promised Molina parole if he will befriend and inform on him. Following the script, Molina draws closer to the robustly heterosexual Arregui and eventually tells him that he loves him. The authorities' plan goes awry, however, when Molina, set free after consummating his sexual relationship with Arregui and obtaining a telephone number from him, is shot by the revolutionaries he has contacted and dies after refusing to betray them in return for medical treatment for his wound. Hurt's Academy Award for playing Molina as a gay pedophile still capable of a heroism inspired by personal loyalty and a dawning revolutionary consciousness marked a new dignity and self-determination in Hollywood's portrayal of gay characters that was confirmed by the Oscar-winning performances of Tom Hanks in *Philadelphia* (1993) and Sean Penn in the title role of *Milk* (2008).

In the Seventies, however, Hollywood portrayals of lesbian and especially gay male characters were an uneasy mix that sought to reach new niche audiences through empathetic bonding even as they had recourse to monstrating stereotypical caricatures in order to mark their empathetic characters as gay. In seeking to attract audiences from both inside and outside the relatively closed communities to whom they were finally opening the doors, the studios were hamstrung by the fact that these two audiences were driven by very different impulses, which might be described as bonding and voyeurism, or empathy and curiosity. The film that most systematically and comprehensively incorporates these apparently irreconcilable impulses is *The Boys in the Band*, William Friedkin's 1970 adaptation of Mart Crowley's 1968 play. Crowley's play had opened a year before the Stonewall riots galvanized the gay community into open resistance against the repressive social order represented by the police. Friedkin, chosen to direct the film adaptation on the basis of his recent adaptation of Harold Pinter's *The Birthday Party* (1968), shot the film in New York City. Refusing to open out Crowley's story of a birthday party that brings together a group of gay friends with a straight outlier who makes waves when he drops in unexpectedly, he staged most of the action in the apartment of Michael (Kenneth Nelson), the party's acerbic host, in a manner whose claustrophobic closeups and group shots and increasingly impressionistic lighting suggested a gay version of *Long Day's Journey into Night*, Sidney Lumet's 1962 adaptation of Eugene O'Neill's one-set 1941 play. The main action, however, was preceded by an opening montage that introduced most of the main characters, coding them as gay in different ways. The most flamboyant of these initial impressions is made by Emory (Cliff Gorman), whose sexual identity is overdetermined by his occupation as the owner of an antique store, his pet poodle, his exaggerated facial expressions, his mincing walk, and the undisguised attention he attracts from other men who watch him as he walks down the street as Harpers Bizarre's cover of Cole Porter's "Anything Goes" plays in the background. Other characters presented in parallel with Emory are less obviously coded, and some of them, like the carefully dressed lawyer Hank (Laurence Luckinbill), would be hard to identify as gay if they were not presented in obvious parallels with Emory.

From the beginning, the film sets up a tension between *identifying with* the characters, a relationship that requires particular compassion and empathy from straight audiences in 1970, and *identifying them* as gay, a process that automatically distances the audience from the group it is categorizing and monstrating. It is not merely the audience that is confronted with this contradiction, for the entire cast, once they have gathered in Michael's apartment, are clearly and painfully under its sway. The partygoers display their painful internalization of this double consciousness by their exceptionally self-conscious performances of themselves as gay. Michael changes from one cashmere sweater to another in the course of the party, and his guests make frequent catty references to each other as fags, girls, queers, and pansies. They wield these epithets in play, antagonizing but never seriously alienating each other, until the unexpected arrival of Michael's straight friend Alan McCarthy (Peter White), who is clearly going through an unexplained emotional crisis, in the middle of the group's spontaneous but joyously and tightly choreographed dance to Martha and the Vandellas' "Heat Wave" (see Figure 8.7). Alan's entrance brings the dance to an abrupt

FIGURE 8.7 *As Donald (Frederick Combs) looks on, Michael (Kenneth Nelson), Bernard (Reuben Greene), Emory (Cliff Gorman), and Larry (Keith Prentice) break into a performance of "Heat Wave" in* The Boys in the Band *(1970).*

end, and later, when in speaking privately to Michael, he calls Emory "a little pansy," Michael is so obviously offended that Alan feels moved to add an awkward apology, just as the word "nigger," freely deployed by the African Americans in Blaxploitation films, carries a different and entirely unacceptable charge when it is used by white characters against them. In performing gay, it seems, Michael's friends are performing only for themselves and each other, not for any straight audiences—except of course for the ones who happen to be watching the film.

The film is driven by its characters' performance as gay, by their loathing of the sexual identity they share, and by their performance of self-loathing. These tropisms all crest in Michael's insistence on playing a game in which each guest must telephone someone he has loved and confess his love over the phone. The game, designed to encourage Alan, whom Michael is convinced is a closeted gay man, backfires when Michael learns that the person Alan has telephoned is his wife, whose separation from him led to the tearful breakdown that encouraged him to seek out Michael's company in the first place. The moral Michael's friend and lover Donald (Frederick Combs) draws from Michael's shocked inability to accept this revelation, is that "maybe we just need to hate ourselves a little bit less." Absent the self-hatred that has fueled the party, the film ends quietly with Michael's departure for Midnight Mass, affirming the religious beliefs that have been savagely ridiculed by Harold (Leonard Frey), who unblinkingly describes himself as "a thirty-two-year-old, ugly, pockmarked Jew fairy," and whose birthday Emory had sought to celebrate by purchasing the favors of Cowboy Tex (Robert La Tourneaux) for his big night.

Vincent Canby, in reviewing the film, praised its direction and its performers, all of whom were reprising their roles from the play's original run, but expressed serious reservations about the "consciously archaic theatricality" of its source material, which he compared to Clare Boothe Luce's *The Women* (1936). "There is something basically unpleasant," he concluded, about the "inspiration of love–hate" in a play that "finally does nothing more than exploit its (I assume) sincerely conceived stereotypes," and added, "Crowley's vision of the world would seem to have been attained from a vantage point about three millimeters above the heads of his characters."[12] All this may be even more apt than Canby realized. MGM's 1939 screen adaptation of *The Women*, whose 150 cast members were all female, purports to give audiences a glimpse into the lives of a substantial cross-section of modern women as men never see them. But Luce's women think of nothing but how to get, keep, and manipulate men. They dress for men, work out for men, scheme against each other for men, and are presented from beginning to end as being defined by men. The opening credits of the film, which display a cameo portrait of each cast member dissolving into an animal—a deer for Mary Haines (Norma Shearer), a wildcat for Crystal Allen (Joan Crawford), a lamb for Peggy Day (Joan Fontaine), and so on—mark them all, in a triumph of identifying over identifying with, as specimen animals confined in a zoo for the delectation of exactly the audiences most likely to identify them as types, an audience of men and self-alienated women. The departure Crowley's play and Friedkin's film make from this earlier pattern, as Canby acutely notes, is that their characters self-consciously internalize these reductive categories and then rage against their inability, which the playwright fully shares, to rise above them.

In seeking to meld the niche audience bonding experience that would attract gay audiences with the minstrel caricatures that would appeal to straight audiences, *The Boys in the Band* reveals more nakedly than any other film about contemporaneous identity politics the paradox at the heart of mass entertainment that attempts to position itself both inside and outside whatever marginalized communities it seeks to represent. Although the film has dated severely, it remains ahead of its time in one strikingly prescient way: in seeing its characters' sexuality as a performance, or a series of performances, by both the actors, all of them simultaneously playing individual characters and readily understood caricatures even as they recreate their stage performances for the screen, and the characters, all of them constantly and self-consciously playing themselves. Unlike Canby, who expresses discomfort because the characters make no attempt to present external behavior that will ultimately reveal a unitary, unadulterated subjectivity, the filmmakers reject the possibility of such a sincere subjectivity out of hand.

Defining identity as performance reveals a gay version of the double consciousness W.E.B. Du Bois ascribed to African Americans compelled to be "always looking at oneself through the eyes of others" and "longing to attain self-conscious manhood" without sacrificing either their African or their American roots.[13] This time, however, there is an important difference. Unlike blackness, which is universally recognized by both insiders and outsiders who are not blind, both public and private displays of gay identity can be to a great extent chosen, modulated, and performed. So the film's view of sexual identity as performance suggests that the paradoxical relationship between identifying as and identifying with is at the heart of both identity perception and identity formation.

This paradox finds a surprisingly close echo in making and studying adaptations for audiences who enjoy what Linda Hutcheon calls "an interpretive doubling, a conceptual flipping back and forth between the work we know and the work we are experiencing."[14] An important lesson attempts to screen hitherto silenced populations reveal about adaptation is that, although these two perspectives do indeed involve something like this flipping back and forth, they are neither mutually exclusive nor even dualistic. Like the characters in *The Boys in the Band*, we are never wholly inside the frame—our experience is never identical to that of any of the characters—because with rare and fleeting exceptions, we are always well aware that we are watching a movie, an object of entertainment, and therefore always assume that we have permission to be entertained by travails and misfortunes that we would find deeply distressing if they happened to us. The oscillation Hutcheon describes is not therefore between an experience that depends on an insider's experience of the *Ding an sich* and an outsider's appreciation of its frame, but among many different frames or scripts—our awareness of performers, genres, styles, and allusions, as well as adapted texts—that all depend on our outsider status, our awareness that identification is itself a construction.

The dialectic of empathy and categorical judgment behind *The Boys in the Band* returns ten years later in a film that might seem to be its polar opposite: *Ordinary People*, the 1980 adaptation of Judith Guest's best-selling 1976 debut novel. Everything about the film, which marked the directorial debut of Hollywood star Robert Redford, seems to set its face against counterculture filmmaking. Its painterly lighting and cutting, like those of Woody Allen's *Interiors* (1978), suggest the closest American mainstream cinema had yet approached to the filmmaking style of Ingmar Bergman. So do its deliberate pacing, its dependence on studied understatements, silences, and refusals to engage in open conflict, and its casting of frequent counterculture star Donald Sutherland as Calvin Jarrett and television star Mary Tyler Moore as his wife Beth, who have yet to come to terms with the death of their son Buck in a boating accident a year before the story begins when their surviving son, Conrad (Timothy Hutton), crippled by survivor's guilt and post-traumatic stress disorder, is released from the hospital to which he was sent after attempting to kill himself.

The film insists that the Jarretts are ordinary people suffering under the weight of an extraordinary tragedy. But its title is ironic, not only because the Jarretts are anything but ordinary, but also because they are persistently coded as white Anglo-Saxon Protestants. Although Conrad tells Jeannine Pratt (Elizabeth McGovern), his tentative new girlfriend, that he does not believe in God, the Jarretts are firmly established as secular Christians by their determined celebration of Christmas, the film's steady diet of religious choral music, and the family's marking of Dr. Tyrone Berger (Judd Hirsch), the psychiatrist Conrad agrees to see, as "Jewish, or maybe just German." Calvin and Beth attend a community theater's presentation of a couple that unwittingly burlesques their own decorous emotional estrangement. Conrad, reading *Jude the Obscure* for an English class, seems to be the only student in the room who takes its oppressive fatalism seriously. Calvin jogs with business associates. Beth shops at a suburban mall near the family home in Lake Forest, Illinois. Conrad takes Jeannine bowling on their first date. Conrad and Beth take time away from home to play golf with her relatives in Houston. Conrad recalls the time Beth enjoined him to change the blue shirt he had chosen for Buck's funeral to a white shirt. The cumulative effect of these details, most of them quite unobtrusive, is to insinuate a correlation between the family's apparent cultural privilege as members of the WASP establishment and their incapacity for emotional connection as profound as that of Michael and the partygoers in *The Boys in the Band*. The banality of the characters' conversation is emphasized equally by their habit of repeating phrases they volley back and forth to fill the silence that hovers over their dining-room table and the vacuous snippets of dialogue floating up from a party Beth and Calvin attend (see Figure 8.8).

The film's oscillation between soliciting sympathy for the Jarretts in their devastating loss and adopting an anthropological perspective on their grieving, or refusing to grieve, is resolved by its handling of Dr. Berger, who eventually persuades Conrad to express and manage his unwelcome emotions rather than seeking to suppress them, as the film's most trustworthy voice; Beth, who refuses to acknowledge her own emotions or anyone else's, as his antagonist; and Conrad, who emerges early on as the primary focus of the film, the person whose story this will be. After a series of harrowingly muted scenes in which Beth finds herself unable to return Conrad's loving embrace and hears a tearful Calvin tell her, "We would have been all right if there hadn't been any mess. But you can't handle mess. You need everything neat and easy," she retreats to their bedroom and gets ready to pack her suitcases for her departure from her husband and son when suddenly her face is contorted, as if by some unseen power within, by wave after wave of the violent grief she had forbidden to come to the surface. The most ordinary people, the film suggests, are subject to extraordinary emotional pressures, but the hegemony of WASP culture has depended on repressing them, and

FIGURE 8.8 *A typical morning in* Ordinary People *(1980) reveals Calvin (Donald Sutherland), Conrad (Timothy Hutton), and Beth (Mary Tyler Moore) already quietly but imperviously estranged from each other.*

Calvin and Conrad, sharing a heartfelt embrace the next morning, can only count themselves lucky to have escaped the stifling cultural imperatives the departed Beth decreed they perform.

Monstrating the short story

It might seem that the WASP family *Ordinary People* examines with such anthropological detachment closes the circle on the range of marginalized groups—the counterculture, African Americans, members of other minority groups, second-wave feminists, other-abled populations, and the gay community—during the 1970s and 1980s. But film adaptations during the era are also notable for two other attempts to screen the silenced, although in both cases what has hitherto been silenced is not populations but genres: one surprisingly respectable literary genre Hollywood had largely ignored, and the other a notoriously disreputable film genre newly revitalized by adaptation.

The first of these is the American short story. To read the roll call of classic American short stories—Nathaniel Hawthorne's "My Kinsman, Major Molineux," Stephen Crane's "The Upturned Face," Henry James's "The Real Thing," Kate Chopin's "Désirée's Baby," Edith Wharton's "A Bottle of Perrier," Sherwood Anderson's "Death in the Woods," Ernest Hemingway's "Hills Like White Elephants," F. Scott Fitzgerald's "A Diamond as Big as the Ritz," Ring Lardner's "Haircut," William Faulkner's "Red Leaves," Katherine Anne Porter's "Pale Horse, Pale Rider," John O'Hara's "The Doctor's Son," Zora Neale Hurston's "The Bone of Contention," Flannery O'Connor's "Good Country People," J.D. Salinger's "A Perfect Day for Bananafish," James Baldwin's "Going to Meet the Man," John Cheever's "The Brigadier and the Golf Widow," Philip Roth's "Defender of the Faith," Donald Barthelme's "Views of My Father Weeping," Raymond Carver's "Fever"—is to uncover one missed opportunity after another, for none of them has ever been adapted to the cinema. When the classic American short stories are filmed, the films are frequently thirty-minute shorts with limited distribution and short shelf lives. Hollywood, which more often seeks literary cachet in adaptations of English or Continental novels than American novels, has long maintained an even greater distance from the American short story.

The industry's neglect of the short story is particularly surprising in view of the unusual pride of place American literature accords the genre. The modern short story, like jazz and the musical theater, is a distinctively American invention that was arguably developed to give voice to a specifically American experience of alienation, uncertainty, and impiety that in important ways was coeval with modernity itself. So it is logical to conclude that "in the tradition of American prose fiction, the short story occupies a much more prominent place than in, for example, British fiction—that it indeed is the unmarked mode of American fiction."[15] Unlike the novel, whose inclusive nature "richly affirm[s] bourgeois individuals of all ages, genders, and temperaments in the richness of their political, social, moral, cultural, sexual, emotional, and psychopathological being," the short story, which "dis-affirms" these categories and the identities based on them, "renders meaning incompatible with existence."[16] The classic American stories from Nathaniel Hawthorne to Raymond Carver neither take the form of improving moral anecdotes nor chart a path from ignorance to wisdom through a sudden inspiring epiphany. When Hawthorne, for example, wishes to point a moral in stories like "The Birthmark" or "Young Goodman Brown," the moral usually requires the death or destruction of the characters who fail to learn it, as in the first of these stories, or learn it all too well, as in the second. Canonical American short stories are shaped instead by a movement from false knowledge to a disillusionment that strips the characters of their certitudes, leaving them wiser, more experienced, but devastated, uprooted, or altogether more fragile, a trajectory unlikely to appeal to an industry whose extreme capital intensiveness encourages it to aim at a mass audience it habitually diagnoses as hungry for uplift. Given Hollywood's even more marked tendency, duly promoted by the enforcement of the Production Code during the heyday of the studio era to foster an official public culture of affirmation, inclusiveness, and happy endings, it is hardly surprising that even when the movies have looked to American literature for material, they have passed over short stories whose import is agnostic, often anti-gnostic.

Not every Hollywood movie, of course, subscribes to an official national culture that prescribes sincerity, hard work, community solidarity, unquenchable optimism, and collective wisdom as the keys to spiritual and material success. The gangster film, as Robert Warshow memorably observed seventy years ago, "express[es] that part of the American psyche which rejects the qualities and demands of modern life, which rejects 'Americanism' itself" by preaching a counter-gospel in which the gangster's unquenchable "drive for success" leads inevitably to "anonymity and death."[17] This line of reasoning would seem to encourage the production of similarly anti-American movies, or at least anti-gospel-of-American-success movies, based on short stories. But although all Dashiell Hammett's novels and all Raymond Chandler's novels spawned film adaptations, Hollywood has ignored their short stories as well, presumably because of the stigma that clung to subliterary venues like *Dime Detective* and *Black Mask*.

Even so, a number of notable Hollywood films have been based on American short stories: *It Happened One Night* (1934), *Bringing Up Baby* (1938), *Stagecoach* (1939), *The Killers* (1946, 1964), *All about Eve* (1950), *High Noon* (1952), *Rear Window* (1954), *A Face in the Crowd* (1957), *Breakfast at Tiffany's* (1962), *The Swimmer* (1968), *Yentl* (1983), *Total*

Recall (1990), *The Shawshank Redemption* (1994), *In the Bedroom* (2001), *Million Dollar Baby* (2004), and *Brokeback Mountain* (2005). Unlike adaptations of American novels from *The Scarlet Letter* to *Cosmopolis*, however, these have been more or less invisible adaptations, most of them based on relatively little-known contemporary stories rather than canonical American short stories. Even as the studios drew obsessively from contemporaneous magazine fiction to feed their voracious appetite for new material, they never looked upon the canonical corpus of American short fiction for consistent nourishment, and when they have adapted American short stories, they have done so, by and large, without advertising them as adaptations or promoting the stories on which they have drawn. Part of the reason for this different treatment is doubtless economic. As the Disney Corporation has abundantly demonstrated, purchasing adaptation rights to a novel, even an unknown novel, offers myriad opportunities for cross-branding that only begin with reprinting the novel in question. But there are no tie-in editions of short stories that have been successfully adapted because no one purchases short stories individually, and it is a rare short story that establishes characters or worlds firmly enough to root profitable franchises.

Apart from Frank Capra's continuing interest in the short stories that provided the basis for *Platinum Blonde* (1933), *Lady for a Day* (1933), *It Happened One Night, Mr. Deeds Goes to Town* (1936), *Meet John Doe* (1941), and *It's a Wonderful Life* (1946), all but the last adapted by the screenwriter Robert Riskin, the other examples in this list are one-offs that do not present themselves as adaptations of short stories, incidental adaptations most audiences do not recognize as adaptations at all. Very few people have read "Night Bus" or "The Tin Star" or "It Had to Be Murder" or "The Wisdom of Eve," or even recognize their titles. And most of those who have read them are struck by how freely their film adaptations depart from them. Rendering short stories invisible by remolding or jettisoning their essential elements or underplaying their importance, even when they have been chosen as source material, is a second strategy Hollywood has used to screen out the American short story.

Still another strategy is illustrated by *Short Cuts* (1993), which adapts the structure of the anthology film to present a bouquet of nine stories by Raymond Carver—"Neighbors," "They're Not Your Husband," "Vitamins," "Will You Please Be Quiet, Please?," "So Much Water So Close to Home," "A Small, Good Thing," "Jerry and Molly and Sam," "Collectors," "Tell the Women We're Going"—and Carver's poem "Lemonade." The principal innovation of the screenplay by director Robert Altman and Frank Barhydt is that instead of presenting the stories in separate sections, in the manner of *O. Henry's Full House* (1952) or Frank and Eleanor Perry's *Trilogy* (1969), which dramatizes three short stories by Truman Capote, it cuts freely from one story to the next, uniting them through visual connections the film supplies (the helicopters spraying insecticide to counter a medfly invasion, the ubiquitous presence of water, the frequent emphasis on the shame or awkwardness of nudity, the climactic earthquake that affects the entire cast, at least briefly, and supplies an unexpected new resolution to one of Carver's plot lines), thematic connections already implicit in Carver's stories (the tendency of banal social occasions to lead to uncomfortable revelations, the breakdown of social rituals that continually betray the feelings they have been developed to protect, the abiding unhappiness of married couples, the remarkable contingency of characters unmoored from the ancient certitudes for which they still hunger), and the deployment of parallel images, characters, and storylines as illustrative analogies of each other that help make Altman's collage of stories feel like a narrative world. *Short Cuts* suggests that a world whose denizens, most of whom remain strangers to each other, have forsaken their roots, their traditions, their formative beliefs, and their trust in each other and the categories that give their lives purpose and meaning is still an intelligible world whose own meaning arises from the relationship between the film's repeated revelation of its thoroughly normative impiety and the accretion of individual and social details that can make that revelation entertaining. Although the film pulled off the rare feat of motivating a tie-in collection of the stories on which it was based, its structure consistently screens out individual stories by subordinating their trajectories to the presentation of a coherent world in the manner of such Altman non-adaptations as *Nashville* (1975), *A Wedding* (1978), *Health* (1980), and *Prêt-à-Porter* (1994).

The most illuminating laboratory for examining two other strategies filmmakers have used to screen out the agnostic, impious, anti-affirmative, anti-teleological, anti-American force of the classic American short story is the two most sustained attempts to film any significant portion of the corpus of classic American short stories. The first of these is the eight Edgar Allan Poe adaptations produced and mostly directed for Universal-International by Roger Corman, the most notable filmmaker since Capra to take a sustained interest in the short story, in the early 1960s. Taken together, these eight films—*House of Usher* (1960), *Pit and the Pendulum* (1961), *Premature Burial* (1962), *Tales of Terror* (1962), *The Raven* (1963), *The Haunted Palace* (1963), *The Masque of the Red Death* (1964), and *The Tomb of Ligeia* (1964)—are most often remembered as a landmark, not in the history of adaptation or even of Poe adaptation, but in the history of exploitation cinema. Corman's films increasingly jettison the narrative armature of Poe's tales in order to monstrate sensationalistic, taboo-busting situations and tableaux, marked most clearly by the systematic sexualizing of the stories (and of the poems "The Raven" and "The Haunted Palace"). These films, most of them widescreen color spectaculars that handle the events of Poe's stories and poems with a predictably free hand, mine their nominal sources for scenes of suspense and violence and emphasize or add sexual subtexts—the same thing Corman does when he adapts three Hawthorne stories in *Twice-Told Tales* (1963).

If these examples suggest that Hollywood has not so much neglected as betrayed the American short story through unfaithful adaptations that screen out Poe's most challenging elements in favor of sensationalistic situations and provocative images, a convenient counterexample or corrective way of achieving the same result is provided by the twenty-one installments in *The American Short Story Collection* Robert Geller's company Learning in Focus produced some twenty years later. These forty-five-minute films—*The Music School* (1974), based on the story by John Updike; *Parker Adderson, Philosopher* (1974), by Ambrose Bierce; *The Jolly Corner* (1975), by Henry James; *Almos' a Man* (1976), by Richard Wright; *Bernice Bobs Her Hair* (1976), by F. Scott Fitzgerald; *I'm a Fool* (1977), by Sherwood Anderson; *The Blue Hotel* (1977), by Stephen Crane; *The Displaced Person* (1977), by Flannery O'Connor; *Soldier's Home* (1977), by Ernest Hemingway; *The Golden Honeymoon* (1980), by Ring Lardner; *The Man That Corrupted Hadleyburg* (1980), by Mark Twain; *The Greatest Man in the World* (1980), by James Thurber; *The Jilting of Granny Weatherall* (1980), by Katherine Anne Porter; *Barn Burning* (1980), by William Faulkner; *Paul's Case* (1980), by Willa Cather; *Rappaccini's Daughter* (1980), by Nathaniel Hawthorne; *The Sky Is Gray* (1980), by Ernest J. Gaines; *Pigeon Feathers* (1988), by John Updike; *The Revolt of Mother* (1988), by Mary E. Wilkins Freeman; *Love and Other Sorrows* (1989), by Harold Brodkey; and *The Hollow Boy* (1990), by Hortense Calisher—treat their source material in the opposite way from Corman, choosing the most unexceptionable stories from the oeuvres of canonical American storytellers, muting the more disturbing challenges the stories' material might pose to student audiences to think outside the box, moralizing their endings, and softening their more radical attacks on the possibility of a stable, knowable personal identity and a coherent world.

Unlike Corman's Poe adaptations, these films, financed by PBS and intended in large part for classroom use, are not disfigured by lurid interludes of the sex or violence Corman injects, or indeed by the impious challenges to official American verities that marked the most characteristic stories of the authors under adaptation. Instead, their source stories seem to have been chosen specifically to avoid such moments. Hemingway is represented by "Soldier's Home" instead of "Hills Like White Elephants," Faulkner by "Barn Burning" instead of "A Rose for Emily," Porter by "The Jilting of Granny Weatherall" instead of "Flowering Judas," O'Connor by "The Displaced Person" instead of "A Good Man Is Hard to Find." But Geller's films, which come across as literary to a fault, are equally unfaithful, although in the opposite way. Instead of pumping the stories up with lurid intimations of sex and violence, they clean them up, homogenizing and monstrating them as classics to be properly reverenced, museum exhibitions of the American short story for the classroom. Several of the stories adapted—"I'm a Fool," "Bernice Bobs Her Hair," "Barn Burning," "The Hollow Boy," "The Sky Is Gray"—were evidently chosen because they were coming-of-age fables likely to appeal, or at least to offer admonition, to school-age audiences; others, like "Rappaccini's Daughter," "Soldier's Home," "Almos' a Man," and "Pigeon Feathers," have been recast as coming-of-age stories, with decidedly mixed results.

The ending of *Rappaccini's Daughter*, for example, cuts Professor Pietro Baglioni, the mentor and confidant who has supplied Giovanni Guasconti with the alleged antidote he fatefully urges the poisoned and poisonous Beatrice Rappaccini to take, from the film's final scene. As a result, the audience no longer hears Baglioni's profoundly equivocal final speech, delivered "in a tone of triumph mixed with horror": "Rappaccini! Rappaccini! And is *this* the upshot of your experiment?," or, for that matter, the last words Hawthorne supplied for Beatrice to Giovanni: "Oh, was there not, from the first, more poison in thy nature than in mine?"[18] Instead, the film ends on a more reassuringly sentimental note, as Beatrice dies without a word of reproach crossing her lips or a word of charged commentary from an observer whose lack of objectivity suddenly becomes monstrously clear.

Two questions in the Study Guide supplied on the DVD release of *Pigeon Feathers* frame the series' approach to the American short story with particular clarity. One of them, "How does the narrative perspective influence your understanding of the story?,"[19] implies that the narrative perspective of the story and its film adaptation are identical, even though the story ends with a revelation that is both more intimate—after shooting the pigeons that have invaded his family's barn, Updike's agnostic teenager David Kern never speaks aloud his newfound conviction that "the God who had lavished such craft upon these worthless birds would not destroy His whole Creation by refusing to let David live forever"[20]—and more equivocal in its very certainty than the conclusion of the film's David (Christopher Collet): "They *are* God's creatures. [...] Maybe we *don't* die" (see Figure 8.9). The other, "Is David's destruction of the birds necessary for his salvation? Is Updike trying to be ironic? Explain,"[21] encourages viewers to decide either that Updike is being ironic by indicating that because the killing of the birds is not necessary to David's salvation, he has simply reached a false conclusion, or the ending can be taken at face value because Updike is not being ironic. Updike's story is certainly ironic, but its ironies, softened into a warmer, less confrontational hypothetical in the film, are considerably more complicated than this either-or question suggests.

Despite the "dedication to the original stories" the DVD notes on *The American Short Story Collection* describes as central, its deeply contradictory goals are better encapsulated by Geller when he recalls in an

FIGURE 8.9 *The care God has lavished on the pigeons he has just shot helps assure David Kern (Christopher Collet) about the prospect of his own immortality in* Pigeon Feathers *(1988).*

interview whose transcript is also reproduced on the DVDs that he wanted in adapting "Soldier's Home" "to make sure that Hemingway came alive and at the same time, hoping it could be an entertaining film experience." To the twin scripts of faithfulness to the stories and faithfulness to the demands of entertainment the National Endowment for the Humanities, which provided financing for the series' first productions, added the charge to "select stories which characterized American values and American history over a hundred year period. Those hundred years were to be reflected as part of a celebration for America's bicentennial." It is not clear exactly when this hundred-year period occurred, but it includes both "Rappaccini's Daughter" (1844) and "The Sky Is Gray" (1963), although not any stories by Poe, presumably because his stories have insufficient affinities with American values and American history. As much as the Hollywood system to which it offers such a bracing alternative, *The American Short Story Collection* screens out transgressive themes, techniques, and figures in the American short story because it is even more deeply committed to a more exigent script, a quasi-official American ideological narrative.

Adaptations for adults

At the same time that Hollywood adaptations of the period were both screening in and screening out the classic American short story, the cinema, in an even more transgressive efflorescence of the development that produced Roger Corman's Poe exploitations, offered a new take on the widely execrated genre of the pornographic film. The success of Andy Warhol's 1969 *Blue Movie*, the first sexually explicit film to be widely released in American movie theaters, ushered in what is still called the Golden Age of Porn, a brief period during which sexually explicit features often played outside the circuit of adults-only theaters and were advertised and reviewed in major newspapers. *Behind the Green Door* (1972) was entered in the Cannes Film Festival; *The Devil in Miss Jones* (1973) was compared to Jean-Paul Sartre's 1944 play *No Exit*; and *Deep Throat* (1973) was discussed by such mainstream commentators as Martin Scorsese, Brian De Palma, Jack Nicholson, Johnny Carson, Frank Sinatra, and Spiro Agnew.

Even in an era during which they were marked by higher production values and more prominent and coherent narratives, few pornographic features were framed as literary adaptations. Although they often borrow narratives as armatures on which to scaffold the attractions—that is, the sex scenes—audiences have come to see, adult films have rarely sought to legitimize themselves by trading on the cultural capital of the texts they adapt. Like Blaxploitation films, their hypotextual universe tends to be cinematic rather than literary, and most of the notable pornographic adaptations to date have been parodies, spoofs, or exploitations of Hollywood movies. Yet Kyle Meikle, noting "adaptation scholars' tendency to define pornographic adaptations in the language of interpretation and intertextuality," has proposed "consider[ing] pornographic adaptation as both an industrial strategy and fannish tactic that calls for the language of interactivity instead."[22]

Unsurprisingly, the literary adaptations that emerged from the adult film industry during the golden age of porn overwhelmingly chose British, not American, works to adapt: *Dorian Gray* (1970), based on a property that seemed made for precisely this treatment; *The Passions of Carol* (1975), based on *A Christmas Carol*; *Alice in Wonderland: An X-Rated Musical Comedy* (1976); *The Autobiography of a Flea* (1976); and *The Amorous Adventures of Fanny Hill* (1983). Richard Burt has identified a surprisingly prevalent strain of "Bardcore," pornographic films more or less loosely based on Shakespeare: *A Midsummer Night's Cream*, *X Hamlet*, *Othello: Dangerous Desire*, *Taming of the Screw*, *Juliet and Romeo*, *In the Flesh* (cf. *Macbeth*).[23]

The most prominent adapter of literary texts to adult films was Radley Metzger. Beginning with *Carmen, Baby* (1967), which updated Prosper Merimee's 1845 novella, he interspersed his other films with a string of increasingly high-toned erotic adaptations: *Therese and Isabelle* (1967), based on Violette Leduc's 1966 novel; *Camille 2000* (1969), based on Alexandre Dumas *fils*'s 1848 novella *La dame aux camélias; Score* (1974), based on Jerry Douglas's off-Broadway 1971 play; and, as Henry Paris, *Naked Came the Stranger* (1975), based on the serial novel attributed to Penelope Ashe; *The Image* (1975), based on the 1956 novel by Catherine Robbe-Grillet writing as Jean de Berg; and *The Opening of Misty Beethoven* (1976), an adaptation of George Bernard Shaw's 1913 play *Pygmalion* by way of Alan Jay Lerner and Frederick Loewe's 1956 Broadway musical *My Fair Lady*. Despite generating any number of titles that paid tongue-in-cheek homage to their putative progenitors, from Russ Meyer's *Beyond the Valley of the Dolls* (1970) to Wakefield Poole's *Boys in the Sand* (1971), the first explicit gay film to display its production credits, to *Lust Horizons* (1976), adult films continued to treat their allusions to literary texts as throwaway jokes. It was only a generation later, long after the rise of home video had ended the golden age of porn, that audiences with a taste for both erotica and adaptation could find *Secretary*, Steven Shainberg's 2002 adaptation of Mary Gaitskill's 1988 short story, and *Fifty Shades of Grey* (2015), *Fifty Shades Darker* (2017), and *Fifty Shades Freed* (2018), Sam Taylor-Johnson's adaptations of the three novels Erika Mitchell published as E.L. James in 2011–12.

On the whole, pornographic films have avoided American literature for many of the same reasons Blaxploitation films have. Canonical American novels and plays and stories, few of which include explicit sex scenes, would have to be radically retooled to accommodate the desires of the target audience. The universe within which porn situates itself, like that of the film-school generation of directors, is demarcated by movies, not books or plays. And the relatively small number of adult films that have taken pains to model themselves, however casually, on literary originals have found in English and French literature a greater potential for the kind of taboo-busting meta-narrative that drives the market by positioning the films both inside and outside the mainstream. By providing the material for what Meikle calls "an erotics of adaptation," "a physiological model of adaptation" that asks "how viewers pleasure themselves to adaptations,"[24] pornographic adaptations recall in an unexpectedly provocative way the irreducibly liminal status of pornography, adaptation, and American literature.

Notes

1 Donald Bogle, *Toms, Coons, Mulattoes, Mammies, and Bucks: An Interpretive History of Blacks in American Films*, 5th ed. (New York: Bloomsbury, 2016), p. xxiv.

2 Vincent Canby, "Ossie Davis's *Cotton Comes to Harlem*," *New York Times*, June 11, 1970, p. 50.
3 Barbara Tepa Lupack, *Literary Adaptations in Black American Cinema: From Micheaux to Morrison* (Rochester: University of Rochester Press, 2002), pp. 344–56.
4 Greg M. Colón Semenza and Bob Hasenfratz, *The History of British Literature on Film, 1895–2015* (New York: Bloomsbury, 2015), p. 285.
5 Lupack, *Literary Adaptations in Black American Cinema*, p. 328.
6 Ed Guerrero, *Framing Blackness: The African American Image in Film* (Philadelphia, PA: Temple University Press, 1993), p. 123.
7 Molly Haskell, *From Reverence to Rape: The Treatment of Women in the Movies*, 2nd ed. (Chicago: University of Chicago Press, 1987), p. 153.
8 Sharon L. Snyder and David T. Mitchell, "Body Genres: An Anatomy of Disability in Film," in *The Problem Body: Projecting Disability on Film*, ed. Sally Chivers and Nicole Markotic (Columbus: Ohio State University Press, 2010), p. 181.
9 Paul K. Longmore, "Screening Stereotypes: Images of Disabled People," in *Screening Disability: Essays on Cinema and Disability*, ed. Christopher R. Smit and Anthony Enns (Lanham, MD: University Press of America, 2001), p. 7.
10 Martin F. Norden, *The Cinema of Isolation: A History of Physical Disability in the Movies* (New Brunswick: Rutgers University Press, 1994), pp. 288–89.
11 Roger Ebert, "Children of a Lesser God," *Chicago Sun-Times*, October 3, 1986, http://www.rogerebert.com/reviews/children-of-a-lesser-god-1986.
12 Vincent Canby, "Screen: 'Boys in the Band': Crowley Study of Male Homosexuality Opens," *New York Times*, March 18, 1970, http://www.nytimes.com/movie/review?_r=3&res=9E00E6D8173EE034BC4052DFB56683B669EDE.
13 W.E.B. DuBois, *The Souls of Black Folk* (1903; rpt. New York: Oxford University Press, 2007), pp. 8, 9.
14 Linda Hutcheon, with Siobhan O'Flynn, *A Theory of Adaptation*, 2nd ed. (New York: Routledge, 2013), p. 139.
15 Thomas Leitch, "The Debunking Rhythm of the American Short Story," in *Short Story Theory at a Crossroads*, ed. Susan Lohafer and Jo Ellyn Clarey (Baton Rouge: Louisiana State University Press, 1989), p. 147.
16 David Trotter, "Dis-enablement: Subject and Method in the Modernist Short Story," *Critical Quarterly* 52.2 (2010): 4, 6.
17 Robert Warshow, "The Gangster as Tragic Hero," in *The Immediate Experience: Movies, Comics, Theatre and Other Aspects of Popular Culture* (1952; rpt. New York: Atheneum, 1975), pp. 130, 132.
18 Nathaniel Hawthorne, *Tales and Sketches* (New York: Library of America, 1982), p. 1005.
19 Study Guide, *Pigeon Feathers* DVD (Monterey Video, 2007).

20 John Updike, *Pigeon Feathers* (New York: Knopf, 1962), p. 150.
21 Study Guide, *Pigeon Feathers* DVD.
22 Kyle Meikle, "Pornographic Adaptation: Parody, Fan Fiction and the Limits of Genre," *Journal of Adaptation in Film and Performance* 8.2 (June 2015): 124–25.
23 Richard Burt, "What the Puck?: Screening the (Ob)Scene in Bardcore *Midsummer Night's Dreams* and the Transmediatic Technologies of Tactility," in *Shakespeare on Screen: A Midsummer Night's Dream*, ed. Sarah Hatchuel and Nathalie Vienne-Guerrin (Havre: Publications de l'Université Rouen, 2004), p. 58.
24 Meikle, "Pornographic Adaptation," p. 137.

9

1989–2007: Adapt or Die

Watching the skies, and looking within

Although the history of American cinema is to a very great extent a history of popular genres like the Western, the gangster film, and the romantic comedy, surprisingly few genres are themselves American. Jazz is an American invention; so is musical theater, derived from but still quite distinct from the light operas and operettas popular in Europe. And a case can readily be made for the Americanness of Hollywood romantic comedies, gangster films, and especially Westerns. The history of American literature on film since 1989 has been largely driven by adaptations of two other popular genres, science fiction and comic books. The first of these is itself an adaptation of the Anglo-European science fiction of nineteenth-century writers like Jules Verne and H.G. Wells; the second depends on a quintessentially American genre coeval with the birth of the cinema. Both genres broke into Hollywood many years after the Western, the gangster film, and the American comedy.

If we count the prodigious output of Georges Méliès, the science fiction film is as old as the cinema. *A Trip to the Moon* (1902) is only the best-known of dozens of Méliès shorts that revolve around visionary voyages to exotic places, encounters with strange and wonderful aliens, and other scientific impossibilities the films dreamed into life with the help of elaborate makeup and stop-motion special effects. But despite occasional features like Fritz Lang's *Metropolis* (1926) and *Woman in the Moon* (1929), William Cameron Menzies's *Things to Come* (1936), based on a novel and screenplay by Wells, and twelve-episode serials like *Buck Rogers in the 25th Century* (1939), *Flash Gordon Conquers the Universe* (1940), and the odd science fiction Western *The Phantom Empire* (1935), in which singing Western star Gene Autry takes on the robots of the futuristic kingdom of Murania, the tradition of science fiction as a continuously popular genre dates from 1950, when the decline of the serial, the dramatic rise in the sale of televisions, a rash of variously publicized sightings of unidentified flying objects, and a generous dose of Cold War paranoia produced in rapid succession a cycle of science fiction films ostensibly about travel through outer space—tracing trajectories either *From the Earth to the Moon*, as the title of Byron Haskin's 1958 adaptation of Jules Verne's novel had it, or in the opposite direction, as in Menzies's *Invaders from Mars* (1953)—that incarnated the American audience's fears about technology in general and the atomic bomb in particular.

Science fiction films have always had a fraught relation to technology. Ever since Méliès, they have depended on cutting-edge technologies to realize their visions of imaginary creatures and their worlds and the devices necessary to explore, conquer, and if necessary defend against those worlds and creatures. Just as Hollywood musicals depended on synchronized sound and Westerns flourished in the era of Technicolor and widescreen processes, science fiction films have been driven by the technological advances that have made them more compelling, from the painstaking stop-motion effects of Ray Harryhausen in adaptations like Eugène Lourié's *The Beast from 20,000 Fathoms* (1953) and Nathan Juran's *The First Men in the Moon* (1964) to the digital effects of James Cameron films like *Terminator 2: Judgment Day* (1991) and *Avatar* (2009). At the same time, science fiction films have from the beginning taken as their subject the heightened ambivalence toward the promise and menace of futuristic technologies capable of spawning both utopian dreams and dystopian nightmares.

The groundwork for Hollywood's love–hate relationship to the technologies of the future was laid by Irving Pichel's 1950 film *Destination Moon*, which screenwriter Robert B. Heinlein adapted into a novella three months after the film's debut. The film is most noteworthy for basing its story of rocket travel to the moon on the best available scientific calculations, a strategy that gave a significant edge to its leading complication: after miscalculating the amount of fuel required to make the journey, the crew must determine which of its members to leave behind in order to make their ship light enough to return to Earth. *Destination Moon*, already preceded by Kurt Neumann's *Rocketship X-M* two months earlier, was followed by a cycle of adaptations about space exploration: *Flight to Mars* (1951), *Project Moon Base* (1953), *Forbidden Planet* (1956), *The Angry Red Planet* (1959), *The First Men in the Moon*. At the same time earthlings were encountering a wide variety of aliens and robots in their adventurous travels, other aliens were traveling to Earth in *The Thing from Another World* (1951), based on John W. Campbell's story, *The Day the Earth Stood Still* (1951), *It Came from Outer Space* (1953), *Invaders from Mars*, *The War of the Worlds* (1953), *This Island Earth* (1955), *Earth vs. the Flying Saucers* (1956), *Kronos* (1957), and *Robinson Crusoe on Mars* (1964). The two vectors were combined in *Flight to Mars* (1951), in which astronauts landing on Mars discover apparently friendly natives who secretly plot to use the visitors' spaceship to launch an invasion of Earth, and *When Worlds Collide* (1951), in which earthlings threatened by a new star hurtling toward Earth scramble to raise money for a rocket that will transport a nucleus of survivors to the planet orbiting that star.

Audiences who followed the closing injunction of *The Thing from Another World*—"Keep watching the skies!"—were motivated by a combination of excitement about the very real possibilities of space travel new technologies had opened and the fear of what earthlings might find or what might find them. The obvious fear these films expressed focused on the nuclear devices that had ended the war with Japan but now threatened all life on Earth, a fear expressed most directly in *Fail-Safe*, Sidney Lumet's 1964 adaptation of Eugene Burdick and Harvey Wheeler's 1962 novel, and *Dr. Strangelove, or How I Learned to Stop Worrying and Love the Bomb*, Stanley Kubrick's 1964 black comedy, adapted from Peter George's decidedly non-comic 1958 novel *Red Alert*, which Kubrick refocused on the insanely picayune inability of American statesmen and servicemen to look beyond their petty personal and national interests to grasp the magnitude of the threat the bomb posed to life on earth. Fear of the bomb and its potentially devastating effects inspired such movies as *Them* (1954), in which extraterrestrial invaders were replaced by giant spiders mutated by their exposure to nuclear radiation, and *Godzilla* (1956), the Japanese film whose monster, a similarly irradiated giant lizard, was soon joined by a host of other monsters. An equally potent and durable trope of science fiction movies of the period was the threat that aliens landing on Earth might disguise themselves as earthlings or colonize the bodies of earthlings. This threat was most memorably incarnated in *It Came from Outer Space, Invaders from Mars,* and *Invasion of the Body Snatchers*, whose paranoia has been widely interpreted as a reaction to contemporaneous politics—though "nobody has established whether *Invasion* is a protest against the political and social conformity called for by right-wing anti-Communists or that demanded by pro-Soviet collectivists."[1]

Most of these films were based on original screenplays rather than previously published material, partly because they aimed, like the combat films released during the Second World War, for a ripped-from-the-headlines urgency they were unlikely to find in genre fiction and partly because the leading American periodicals that published stories in the genre—*Weird Tales, Amazing Stories,* and *Astounding Science Fiction*—were pulp magazines that focused on precisely the kinds of sensational, cartoonish plots and characters *Destination Moon* had sought to leave behind. An important force in the science fiction film's rise to prominence in the 1950s was the appearance of the more literary and respectable *Magazine of Fantasy & Science Fiction*, originally *The Magazine of Fantasy*, in 1949. Almost immediately, *F&SF*, as fans dubbed it, began to supply new material suitable for Hollywood adaptations. Even so, the most notable science fiction adaptations of the period found their inspiration outside *F&SF. Robinson Crusoe on Mars* isolated Daniel Defoe's shipwrecked hero on the red planet;

Invasion of the Body Snatchers was based on Jack Finney's *Collier's* serial; *Forbidden Planet* updated the story of William Shakespeare's play *The Tempest*; *The War of the Worlds* was based on H.G. Wells's 1897 novel; *When Worlds Collide* adapted a novel by Edwin Balmer; and *It Came from Outer Space* took its inspiration from Ray Bradbury's unpublished short story treatment "The Meteor," a tale of aliens who took human form that also played an important role in inspiring *Invaders from Mars* and *Invasion of the Body Snatchers* as well.

Unlike the other leading lights of his generation of science fiction writers—Robert Heinlein, Isaac Asimov, and Arthur C. Clarke, whose work was adapted sporadically, sometimes many years after its original publication—Bradbury, whose obituary in the *New York Times* identified him as "the writer most responsible for bringing modern science fiction into the literary mainstream,"[2] was eagerly adapted as early as 1951. Following six television segments based on his work between 1951 and 1953 and *It Came from Outer Space*, *The Beast from 20,000 Fathoms* included a scene based on his story "The Fog Horn." Bradbury's early work, especially the stories collected in *The Martian Chronicles* (1950), used outer space as a new arena for staging age-old questions about the unquenchable appetite for exploration, the ability of new worlds to reawaken their visitors to the beauty of life, the often casual cruelty of colonization, difficulties in communicating that are exacerbated rather than resolved by telepathic communication, the troubled relations between different cultures, and the futile attempt to recreate a sense of home in other locations. Bradbury's explorers, whose continued longing for signs of their native culture wherever they travel makes them all too vulnerable to Martians masquerading as earthlings or presenting seductive simulacra or their culture, must adapt or die.

In 1953 John Huston invited Bradbury to write the screenplay for his adaptation of Herman Melville's novel *Moby-Dick*, an epic story of another monstrous menace an obsessive hero is driven to encounter. Following the film's release in 1956, Bradbury returned to television work, sometimes writing original teleplays, sometimes providing material for others' adaptations, for a period of forty years, bridging the gap between the stories of space exploration, colonization, and invasion that had provided the basis for so many science fiction films of the 1950s and more direct confrontations with the psychological demons his early space operas had revealed. *Fahrenheit 451* (1966), François Truffaut's first English-language film, developed the fear of censorship Bradbury had already expressed in "Usher II," a story in *The Martian Chronicles*, into a paranoid nightmare in which crews of firefighters travel the countryside not to put out fires but to start them, burning books, especially novels, wherever they find them, and encouraging in response every member of an underground community that still treasures literature to memorize the single book most important to him or her, so that instead of adapting books to their own ends, people adapt themselves to books. By contrast, Jack Smight's *The Illustrated Man* (1969) uses the florid illustrations—"They're not tattoos!" he repeatedly insists to the young man he meets on the road—that cover the body of Carl (Rod Steiger) to blur the line between Carl's love and hatred for Felicia (Claire Bloom), the woman who provided the painstaking illustrations that periodically come alive, between fantasy and reality, and between present, past, and future (see Figure 9.1). By allowing his body to become adapted into a text, Carl has forfeited his own happiness and threatens that of everyone whose path crosses his.

Perhaps the most highly regarded film based on Bradbury's fiction is Jack Clayton's *Something Wicked This Way Comes* (1972; remade in 1983), the story of an otherworldly carnival that comes to a small American town where two young boys live—a story Bradbury had originally written for the screen in 1958 and then, when the project languished, converted into a novel in 1962. Among the hundred other adaptations of Bradbury's work, the one that stands as his most distinctive achievement is *The Ray Bradbury Theatre*, a Canadian television series (1985–92) whose fifty-nine episodes mark the most sustained attempt to present televised adaptations of a single author's work since the 149 episodes of *Zane Grey Theatre* (1956–61) and the 271 episodes of *Perry Mason* (1957–66). Unlike both of these series, whose weekly schedule soon obliged them to complement their adaptations of Zane Grey and Erle Stanley Gardner with original teleplays, Bradbury not only introduced but provided material for every episode of *The Ray Bradbury Theatre*, often basing his teleplays on his earlier novels and stories whose writing process his voiceover introduction emphasized.

FIGURE 9.1 *Carl (Rod Steiger) is haunted by his own history and fantasies the illustrations—they're not tattoos—all over his body represent in* The Illustrated Man *(1969).*

More explicitly than any of the space operas of the 1950s, *Fahrenheit 451* marked a generic shift from stories of exploration fueled equally by the excitement of new discoveries and the fear of the dissolution or annihilation of human culture to the representation of futuristic dystopias in the mold of Aldous Huxley's *Brave New World* (1932) and George Orwell's *Nineteen Eighty-Four* (1949). A pivotal film in this transition was Stanley Kubrick's *2001: A Space Odyssey* (1968), which presents the dystopia that arises from the collision of human explorers with the computers their missions require as being right around the corner. Many of the film's early viewers reported frustration with its elliptical, often obscurantist storytelling, but no one complained about its visionary mise-en-scene, which celebrated the power of cinema to dream a harrowing future in compelling new terms. The famously exacting Kubrick spent two years personally supervising the film's postproduction work, with special attention to the traveling mattes that rooted its story of space exploration in realistic visuals. The result was a film whose state-of-the-art visuals still command respect from special-effects specialists fifty years after its release and thirty years after its traveling mattes have been replaced by digital effects.

Many later science fiction films from the *Star Wars* franchise, which began in 1977, to the *Alien* franchise, which began in 1979, would follow *It Came from Outer Space*, Universal–International's first release in 3-D, *The Beast from 20,000 Fathoms*, and *2001: A Space Odyssey* in rooting their appeal in striking monstrations against which they set ever more urgent questions about the nature and knowability of human identity. The most influential of this new generation of visually stunning internal explorations was *Blade Runner*, "the key postmodern science fiction film."[3] Directed in 1982 by Ridley Scott, who had made the first of the *Alien* movies, the film was based on Philip K. Dick's 1968 short story "Do Androids Dream of Electric Sheep?" Dick was in many ways Bradbury's opposite. Despite his near-lifelong financial straits, he remained a reclusive figure who disdained Hollywood, had little interest in licensing the rights to his work, was highly skeptical of any adaptations that were made, and declined a $400,000 fee to write a novelization of *Blade Runner* aimed at a youth audience. The only two adaptations of Dick's fiction before *Blade Runner* were two television segments that appeared in 1962 and 1981. Going further than Bradbury, who used the backdrops of outer space to explore the age-old moral and psychological problems of his human heroes and villains, Dick's fiction focused almost exclusively on alternate realities and the relations between the human and the non-human, the real and the non-real. The key figure in Dick is the cyborg or replicant, one of the many robotic machines built to work in the off-planet industrial colonies humans have established. As in the sequels to *Alien*, the threat of this non-human life-form is set against the equally serious threat of a faceless, ultimately antihuman industrial conglomerate—the Weyland-Tutani Corporation, which sponsors and monitors the calamitous space journeys in the *Alien* films, and the Tyrell Corporation, which manufactures and polices the rebellious replicants in *Blade Runner*. The replicants that escape to 2019 Los Angeles in *Blade Runner* have become so difficult to distinguish from humans like Rick Deckard (Harrison Ford), the operative charged with hunting them down and "retiring" them, that they threaten human identity even as they, like Hal, develop remarkably human-seeming problems of their own, from their hopeless aspiration to enjoy the freedoms and privileges reserved for their masters to their tragic uncertainty about who and what they really are. Unlike *The Thing*, which John Carpenter remade in the same year as *Blade Runner*, Scott's film follows Dick's story in rooting its alien life-forms firmly in human agency—people have deliberately created the replicants that they now see as threatening them—and endowing each of them with a poignant interiority that gives the bleakly dystopian world of *Blade Runner* a strong undercurrent of pathos that continues in a different vein in *Blade Runner 2049* (2017), whose replicant operative KD6-3.7 (Ryan Gosling), reversing the trajectory of the earlier film, comes to suspect that he is actually the human descendant of Deckard.

Dick suffered a fatal stroke at the age of fifty-three a few months before Scott's film was released, and *Blade Runner*, which received mixed reviews and performed indifferently at the box office, did not immediately inspire imitations. But its growing status as a cult film and visionary bleakness of its neo-noir Los Angeles cityscapes (see Figure 9.2) eventually inspired imitations as diverse as the television series *Battlestar Galactica* (1978–79), the manga and film franchise *Ghost in the Shell* (1989–2015), and the video

FIGURE 9.2 *The Los Angeles of* Blade Runner *(1982) is full of garish commercial signs, dreary weather, and echoes of film noir.*

game *Deus Ex* (2000). Dick's own greatest success in Hollywood came only years after his death. *Total Recall*, Paul Verhoeven's 1990 adaptation of Dick's 1966 short story "We Can Remember It for You Wholesale," uses the conceit of cyber-vacations that seek to implant experiences and memories of trips vacationers have never actually taken in their brains, continuing Dick's exploration of the relation between reality and its commercially created counterparts. So does Steven Spielberg's *Minority Report* (2002), based on Dick's 1956 short story, which uses the conventions of the futuristic action film to examine the moral dilemmas arising from the state's ability to use "precogs" to predict crimes before they happen and neutralize potential evildoers before they do any evil by exposing its hero, Precrime Division head John Anderton (Tom Cruise), to a perversion of the system by a colleague who has failed to reckon with the fact that once people can see their future, they have the power to change it. Richard Linklater's *A Scanner Darkly* (2006), based on Dick's 1977 novel, uses the unending drug wars in the United States as the basis for a dark parable about Bob Arctor (Keanu Reeves), an undercover cop who allows himself to get addicted to the powerful hallucinogenic Substance D in order to infiltrate the supply chain but discovers that Substance D is being manufactured and distributed by New-Path, a corporation whose rehab clinics are supposed to wean users from the drug but actually depend on them to work the fields in which the crops from which Substance D is derived are raised. Linklater puts a new visual spin on Dick's customary opposition between alternate reality and capitalism by shooting in digital video and then rotoscoping the entire film, turning its live-action visuals into highly stylized animation. More recent adaptations of Dick's work—*The Adjustment Bureau* (2011), *Blade Runner 2049*, and the television series *Minority Report* (2015), *The Man in the High Castle* (2015–19), and *Philip K. Dick's Electric Dreams* (2017–18), all emphasize the allure of his leading theme: the construction of, dependence on, and frequent collapse of artificial realities that both extend and challenge the reach of human consciousness. If Bradbury's heroes must adapt or die, adaptation itself becomes equally dangerous to Dick's characters, whose identities end up fatally compromised by the illusions to which they have submitted.

Heroes without canons

The science fiction film represents a late-blooming genre heavily dependent on the technology that was both its enabler and its subject. The superhero comic book adaptation, the other genre most representative of the 1990s, enjoyed an even more meteoric rise. Like science fiction films, comic book adaptations had been cropping up sporadically for years before they bloomed into a full-grown genre. Felix the Cat, the cartoon hero created by Pat Sullivan and Otto Messmer, had appeared in some fifty animated shorts even before his 1923 debut in the comic strips. Disney staples like Mickey Mouse and Donald Duck freely flitted between comic books and movies beginning in 1928. Li'l Abner Yokum, the hillbilly hero of Dogpatch, U.S.A., created in 1934 by cartoonist Al Capp, anchored a live-action feature film released by RKO as early as 1940 and an elaborate Paramount musical adaptation of the 1956 Broadway musical *Li'l Abner* in 1959. Superman, who made his comic book debut in 1938, appeared in a series of seventeen short animated films as early as 1941–43, the first nine produced by Fleischer Studios and the following eight by Famous Studios, a fifteen-part Columbia live-action serial in 1948, and a 1951 feature, *Superman and the Mole Men*, before settling into *Adventures of Superman*, a live-action television series of 104 episodes from 1952 to 1958. Batman, who had first appeared in *Detective Comics* a year after Superman, starred in two fifteen-part live-action Columbia serials, *Batman* (1943) and *Batman and Robin* (1949), before landing his own television show, whose 120 episodes unfolded in ABC-TV over three seasons, initially twice a week, then once a week, between 1966 and 1968. Ten years later, after Ellie Wood Walker had played the title character in a four-minute 1967 short, *Wonder Woman: Who's Afraid of Diana Prince?*, Cathy Lee Crosby starred as Wonder Woman in an abortive 1974 television pilot before being replaced with Lynda Carter in fifty-eight episodes of *Wonder Woman*, the first season, set during the time of the heroine's comic book debut, in the 1940s, airing on ABC from 1976 to 1977, the latter two, updated to the present day and renamed *The New Adventures of Wonder Woman*, on CBS from 1977 to 1979.

For better or worse, the ABC *Batman* is far better remembered than either *Adventures of Superman* or *Wonder Woman*. From its opening episode, it aimed for a self-consciously jokey tone through its eye-popping color scheme, its gallery of high-profile guest villains—Burgess Meredith as the Penguin, Frank Gorshin as the Riddler, Cesar Romero as the Joker, Julie Newmar as Catwoman—and its often self-mocking dialogue (offered a restaurant booth while Robin, a minor, waits outside in the Batmobile, Batman says he'll sit at the bar instead because "I don't want to appear conspicuous"). The series, hailed and reviled as a camp classic, provided an unintended but surprisingly pervasive antitype for the superhero features that would follow.

The first of these movies, *Superman*, was released by Warner Bros. in 1978. The film, budgeted at $55 million, was at the time the most expensive ever produced anywhere. As originally conceived, it boasted a 550-page combined shooting script for *Superman* and *Superman II* by Mario Puzo, who had written the 1969 novel *The Godfather* and collaborated with Francis Ford Coppola on the screenplay for its 1972 Paramount adaptation, and a cast including Marlon Brando as Jor-El and either Al Pacino, James

Caan, Steve McQueen, Clint Eastwood, Dustin Hoffman, or Muhammed Ali as his son Superman. When Richard Donner was brought in to replace Guy Hamilton as director, he cast the unknown actor Christopher Reeve in the title role, objected to the Puzo script as too campy, in the manner of the *Batman* TV series, and brought in Tom Mankiewicz for an extensive rewrite.

The result was the most reverential treatment imaginable of a comic book superhero, a film whose tone could easily have been mistaken, especially in its opening forty-five minutes, for that of *The Greatest Story Ever Told* (1965). Instead of apologizing for its comic book origins or self-consciously satirizing them, as the *Batman* television series had done, the film focuses on the underlying events they portray, which are inflated to the status of monumental myths by the film's deliberate pacing (it has a running time of 143 minutes), the straight-faced self-seriousness of Brando's Jor-El and Glenn Ford's Jonathan Kent, who tells his foster son Clark, whose superpowers he has seen in action, "You're here for a reason …. It's not to score touchdowns," and Superman himself, whose flying scenes with Lois Lane (Margot Kidder) are turned into a running joke that contrasts her wisecracking realism and her amatory pursuit by the comically inept Clark Kent, Superman's alter ego, with the grave self-assurance of Superman, who tells Lois after he first rescues her, "I hope this hasn't put you off flying. Statistically, it's still the safest way to travel" (see Figure 9.3).

The film consistently sets Superman's mythic sense of himself and the mission to help humankind inculcated in him by both his father figures against the broad comedy of the scenes at the *Daily Planet*, where Clark and Lois work as reporters, and the even more farcical performances of Gene

FIGURE 9.3 *Throughout* Superman *(1978), Lois Lane (Margot Kidder) clings with a variety of emotions to Superman (Christopher Reeve).*

Hackman as villainous Lex Luthor and Ned Beatty and Valerie Perrine as his incompetent, long-suffering sidekicks. The film's basic narrative strategy is to encourage audiences to anticipate obligatory moments and motifs *Superman* comics have already made familiar to them and then remind them of this familiarity when they arrive. It builds suspense by delaying Superman's initial entrance for forty-seven minutes while it cycles through the obligatory backgrounds of the infant Kal-El's escape from the doomed planet Krypton, his voyage to Earth, his discovery and adoption by Martha and Jonathan Kent, and his journey to the Fortress of Solitude to confront and absorb the teachings of his long-dead father. It plays with the audience's expectations by showing Clark Kent, looking for a place to change into Superman, briefly eying an open-air phone booth before moving on to a revolving door as offering greater concealment. More generally, the film pits a self-serious mythology of Superman, which it presents as normative, against the everyday routine of the *Daily Planet*, Clark's pursuit of Lois, and Luthor's felonious plots, which it presents as variously goofy and comically aberrant. The sequels that followed—*Superman II* (1980), *Superman III* (1983), and *Superman IV: The Quest for Peace* (1987)—were marked by gradually diminishing budgets and, in the case of *Superman III*, which began with an opening sequence out of Rube Goldberg and presented a hapless lead villain played by comedian Richard Pryor, a more consistently comic tone. These three sequels successively downplayed the mythic, quasi-religious overtones of the initial film but continued to oppose Superman's fundamental self-serious gravity to the frivolity of the scenes involving his alter ego and his antagonists.

Although *Superman* was a notable success at the box office, grossing over $134 million, that gross dropped for each of its three sequels: $108 for *Superman II*, $60 million for *Superman III*, $16 million for *Superman IV: The Quest for Peace*.[4] The relatively modest impact of the comic book movies that followed—only Robert Altman's *Popeye* (1980) and John Huston's *Annie* (1982) approached the financial success of the franchise, grossing $50 million and $57 million, respectively—made comic book adaptations seem like a brief, self-limiting cycle that would peter out unless something happened to bring them into the Hollywood mainstream.

That something was *Batman*, the monumentally influential 1989 adaptation in which Tim Burton set the pattern for dozens of superhero movies to come. The film's visionary production design for Gotham City, rejecting the high-key lighting and brightly saturated colors of *Superman* for a more stylized, neo-noir look clearly influenced by that of *Blade Runner*'s futuristic Los Angeles, set the standard for a generation of comic book adaptations. Surveying the relative critical and financial failure of *Popeye*, Warren Beatty's *Dick Tracy* (1990), and Ang Lee's *Hulk* (2003), Dan Hassler-Forest has noted the determination of all three of them to incorporate different features of the comic books they were adapting into their visuals—stylized movements and apparently two-dimensional sets in *Popeye*, a palette limited to bright primary colors in *Dick Tracy*, the explicit invocation of discrete comic book frames in *Hulk*—and concluded that all three strategies limited the films' appeal by ignoring "the unspoken demand that the films' relationship to comic books be one in which the characters and narratives are fully absorbed by Hollywood cinema, while comic books' formal features are either ignored or in a few cases reduced to the occasional iconic image reproduced in one of the film's shots."[5] The obvious moral to draw is that although audiences are happy to be reminded that they are watching superhero movies, they are much less happy to be reminded that they're watching comic book movies—a moral clearly underlined by the surprising fan backlash against Zack Snyder's *Watchmen* (2009), together with Robert Rodriguez's *Sin City* (2005) the most slavishly literal of all comic book adaptations in its invocation of its source text's visual style. Unlike *Sin City*, whose distinctive visual style of essentially black-and-white images contrasted with a relatively small area or a single object highlighted in a single color in each shot focused on evoking the style of Frank Miller's graphic novels, *Watchmen*'s compositions, often copied frame by frame from Dave Gibbons's graphic novel, make the film look less like a graphic novel than like a more downscale comic book. Adult and adolescent audiences looking to escape into the kinds of mythmaking they enjoyed as children evidently do not want their repackaged myths to address them as children.

The influentially neo-noir cityscape of *Batman*, which takes as anti-scripts both the *Superman* movies and the *Batman* TV show, encouraged filmgoers of all ages to savor its stylized world without fearing that they were being condescended to. By building the mythic dimension *Superman* had reserved to its hero's sense of mission into the everyday reality of Gotham City, *Batman* allowed the rebalancing of its leading conflict into an epic struggle between two equally mythic figures, Batman (Michael Keaton) and the Joker (Jack Nicholson) (see Figure 9.4). Instead of leading with its hero's obligatory origin story, as *Superman* does, Burton postpones the story of the murder of young Bruce Wayne's parents by a mugger before his eyes to a dramatically fraught moment when it can serve both as a punch line, explaining its hero's motivations for his anonymous fight for justice, and as setup line, preparing the later identification of the mugger as the Joker. Although Nicholson's Joker, befitting his sobriquet, laughs even more than Gene Hackman's Lex Luthor, his is a dark laughter that has the opposite effect from comic relief. Nicholson's performance, over the top in its intensity rather than its risibility, not only prepares for the even darker intensity of Heath Ledger's performance as the Joker in Christopher Nolan's *The Dark Knight* (2008) but creates a more general precedent for A-list actors and actresses like Michelle Pfeiffer, Danny DeVito, Tommy Lee Jones, Jim Carrey, Arnold Schwarzenegger, and Uma Thurman to play

FIGURE 9.4 *Batman (Michael Keaton) confronts the Joker (Jack Nicholson), a villain as mythically compelling as he is, in* Batman *(1989).*

villainous antagonists in comic book adaptations without fearing that they will undercut their own screen personas.

Encouraged by the success of *Batman* and its sequels—*Batman Returns* (1992), *Batman Forever* (1995), and *Batman and Robin* (1997)—other studios began to eye superhero franchises with new respect. The same year that Buena Vista released *Dick Tracy*, New Line released the even more successful *Teenage Mutant Ninja Turtles* (1990), aimed squarely at the pre-teen market, following it with two sequels in 1991 and 1993, and *The Mask* in 1994. Although all these films were profitable, the genre also had its share of duds. United Artists' *Tank Girl* (1995) eked out barely $4 million at the box office and Grammercy's *Barb Wire* (1996) even less. Pamela Anderson, who played the title character in David Hogan's film, won a 1997 Golden Raspberry Award as the Worst New Star of the year, perhaps in part because the ferociously sexualized character of Barb Wire, like the equally willing bad girls Mae West played two generations earlier, promised so few possibilities for narrative complications that a criminal plot had to be grafted onto her character. Paramount's *The Phantom* (1996) returned less than half of its $45 million budget. Although New Line was more successful with *Blade* (1998) and *Blade II* (2002), which grossed $70 million and $82 million, respectively, the *Blade* films are now remembered mainly as a missed opportunity for their star, Wesley Snipes, who was drawn into the first of them because of his interest in playing Black Panther but ended up playing the vampire hunter Blade, whose comic book adventures he had never read, as a survivor from the Blaxploitation films of the 1970s. It was not until Columbia's *Men in Black* (1997), directed by Barry Sonnenfeld, that a new comic book franchise arose that seriously rivaled *Batman* in critical and financial success and staying power. In addition to featuring a perfectly matched salt-and-pepper pair of heroes, Agents K (Tommy Lee Jones) and J (Will Smith), *Men in Black* benefited from an irresistible and eminently recyclable hook: a straitlaced US government agency treats alien invasions as criminal acts and deals with them in terms that might have been drawn from the venerable television series *Dragnet* (1951–59), strategically adding alien bugs, laser cannons, and blue goo.

The new superhero franchises depended just as completely as science fiction adaptations on recent technological developments. The development of the ever more realistic computer-generated imagery displayed to spectacular effect in *Terminator 2: Judgment Day* (1991) and *Jurassic Park* (1993) increasingly allowed Batman to leave Superman's already-dated flying sequences behind. As VHS videotapes gave new life to old movies, superhero franchises benefited from the rise of home video, which allowed audiences the ability to time-shift their television viewing, to archive and curate their own video libraries, and to watch their favorite movies, in whole or in part, over and over again. At the same time the rise of home video ended the Golden Age of Porn by allowing independent producers and amateurs to release adult videos audiences could watch in the privacy of their own homes, it encouraged the proliferation of entertainment franchises arrayed around tentpole feature films that spread to direct-to-video sequels and prequels, tie-in merchandise, and of course more comic books. All these developments provided a fertile ground for new adaptations even as they called into question long-accepted assumptions about origins.

Superhero movies increasingly built these questions about origins into their stories. Influential as the Batman films have been on later superhero franchises, which have routinely used them rather than the Superman films as models for their stories, their tone, and their visual styles, they have been even more broadly influential in establishing canons of adaptation at the turn of the twenty-first century. But the Batman canon is itself noncanonical, even anti-canonical. Will Brooker has observed that "although a Batman film could in theory adapt a single specific text—along the lines of *300* (2007) or *Watchmen*—none of the ten Batman films released in theatres since 1943 has done so."[6] This remark makes it sound as if it just happens to be the case that none of the ten Batman films to date have been based on a single specific text, as other comic book adaptations have been. But the normal procedure for adapting comic books, like the normal procedure for writing and illustrating new comic book installments of a given franchise, is to imagine more adventures for an established hero, not to recycle adventures with which the audience is already familiar. Even the 1976

Superman, once it got beyond the long opening movement that presented the familiar story of Superman's early years, devoted itself to a new story involving a confrontation between Superman and his familiar antagonist Lex Luthor, putting a new spin on the relation between them just as it put a new spin on the relation between Superman and Lois Lane. For this reason, the counterexamples Brooker cites, *300* and *Watchmen*—to which he might have added *V for Vendetta* (2006) and *Kick-Ass* (2010)—are outliers, special cases in which a single text offers itself as an obvious adaptation target because it has achieved canonical status. The reason that no Batman film has sought to adapt a single specific text is that no single Batman adventure has achieved canonical status: the franchise itself has become a canon without a center, a status it shares with virtually every other comic book franchise.

This development was already obvious to insiders before Tim Burton ever came on the scene. Liam Burke has recalled that despite his reservations about "strict continuity in comics," Dennis O'Neil, on becoming editor of DC Comics' Batman titles in 1986,

> introduced the Bat-bible. The Bat-bible summarized the fundamental aspects of the character for comic book creators, thereby ensuring greater consistency between the many titles. [...] Among the key guidelines stated in the document are: "His determination to stop crime is exceeded only by his compassion for crime's victims"; "Wayne/Batman is not insane"; "He is celibate .... He appreciates women .... but he cannot afford intimacy"; and "He never kills. Let's repeat that for the folks in the balcony: Batman never kills."[7]

As Burke points out, the Bat-bible, first written and distributed to DC Comics writers in 1986, has required repeated updates as the Batman canon has expanded and changed; the version Burke himself quotes is dated 2010. In addition, "the rules of the Bat-bible were flouted" as early as Burton's 1989 film, which shows Batman declining to interrupt a mugging, threatening the Joker, "You wanna get nuts? Come on! Let's get nuts!," consummating a sexual relationship with reporter Vicki Vale (Kim Basinger), and killing the Joker and several other adversaries.[8] So it seems clear that the Batman franchise is a canon in only a very limited or aspirational sense. A primary feature that makes the Batman universe feel like a canon even though it is not is the hero's origin story, the ur-myth that explains how Batman came to be and authorizes all later Batman stories by providing their rules: Batman lives in Gotham City; he is the son of Thomas and Martha Wayne; their fatal shooting before his eyes when he was still a boy moved him to become a crime fighter; after years of preparation, he decided to assume the costume of a bat because superstitious criminals would find this disguise frightening. This origin story normalizes Batman's core identity and behavior so that they do not have to be explained or motivated anew in every Batman adventure.

It is tempting to call Batman's origin story the canonical source text each of his adventures adapts, the cause of their effects. But in fact the causality operates precisely the other way around. Origin stories are effects, not causes, of superhero franchises. That is why Batman could get along perfectly well for the six months following his debut in May 1939 without any origin story at all. Christopher Nolan's 2005 film *Batman Begins*, whose origin story supplements the brief account that first appeared in *Detective Comics* #33 in November 1939 with material drawn from Frank Miller's *Batman: Year One*, which elaborates in turn on material in Miller's *The Dark Knight Returns* (1986), alters so many details of Batman's origins that it is commonly considered a reboot rather than a continuation of the franchise. Burton's 1989 film had already revised the earlier origin story by identifying the Joker as the criminal who killed Thomas and Martha Wayne. Even before then, contradictory details had crept into the story. The adult Batman recognizes Joe Chill as the criminal who had shot his parents during a holdup (*Batman* #47, June/July 1948); Martha Wayne had not been shot by Joe Chill but had died on the scene of a heart attack (*Detective Comics* #190, Dec. 1952); Chill, now identified as Joey Chill, had only pretended to be a holdup man but was actually a hired killer working for Lew Moxon, whom Thomas Wayne had helped convict of bank robbery (*Detective Comics* #235, Sept. 1956).[9] The goal in each revision of Batman's origin story is clearly to provide greater coherence to the whole franchise, but this coherence is inevitably retrospective, for later franchise installments construct and develop Batman's origin stories, or the versions of his origin story, that best suit their own interests, like the belated origin stories in *Young Sherlock Holmes* (1985) and *Hannibal Rising* (2007) that explain the behavior of franchise heroes or villains the world has known only as adults by discovering evidence of their most distinctive traits in their childhood avatars.

In addition, the origin stories that might seem to establish the canonical features of a franchise are introduced to franchises only when they are deemed necessary. In 1948, the Riddler is given an origin story as orthodox in its way as Batman's, even though there is less about him to explain. The Joker, by contrast, had appeared nearly ten years earlier without an origin story, though this absence has not stopped fans from supplying their own. A prison guard describes the Penguin in 1949–50 as "a villain who has 'never killed anybody!'" (*Batman* #56, Dec. 1949–Jan. 1950),[10] despite the fact that the Penguin's earlier history, which does not include a formal origin story, includes many murders. Nolan's 2008 film *The Dark Knight* changes and darkens Two Face's origin story by making his alter ego, District Attorney Harvey Dent, the boyfriend of Rachel Dawes, Batman's childhood sweetheart. Alfred, Batman's loyal retainer, was originally stout and clean-shaven in the comic books; it was not until he was played in the 1949 serial *Batman and Robin* by the slim, mustachioed Eric Wilton, who played dozens of other butlers before and after this one, that this new physical type became normative for future Alfreds. Like Batman himself, Alfred is given multiple origin stories, sometimes beginning as Thomas Wayne's butler, sometimes applying to Batman for a job instead of inheriting it, sometimes, as in the 1965 television series, appearing simply as one more item in the franchise's furniture.

There is nothing at all unusual about this lack of regularity. Comic book characters from Blondie to Bazooka Joe do not have origin stories, though sometimes pivotal moments in their adventures, like the flapper Blondie Boopadoop's marriage to Dagwood Bumstead, are dramatized at length. Sherlock Holmes and Philo Vance are given origin stories at the beginning of their opening installments, but Nero Wolfe and Philip Marlowe are not, and *Maigret's First Case* (1948), produced midway through Georges Simenon's cycle of novels about Inspector Jules Maigret of the Parisian Sureté, is nothing more than the story of Maigret's first case. Even James Bond is not presented with an origin story in his first appearance, Ian Fleming's novel *Casino Royale* (1953): only in the 2006 reboot of *Casino Royale* is his origin story marked as an origin story, and now precisely because it explicitly contradicts earlier hints of his origins. The characters most consistently provided with origin stories are superheroes, who need origin stories to root their fantastical experience in some sort of lived quasi-scientific reality, like the myth that before he became Spider-Man, Peter Parker received superpowers from the bite of a radioactive spider. Indeed the very term "origin stories" is relevant only to multiple versions and franchises. Despite the repeatedly filmed stories of Elizabeth Bennet, Judah Ben-Hur, and the Brothers Karamazov, it makes no sense to ask about their origin stories—at least not yet—and the origin story of Frankenstein's monster becomes recognized as such only when Mary Wollstonecraft Shelley's novel becomes a franchise.

Like the characters they purport to explain, origin stories are subject to change. More precisely, a large audience for superhero franchises is capable of entertaining multiple origin stories simultaneously without any sense of fundamental contradiction. This negative capability is hardly surprising in the light of the exercise superhero franchises give their audiences in entertaining what might ordinarily seem to be mutually exclusive features. The proclivity of comic books to threaten their superheroes with apparently irreversible dangers or calamities, like the death of Superman or his marriage to Lois Lane, often leads them to show their heroes undergoing transformations that leave no lasting impact on the saga as a whole. Hence *Giant Batman Annual* #5 collects, among other "Strange Lives of Batman and Robin," Zebra Batman, Phantom Batman, Rip Van Batman, and Merman Batman. In *Batman* #217 (May 1969), Dick Grayson goes off to college, and Batman responds by downsizing, moving out of Wayne Manor into an apartment in downtown Gotham City.

More recent versions of Batman have taken increasingly broad liberties with the character and his storyworld. Sometimes these alternative versions of the Caped Crusader are embedded in the orthodox or Cartesian Batman universe by revealing that Batman's marriage to Batwoman has been the dream of Dick Grayson (*Batman* #122) or by explaining the stories of Grayson's career as Batman II with his own Robin II—the son, naturally, of Batman and Batwoman—as the inventions of Alfred, Bruce Wayne's longtime butler, as he indulges his own speculations about the franchise's possible future. Other stories, like Batman's marriage to Lois Lane (*Lois Lane* #89), or Batman's last case (*Batman* #300), or the alternative origin story in which Bruce Wayne suspects Superman of complicity in his father's death and becomes Batman in order to bring him to justice (*World's Finest* #153), are true imaginary stories without any motivation in what might be called the story's main universe if the success of Frank Miller's graphic novels and Christopher Nolan's movies about Batman had not called the primacy of that comic book universe into question. In sum, not only has the canonical Batman universe been supplemented by many alternative Batman universes, but there are no clear guidelines demarcating these alternative versions as imaginary and no clear rules about how and when a given offshoot enters or supersedes the Bat-canon. For all these reasons, "Bat-bible," with its implications of anteriority, canonicity, and scriptural authority, was exactly the wrong term for Dennis O'Neil to have coined in describing the document he circulated to DC Comics writers about the rules for writing new Batman adventures. A much more precise term would have been "Bat-script," in parallel with all the many, diverse, and often contradictory scripts all adaptations are invited or commanded to follow. It is certainly understandable that O'Neil avoided this term because he wished to claim greater authority for his script than for the hundreds of competing scripts in Batman comics. The futility of his attempt to regulate and normalize the Batman universe once and for all is eminently characteristic of all adaptations, whether or not they make reference to any canonical works.

Although the explosion of online superhero fan fiction has multiplied the fractures in whatever remains of the stable, unmarked, or normal Batman universe, that universe was from its earliest pre-cinema days already a multiverse that supported divergent, alternative, often blankly contradictory versions of its franchise hero, some of them clearly marked as more imaginary than the avowedly canonical core universe, often with no clear indications or rules that would determine which versions are imaginary and which versions canonical, precisely because comic books and comic strips, by virtue of their potentially endless capacity for serialization, are not only noncanonical but anti-canonical. The very word "universe" is etymologically paradoxical, combining *uni-*, "one," with *verse*, "turned or combined." A universe—it is interesting that putting "a" before "universe" makes perfect sense, just as it makes sense to give its plural as "universes"—represents a coherence that is manufactured or perceived.

For this reason, the Batman universe, like the DC Comics universe or the superhero universe or the universe of discourse, is better described as a textual multiverse that is largely constructed by divergent adaptations, whether these cross the border into different media like television and cinema or remain within the same medium like the different comic book accounts of Batman's origin story. Just as the adaptations that construct new rooms in Wayne Manor must choose their sources from among competing sub-universes, adaptations reveal that the textual universes they adapt, whether they are superhero franchises, fictional franchises, or canonical texts like *Tristram Shandy* that have never before been adapted, are always already multiverses whose multivalence it is the business of adaptation to release and multiply. Like adaptations generally, superhero franchises, with their multiple origin stories, imaginary universes, mutually exclusive versions, and proclivity for endless rebooting, remind their audiences that every world they can possibly imagine, including the world they imagine they inhabit, is an alternative world.

No room for heritage

The rise of Hollywood science fiction and superhero franchises coincided with the decline of the American literary canon as a bankable set of scripts, even for niche movies offered as counterprogramming to summer blockbusters. When John Pierson identifies 1989 as "The Year It All Changed," the game-changing film he emphasizes is not *Batman* or *Driving Miss Daisy*, Bruce Beresford's Oscar-winning adaptation of Alfred Uhry's 1987 play, but Steven Soderbergh's *sex, lies, and videotape*, which, like Jim Jarmusch's *Mystery Train* and Spike Lee's *Do the Right Thing*, the other American films that found receptive audiences at the Cannes Film Festival that year, was based on an original screenplay.[11] So in the midst of Hollywood's deepening attachment to superhero franchises, during a period when even niche films seemed to shun literary cachet, one development stood out in startling contrast: the Jane Austen year. Ever since the success of *The Graduate* and *Bonnie and Clyde* in 1967 had led the movies to consider the youth audience as a significant demographic and the American industry's decision to replace the Shurlock Office with the Ratings Code in 1969 had allowed the studios to make films that particularly targeted different audiences instead of aiming every time to please an audience that included every filmgoer in America, Hollywood had focused with ever greater determination on the youth demographic, which it identified with male audiences between the ages of 12 and 21, as the economically leading segment of the movie audience.

The result was to separate mainstream films, those targeting teenaged boys, from niche films, those targeting children, teenaged girls, or anyone over 21. The success of blockbuster adaptations like *Jaws* (1975) and the *Star Wars* franchise confirmed the studios in their pursuit of young male audiences to the virtual exclusion of everyone else. Mainstream films, as the label implies, had higher production and publicity budgets, wider distribution, and greater market saturation. Niche films required special handling, often being rolled out in a small number of theaters until word of mouth could build enough to justify their wider release. Unlike failed mainstream films like *Heaven's Gate* (1980), *Ishtar* (1987), *The Adventures of Baron Munchausen* (1988), *The Bonfire of the Vanities* (1990), *Hudson Hawk* (1991), *North* (1994), *Cutthroat Island* (1995), *The Scarlet Letter* (1995), *Waterworld* (1995), *The Postman* (1997), *Meet Joe Black* (1998), *Battlefield Earth* (2000), *Red Planet* (2000), *Glitter* (2001), *The Adventures of Pluto Nash* (2002), *Gigli* (2003), *Timeline* (2003), *Alexander* (2004), *Around the World in 80 Days* (2004), *Catwoman* (2004), *A Sound of Thunder* (2005), and *All the King's Men* (2006), which flamed out spectacularly under the public's fascinated eyes, most niche films, many of them literary adaptations assumed to have little appeal to the youth audience, died quiet deaths without going into wide release.

It was all the more remarkable, then, that 1995–96 suddenly emerged as the year of Jane Austen. The year was anchored by the BBC's five-hour, six-episode miniseries *Pride and Prejudice*, which was so popular that Helen Fielding's fictional diarist Bridget Jones, settling in to watch the latest installment, confided in Fielding's 18 October 1995 column for the *Independent*: "Just nipped out for fags ready for Pride and Prejudice. Hard to believe there are so many cars out on the roads. Shouldn't they be at home getting ready?"[12] The miniseries was joined by other Austen adaptations: Ang Lee's *Sense and Sensibility* (1995), starring Emma Thompson, who also wrote the screenplay; Douglas McGrath's *Emma* (1996), starring Gwyneth Paltrow; and Diarmuid Lawrence's television movie *Emma* (1996), starring Kate Beckinsale. All these projects were duly marketed as Jane Austen adaptations aimed specifically at niche audiences that would recognize their status as literary adaptations as one of their main attractions. The opposite was the case, however, with *Clueless* (1995), in which writer-director Amy Heckerling recreated the plot of *Emma* for Alicia Silverstone in contemporary Beverly Hills. Launched by the remarkable box-office strength of *Clueless*, which attracted millions of teenagers who had no idea they were watching an adaptation of Austen, whose name was nowhere listed in the credits, and the unstinting loyalty inspired by the BBC *Pride and Prejudice*, the Jane Austen year was such a widely recognized phenomenon that Emma Thompson could openly joke about it in her speech on 26 March 1996 accepting the Academy Award for Best Adapted Screenplay: "Before I came I went to visit Jane Austen's grave in Winchester

Cathedral to pay my respects, you know, and to tell her about the grosses. And I don't know how she would react to an evening like this, but I do hope, I do hope she knows how big she is in Uruguay."[13] While the 1995 *Pride and Prejudice* miniseries was the ultimate "heritage adaptation," to use the term established by Andrew Higson and Ginette Vincendeau,[14] the complementary success of *Clueless* indicated how well Austen's wit and romance could travel to cultural moments quite remote from the heritage cinema of the United Kingdom. Two hundred years after she lived, Austen enjoyed a stunning victory lap around the English-speaking world.

The success of this kind of niche counterprogramming offered an irresistible hook for entertainment reportage, particularly among observers who had grown tired of Hollywood's tireless focus on teenaged audiences. So it came as no surprise to contemporaneous observers that "as the craze for Hampshire's Jane Austen began to subside, the New York–born Henry James (1843–1916), who settled in next-door Sussex in 1898, has been edging forward as the current classic literary adaptee of choice for the English-speaking film world."[15] All three of the new James adaptations—*The Portrait of a Lady* (1996), *Washington Square* (1997), and *The Wings of the Dove* (1997)—were period costume dramas directed by non-American filmmakers: Australian Jane Campion, Polish Agnieszka Holland, and English Iain Softley. All were respectfully reviewed. Even critics who were impatient with the slow pace of *The Portrait of a Lady* or who found Nicole Kidman and John Malkovich miscast as Isabel Archer and Gilbert Osmond were impressed with the risks Jane Campion took in boldly infusing *The Portrait of a Lady* with more explicit sexuality. *Washington Square* and *The Wings of the Dove* met an even more enthusiastic critical reception, often by contrast with *The Portrait of a Lady*, even when the grounds for this contrast were obscure. Edward Guthmann, reviewing *The Wings of the Dove* on its first release, observed mysteriously that *The Wings of the Dove*, the 1902 novel that is one of the capstones of James's career, was "a minor literary work that manages on screen to upstage both 'Washington Square' and 'The Portrait of a Lady,' two superior Henry James novels that came off as stiff and deliberate in recent film translations."[16] All three films were implicitly or explicitly acknowledged as niche films, as in Marc Savlov's representative assessment in reviewing *The Wings of the Dove*, that "the only reason James is being brought to the screen so frantically of late (*Washington Square* et al.) is that the national supply of Jane Austen is running thin, and we have to have something without Bruce Willis up there."[17] Yet none of them was successful at the box office; none of them had anything like the impact of the Austen adaptations from the year before; and none of them was even recognized as fulfilling the prophecy of a Henry James year.

The reasons for the collective failure to establish anything like an American counterpart to English heritage cinema are revealing. James was at best a highly equivocal American, a writer who had been born in New

York but had spent most of his adult life in Europe, eventually settling in England and taking out British citizenship the year before his death in 1916 to protest the failure of the United States to enter the Great War. So he would never have been the obvious anchor for an American heritage cinema that offered a significant alternative to English heritage cinema. Indeed, when London Weekend Television produced *Affairs of the Heart*, a series of thirteen-hour-long James television adaptations, in 1974–75, they had no trouble making James look English because most of the stories they chose to dramatize—"The Marriages," "Covering End," "Glasses," "The Tone of Time," "Lord Beaupre," "The Bench of Desolation," "Nona Vincent," "The Great Condition"—were already set in England, and most of the ones that were not—"The Aspern Papers," *The Wings of the Dove*, "An International Episode," and "Daisy Miller"—were chosen from among the stories James described as his "international" fiction, tales that examined clashes between American and European values in close, lucid, and evenhanded terms. The only all-American episode of the series was "Catherine," based on *Washington Square*, a novel James had excluded from the twenty-three volume New York Edition of his collected works published by Scribner in 1907–09, and even this episode, while retaining its nominally American setting, was reframed as universal in its matrix of moral values.

Nor did James have anything like the core audience of Jane Austen that could be counted on to turn out for Jamesian film adaptations in America or anywhere else. None of James's novels or stories is remotely comparable to *Pride and Prejudice*, which provides a zero-degree model for witty, literate romantic comedy. Beneath their evocation of the moneyed veneer of the privileged classes, their focus is relentlessly, and for many readers punishingly, analytical. They are full of great settings and ideas, but not of memorable characters, sparkling conversations, or unforgettable scenes. If Austen can generate niche adaptations, and the occasional non-niche adaptation like *Clueless*, notable for their literateness, James's literateness is altogether more formidable, more of an issue to be grappled with and overcome. It would be going too far to say that James is unfilmable. Ismail Merchant and James Ivory's 2000 adaptation of *The Golden Bowl*, the 1904 novel that was the last James completed, may have been nothing more than "the most visually accomplished of the Ivory soaps,"[18] or "a sort of handsomely illustrated Cliffs Notes version of the novel,"[19] but its very existence suggested that no James novel was unfilmable: not *What Maisie Knew*, which Scott McGehee and David Siegel adapted in 2012, forty-four years after the BBC's 1968 miniseries, and presumably not *The Awkward Age* or *The Sacred Fount*, which still await adaptation. But although James is certainly filmable, no one has yet found a way to film him that leads to consistent commercial success.

All three of the adaptations from the abortive Henry James year point to a particular problem in adapting James: his legendary reticence about sex. Given the amount of time and energy James's characters invest in amatory entanglements, they think remarkably little about the sexual aspect of their relationships. Still less are they shown as motivated by their libidos. Since Hollywood famously adds heterosexual romance to genres as different as the gangster film and the Western in order to appeal to female audiences, it would be unthinkable to film James in the 1990s without more open intimations of sex than he provides. The three adaptations rise to this challenge in three different ways. In *The Portrait of a Lady*, Isabel's fantasies are as florid as her behavior is abstemious. In the film's most notorious scene, she lies fully clothed on a bed surrounded by the three suitors she has otherwise kept at arm's length, all of whom indulge in a decorous groping session that makes her hidden desires—not so much the desire for sexual fulfillment as the desire to be desired—manifest to the audience while concealing them from the other characters (see Figure 9.5). In *The Wings of the Dove*, the implicit sexual bargain Kate Croy (Helena Bonham Carter) offers her secret fiancé Merton Densher (Linus Roache) in return for his courtship of the orphaned, mortally ill American heiress Milly Theale (Allison Elliott), whom she hopes will fall in love with Densher, leave him her fortune, and so pave the way for his marriage to Kate is both literalized and displaced onto two sex scenes, one in a Venetian alley when Kate has just begun to become jealous of Milly, the other after Milly's death, in between the moment when Densher tells Kate that he will not accept Milly's legacy and the moment when she demands that he assure her he is no longer in love with Milly and leaves him when he cannot give this assurance. Sex in Softley's film becomes the exchange commodity Kate uses in the ultimately futile attempt to secure Densher's exclusive devotion. In addition, however, the period settings and costumes of *The Wings of*

FIGURE 9.5 *In the most notorious scene in* The Portrait of a Lady *(1996), Isabel Archer (Nicole Kidman) fantasizes her simultaneous embrace by three suitors: Caspar Goodwood (Viggo Mortenson), Lord Warburton (Richard E. Grant), and Ralph Touchett (Martin Donovan).*

the Dove, whose date was changed from 1902 to 1910 to allow costume designer Sandy Powell to create a more distinctive wardrobe for Kate and Milly, is everywhere drenched in a claustrophobic sensuality that makes the film seem both decorous and decadent. *Washington Square*, by contrast, associates sex appeal exclusively with Morris Townsend (Ben Chaplin), the fortune-hunting suitor who pursues homely heiress Catherine Sloper (Jennifer Jason Leigh) over the mounting objections of Dr. Sloper (Albert Finney). Handsome, callow Morris, like Montgomery Clift in *The Heiress* nearly fifty years earlier, represents a sexual fulfillment Catherine becomes heartrendingly aware of but then deliberately denies herself. Unlike both James's Catherine, who resigns herself to spinsterhood with mild placidity, and Olivia de Havilland's steely Catherine in *The Heiress*, Leigh's Catherine ends by finding at least partial fulfillment elsewhere: the closing sequence of the film shows her presiding over what looks like a remarkably forward-looking daycare for young children, replacements for the children she will never bear herself. This incongruously sudden emergence of James's heroine as a career woman follows a script that seeks to make her portrayal palatable to a late-twentieth-century audience rather than James's own script, which finds grace in both Catherine and Densher's renunciations. It is easy to see why none of these strategies for representing sexual desire carried anything like the force of Darcy's wet shirt in the BBC *Pride and Prejudice*, which had gone so far to reconcile Jane Austen's decorum with its audience's sense of sexual desire, sexual propriety, and sexual identity.

One final reason for the failure of the Henry James year is the prophetic determination of James's fiction to elude generic categories. He seems to delight in predicting the leading Hollywood genres and then turning them inside out. James wrote dozens of ghost stories, but except for "The Turn of the Screw," which has been adapted to film or television at least twenty-one times, few of them have been filmed because they are not very scary—or at least not Hollywood-scary, devoid as they are of fatalities, gruesome spectacles, and jump-scares. If James's ghost stories are better described, in Tzvetan Todorov's terms, as tales of the fantastic marked by "that hesitation experienced by a person who knows only the laws of nature, confronting an apparently supernatural event,"[20] his romances are more often anti-romances in which love pointedly fails to conquer all. Since James's characters seem to have well controlled sexual appetites, and since, with rare exceptions like Kate Croy, they rarely have to worry about money, their romances, unlike those of Edith Wharton's heroines in *The House of Mirth* (1905; adapted by Terence Fisher in 2000) and *The Age of Innocence* (1920; adapted by Wesley Ruggles in 1924, by Philip Moeller in 1934, and by Martin Scorsese in 1993) can come across as hermetic, dispassionate, and lifeless on-screen (see Figure 9.6). Although it would be facile to say that James is too literate for the silver screen, his resolute focus on the psychological complexities of his conflicted characters, whose most signal achievement is often to keep a

FIGURE 9.6 *In* The Age of Innocence *(1993), passion flares decorously but realistically between Ellen Olenska (Michelle Pfeiffer) and Newland Archer (Daniel Day-Lewis).*

stiff upper lip, has limited both the success of individual James adaptations and prevented the launch of anything like a Henry James brand.

In search of the middle

The failure of Henry James to achieve the escape velocity of Jane Austen did not mean that audiences were no longer interested in adaptations of American literature that did not happen to take the form of comic books or graphic novels. It simply meant that American literary adaptations could not rely so largely on the canonical prestige of their source material, that successful adaptations would probably be more amenable to the generic conventions that promised certain predictable pleasures even if they made others less likely, and that these adaptations would have to be more carefully marketed than *The Portrait of a Lady*, *Washington Square*, and *The Wings of the Dove*. Gone were the days when studios would make loss leaders like *The Wizard of Oz* for the value of the prestige they gave the entire studio's offerings; now every adaptation was expected to pay its own way. And the way for adaptations counterprogrammed to superhero franchise entries, summer action movies, and other blockbusters was increasingly seen as a middle way that specifically counterpointed those mainstream offerings without veering too far in the direction of literary adaptation.

A textbook case of the ability of middlebrow adaptations of a middlebrow author to adapt to this new pattern is film versions of the novels of Larry McMurtry. McMurtry's career combined impeccable literary credentials with a strong generic affiliation. As a Wallace Stegner Fellow at Stanford University's Creative Writing Center, he studied with Frank O'Connor and Malcolm Cowley. After completing his fellowship year, he taught English at Texas Christian University and Rice University. Years after becoming a successful novelist, he co-founded Booked Up, a chain of bookstores. His numerous literary honors included a Guggenheim Fellowship and three Jesse H. Jones Awards from the Texas Institute of Letters, affirming his close ties to his native state, where all his novels have been set, and which clearly influenced the apparel—a dinner jacket, blue jeans, and cowboy boots—in which he accepted the Academy Award he shared with Diana Osseana for writing the screenplay of *Brokeback Mountain*, Ang Lee's 2005 adaptation of E. Annie Proulx's 1997 short story, whose existence he took the opportunity to remind the audience of in his acceptance speech. McMurtry's first three novels—*Horseman, Pass By* (1961), *Leaving Cheyenne* (1963), and *The Last Picture Show* (1966)—comprised a trilogy examining the problems of life in the fictitious North Texas town of Thalia in the years after the Second World War. All three of them were filmed, *Horseman, Pass By* by Martin Ritt as *Hud* (1963); *The Last Picture Show* by Peter Bogdanovich in 1971; and *Leaving Cheyenne* by Sidney Lumet as *Lovin' Molly* in 1974. Both *Hud* and *The Last Picture Show* were notably successful. *Hud* was nominated for seven Academy Awards and won three: Patricia Neal for Best Actress, Melvyn Douglas for Best Supporting Actor, and James Wong Howe for Best Cinematography. Eight years later, Cloris Leachman won an Oscar for Best Supporting Actress and Ben Johnson for Best Supporting Actor in *The Last Picture Show*, whose eight Academy Award nominations confirmed the status of Bogdanovich, hitherto best known as a journalist and film historian, as a mainstream filmmaker after his striking horror/docudrama feature debut *Targets* (1968).

Bogdanovich would remain a critical darling for only a few years. *Paper Moon*, his 1973 adaptation of Joe David Brown's Depression-era novel *Addie Pray* (1971), was greeted with critical and box-office success and a Best Supporting Actress Oscar for ten-year-old Tatum O'Neill, the youngest person ever to win a competitive Academy Award. His fortunes began to slide with his widely derided adaptation *Daisy Miller* (1974), in which critics unanimously agreed that his girlfriend, former model Cybill Shepherd, who had made such a striking debut as the hometown heartbreaker Jacy Farrow in *The Last Picture Show*, was out seriously past her depth as Henry James's flirtatious, doomed heroine. But McMurtry's greatest film achievements lay still ahead of him. When James L. Brooks adapted his tear-jerking

1975 family romance *Terms of Endearment* in 1983, the film, budgeted at $8 million, grossed a spectacular $108 million and was nominated for eleven Academy Awards, winning Oscars for Shirley MacLaine as Best Actress, Jack Nicholson as Best Supporting Actor, Best Direction and Best Adapted Screenplay for Brooks, who had created Nicholson's character, astronaut Garrett Breedlove, specifically for the screenplay, and Best Picture. McMurtry's 1985 novel *Lonesome Dove*, which won the Pulitzer Prize for Fiction in 1986, was made into a historically successful four-episode television miniseries that aired on CBS in 1989. The series was nominated for a remarkable eighteen Prime Time Emmy Awards and won seven. Its surprisingly large audience, estimated at 26 million, went a long way toward reversing the fortunes of two declining genres, the miniseries, which had languished since the historic success of *Roots* in 1977, and the Western, which had been pronounced dead despite repeated attempts like Clint Eastwood's spectral morality play *Pale Rider* and Lawrence Kasdan's pastiche *Silverado* (both 1985) to revive it. This last was especially ironic because *Lonesome Dove*, like most of McMurtry's fiction, is as much anti-Western as Western. Although its 1870s setting departs from the contemporary Texas settings of *Horseman, Pass By* and *The Last Picture Show*, the attitude it adopts toward its flawed heroes and their self-ordained missions is strikingly nuanced and modern, balancing a deep appreciation of the mythic potential of the Old West with an elegiac certainty that this potential has largely been buried beneath the needs of everyday life for characters determined to survive and leave their imprint on a land they feel is no longer theirs. The popularity of the miniseries encouraged McMurtry to write a sequel, *Streets of Laredo* (1993), and two prequels, *Dead Man's Walk* (1995) and *Comanche Moon* (1997), all of them also adapted as television miniseries (see Figure 9.7). At the same time, however, it drove McMurtry to some seriously critical deliberation on the nature of his achievement. In his Preface to a 2000 Simon and Schuster reprint of *Lonesome Dove*, he reflects:

> I thought I had written about a harsh time and some pretty harsh people, but, to the public at large, I had produced something nearer to an idealization; instead of a poor-man's *Inferno,* filled with violence, faithlessness, and betrayal, I had actually delivered a kind of *Gone with the Wind* of the West, a turnabout I'll be mulling over for a long, long time.[21]

McMurtry's recipe for the Texas-based novels that were adapted so successfully into movies and television miniseries—to treat the Western genre as one among many competing scripts rather than to remain unquestioningly within its formula—was further developed by the novelist Cormac McCarthy. McCarthy's literary credentials were as impeccable as McMurtry's. In the early years of his career, he won a traveling award

FIGURE 9.7 *Driven by the adventures of Texas Rangers Gus McCrae (Robert Duvall) and Woodrow Call (Tommy Lee Jones),* Lonesome Dove *(1989) led to a resurgence of the television miniseries.*

from the American Academy of Arts and Letters, a Rockefeller Foundation Grant, and a MacArthur Foundation Fellowship. At Random House, which published his first five novels, he inherited the services of Albert Erskine, who had been William Faulkner's editor. His early novels, set in his native Appalachia, were slow to gain readership, largely because of his uncompromisingly sparse punctuation, which eschewed many commas and all quotation marks. But *Blood Meridian* (1985), his fifth novel and his first with a Western setting, gradually assumed outsized status: a 2006 poll conducted by the *New York Times* named it the third most important work of American fiction published in the past twenty-five years, behind only Toni Morrison's *Beloved* (1987) and Don DeLillo's *Underworld* (1997). At the same time his literary star rose among respected critics, McCarthy made no secret of his impatience with novelists like Henry James and Marcel Proust, preferring to read writers who "deal with issues of life and death."[22]

McCarthy's breakout novel, *All the Pretty Horses* (1992), won both the National Book Award and the National Book Critics' Circle Award. Several years after McCarthy followed it with *The Crossing* (1994) and *Cities of the Plain* (1998), Billy Bob Thornton adapted *All the Pretty Horses* to a 2000 movie starring Matt Damon and Penelope Cruz. The film, recounting the adventures of two Texas cowboys riding into 1940s Mexico in search of adventure and finding chaos, cruelty, romance, and violent death, failed at the box office. It was not until the adaptation of his 2005 novel *No Country for Old Men* that McCarthy established himself as a force to be reckoned with in Hollywood. That 2007 adaptation, written and directed by Joel and Ethan Coen, was immediately recognized as one of the most distinguished in the long series of anti-Westerns from William Wellman's anti-lynching parable *The Ox-Bow Incident* (1943), based on Walter Van Tilburg Clark's 1940 novel, to Ron Howard's *The Missing* (2003), based on Thomas Eidson's 1996 novel *The Last Ride.*

No Country for Old Men goes well beyond its anti-Western forbears, setting new records for random-seeming violence, amorality, bleakness, and a pitiless refusal to follow the moral codes of the Western. All its most sympathetic figures, whether they are leading or supporting characters, are murdered, one at a time, with little fanfare, and its villain, the dead-eyed Anton Chigurh, exudes a truly apocalyptic menace (see Figure 9.8). Although the Coen brothers' previous films had included at least two sort-of-adaptations, *Miller's Crossing* (1990), which borrowed important elements from Dashiell Hammett's *Red Harvest* (1929) and much of the plot of Hammett's *The Glass Key* (1931) without acknowledgment, and *O Brother, Where Art Thou?* (2000), a waggishly Southern tale based very loosely indeed on the *Odyssey*, their work was more notable for original screenplays than adaptations. The film changes the focus of McCarthy's novel, which spends considerably more time on Sheriff Ed Tom Bell, played in the movie by Tommy Lee Jones, but follows the novel's plot in almost every detail and, in a significant departure from intermittently playful films like *Fargo* (1996) and *The Ladykillers* (2004), maintains an unremittingly bleak tone. In this regard it is materially assisted not only by the Coen brothers' expertise and that of their longtime collaborators,

FIGURE 9.8 *The baleful figure of Anton Chigurh (Javier Bardem) sets the tone for the pitch-black comedy of* No Country for Old Men *(2007).*

cinematographer Roger Deakins and composer Carter Burwell, but by the Coen brothers' brand. From their first two films, *Blood Simple* (1984) and *Raising Arizona* (1987), the Coens had alternated between crime dramas with unsettlingly comical elements and knockabout comedies about crime. By the time they made *No Country for Old Men*, their brand was firmly established as black comedy, with predominantly comical crime films like *The Big Lebowski* (1997) alternating with straight-faced crime films with a disturbingly comical edge like *The Man Who Wasn't There* (2001). Laying claim to McCarthy's novel allowed the Coens to rebrand their noir Western horror film as a pitch-black comedy, with its comical strokes limited to conceptual features like the arbitrariness of its violence and the failure of the three characters ever to meet, this last element an elaboration of the central irony in *Blood Simple*. Instead of battling or vitiating the strongly conflicting narrative elements in McCarthy's novel, the Coens provided a script that implicitly promised to package these elements as predictably unpredictable entertainment.

After *No Country for Old Men* won Oscars for Best Picture, Best Direction, and Best Adapted Screenplay, McCarthy and the Coens went their separate ways, McCarthy to publish *The Road* in 2006, the Coens to make several more films based on original screenplays and a single additional adaptation, *True Grit* (2010). Based, like Henry Hathaway's 1968 film that won John Wayne his Academy Award for Best Actor, on Charles Portis's 1968 novel, the Coens' adaptation remythologized Western myths of professionalism and revenge that Hathaway's film had attacked with a relish best exemplified in Wayne's uncharacteristically boozy portrayal of hired gunman Rooster Cogburn. The Coens' film did not need *Superman*'s self-seriousness to rehabilitate Western myths; it simply needed to present those myths straight. So the film's surprising lack of irony in its adaptation of Portis's novel provided an additional layer of irony when it was read, as virtually all reviewers read it, against Hathaway's more broadly ironic film, and it was perfectly logical when it surpassed *No Country for Old Men* as their top-grossing film to date.

As for McCarthy, the even more nihilistic, despairing tone of *The Road* would have seemed like an unlikely vehicle for film adaptation if *No Country for Old Men* had not done so much to develop his own brand. His tale of an unnamed man and his son's stoic journey to the sea following the destruction of most of humankind in an unspecified apocalyptic disaster would have seemed to have limited entertainment value if two new genres had not arisen to provide scripts for both the film and its audience. The first of these was the post-apocalyptic survival film represented by Francis Lawrence's *I Am Legend* (2007), based on Richard Matheson's 1954 novel, which had already generated Ubaldo Ragona and Sidney Salkow's Italian-American adaptation *The Last Man on Earth* (1964) and Boris Sagal's *The Omega Man* (1971), and the Mad Max movies, which featured elemental conflicts, brutal action sequences, and somber reflections on the present day. The second was the Cormac McCarthy adaptation, which promised sparse dialogue, an absence of moralizing, and a bleak worldview. The dissonances between these two genres allowed *The Road* to play with the scripts supplied by both of them even as its protagonists struggled to survive in the face of death.

The adaptation that was most ingenious in finding the middle ground was *The Bridges of Madison County* (1995). Robert James Waller's first novel, which the author, on leave from teaching business management at the University of Northern Iowa, had written in two weeks, had become an unprecedented publishing phenomenon in 1992, eventually outselling *Gone with the Wind*. The novel, chronicling the affair between 45-year-old Iowa farm wife Francesca Johnson and 52-year-old *National Geographic* photographer Robert Kincaid during the four days in 1965 when her husband and teenaged son and daughter are at the state fair exhibiting their prize steer, had been roundly lambasted by critics for its overblown prose, beginning with its opening line, "There are songs that come free from the blue-eyed grass, from the dust of a thousand country roads,"[23] and pronounced by Oprah Winfrey a gift to the country. Amblin Entertainment, the Steven Spielberg company that bought the adaptation rights, hired Richard LaGravenese to write the screenplay and Bruce Beresford to direct. Beresford promptly called for another screenwriter to rework the script. But when Beresford pressed to have the Italian-born Francesca played by a foreign actress, he was dismissed from the project and replaced by its star, Clint Eastwood. LaGravenese returned, and Meryl Streep, who had "'fought long and hard not to do this movie' because she found the book overwrought,"[24] agreed to play Francesca.

As the film, shot in sequence to help Eastwood and Streep immerse themselves in their characters' limited-time romance, took shape, columnists buzzed with wonderment about the unlikely mix of Clint Eastwood, Meryl Streep, and a sentimental tearjerker that would seem to take both of them well out of their comfort zones. *New York Times* movie reviewer Janet Maslin's speculations are typical: "When the immovable object is a book that's been parked on the best-seller list for nearly three years, and the irresistible force is Clint Eastwood, it's natural to wonder what will give. At the very least, 'The Bridges of Madison County' will test the maxim that Hollywood finds better movie material in bad books than good ones."[25] But the film was unusually successful in capitalizing on the multiple scripts whose very contradictions might have seemed to doom it.

The first of these scripts is of course Waller's best-selling novel, whose central situation—following an unlikely four-day midlife romance, the lovers never saw each other again—had appealed to millions of readers despite, or because of, its overripe prose. Waller's script dictated a sweepingly romantic story that would end with a renunciation that would assure its audience members that their unremarkable everyday lives were suffused with the passion of their high-flown memories of lost love and dreams of undiscovered love. A less widely remarked script was LaGravenese's screenplay, which pruned away most of Waller's purple prose, oriented the story more firmly as Francesca's—after every scene involving the two leads ends, the camera remains on Francesca to record her reactions while providing only one sequence showing Robert without her—and added a framework showing her adult children reading her account of her love after her death and struggling to come to terms with it. LaGravenese, best known for writing the original screenplay for *The Fisher King* (1991), had been deeply shaken when Beresford replaced him on the project, but emerged by the end of 1995 as an acknowledged master of adaptation for *A Little Princess*, *Unstrung Heroes*, and *The Bridges of Madison County*.

Far more widely publicized were the scripts provided by the film's celebrated lead performers. Eastwood, who had made his mark as the hero of Sergio Leone's spaghetti Westerns *A Fistful of Dollars* (1964), *For a Few Dollars More* (1965), and *The Good, the Bad, and the Ugly* (1966), had turned to directing with *Play Misty for Me* (1971) and racked up a long series of action films as the director and star. By the time he signed on to direct *The Bridges of Madison County*, his well-established persona, and the script it projected, suggested late middle age (he was sixty-four at the time of filming), bedrock professionalism, wide-ranging experience, laconic and sometimes scowling stoicism, and, ever since he had directed *Bird* (1988), a fondness for the blues. Eastwood's peculiar status in the movies was aptly summarized by Sergio Leone when he was invited by journalist Pete Hamill after making *Once Upon a Time in America* (1984) to compare its star, Robert De Niro, to Eastwood: "Bobby, first of all, is an actor. Clint, first of all, is a star. Bobby suffers. Clint yawns."[26]

Streep, who was already well on her way to becoming the most honored cinema performer of her generation, enjoyed a contrasting reputation as an unexcelled technician. Although her most recent roles in *Death Becomes Her* (1992) and *The River Wild* (1994) had introduced her to the special-effects carnival and the action-adventure film, she was connected more closely with a series of high-profile adaptations—*Kramer vs. Kramer* (1979), *The French Lieutenant's Woman* (1981), *Sophie's Choice* (1982), *Out of Africa* (1985), *Heartburn* (1986), *Ironweed* (1987), *Postcards from the Edge* (1990)—for which she adopted a wide range of different attributes and accents. When she appeared in *The Bridges of Madison County*, Streep's persona was middle-aged (like Francesca, she was forty-five at the time of shooting) and noted for decorum, rectitude, emotional reserve, untapped depths, and an endless capacity for psychological and emotional development. Like Eastwood, Streep was a consummate professional. But her professionalism was that of a protean star who could submerge herself in any role and suggest hidden depths in any character.

The collision between Eastwood's and Streep's scripts, which seemed to come from two different worlds, marked any romance between their characters as unthinkable. But it also made Francesca's forbidden romance acceptable both narratively, because it would fulfill many audience members' own fantasies, and thematically, because it would make Francesca's climactic renunciation inevitable. Francesca would change more deeply than Robert because she would have to and she would be able to do so. At the same time, the script provided not simply by Waller's novel but by the film's status as the adaptation of a mega-selling novel sanctioned its unlikely romance as exactly what its target audience wanted and demanded, the image of a universal dream almost as universally denied.

Although a traveling photographer's affair with a Midwestern housewife might have seemed the basis for a joke about the traveling salesman and the farmer's daughter, the film takes exceptional pains to integrate its conflicting scripts in ways that encourage the audience to take these conflicts seriously as both obstacles to be overcome and signs of how remarkable and precious the four-day affair is and remains. A newly invented scene, the discovery of Francesca's journals by her daughter Carolyn (Annie Corley) and her son Michael (Victor Slezak), who are both scandalized by the request in her will that her body be cremated and the ashes scattered from the Roseman Bridge, frames the long flashback to 1965 by establishing Carolyn and Michael as surrogates who will anticipate and model the audience's reactions. On the morning Francesca, wearing a nondescript shirtwaist dress, first meets Robert, in jeans and a t-shirt, when he stops at her house to ask directions, he asks where she is from, and she is surprised to hear that he once visited Bari, her birthplace in Italy, and even more surprised that when he passed through it years ago, he stayed "a few days" on a whim "because it looked pretty." After she offers to ride along in his truck to direct him to the bridge, he demonstrates his old-fashioned courtesy by picking her a bouquet of wildflowers in thanks, and she demonstrates her unexpected sense of humor by telling him that they're poisonous, a revelation that makes him drop the bouquet before she confesses that she's just teasing him (see Figure 9.9).

Over the dinner Francesca cooks for him after taking him to the Roseman Bridge, Robert tells a story about being ogled during a trip to Africa by a gorilla who gave him "the most lascivious look you've ever seen on any creature with that much hair," establishing his own sense of humor and foreshadowing his unlikely affair with Francesca. After they talk about the poet William Butler Yeats and he leaves, she is shown reading a volume of Yeats alone, and the next day she tacks an unsigned invitation to him to come to dinner that night on the bridge. Eating lunch at a local diner, Robert encounters Lucy Redfield (Michelle Benes), whom the townsfolk have shunned after learning of her adulterous affair, and phones Francesca offering to cancel their dinner because he doesn't want to subject her to

FIGURE 9.9 *Robert Kincaid (Clint Eastwood) begins his adulterous affair with Francesca Johnson (Meryl Streep) in* The Bridges of Madison County *(1995) with one of the most traditional of courtship rituals.*

gossip. Thoroughly entranced by him, however, Francesca insists that she wants to see him again. They spend the afternoon together on a second bridge where he surprises her by snapping several pictures of her, then return to her house, where, as she lies in the bathtub in whose water he's just showered, she reflects, "Almost everything about Robert Kincaid had begun to seem erotic to me." After they share dinner, some slow dancing, and some gently pointed dialogue about whether he's forcing himself on her, a slow fade to black leads to a cutaway to Carolyn and Michael reading Francesca's journal. Michael announces that he needs some air and stalks out of the room; Carolyn is clearly enthralled by her mother's confession.

The story returns to Francesca and Robert lying in a postcoital embrace sharing memories of Bari that mark them as secret soulmates even as Francesca's journal establishes Robert more and more firmly as a Gothic hero as wild yet sensitive as Emily Brontë's Heathcliff. That evening, he takes her to a blues club "off the Interstate—a place, he assured me, where no one I knew would see us"—and they drink beer, slow dance, and return to her house for sex. Another decorous cutaway to Francesca's children finds Michael returning from a bar to announce, "I feel like she cheated on me," and Carolyn, obviously unhappy in her own marriage, sneaking quick peeks at a divorce lawyer's business card. Back in 1965 the following day, Francesca accuses Robert of treating her as just one more adventure in an endless series of adventures, and the two, in a scene invented by LaGravenese, settle into their most serious quarrel before Robert ends it by saying, "It seems to me that all I've been doing in my life is making my way to you" and asking her to come away with him. Although the film shows her, wearing a red dress, packing two suitcases, he asks her at their last dinner together, "You're not coming with me, are you?" and she replies, "It doesn't seem like the right thing—for anyone," setting up the film's surprisingly long last act, which aims to make the lovers' renunciation of their love as beautiful as the pursuit and consummation of it. If it is less desirable to give up love than to embrace it, their dialogue suggests, it is incomparably more noble, as Robert makes clear in his final line of dialogue: "I'll only say this once. I've never said it before. This kind of certainty comes but once in a lifetime." The closing scenes of the film focus on establishing and legitimizing the legacy of the lovers' magical four days. "What Robert and I shared couldn't continue if we were together," Francesca confides in the journal her children will later read. She befriends Lucy Redmond, finding in their closeness welcome comfort and affirmation, and ministers lovingly to her husband Richard (Jim Haynie) on his deathbed, as he tells her: "Franny, I just want to say I know you've had your own dreams. I'm sorry I couldn't give them to you. I love you so very much." Unable to track down Robert, who has left *National Geographic*, Francesca revisits the bridges that have become talismans to her on her birthday every year. Back in the present, Carolyn, strengthened by her mother's story, phones her husband to start arrangements for their divorce, and Michael, who finally gets it, returns to the wife who wonders angrily where he's been all night and asks her: "Do I make you happy, Betty? Because I want to—more than anything." Thoroughly enlightened about why Francesca made her last wish, they scatter her ashes from the bridge in the film's final shot.

In its own way, *The Bridges of Madison County* is every bit as formulaic as the summer blockbusters, with or without superheroes, to which it poses as counterprogramming. What makes it remarkable is not its originality, its sentimentality, or its psychological insight, but its dexterity in juggling the conflicting scripts provided by its source novel, its screenplay, its screenwriter, its director, and its two very different stars, which combine to give its commonplace story of forbidden love a sense of taboos decorously but deliciously violated, the satisfaction of an impossible union consummated, the nobility of the characters' renunciation, the assurance that their affair has changed them permanently for the better, and the invitation to the audience to live vicariously through dreams that remain ever more distant memories for the film's heroine. Like Eastwood and Streep and the characters they play, the film is a valentine to adaptation that celebrates both the surrender to love and the decision to put it behind, secure in the faith that whatever its vicissitudes it will take lasting root.

Notes

1. Steven M. Sanders, "Picturing Paranoia: Interpreting Invasion of the Body Snatchers," in *The Philosophy of Science Fiction Film*, ed. Steven M. Sanders (Lexington: University Press of Kentucky, 2008), p. 59.
2. Gerald Jonas, "Ray Bradbury, Who Brought Mars to Earth with a Lyrical Mastery, Dies at 91," *New York Times*, June 6, 2012, https://www.nytimes.com/2012/06/07/books/ray-bradbury-popularizer-of-science-fiction-dies-at-91.html.
3. J.P. Telotte, *Science Fiction Film* (Cambridge: Cambridge University Press, 2001), p. 57.
4. The figures in this paragraph are all taken from Liam Burke, *The Comic Book Film Adaptation: Exploring Modern Hollywood's Leading Genre* (Jackson: University Press of Mississippi, 2015), p. 271.
5. Dan Hassler-Forest, "Roads Not Taken in Hollywood's Comic Book Movies: Popeye, Dick Tracy, and Hulk," in *The Oxford Handbook of Adaptation Studies*, ed. Thomas Leitch (New York: Oxford University Press, 2017), p. 421.
6. Will Brooker, *Hunting the Dark Knight: Twenty-First Century Batman* (London: Taurus, 2012), p. 49.
7. Burke, *The Comic Book Film Adaptation*, p. 163.
8. Burke, *The Comic Book Film Adaptation*, p. 164.
9. Michael L. Fleisher, assisted by Janet E. Lincoln, *The Original Encyclopedia of Comic Book Heroes, Volume 1: Featuring Batman* (New York: DC Comics, 2007), pp. 176, 378.
10. Fleisher, *The Original Encyclopedia of Comic Book Heroes, Volume 1*, p. 295.
11. See John Pierson, *Spike, Mike, Slackers and Dykes: A Guided Tour across a Decade of American Independent Cinema* (New York: Hyperion, 1996), pp. 126–32.
12. Helen Fielding, "Bridget Jones's Diary," *Independent*, 1995–97, http://bridgetarchive.altervista.org/index1995.htm.
13. Emma Thompson, "1995 Acceptance Speech for Writing (Screenplay Based on Material Previously Produced or Published)," *Academy Award Acceptance Speech Database*, http://aaspeechesdb.oscars.org/link/068-23/.
14. See Andrew Higson, "Re-presenting the National Past: Nostalgia and Prejudice in the Heritage Film," in *Fires Were Started, British Theater and Thatcherism*, ed. Lester Friedman (Minneapolis: University of Minnesota Press, 1993), pp. 91–109, and Ginette Vincendeau, "Introduction," in *Film/Literature/Heritage: A Sight and Sound Reader*, ed. Ginette Vincendeau (London: BFI, 2001), pp. xvii–xix.
15. Philip Horne, "The James Gang," *Sight and Sound* 8.1 (1998): 16.
16. Edward Guthmann, "The Wings of the Dove," *San Francisco Chronicle*, November 14, 1997, https://www.sfgate.com/movies/article/Gorgeous-Wings-Takes-Fresh-Flight-Bonham-2822972.php.

17 Marc Savlov, "*The Wings of the Dove*," *Austin Chronicle*, November 21, 1997, https://www.austinchronicle.com/events/film/1997-11-21/the-wings-of-the-dove/.

18 Jessica Winter, "Mondo Trasho and Desperate Living," *Village Voice*, April 24, 2001, https://www.villagevoice.com/2001/04/24/mondo-trasho-and-desperate-living/.

19 Jay Carr, "The Gleam of a Gilded Cage," *Boston Globe*, May 18, 2001, p. D5.

20 Tzvetan Todorov, *The Fantastic: A Structural Approach to a Literary Genre*, trans. Richard Howard (Ithaca, NY: Cornell University Press, 1975), p. 25.

21 Larry McMurtry, Introduction to *Lonesome Dove* (1985; rpt. New York: Simon and Schuster, 2000), p. 11.

22 Richard Woodward, "Cormac McCarthy's Venomous Fiction," *New York Times Magazine*, April 18, 1992, https://www.nytimes.com/1992/04/19/magazine/cormac-mccarthy-s-venomous-fiction.html.

23 Robert James Waller, *The Bridges of Madison County* (New York: Warner, 1992), p. vii.

24 Maureen Dowd, "Go Ahead, Make Him Cry," *New York Times*, March 25, 1995, https://www.nytimes.com/1995/03/26/movies/go-ahead-make-him-cry.html.

25 Janet Maslin, "What the Critics Can't Wait to See," *New York Times*, May 14, 1995, https://www.nytimes.com/1995/05/14/movies/film-what-the-critics-can-t-wait-to-see-676895.html.

26 Quoted in Richard Schickel, *Clint Eastwood: A Biography* (New York: Knopf, 1996), p. 149.

10

2007–18: Entertainment for Me

The decline of the literary adaptation

Despite the box office success of *The Bridges of Madison County* and the continued domination of the Academy Awards by films whose screenplay was based on material that had originally been presented, in the phrase the Academy itself adopted from 1957 through 1990, in another medium, it became clear by the opening years of the twenty-first century that the most commercially successful Hollywood adaptations had even less to do with traditional canons of American literature than Robert James Waller. In 1991, the year the Academy changed its designation for adapted screenplays to those based on material previously produced or published, the Oscar had gone to *The Silence of the Lambs*, followed by *Howards End* (1992), *Schindler's List* (1993), *Forrest Gump* (1994), *Sense and Sensibility* (1995), *Sling Blade* (1996), *L.A. Confidential* (1997), *Gods and Monsters* (1998), and *The Cider House Rules* (1999). Most of these films were rooted in either canonical literary classics or contemporary best-selling novels. The Oscars that followed, however, reflected new trends. The winners of Academy Awards for Best Screenplay based on material previously produced or published included *Traffic* (2000), *A Beautiful Mind* (2001), *The Pianist* (2002), *The Lord of the Rings: The Return of the King* (2003), *Sideways* (2004), *Brokeback Mountain* (2005), *The Departed* (2006), *No Country for Old Men* (2007), *Slumdog Millionaire* (2008), *Precious* (2009), *The Social Network* (2010), *The Descendants* (2011), *Argo* (2012), *12 Years a Slave* (2013), *The Imitation Game* (2014), *The Big Short* (2015), *Moonlight* (2016), and *Call Me by Your Name* (2017). *Sideways, No Country for Old Men, Slumdog Millionaire, The Descendants*, and *Call Me by Your Name* continued the tradition of adapting the kinds of middlebrow novels Hollywood had been filming for many years. Although Rex Pickett's *Sideways* (2004) and Kaui Hart Hemmings's *The Descendants*

(2007), the two novels Alexander Payne had chosen to film, were relatively little known before the films were released, they were just as representative of long-standing trends in Hollywood adaptation as Cormac McCarthy's better-known 2005 novel *No Country for Old Men*, André Aciman's prize-winning 2007 novel *Call Me by Your Name*, and Vikas Swarup's 2005 novel *Q and A*, the source for *Slumdog Millionaire*. *The Lord of the Rings* was based on a celebrated novel that had never achieved either broad popularity or canonical status before Peter Jackson's adapted trilogy, and *Brokeback Mountain* on E. Annie Proulx's 1997 short story, exactly the kind of material on which Hollywood had drawn so freely in the studio era. But the other Oscar winners drew on very different kinds of material. *A Beautiful Mind*, *The Pianist*, *The Social Network*, and *The Imitation Game* were based on memoirs, biographies, and other nonfictional works. *Argo* and *The Big Short* were based on journalistic accounts of events from recent history. *Traffic* was based on a television miniseries. *The Departed* was a remake of the 2002 Hong Kong film *Internal Affairs*. *Moonlight* was based on *In Moonlight Black Boys Look Blue*, an unpublished, unproduced play that Tarell Alvin McCraney had written as a drama school project. Like *Precious* and *12 Years a Slave*, it provided an account of the African American experience that had heretofore been barred from the canon, and in all three cases the success of the film was widely considered a legitimation of its source material. By the time Lee Daniels made *Precious*, he felt entitled, or obliged, to release it first under the title *Push: Based on the Novel by Sapphire*, and then, to avoid its confusion with the science-fiction film *Push* (2009), as *Precious: Based on the novel "Push" by Sapphire*.

The decisive shift away from classic and best-selling novels and popular plays, the kinds of material Hollywood had originally mined for its most prestigious adaptations, involves both technological changes and changes in literary and cultural tastes that together produced a revolution in notions of what counted as American literature and culture in the new century. Hollywood's treatment of the novels of Philip Roth is particularly revealing. Roth had first made his mark as a chronicler of the American Jewish experience in his novella *Goodbye, Columbus* (1959) and his wildly satirical novel *Portnoy's Complaint* (1969). Unsatisfied with his identification as an ethnic novelist, the "alarmingly protean"[1] Roth embarked on a period of experimentation with modes as different as *Our Gang (Starring Tricky and His Friends)*, his 1971 satire of Richard Nixon; *The Breast*, a 1972 novella that invited comparisons to Franz Kafka's story "The Metamorphosis"; and *The Great American Novel*, the 1973 novel that chronicles the wartime vicissitudes of the Patriot Baseball League, which is ultimately dissolved and forgotten because it has become a shadow arm of the American Communist Party. In *My Life as a Man* (1974), Roth discovered what would become one of the central themes of his career: his male protagonists' obsession with establishing and maintaining their masculinity in a social culture that everywhere diminishes manhood as they face a biological mortality that is bound to extinguish it. In *The Ghost Writer* (1979), which plays with the possibility that the young diarist Anne Frank actually survived the Second World War, he introduced Nathan Zuckerman, who would return in eight more novels. In the five parts of *The Counterlife* (1986), the fifth Zuckerman novel, Roth, who had heretofore been noted for his resistance to fashionable strains of postmodernism, produced an aggressively self-contradictory, self-critical, self-referential series of narratives that suggested that no human life can be comprehensively and authoritatively known and indeed that every life may be a counterlife.

The ferocious postmodern carnival of *The Counterlife* finds a broader canvas in the novels that follow. *Operation Shylock: A Confession* (1993) follows a narrator named Philip Roth, whose habitual use of Halcion renders the accuracy of his memories highly suspect, on a trip to Israel that turns into a secret mission for the Israeli intelligence service Mossad, an account the narrator insists both is and is not fictional. *Sabbath's Theater* (1995) is the playfully tormented confession of unemployed puppeteer Mickey Sabbath, a self-styled dirty old man. The life of the respectable Newark family man of *American Pastoral* (1997) is plunged into chaos by his country's involvement with the Vietnam War, sharpened by his own daughter's identification as a domestic terrorist. *The Human Stain* (2000) tells the story of Zuckerman's neighbor Coleman Silk, an accused racist who turns out to be an African American passing as a Jew. *The Plot against America* (2004), like Philip K. Dick's *The Man in the High Castle*, proposes a dystopian alternative history of the Second World War. In Roth's telling, Franklin D. Roosevelt is unseated as President by celebrated aviator Charles Lindbergh, whose administration enforces an anti-Semitic regimen that has a nightmarish impact on the family of young Philip Roth. The furious energy of these novels did not so much abate as find a more classical subject in *The Dying Animal* (2001), *Exit Ghost* (2007), and the four short novels Roth called "Nemeses": *Everyman* (2006), *Indignation* (2008), *The Humbling* (2009), and *Nemesis* (2010), all of them elegiac meditations on mortality.

Widely paired with Saul Bellow as one of the two greatest American novelists of his generation, the prolific Roth garnered many literary awards, lived to see his leading novels collected in nine volumes published by the Library of America (a tenth volume of his nonfiction appeared just before his death), and was frequently mentioned as the leading American contender for the Nobel Prize in Literature. When songwriter Bob Dylan won the prize in 2016, many commentators expressed bewilderment or outrage that Roth had been passed over, and his failure to win a Nobel prize was a common theme in the obituaries that greeted his death two years later. Considering the breadth, depth, ambition, and resourcefulness of Roth's work, his relative neglect by the movies is equally surprising. Roth is not a niche novelist like William Kennedy, whose 1983 novel *Ironweed* was filmed by Héctor

Babenco in 1987, or, despite his frequent flirtations with metafictionality, a self-consciously hermetic novelist like Don DeLillo, whose 2003 novel *Cosmopolis* was filmed by David Cronenberg in 2012. Even his knottiest novels are extroverted, clearly written, and engaged with social problems of urgent import. In an earlier period, they might have seemed tailor-made for film adaptation. But Hollywood has produced only a handful of Roth adaptations, and the critical and economic failure of these films provides ample reason for why there have not been more. The early film adaptations of *Goodbye, Columbus* (1969) and *Portnoy's Complaint* (1972) gave Roth's name wider publicity without bolstering his reputation. Following a thirty-year gap with no film adaptations, a more modest Roth wave began in 2003 with Robert Benton's adaptation of *The Human Stain*, followed at length by *Elegy*, Isabel Coixet's 2008 adaptation of *The Dying Animal*; Barry Levinson's *The Humbling* (2016); James Schamus's *Indignation* (2016); Ewan McGregor's *American Pastoral* (2016); and Irene Pavlásková's *The Prague Orgy* (2019).

None of this latest wave put Roth firmly on the Hollywood map for reasons the first of them, *The Human Stain*, makes perfectly clear. The hero of Roth's novel, Coleman Silk, is a distinguished professor of classics at a New England college he has helped to raise to eminence who refers to two students who have never shown up in his class as spooks, unaware that they are African American. When they lodge complaints against Silk for racism, he resigns his position in protest, and his wife dies of a coronary embolism hours later. Silk hopes to avenge himself by telling his story to Nathan Zuckerman, a writer who has retreated from the world to live in the woods nearby, and encouraging him to use it as the basis for a novel. Although Zuckerman declines, the two men become friends, and Silk confides that he has begun an affair with Faunia Farley, a beautiful janitor at the college who is half his age. What he does not tell Zuckerman is that he is himself a light-skinned African American who has passed as white ever since he forswore his family and enlisted in the Navy. Against the background of repeated flashbacks to Silk's early years of struggle with his racial identity and excurses on President Bill Clinton's 1998 affair with White House intern Monica Lewinsky, Roth unfolds the story of Silk's unlikely May-December relationship with the illiterate Faunia, whose own background includes childhood abuse by her wealthy stepfather, the deaths of her two children in an accidental fire for which her deranged ex-husband Les blames her, and a suicide attempt. Hours after Silk confesses his secret to the lover who with the help of Viagra has awakened his fiercely wintry carnality, Les uses his truck to run the lovers off the road in a staged accident that leaves them both dead and Silk's secret secure from everyone but Zuckerman, who does not learn the truth until after Silk's death.

The film, scripted by Nicholas Meyer, was a box office failure that recouped only $25 million of its $30 million production budget.

Contemporaneous reviews of the film agree on the reasons why. Unlike the novel, which reviewers described as passionate, ambitious, and unbridled, the film was suffocatingly tasteful in its presentation of Silk's last love and overly reverential toward Roth's novel, to which it strained to be faithful despite the unavoidable absence of many of its incidents—the film boiled the first hundred pages of Roth's 350-page novel down to ten minutes—and of Nathan Zuckerman's voice, by turns restless, inquiring, and self-lacerating.

Although many reviewers admired the performances of Nicole Kidman as Faunia and especially Anthony Hopkins as Silk, most of them found both leading roles fatally miscast, with little sexual chemistry between the performers and no conceivable continuity between Wentworth Miller, the young mixed-race actor who played the young Coleman Silk, and Hopkins, who played the man he would grow up to become. No wonder, as the review aggregator Rotten Tomatoes concluded years later in summarizing these opinions, "the story is less powerful on screen than on the page."[2]

These reviewers' strictures are both judicious and eminently predictable because something like them gets leveled at so many recent film adaptations. A closer look at the reviewers' judgments shows in illuminating detail the challenges the filmmakers faced in adapting Roth's novel. The novel had itself been generated by a rich mixture of explosive scripts: the volume's position as the third volume of a trilogy about American public life whose earlier volumes had been *American Pastoral* (1997) and *I Married a Communist* (1998); Roth's continuing anatomy of the relations among masculinity, eros, and mortality, themes he had already explored in *My Life as a Man* (1974), *The Professor of Desire* (1977), *Deception* (1990), and *Sabbath's Theater* (1995); Roth's continuing use of the narrator Nathan Zuckerman as an confessional alter ego who observed and often passed judgment on himself and other Roth alter egos; Roth's continuing attack on political correctness and other taboos, dating back as far as *Portnoy's Complaint* (1969), written long before the term "political correctness" was coined, and focused and intensified here by analogy to both President Clinton's adulterous dalliance with a much younger woman and what Zuckerman called "the summer of an enormous piety binge, a purity binge,"[3] that greeted the revelations of his affair; and the persistent rumor, repeatedly denied by Roth, that Coleman Silk was based at least partly on the mixed-race *New York Times* reviewer and literary editor Anatole Broyard, who had also passed for most of his adult life as white—although Roth repeatedly and heatedly insisted that Silk had been based instead on the figure of his friend Melvin Tumin, a Princeton sociologist.[4]

The film explored some of these scripts while ignoring others. The clearest imperative it shared with the novel was the attack on political correctness and the determination to explore taboo behavior sympathetically. Roth's name remained attached to the film, but it now signified something quite different. In the absence of any reference to the earlier novels in Roth's trilogy, to any other Roth novels, or to any of Roth's long-standing thematic concerns as particular to Roth, the film transforms the author from an ongoing presence into a brand name associated with an elite literary establishment. The film retained numerous analogies to the Monica Lewinsky affair, but now, as A.O. Scott points out, that is "a moment in the recent past that history has conspired to make more distant than it might otherwise be" whose former urgency is transmuted into nostalgia.[5]

The film added several unavoidable scripts to Roth's rich stew. In order to secure funding for the project, Lakeshore Entertainment and Miramax sought top box office stars for the roles of Silk and Faunia. The casting of Anthony Hopkins introduced several new scripts rooted in his persona as an experienced and versatile performer who was not afraid to step outside his comfort zone to play characters as different as Hannibal Lecter and Richard Nixon. But although he was helped by several scenes bathed in subdued reddish light and publicity posters that cast his profile in convenient shadow, the Welsh Hopkins made no attempt to look African American or even sound American. Nicole Kidman, who had most recently appeared in an Oscar-winning performance as the novelist Virginia Woolf in *The Hours* (2002), Stephen Daldry's adaptation of Michael Cunningham's 1998 novel, and as hard-used public sex toy Grace Margaret Mulligan in Lars Von Trier's *Dogville* (2003), was cast once again against the glamorous, pristine persona that had characterized her earlier roles and delivered a performance as the tattooed, red-haired Faunia that reviewers found more conscientious than convincing. Mick LaSalle, noting that "good actors (Anthony Hopkins, Nicole Kidman) and a good director (Robert Benton) do their best to put over a good book by a major American novelist (Philip Roth)," expressed impatience with the complications introduced by the film's casting:

> That a black man from Newark, N.J., pretending to be a white man from Newark would adopt an English accent adds a whole layer of artifice that Roth never anticipated. One could argue that it takes the character of Coleman Silk and renders him finally and completely crazy, but that's not how we experience it. Instead we experience "The Human Stain" as a movie about Hopkins and Kidman kissing.[6]

Gary Sinise, who was cast as Zuckerman, offered no continuity with either Mark Linn Baker, who had played Zuckerman in a 1984 television adaptation of *The Ghost Writer* for *American Playhouse*, or David Strathairn, who would play the character in Ewan McGregor's 2016 film adaptation of *American Pastoral*. The one performer whom reviewers singled out for unanimous praise was Wentworth Miller, the only leading performer who brought no new scripts of his own to the movie except for the imperative to look like Hopkins, a challenge he could hardly be faulted for failing to meet (see Figures 10.1 and 10.2).

FIGURES 10.1 AND 10.2 *Audiences for* The Human Stain *(2003) could not accept the premise that the young Coleman Silk (Wentworth Miller), who is teaching Steena Paulsson (Jacinda Barrett) to box, would grow up to become the older Silk (Anthony Hopkins), shown here with his lover Faunia Farley (Nicole Kidman).*

More formidable challenges were posed by the film's inescapable closeness to Roth's novel, which became both a selling point and a stumbling block for a film marketed with the tag line, "How far would you go to escape the past?" Because the best-selling success of Roth's novel had made its central conceit, the secret of Silk's racial identity, considerably less secret, reviewers of the film felt free to disclose this information in their reviews even as they complained about what LaSalle called "a pervading inevitability" that gives the film "not much on which to hang a compelling dramatic story."[7] More generally, they criticized the film for its reverence toward Roth's defiantly irreverent novel. A.O. Scott called the film

> an honorable B+ term paper of a movie: sober, scrupulous and earnestly respectful of its literary source. This is precisely the problem: that source, Philip Roth's 2000 novel, is not especially sober, scrupulous or respectful. It is an angry, ungainly squall of a book, a clamorous defense of sexual vitality in an age of Puritan censoriousness and a lyrical inquiry into the mysteries of race, old age and recent American history.[8]

David Edelstein observes:

> Philip Roth's later novels are practically the antithesis of mainstream American cinema: The narrator doesn't seem to be telling a story so much as teasing one out of his own labyrinthine musings—churning thought before our eyes into narrative. It's difficult to imagine a perfect compromise between the author's voice and the language of the average studio film, but in *The Human Stain* (Miramax), director Robert Benton and screenwriter Nicholas Meyer have found what seems to me to be the exact midway point between the two—and thereby shown what an unsatisfying place that is to be.[9]

LaSalle adds that "compounding the problem more than anything else is the esteem in which the book is held, which prevents the filmmakers from wholesale additions to the story. They'd have had more freedom with a so-so book and might have made a better movie."[10] In other words, the film, whatever its incidental accomplishments or shortcomings, was doomed by its failure to be just like the book, although reviewers recognized that it could not possibly have been just like the book and they would not have approved if it had been. Although its lukewarm reception did not prevent Nicholas Meyer from writing a screenplay based on Roth's 2001 novel *The Dying Animal* that ultimately became the basis of Isabel Coixet's 2008 film *Elegy*, it did nothing to encourage a year of Philip Roth or any more pronounced interest in adapting the author's work generally. Instead it fell victim to the burden of too many scripts whose contradictory demands it could not reconcile, transcend, or otherwise manage.

The care and feeding of franchises

It would be easy to dismiss Hollywood's neglect of Philip Roth, or the indifferent success of the Roth adaptations that have made it to the screen, as an isolated case if it were not so characteristic of a broader tendency in twenty-first-century film adaptations. Hollywood is as eager as ever to acquire presold properties whose name recognition will guarantee a certain level of prospective interest and offer the promise of economic success. But the industry, which never focused its search for those properties primarily on American literature, has become even more indifferent to American literary sources in recent years. Or, to put it more precisely, its view of the kinds of American literature most likely to supply its needs for marketable product has undergone a rapid and dramatic change. The industry had little use for highbrow adaptations represented by its brief flirtation with Henry James, and the studios passed on adapting Roth's later novels in their pursuit of middlebrow properties that could attract a mass audience increasingly composed of young people. Forty years after the unexpected success of *Bonnie and Clyde* and *The Graduate* among younger audiences in 1967 alerted the studios to the existence of a statistically vital youth demographic that encouraged them to begin producing and marketing films specifically for that demographic, they turned increasingly for source material to a literature that had also been created and marketed specifically for that demographic as well.

A pivotal figure in the transition to a new American canon was Susan Eloise Hinton, whose first novel, *The Outsiders*, written when she was still a student in an Oklahoma high school, was published under the byline S.E. Hinton in 1967. *The Outsiders*, as well as her next three books, *That Was Then, This Is Now* (1971), *Rumble Fish* (1975), and *Tex* (1979), were all YA (Young Adult) novels set in Oklahoma and aimed at high school readers. The feature that set Hinton's novels apart from most YA fiction was that instead of seeking to teach and prepare their readers for their responsibilities they were to assume as adults, she emphasized a sympathetic portrayal of the pain and confusion that marked their present-day lives. All four of these novels were made into movies that targeted the same demographic, by now the unmarked audience for Hollywood movies. Tim Hunter filmed *Tex* in 1982, Francis Ford Coppola *The Outsiders* and *Rumble Fish* in 1983, and Christopher Cain *That Was Then ... This Is Now* in 1985. Matt Dillon, who starred in the first three of these films, established himself as a teenaged heartthrob, not by any means a literary personage, before moving on to a long and varied career in which adaptations played only an incidental role.

A generation of YA novels, encouraged by the runaway success of John Hughes's teen movies—*Sixteen Candles* (1984), *The Breakfast Club* (1985), *Weird Science* (1985), *Pretty in Pink* (1986), *Ferris Bueller's Day Off* (1986), and *Some Kind of Wonderful* (1987), all of them based on Hughes's original screenplays—followed Hinton to Hollywood: Mary Rodgers's *Freaky Friday* (1972, filmed 2003), Lois Duncan's *I Know What You Did Last Summer* (1973, filmed 1997), Natalie Babbitt's *Tuck Everlasting* (1975, filmed 1981 and 2002), Catherine Paterson's *Bridge to Terabithia* (1977, filmed 1985), Gail Carson Levine's *Ella Enchanted* (1997, filmed 2004), Dyan Sheldon's *Confessions of a Teenage Drama Queen* (1999, filmed 2004), Neil Gaiman's *Stardust* (1999, filmed 2007), Stephen Chbosky's *The Perks of Being a Wallflower* (1999, filmed 2012), Meg Cabot's *The Princess Diaries* (2000, filmed 2001), Ann Brashares's *The Sisterhood of the Traveling Pants* (2001, filmed 2005), Jodi Picoult's *My Sister's Keeper* (2004, filmed 2009), Rachel Cohn's *Nick and Norah's Infinite Playlist* (2006, filmed 2008), Brian Selznick's *The Invention of Hugo Cabret* (2007, filmed 2011), John Green's *The Fault in Our Stars* (2012, filmed 2014), Jesse Andrews's *Me and Earl and the Dying Girl* (2012, filmed 2015), R.J. Palacio's *Wonder* (2012, filmed 2017), and a long series of best-selling novels by Nicholas Sparks. Most of these adaptations enjoyed enough success to feed the trend toward filming YA novels further. But Hollywood's real preference, already forecast by the superhero adaptations of the 1980s and 1990s, was increasingly for fictional franchises that could both generate a whole series of novels and serve as a tentpole for a much wider series of branded merchandise, from video games to apparel to children's toys. Given the industry's long-standing preference for British over American novels as avatars of cultural cachet, it may come as no surprise that so many of these franchises were British. But the best-known of these—C.S. Lewis's Chronicles of Narnia, J.K. Rowling's Harry Potter novels, Philip Pullman's *His Dark Materials* novels, E.L. James's *Fifty Shades of Grey* trilogy—seemed to move further and further from the cultural orbit of the England Hollywood had fetishized for so long, and they comported easily with adaptations of such American works as George R.R. Martin's *Game of Thrones* (1996) and the historical fantasies that followed in his series *A Song of Ice and Fire* (adapted for television beginning in 2011), the *Series of Unfortunate Events* (1999–2006, filmed 2004, adapted for television 2017–19) Daniel Handler chronicled under the pen name Lemony Snicket, Stephenie Meyer's *Twilight* quartet of teen vampire romances (2005–08, filmed 2008–12), Rick Riordan's books about Percy Jackson and the Olympians (2005–09, filmed 2010–13), Suzanne Collins's dystopian *The Hunger Games* (2008–10, filmed 2012–15), Jeff Kinney's *Diary of a Wimpy Kid* and its sequels (2007–18, filmed 2010–17), and Veronica Roth's *Divergent* series (2011–18, filmed 2014–16).

The turn toward youth-oriented adaptations of youth-oriented novels—novels rather than plays, because teenagers rarely went to the theater—was a logical extension of Hollywood's original discovery of the youth market. Half a century earlier, when the movies' economic dominance had been threatened by the rise of television, the studio chiefs had tried to distinguish their product from television series by a series of technical innovations TV could not match. 3-D projection enjoyed a brief vogue in 1953, the same year that CinemaScope and several rival wide-screen processes debuted and that Eastmancolor, a more inexpensive and realistic alternative to Technicolor, had been widely available, unleashing an unprecedented number of color films in 1954. In addition, the studios fought back by adapting best-selling novels from *Peyton Place* (1956, filmed 1957) to *The Carpetbaggers* (1961, filmed 1964) too racy for television to air. None of these strategies prevented paying attendance at American cinemas from falling from a high of $4.5 billion in 1946 to a low of $820 million in 1972 before a modest recovery. What ultimately saved Hollywood was not glorious Technicolor, breathtaking Cinemascope, stereophonic sound, or even weaponizing best sellers but the assiduous cultivation of the teenage audience that soon became its mainstay.

At the turn of the century, the studios still sought to appeal to this audience through a variety of action films, teen romances, and comedies. Within a few years, however, the industry's focus had narrowed to what Liam Burke has called "Hollywood's leading genre,"[11] the comic book adaptation. Burke has summarized three reasons for the increasing dominance of comic book adaptations: "cultural traumas and the celebration of the hero following real-life events, in particular the 9/11 terrorist attacks; technological advancements, most notably digital film techniques, which allow the source to be recreated more faithfully and efficiently on screen; and finally contemporary filmmaking paradigms that favor content with a preexisting fan base and an amenability to franchise opportunities."[12] Despite the high cost of producing films whose comic book heroes established their status by their ability to break the laws of the physical world, successful superhero movies carried the potential to offset their outsized production budgets in at least three ways. They could attract repeat customers who would pay more than once to see the same film; they could generate sequels whose built-in fan base would make them far easier to market; and they could spawn extra-cinematic franchises based on video releases, video games, and other affiliated merchandise. Since the studios licensed rather than producing these franchise offshoots, any revenue they generated was pure profit, allowing Batman and Spider-Man to punch far above their weight.

In one sense, this new era marked the close in the long history of Hollywood's dependence on literary adaptations. In another, however, the studios' increasing dependence on superhero franchises marked the first time in Hollywood history in which adaptations of American literature, broadly defined, were central to the industry's economic model. The new generation of superhero adaptations posed specific problems stemming from their status as franchises. The first of these was the age-old question of fidelity. With rare exceptions like *Gone with the Wind* (1939), the studios had treated the literary sources they adapted as so much raw material that did not require film adaptations to follow them faithfully. But the active fan bases for comic book heroes, energized and linked by social media, were both more watchful and more demanding than even the most devoted readers of Harriet Beecher Stowe and Henry James. The problem was intensified by the fact that superhero adaptations, because they never chose to adapt a single story that had already appeared in a comic book, incurred the demanding responsibility to remain faithful to a text that amounted to the textual universe of Superman or the Avengers or the X-Men.

Will Brooker has described the daunting problems Christopher Nolan faced in fashioning *Batman Begins* (2005) as a reboot that would remain faithful to the Batman universe, even though it could not possibly incorporate all the features of that universe, while marking a distinctive new chapter that would renew the franchise and incidentally make millions of dollars (see Figure 10.3). Parsing the slippery relationship between words and images in the DVD supplement "Genesis of the Bat," Brooker traces the process by which Nolan and his co-writer David Goyer, beginning with a determination to avoid the fate of Joel Schumacher's free-wheeling *Batman Forever* (1995) and *Batman and Robin* (1997), approached the task of "adapting 'Batman' in his 66-year complexity" by cutting it down to "adapting Batman since the early 1970s," ultimately focusing on three sources: Jeph Loeb and Tim Sale's *The Long Halloween* (1996–97), which introduced the gang leader Carmen Falcone; Dennis O'Neil's tales of Ra's al Ghul (1971) and his 1989 story "The Man Who Falls," which imagined Bruce Wayne traveling the world after his parents' murders before returning home to Gotham City to become Batman; and Frank Miller's *Batman: Year One* (1987), which focused on Batman's origins and his early relationship with Lieutenant James Gordon (61). Brooker concludes:

FIGURE 10.3 *The subdued graphics and an unusually brooding Batman (Christian Bale) help* Batman Begins *(2005) in marking a new era in superhero franchise adaptations.*

Although the production notes and documentaries stress romantic notions of loyalty, reverence and fidelity in an attempt firmly to position Nolan's Batman as distinct from Schumacher's and win the approval of the fan audience, the process of adaptation even from a relatively small set of source texts still fits the more promiscuous poststructuralist model, with the film occupying one node in an interlinked network, rather than a more traditional view of "original" and "copy." Rather than the faithful pairing implied by both the film crew and the comic book creators, *Batman* entered a matrix.[13]

An earlier generation of movies about Superman and Batman had already raised the question of how a franchise could become a canon without a center, a single authoritative source that provides a basis for later avatars. Nolan's ambitious reboot raised the stakes by asking implicitly what makes a franchise a franchise.

Whether or not the discussion is governed by Henry Jenkins's definition of a franchise as "the coordinated effort to brand and market fictional content within the context of media conglomeration,"[14] it is clear that franchises include multiple instances of a particular storyworld, often across several media platforms, variously coordinated. Jenkins's emphasis on coordination and conglomeration emphasizes the coherence of this storyworld across different versions and platforms, but it is equally appropriate to emphasize the diversity of different instances, which would otherwise require only replication, not coordination. The very effort to fashion franchises attests to the diversity of offerings within the franchises; Jenkins's convergence culture marks a series of sustained, top-down attempts to franchise what would otherwise be instances of a divergence culture. The Batman franchise, to stick with Brooker's example, is not a canon but a network, in Jenkins's terms, or a matrix, in Brooker's.

Along with the heady possibilities of building superhero networks or matrices through a process of theoretically infinite expansion, the problems Nolan faced marked a pivotal new stage in the development of superhero franchises, a moment when the problems of such dramatic expansion would become more and more obvious and the bill for the program would come due. The most obvious of these problems was the best way to launch new superheroes into a universe, or a series of competing universes, or a summer release schedule that was already crowded with them. If fans had grown tired of Superman and Batman movies, what did they want instead? Nolan and Warner Bros. gambled that what they wanted was a new, darker, more intense take on the Dark Knight; other studios bet that they wanted fresh, though familiar, blood.

The situation was further complicated by the emergence of two competing universes: the DC Universe, home to Superman, Batman, and other foursquare members of the Justice League of America, and the Marvel

Universe, whose distinctly more offbeat roster of heroes included Spider-Man, Iron Man, the Incredible Hulk, the Fantastic Four, Captain America, Sub-Mariner, and the Mighty Thor. Each of the Marvel heroes had anchored an animated television series beginning in 1966 (except for Spider-Man, who had debuted in 1967), and Spider-Man, who had appeared in the Turkish features *3 Dev Adam* (1973) and *Örümcek Adam* (1966) and the tokusatsu series *Supaidâman* (1978–79) for Japanese television, had returned to American television in the live-action *The Amazing Spider-Man* (1977–79) and the animated series *Spider-Man* (1981–82), a year before *The Incredible Hulk* (1982–83). But the legal and financial vicissitudes of Marvel Productions, which passed from the control of one media conglomerate to another during the 1980s and 1990s, delayed the arrival of its products on the big screen until *Blade* (1998), released while the fate of Marvel Enterprises, which focused less on producing film adaptations than on acquiring other media outlets from Artisan Entertainment to Cover Concepts, was still uncertain. The success of *Blade* and the even greater success of *X-Men* (2000) encouraged the company to launch a longer list of superhero movies: *Blade 2* and *Spider-Man* in 2002; *Daredevil*, *X2*, and *Hulk* in 2003; *The Punisher*, *Spider-Man 2*, and *Blade: Trinity* in 2004; *Elektra*, *Man-Thing*, and *Fantastic Four* in 2005. During this last year, the company reorganized itself as Marvel Entertainment to indicate its new focus on producing feature films like *Ghost Rider* (2007) and its sequels, *The Wolverine* (2013), *Fantastic Four* (2015), and *Logan* (2017).

Almost without exception, the Marvel films performed prodigiously at the box office. Under the direction of Sam Raimi, the Spider-Man franchise was especially successful: *Spider-Man* (2002) grossed $822 million, *Spider-Man 2* (2004) $784 million, and *Spider-Man 3* (2007) $891 million worldwide. More clearly perhaps than any other hero of the Marvel Universe, Spider-Man illustrated the distinctive nature of Marvel heroes. An accidental recipient of superpowers from the bite of a genetically modified spider, Peter Parker (Tobey Maguire) is a decidedly reluctant superhero who resists using his powers to apprehend criminals until one of them kills his beloved Uncle Ben (Cliff Robertson) and then finds himself caught in the toils of his teenaged romance with Mary Jane Watson (Kirsten Dunst) and squaring off against Green Goblin (Willem Dafoe), the father of his best friend Harry Osborn (James Franco) (see Figure 10.4). Everything about Spider-Man, from his casting to his dialogue to his relations to other characters, expresses his self-conscious neuroses, his constant self-doubt, his wry discomfort with his world and his mission, and his essential Everyman normalcy, all of which generate a touching, often cheeky dissonance between his superhero status and his secret identity that other Marvel superheroes from Iron Man to the Hulk exploit in different ways.

For all his success at the movies, Spider-Man would soon become an example of a problem that emerged as central in the second wave of

FIGURE 10.4 Spider-Man *(2002) puts a superhero spin on the otherwise conventional teen romance between Spider-Man (Tobey Maguire) and Mary Jane Watson (Kirsten Dunst).*

superhero adaptations: how to manage the tricky business of rebooting a popular franchise. "Rebooting," a term borrowed from the different ways to restart a computer whose operations had developed problems, involved breaking the continuity of an existing fictional franchise, returning to its roots, and restarting it on a different basis. Although DC Comics had begun rebooting its superhero franchises as early as 1956, giving Green Lantern, for example, a new costume, a new secret identity, and a new origin story in *Showcase* 22 (September–October 1959), the practice became more common, and the use of the term more widespread, after

> the release of Gus Van Sant's 1998 "replica" of *Psycho* (1960) not only antagonized critics, but also initiated a broad discursive shift away from the term "remake" toward a host of remake euphemisms—reworking, refitting, retooling, retread, replay, redo, and others—that have come to dominate review articles and criticism in the new millennium. Associated industry discourses—in particular, official film websites—began to frame publicity *positively* around a new film's "remake" status, ascribing value to an earlier version and then identifying various filters—technological, cultural, authorial—through which that property had been transformed. This trend, which has increasingly led to (authorized) remakes that bear only a generic resemblance to their precursors, seems to have found its apotheosis in the "reboot": a (legally sanctioned) version that attempts to disassociate itself textually from previous iterations while at the same time having to concede that it does not replace—but adds

new associations to—an existing (serial) property. As much a critical or discursive formation as an industrial or textual one, the category of the reboot thus re-imagines not simply a specific film (or films) but the concept of the remake for the new millennium. For instance, asked what appealed to him about "rebooting a series that had already been interpreted," Christopher Nolan replied that when he undertook *Batman Begins* (2005), the first installment in Warner Bros.' Dark Knight trilogy, "there was no such thing conceptually as a 'reboot.' That idea didn't exist."[15]

Batman Begins quickly established the gold standard for reboots. Nolan and screenwriter David S. Goyer returned to the model of the 1978 *Superman*—extended exploration of the superhero's roots, mythopoetic self-seriousness, all-star supporting players, a reliance on traditional stunts and miniature shots supplemented by minimal CGI effects—but with the consistently darker, more brooding tone established most influentially by Frank Miller's *Batman: The Dark Knight Returns* (1986). Nolan's film and its two sequels, *The Dark Knight* (2008) and *The Dark Knight Rises* (2012), succeeded by inviting their audience to a personal investment in Batman, his alter ego Bruce Wayne, Gotham City, and the villains they battled, every element highly stylized but none of them cartoonish. *Spider-Man*, by contrast, was invincibly cartoonish in both his comic book and his film appearances: a nerdy high school kid with money problems, school problems, work problems, and girl problems who just happens to have superpowers he uses to fight evil. So when Sony Pictures decided that instead of making *Spider-Man 4*, which had been stalled because Raimi and his writers had not been able to come up with a compelling story, they would reboot the franchise with a new star and a new creative team, they faced serious challenges, for injecting mythopoetic self-seriousness into Peter Parker would neuter the character and perhaps kill the franchise. The selling point of the reboot was that instead of developing Spider-Man further, it would return to his roots and present another version of the coming-of-age story at its heart.

Accordingly, *The Amazing Spider-Man* (2012) supplied its hero, now played by Andrew Garfield, with a new origin story, a new girlfriend, a new antagonist, and a newly developed set of superpowers in order to fulfill director Marc Webb's concept of the film as presenting "a different universe and a different story with different characters"[16] (see Figure 10.5). The goal, in other words, was not to present a definitive Spider-Man like Nolan's Batman who would eclipse all earlier iterations of the character but to embrace the multiplicity of the franchise and present one more adaptation of its defining moment, Peter Parker's reluctant acceptance of his superhero vocation. The strategy paid off not only in the financial success of Webb's reboot, which grossed $758 million worldwide, but in its ability to generate both the obligatory sequel, *The Amazing Spider-Man 2*, which grossed $709

FIGURE 10.5 *Because it is a reboot rather than a sequel,* The Amazing Spider-Man *(2012) can choose to include very much the same material in new guises, like this moment between Spider-Man (Andrew Garfield) and Gwen Stacy (Emma Stone).*

million upon its release in 2014, and yet another reboot in remarkably short order. *Spider-Man: Homecoming* (2017) followed *Captain America: Civil War* (2016) in embedding the hero more firmly within the Marvel Comics Universe by emphasizing his apprenticeship to the Avengers, who consider him not yet seasoned enough for full membership. Despite fans' skepticism about a second reboot only five years after the first, *Spider-Man: Homecoming*'s worldwide gross of $880 million showed the promise of reboots that positioned themselves as just the latest in a potentially endless series of readaptations of the same material.

Sony's decision to integrate Spider-Man, a Marvel Comics superhero, more closely with the Marvel Universe of the Avengers indicates a second problem for the new generation of superhero adaptations: the challenges of melding and expanding often familiar stories about individual heroes into ensemble adventures that will be original and compelling enough to bring audiences back. The obvious temptation is to make all these group adventures alike, gathering a stable of variously gifted but limited superheroes in order to defeat a single apocalyptic threat. Yielding to this temptation not only threatens to make all ensemble adventures homogeneous but poses the more specific problem of providing sequels to particular group franchises that will not simply recapitulate the stories with factitiously raised stakes, producing a franchise as monotonous as it is overscaled. The paradigmatic ensemble adaptation, Bryan Singer's *X-Men*, deals with this challenge in several ways. It doles out fragments of the obligatory origin stories and backstories of heroes like Wolverine (Hugh Jackman) and Rogue (Anna Paquin) slowly, teasingly, and incompletely, making the exposition of them as playfully rewarding as the forward trajectory of their epic confrontation with the villainous Magneto (Ian McKellan). It complements the monumental conflict between the X-Men, under the command of wheelchair-bound telepath Dr. Charles Xavier (Patrick Stewart), and Magneto and his underlings with a series of vignettes emphasizing the running conflicts among the X-Men themselves. It leavens its winner-take-all battle with constant metafictional references to its cultural dubious status as a comic book adaptation, as when Wolverine, scornfully regarding the regalia worn by Cyclops (James Marsden), asks him, "You actually go outside in these things?" and Cyclops replies, "What would you prefer—yellow spandex?" And it ends with an extended battle sequence that still hints at a possible sequel in which Wolverine will learn more about his troubled past, Magneto will break out of "this plastic prison" in which he has been confined, and another epic battle will ensue.

These tendencies are further developed in *The Avengers* (2012). Joss Whedon's film consistently subordinates the battles between the superhero Thor (Chris Hemsworth) and his allies and the supervillain Loki (Tom Hiddleston) and his minions to semicomic frictions between the heroes themselves, an uneasy rapport of frenemies openly mocked by the sudden eruption of the Hulk (Mark Ruffalo) and Dr. Strange (Benedict Cumberbatch) from their remote corners of the Marvel Universe into the world of Taika Waititi's *Thor: Ragnarok* (2017) (see Figure 10.6). Apart from the Hulk

FIGURE 10.6 The Avengers *(2012) faces the challenge of integrating the stories of Black Widow (Scarlett Johansson), Thor (Chris Hemsworth), Captain America (Chris Evans), Hawkeye (Jeremy Renner), Iron Man (Robert Downey, Jr.), and the Hulk (Mark Ruffalo).*

(Mark Ruffalo), each of the headline Avengers gets an opportunity to lead the team, and each displays a different leadership style. Thor repeatedly solicits Loki's cooperation for the good of humanity only to be repeatedly rebuffed. Captain America (Chris Evans), a white-bread hero like Superman, directs his own pleas to the Avengers, whom he begs to cooperate with each other. Iron Man (Robert Downey, Jr.) is acerbic, abrupt, and sarcastic, a wealthy industrialist turned hero accustomed to dictatorial power. Black Widow (Scarlett Johansson) is more empathetic and ingratiating. And Nick Fury (Samuel L. Jackson), not an Avenger but a summoner and coordinator, is cool, strategic, and so calculating that during the climactic battle he overrides a military command to step down and relinquish control of the Avengers and orders the troops under his control to shoot down an American bomber fitted with a nuclear device aimed at Manhattan. Fury's action shows the remarkably limited roles ordinary human beings have in the millennial soap opera of *The Avengers*. Humans who do not happen to be the alter egos of superheroes are little more than animated scenery whose collective casualties indicate the high stakes of every battle. Their functions are limited to screaming, fleeing en masse, getting rescued, and dying en masse. Very few of them even enter into dialogue with the Avengers, and those that do swiftly resign themselves to their roles as walk-ons or ad hoc helpers.

The one great exception to the unimportance of human characters is Stan Lee, the longtime mainstay of Marvel Comics who co-created the Fantastic Four, the Hulk, Thor, Iron Man, the X-Men, Daredevil, Dr. Strange, and Spider-Man, and who spearheaded Marvel's transformation from a comic book publisher to a dominant multimedia corporation. Beginning with *X-Men*, Lee, who had already appeared as the jury foreman in the 1989 television movie *The Trial of the Incredible Hulk*, took cameo roles in each of the Marvel features. Lee's cameos are often compared to Alfred Hitchcock's, but the differences between the two sets of attractions are more telling than their similarities. Hitchcock's cameos are always walk-ons who never speak, typically appear in only one shot, and cannot truly be called characters. Lee plays more (though not much more) consequential figures who interact with other characters and occasionally with superheroes. In *Thor: Ragnarok*, for example, he is the barber sent to cut the captured Thor's hair, and in Joss Whedon's *Avengers: Age of Ultron* (2015), he is a Second World War veteran who is carried out drunk from the Avengers' victory party after accepting a shot of Asgardian liquor from Thor. Lee's cameos establish him, like Hitchcock, as their stories' creator, but they do so by emphasizing his intertextual status as the creator and monstrator of earlier versions of the stories, a visitor, however privileged, to the new world at hand. Both Lee's and Hitchcock's cameos reveal and invite a double consciousness focusing on authority figures, but in Hitchcock's case the double consciousness focuses on the relation between the created world and its creator, in Lee's case on the relation between the present version of the storyworld and the earlier versions this one adapts.

More than any other single feature of the Marvel Universe, Lee's cameos illustrate a third challenge for the second generation of superhero adaptations: the need to balance the mythological pretensions of their epic battles against their snarky self-consciousness about their own status as both lowbrow fiction and metafiction. Different superhero movies have struck a balance between these two impulses in many different ways. *Superman* and *Watchmen* (2009) opt for self-seriousness, *Batman Begins* for psychological self-criticism, and *Wonder Woman* (2017) and *Black Panther* (2018) for a contemporary revisionist take on myths of feminine and African American empowerment. *Kick-Ass* (2010), whose all-too-human hero strives to play the role of superhero, produces naturalistically rooted, dark-tinged comedy; *Suicide Squad* (2016), which follows the exploits of a team of supervillains freed from prison in the hope of saving the world, black comedy; *The Lego Batman Movie* (2017) an unbridled satire that reveals just how thin a line separates the superhero universe from the universe of comically inexpressive Lego figures. Tim Miller's *Deadpool* seemed on its 2017 release to mark a new extreme in throwaway self-referentiality from its opening credits, which indicated that the film, "produced by asshats" and "directed by an overpaid tool," starred "God's perfect idiot," "a hot chick," "a British villain," "the comic relief," "a moody teen," "a CGI character," and "a gratuitous cameo," to the jaundiced disaffection of its scarred, murderous, foul-mouthed hero (Ryan Reynolds), who supplies a relentlessly impertinent voiceover that makes it hard to take even the most suspenseful scenes seriously. By the time David Leitch's *Deadpool 2* was released in 2018, however, these devices had already come to seem like signs of a new normal in superhero movies that depended increasingly on a combination of self-serious, world-threatening conflicts and self-mocking metafictionality. Far from departing from the norms of classic American novels like *Moby-Dick* and *V.*, however, these tonal conflicts marked a resurgence of a central motif in American fiction, as if an indispensable ingredient of successful superhero franchises were an ability to arouse and reward precisely the same appetites as those traditionally associated with a modernist view of American literature, driven as it was from its beginnings by multiple, often openly competing scripts that prevented its audience from accepting any one view of reality or its fictional avatars.

Whither the youth audience?

Even as Hollywood settled in to make movies mainly directed more and more exclusively at young people, its target audience had begun to contract.

Writing in June 2016, Derek Thompson notes that franchise films and sequels had come to monopolize the American box office:

> Twenty years ago, in 1996, none of the 10 biggest films were sequels or superhero movies. Films based on comics accounted for just 0.69 percent of the box office. [...] This year, out of the 371 movies released, 4 superhero films—*Captain America: Civil War, Deadpool, Batman vs. Superman,* and *X-Men: Apocalypse*—accounted for 29 percent of the box office. In the biggest picture, Hollywood is in the business of telling stories that people want to see, and when people go to the movies, by and large they want to see sequels of their favorite heroes.[17]

The race to make more and more franchise movies about familiar superheroes is best illustrated by Marvel Studios, whose release of Peyton Reed's *Ant-Man and the Wasp* (2018) marked the twentieth consecutive time a Marvel film had opened in the number one position in the American box office. Observing the appeal of superhero franchises for young audiences, Thompson concludes: "The problem for Hollywood is that audiences are ignoring *everything that isn't a sequel, adaptation, or reboot*. The market for films based on stories that aren't already famous is threadbare. These sorts of stories exist in entertainment, but audiences are looking for them outside of darkened theaters."[18] Noting that most Americans go to the movies only four or five times a year, Thompson emphasizes the dependence of Hollywood's business model on audience members, most of them between 18 and 39 years old, who go at least once a month, and then, reprinting a chart from the annual MPAA report in box office statistics,[19] indicates that "Hollywood's young fanatics are getting less fanatical by the year. [...] The most important demographic to Hollywood, 18-to-24-year-olds, is also abandoning Hollywood faster than any other group," and concludes that "Hollywood is losing its grip on young people" whose "attention is pouring into mobile devices and apps, like Netflix and premium cable apps (where many Hollywood auteurs have decamped), YouTube, Facebook, and Snapchat. In the last five years, as young people have trickled away from movies, mobile has taken attention share from every other major category."[20]

Young audiences have been abandoning movie theaters for several reasons. The desire of teenagers to escape from their parents' houses to spend time with the people they were dating, one of the primary drivers of the youth audience first widely recognized in the later 1960s, has waned dramatically because so few millennials go on dates. *USA Today* business columnist Paul Carrick Brunson estimated that the endless proliferation of dating apps, the cheapening of sex, the decreased commitment to marriage, and the lack of faith that dating necessarily leads to romantic courtship or anything else mean that "80% of Singles will NOT Go on One Date in 2017."[21] Millennials who seek not the experience of dating but video entertainment per se can access thousands of hours of material online through streaming services or video sites like YouTube, material they are much more likely to find searchable and responsive to their immediate interests than whatever happens to be playing at the nearest multiplex. And their attachment to the smartphones with which they have grown up makes them much less willing to surrender their personal preferences about their behavior to the social decorum of shared viewing spaces, as any filmgoer who has listed in exasperation to the unquenchable chatter of the surrounding cinephiles knows.

Like so many other momentous social shifts in cinema history, this one is largely driven by technology. Thomas Friedman has identified 2007 as a watershed year in recent history because it saw the introduction or the global dissemination of Facebook, Change.org, the Android, Bitcoin, the Kindle, and the cognitive computer Watson. Each of these developments made online communications faster, easier, and more appealing. Perhaps the most important of all the technologies released in 2007 was the iPhone, which, as internet pioneer Vint Cerf maintains, "made the Internet more valuable, because it became all the more accessible," at the same time the internet "also made the smartphone more valuable."[22] The future Friedman sees for human culture will be driven not by the monuments of canonical culture but by the proliferating platforms and affordances of digital technology and the present generation's abilities to adapt, and to adapt to, that technology to solve global problems.

This millennial view of technology may seem to have little room for any activity as apparently marginal as film adaptation. But it has crucial implications for the future of American literature on film. The first of these is the irreversible decline of the archival culture representing by Hollywood adaptations of classic American novels and plays. Contemporary filmgoers are simply not particularly invested in such adaptations, and generations to come are not likely to return to them. Thirty years ago, E.D. Hirsch called for a renewed attention to a cultural literacy based on familiarity with such common cultural topoi as Shakespeare, the Bible, and the American Civil War. Because "these stable elements of the national vocabulary are at the core of cultural literacy," Hirsch argued, it was only through education in those elements, rather than "the terms that ebb and flow," that citizens could communicate with each other in a kind of referential shorthand that made it unnecessary for them to reinvent the wheel in every conversation.[23] A generation later, it is clear that although communication does indeed depend on common cultural referents, those referents are increasingly drawn not from the archival culture Hirsch insisted was necessary to guarantee a continuity of references from decade to decade but from a popular culture as evanescent as it is ubiquitous. A recent Google search for "Shakespeare" turned up 158 million hits, a search for "Kardashian" 284 million hits. Of course Shakespeare maintains a decisive lead over the Kardashian clan in libraries around the globe, but the power of that lead depends on the assumption that more people, and more broadly influential people, spend time reading material available in libraries rather than online. The way forward for movie adaptations is clearly indicated by Bollywood, the Indian filmmaking industry in which "adaptation is a pervasive cultural and industrial practice" even though it "produces few literary adaptations and the status of the adaptation as a film genre in the sense of a contract between producer and spectators is weak."[24]

The view of American literature that emerges from this shift is of a corpus of unread, dimly sensed monuments that are marginal and largely irrelevant to contemporary American culture, even if the literary works themselves are as recent as Ntozake Shange's 1980 play *For Colored Girls Who Have Considered Suicide When the Rainbow Is Enuf*, adapted in 2010; Toni Morrison's 1987 novel *Beloved*, adapted in 1998; and Alice Sebold's 2002 novel *The Lovely Bones*, adapted in 2009. Despite the participation of well-known performers from Whoopi Goldberg to Rachel Weisz, and the star directors Jonathan Demme, Peter Jackson, and Tyler Perry, who wrote, directed, and produced *For Colored Girls* through his own company, Tyler Perry Productions, where it nested along with *Precious* (2009) amid a list that included *Diary of a Mad Black Woman* (2005), *Why Did I Get Married Too?* (2010), and *Boo! A Madea Halloween* (2016), none of these latter-day literary adaptations was well reviewed or financially successful, and none of them created any demand for further adaptations of the authors' work. This neglect is especially remarkable in the case of Morrison, a much-honored novelist who as early as 1993 had been awarded the Nobel Prize for Literature that continued to elude Philip Roth till the end of his life.

Roth himself had repeatedly prophesied the decline of American literary culture. Interviewed by Robert McCrum in 2001, he said, "I'm not good at finding 'encouraging' features in American culture. [...] I doubt that aesthetic literacy has much of a future here."[25] Eight years later, he told another interviewer, Tina Brown, that his earlier prediction that "novels are [not] going to be read 25 years from now" had been overly "optimistic": "I think it's going to be cultic. I think always people will be reading them but it will be a small group of people. Maybe more people than now read Latin poetry, but somewhere in that range." The object of the book itself, Roth opined, presented an increasing challenge to contemporary culture: "To read a novel requires a certain amount of concentration, focus, devotion to the reading. [...] I think that kind of concentration and focus and attentiveness is hard to come by—it's hard to find huge numbers of people, large numbers of people, significant numbers of people, who have those qualities" in the age of ubiquitous screens: "The book can't compete with the screen. It couldn't compete beginning with the movie screen. It couldn't compete with the television screen, and it can't compete with the computer screen."[26]

Divergence culture

The battle between books and screens has provoked considerable speculation and ongoing debate among adaptation scholars. In her 2013 Preface to the second edition of *A Theory of Adaptation,* Linda Hutcheon, considering the impact of emerging digital media and platforms on the practice of adaptation, asks, "For adaptation studies, is ours a transitional time or are we facing a totally new world?"[27] After surveying the evidence, she concludes that what Henry Jenkins has called convergence culture does indeed change the adaptation game in fundamental ways, a conclusion that is echoed by Siobhan O'Flynn's Epilogue to this second edition, which concludes:

> What is probably the most significant shift since the 2006 publication of *A Theory of Adaptation* is that where media conglomerates and IP holders once controlled the production and distribution of adaptations, with limited temporal, geographic or product releases, audiences now claim all aspects of ownership over content that they identify with, immerse themselves in, adapt, remix, reuse, and share.[28]

Citizens of the digital era have been told over and over again that they live in an era of convergence culture unprecedented in human history, an era made possible by new digital modes of creation and communication and unique new opportunities for consumers to participate actively in that culture by systematically blurring the borders between producers and consumers of culture, turning themselves into what Alvin Toffler has called "prosumers."[29] Convergence culture is everywhere: in fan fiction; in unauthorized franchise sequels; in YouTube videos of cats, babies, and household accidents; and in all the retitled scenes showing Hitler ranting in his bunker at targets the makers of the film *Downfall* never imagined. In the words of Henry Jenkins, who is largely responsible for the term's currency, "convergence culture represents a paradigm shift—a move from medium-specific content toward content that flows across multiple media channels, toward the increased interdependence of communications systems, toward multiple ways of accessing media content, and toward ever more complex relations between top-down corporate media and bottom-up participatory culture."[30]

The hallmark of convergence culture, the phenomenon that gives it its name, is the construction of storyworlds like that of *The Matrix* whose entry points are distributed over a wide range of media and whose creators increasingly tolerate and sometimes actively solicit fan participation in the construction of a world whose full understanding depends on consumption and participation across media. *The Matrix* is the crown jewel in the theory of convergence culture promulgated by Jenkins, a noted academic who also describes himself as a fanboy, someone who both blogs and writes for quarterlies, an observer whose analysis of convergence culture has been spectacularly successful. But convergence culture as Jenkins describes it exists mainly as a prophecy and coterie phenomenon, not as a game-changing present-tense phenomenon. Emerging technologies of production and communication have profoundly influenced contemporary culture, but these are only new technological upgrades on cultural products and habits that have already existed, and they are not aptly described by the label "convergence culture."

Other observers have already confirmed a good deal of what Jenkins describes: multiply sourced adaptations, franchises that blur the line between official productions and fan productions, the rise of reboots that resuscitate the fictional franchises of *Star Trek*, *RoboCop*, and Batman by seeking "to disavow and render inert [their] predecessors' validity."[31] But other aspects of convergence culture remain limited in their range and impact. As Marie-Laure Ryan notes,

> Jenkins's definition of transmedia storytelling presupposes a top-down planning process that distributes narrative information into multiple documents, so that users will have to consume many of these documents for *a unified and coordinated entertainment experience*. Yet in practice, most franchises grow from the bottom up, through a process of aggregation that adds more and more documents to a storyworld that has already achieved popularity and coherence independently of any transmedia buildup. This bottom-up process will, however, be followed by top-down development when media conglomerates adopt a best-seller and build around it a systematic advertising campaign that covers many platforms. Transmedia projects that are conceived top-down from the very beginning are the exception rather than the rule.[32]

The transmedia landscape created around *The Matrix*—three feature films (1999, 2001, 2003), a series of animated shorts, two popular video games, and a series of graphic novels—has inspired no equally ambitious imitators. Instead, recent comic book adaptations have simply reconfigured DC and Marvel Comics from producers of superhero comics to providers of licensed content for tentpole films that reach a wider audience and generate more revenue than the comics ever did. Shifting the tentpole from one media platform to another does not in itself foster convergence culture.

Siobhan O'Flynn, following an announcement by the Producers Guild of America about the Transmedia Producers Credit, asserts that "a transmedia production exists across multiple platforms and discrete components understood together [to] comprise an integrated, interconnected narrative whole, though they are encountered separately."[33] Claire Parody, however, points out that "where franchise production is diasporic and development un-coordinated, canonicity, authority, and continuity become problematic concepts, constantly re-negotiated; many franchise multitexts come together as an 'array' (Collins 164) of versions, origin points, co-existing, overlapping, and contradictory narrative realities, rather than a master narrative and stable textual corpus."[34] Parody's distinction reveals contemporary capital-intensive official culture less as a series of convergence networks that reveal coherent worlds than as a realm of licensed tentpole franchises designed to encourage active participation. As Raffi Khatchatdourian puts it: "Interactive films might have seemed like a stunt in the nineties, but for an audience in the age of Netflix personalized content has become an expected norm; L.C.D. screens increasingly resemble mirrors, offering users opportunities to glimpse themselves in the content behind the tempered glass."[35]

The range of participatory activities contemporary interactive culture licenses can be surprisingly limited and even old-fashioned. As Kyle Meikle has pointed out in his response to O'Flynn's celebration of Trilogy Studios' 2011 iBook adaptation of Crocker Johnson's 1955 children's book *Harold and the Purple Crayon*, an adaptation whose "illustrations are designed to invite interactivity,"[36] *Harold and the Purple Crayon* had always invited participation from every young reader armed with a purple crayon. So the iBook adaptation "doesn't so much innovate new modes of interactivity as it does make explicit the modes of interactivity that were in place all along."[37] The leading fashions in the contemporary mediascape involve not transmedia storyworlds but a new ferment of variously transgressive independent production that can be readily disseminated across new media platforms until a small fraction of this production ends up attracting a disproportionate audience.

Adaptation assumes a prominent but problematic role in this brave new world. O'Flynn observes that "the promotion of world building" is "an essential component of developing a brand identity that can be extended across platforms."[38] Beneath this confident assertion is a series of hard questions. What exactly do we mean by a world? Is it a coherent textual universe or an array of variant and often contradictory texts across multiple platforms? Does it encourage immersion or metacriticism? Is it universally available, endorsed, and consumed, or given currency only by a coterie or cult whose intense devotion is balanced by their limited impact? Does it require logical causality, narrative consistency, or simply recognizable branding? And since narrative worlds, whether they depend on single texts or intermedial platforms, are clearly not congruent with what we sometimes call "the world," what makes each of their worlds a world?

Jenkins's observation that "media industries are embracing convergence for a number of reasons: because convergence-based strategies exploit the advantages of media conglomeration; because convergence creates multiple ways of selling content to consumers; because convergence cements consumer loyalty at a time when the fragmentation of the marketplace and the rise of file sharing threatens old ways of doing business"[39] indicates that what is converging in his account is not individual versions of particular stories like

Star Wars and *The Matrix* but different media as such. At the level of individual storyworlds, ours is not a convergence culture but a divergence culture whose patrons feel increasingly licensed to sample whatever they like, whether or not their millions of downloads of songs and videos are in fact licensed, whether or not they are building or even entering a world outside their own.

The millennials who have followed Jenkins have been eager to confer the label of convergence culture on a public culture that is clearly fractured, fragmentary, and divergent because of the widespread embrace of digital media as a game changer that transfers the power to produce and distribute branded texts from corporations to fans. Adaptation scholars have increasingly accepted Jenkins's account of convergence culture because it validates the field's intertextual tendency to redefine each source text as nothing more than a signature attraction, empowering both adaptations and those who love them. Jenkins, who describes himself as "a critical utopian,"[40] makes no secret of his pleasure in announcing that convergence culture is rapidly transferring power to its users by democratically remaking the relationship between the parties the BBC's Ashley Highfield has characterized as the "monologue broadcaster" and the "grateful viewer."[41] More generally, theorists who share Jenkins's utopian bent are always happy for signs that post-national, bottom-up cultures are triumphing over cultural imperialism. As the subtitle of *Convergence Culture: When Old and New Media Collide* accurately indicates, however, what happens when old and new media collide is not the consistent world-building celebrated by utopian theorists but innumerable versions clamoring for attention, not a convergence culture marked by "consumption as a networked practice"[42] but a divergence culture marked by endless collisions of microcommunities whose hold on their collective identity depends in large part on ignoring the works and utterances of other communities.

To the extent that it concerns either the postindustrial production of texts or the phenomenological reception of texts, convergence culture has existed as long as poets and painters have imitated other poets and painters, and patrons have browsed library stacks looking for books in the neighborhood of specific titles. Clearly, however, theorists of contemporary convergence culture are responding to something new. That something is not yet the decentering of corporate power over branding or the de-hierarchizing of different versions. The Disney Corporation's long-standing hegemony over the use of its branded characters suggests precisely the opposite development. Nor is it yet the decline of cinema as a tentpole medium that can insure the broad penetration of fictional franchises. Even if cinema is no longer the most important art, as V.I. Lenin reportedly called it, its capital-intensive model continues to drive many intermedial franchises. The latest developments in the long history of divergence culture are three emerging trends that point toward a disruption of the status quo both less and more radical than Jenkins has discerned.

The first is the rise of an exhibitionist culture that lives on Facebook, Snapchat, Twitter, and the social media app du jour, producing and consuming ever more telegraphic, disjointed personal utterances. Members of this online community, instead of becoming prosumers, are turning from passive consumers into self-displaying writers, bloggers and diarists so driven to document their every movement and opinion that many of them have neither the time nor the inclination to assimilate and digest the outpourings of anyone else. This development marks not a convergence culture but a frankly and proudly divergence culture that rejects the traditional aesthetic values of consonance, consistency, and coherence in favor of the kind of timeliness that requires constant updates. Participants in this culture never have to give any of their productions definitive form because they never face deadlines. The impetus toward timeliness at the expense of coherence produces the culture of Facebook updates, photos of users' pets and latest restaurant meals, and selfies they can send their friends confident that even their most indiscreet photos and videos will self-destruct as soon as they are viewed. Instead of collecting photographs in albums for use a generation later to prod failing memories, the average smartphone user snaps one selfie a day—material for a series of impossibly capacious albums that will never be archived. Whether intentionally or not, this impetus sets itself squarely against the curatorial impetus behind an official culture organized around a series of timeless, aspirational artistic monuments that has pinned its pretensions to the ideals of transnational unity, endurance, and universality. Writ large, divergence culture, which can be even more far-ranging geographically, sets itself apart from history, bringing its participants together not across generations but in a series of communal moments—clicker moments, they might be called—as highly charged as they are evanescent.

The second trend is the embrace of what we might call Entertainment for Me. Twenty years after the rise of wide-screen television sets and ten years after the rise of wide-screen computer monitors that were advertised as presenting audiovisual entertainment in all its glory, viewers turned more and more frequently from their state-of-the-art home entertainment systems to watch television shows and movies and stream video on their smartphones, deliberately choosing customization and convenience over beauty, immersiveness, and auditory or visual impact. The look and sound of the program material matters much less to these viewers than their ability to consume it on their own terms as they walk down the street or wait for a bus, sliced into as many pieces as suit their schedules.

In a recent column in the *New York Times*, Tim Wu posits a longer historical context for "the dream of convenience," originally "premised on the nightmare of physical work," which led to a "convenience revolution" that faded by the 1960s, when champions of individualism, fueled by the counterculture, decided that "convenience meant conformity." Given the consensual search for individuality, Wu argues, it was inevitable that the second wave of convenience technologies—the period we are living in—would co-opt this ideal. It would conveniencize individuality.

You might date the beginning of this period to the advent of the Sony Walkman in 1979. With the Walkman we can see a subtle but fundamental shift in the ideology of convenience. If the first convenience revolution promised to make life and work easier for you, the second promised to make it easier to *be you*. The new technologies were catalysts of selfhood. They conferred efficiency on self-expression.

Consider the man of the early 1980s, strolling down the street with his Walkman and earphones. He is enclosed in an acoustic environment of his choosing. He is enjoying, out in public, the kind of self-expression he once could experience only in his private den. A new technology is making it easier for him to show who he is, if only to himself. He struts around the world, the star of his own movie.[43]

The goal of such recent technologies as the VCR, the playlist, the Facebook page, and the Instagram account—to which Wu might have added the smartphone and the television remote control—is to "minimize[e] the mental resources, the mental exertion, required to choose among the options that express ourselves. [...] The ideal is personal preference with no effort." Wu's unsettling conclusion is that

> today's technologies of individualization are technologies of mass individualization. Customization can be surprisingly homogenizing. Everyone, or nearly everyone, is on Facebook: It is the most convenient way to keep track of your friends and family, who in theory should represent what is unique about you and your life. Yet Facebook seems to make us all the same. Its format and conventions strip us of all but the most superficial expressions of individuality.[44]

The constant search for greater convenience is both homogenizing and fragmenting because like hypertext browsing and watching videos on handheld devices, multitasking approaches communication culture piecemeal, like a buffet in which every single bite has to be tasty enough to justify its consumption for diners who habitually hold a fork in one hand and a remote control in the other. Instead of asking what they can do for the larger culture, students ask, not unreasonably, what culture can do for them. As technological developments have made it successively easier to archive treasured materials, the communal power of the archive has surrendered to the imperatives of convenience, individuality, and self-display, with millions of individually curated archives competing for attention. Just as the rise of digital search engines has largely supplanted reference desks at public libraries, the widespread availability of video streaming services has radically reshaped, updated, and abridged the cinematic canon. Kate Hagen, reflecting on the implications of the vanishing of video rental outlets, notes that "the stability of what media is available online (and how long it stays there) is quite tenuous."[45] She cites Yoni Heisler's observation that the number of movie titles the streaming service Netflix, whose chief content officer Ted Sarandos told Heisler in 2016 that "66% of all Netflix subscribers don't even watch movies," made available to its subscribers dropped from 6755 in 2010 to 4010 in 2018.[46] Hagen points out that "no streaming service has been able to match the breadth and depth of a decades-old video store." Instead of archiving old, arguably classic films, streaming services focus on providing new content; of the 4010 films currently available on Netflix, only 98 of them were produced before 1990. Even Amazon Prime, whose catalogue of 14,214 films available for free streaming to Prime members dwarfs Netflix's, maintains a list of titles 59 percent of which have been released in the past ten years.[47] The result is a cinematic canon that is recent, popular, and constantly changing—exactly the opposite tendencies of traditional archives.

The third trend that indicates a radical disruption of business as usual in the world of social media, data-mining, entertainment, and adaptation concerns the realm that corresponds most closely to the model of Jenkins's convergence culture, a realm whose entry points are dispersed over a wide range of media, a realm in which stories and worlds not only compete with each other but supplement each other for consumers who move incessantly from one media outlet to another in search of new insights. That realm is not that of *The Matrix* or any other fictional franchise but the avowedly nonfictional realm of what used to be called the daily news. It is no accident that the closing chapters of *Convergence Culture* and Jenkins's 2008 Epilogue focus on nonfictional rather than fictional worlds. Increasingly during the 2016 election season, Americans found themselves constantly checking and rechecking online news sources in search of the most up-to-the-minute stories and polling information, whether they were seeking information, reassurance, or bonding with like-minded souls. Jenkins finds evidence of convergence in interactive news sources like Slashdot and the abortive Current TV channel; evidence of a countervailing divergence can readily be found across innumerable micro-cultures that resist all attempts to synthesize disparate worldviews that can only be aggregated by meta-sites like Five Thirty Eight, Rotten Tomatoes, and Google. As early as 1995 MIT Media Lab founder Nicholas Negroponte coined the term *"The Daily Me"* for an online daily newsfeed each individual reader could shape according to his or her preferences about what to include, prioritize, and omit.[48] Since 2005 the website DailyMe.com has provided just such a service for subscribers who wish to curate their own news instead of letting someone else do it for them, encouraging ever greater fragmentation, or what might be called greater self-adaptability, in what the larger public considers the news.

Jenkins ends the first edition of *Convergence Culture* with a utopian flourish: "Welcome to convergence culture, where old and new media collide, where grassroots and corporate media intersect, where the power of the media producer and the power of the media consumer interact in unpredictable ways."[49] Ten years of hindsight have validated every word of this description, but with a very different spin than Jenkins puts on the words *unpredictable, interact, intersect,* and *collide.* The most valuable lesson the twenty-four-hour news cycle teaches is not that cultural productions, official culture, the culture of the real, and cultural producers and participants are all best approached as works in progress—adaptation scholars had already been preaching that lesson for ten years before Jenkins—but that the most distinctive product of the convergence culture so enthusiastically hailed by Jenkins and other social utopians is a series of codependent microcultures that are as alienating as they are addictive. Audiences' increasingly fragmentary experiences of both specific beloved cultural artifacts and culture in general have produced not a convergence culture that brings different stakeholders' interests into alignment but a radical divergence culture whose rise and spread offers individually customized cultural experiences as compelling as the false memories of *Total Recall* (1990) at the price of forgoing the communal experience that has been the principal rationale for culture since its beginnings.

A new canon rising

Despite the well-documented fears of Philip Roth, divergence culture has not brought an end to American literature or to cinematic adaptations of American literature. Instead, it has heralded the latest in a long series of updated notions about what Hollywood considers American literature. At the head of contemporary Hollywood adaptation culture, in terms of box office performance if not yet of honors from the Academy and elsewhere, is comic book adaptations of the DC and Marvel Universes. Behind them are non-comic franchises like *Game of Thrones* and *The Hunger Games*, adaptations of best-selling novels like Dan Brown's *The Da Vinci Code* (2003, filmed 2006) and Gillian Flynn's *Gone Girl* (2012, filmed 2014) and adaptations of nonfictional sources from *12 Years a Slave* to *The Big Short*. Adaptations of contemporary best sellers continue to proliferate, and if most of these, like *The Da Vinci Code* and *Gone Girl*, turn out to be unrepeatable one-offs, that is eminently in keeping with such American classics as *The Red Badge of Courage* and Kate Chopin's *The Awakening*, adapted in Mary Lambert's film *Grand Isle* (1991). This range of sources, which may seem remote from traditional definitions of literature as an aesthetically elitist medium, is rounded out by novelists who have succeeded in making themselves into franchises, not because they tell a continuing story in a single proliferating storyworld but because they have established commanding positions in genres they have made their own. Hollywood courtroom dramas are increasingly cast in the mold of John Grisham, Hollywood romances in the mold of Nicholas Sparks, Hollywood crime comedies in the mold of Elmore Leonard, and Hollywood cat-and-mouse thrillers in the mold of James Patterson. Each of these authors has made a home in a popular genre they have tailored to their own ends without significantly changing it, enlarging its boundaries, or transcending its limitations. Many of Patterson's novels revolve around the criminal investigations of psychologist Alex Cross, and Grisham's lawyer heroes, although they have different names and backstories, bear strong enough resemblances to one another to make them instantly recognizable from one tale to the next. But one last American storyteller demands special attention because he has become such a dominant figure in contemporary adaptation that he has come to represent a genre that has largely become defined by his own work, like Alfred Hitchcock's thrillers: Stephen King.

King is still widely identified with the horror genre, and many of his most characteristic novels are tales of horror, including the three novels that launched his career: *Carrie* (1973), whose heroine, a telekinetic high school student, takes a terrible vengeance on the fellow students who humiliate her on prom night; *Salem's Lot* (1975), in which a man returning to his childhood home gradually realizes that many of its inhabitants have become vampires; and *The Shining* (1977), the story of Jack Torrance, a family man who gradually descends into homicidal madness after he accepts the position of off-season caretaker at Colorado's isolated Overlook Hotel. All three of these novels reveal an important basis for King's achievement: his ability to root traditional horror tropes in such ordinary fears as ostracism by the adolescent in-crowd (*Carrie*), distrust of the government (*Salem's Lot*), and the professional anxiety of aspiring writers (*The Shining*). Suspense novelist Jeffery Deaver contends that King "single-handedly made popular fiction grow up" by the way he "brought reality to genre novels. He's often remarked that *Salem's Lot* (1977) was '*Peyton Place* meets *Dracula*.' And so it was."[50] All three of these early novels were adapted to the screen. Both Tobe Hooper's 1979 television miniseries and Mikael Salomon's 2004 miniseries based on *Salem's Lot* were nominated for Prime-Time Emmys. Triumphing over its anemic $1.8 million budget and its pigeonholing as a horror film, Brian De Palma's 1976 film adaptation of *Carrie*, the first of four films that would be based on King's debut novel, earned Academy Award nominations for Sissy Spacek, who played the title character, and Piper Laurie, who played her mother, en route to notable financial success (see Figure 10.7). And Stanley Kubrick's 1980 film adaptation of *The Shining* became a landmark horror film despite lukewarm opening reviews and King's own disapproval of its many departures from his novel, which he addressed when he wrote the teleplay for a 1997 miniseries remake under the same title (see Figure 10.8).

FIGURE 10.7 *Carrie White (Sissy Spacek) is pressed by her fundamentalist mother Margaret (Piper Laurie) to join her in prayer moments before the two try to kill each other in* Carrie *(1976), the film that introduced Stephen King to Hollywood.*

FIGURE 10.8 *The iconic moment in* The Shining *(1980) when the madness that has claimed Jack Torrance (Jack Nicholson) leads him to attack his wife and son.*

Although King has long acknowledged his debts to horror writers from Joseph Payne Brennan to Robert Bloch to Richard Matheson, he has become a household name in ways they never have. There are several keys to his success. The most obvious is his vast output of fifty-nine novels and over two hundred short stories, a volume of work that has driven his sales over 350 million copies. King's eight-volume franchise *The Dark Tower* (1982–2004) illustrates his ability to weave together scripts from such disparate genres as horror, fantasy, alternate reality, and the Western, while his trilogy *Mr. Mercedes* (2014), *Finders Keepers* (2015), and *End of Watch* (2016) builds a franchise uniquely his own. Even more influentially, King has become his own franchise. As Deaver points out, King is particularly adept in anchoring pop-culture nightmares in the fears of Everyman heroes, especially adolescent and preadolescent heroes and heroines, and the rhythms and details of daily life, presenting a family dog stricken with rabies (*Cujo*, 1981, filmed 1983), a used car possessed by demons (*Christine*, 1983, filmed 1983), and cell phones that turn the users who are hooked on them into mindless killers (*Cell*, 2006, filmed 2016). So King has come to occupy three different positions—master of the horror genre, genre-bending deviser of genre hybrids like *The Dark Tower*, and anatomist of the frontier where ordinary fears shade into pop-culture nightmares—even as his carnivalesque energy enriches them all by constantly tacking between them and infusing each set of genre conventions with enough intimations of other genres to prevent any of them from becoming reassuringly predictable.

In addition to fifteen Bram Stoker awards for horror, King has been the recipient of several more mainstream honors. The American Library Association named *Salem's Lot* and *Firestarter* (1981) the Best Young Adult Books of the Year. King's story "The Man in the Black Suit," originally published in the *New Yorker*, received the 1996 O. Henry Award as the Best Short Story of the Year. In 2003 King was awarded the Medal of Distinguished Contribution to American Letters by the National Book Foundation. Despite the inevitable backlash against these accolades from such guardians of the canon as Harold Bloom, who called the last of these honors, which should have gone to one of the "four living American novelists I know of who are still at work and who deserve our praise"—Thomas Pynchon, Philip Roth, Cormac McCarthy, and Don DeLillo—"another low in the shocking process of dumbing down our cultural life,"[51] these credentials have served King well in Hollywood, where he has become the most frequently adapted American author since Edgar Allan Poe, with 244 films and television segments to Poe's 351. Since thirty-three more projects based on King's work have been announced or are in production, compared to eleven in the Poe pipeline, King, who unlike Poe is still writing, can expect to overtake his master by 2025. Ever since the release of *Carrie* in 1976, there have been only four years—1977, 1978, 1981, and 1988—that have passed without a new Stephen King movie, and the pace of these adaptations has greatly increased in recent years.

Like Stan Lee, King has kept his name and face before the screen audience by appearing in two dozen of the hundreds of films based on his work, usually in cameos, occasionally in more substantial roles. His twenty-year stint as a guitarist with the Rock Bottom Remainders, a band in which he joined fellow authors Dave Barry, Matt Groening, Ridley Pearson, Amy Tan, and Scott Turow, maintained his brand while extending his range. William Goldman has noted that King is unfairly criticized for writing only scary stories, since apart from *Carrie* and *The Shining*, none of the best movies based on his work is all that scary. Rob Reiner's *Stand by Me* (1986, based on King's 1982 novella "The Body") follows four tween boys on a hike in search of a schoolmate's dead body rumored to be lying abandoned along an isolated Maine road. Reiner's *Misery* (1990, based on King's 1987 novel) strands a novelist whose car has been wrecked in an accident with the initially worshipful fan from hell. Taylor Hackford's *Dolores Claiborne* (1995), based on King's 1992 novel, shows a reporter's attempts to probe the accusation made against her troubled mother of killing the elderly, paralyzed woman she lives with. And the two King adaptations directed by Frank Darabont, *The Shawshank Redemption* (1994), based on King's 1982 novella "Rita Hayworth and the Shawshank Redemption," and *The Green Mile* (1999), based on King's 1996 novel, immerse themselves in the numbingly routine worlds of men held in prisons for crimes they have not committed before allowing them moments of salvation and transcendence. Although most of these films include brief scary sequences, none of them is a horror film.

In addition to inhabiting a popular genre, tailoring it to his measure, exploring its borders with other genres, and infusing judicious hints of it into highly regarded mainstream adaptations, King is a stellar example of Entertainment for Me. He has experimented with a wide array of nontraditional publishing models. He contributed to the comic book *Heroes for Hope Starring the X-Men* (1985). *The Green Mile* was originally published in serial form as six separate paperback volumes in 1996. Four years later, King began *The Plant* as an online serial project but never completed it. His novella "Riding the Bullet" first appeared online in 2000 and his novella *Ur* as a project for the Amazon Kindle in 2009. Perhaps the most distinctive feature of King's hyperadaptability is his open invitation to amateur filmmakers to adapt his short stories, a process for which he charges only one dollar, as he did for each of the eight short adaptations of his 1977 short story "The Man Who Loved Flowers." Of the thirteen King adaptations that premiered in 2011, only three—Joel Soisson's *Children of the Corn: Genesis* and the two television episodes of *Bag of Bones*—were commercially produced; the others were all shorts made by nonprofessional filmmakers. It would be easy to lampoon this spate of amateur productions as a blot on King's reputation. But his wholehearted outreach to potential adapters is not only an invitation to the Entertainment for Me generation to make his stories their own but a telling echo of the enduring incompleteness of the American literary canon, which has always been less a treasured archive than a storehouse of material for adaptive performances. King remains an enduring and wonderfully productive master of the art of surfing multiple and often contradictory scripts. More than any other living author, he epitomizes a divergence culture that reflects long-standing currents in American literature ever since Poe, which its film adaptations have delighted in pointing out from the beginning.

Even though *The Shawshank Redemption*, the top-rated movie among the thousands listed on the Internet Movie Database, was nominated for seven Academy Awards and *The Green Mile* for four, and even though Kathy Bates won the Best Actress award for playing Annie Wilkes in *Misery*, few filmgoers think of Stephen King movies as Oscar bait. But that may change with the Academy's proposed creation of a new category to honor the Best Popular Film. The new award was widely perceived as a sop to *Black Panther*, which observers feared might be omitted from the ten possible Best Picture nominees despite strong reviews that earned it a Metascore of 88 out of 100 on metacritic.com and a box office gross reaching over $700 million in the United States and over $1.3 billion worldwide (see Figure 10.9). *Atlantic* blogger David Sims dubbed the new category "The Black Panther Memorial Award for Movie That We're Afraid Won't Get a Best Picture Nomination."[52] CNN blogger Frank Pallotta, noting that nine of the ten all-

FIGURE 10.9 *Skeptics complained that the new Academy Award category for Best Popular Film was created as a consolation prize for movies like* Black Panther *(2018).*

time top grossing films, from *Gone with the Wind* (1939) to *The Exorcist* (1973), had won or been nominated for Best Picture, concluded, "Popular films are films!"[53] Vulture blogger Mark Harris derided the redundancy of the new award within a galaxy of awards designed to raise the profile of American filmmaking: "There is already an award for popular films. It's called 'money.'"[54]

Only a month after proposing this new separate-yet-equal category, the Academy delayed its implementation for at least a year in order to "examine and seek additional input regarding the new category."[55] Whether or not Oscars will ever be awarded for Outstanding Achievement in Popular Film, its very proposal is only the most recent sign of a generational shift in Hollywood's attitude toward an American literature increasingly viewed as split between canonical books no one reads and popular books no one admits to reading. The *Hollywood Reporter*'s Scott Feinberg points out that "the gulf between what the public buys tickets to see and what the Academy nominates and awards has never been greater."[56] Ani Bundel, writing for NBC News, agrees that "the gap—between the films people want to see and the films the academy wants to reward—is still widening. Filmmakers simply aren't making the lush, middlebrow dramas that were once the Best Picture category's bread and butter."[57] Whether or not the ascendancy of Stephen King marks a decisive shift in the pantheon of Hollywood adaptations, it is only the latest in the cinema's long series of reminders that like American culture, American literature remains, as it has always been, a work in progress.

Notes

1 Reynolds Price, quoted by Mike Harris, "*My Life as a Man*," *Daily Iowan*, September 12, 1974, p. 7.
2 "*The Human Stain*," *Rotten Tomatoes*, https://www.rottentomatoes.com/m/human_stain/.
3 Philip Roth, *The Human Stain*, in Roth, *The American Trilogy, 1997–2000* (New York: Library of America, 2011), p. 706.
4 When the Wikipedia entry on *The Human Stain* repeated the rumor that Coleman Silk was based on Anatole Broyard, Roth attempted to correct the entry but was told that "I, Roth, was not a credible source" because "we require secondary sources." In response to his dismissal as an authority about the books he had written, Roth wrote a famous open letter to Wikipedia asserting that "*The Human Stain* was inspired by an unhappy event in the life of my great friend Melvin Tumin." This letter, which also appeared in the *New Yorker* blog of September 6, is reprinted as "Errata," in Roth, *Collected Nonfiction, 1960–2013* (New York: Library of America, 2016), pp. 349–63; the quoted passages appear on page 349. The Wikipedia entry (https://en.wikipedia.org/wiki/The_Human_Stain) was eventually changed to reflect Roth's corrections.

5   A.O. Scott, "Film Review: Secrets of the Skin, and of the Heart," *New York Times*, October 31, 2003, https://www.nytimes.com/2003/10/31/movies/film-review-secrets-of-the-skin-and-of-the-heart.html.

6   Mick LaSalle, "'Human Stain' Doesn't Quite Wash/Philip Roth Adaptation a Nice Effort but Ultimately Unbelievable," *San Francisco Chronicle*, October 31, 2003, https://www.sfgate.com/movies/article/Human-Stain-doesn-t-quite-wash-Philip-Roth-2579824.php.

7   LaSalle, "'Human Stain' Doesn't Quite Wash/Philip Roth Adaptation a Nice Effort but Ultimately Unbelievable."

8   Scott, "Film Review: Secrets of the Skin, and of the Heart."

9   David Edelstein, "All Too Human: The Perils of Filming Philip Roth," *Slate.com*, October 31, 2003, http://www.slate.com/articles/arts/movies/2003/10/all_too_human.html.

10 LaSalle, "'Human Stain' Doesn't Quite Wash/Philip Roth Adaptation a Nice Effort but Ultimately Unbelievable."

11 Liam Burke, *The Comic Book Film Adaptation* (Jackson: University Press of Mississippi, 2015), p. 267.

12 Burke, *The Comic Book Film Adaptation*, pp. 23–24.

13 Will Brooker, *Hunting the Dark Knight: Twenty-first Century Batman* (London: Taurus, 2012), p. 62.

14 Henry Jenkins, *Convergence Culture: Where Old and New Media Collide* (New York: New York University Press, 2006), p. 326.

15 Constantine Verevis, "The Cinematic Return," *Film Comment* 40.1 (January 2016), https://quod.lib.umich.edu/f/fc/13761232.0040.134/–cinematic-return?rgn=main;view=fulltext. The quoted passage is from Scott Foundas, "Cinematic Faith: Interview with Christopher Nolan," *Film Comment*, Special Supplement (Winter 2012/13): 7.

16 Marc Webb, quoted by Ethan Anderton, "Marc Webb Talks New Story & Universe in 'The Amazing Spider-Man,'" *FirstShowing.net*, December 19, 2011, http://www.firstshowing.net/2011/marc-webb-talks-new-story-universe-in-the-amazing-spider-man/.

17 Derek Thompson, "Hollywood Has a Big Millennial Problem," *Atlantic*, June 8, 2016, https://www.theatlantic.com/business/archive/2016/06/hollywood-has-a-huge-millennial-problem/486209/.

18 Thompson, "Hollywood Has a Big Millennial Problem."-

19 "Theatrical Market Statistics 2015," *Motion Picture Association of America*, https://www.mpaa.org/wp-content/uploads/2016/04/MPAA-Theatrical-Market-Statistics-2015_Final.pdf.

20 Thompson, "Hollywood Has a Big Millennial Problem."

21 Paul Carrick Brunson, "80% of Singles Will NOT Go on One Date in 2017," *LinkedIn Pulse*, https://www.linkedin.com/pulse/80-singles-go-one-date-2017-paul-carrick-brunson.

22 Vint Cerf, quoted by Thomas Friedman, *Thank You for Being Late: An Optimist's Guide to Thriving in the Age of Accelerations* (New York: Farrar, Straus, and Giroux, 2016), p. 20.
23 E.D. Hirsch, Jr., *Cultural Literacy: What Every American Needs to Know*, updated and expanded edition (New York: Vintage, 1988), p. 29.
24 Lucia Krämer, "Adaptation in Bollywood," in *The Oxford Handbook of Adaptation Studies*, ed. Thomas Leitch (New York: Oxford University Press, 2017), p. 262.
25 Robert McCrum, "A Conversation with Philip Roth," *Guardian Observer*, June 30, 2001, https://www.theguardian.com/books/2001/jul/01/fiction.philiproth1.
26 Tina Brown, "Philip Roth Unbound: This Is How I Write," *Daily Beast*, October 30, 2009, https://www.thedailybeast.com/philip-roth-unbound-interview-transcript.
27 Linda Hutcheon, with Siobhan O'Flynn, *A Theory of Adaptation*, 2nd ed. (New York: Routledge, 2013), p. xix.
28 Hutcheon with O'Flynn, *A Theory of Adaptation*, p. 206.
29 Alvin Toffler, *The Third Wave* (New York: Morrow, 1980), p. 283.
30 Jenkins, *Convergence Culture*, p. 254.
31 William Proctor, "Regeneration and Rebirth: Anatomy of the Franchise Reboot," *Scope* 22 (February 2012), https://www.nottingham.ac.uk/scope/documents/2012/february-2012/proctor.pdf.
32 Marie-Laure Ryan, "Transmedia Storytelling as Narrative Practice," *The Oxford Handbook of Adaptation Studies*, ed. Thomas Leitch (New York: Oxford University Press, 2017), p. 530.
33 Hutcheon with O'Flynn, *A Theory of Adaptation*, p. 181.
34 Claire Parody, "Franchising/Adaptation," *Adaptation* 4.2 (September 2011): 212. The parenthetical reference is to Jim Collins, "Batman: The Movie, Narrative: The Hyperconscious," in *The Many Lives of the Batman: Critical Approaches to a Superhero and His Media*, ed. Roberta E. Pearson and William Uricchio (New York: Routledge, 1991), pp. 164–81.
35 Raffi Khatchatdourian, "Alternate Endings: Moves That Allow You to Decide What Happens Next," *New Yorker*, January 30, 2017, p. 53.
36 Hutcheon with O'Flynn, *A Theory of Adaptation*, p. 202.
37 Kyle Meikle, "Adaptation and Interactivity," in *The Oxford Handbook of Adaptation Studies*, ed. Thomas Leitch (New York: Oxford University Press, 2017), p. 543.
38 Hutcheon with O'Flynn, *A Theory of Adaptation*, p. 196.
39 Jenkins, *Convergence Culture*, p. 254.
40 Jenkins, *Convergence Culture*, p. 258.
41 Ashley Highfield, "TV's Tipping Point: Why the Digital Revolution Is Only Just Beginning," October 7, 2003, *BBC.co.uk*, http://www.bbc.co.uk/pressoffice/speeches/stories/highfield_rts.shtml.

42 Jenkins, *Convergence Culture*, p. 255.
43 Tim Wu, "The Tyranny of Convenience," *New York Times*, February 16, 2018, Sunday Review, https://www.nytimes.com/2018/02/16/opinion/sunday/tyranny-convenience.html.
44 Wu, "The Tyranny of Convenience."
45 Kate Hagen, "In Search of the Last Great Video Store," *The Black List*, https://blog.blcklst.com/in-search-of-the-last-great-video-store-efcc393f2982.
46 Yoni Heisler, "Netflix's Movie Library Is Shrinking Rapidly as Focus on TV Continues," *BGR.com*, https://bgr.com/2018/02/23/netflixs-movie-library-is-shrinking-rapidly-as-focus-on-tv-continues/.
47 Hagen, "In Search of the Last Great Video Store."
48 Nicholas Negroponte, *Being Digital* (New York: Knopf, 1995), p. 153.
49 Jenkins, *Convergence Culture*, p. 270.
50 Jeffery Deaver, *A Century of Great Suspense Stories* (New York: Berkley, 2001), p. 200.
51 Harold Bloom, "Dumbing Down American Readers," *Boston Globe*, September 24, 2003, http://archive.boston.com/news/globe/editorial_opinion/oped/articles/2003/09/24/dumbing_down_american_readers/.
52 David Sims @davidlsims, quoted in Christi Carras, "Twitter Reacts to New Oscars Popular Film Category: 'This Is So Lazy,'" *Variety*, August 8, 2018, https://variety.com/2018/film/news/twitter-reacts-new-oscars-popular-film-category-academy-1202899436/.
53 Frank Pallotta @frankpallotta, quoted in Adam Holmes, "People Are Not Happy about the New Popular Movie Oscar Category," *Cinemablend*, August 8, 2018, https://www.cinemablend.com/news/2455373/people-are-not-happy-about-the-new-popular-movie-oscar-category.
54 Mark Harris, @MarkHarrisNYC, quoted in Carras, "Twitter Reacts to New Oscars Popular Film Category."
55 Gregg Kilday, "Academy Postponing New Popular Oscar Category," *Hollywood Reporter*, September 6, 2018, https://www.hollywoodreporter.com/news/academy-postponing-new-popular-oscar-category-1140423.
56 Scott Feinberg, "Oscars Won't Televise All Awards Live, Adds 'Popular' Film Category," *Hollywood Reporter*, August 8, 2018, https://www.hollywoodreporter.com/race/academy-plans-three-hour-oscars-telecast-adds-popular-film-category-1133138.
57 Ani Bundel, "Oscars Adds New 'Popular Film' Award Category to Appear Less Elitist and Boost Ratings. It Won't Work," *NBC News*, nbcnews.com/think/opinion/oscards-adds-new-popular-film-category-attempt-appear-less-elitist-ncna899001.

BIBLIOGRAPHY

Altman, Rick. "Dickens, Griffith, and Film Theory Today." *South Atlantic Quarterly* 88.2 (1989): 321–59.
Altman, Rick. *Film/Genre*. London: British Film Institute, 1999.
Anderton, Ethan. "Marc Webb Talks New Story & Universe in 'The Amazing Spider-Man.'" *FirstShowing.net*. Dec. 19, 2011. http://www.firstshowing.net/2011/marc-webb-talks-new-story-universe-in-the-amazing-spider-man/.
Andrew, Dudley. *Mists of Regret: Culture and Sensibility in Classic French Film*. Princeton, NJ: Princeton University Press, 1995.
Anon. "Best Seller on Film [Review of *Peyton Place*]." *Newsweek*. Dec. 23, 1957: 76.
Anon. "Dickens in Pictures." *Moving Picture World* 3.22 (Nov. 28, 1908): 431.
Anon. "Giving Credit Where Credit Is Due." *Moving Picture World* 6.10 (Mar. 12, 1910): 369–70.
Anon. "Review of *After Many Years*." *Moving Picture World* 3.19 (Nov. 7, 1908): 364.
Anon. "Review of *L'Arlesienne*." *Moving Picture World* 3.22 (Nov. 28, 1908): 433.
Anon. "Review of *The Face on the Barroom Floor*." *Moving Picture World* 3.4 (July 25, 1908): 67.
Anon. "Review of *For the Love of Gold*." *Moving Picture World* 3.8 (Aug. 22, 1908): 142.
Anon. "Review of *The Lady or the Tiger*." *Moving Picture World* 3.22 (Nov. 28, 1908): 430.
Anon. "Review of *Puss in Boots*." *Moving Picture World* 3.20 (Nov. 14, 1908): 408.
Anon. "Review of *Uncle Tom's Cabin*." *Moving Picture World* 7.6 (Aug. 6, 1910): 298.
Anon. "Robbins'-Egg Blue [Review of *The Carpetbaggers*]." *Newsweek*. July 6, 1964: 76.
Auerbach, Erich. *Mimesis: The Representation of Reality in Western Literature*. Trans. Willard R. Trask. Princeton, NJ: Princeton University Press, 1953.
Bailey, Jonathan. "Dracula vs. Nosferatu: A True Copyright Horror Story." *Plagiarism Today*. Oct. 17, 2011. http://www.plagiarismtoday.com/2011/10/17/dracula-vs-nosferatu-a-true-copyright-horror-story/.
Bakhtin, M.M. *The Dialogic Imagination: Four Essays*. Ed. Michael J. Holquist. Trans. Caryl Emerson and Michael J. Holquist. Austin: University of Texas Press, 1981.
Basinger, Jeanine. *The World War II Combat Film: Anatomy of a Genre*, with an updated Filmography by Jeremy Arnold. Middletown, CT: Wesleyan University Press, 2003.
Baum, L. Frank. *The Emerald City of Oz*. Chicago, IL: Reilly & Lee, 1910.

Baum, L. Frank. *The Patchwork Girl of Oz*. Chicago, IL: Reilly & Lee, 1913.
Belton, John. *American Cinema/American Culture*. Englewood Cliffs, NJ: McGraw–Hill, 1994.
Benjamin, Walter. "The Work of Art in the Age of Mechanical Reproduction." In Benjamin, *Illuminations*, ed. Hannah Arendt, trans. Harry Zohn, 217–52. 1968; rpt. New York: Schocken, 1969.
Bergan, Ronald. *The United Artists Story*. New York: Crown, 1986.
Biskind, Peter. *Easy Riders, Raging Bulls: How the Sex-Drugs-and-Rock 'n' Roll Generation Saved Hollywood*. New York: Simon and Schuster, 1998.
Black, Gregory D. *The Catholic Crusade against the Movies, 1940–75*. New York: Cambridge University Press, 1997.
Bloom, Harold. "Dumbing Down American Readers." *Boston Globe*. Sept. 24, 2003. http://archive.boston.com/news/globe/editorial_opinion/oped/articles/2003/09/24/dumbing_down_american_readers/.
Bluestone, George. *Novels into Film*. Baltimore, MD: Johns Hopkins University Press, 1957.
Bogle, Donald. *Toms, Coons, Mulattoes, Mammies, and Bucks: An Interpretive History of Blacks in American Films*, 5th edn. New York: Bloomsbury, 2016.
Boozer, Jack, ed. "Introduction: The Screenplay and Authorship in Adaptation." In *Authorship in Film Adaptation*, ed. Jack Boozer, 1–30. Austin: University of Texas Press, 2006.
Borde, Raymond, and Étienne Chaumeton. *A Panorama of American Film Noir, 1941–1953*. Trans. Paul Hammond. San Francisco, CA: City Lights, 2002.
Boswell, Parley Ann. *Edith Wharton on Film*. Carbondale: Southern Illinois University Press, 2007.
Bottalico, Michele. "A Place for All: Old and New Myths in the Italian Appreciation of American Literature." In *As Others Read Us: International Perspectives on American Literature*, ed. Huck Gutman, 148–60. Amherst: University of Massachusetts Press, 1991.
Bowser, Eileen. *The Transformation of Cinema, 1907–1915 [History of the American Cinema 2]*. New York: Scribner's, 1990.
Brackett, Charles. Letter to John O'Hara. Mar. 11, 1957. Charles Brackett papers. Folder 5.f-[53]. Margaret Herrick Library, Academy of Motion Picture Arts and Sciences.
Bray, William, and R. Barton Palmer, eds. *Modern American Drama on Screen*. Cambridge: Cambridge University Press, 2013.
Breen, Joseph I. Letter to Will Hays. Dec. 18, 1935. Motion Picture Association of America, Production Code Administration records, Margaret Herrick Library.
Breen, Joseph I. Letter to Louis B. Mayer. Jan. 31, 1936. Motion Picture Association of America, Production Code Administration records, Margaret Herrick Library.
Breen, Joseph I. Letter to Louis B. Mayer. Mar. 22, 1939. Production Code Administration records, Margaret Herrick Library.
Breen, Joseph I. Letter to Louis B. Mayer. June 2, 1939. Production Code Administration records, Margaret Herrick Library.
Brooker, Will. *Hunting the Dark Knight: Twenty-First Century Batman*. London: Taurus, 2012.

Brown, Tina. "Philip Roth Unbound: This Is How I Write." *Daily Beast*. Oct. 30, 2009. https://www.thedailybeast.com/philip-roth-unbound-interview-transcript.
Brunson, Paul Carrick. "80% of Singles Will NOT Go on One Date in 2017." *LinkedIn Pulse*. https://www.linkedin.com/pulse/80-singles-go-one-date-2017-paul-carrick-brunson.
Bundel, Ani. "Oscars Adds New 'Popular Film' Award Category to Appear Less Elitist and Boost Ratings. It Won't Work." *NBC News*. Aug. 8, 2018. nbcnews.com/think/opinion/oscards-adds-new-popular-film-category-attempt-appear-less-elitist-ncna899001.
Burke, Liam. *The Comic Book Film Adaptation: Exploring Modern Hollywood's Leading Genre*. Jackson: University Press of Mississippi, 2015.
Burt, Richard. "What the Puck? Screening the (Ob)Scene in Bardcore *Midsummer Night's Dreams* and the Transmediatic Technologies of Tactility." In *Shakespeare on Screen: A Midsummer Night's Dream*, ed. Sarah Hatchuel and Nathalie Vienne-Guerrin, 57–86. Havre: Publications de l'Université Rouen, 2004.
Calhoun, John C. *Speeches of John C. Calhoun, Delivered in the House of Representatives and in the Senate of the United States [The Works of John C. Calhoun, Volume II]*. Ed. Richard K. Crallé. New York: Appleton, 1853.
Canby, Vincent. "Ossie Davis' *Cotton Comes to Harlem*." *New York Times*, June 11, 1970: 50.
Canby, Vincent. "Screen: 'Boys in the Band': Crowley Study of Male Homosexuality Opens." *New York Times*, Mar. 18, 1970: 36.
Carr, Jay. "The Gleam of a Gilded Cage." *Boston Globe*. May 18, 2001: D5.
Carras, Christi. "Twitter Reacts to New Oscars Popular Film Category: 'This Is So Lazy.'" *Variety*. Aug. 8, 2018. https://variety.com/2018/film/news/twitter-reacts-new-oscars-popular-film-category-academy-1202899436/.
Cattrysse, Patrick. *Descriptive Adaptation Studies: Epistemological and Methodological Issues*. Antwerp: Garant, 2014.
Chandler, Raymond. *Later Novels and Other Writings*. New York: Library of America, 1995.
Chandler, Raymond. *Raymond Chandler Speaking*. Ed. Dorothy Gardiner and Kathrine Sorley. London: Hamish Hamilton, 1962.
Chartier, Jean-Pierre. "Les Américains aussi font des films 'noirs'." *Revue du cinéma* 2 (1946): 67–70.
Chase, Richard. *The American Novel and Its Tradition*. Garden City, NY: Doubleday, 1957.
Chénetier, Marc. "American Literature in France: Pleasures in Perspective." In *As Others Read Us: International Perspectives on American Literature*, ed. Huck Gutman, 79–95. Amherst: University of Massachusetts Press, 1991.
Ciment, Michael. "Two Encounters with John Huston." In *John Huston Interviews*, ed. Robert Emmet Long, 135–49. Jackson: University Press of Mississippi, 2001.
Collins, Jim. "Batman: The Movie, Narrative: The Hyperconscious." In *The Many Lives of the Batman: Critical Approaches to a Superhero and His Media*, ed. Roberta E. Pearson and William Uricchio, 164–81. New York: Routledge, 1991.
Cook, David A. *A History of Narrative Film*, 4th edn. New York: Norton, 2004.
Countryman, Edward. "John Ford's *Drums along the Mohawk*: The Making of an American Myth." *Radical History Review* 24 (1980): 93–112.

Crafton, Donald. *The Talkies: American Cinema's Transition to Sound, 1926–1931* [*History of the American Cinema 4*]. New York: Scribner's, 1997.

Crowther, Bosley. "The Screen: Drama in 'Peyton Place.'" *New York Times*, Dec. 13, 1957: 35.

Davis, Tracy C., and Stefka Mihaylova, eds. *Uncle Tom's Cabins: The Transnational History of America's Most Mutable Book*. Ann Arbor: University of Michigan Press, 2018.

Deaver, Jeffery, ed. *A Century of Great Suspense Stories*. New York: Berkley, 2001.

DeBona, Guerric. *Film Adaptation in the Hollywood Studio Era*. Urbana: University of Illinois Press, 2010.

Decherney, Peter. *Hollywood's Copyright Wars: From Edison to the Internet*. New York: Columbia University Press, 2012.

Doctorow, E.L. "Wakefield." *New Yorker*, Jan. 14, 2008: 60–74.

Doherty, Thomas. *Hollywood's Censor: Joseph I. Breen and the Production Code Administration*. New York: Columbia University Press, 2007.

Dowd, Maureen. "Go Ahead, Make Him Cry." *New York Times*. Mar. 25, 1995. https://www.nytimes.com/1995/03/26/movies/go-ahead-make-him-cry.html.

DuBois, W.E.B. *The Souls of Black Folk*. 1903; rpt. New York: Oxford University Press, 2007.

Ebert, Roger. "Children of a Lesser God," *Chicago Sun-Times*. Oct. 3, 1986. http://www.rogerebert.com/reviews/children-of-a-lesser-god-1986.

Edelstein, David. "All Too Human: The Perils of Filming Philip Roth." *Slate.com*. Oct. 31, 2003. http://www.slate.com/articles/arts/movies/2003/10/all_too_human.html.

Eisenstein, Sergei. "Dickens, Griffith, and the Film Today." 1944. *Film Form: Essays in Film Theory*. Ed. and trans. Jay Leyda, 195–255. New York: Harcourt, Brace, and World, 1949.

Eldridge, Judith A. *James Oliver Curwood: God's Country and the Man*. Bowling Green: Bowling Green State University Popular Press, 1993.

Evans, Robert. *The Kid Stays in the Picture*. New York: Hachette, 1994.

Eyman, Scott. *Empire of Dreams: The Epic Life of Cecil B. DeMille*. New York: Simon and Schuster, 2010.

Eyman, Scott. *Print the Legend: The Life and Times of John Ford*. New York: Simon and Schuster, 1999.

Eyman, Scott. *The Speed of Sound: Hollywood and the Talkie Revolution, 1926–1930*. New York: Simon and Schuster, 1997.

Feidelson, Charles, Jr. *Symbolism and American Literature*. Chicago: University of Chicago Press, 1953.

Feinberg, Scott. "Oscars Won't Televise All Awards Live, Adds 'Popular' Film Category." *Hollywood Reporter*. Aug. 8, 2018. https://www.hollywoodreporter.com/race/academy-plans-three-hour-oscars-telecast-adds-popular-film-category-1133138.

Field, Syd. *Screenplay: The Foundations of Screenwriting*. Rev. and expanded edition. New York: Dell, 1984.

Fielding, Helen. "Bridget Jones's Diary." *Independent*. 1995–97. http://bridgetarchive.altervista.org/index1995.htm.

Fitzgerald, F. Scott. *Three Novels: The Great Gatsby, Tender Is the Night, The Last Tycoon*. New York: Scribner, 1953.

Fleisher, Michael, assisted by Janet E. Lincoln. *The Original Encyclopedia of Comic Book Heroes, Volume 1: Featuring Batman*. New York: DC Comics, 2007.
Fordin, Hugh. *MGM's Greatest Musicals: The Freed Unit*. New York: Da Capo, 1996.
Foundas, Scott. "Cinematic Faith: Interview with Christopher Nolan." *Film Comment*, Special Supplement (Winter 2012/13): 7–11.
Frank, Nino. "Un nouveau genre 'policier': L'aventure criminelle," *L'écran français* 61 (Aug. 28, 1946): 14–16.
Frei, Hans W. *The Eclipse of Biblical Narrative: A Story in Eighteenth and Nineteenth Century Hermeneutics*. New Haven, CT: Yale University Press, 1974.
Frick, John W. *Uncle Tom's Cabin on the American Stage and Screen*. Houndmills: Palgrave Macmillan, 2012.
Friedman, Thomas. *Thank You for Being Late: An Optimist's Guide to Thriving in the Age of Accelerations*. New York: Farrar, Straus, and Giroux, 2016.
Genette, Gérard. *Palimpsests: Literature in the Second Degree*. Trans. Channa Newman and Claude Doubinsky. Lincoln: University of Nebraska Press, 1997.
Gifford, Denis. *Books and Plays in Film 1896–1915: Literary, Theatrical and Artistic Sources of the First Twenty Years of Motion Pictures*. London: Mansell, 1991.
Gish, Lillian, with Ann Pinchot. *The Movies, Mr. Griffith, and Me*. Englewood Cliffs, NJ: Prentice Hall, 1969.
Gleason, Ralph J. "Joan's Conscience Honors Us All." "On the Town," *San Francisco Chronicle*. Nov. 18, 1964: 43.
Goldman, William. *Adventures in the Screen Trade: A Personal View of Hollywood and Screenwriting*. New York: Warner, 1983.
Goldstein, Laurence. *The American Poet at the Movies: A Critical History*. Ann Arbor: University of Michigan Press, 1994.
Gomery, Douglas. *Movie History: A Survey*. Belmont, CA: Wadsworth, 1991.
Gorbman, Claudia. *Unheard Melodies: Narrative Film Music*. Bloomington: Indiana University Press, 1987.
Grant, Catherine. "Recognizing *Billy Budd* in *Beau Travail*: Epistemology and Hermeneutics of an Auteurist 'Free' Adaptation." *Screen* 43.1 (2002): 57–73.
Greco, John. "*Ossessione* (1943)/Luchino Visconti." *Twenty Four Frames: Notes on Film*. July 11, 2012. http://twentyfourframes.wordpress.com/2009/07/11/ossessione-1943-visconti/.
Green, Jesse. "Big Laughs and Then a Shift in Culture." *New York Times*, Aug. 27, 2018: C1, C4.
Griffin, Susan M. *Henry James Goes to the Movies*. Lexington: University Press of Kentucky, 2015.
Grissom, Candace Ursula. *Fitzgerald and Hemingway on Film: A Critical Study of the Adaptations, 1924–2013*. Jefferson, NC: McFarland, 2014.
Grossman, Julie. *Literature, Film, and Their Hideous Progeny: Adaptation and ElasTEXTity*. Houndmills: Palgrave Macmillan, 2015.
Guerrero, Ed. *Framing Blackness: The African American Image in Film*. Philadelphia, PA: Temple University Press, 1993.
Gunning, Tom. "An Aesthetic of Astonishment: Early Film and the (In)Credulous Spectator" 1989; rpt. In *Viewing Positions: Ways of Seeing Film*, ed. Linda Williams, 114–33. New Brunswick, NJ: Rutgers University Press, 1995.

Gunning, Tom. "The Cinema of Attractions: Early Film, Its Spectator, and the Avant-Garde." *Wide Angle* 8.3 (1986): 63–70.

Gunning, Tom. *D. W. Griffith and the Origins of American Narrative Film: The Early Years at Biograph*. Urbana: University of Illinois Press, 1991.

Gunning, Tom. "'Primitive' Cinema—A Frame-up? or The Trick's on Us." *Cinema Journal* 28.2 (Winter 1989): 3–12.

Guthmann, Edward. "*The Wings of the Dove*." *San Francisco Chronicle*. Nov. 14, 1997. https://www.sfgate.com/movies/article/Gorgeous-Wings-Takes-Fresh-Flight-Bonham-2822972.php.

Gutman, Huck, ed. *As Others Read Us: International Perspectives on American Literature*. Amherst: University of Massachusetts Press, 1991.

Hagen, Kate. "In Search of the Last Great Video Store." *The Black List*. https://blog.blcklst.com/in-search-of-the-last-great-video-store-efcc393f2982.

Hammett, Dashiell. *Complete Novels*. New York: Library of America, 1999.

Hand, Richard J. "Radio Adaptation." In *The Oxford Handbook of Adaptation Studies*, ed. Thomas Leitch, 340–55. New York: Oxford University Press, 2017.

Harris, Mark. *Pictures at a Revolution: Five Movies and the Birth of the New Hollywood*. New York: Penguin, 2008.

Harris, Mike. "My Life as a Man." *Daily Iowan*, Sept. 12, 1974: 7.

Harte, Bret. *The Writings of Bret Harte*. 19 volumes. Boston, MA: Houghton Mifflin, 1900.

Haskell, Molly. *From Reverence to Rape: The Treatment of Women in the Movies*, 2nd edn. Chicago: University of Chicago Press, 1987.

Hawthorne, Nathaniel. *Tales and Sketches*. New York: Library of America, 1982.

Hays, Will H. "Statement Issued by Mr. Hays to Newspapers in Connection with IT CAN'T HAPPEN HERE." Feb. 17, 1936. Production Code Administration records, Margaret Herrick Library.

Heath, Joseph, and Andrew Potter. *The Rebel Sell: How the Counterculture Became Consumer Culture*. Chichester: Capstone, 2005.

Henry, O. *The Voice of the City: Further Stories of the Four Million*. Garden City, NY: Doubleday, Page, 1920.

Highfield, Ashley. "TV's Tipping Point: Why the Digital Revolution Is Only Just Beginning." *BBC.co.uk*. Oct. 7, 2003. http://www.bbc.co.uk/pressoffice/speeches/stories/highfield_rts.shtml.

Higson, Andrew. "Re-presenting the National Past: Nostalgia and Prejudice in the Heritage Film." In *Fires Were Started: British Theater and Thatcherism*, ed. Lester Friedman, 91–109. Minneapolis: University of Minnesota Press, 1993.

Hirsch, E.D., Jr. *Cultural Literacy: What Every American Needs to Know*, updated and expanded edition. New York: Vintage, 1988.

Hofstadter, Richard. *Anti-Intellectualism in American Life*. New York: Knopf, 1963.

Holmes, Adam. "People Are Not Happy about the New Popular Movie Oscar Category." *Cinemablen*. Aug. 8, 2018. https://www.cinemablend.com/news/2455373/people-are-not-happy-about-the-new-popular-movie-oscar-category.

Horak, Jan-Christopher. "Maurice Tourneur's Tragic Romance." In *The Classic American Novel and the Movies*, ed. Gerald Peary and Roger Shatzkin, 10–19. New York: Ungar, 1977.

Horne, Philip. "The James Gang." *Sight and Sound* 8.1 (1998): 16–19.
"*The Human Stain.*" *Rotten Tomatoes*. https://www.rottentomatoes.com/m/human_stain/.
"*The Human Stain.*" *Wikipedia*. https://en.wikipedia.org/wiki/The_Human_Stain.
Hutcheon, Linda, with Siobhan O'Flynn. *A Theory of Adaptation*. 2nd edn. New York: Routledge, 2013.
Isherwood, Charles. "A Broadway Master Who Paved the Way for a Sitcom Explosion." *New York Times*. Aug. 27, 2018: A1, A14–A15.
James, Henry. *Literary Criticism: French Writers, Other European Writers, The Prefaces to the New York Edition*. New York: Library of America, 1984.
Jenkins, Henry. *Convergence Culture: Where Old and New Media Collide*. New York: New York University Press, 2006.
Jessel, George. *So Help Me: The Autobiography of George Jessel*. Whitefish, MT: Kessinger, 1943.
Jonas, Gerald. "Ray Bradbury, Who Brought Mars to Earth with a Lyrical Mastery, Dies at 91." *New York Times*. June 6, 2012. https://www.nytimes.com/2012/06/07/books/ray-bradbury-popularizer-of-science-fiction-dies-at-91.html.
Kael, Pauline. *5001 Nights at the Movies*. New York: Holt Rinehart and Winston, 1982.
Kawin, Bruce F. *Faulkner and Film*. New York: Ungar, 1977.
Khatchatdourian, Raffi. "Alternate Endings: Moves That Allow You to Decide What Happens Next." *New Yorker*. Jan. 30, 2017: 46–55.
Kilday, Gregg. "Academy Postponing New Popular Oscar Category." *Hollywood Reporter*. Sept. 6, 2018. https://www.hollywoodreporter.com/news/academy-postponing-new-popular-oscar-category-1140423.
Koszarski, Richard. *An Evening's Entertainment: The Age of the Silent Feature Picture, 1915–1928 [History of the American Cinema 3]*. New York: Scribner's, 1990.
Krämer, Lucia. "Adaptation in Bollywood." In *The Oxford Handbook of Adaptation Studies*, ed. Thomas Leitch, 251–66. New York: Oxford University Press, 2017.
LaSalle, Mick. "'Human Stain' Doesn't Quite Wash/Philip Roth Adaptation a Nice Effort but Ultimately Unbelievable." *San Francisco Chronicle*. Oct. 31, 2003. https://www.sfgate.com/movies/article/Human-Stain-doesn-t-quite-wash-Philip-Roth-2579824.php.
Laurence, Frank M. *Hemingway and the Movies*. Jackson: University Press of Mississippi, 1981.
Lawson, Robert. "Dean Acheson and the Potato Head Blues; Or, British Academic Attitudes to America and Its Literature." In *As Others Read Us: International Perspectives on American Literature*, ed. Huck Gutman, 17–33. Amherst: University of Massachusetts Press, 1991.
Leff, Leonard J., and Jerold L. Simmons. *The Dame in the Kimono: Hollywood, Censorship, and the Production Code*, rev. edn. Lexington: University Press of Kentucky, 2001.
Leitch, Thomas. "Adaptation, the Genre." *Adaptation* 1.2 (2008): 106–20.
Leitch, Thomas. "The Debunking Rhythm of the American Short Story." In *Short Story Theory at a Crossroads*, ed. Susan Lohafer and Jo Ellyn Clarey, 130–47. Baton Rouge: Louisiana State University Press, 1989.

Leitch, Thomas. *Film Adaptation and Its Discontents: From Gone with the Wind to The Passion of the Christ*. Baltimore, MD: Johns Hopkins University Press, 2007.

Leitch, Thomas. "Jekyll, Hyde, Jekyll, Hyde, Jekyll, Hyde, Jekyll, Hyde: Four Models of Intertextuality." In *Victorian Literature and Film Adaptation*, ed. Abigail Burnham Bloom and Mary Sanders Pollock, 27–49. Amherst: Cambria, 2011.

Leitch, Thomas, ed. *The Oxford Handbook of Adaptation Studies*. New York: Oxford University Press, 2017.

Leitch, Thomas. "The Pulitzers Go to Hollywood." In *Adaptation, Awards Culture, and the Value of Prestige*, ed. Colleen Kennedy-Karpat and Eric Sandberg, 23–39. Houndmills: Palgrave Macmillan, 2017.

Leitch, Thomas. "The Texts behind *The Killers*." In *Twentieth-Century American Fiction on Screen*, ed. R. Barton Palmer, 26–44. Cambridge: Cambridge University Press, 2007.

Leitch, Thomas. *What Stories Are: Narrative Theory and Interpretation*. University Park: Pennsylvania State University Press, 1986.

Leitch, Thomas. "You Talk Like a Character in a Book: Film Dialogue and Adaptation." In *Film Dialogue*, ed. Jeff Jaeckle, 85–100. London: Wallflower, 2013.

Lennig, Arthur. "Myth and Fact: The Reception of *Birth of a Nation*." *Film History* 16.2 (2004): 117–41.

Lev, Peter. "How to Write Adaptation History." In *The Oxford Handbook of Adaptation Studies*, ed. Thomas Leitch, 661–78. New York: Oxford University Press, 2017.

Lewton, Val. Letter to Joseph I. Breen. June 8, 1936. Production Code Administration records, Margaret Herrick Library.

Longmore, Paul K. "Screening Stereotypes: Images of Disabled People." In *Screening Disability: Essays on Cinema and Disability*, ed. Christopher R. Smit and Anthony Enns, 1–17. Lanham, MD: University Press of America, 2001.

Luhr, William. *Raymond Chandler and Film*. Tallahassee: Florida State University Press, 1991.

Lundén, Rolf. "The Dual Canon: A Swedish Example." In *As Others Read Us: International Perspectives on American Literature*, ed. Huck Gutman, 236–50. Amherst: University of Massachusetts Press, 1991.

Lupack, Barbara Tepa. *Literary Adaptations in Black American Cinema: From Micheaux to Morrison*. Rochester: University of Rochester Press, 2002.

Lupack, Barbara Tepa. *Nineteenth-Century Women at the Movies: Adapting Classic Women's Fiction to Film*. Bowling Green: Bowling Green State University Press, 1999.

Lurie, Peter, and Ann J. Abadie, eds. *Faulkner and Film*. Jackson: University Press of Mississippi, 2014.

Macdonald, Dwight. *Against the American Grain: Essays on the Effects of Mass Culture*. New York: Random House, 1962.

Marx, Samuel. *A Gaudy Spree: The Literary Life of Hollywood in the 1930 When the West Was Fun*. New York: Franklin Watts, 1987.

Marx, Samuel. "Looking for a Story." In *We Make the Movies*, ed. Nancy Naumberg, 16–31. New York: Norton, 1937.

Maslin, Janet. "FILM; What the Critics Can't Wait to See." *New York Times*. May 14, 1995. https://www.nytimes.com/1995/05/14/movies/film-what-the-critics-can-t-wait-to-see-676895.html.
Mast, Gerald, and Bruce F. Kawin. *A Short History of the Movies*, 9th edn. New York: Pearson, 2006.
Matthiessen, F.O. *American Renaissance: Art and Expression in the Age of Emerson and Whitman*. Oxford: Oxford University Press, 1941.
McAleer, Jon. *Rex Stout: A Biography*. Boston, MA: Little, Brown, 1977.
McCoy, Horace. "*They Shoot Horses, Don't They?*" 1935; rpt. In *Crime Novels: American Noir of the 1930s and 1940s*, ed. Robert Polito, 97–213. New York: Library of America, 1997.
McCrum, Robert. "A Conversation with Philip Roth." *Guardian Observer*. June 30, 2001. https://www.theguardian.com/books/2001/jul/01/fiction.philiproth1.
McFarlane, Brian. *Novel to Film: An Introduction to the Theory of Adaptation*. Oxford: Clarendon Press, 1996.
McKee, Robert. *Story: Substance, Structure, Style, and the Principles of Screenwriting*. New York: Regan, 1997.
McMurtry, Larry. *Lonesome Dove*. 1985; rpt. New York: Simon and Schuster, 2000.
Meer, Sarah. *Uncle Tom Mania: Slavery, Minstrelsy and Transatlantic Culture in the 1850s*. Athens: University of Georgia Press, 2005.
Meikle, Kyle. "Adaptation and Interactivity." In *The Oxford Handbook of Adaptation Studies*, ed. Thomas Leitch, 542–56. New York: Oxford University Press, 2017.
Meikle, Kyle. "Phenomenal Adaptations." University of Delaware dissertation, 2015.
Meikle, Kyle. "Pornographic Adaptation: Parody, Fan Fiction and the Limits of Genre." *Journal of Adaptation in Film and Performance* 8.2 (June 2015): 123–40.
Merrill, Sam. "Mason Hoffenberg Gets in a Few Licks." *Playboy*. Nov. 1973. http://theband.hiof.no/articles/mason_hoffenberg_gets_in_a_few_licks.html.
Merritt, Russell. "Dixon, Griffith, and the Southern Legend." *Cinema Journal* 12.1 (Autumn 1972): 26–45.
Metalious, Grace. *Peyton Place*. 1956; rpt. Boston, MA: Northeastern University Press, 1999.
Metz, Walter. "'Signifying Nothing?': Martin Ritt's *The Sound and the Fury* (1959) as Deconstructive Adaptation." *Literature/Film Quarterly* 27.1 (1999): 21–31.
Miller, Frank, with Klaus Janson and Lynn Varley. *Batman: The Dark Knight Returns*. New York: DC Comics, 1986.
Miller, Frank. *Batman: Year One*. New York: DC Comics, 1987.
Miller, Neil. *Banned in Boston: The Watch and Ward Society's Crusade against Books, Burlesque, and the Social Evil*. Boston, MA: Beacon, 2010.
Miller, Renata Kobetts. "Nineteenth-Century Theatrical Adaptations of Novels: The Paradox of Ephemerality." In *The Oxford Handbook of Adaptation Studies*, ed. Thomas Leitch, 53–70. New York: Oxford University Press, 2017.
Monger, James Christopher. "Rachel Portman, *The Human Stain*." *AllMusic Review*. https://www.allmusic.com/album/the-human-stain-mw0000324608.

Mooney, William H. *Dashiell Hammett and the Movies*. New Brunswick, NJ: Rutgers University Press, 2015.
Murray, Kathleen. "*To Have and Have Not*: An Adaptive System," In *True to the Spirit: Film Adaptation and the Question of Fidelity*, ed. Colin MacCabe, Kathleen Murray and Rick Warner, 91–113. New York: Oxford University Press, 2011.
Murray, Simone. *The Adaptation Industry: The Cultural Economy of Contemporary Literary Adaptation*. New York: Routledge, 2012.
Musser, Charles. Commentary on *Life of an American Policeman*. Edison: The Invention of the Movies. Kino DVD, 2005.
Naremore, James. *More Than Night: Film Noir in Its Contexts*, updated and expanded edition. Berkeley: University of California Press, 2008.
Negroponte, Nicholas. *Being Digital*. New York: Knopf, 1995.
Nevins, Francis M., and Martin Grams, Jr. "The Radio Adventures of Ellery Queen: The First Season." http://www.otrr.org/FILES/Articles/Martin_Grams_Jr_Articles/Adventures_Of_Ellery_Queen.htm.
Norden, Martin F. *The Cinema of Isolation: A History of Physical Disability in the Movies*. New Brunswick, NJ: Rutgers University Press, 1994.
"Notes for *Tobacco Road* (1941)." *Turner Classic Movies*. http://www.tcm.com/tcmdb/title/93489/Tobacco-Road/notes.html.
O'Flynn, Siobhan. "Epilogue." Linda Hutcheon, with Siobhan O'Flynn. *A Theory of Adaptation*. 2nd edn., 179–206. New York: Routledge, 2013.
O'Hara, John. Letter to Charles Brackett. Mar. 13, 1957. Charles Brackett papers. Folder 5.f [53]. Margaret Herrick Library, Academy of Motion Picture Arts and Sciences.
Orlandello, John. *O'Neill on Film*. Teaneck, NJ: Fairleigh Dickinson University Press, 1982.
Othman, Frederick C. "'Tobacco Road' Cleaned Up for Production as Movie." *St. Petersburg Times*. Dec. 15, 1940: B9.
Owens, Mitchell. "Rona Jaffe—Popular Novelist." *New York Times*, Jan. 1, 2006. *SFGate*. http://sfgate.com/cgi-bin/article.cgi?file=/c/a/2006/01/01/BAGDCGG18V1.DTL.
Palmer, R. Barton, ed. *Nineteenth-Century American Fiction on Screen*. Cambridge: Cambridge University Press, 2007.
Palmer, R. Barton, ed. *Twentieth-Century American Fiction on Screen*. Cambridge: Cambridge University Press, 2007.
Parody, Claire. "Franchising/Adaptation." *Adaptation* 4.2 (2011): 210–18.
Patsalidis, Savas. "(Mis)Understanding America's Literary Canon: The Greek Paradigm." In *As Others Read Us: International Perspectives on American Literature*, ed. Huck Gutman, 114–30. Amherst: University of Massachusetts Press, 1991.
Patterson, Frances Taylor. *Cinema Craftsmanship: A Book for Photoplaywrights*. New York: Harcourt, Brace and Howe, 1920.
Peary, Gerald, and Robert Shatzkin, eds. *The Classic American Novel and the Movies*. New York: Ungar, 1977.
Peary, Gerald, and Robert Shatzkin, eds. *The Modern American Novel and the Movies*. New York: Ungar, 1978.
Pendo, Stephen. *Raymond Chandler on Screen: His Novels into Film*. Metuchen, NJ: Scarecrow, 1976.

Phillips, Gene D. *Fiction, Film, and Faulkner: The Art of Adaptation*. Knoxville: University of Tennessee Press, 1988.
Phillips, Gene D. *Hemingway and Film*. New York: Ungar, 1980.
Pierson, John. *Spike, Mike, Slackers and Dykes: A Guided Tour across a Decade of American Independent Cinema*. New York: Hyperion, 1996.
Pigeon Feathers. DVD. Monterey Video, 2007.
Poe, Edgar Allan. *Poetry and Tales*. New York: Library of America, 1984.
Prince, Michael J. *Adapting the Beat Poets: Burroughs, Ginsberg, and Kerouac on Screen*. Lanham, MD: Rowman and Littlefield, 2016.
Proctor, William. "Regeneration and Rebirth: Anatomy of the Franchise Reboot." *Scope* 22 (Feb. 2012). https://www.nottingham.ac.uk/scope/documents/2012/february-2012/proctor.pdf.
Rahv, Philip. "Paleface and Redskin." *Kenyon Review* 1.3 (Summer 1939): 251–56.
Raker, James. Memo to Eddie Lawrence, MGM. James Raker papers. Folder 1.f-64. Margaret Herrick Library, Academy of Motion Picture Arts and Sciences.
Rapf, Joanna E. "Classical Hollywood, 1928–1946." In *Producing*, ed. John Lewis, 36–62. New Brunswick, NJ: Rutgers University Press, 2016.
Raskin, Victor. "Semantic Mechanisms of Humor." *Proceedings of the Fifth Annual Meeting of the Berkeley Linguistics Society* (1979): 325–35.
Rathner, Harry. Letter to Joseph I. Breen, Apr. 8, 1937. Production Code Administration records, Margaret Herrick Library.
Raw, Laurence. *Adapting Henry James to the Screen: Gender, Fiction, and Film*. Lanham, MD: Scarecrow, 2006.
Raw, Laurence. *Adapting Nathaniel Hawthorne to the Screen: Forging New Worlds*. Lanham, MD: Scarecrow, 2008.
Reising, Russell. *The Unusable Past: Theory and the Study of American Literature*. New York: Methuen, 1986.
Robinson, Dorothy. Reader's report on Edna Ferber, *So Big*. May 23, 1936. Jean and Dusty Negulesco papers, Margaret Herrick Library, 65.f-1043.
Ross, Lillian. *Picture: A Story about Hollywood*. New York: Rinehart, 1952.
Roszak, Theodore. *The Making of a Counter Culture: Reflections on the Technocratic Society and Its Youthful Opposition*. Garden City, NY: Doubleday, 1969.
Roth, Philip. *The American Trilogy, 1997–2000*. New York: Library of America, 2011.
Roth, Philip. *Collected Nonfiction, 1960–2013*. New York: Library of America, 2016.
Rubenstein, Hal. "New Again: Demi Moore." *Interview*. Mar. 2, 2017. https://www.interviewmagazine.com/culture/new-again-demi-moore.
Ryan, Marie-Laure. "Transmedia Storytelling as Narrative Practice." In *The Oxford Handbook of Adaptation Studies*, ed. Thomas Leitch, 527–41. New York: Oxford University Press, 2017.
Sanders, Steven M. "Picturing Paranoia: Interpreting *Invasion of the Body Snatchers*." In *The Philosophy of Science Fiction Film*, ed. Steven M. Sanders, 55–72. Lexington: University Press of Kentucky, 2008.
Sarris, Andrew. *The American Cinema: Directors and Directions, 1929–1968*. New York: Dutton, 1969.
Savlov, Mark. "*The Wings of the Dove*." *Austin Chronicle*. Nov. 21, 1997. https://www.austinchronicle.com/events/film/1997-11-21/the-wings-of-the-dove/.
Scharnhorst, Gary. Commentary on *Salomy Jane*. *Treasures from American Film Archives 5: The West, 1898–1938*. Image DVD.

Schatz, Thomas. *Boom and Bust: American Cinema in the 1940s [History of the American Cinema, Volume 6]*. Berkeley: University of California Press, 1987.

Schatz, Thomas. *The Genius of the System: Hollywood Filmmaking in the Studio Era*. New York: Pantheon, 1988.

Scheuer, Philip K. "'No Down Payment' Certain to Cause a Sensation/'No Down Payment' Filled with Disturbing Drama." *Los Angeles Times*. Oct. 6, 1957: E1.

Schickel, Richard. *Clint Eastwood: A Biography*. New York: Knopf, 1996.

Schneider, Rebecca. "Performance Remains." *Performance Research* 6.2 (2001): 100–08.

Schrader, Paul. "Notes on Film Noir." *Film Comment* 10.1 (Jan.–Feb. 1974): 30–35. Rpt. in *Film Noir Reader*, ed. Alain Silver and James Ursini, 53–64. New York: Limelight Editions, 2004.

Schwager, Jeff. "*The Past* Rewritten." *Film Comment* 27.1 (Jan.–Feb. 1991): 12–17.

Scott, A.O. "Film Review: Secrets of the Skin, and of the Heart." *New York Times*. Oct. 31, 2003. https://www.nytimes.com/2003/10/31/movies/film-review-secrets-of-the-skin-and-of-the-heart.html.

Selznick, David O. *Memo from David O. Selznick*. Ed. Rudy Behlmer. New York: Viking, 1972.

Semenza, Gregory M. Colón and Bob Hasenfratz. *The History of British Literature on Film*. New York: Bloomsbury Academic, 2015.

"Sensational Screen Play Comes Thurs. to Fox California." *San Jose Evening News*. Mar. 12, 1941: 13.

Smith, Stephen. "Radio: The Internet of the 1930s." *American RadioWork*, Nov. 10, 2014. http://www.americanradioworks.org/segments/radio-the-internet-of-the-1930s/.

Smyth, J.E. *Edna Ferber's Hollywood: American Fictions of Gender, Race, and History*. Austin: University of Texas Press, 2010.

Snyder, Sharon L., and David T. Mitchell. "Body Genres: An Anatomy of Disability in Film." In *The Problem Body: Projecting Disability on Film*, ed. Sally Chivers and Nicole Markotić, 179–204. Columbus: Ohio State University Press, 2010.

Sobchack, Vivian C. "The Grapes of Wrath: Thematic Emphasis through Visual Style," *American Quarterly* 31.5 (Winter 1979): 596–615. Rpt. in *Literature and Film: A Guide to the Theory and Practice of Film Adaptation*, ed. Robert Stam and Alessandra Raengo, 111–25. Malden, MA: Blackwell, 2005.

Sontag, Susan. "The Decay of Cinema." *New York Times*, Feb. 25, 1996. http://www.nytimes.com/books/00/03/12/specials/sontag-cinema.html.

Stam, Robert. "Introduction: The Theory and Practice of Adaptation." In *Literature and Film: A Guide to the Theory and Practice of Film Adaptation*, ed. Robert Stam and Alessandra Raengo, 1–52. Malden, MA: Blackwell, 2004.

Stamp, Shelley. *Lois Weber in Early Hollywood*. Berkeley: University of California Press, 2015.

Stowe, Harriet Beecher. *Three Novels*. New York: Library of America, 1982.

"Stowe's Global Impact: Her Words Changed the World." *Harriet Beecher Stowe Center*. https://www.harrietbeecherstowecenter.org/harriet-beecher-stowe/her-global-impact/.

Telotte, J.P. *Science Fiction Film*. Cambridge: Cambridge University Press, 2001.
"Theatrical Market Statistics 2015." *Motion Picture Association of America*. https://www.mpaa.org/wp-content/uploads/2016/04/MPAA-Theatrical-Market-Statistics-2015_Final.pdf.
Thompson, David, ed. *Altman on Altman*. London: Faber and Faber, 2006.
Thompson, Derek. "Hollywood Has a Huge Millennial Problem." *Atlantic*, June 8, 2016. https://www.theatlantic.com/business/archive/2016/06/hollywood-has-a-huge-millennial-problem/486209/.
Thompson, Emma. "1995 Acceptance Speech for Writing (Screenplay Based on Material Previously Produced or Published)." *Academy Award Acceptance Speech Database*. http://aaspeechesdb.oscars.org/link/068-23/.
Thompson, Kristin, and David Bordwell. *Film History: An Introduction*. New York: McGraw–Hill, 1994.
Tibbetts, John C., and James M. Welsh, eds. *Encyclopedia of Novels into Film*. 2nd edn. New York: Facts on File, 2005.
Tibbetts, John C., and James M. Welsh, eds. *Encyclopedia of Stage Plays into Film*. New York: Facts on File, 2001.
Todorov, Tzvetan. *The Fantastic: A Structural Approach to a Literary Genre*. Trans. Richard Howard. Ithaca, NY: Cornell University Press, 1975.
Toffler, Alvin. *The Third Wave*. New York: Morrow, 1980.
Toth, Emily. *Inside Peyton Place: The Life of Grace Metalious*. Garden City, NY: Doubleday, 1981.
Trotter, David. "Dis-enablement: Subject and Method in the Modernist Short Story." *Critical Quarterly* 52.2 (2010): 4–13.
Twain, Mark. *Mississippi Writings*. New York: Library of America, 1982.
Updike, John. *Pigeon Feathers*. New York: Knopf, 1962.
Vasey, Ruth. *The World According to Hollywood, 1918–1939*. Madison: University of Wisconsin Press, 1996.
Verevis, Constantine. "The Cinematic Return." *Film Comment* 40.1 (Jan. 2016). https://quod.lib.umich.edu/f/fc/13761232.0040.134/-cinematic-return?rgn=main;view=fulltext.
Vest, Jason P. *Future Imperfect: Philip K. Dick at the Movies*. Westport, CT: Praeger, 2007.
Vincendeau, Ginette, ed. *Film/Literature/Heritage: A Sight and Sound Reader*. London: BFI, 2001.
"Wakefield." *Rotten Tomatoes*. https://www.rottentomatoes.com/m/wakefield.
Waller, Robert James. *The Bridges of Madison County*. New York: Warner, 1992.
Warshow, Robert. "The Gangster as Tragic Hero." In *The Immediate Experience: Movies, Comics, Theatre and Other Aspects of Popular Culture*, 127–33. 1952; rpt. New York: Atheneum, 1975.
Wead, George. "Frank Norris: His Share of *Greed*." In *The Classic American Novel and the Movies*, ed. Gerald Peary and Roger Shatzkin, 143–51. New York: Ungar, 1977.
Weinberg, Herman G. *The Complete Greed of Erich von Stroheim*. New York: Arno, 1972.
Wexman, Virginia Wright. *A History of Film*, 7th edn. Boston, MA: Allyn & Bacon, 2010.

Winter, Jessica. "Mondo Trasho and Desperate Living." *Village Voice*. Apr. 24, 2001. https://www.villagevoice.com/2001/04/24/mondo-trasho-and-desperate-living/.

Wood, Michael. *America in the Movies, or "Santa Maria, It Had Slipped My Mind."* New York: Basic, 1975.

Woodward, Richard. "Cormac McCarthy's Venomous Fiction." *New York Times Magazine*. Apr. 18, 1992. https://www.nytimes.com/1992/04/19/magazine/cormac-mccarthy-s-venomous-fiction.html.

Wu, Tim. "The Tyranny of Convenience." *New York Times*. Sunday Review. Feb. 16, 2018. https://www.nytimes.com/2018/02/16/opinion/sunday/tyranny-convenience.html.

Wylie, I.A.R. "An Impression of 'Four Sons' by Its Author." Souvenir Program for *Four Sons*, rpt. and included with the DVD release *Ford at Fox*. Twentieth Century Fox, 2007.

Wyllie, Barbara. *Nabokov at the Movies: Film Perspectives in Fiction*. Jefferson, NC: McFarland, 2003.

Yagoda, Ben. *Will Rogers: A Biography*. New York: Knopf, 1993.

Zanuck, Darryl F. Memo to Julian Johnson, David Brown, and Joseph Moskowitz. July 5, 1952. Henry King papers. Folder 8.f-138. Margaret Herrick Library, Academy of Motion Picture Arts and Sciences.

Zimmerman, Paul D. "The City Game." *Newsweek*. Feb. 15, 1971: 82.

Zuckoff, Mitchell. *Robert Altman: The Oral Biography*. New York: Knopf, 2009.

INDEX

Note: **Boldface** numbers refer to illustrations.

Abadie, Ann J. 27
Abbott, George 74, 122
Abby (1974) 273
Abe Lincoln in Illinois (1940) 117
Abe Lincoln in Illinois (TV, 1950) 202
Abie's Irish Rose (1928) 80
Abie's Irish Rose (1946) 80
Academy Awards 4, 93, 118, 119, 146, 149, 157, 158, 191, 192, 194, 199, 204, 212, 213, 216, 231, 243, 245, 251, 257, 259, 269, 272, 278, 282, 284, 320–1, 326, 327, 330, 339–40, 344, 370, 374–5
Aciman, André
  Call Me by Your Name 340
Ackroyd, Dan 276
Across 110th Street (1972) 272
Adams, Samuel Hopkins
  "Night Bus" 146, 292
adaptation
  as adaptation 35, 159
  and anti-adaptation 257
  antitypes 309, 312
  as attraction 35–40
  canons of 314
  central to Hollywood's economic model 349
  daisy-chain model of 80–1
  dangerous 308
  fetishizing 196
  foreign 27–8, 169–72
  heritage 319–25
  of heroes 254–5
  vs. history 187
  and interpretive doubling 287

  invisible 172–81, 186–90, 192–3
  literary 339–40
  niche 322
  ostensive 166, 187, 225, 227, 263
  of people to books 304–5
  pornographic 297–8
  the same but different 44, 45, 79
  unacknowledged 186–7
  unfaithful 294
Ade, George 38
  The County Chairman 277
Adjustment Bureau, The (2011) 308
Adventure of the Hasty Elopement, The (1914) **39**
Adventures of Baron Munchausen, The (1988) 320
Adventures of Ellery Queen, The (radio program) 133
Adventures of Huckleberry Finn, The (1939) 136, 173
Adventures of Mark Twain, The (1944) 174
Adventures of Pluto Nash, The (2002) 320
Adventures of Robin Hood, The (1938) 148, 156, 163, 209
Adventures of Superman (TV, 1952–8) 309
Adventures of Tom Sawyer, The (1938) 136
Adventures of Tom Sawyer, The (TV, 1951) 201
Advise and Consent (1962) 283
aesthetic
  novelistic 137–40, 142–51
  theatrical 113, 137

INDEX

Affairs of the Heart (TV, 1974–5) 25, 322
African American cinema 143–5, 263, 269–76, 286, 340, 358
African Queen, The (1951) 157, 195
After Many Years (1908) 37
After the Thin Man (1936) 130
Age for Love, The (1931) 117
Age of Innocence, The (1924) 324
Age of Innocence, The (1934) 11, 138, 324
Age of Innocence, The (1993) 261, 324, **325**
Agnew, Spiro 297
Ahearne, Brian 220
Ahern, Lassie Lou 95
Ah, Wilderness! (1935) 23, 116
Aiken, George L. 40
Airport (1970) 262
Aitken, Spottiswoode 64, **66**
Akerman, Chantal 277
Albee, Edward 16
Alcott, Louisa May 11
   Little Women 157
Aldrich, Bess Streeter 173
Aleong, Aki 218
Alexander (2004) 320
Alfred 316, 317, 318
Alfred Hitchcock Hour (TV, 1962–5) 203
Alfred Hitchcock Presents (TV, 1955–62) 203
Algren, Nelson
   The Man with the Golden Arm 204
Ali, Muhammed 310
Alias (TV, 2001–6) 3
Alias Jimmy Valentine (1915) 83
Alias Jimmy Valentine (1920) 83
Alibi Ike (1935) 113, 156
Alice Adams (1935) 157
Alice Doesn't Live Here Anymore (1974) 277
Alice in Wonderland: An X-Rated Musical Comedy (1976) 297
Alice's Restaurant (1969) 242–3, 249, 250, 254, 255, 256, 264
Alien (1979) 306, 307
Alien, The (1967) 263

Alison's House (TV, 1951) 202
All about Eve (1950) 192, 193, 212–13, 291
Allen, Hervey
   Anthony Adverse 146
Allen, Woody 288
All Quiet on the Western Front (1930) 91, 116, 135
All That Heaven Allows (1955) 221
All the King's Men (1949) 155, 190, 191
All the King's Men (2006) 320
All the Pretty Horses (2000) 328
All This, and Heaven Too (1940) 145
Almos' a Man (1976) 294
Altman, Rick 120, 122, 152 n.25, 154 n.58, 154 n.59
Altman, Robert 37, 256–9, 292, 293, 311
Amazing Spider-Man, The (TV, 1977–9) 352
Amazing Spider-Man, The (2012) 354, 355
Amazing Spider-Man 2, The (2014) 354–5
Amazon Prime 201, 368
Amblin' (1968) 261
Amblin Entertainment 331
American Broadcasting Company (ABC) 309
American Film Institute (AFI) 120
American Film Theatre (1973–5) 24
American Gigolo (1980) 261
American Graffiti (1973) 260
American International Pictures 273
Americanism 291
American literature
   vs. American national identity 76
   as archive of canonical texts 27, 79–81, 239, 374
   as attraction 52
   vs. British literature 7–8, 9–10, 14–15
   as collection of stories in the public domain 52
   defining 25–6, 28
   as export commodity 169–72
   future of 369

history of 25
Hollywood's attitudes toward 8, 191–7, 340, 347, 358
  as licensed inspiration and competitor 52
  as raw material 6
  study of 10–11
  a work in progress 375
American Mutoscope Company 31, 33
American mythology 13
American Pastoral (2016) 342, 344
American Playhouse (TV, 1981–94) 23, 274, 344
Americans
  abroad 87–9
  ethnic 278–9
  prototypical 106, 136
American Short Story Collection, The (TV, 1974–90) 24, 294–6
American Tragedy, An (1931) 12, 120, 138, 140
Amorous Adventures of Fanny Hill (1983) 297
Anatomy of a Murder (1959) 207
Anderson, Edward
  Thieves Like Us 175
Anderson, James 204
Anderson, Maxwell 116, 232
  Both Your Houses 116
  Joan of Lorraine 187
  Key Largo 195
  Mary of Scotland 202
  What Price Glory? 80
Anderson, Pamela 313
Anderson, Sherwood 6, 170
  "Death in the Woods" 290
  "I'm a Fool" 294, 295
Anders, Paul 247
Anderton, Ethan 376 n.16
Andrew, Dudley 137
Andrews, Jesse
  Me and Earl and the Dying Girl 348
Andrews, Mary Raymond Shipman
  "The Unbeliever" 87
Android 360
Angelou, Maya 23
Angels in America (2003) 27

Angry Red Planet, The (1959) 302
Animal Crackers (1930) 119, 138, **139**
Animal Kingdom, The (1932) 135
Anna Christie (1923) 79
Anna Christie (1930) 114–15, 116, 206
Anna Karenina (1935) 136, 137
Annaud, Jean-Jacques 38
Annie (1982) 203, 311
Annie Get Your Gun (musical) 173
Another Thin Man (1939) 134
Another Time, Another Place (1958) 205
anthology adaptations 199–200
Anthony Adverse (1936) 146, 148, 156, 209
antiheroes 254–5
anti-Semitism 188, 283, 341
Ant-Man and the Wasp (2018) 359
Arena, The (1974) 277
Argo (2012) 339, 340
Arkin, Alan 243, 249
Armstrong, Charlotte
  The Balloon Man 170
  The Chocolate Cobweb 171
Armstrong, Paul 76, 83
Armstrong, William H.
  Sounder 274
Arnold, Edward 127
Arnold, Jeremy 165
Around the World in 80 Days (2004) 320
Arper, Clarence 77
Arrowsmith (1931) 116
Arsenic and Old Lace (1944) 117
Artisan Entertainment 352
Arzner, Dorothy 277
Ashe, Penelope
  Naked Came the Stranger 298
Asher, Jane 21
Ashley, Elizabeth 224
As I Lay Dying (2013) 4–5, **5**
Asimov, Isaac 304
Asphalt Jungle, The (1950) 185, 195, 203
Astaire, Fred 118, 157, 173, 259
Astor, Mary 181, 182, **192**
Atkins, Zoë
  Morning Glory 157

attractions 33–4, 46, 50, 54, 66, 78–9
   auditory 115–16
   visual 63
Auerbach, Erich 139
Aulin, Ewa 247
aura 209
   vs. fidelity 226
Austen, Jane 6, 7, 9, 19, 24, 25, 138, 139, 239, 319, 320–1, 322, 324, 325
   Pride and Prejudice 7, 138
Austenland (2013) 7, 22
authors, film treatments of 179–81, 186–90
Autobiography of a Flea, The (1976) 297
Avatar (2009) 302
Avengers, the 350, 355, 357
Avengers, The (2012) 356–7, **356**
Avengers: Age of Ultron (2015) 357
Avenging Conscience, The (1914) 63–6, 115
Aventures dans le Grand Nord (TV, 1995) 38
Averty, Jean-Christophe 169
Aviator, The (2004) 261
Awful Truth, The (1937) 146
Ayres, Lew 281

Babbitt (1924) 83
Babbitt, Natalie
   Tuck Everlasting 348
Babenco, Héctor 283, 341–2
Babes in Arms (1939) 118, 173
Baby Doll (1956) 207, 208
Baby Mine (1917) 79
Baby Mine (1928) 79
Baby's Breakfast (1895) 43
Bacall, Lauren 36, 183
Bach, Johann Sebastian 251
Back Street (1932) 221
Back Street (1941) 221
Back Street (1961) 221
Back to the Future (1985) 267
Backus, Jim 243
Bacon, Frank
   Lightnin' 79–80
Badham, Mary 204

Badlands (1973) 261
Bad Seed, The (1956) 116
Baez, Joan 235
Bag of Bones (TV, 2011) 373
Bailey, Jonathan 198 n.20
Baker, Carroll 224, **225**, 225
Baker, Diane 219
Baker, Mark Linn 344
Bakhtin, Mikhail 137, 138
Bakshi, Ralph 248
Baldwin, Faith 200
Baldwin, James 23
   "Going to Meet the Man" 290
   Go Tell It on the Mountain 274
Bale, Christian **350**
Balin, Ina 222
Balmer, Edwin
   When Worlds Collide 304
Balzac, Honoré de 139
Band, Albert 195
Band à part (1964) 171
Barbarian and the Geisha, The (1958) 203
Barb Wire (1996) 313
Bardcore 297
Bardem, Javier **329**
Barefoot in the Park (1963) 232
Barhydt, Frank 292
Barker, Lex 124
Barn Burning (1980) 294
Barrett, Jacinda **345**
Barry, Dave 373
Barrymore, John 37, **121**, 157
Barry, Philip
   The Animal Kingdom 135
   Holiday 157
   The Philadelphia Story 146, 157
Barthelme, Donald
   "Views of My Father Weeping" 290
Barthes, Roland 41
Barton Fink (1991) 10, 117
Basinger, Jeanine 165
Basinger, Kim 315
Bat, The (1926) 80
Bat-bible 315, 318
Bates, Kathy 374
Batman 107, 108, 309, 314, 316–19, 350–1, 354, 363

Batman (1943) 309
Batman (TV, 1966–8) 309, 310, 312
Batman (1989) 311–13, **313**, 316
Batman and Robin (1949) 309, 316
Batman and Robin (1997) 313, 350
Batman Begins (2005) 316, 350, **350**, 354, 358
Batman Forever (1995) 313, 350
Batman Returns (1992) 313
Batman vs. Superman: Dawn of Justice (2016) 359
Battlefield Earth (2000) 320
Battle of San Pietro, The (1945) 195
Battlestar Galactica (TV, 1978–9) 307
Bat Whispers, The (1930) 80
Batwoman 318
Baum, L. Frank 53, 54, 55, 56, 58, 59, 62
  The Emerald City of Oz 54
  The Marvelous Land of Oz 53, 55
  Ozma of Oz 53, 56
  The Patchwork Girl of Oz 54
  Queen Zixi of Ix 56
  The Road to Oz 58
  The Scarecrow of Oz 58
  Sky Island 58
  The Tik-Tok Man of Oz 56
  Tik-Tok of Oz 56
  The Wonderful Wizard of Oz 53, 58, 274
Baum, Vicki
  Menschen im Hotel 120–1
Bazin, André 187
Bazooka Joe 317
Beach, Rex Ellingwood 39
Bear, The (1988) 38
Beast from 20,000 Fathoms, The (1953) 302, 304, 306
Beatles, the 235, 251
Beatty, Ned 311
Beatty, Warren 311
The Beautiful and Damned (1922) 83
Beautiful Mind, A (2001) 339, 340
Beckinsale, Kate 320
Becoming Jane (2007) 10
Bedford, Barbara 84, **84**
Beery, Noah 102, 103
Beggar on Horseback (1925) 119

Behind That Curtain (1929) 127, 128
Behind the Green Door (1972) 297
Belasco, David 39
Bellaman, Harry 195
  Kings Row 174
Bellamy, Ralph 133
Bell for Adono, A (1945) 174
Bellow, Saul 6, 341
Beloved (1998) 23, 361
Belton, John 246
Belushi, John 276
Benchley, Peter
  Jaws 262
Benedictus, Michael
  You're a Big Boy Now 259
Benes, Michelle 333
Ben Hur (1907) 50–1
Ben-Hur (1925) 12
Ben-Hur (1959) 149
Benjamin, Walter 209
Benton, Robert 342, 344, 346
Beresford, Bruce 331, 332
Bergen, Candice 247
Bergman, Ingmar 257, 288
Bergman, Ingrid 137, 204
Bergman, Ronald 109 n.20
Berkeley, Busby 118, 173
Berlin, Irving 118, 166, 167
  The Cocoanuts 80
  This Is the Army 166
  Yip, Yip, Yaphank 166, 167
Berne Convention 172
Bernice Bobs Her Hair (1976) 294
Bernstein, Elmer 224
Bernstein, Leonard
  West Side Story 241
Besserer, Eugénie 114, **115**
Best of Everything, The (1959) 219–20, **220**, 224, 226, 227
Best People, The (1925) 80
best sellers, adaptations of 203–28, 278, 280, 288
Best Years of Our Lives, The (1946) 146, 187, 188, 192
Beyond the Forest (1949) 156
Beyond the Horizon (TV, 1959) 79
Beyond the Valley of the Dolls (1970) 298

BFG, The (2016) 263
Bierce, Ambrose
    "Parker Adderson, Philosopher"
    294
Biggers, Earl Derr 127, 128, 134
    The House without a Key 127
Big Heat, The 245
Big Knife, The (1955) 117
Big Lebowski, The (1997) 330
Big Parade, The (1925) 12
Big Short, The (2015) 62, 339, 340,
    369
Big Sleep, The (1946) 183, 258
Big Tree, Chief 162
Bill of Divorcement, A (1932) 135,
    136, 157
Biograph Company 38
biopics 135, 151
Birds, The (1963) 12, 246
Birthday Party, The (1968) 284
Birth of a Nation, The (1915) 12,
    69–73, **71**, 83
Birthright (1924) 144
Birthright (1938) 144, **145**
Biskind, Peter 265 n.16, 266 n.30
Bitcoin 360
Bitzer, Billy 32
Black Angel (1946) 177, 178, 179,
    188–9, **189**
Black Belt Jones (1974) 273
Blackboard Jungle, The (1955) 235,
    241, 246
Black Caesar (1973) 273, 276
Black Cat, The (1934) 20
black comedy 330
Blackenstein (1973) 273
blackface 42, 43, 71, 94, 114, 123,
    145, 276. *See also* minstrelsy
Black Fury (1935) 187
Black Godfather, The (1974) 273, 276
Blackie, Boston 122
Black Mama White Mama (1972) 273
Black Panther 313
Black Panther (2018) 358, 374–5, **374**
Black Power 274
Black Rose, The (1950) 157
Black Samurai (1977) 272
Black Shampoo (1975) 273

Black Swan, The (1942) 157
Black Widow 357
Blacula (1972) 273–4
Blade 314
Blade (1998) 352
Blade (1998) 313
Blade II (2002) 313, 2002
Blade Runner (1982) 306–8, **307**, 311
Blade Runner 2049 (2017) 307, 308
Blade: Trinity (2004) 352
Blair, Linda 250, **251**
Blair Witch Project, The (1999) 37
Blake, A.D. 99
Blane, Torchy 128, 132, 173
Blatty, William Peter
    The Exorcist 250
Blaxploitation 268, 272–4, 277, 280,
    286, 297, 298, 314
Blind Alley (1939) 185
Bloch, Robert 372
blockbusters 7, 69, 119, 259, 262–3,
    267, 319, 320, 325, 335
Blonde Inspiration (1941) 173
Blood and Sand (1941) 157
Blood Relatives (1978) 171
Blood Simple (1984) 330
Bloom, Claire 305
Bloom, Harold 372
Blow Out (1981) 261
Blue Collar (1978) 261
Blue Hotel, The (1977) 294
Blue Movie (1969) 297
Blues Brothers, The (1980) 276
Bluestone, George 27, 122
Blyth, Harry. *See* Meredith, Hal
Bodeen, DeWitt 261
Body Double (1984) 261
Body Heat (1981) 187
Bogart, Humphrey 36, 181, 182, **182**,
    183, 258
Bogart, Paul 258
Bogdanovich, Peter 259, 326
Bogle, Donald 298 n.1
Bollywood 361
Bolton, Guy
    Rio Rita 80
Bond, James 22, 132
Bond, Ward 161

Bonfire of the Vanities, The (2000) 320
Bonham Carter, Helena 323
Bonner, Priscilla 100
Bonnie and Clyde (1967) 231, 235, 245, 251, 319, 347
Boo! A Medea Halloween (2016) 361
Booth, Margaret 241
Boozer, Jack 36
Borde, Raymond 171, 198 n.17
Bordwell, David 264 n.6
Borzage, Frank 19, 91, 93, 140
Bostonians, The (1984) 14
Boswell, Parley Ann 26–7
Bosworth Company 52
Bottalico, Michele 170
Boucicault, Dion 32, 35, 36
Bouton, Jim 258
Bow, Clara 93, 105
Bowery Boys 122
Bowser, Eileen 92
Boxcar Bertha (1972) 261
Boy Cried Murder, The (1966) 178
Boyd, Stephen 220
Boyer, Charles 167
Boys from Syracuse, The (1940) 118
Boys in the Band, The (1970) 284–7, **285**, 288, 289
Boys in the Sand (1971) 298
Brackett, Charles 222
Bradbury, Ray 304–5, 306, 308
  Fahrenheit 451 170
  "The Fog Horn" 304
  The Martian Chronicles 304
  "The Meteor" 304
  "Usher II" 304
Brady, Cyrus Townsend 39
Brady, Matthew 195
Bram Stoker Award 372
branding 55, 158, 263, 344, 365
Brand, Max
  "Internes Can't Take Money" 122
Brando, Marlon 194, 259, **260**, 309
Brashares, Anne
  The Sisterhood of the Traveling Pants 348
Bray, William Robert 27
Breach, The (1970) 170
Breakfast at Tiffany's (1962) 291

Breakfast Club, The (1985) 347
Breaking Bad (TV, 2008–13) 2–3, 201
Break of Hearts (1936) 157
Breathless (1959) 171
Breen, Joseph I. 139, 159, 179, 209
Breen Office 156, 159, 179, 180, 188, 194, 206, 207–8, 209
Breese, Edmund 104
Brennan, Joseph Payne 372
Brewer, Sherri 271
Brewster McCloud (1970) 257
Brice, Fanny 278
Bride of Frankenstein, The (1935) 20
Bride Wore Black, The (1968) 170, 178
Bridges of Madison County, The (1995) 331–5, **334**, 339
Bridge to Terabithia (1985) 348
Brighton Beach Memoirs (1986) 232
Bright Star (2009) 10
Bright Victory (1951) 165
Bringing Out the Dead (1999) 261
Bringing Up Baby (1938) 157, 291
British Broadcasting Corporation (BBC) 24, 25, 320, 322, 324, 365
Brit-Lit 27, 274
  vs. Am-Lit 7–8
Broadway Melody, The (1929) 116, 118
Broderick, Helen 131
Broderick, James 242
Brodkey, Harold
  "Love and Other Sorrows" 294
Brokeback Mountain (2005) 292, 326, 339, 340
Brontë, Emily
  Wuthering Heights 7, 15, 334
Brooker, Will 314, 315, 350–1
Brooks, Eunice 143, 144
Brooks, James L. 326, 327
Brooks, Richard 221, 280
  The Brick Foxhole 188, 283
Brotherhood, The (1968) 259
Brown, Buster 40, 53
Brown, Charles Brocken 6, 13, 238
  Wieland 40

Brown, Clarence 23, 83, 84, 85, 253
Brown, Dan
  The Da Vinci Code 369
Brown, David 204
Brown, Joe David
  Addie Pray 326
Brown, Joe E. 113
Brown, Tina 361
Brown, William F. 274
Browning, Tod 253, 268
Broyard, Anatole 343
Brunson, Paul Carrick 359
Buck, Pearl S.
  The Good Earth 113, 147
Buck Rogers in the 25th Century (1939) 301
Buena Vista Pictures 313
Buffalo Bill and the Indians (1976) 257
Bugliosi, Vincent
  Helter Skelter 240
Bullets or Ballots (1937) 187
Bullitt (1968) 245
Bumstead, Blondie Boopadoop 122, 317
Bumstead, Dagwood 122, 317
Bundel, Ani 375
Burdick, Eugene
  Fail-Safe 303
Burke, Liam 315, 336 n.4, 349
Burnham, Beatrice 101
Burroughs, Edgar Rice 123
  The Return of Tarzan 123
  Tarzan of the Apes 123
  Tarzan the Untamed 123
Burstyn, Ellen 250
Burton, Clarence 93
Burt, Richard 297
Burton, Tim 311, 315, 316
Burwell, Carter 330
Busch, Niven 195
  Duel in the Sun 190
Bushman, Francis X. 90
BUtterfield 8 (1960) 221, 222, 224, 226, 227
By Love Possessed (1961) 205, 221, 224, 226, 227, 255

Caan, James **260**, 309–10
A Cabana do Pai Tomás (1909) 169
A Cabana do Pai Tomás (TV, 1969–70) 169
Cabinet of Dr. Caligari (1920) 184
Cabin in the Cotton, The (1933) 156
Cabin in the Sky (1943) 174
Cabot, Meg
  The Princess Diaries 348
Cahan, Abraham
  Yekl: A Tale of the New York Ghetto 279
Cain, Christopher 347
Cain, James M. 155–6, 170, 179–81
  Double Indemnity 140, 179, 183, 213
  Mildred Pierce 179
  The Postman Always Rings Twice 140, 172, 175, 179, 180
  Serenade 140
Calamity Jane 76
Caldwell, Erskine 170, 195
  Tobacco Road 159–61, 188
Calhoun, John C. 237
California Split (1974) 257
Calisher, Hortense
  "The Hollow Boy" 24, 294, 295
Calling Dr. Gillespie (1942) 185
Call Me by Your Name (2017) 349
Cambridge, Godfrey 269, 270, **270**, 271
cameo appearances 357–8, 373
Cameron, Anne
  "Green Dice" 126
Cameron, James 302
Camille (1936) 252
Camille 2000 (1969) 298
Campbell, John W.
  "The Thing from Another World" 302
Campbell, Joseph 260
Campion, Jane 321
Canary Murder Case, The (1929) 127
Canby, Vincent 271, 286–7
Candy (1968) 244, 247–8, 249, 255
Cannes Film Festival 319
canons
  franchise 314–19
  literary 7–8

INDEX

Cape Fear (1991) 261
Capote (2005) 10
Capote, Truman 292
Capp, Al 309
Capra, Frank 119, 292
Captain America 352, 357
Captain America: Civil War (2016) 355, 359
Captain Blood (1935) 156
Captain from Castille (1947) 157
Cardinal, The (1963) 190
Carefree (1938) 185
Carewe, Arthur Edmund 94–5
Carmen, Baby (1967) 297
Caron, Leslie 241
Carousel (musical) 173
Carpenter, John 307
Carpetbaggers, The (1964) 223–5, 349
Carr, Jay 337 n.19
Carradine, John 162
Carrie (1976) 261, 370, **371**, 372, 373
Carson, Johnny 297
Carter, Lynda 309
Carter, Nick 39, 40
Cartmell, Deborah 8
Carver, Raymond 291, 292, 293
  "Collectors" 292
  "Fever" 290
  "Jerry and Molly and Sam" 292
  "Lemonade" 292
  "Neighbors" 292
  "A Small, Good Thing" 292
  "So Much Water So Close to Home" 292
  "Tell the Women We're Going" 292
  "They're Not Your Husband" 292
  "Vitamins" 292
  "Will You Please Be Quiet, Please?" 292
Casablanca (1942) 36, 155
Case of the Black Cat, The (1936) 132
Case of the Curious Bride, The (1935) 132
Case of the Howling Dog, The (1934) 127
Case of the Lucky Legs (1935) 132

Case of the Stuttering Bishop, The (1937) 132
Case of the Velvet Claws, The (1936) 132
Casino (1995) 261
Casino Murder Case, The (1935) 130, 133
Casino Royale (2006) 317
Caspary, Vera 192, 211
Cass Timberlaine (1947) 204
Castle, William 37
Catch-22 (1970) 244, 245, 246, 249, 254, 255
Cather, Willa 6
  "Paul's Case" 294
Cat People (1942) 261
Cat People (1982) 261
Cattrysse, Patrick 17, 186
Catwoman 309
Catwoman (2004) 320
Cayatte, André 278
Cazale, John 260
Cell (2016) 372
censorship 52, 180, 234
Cerf, Vint 360
Chabrol, Claude 170–1
Chan, Charlie 16, 122, 127, 128–9, 131, 133, 134, 135, 145, 175, 181, 183
Chandler, Raymond 34, 41, 176, 182, 291
  The Big Sleep 258
  The Long Goodbye 258
  Raymond Chandler Speaking 258
Change.org 360
Chaplin, Ben 324
Chaplin, Charlie 59, 60–1, 105
Chapman Report, The (1962) 207
Chapter Two (1979) 232
Charge of the Light Brigade, The (1936) 148, 156
Charles, Nick 127, 129–30, 131, 132, 134, 173, 181, 183
Charles, Nora 127, 130, 131, 132, 134, 173, 181, 183
Charlie Chan at Monte Carlo (1937) 128

Charlie Chan at Ringside (uncompleted) 128–9
Charlie Chan Carries On (1931) 127
Charlie Chan in London (1934) 128
Charlie Chan in Paris (1935) 133
Charlie Chan's Chance (1932) 128
Charlie Chan's Courage (1934) 128
Charlie Chan's Greatest Case (1933) 128
Charly (1968) 280, 281
Chartier, Jean-Pierre 171, 197 n.16
Chase, The (1946) 177, 179, 185
Chase, Mary 195
   Harvey 190
Chase, Richard 14, 15
Chaumeton, Étienne 171, 198 n.17
Chbosky, Stephen
   The Perks of Being a Wallflower 348
Cheap Detective, The (1978) 232
Cheat, The (1915) 70–3, **72**, 98
Cheers for Miss Bishop (1941) 173
Cheever, John 200
   "The Brigadier and the Golf Widow" 290
   "The Country Husband" 202
Chenal, Pierre 23, 274
Chénetier, Marc 197 n.11
Chesnutt, Charles W.
   The House behind the Cedars 143
Chester, George 39
Chevrolet Tele-Theatre (TV, 1948–50) 201
Children of a Lesser God (1986) 281–2, **281**
Children of the Corn: Genesis (2011) 373
Children's Hour, The (1961) 277, 283
Chill, Joe 316
Chinatown Nights (1929) 135
Chinese Parrot, The (1928) 127, 128
Chopin, Kate 6, 14
   The Awakening 369
   "Désirée's Baby" 290
Christine (1983) 372
Christmas Carol, A (1938) 120
Christopher Strong (1933) 135
Chu, Louis
   Eat a Bowl of Tea 279

Cider House Rules, The (1999) 339
Cimarron (1931) 138, 146
Ciment, Michael 228
Cinderella (1914) 92
Cinderella (1957) 119
cinema of attractions 33
cinema of narrative recognition, *vs.* cinema of narrative generation 51–2
CinemaScope 205, 206, 218, 219, 349
Cinerama 37, 206
Cioffi, Charles 272
Citizen Kane (1941) 176, 185, 191
Clark, Petula 259
Clark, Walter Van Tilburg
   The Ox-Bow Incident 329
Clash by Night (1952) 12, 117
Clash by Night (TV, 1957) 202
Claudia (1943) 137
Clayton, Jack 11, 305
Clements, Flo 143
Cleopatra (1963) 234
Cleopatra Jones (1973) 277
Clift, Denison 25
Clift, Montgomery 324
Clinton, Bill 342, 343
Close Encounters of the Third Kind (1977) 263, 267
Clueless (1995) 320, 321, 322
Clurman, Harold 178
Coad, Joyce 85
Cobb, Irvin S. 126
Coburn, James 248
Cocoanuts, The (1929) 80, 119
Code of Practice for Television Broadcasters 206
Coe, Barry 214, **215**
Coen, Ethan 10, 117, 187, 329–30
Coen, Joel 10, 117, 187, 329–30
Coffy (1973) 277
Cohan, George M. 119
Cohn, Harry 234
Cohn, Rachel
   Nick and Norah's Infinite Playlist 348
Coixet, Isabel 342, 346
Colbert, Claudette 162
Collet, Christopher 295, **296**

Collins, Jim 377 n.34
Collins, Joan 204
Collins, Suzanne 23
   The Hunger Games 348
Collison, Wilson
   Getting Gertie's Garter 80
   Up in Mabel's Room 80
Colonial Company 53
Colorado Territory (1949) 187
Color of Money, The (1986) 261
Color Purple (1985) 263, 268
Columbia Broadcasting System (CBS) 142, 309, 326
Columbia Pictures 112, 132, 133, 159, 179, 190, 234, 309, 314
Comanche Moon (TV, 2008) 327
Combs, Frederick **285**, 286
Come and Get It (1936) 146, 191
Come Back Charleston Blue (1972) 271, 273
comic book adaptations 308–19, 349–58, 363, 369
comic books 301, 311–12, 325
Compulsion (1959) 283
Confessions of a Nazi Spy (1939) 166
Confessions of a Teenage Drama Queen (2004) 348
Connecticut Yankee in King Arthur's Court, A (1921) 81
Connelly, Marc 117
   Beggar on Horseback 119
   Merton of the Movies 119
Connolly, Walter 128
Conroy, Pat
   The Prince of Tides 278
Constant Woman, The (1933) 116
Contempt (1963) 171
Cook, David A. 234
Cook, Donald 127
Cook, Elisha, Jr. 181
Cook, Fielder 23
Cook, Lawrence 276
Cool Hand Luke (1967) 244, 254, 255
Cooper, Gary 140, 222
Cooper, James Fenimore 6, 11, 13, 239
   The Last of the Mohicans 11, 26, 84–5, 140, 169
   Leatherstocking Tales 15, 84, 85

Coppola, Francis Ford 259–60, 309, 347
Corey, Jeff 247
Corley, Annie 333
Corman, Roger 21, 22, 293–4, 297
Corner in Wheat, A (1909) 61–2, 81
Corn Is Green, The (1945) 156
Cortez, Ricardo 131–2
Costello, Dolores 37
Cotton Comes to Harlem (1970) 269–71, **270**, 272, 276
Counsellor at Law (1933) 116, 191
Countdown (1968) 257
counterculture 235–59, 264
   and dominant culture 236–43, 256–64
counterprogramming 325, 335
Country Girl, The (1954) 117
Country Husband, The (TV, 1956) 202
Countryman, Edward 163
County Chairman, The (1935) 277
Court, Hazel 21
Courtot, Marguerite 88, **88**
Cover Concepts 352
Covered Wagon, The (1923) 101
Cover Girl (1944) 185
Cowan, Jerome 182
Cozzens, James Gould
   By Love Possessed 221
   The Just and the Unjust 202
   The Last Adam 126
Crabbe, Buster 123
Crafton, Donald 113, 152 n.34
Craig's Wife (1936) 79
Craig's Wife (TV, 1947) 201
Crain, William 273
Crane, Cheryl 227
Crane, Stephen 6, 11, 13, 14, 25
   "The Blue Hotel" 294
   The Red Badge of Courage 14, 15, 138, 139, 195–6, 369
   "The Upturned Face" 290
Cranston, Brian **2**, 2–3
Crawford, Broderick 191
Crawford, Joan 135, 157, 220, 286
Criss Cross (1949) 183
Cronenberg, David 10, 342
Crosby, Cathy Lee 309
Crosland, Alan 87

Crossfire (1947) 187, 188, 283
Crowley, Mart
  The Boys in the Band 284, 286
Crowther, Bosley 215
Croy, Homer
  They Had to See Paris 116
Cruise, Tom 308
Crumb, Robert 248
Cruz, Penelope 328
Cruze, James 101
Cry "Havoc" (1943) 165
Cry of the Owl, The (1978) 171
Cujo (1983) 372
cultural tourism 238
culture
  adaptation 369
  American 7, 14, 15, 26, 69, 72, 140, 169, 170, 171, 191, 217, 375
  archival 360, 367–8
  British 7
  convergence 351, 365, 366, 368, 369
  divergence 362–9, 374
  exhibitionist 366
  foreign 72, 169
  high 226, 227
  interactive 364
  literary 9, 195, 213, 225
  Native American 85
  official 364, 369
  popular 23–4, 231, 372
  slave 44
Cumberbatch, Benedict 356
Cummins, Peggy 209
Cunningham, John W.
  "The Tin Star" 292
Cunningham, Michael
  The Hours 344
Curious Case of Benjamin Button, The (2008) 2
Current TV 368
Curtis, Tony 273
Curwood, James Oliver 38
Cutthroat Island (1995) 320
Cyclops 356

DaCosta, Morton 119
Daddy-Long-Legs (1919) 83
Dafoe, Willem 352

Dailey, Dan 211
DailyMe.com 368
Daisy Kenyon (1947) 155
Daisy Miller (1974) 326
Daldry, Stephen 344
Damon, Matt 328
Dance of Life, The (1929) 135
Dane, Karl 87
Dangerous (1935) 156
Daniels, Lee 340
Dannay, Frederic 132
Dante Alighieri
  The Inferno 327
Darabont, Frank 373
Darby's Rangers (1958) 165
d'Arcy, Hugh Antoine
  "The Face on the Barroom Floor" 60
Daredevil 357
Daredevil (2003) 352
Dark Knight, The (2008) 312, 316, 354
Dark Knight Rises, The (2012) 354
Darktown Strutters (1975) 273
Dark Victory (1939) 156, 252
Darley, Gabrielle 100, 101
Darnell, Linda 209, **210**
Darwell, Jane 160
Daudet, Alphonse 37
Davenport, Dorothy 100
David and Bathsheba (1951) 213
David and Lisa (1962) 280
David Copperfield (1935) 11, 23, 135, 137
David Harum (1934) 125–6, **126**, 127, 148
Davies, Terence 13
Da Vinci Code, The (2006) 369
Davis, Bette 111, 122, 145, 156, 159
Davis, Donald
  The Good Earth 147
Davis, Jack 258
Davis, Ossie 269, 271
Davis, Owen 116, 232
  The Good Earth 147
  Icebound 79, 116, 201
  Jezebel 148, 192
  Lazybones 80, 91
  The Nervous Wreck 80
  Whoopee! 80

Davis, Richard Harding 38
Davison, Bruce 246
Dawes, Rachel 316
Day at the Races, A (1937) 119
Day in the Country, A (1936) 172
Day-Lewis, Daniel 85, **325**
Days of Heaven (1978) 261
Days of Wine and Roses (TV, 1958) 202
Day the Earth Stood Still, The (1951) 301
DC Comics 315, 318, 353, 363
DC Universe 351, 369
Dead End (1937) 148, 192
Deadline at Dawn (1946) 117, 177, 178, 179, 213
Dead Man's Walk (TV, 1996) 327
Dead of Night (1945) 199
Deadpool (2017) 358, 359
Deadpool 2 (2018) 358
Deakins, Roger 330
Dean, Jack 71
Dean, James 243
Death Becomes Her (1992) 332
Deaver, Jeffery 370, 372
de Berg, Jean
  The Image 298
DeBona, Guerric 11
Deception (1946) 156
Decherney, Peter 68 n.29, 68 n.30, 68 n.32
Dee, Frances 140
Deerslayer, The (1943) 173
Defiant Ones, The (1958) 273
Defoe, Daniel
  Robinson Crusoe 303
De Havilland Law 156
de Havilland, Olivia 113, 148, 156–7, 159, 192, 324
de la Cruz, Juan 99
DeLillo, Don 6, 22, 372
  Cosmopolis 292, 342
  Underworld 328
Del Ruth, Roy 182
Dementia 13 (1963) 259
DeMille, Cecil B. 31, 70, 71, 73, 74, 81, 203, 217
deMille, William 74, 93

Demme, Jonathan 23, 361
demographics 319–20
De Niro, Robert 332
Dent, Harvey 316
De Palma, Brian 260–1, 297, 370
Departed, The (2006) 261, 339, 340
Descendants, The (2011) 339
Destination Moon (1950) 302, 303
DeSylva, B.G.
  Good News 80
detective films 127–35, 181–3
Detective Story (1951) 186
Deus Ex (video game, 2000) 307–8
Devil in Miss Jones, The (1973) 297
Devil Is a Woman, The (1935) 140
Devil Wears Prada, The (2006) 220
DeVito, Danny 312
Devotion (1946) 10
Dial M for Murder (1953) 12
dialogue, literary 15–16, 176, 177
Diana of the Crossways (1922) 25
Diary of a Mad Black Woman (2005) 361
Diary of a Mad Housewife (1970) 277
Diary of a Wimpy Kid (2010) 348
Dick, Philip K. 306–8
  "Do Androids Dream of Electric Sheep?" 306
  The Man in the High Castle 341
  A Scanner Darkly 308
  "We Can Remember It for You Wholesale" 308
Dickens, Charles 6, 7, 9, 19, 22, 24, 25, 37–8, 39, 139, 239
  A Christmas Carol 38, 213, 297
  David Copperfield 196
  Little Dorrit 14
  Nicholas Nickleby 42
  Oliver Twist 7
Dickinson, Emily 9, 11
Dickson, William Kennedy Laurie 31, 32
Dick Tracy (1990) 311–12, 313
Didion, Joan 278, 280
Dieterle, William 24
Dietrich, Marlene 157
Dillon, Matt 347
Dim Sum (1985) 279

Dinner at Eight (1933) 119, 121, 135, 146
Dinner at Eight (television, 1948) 201
Dionysus in '69 (1970) 260
Directors Guild of America (DGA) 203
Dirks, Rudolph 39, 40
Dirty Hands (1975) 170
disability cinema 269, 280–2
disaster cycle 262
disavowal 34, 44, 177, 203, 209, 237
Dishonored Lady (1947) 186
Disney Corporation 292, 309, 365
Disney, Walt 199, 263
Displaced Person, The (1977) 294
display 32, 33, 34, 36, 41, 42, 45, 50, 52, 54, 56, 57, 58, 62, 65, 66, 67 n.12, 72, 73, 84, 135, 138, 148, 158, 160, 167, 183, 216, 256, 258, 268, 280, 285, 286, 287, 314. *See also* monstration
Divergent (2011) 348
Dix, Richard 102, 104
Dixon, Ivan 276
Dixon, Thomas F., Jr.
  The Clansman 69–70, 73
  The Leopard's Spots 69–70
  The Traitor 70
Dmytryk, Edward 283
Doctor Bull (1933) 126, 127
Doctor Doolittle (1967) 231, 232, 234
Doctorow, E.L.
  Billy Bathgate 3
  The Book of Daniel 3
  Ragtime 3
  "Wakefield" 3, 4
  Welcome to Hard Times 3
documentaries 165, 195, 279
Dodd, Claire 132
Dodsworth (1936) 116, 127, 191
Dogville (2003) 344
Doherty, Thomas 204
Dolores Claiborne (1995) 373
Donald Duck 309
Donnelly, Dorothy
  Poppy 83
Donner, Richard 310
Donovan, Martin 323
Donovan Affair, The (1929) 116

Don Q, Son of Zorro (1925) 107
Don't Change Your Husband (1919) 81
Don't Ever Open That Door (1952) 178
Dorian Gray (1970) 297
Dorothy and the Scarecrow in Oz (1910) 55
Dos Passos, John 22, 170
  U.S.A. 140
Dostoevsky, Fyodor 139
  Notes from Underground 138
Do the Right Thing (1989) 319
double consciousness 285, 287, 357–8
Double Indemnity (1944) 156, 171, 175, 176, 183
Douglas, Jerry
  Score 298
Douglas, Kirk 175, 186
Douglas, Lloyd C.
  Magnificent Obsession 221
Douglas, Melvyn 326
Dourif, Brad 245
Dove, Billie 103
Dowd, Maureen 337 n.24
Downey, Robert, Jr. **356**, 357
Downey, Robert [Sr.] 276
Downfall (2004) 362
Down to Earth (1932) 126
Downton Abbey (TV, 2010–15) 24
Doyle, Sir Arthur Conan 6, 53–4
Dracula 132, 274
Dracula's Daughter (1936) 283
Dragnet (TV, 1951–9) 314
Dragonwyck (1946) 193
Drake, William Absalom
  Grand Hotel 121
Dranet, Leontine 55
Dr. Black, Mr. Hyde (1975) 273
Dreiser, Theodore
  An American Tragedy 13, 140
Dream Girl (1948) 116
Dream of a Rarebit Fiend, The (1906) 48–50, **50**
Dressed to Kill (1980) 261
Dressler, Marie 59–60
Drew, Nancy 128, 132, 173
Dreyfuss, Richard **262**
Dr. Gillespie's Criminal Case (1943) 185

Dr. Gillespie's New Assistant (1942) 185
Driving Miss Daisy (1989) 319
Dr. Jekyll and Mr. Hyde (1932) 120
Dr. Jekyll and Mr. Hyde (1941) 204
Dro itsureb gantiadisas (1965) 178
Dr. Strangelove, or How I Learned to Stop Worrying and Love the Bomb (1964) 303
Drums along the Mohawk (1939) 155, 162–3
Dryden, John 9
Du Bois, W.E.B. 287
Du Crow, Tote 107
Duel (1971) 261
Duel in the Sun (1946) 190
Duhamel, Marcel 175
Dullea, Keir 282, **283**
Dumas, Alexandre *fils*
   La dame aux camélias 298
Duncan, Lois
   I Know What You Did Last Summer 348
Dunne, John Gregory 278
Dunne, Philip 85, 221
Dunst, Kirsten 352, **353**
Duvall, Robert 18, **328**
Dwan, Allan 277
Dylan, Bob 235, 341

Ealing Studios 199
Earth vs. the Flying Saucers (1956) 302
Earth, Wind & Fire 271
Eason, B. Reeves 84
Eastmancolor 205, 206, 349
Eastwood, Clint 310, 327, 331–5, **334**
Easy Rider (1969) 234–5, 256
Eat a Bowl of Tea (1989) 279
Ebert, Roger 282
Éclair Company 52
Edelstein, David 346
Edgar Allen Poe (1909) 10, 64
Edgar Allen Poe's The Haunted Palace (1963) 21
Edge of Darkness (1943) 165
Edison Studios 38, 39, 40, 87
Edmonds, Walter D.
   Drums along the Mohawk 162, 163

Egg and I, The (1947) 155
Eidson, Thomas
   The Last Ride 329
Eisenstein, Sergei M. 24, 122, 140
Eldridge, Judith A. 68 n.21
Eleanor of Aquitaine 278
Electric Company, The (TV, 1971–7) 249
Electronic Labyrinth THX 1138 4EB (1967) 260
Elegy (2008) 342, 346
Elektra (2005) 352
Eliot, George 24
   Middlemarch 14
Eliot, T.S. 23
Ella Enchanted (2004) 348
Ellery Queen, Master Detective (1940) 133
Elliott, Allison 323
Ellison, Ralph 14
Eloise (TV, 1956) 202
Emerson, Ralph Waldo 11, 170
Emma (1996) 320
Emma (TV, 1996) 320
Emmanuelle (1974) 213
Emperor Jones, The (1933) 116
Empire Strikes Back, The (1980) 267
Enemy Below, The (1957) 165
Epstein, Rob 10
Erickson, Leif 224
Erlanger, A.L. 51
Erskine, Albert 328
Escapade (1957) 178
Establishment, the 235, 240, 252
E.T. The Extra-Terrestrial (1982) 263, 267
Euripides
   The Bacchae 260
Europeans, The (1979) 14
Evans, Chris **356**, 357
Evans, Robert 220, 259
Everett, John 144
Exile, The (1931) 143
Exorcist, The (1973) 250, 255, 262, 273, 375
exoticism 69–108
   of African Americans 94–5, 144–5
   of American literature 169

and defamiliarization 91
of disabled characters 280
and empathy 87
vs. familiarity 78
of heroes 134
home-grown 95
vs. homeliness 76
of monsters 100
of settings 134, 155, 174
of subcultures 94
exploitation cinema 293
expressionism 181–6
Eyman, Scott 108 n.4, 151 n.7, 228 n.1

Fable of the Brash Drummer and the Nectarine, The (1914) 38
Fable of the Girl Who Took Notes and Got Wise and Then Fell Down, The (1917) 38
Facebook 359, 360, 366, 367
Face in the Crowd, A (1957) 291
Face on the Barroom Floor, The (1908) 38
Face on the Barroom Floor, The (1914) **59**, 59–60
Fahrenheit 451 (1966) 170, 304–5, 306
Fail-Safe (1964) 303
Fair and Warmer (1919) 80
Fairbanks, Douglas [Sr.] 105–7, **107**
Falcone, Carmen 350
Fall Guy (1947) 177
Falling Leaves (1912) 59
Family Plot (1976) 12
Famous Players–Lasky 79, 101. See also Paramount Pictures
Famous Studios 309
Fantasia (1940) 199
Fantastic Four 352, 357
Fantastic Four (2005) 352
Fantastic Four (2015) 352
Farewell to Arms, A (1932) 19, 120, 155
A Farewell to Arms (1957) 19, 140, 221
Fargo (1996) 329
Farrell, Charles 91, 92
Farrell, Glenda 128

Farrell, Henry
Such a Gorgeous Kid Like Me 170
Farrell, James T. 181
Farrow, Mia 250
Fast, Howard
Spartacus 268
Fast and Loose (1930) 80
Fat City (1972) 203
Father Knows Best (TV, 1954–60) 217
Faulkner, William 6, 14, 25, 36, 139, 200, 221, 238, 328
Absalom, Absalom! 23, 273
As I Lay Dying 4–5
"Barn Burning" 294, 295
Go Down, Moses 273
The Hamlet 225
"Old Man" 202
Pylon 221
"Red Leaves" 290
"A Rose for Emily" 294
Sanctuary 225
The Sound and the Fury 6, 14, 225, 273
"Tomorrow" 202
Fault in Our Stars, The (2014) 348
Fearing, Kenneth
The Big Clock 175
Fear in the Night (1947) 177
Feidelson, Charles 15
Feiffer, Jules
Little Murders 249, 254
Feinberg, Scott 375
Felix the Cat 309
Fellowes, Rockliffe 96, **96**
feminism 236, 277–8
Fenton, Frank 176
Ferber, Edna 146, 149, 221
Cimarron 146
Come and Get It 146, 191
Dinner at Eight 119, 135, 146
Giant 146, 221
Ice Palace 146
The Royal Family 119, 146, 202
Saratoga Trunk 146
Show Boat 80, 118
So Big 111, 146
Stage Door 119, 139, 146, 157
Ferguson, Helen 94

Ferris Bueller's Day Off (1986) 347
fetishism 196, 212, 213, 215, 219, 227, 228, 348
Fey, Tina 10
fidelity 16–19, 55–6, 64, 81, 83, 84, 90, 112, 119, 123, 164, 178, 180, 188, 194, 210, 217, 226, 227, 238, 245, 257, 294, 296, 343, 349–51
Field, Betty 216
Field, Rachel
  All This and Heaven Too 145
Field, Salisbury
  Twin Beds 79
Field, Syd 121
Fielding, Helen 320
Fields, Herbert
  Hit the Deck 80
Fields, Robert 250–1
Fifty Shades Darker (2015) 298
Fifty Shades Freed (2018) 298
Fifty Shades of Grey (2015) 298
Film Johnny, A (1914) 61
film noir 17, 171–2, 174–81, 187, 195, 211, 212, 307
film-school generation 259–64
Finian's Rainbow (1968) 259
Finney, Albert 324
Finney, Jack
  Invasion of the Body Snatchers 304
First Men in the Moon, The (1964) 302
First World War 102, 140, 144, 161, 165, 166, 167, 168, 187
Fischer, Margarita 94
Fisher, Bud 39, 40
Fisher, Terence 324
Fisher King, The (1991) 332
Fistful of Dollars, A (1964) 332
Fitch, Clyde 39
Fitzgerald, F. Scott 6, 7, 14, 247
  The Beautiful and Damned 83
  "Bernice Bobs Her Hair" 294, 295
  "A Diamond as Big as the Ritz" 290
  The Great Gatsby 6, 8, 13, 79, 116, 202, 247, 273
  The Last Tycoon 201, 202
  Tender Is the Night 225, 247
  "Winter Dreams" 202

Five Graves to Cairo (1943) 179
Five Thirty Eight 368
Flame and the Flesh, The (1954) 204
Flash Gordon Conquers the Universe (1940) 301
Flaubert, Gustave
  Madame Bovary 122, 139
Fleischer Studios 309
Fleisher, Michael L. 336 n.9
Fleming, Ian
  Casino Royale 317
Fleming, Victor 93, 105, 158, 204, 274
Fletcher, Louise 244
Flight to Mars (1951) 302
Florey, Robert 20
Flying Down to Rio (1933) 118
Flynn, Emmett J. 81
Flynn, Errol 148, 156
Flynn, Gillian
  Gone Girl 369
Follow the Fleet (1936) 118
Fonda, Henry 160, 162
Fonda, Jane 250, **252**
Fonda, Peter 235, 237
Fontaine, Joan 136, 286
Fontanne, Lynn 167
Fool's Highway (1924) 98
Footlight Parade (1933) 118
For a Few Dollars More (1965) 332
Forbidden Planet (1956) 302, 304
For Colored Girls (2010) 361
Ford, Glenn 310
Ford, Harrison 307
Fordin, Hugh 265 n.17
Ford, John 89, 101, 127, 144, 159, 160, 162, 165, 203
Foreign Correspondent (1940) 12
Forever Amber (1947) 209–11, **210**, 213, 227
Forman, Milos 241, 244
Forman, Tom 75
Forrest Gump (1994) 339
Forster, E.M. 13
For the Love of Gold (1908) 38
Forty Naughty Girls (1937) 131
42nd Street (1933) 118, 173
For Whom the Bell Tolls (1943) 155
For Whom the Bell Tolls (TV, 1959) 202

400 Blows, The (1959) 239
Four Sons (1928) 89–91, **89**, 165
Four Sons (1940) 165, 174
Fowler, Karen Joy
    The Jane Austen Book Club 2
Fox, The (1967) 283
Foxe, Earle 90
Fox Film Corporation 81, 91, 101, 112. *See also* Twentieth Century Fox
Fox, Mardou 241
Foxx, Redd 270
Foxy Brown (1974) 277
franchises 19–23, 53–9, 80, 120–34, 145, 150, 246, 270, 306, 308–19, 320, 325, 347–58, 363, 368, 369, 370, 372
Franco, James 4–6, **5**, 23, 352
Frank, Anne 341
Frankau, Gilbert
    Christopher Strong 135
Frankenstein 132
Frankenstein (1931) 116
Frank, Nino 171, 175, 197 n.16
Freaks (1932) 268
Freaky Friday (2003) 348
Fredericks, Arnold. *See* Kummer, Frederick Arnold
Freeman, Jerrold 274
Freeman, Mary E. Wilkins
    "The Revolt of Mother" 294
Frei, Hans W. 197 n.7
French Connection, The (1971) 245
French Lieutenant's Woman, The (1981) 332
French Line, The (1953) 208
Frenzy (1972) 12
Frey, Leonard 286
Frick, John W. 109 n.16
Friedkin, William 245, 250, 284, 287
Friedlander, Louis 20
Friedman, Jeffrey 10
Friedman, Thomas 360
Friml, Rudolf
    The Vagabond King 80
Fritz the Cat (1972) 248–9, 255, 256
From the Earth to the Moon (1958) 302

From the Terrace (1960) 221, 224, **226**, 227, 255
Front Page, The (1931) 186
Front Page, The (1974) 186
Fu Manchu 122
Funny Face (1957) 80
Funny Girl (1968) 278
Fury, Nick 357
Fuzz (1972) 246

Gable, Clark 112, 135, 138
Gaiman, Neil 22
    Stardust 348
Gaines, Ernest J.
    "The Sky Is Gray" 294, 295, 296
Gainsborough Studios 199
Gaitskill, Mary
    "Secretary" 298
Gale, Zona
    Miss Lulu Bett 79, 93
Gallimard 175
Gambler, the Nun, and the Radio, The (TV, 1960) 202
Game of Thrones (TV, 2011–19) 348, 369
Gang's All Here, The (1943) 173
Gangs of New York (2002) 261
gangster films 33, 146, 175, 183, 185, 291, 301, 323
Garbo, Greta 115, **121**, 122, 135, 145, 157, 206
Garcia, Al 75
Gardenia, Vincent 249
Garden of Allah, The (1936) 136
Garden of Eden, The (1928) 80
Gardner, Ava 207, **208**
Gardner, Erle Stanley 131, 305
    The Case of the Velvet Claws 127
Garfield, Andrew 352, **355**
Garfield, John 190
Garland, Judy 150
Garner, James 258
Garner, Jennifer 3
Garnett, Tay 204
Garrett, Oliver H.P. 190
Garson, Greer 174
Gates, Eleanor
    Poor Little Rich Girl 92

Gaudreault, André 33
gay cinema 283–7, 288
Gay Divorcee, The (1934) 118
Gaynor, Janet 91, 92–3
Gazzo, Michael V.
    A Hatful of Rain 208
Geller, Robert 294, 295–6
General Died at Dawn, The (1936) 117
Genette, Gérard 9, 17
genres 17, 23, 33–4, 112, 146, 258, 262, 276, 290, 301, 324, 327, 330, 331, 349, 370, 372, 373.
    See also specific genres
    and anti-genres 257
Gentleman's Agreement (1947) 187, 188
Gentry, Curt
    Helter Skelter 240
George, Peter
    Red Alert 303
George Washington Slept Here (1942) 119
Gershwin, George
    Funny Face 80
    Porgy and Bess 80
Gershwin, Ira
    Funny Face 80
    Porgy and Bess 80
Get Christie Love! (1974) 277
Getting Gertie's Garter (1927) 80
Getting Straight (1970) 246–7, **248**, 249, 255, 256
Ghost Goes West, The (1935) 117
Ghost in the Shell (manga and film franchise, 1989–2015) 307
Ghost Rider (2007) 352
ghost stories 324
Ghost Writer, The (TV, 1984) 344
Giant (1956) 146, 221
Gibson, Hoot 135
Gibson, William
    The Miracle Worker 202
Gideon of Scotland Yard (1958) 203
Gifford, Denis 68
Gigli (2003) 320
Gilbert, John 115
Girl from Chicago, The (1932) 144

Gish, Dorothy 171
Gish, Lillian 61, 85, 86, **86**, 87, 115, 171
Give My Regards to Broadway (musical) 192
Glasgow, Ellen 6
Glaspell, Susan
    Alison's House 202
Glass Key, The (1935) 187
Glass Key, The (1942) 187
Glass, Sydney A. 261
Gleason, James 127
Gleason, Ralph J. 264 n.5
Glitter (2001) 320
Glyn, Eleanor
    It 93
Godard, Jean-Luc 171
Goddard, Mark 223, **223**
Godfather, The (1972) 251, 259–60, **260**, 262, 263, 278
Godfather: Part II, The (1974) 278
Gods and Monsters (1998) 339
Godzilla (1956) 303
Goetz, Augustus
    The Heiress 192
Goetz, Ruth
    The Heiress 192
Goldberg, Whoopi 361
Gold Diggers, The (1923) 80, 118
Gold Diggers of Broadway (1929) 80
Gold Diggers of 1933 (1933) 80, 118
Gold Diggers of 1935 (1935) 80, 118
Gold Diggers of 1937 (1936) 80, 118
Gold Diggers in Paris (1938) 118, 173
Golden Age of Porn 297, 298, 314
Golden Age of Television 201–3
Golden Bowl, The (2000) 14, 322
Golden Boy (1939) 117, 148
Golden Honeymoon, The (1980) 294
Golden Raspberry Awards 313
Goldman, James
    The Lion in Winter 278
Goldman, William 234, 373
Goldstein, Lawrence 26
Goldwyn, Samuel 79, 80, 112, 191, 234
Gomery, Douglas 235
Gone Girl (2014) 369

Gone with the Wind (1939) 116, 136, 149, **150**, 155, 156, 158, 190, 209, 327, 349, 375
Good, the Bad, and the Ugly, The (1966) 332
Goodbye, Columbus (1969) 342
Goodbye Girl, The (1977) 232
Goodbye, Mr. Chips (1939) 165, 173, 174
Good Earth, The (1937) 11, 147, **147**, 148, 149
Goodfellas (1990) 261
Goodis, David
   Down There 170, 175
Goodman, Daniel Carson 39
Good News (1930) 80
Good News (1947) 80
Goodwin, Archie 127
Google 360, 368
Gorbman, Claudia 256
Gordon, Lt. James 350
Gordon, Michael 211
Gorman, Cliff 284, **285**
Gorshin, Frank 309
Gosling, Ryan 307
Go Tell It on the Mountain (TV, 1985) 23, 274
Gould, Bobbie 55
Gould, Elliott 247, **248**, 249, 258
Gowland, Gibson 81, **82**
Goyer, David 350, 352
Graduate, The (1967) 231, 235, 243, 244, 245, 253, 254, 255, 319, 347
Graham, Sheilah 247
Grammercy Pictures 313
Grams, Martin, Jr. 152 n.31
Grand Hotel (1932) 117, 120–1, **121**, 204
Grand Isle (1991) 369
Grandon, Francis J. 62
Grant, Catherine 186
Grant, Richard E. **323**
Granville, Bonita 128
Grapes of Wrath, The (1940) 23, 27, 127, 144, 155, 158, 159, 160, 161
Grapewin, Charley 159, **160**
graphic novels 325

Grau, Albin 172
Grauman, Walter 221–2
Graves, Taylor 94
Gray, Mona 95
Grayson, Dick 317, 318
Gray, Virginia 95
Greatest Man in the World, The (1980) 294
Greatest Question, The (1919) 83
Greatest Story Ever Told, The (1965) 310
Great Gatsby, The (1926) 79
Great Gatsby, The (1949) 116
Great Gatsby, The (TV, 1958) 202
Great Gatsby, The (1974) 11, 13
Great Lie, The (1941) 156
Great Train Robbery, The 33, 48
Greed (1924) 12, 81–3, **82**, 140
Greenberg, Joanne. *See* Green, Hannah
Green Dolphin Street (1947) 204
Greene, Reuben **285**
Green Goblin 352
Green, Hannah
   I Never Promised You a Rose Garden 280
Green, Jesse 264 n.4
Green, John
   The Fault in Our Stars 348
Green Lantern 353
Greenlee, Ben
   The Spook Who Sat by the Door 276
Green Mile, The (1999) 373, 374
Green, Paul
   In Abraham's Bosom 79
Green Room, The (1978) 170
Greenstreet, Sydney 181
Greer, Jane 175
Greetings (1968) 260
Gresham, William Lindsay
   Nightmare Alley 158, 175
Grey, Zane 101, 304
Grier, Pam 273
Griffin, Susan M. 27
Griffith, D.W. 10, 37, 61–6, 69, 70, 105
Grisham, John 370
Grissom, Candace Ursula 27

INDEX

Griswold, Rufus 10, 11
Groening, Matt 373
Grossman, Julie 43–4
Guadalcanal Diary (1943) 166
Guerrero, Ed 299 n.6
Guess Who's Coming to Dinner (1967) 231
Guest, Judith
   Ordinary People 288
Guilty, The (1947) 177
Gunga Din (1939) 148
Gung Ho (1943) 166
Gunning, Tom 33, 34, 36
Gunn, Moses 271
Gunsmoke (TV, 1952–61) 203
Guthmann, Edward 321
Guthrie, Arlo 242, 255
Guthrie, Woody 235
Guy-Blaché, Alice 59
Guys and Dolls (1955) 119

Hackathorne, George 85
Hackford, Taylor 373
Hackman, Gene 254, 310–11, 312
Hagen, Kate 368
Hahn, Virginia K. Bridger Wachsman 101
Haines, Randa 281
Hair (1979) 241, 242, 244, 250, 254
Hairy Ape, The (1944) 213
Hale, Edward Everett
   "The Man without a Country" 83
Hale, William
   The Greatest Question 83
Half-Naked Truth, The (1932) 135
Hallelujah, I'm a Bum (1933) 118
Hall, Franklin 98
Hall, James 90
Hamill, Pete 332
Hamilton, Guy 310
Hammerstein, Oscar II 118–19
   Carousel 119
   Flower Drum Song 119
   The King and I 119
   Oklahoma 119
   Show Boat 80
   The Sound of Music 119
   South Pacific 119

Hammett, Dashiell 291
   The Glass Key 187, 329
   The Maltese Falcon 156, 179, 181, 182, 186
   Red Harvest 329
   The Thin Man 127, 129–31, 179
Hammond, C. Norman 99
Handler, Daniel. *See* Snicket, Lemony
Hand, Richard 153 n.52
Hand That Rocks the Cradle, The 100
Hanks, Tom 284
Hannibal Rising (2007) 316
Hanson, Lars 85, 86, 87, 115
Harbach, Otto
   No, No, Nanette 80
   Up in Mabel's Room 80
Harbaugh, Carl 96
Harburg, E.Y.
   Finian's Rainbow 259
Hardcore (1979) 261
Hardy, Andy 122
Hardy, Thomas 15, 25
   Jude the Obscure 288
Harlem Renaissance 23
Harlow, Jean 135
Harold and the Purple Crayon (iBook, 2011) 364
Harolde, Ralf 183
Harper and Brothers 51
Harris, Mark 231, 232, 375
Harris, Mike 375 n.1
Harris, Mildred 57, 58
Harrison, Joan 277
Harryhausen, Ray 302
Harte, Bret 39, 40, 78, 79
   "Salomy Jane's Kiss" 76, 77
Hart, Lorenz 118
   Pal Joey 190
Hart, Moss
   George Washington Slept Here 119
   I'd Rather Be Right 119
   The Man Who Came to Dinner 119
   Merrily We Roll Along 119
   Once in a Lifetime 119
   You Can't Take It with You 119, 202
Harvey (1950) 190
Harvey, Anthony 278

Harvey, Laurence 226
Hasenfratz, Bob 7, 8, 27, 274
Haskell, Molly 299 n.7
Haskin, Byron 302
Hassler-Forest, Dan 311
Hatful of Rain, A (1957) 204
Hathaway, Henry 330
Haunted Palace, The (1963) 293
Haunting, The (1963) 280
Hawks, Howard 19, 36, 183, 186, 191, 258
Hawthorne, Nathaniel 13, 14, 25, 170, 237, 294
  "The Birthmark" 291
  House of the Seven Gables, The 4, 201, 203
  "My Kinsman, Major Molineux" 4, 290
  "Rappaccini's Daughter" 4, 24, 294, 295, 296
  Scarlet Letter, The 4, 14, 15, 18–19, 85, 139, 169, 202, 238, 273, 292
  "Wakefield" 3–4
  "Young Goodman Brown" 4, 291
Hayakawa, Sessue 71, **72**
Haydn, Richard 210
Hayes, Helen 140
Hayes, Isaac 272
Hayes, John Michael 215
Haynie, Jim 335
Hays Office 140, 141, 204, 216–17, 277
Hays, Will H. 141
Hayward, Susan 211, 226
Hayworth, Rita 185
Health (1980) 293
Hearst, Patricia 261
Heartbreak Kid, The (1972) 232
Heartburn (1986) 332
Heat and Dust (1983) 13
Heatherton, Joey 227
Heath, Joseph 264
Heaven Can Wait (1943) 12
Heaven Knows, Mr. Allison (1957) 203
Heaven's Gate (1980) 320
Hecht, Ben
  The Front Page 186
Heckerling, Amy 320

Heggen, Thomas
  Mister Roberts 190
Heinlein, Robert B. 304
  Destination Moon 302
Heiress, The (1949) 15–16, 157, 191–2, 324
Heisler, Stuart 187
Heisler, Yoni 368
Heller, Joseph
  Catch-22 165, 244, 245
Hellinger, Mark 185
Hellman, Lillian
  The Children's Hour 191
  The Little Foxes 192
  These Three 277–8
  Watch on the Rhine 165
Hello, Dolly! (1968) 278
Hemingway, Ernest 6, 8, 14, 19, 22, 155, 158, 170, 200, 203–4, 221
  A Farewell to Arms 14, 140, 221, 239, 273
  For Whom the Bell Tolls 169, 202
  "The Gambler, the Nun, and the Radio" 202
  "Hills Like White Elephants" 290, 294
  "The Killers" 16
  The Old Man and the Sea 203
  "Soldier's Home" 294, 295, 296
  "The Snows of Kilimanjaro" 202, 203, 207
  The Sun Also Rises 203
  To Have and Have Not 36
Hemingway and Gellhorn (2012) 10
Hemmings, Kaui Hart
  The Descendants 339–40
Hemsworth, Chris 356, **356**
Henderson, Lucius 76
Henderson, Ray
  Good News 80
Henry, Buck 244
Henry, O. 39, 40, 52, 199–201
  "The Clarion Call" 199
  "The Cop and the Anthem" 199
  "The Gift of the Magi" 199
  "The Last Leaf" 59, 199
  "The Ransom of Red Chief" 199

"A Retrieved Reformation" 83
"Transients in Arcadia" 74–5
Henry and June (1990) 10, 234
Henry II 278
Henry V (1944) 174
Hepburn, Katharine 136, 157, 278, 280
Herbert, Henry 25
Herbert, Holmes 83
heritage adaptations 13, 319–25
Herman, Jerry 278
Heroes for Hope Starring the X-Men (comic book) 373
Hersholt, Jean 81, **82**
Hester Street (1975) 279
heteroglossia 138, 142, 145, 185
Heyward, Dorothy
  Porgy (play) 80
Heyward, DuBose
  Porgy (novel) 80
  Porgy (play) 80
Hiawatha: The Indian Passion Play (1913) 53
Hickok, Wild Bill 76
Hidden Fortress, The (1958) 260
Hiddleston, Tom 356
Higher and Higher (1943) 118
Highfield, Ashley 365
High Noon (1952) 291
High Sierra (1941) 181, 187
Highsmith, Patricia
  The Cry of the Owl 171
  Strangers on a Train 12
  The Talented Mr. Ripley 175
Higson, Andrew 321
Hill, George Roy 242
Hill, Georg M. 53
Hiller, Arthur 252
Himes, Chester 270, 271, 273
  Cotton Comes to Harlem 269
  If He Hollers Let Him Go 273
  A Rage in Harlem 273
  The Real Cool Killers 175
Hi, Mom! (1970) 260
Hingle, Pat 218
Hinnant, Skip 249
Hinton, S.E. 347, 348
  The Outsiders 347
  Rumble Fish 347

Tex 347
That Was Then, This Is Now 347
Hirsch, E.D. 360
Hirsch, Judd 288
His Girl Friday (1940) 186
His Majesty the American (1920) 105–6
His Majesty, the Scarecrow of Oz (1914) 58–9
Hitchcock, Alfred 12, 137, 158, 261, 263, 357, 370
Hitchens, Dolores 171
Hit the Deck (1930) 80
Hit the Deck (1955) 80
Hit Man (1972) 273
Hoffe, Monckton 91
Hoffenberg, Mason
  Candy 244
Hoffman, Dustin 243, 310
Hofstadter, Richard 10
Hogan, David 313
Hold Back the Dawn (1941) 156
Holiday (1938) 157
Holiday Inn (1942) 116
Holland, Agnieszka 321
Hollow Boy, The (1990) 294
Hollywood Canteen (1944) 166
Hollywood Revue of 1929 (1929) 118
Holm, Eleanor 124
Holmes, Oliver Wendell 51
Holmes, Phillips 140
Holmes, Sherlock 22, 173, 317
Holocaust 263
Holt, Jack 102
Home Box Office (HBO) 180, 201
Home of the Brave (1949) 187, 188
Homer
  The Odyssey 329
Homesteader, The (1919) 143
homophobia 188, 283
Hoodlum, The (1919) 92
Hook (1991) 263
Hooker, Brian
  The Vagabond King 80
Hooker, Richard
  M*A*S*H 257
Hooligan, Happy 40, 53
Hooper, Tobe 370

Hoover, J. Edgar 276
Hopkins, Anthony 343, 344, **345**
Hopley, George. *See also* Woolrich, Cornell
   Fright 177
   Night Has a Thousand Eyes 177
Hopper, Dennis 235, 237
Hopwood, Avery
   The Bat 80
   The Best People 80
   Fair and Warmer 80
   The Garden of Eden 80
   Getting Gertie's Garter 80
   The Gold Diggers 80
   Ladies' Night 80
Horak, Jan-Christopher 108 n.11
Horne, Philip 336 n.15
horror films 37, 250, 326, 330, 370, 371, 372, 373
Horse Soldiers, The (1959) 203
Hours, The (2002) 344
House behind the Cedars, The (1927) 143
House of Mirth, The (2000) 13, 324
House of Strangers (1949) 213
House of the Seven Gables, The (1940) 173
House of the Seven Gables, The (TV, 1949) 201
House of Usher (1960) 21, 293
House on 92nd Street, The (1945) 166
House without a Key, The (1926) 127, 128
Howard, George Bronson 39
Howard, Ron 329
Howards End (1992) 13, 339
Howard, Sidney 16, 116, 140
   They Knew What They Wanted 79, 116
Howe, James Wong 326
Howells, William Dean 6
How Green Was My Valley (1941) 155
Howl (2010) 10
How to Marry a Millionaire (1953) 219, 220
Hucksters, The (1947) 155
Hud (1963) 326
Hudson Hawk (1991) 320

Hudson, Rock 221
Hughes, Hatcher
   Hell-Bent fer Heaven 79
Hughes, Howard 157, 208, 223
Hughes, John 347
Hugo (2011) 261
Hulk, the 352, 356, 357
Hulk (2003) 311–12, 352
Hulu 201
Human Comedy, The (1943) 174, 253
Human Stain, The (2003) 342–6, **345**
Humbling, The (2016) 342
Humoresque (1946) 117
Hunchback of Notre Dame, The (1939) 24, 148
Hunger Games, The (2012) 348, 369
Hunter, Evan
   The Blackboard Jungle 241, 246
   Last Summer 240, 246
Hunter, Jeffrey 218
Hunter, Kim 194
Hunter, Tim 347
Hurston, Zora Neale 23
   "The Bone of Contention" 290
Hurt, William 281, **281**, 282, 283, 284
Hussey, Ruth 164
Huston, John 181, 182, 195, 203, 304, 311
Huston, Walter 181
Hutcheon, Linda 35, 186, 287–8, 362
Hutton, Timothy 288, **289**
Huxley, Aldous 138
   Brave New World 306
Huyck, Willard 260
Hyer, Martha 220

I Am a Fugitive from a Chain Gang (1932) 187
I Am Legend (2007) 330
I Can Get It for You Wholesale (1951) 211–13
Icebound (1924) 79
Icebound (TV, 1951) 202
Ice Palace (1960) 146
I Confess (1952) 12
identification as construction 288
identifying, *vs.* identifying with 285, 287

identity formation 287–8
identity perception 287
identity politics 260, 268, 269, 283, 287
I Died a Thousand Times (1955) 187
Idiot's Delight (1939) 117, 165
If He Hollers Let Him Go (1968) 273
I Know What You Did Last Summer (1997) 348
I Know Why the Caged Bird Sings (1979) 23
I'll Cry Tomorrow (1955) 213
Illustrated Man, The (1969) 305, **305**
illustration 70
I Love Lucy (TV, 1951–7) 203
I'm a Fool (1977) 294
Image, The (1975) 298
Images (1972) 257
I Married an Angel (1942) 118
Imitation Game, The (2014) 339, 340
Imitation of Life (1934) 209
Imitation of Life (1959) 205, 227
In a Lonely Place (1950) 183
Inconvenient Truth, An (2006) 62
Incredible Hulk, The (TV, 1982–3) 352
Independent Motion Pictures 92
Indiana Jones and the Temple of Doom (1984) 233
Indignation (2016) 342
I Never Promised You a Rose Garden (1977) 280
Inge, William 16
Ingram, Rex 81, 136
Instagram 367
Interiors (1978) 288
Intermezzo (1939) 136, 137
Internal Affairs (2002) 340
Internes Can't Take Money (1937) 122
Internet Movie Database (IMDb) 3, 5
In the Bedroom (2001) 292
In the Flesh (1998) 297
In the Heat of the Night (1967) 231, **232**, 245, 254, 269
In This Our Life (1942) 156
Intruder in the Dust (1948) 187, 188
Invaders from Mars (1953) 302, 303, 304
Invasion of the Body Snatchers (1956) 303, 304

Invention of Hugo Cabret, The (2011) 348
Invisible Man, the 132
iPhone 360
Iris (2001) 10
Irishman, The (2019) 261
Irish, William 179. *See also* Woolrich, Cornell
  After-Dinner Story 177
  The Blue Ribbon 177
  Borrowed Crime 177
  The Dancing Detective 177
  Deadline at Dawn 177
  Dead Man Blues 177
  If I Should Die before I Wake 177
  I Married a Dead Man 175, 177, 178
  I Wouldn't Be in Your Shoes 177
  Phantom Lady 177, 178, 179
  Six Nights of Mystery 177
  Somebody on the Phone 177
  Waltz into Darkness 170, 177, 178
Iron Horse, The (1924) 101
Iron Man 352, 357
Ironweed (1987) 332, 341–2
Irving, George 102
Irving, Washington 11, 12, 39, 40
  "Rip Van Winkle" 32, 35–6, 39, 40, 201
Isherwood, Charles 264 n.3
Ishtar (1987) 320
It (1927) 93
Italianamerican (1974) 279
Italian-American Civil Rights League 259
It Came from Outer Space (1953) 302, 303, 304, 306
It Happened in Paris (1935) 181
It Happened One Night (1934) 146, 232, 245, 291, 292
It's a Wonderful Life (1946) 155, 292
Ivanhoe (1952) 206
Ivory, James 13, 14, 322
I Wanted Wings (1941) 165, 169
I Want to Live! (1958) 213
I Wouldn't Be in Your Shoes (1948) 177

Jack London (1943) 173
Jackman, Hugh 355
Jackson, Helen Hunt
    Ramona 62, 63
Jackson, Michael 275, **275**
Jackson, Percy 348
Jackson, Peter 340, 361
Jackson, Samuel L. 357
Jackson, Shirley
    The Haunting of Hill House 280
Jaeckin, Just 213
Jaffe, Rona
    The Best of Everything 219
Jaffe, Sam 211, 212
James, E.L. 298
    Fifty Shades of Grey 348
James, Henry 6, 11, 15, 25, 27, 79, 139, 142, 169, 170, 228, 237, 252, 321–5, 326, 328, 347, 350
    "The Altar of the Dead" 170
    The Ambassadors 11
    "The Aspern Papers" 322
    The Awkward Age 322
    "The Bench of Desolation" 322
    The Bostonians 14
    "Covering End" 322
    "Daisy Miller" 238, 322, 326
    The Europeans 14
    "Glasses" 322
    The Golden Bowl 138, 238
    "The Great Condition" 322
    "An International Episode" 322
    "The Jolly Corner" 294
    "Lord Beaupre" 322
    "The Marriages" 322
    "Nona Vincent" 322
    The Portrait of a Lady 14, 321
    "The Real Thing" 290
    The Sacred Fount 322
    "The Tone of Time" 322
    "The Turn of the Screw" 324
    Washington Square 138, 192, 321, 322
    What Maisie Knew 322
    The Wings of the Dove 202, 203, 321, 322
Jane Austen Book Club, The (2007) 2
Jane Eyre (1943) 137

Janowitz, Tama
    Slaves of New York 14
Japanese Association of Southern California 71
Jarmusch, Jim 319
Jaws (1975) 262, **262**, 263, 267, 320
jazz 290, 301
Jazz Singer, The (1927) 87, 114, **115**, 116
Jeanne Diehlmann, 23 quai de Commerce, 1080 Bruxelles (1975) 277
Jefferson, Joseph 31, 32, **32**, 35, 36
Jefferson in Paris (1995) 14
Jenkins, Henry 351, 362–5, 368–9
Jennings, Talbot 163
Jensen, Eulalie 95
Jessel, George 116
Jewett, Sarah Orne 6
Jewison, Norman 245
Jezebel (1938) 116, 148, 156, 181, 192
Jilting of Granny Weatherall, The (1980) 294
Joan of Arc (1948) 116, 187
Joffé, Roland 18, 85
Johansson, Scarlet **356**, 357
John Brown's Body. See *Ellery Queen, Master Detective*
Johnson, Ben 326
Johnson, Coffin Ed 269
Johnson, Crocker
    Harold and the Purple Crayon 364
Johnson, Julian 206
Johnson, Nunnally 159
Johnson, Sissyl 101
John the Baptist 76, 77
Joker, the 309, 312, 316
Joliffe-Andoh, Lisa 19
Jolly Corner, The (1975) 294
Jolson, Al 114, **115**
Jonas, Gerald 336 n.2
Jones, Bridget 320
Jones, Buck 91
Jones, Gravedigger 269
Jones, James
    From Here to Eternity 165
    The Thin Red Line 261
Jones, Jennifer 136

Jones, Tommy Lee 312, 314, **328**, 329
Jonson, Ben 24
Jourdain, Louis 220
Joy, Leatrice 73
Joyce, Brenda 124
Joyce, James 23, 122, 139
Joy Luck Club, The (1993) 268, 279
Juarez (1939) 181
Jubilo (1919) 125
Jubilo, Jr. (1924) 125
Judge Priest (1934) 126, 127
Julia, Raúl 283
Juliet and Romeo (2015) 297
Juran, Nathan 302
Jurassic Park (1993) 263, 314
Jurassic Park 2: The Lost World (1997) 263
Jus' Passing Through (1923) 125
Just and the Unjust, The (TV, 1951) 202
Justice League of America 351

Kael, Pauline 221
Kafka, Franz
    "The Metamorphosis" 271, 340
Kalem Company 50–1
Kalem v. Harper Brothers 51
Kane, Bob 107
Kantor, MacKinlay
    Glory for Me 192
Kaper, Bronislau 222
Kaplan, Marvin 211, 212
Kardashian family 360
Karloff, Boris 20, 21, 22, 128
Kasdan, Lawrence 187, 327
Kati Patang (1970) 178
Katzenjammer Kids 40, 53
Katz, Gloria 260
Kaufman, George S. 119
    Animal Crackers 119
    Beggar on Horseback 119
    The Butter and Egg Man 119
    The Cocoanuts 80, 119
    Dinner at Eight 119, 135, 146
    George Washington Slept Here 119
    I'd Rather Be Right 119
    The Man Who Came to Dinner 119
    Merrily We Roll Along 119

Merton of the Movies 119
Once in a Lifetime 119
The Royal Family 119, 146, 202
Stage Door 119, 139, 146, 157
You Can't Take It with You 119, 202
Kaufman, Philip 10
Kaufman, Sue
    Diary of a Mad Housewife 277
Kawin, Bruce F. 26, 265 n.10
Kazan, Elia 174, 193, 194, 199
Keaton, Michael 312, **313**
Keene, Carolyn 132
    The Secret of the Old Clock 128
Keighley, William 186
Kellaway, Cecil 247
Keller, Helen 280
Kelly, Gene 137, 185, 190, 191, 278
Kelly, George 117
    Craig's Wife 79, 201
Keneally, Thomas
    Schindler's List 263
Kennedy, Arthur 214
Kennedy, John 236
Kennedy, Robert 236
Kennedy, William
    Ironweed 341
Kenyon, Charles 101
Kern, Jerome 118
    Show Boat 80
Kerouac, Jack
    The Subterraneans 241
Kerr, Darwin 87
Kershner, Irvin 278
Kesey, Ken
    One Flew Over the Cuckoo's Nest 244, 245
Keyes, Daniel
    "Flowers for Algernon" 280
    Flowers for Algernon 280
Key Largo (1948) 116, 195
Keys of the Kingdom, The (1944) 137, 155
Keystone Cops 61
Keystone Pictures 60
Khatchatdourian, Raffi 364
Kick-Ass (2010) 315, 358
Kidder, Margot 310, **310**

Kidman, Nicole 321, **323**, 343, 344, 345
Kildare, Dr. James 122, 185
Kildare, O.F.
  My Mamie Rose 95
Kilday, Gregg 378 n.55
Killers, The (1946) 16, 19, 155, 183, 184, **184**, 291
Killers, The (TV, 1964) 267, 291
Kindle 360
King, Henry 19
King, Mabel 275
King, Martin Luther 236
King, Rufus 148
King, Stephen 28, 357, 370–4
  "The Body" 373
  Carrie 260, 370
  Cell 372
  Christine 372
  Cujo 372
  The Dark Tower 372
  Dolores Claiborne 373
  End of Watch 372
  Finders Keepers 372
  Firestarter 372
  The Green Mile 373
  "The Man in the Black Suit" 372
  "The Man Who Loved Flowers" 373
  Misery 373
  Mr. Mercedes 372
  The Plant 373
  "Riding the Bullet" 373
  "Rita Hayworth and the Shawshank Redemption" 373
  Salem's Lot 370, 372
  The Shining 370
  Ur 373
King Creole (1958) 223
King Kong (1933) 135
King of Kings, The (1927) 74
Kingsley, Sidney
  Dead End 148, 192
  Detective Story 186
Kings Row (1942) 174, 185, 188
Kinney, Jeff
  Diary of a Wimpy Kid 348
Kiri no minato (1923) 79

Kirkland, Jack
  Tobacco Road 159
Kiss of the Spider Woman (1985) 283
Kitty Foyle (1940) 185
Klaw, Marcus 51
Klempner, John
  "A Letter to Five Wives" 192
Knight, Hilary
  Eloise 202
Knopf, Alfred A. 156, 172
Kolb, Ken
  Getting Straight 247
Korean War 165
Korkes, Jon 249
Korngold, Erich Wolfgang 209
Koszarski, Richard 114
Kotcheff, Ted 186
Kozloff, Sarah 151 n.13
Kraft Television Theatre (TV, 1947–58) 201
Krämer, Lucia 377 n.24
Kramer vs. Kramer (1979) 332
Kremlin Letter, The (1970) 203
Kronos (1957) 302
Kubrick, Stanley 221, 268, 282, 303, 306, 371
Ku Klux Klan 69–70
Kummer, Frederick Arnold 39, 40
Kunen, James Simon
  The Strawberry Statement 246
Kurosawa, Akira 260

La capanna della zio Tom (1918) 169
La case de l'oncle Tom (1963) 169
La Cava, Gregory 104
L.A. Confidential (1997) 339
Ladd, Bernice 143
Ladies' Night (1926) 80
Lady Eve, The (1941) 91
Lady for a Day (1933) 292
Lady from Shanghai, The (1948) 183
Lady in the Dark (1944) 185–6, 280
Lady in the Lake (1946) 183
Ladykillers, The (2004) 329
Lady or the Tiger, The (1908) 38
Lady to Love, A (1930) 79, 116
Laemmle, Carl 92, 135, 234
LaGravenese, Richard 331–2, 334

Lakeshore Entertainment 344
Lambert, Mary 369
Landis, John 276
Land of Oz, The (1910) 55
Lane, Burton 278
Lane, Lois 310, 315, 317, 318
Lange, Hope 214, 219, **220**
Langford, Frances 167
Lang, Fritz 12, 184, 245, 301
Lang, Walter 100
Lardner, Ring
   "Alibi Ike" 113
   "The Golden Honeymoon" 294
   "Haircut" 290
L'Arlesienne (1908) 37
LaSalle, Mick 344, 346
Last Hurrah, The (1958) 203
Last Man on Earth, The (1964) 330
Last of the Mohicans, The (1920) 83–5, **84**, 90
Last of the Mohicans, The (1932) 84
Last of the Mohicans, The (1936) 85
Last of the Mohicans, The (1992) 85
Last of the Red Hot Lovers (1972) 232
Last Picture Show, The (1971) 326
Last Summer (1969) 240, 254
Last Temptation of Christ, The (1988) 261
Last Tycoon, The (TV, 1949) 201
Last Tycoon, The (TV, 1957) 202
Late George Apley, The (1947) 193
Lathan, Stan 23, 274
La Tosca (1940) 172
La Tourneaux, Robert 286
Laughton, Charles 128
Laura (1944) 171, 175
Laurents, Arthur
   West Side Story 241
Laurie, Piper 282, 370, **371**
Lawrence, Diarmuid 320
Lawrence, Eddie 222
Lawrence, Florence (actress) 92
Lawrence, Florence (journalist) 109 n.19
Lawrence, Frank M. 26
Lazybones (1925) 80, 91
Leachman, Cloris 326
League of Frightened Men, The (1937) 127–8

Learning in Focus 294
Learning Tree, The (1969) 274
Leaud, Jean-Pierre 239
Leave Her to Heaven (1945) 174, 188, **189**, 209
Leavis, F.R. 169
Lecter, Hannibal 344
Le dernier tournant (1939) 172
Lederstrumpf (1920) 169
Ledger, Heath 312
Le Divorce (2003) 14
Leduc, Violette
   Therese and Isabelle 298
Lee, Ang 311, 320, 326
Lee, Christopher 22
Lee, Harper 14
   To Kill a Mockingbird 204
Lee, Manfred B. 132
Lee, Spike 319
Lee, Stan 22, 357–8, 373
Leff, Leonard L. 206
Legend of Nigger Charley (1972) 273
Legion of Decency 208, 216
Lego Batman Movie, The (2017) 358
Leibman, Ron 243
Leigh, Jennifer Jason 324
Leigh, Vivien 136, 149, **150**, 194, **194**
Leitch, David 358
Leitch, Thomas 29 n.21, 29 n.23, 68 n.37, 108 n.8, 151 n.15, 153 n.53, 154 n.57, 198 n.26, 299 n.15
Le miroir a deux faces (1958) 278
Leni, Paul 199
Lenin, V.I. 365
Lennart, Isobel
   Funny Girl 278
Lennig, Arthur 108 n.3
LeNoire, Rosetta 249
Leonard, Elmore 370
Leonard, Robert Z. 145, 204
Leone, Sergio 259, 332
Leopard Man, The (1943) 177, 179
Lerner, Alan Jay 278
   My Fair Lady 298
lesbian cinema 277–8
Leslie, Joan 167
Le théatre de la jeunesse (TV, 1963) 169

Letter, The (1940) 156
Letter to Three Wives, A (1949) 192–3
Let There Be Light (1946) 195
Lev, Peter 120
Levien, Sonya 162
Levine, Gail Carson
   Ella Enchanted 348
Levine, Joseph E. 225
Levin, Ira
   Rosemary's Baby 250
Levinson, Barry 342
Lewinsky, Monica 342, 344
Lewis, C.S. 348
Lewis, Edgar 53
Lewis, Ralph 65, **66**
Lewis, Sinclair 6, 141, 170
   Babbitt 83
   Dodsworth 192
   It Can't Happen Here 140–1, 191
   Mantrap 93, 105
Lewton, Val 153 n.47
Life Begins at 40 (1935) 126, 127
Lifeboat (1944) 12, 159
Life of an American Fireman, The
   (1903) 33
Life's Whirlpool (1916) 81
Lightnin' (1925) 80
Lightnin' (1930) 80
Li'l Abner (1940) 309
Li'l Abner (1959) 309
Li'l Abner (musical play) 309
Lilies of the Field (1963) 269
liminal figures 83, 85
Lincoln (2012) 263
Lincoln, Elmo 123
Lincoln, Janet E. 336 n.9
Lindbergh, Charles 341
Lindsay, Margaret 133
Linklater, Richard 308
Lion in Winter, The (1968) 278
Lippmann, Julie Mathilde
   Burkses' Amy 92
Little Big Man (1970) 13
Little Caesar (1931) 175
Little Foxes, The (1941) 156
Little Lord Fauntleroy (1936) 136
Little Murders (1971) 249, 250, 254,
   255, 256

Little Orphan Annie (1932) 135
Little Princess, A (1995) 332
Little Women (1993) 2, 157
Litvak, Anatole 145
Livingston, Margaret 93
Lockhart, Calvin 269
Lockridge, Ross, Jr.
   Raintree County 190
Loeb, Jeph
   The Long Halloween 350
Loesser, Frank
   The Most Happy Fella 79
Loewe, Frederick
   My Fair Lady 298
Logan (2017) 352
Loki 356, 357
Lolita (1962) 18, 221, 243, 282
London, Jack 38, 39, 40, 52, 79
   The Call of the Wild 113
London after Midnight (1927) 253
London Weekend Television 322
Lonesome Dove (TV, 1989) 327, **328**
Long Day's Journey into Night
   (1962) 284
Longest Day, The (1962) 166, 234
Longfellow, Henry Wadsworth 11, 38,
   40
   Hiawatha 53
Long Goodbye, The (1973) 257–9
Long Gray Line, The (1955) 203
Long, Hot Summer, The (1958) 225
Long, Huey 191
Longmore, Paul K. 299 n.9
Long Voyage Home, The (1940) 116
Long, Walter **71**
Looking for Mr. Goodbar (1977) 280
Lord of the Rings: The Return of the
   King, The (2003) 339, 340
Lorraine, Harry 85
Lorre, Peter 21, 128, **129**, 132, 181
Losch, Tilly 147
Lost (TV, 2004–10) 201
lost films 38, 79, 143, 277
Lost Squadron, The (1932) 135
Lost Weekend, The (1945) 171, 175,
   187, 188
Lost World, The (1997) 263
Louis, Joe 167

Lourié, Eugène 302
Louys, Pierre
  The Devil Is a Woman 140
Love and Other Sorrows (1989) 294
Lovecraft, H.P.
  The Case of Charles Dexter Ward 21
Lovejoy, Alec 144, **145**
Lovely Bones, The (2009) 361
Love Me Tonight (1932) 118
Loves of Edgar Allan Poe, The (1942) 173
Love Story (1970) 251–3, **253**, 254, 255
Lovin' Molly (1974) 326
Lowell, James Russell 11, 12
Lower Depths, The (1937) 172
Lowry, Malcolm
  Under the Volcano 201
Loy, Myrna 127, 133
Lubitsch, Ernst 12
Lucas, Charles D. 143
Lucas, George 260
Luce, Clare Boothe
  The Women 286
Luckinbill, Laurence 285
Lugosi, Bela 20, 22, 128, 169
Luhr, William 26
Lukas, Paul 130, 133
Luke, Keye 129, **129**, 133
Lumet, Sidney 202, 245, 284, 303, 326
Lumière, Auguste and Louis 36, 43, 72
Lundén, Rolf 170
Lunt, Alfred 167
Lupack, Barbara Tepa 26, 273
Lupino, Ida 277
Lurie, Peter 27
Lust Horizons (1976) 298
Luthor, Lex 311, 312, 315
Lyon, Sue 282

Mabel's Dramatic Career (1913) 61
MacArthur, Charles
  The Front Page 186
Macdonald, Dwight 249–50
MacDonald, J. Farrell 55, 56
MacDougall, Ranald 179
MacGraw, Ali 252, **253**

Mack, The (1973) 273
MacKaye, Steele
  Hazel Kirke 45, 46
MacLaine, Shirley 327
Macmillan Publishers 209
MacMillan, Violet 55, 56, 58
MacMurray, Fred 176
Macomber Affair, The (1947) 155
Madame Butterfly (1915) 92
Madame Curie (1943) 174
Madame X (1910) 221
Madame X (1916) 221
Madame X (1929) 221
Madame X (1937) 221
Madame X (1966) 205, 221
Made in U.S.A. (1966) 171
Mad Max 330
Mad Men (TV, 2007–15) 201, 220
Madonna 10
Magazine of Fantasy & Science Fiction (F&SF) 303
Magic Cloak, The (1914) 56
Magic Cloak of Oz, The (1914) 56–8, 57
Magneto 356
Magnificent Ambersons, The (1942) 155
Magnificent Ambersons, The (TV, 1950) 202
Magnificent Obsession (1954) 221
Magrill, George 102
Maguire, Tobey 352, **353**
Maigret, Jules 317
Mailer, Norman 6
  The Naked and the Dead 165
mainstream films 320, 326
Mainwaring, Daniel
  Build My Gallows High 176
Major and the Minor, The (1942) 165, 179
Malachi's Cove (1973) 25
Malcolm X 236
Malden, Karl 194
Male Animal, The (1942) 156
Male Animal, The (TV, 1958) 202
Malick, Terrence 261
Malkovich, John 321
Maltese Falcon, The (1931) 181, 182

Maltese Falcon, The (1941) 155, 171, 175, 181–2, **182**, 183
Mamet, David 180
Mamoulian, Rouben 80, 122
Mandarin Mystery, The (1936) 127, 132
Mandel, Frank
   My Lady Friends 80
   No, No, Nanette 80
Man in the Gray Flannel Suit (1955) 207, 227
Man in the High Castle, The (TV, 2015–18) 308
Mankiewicz, Herman 193
Mankiewicz, Joseph L. 119, 136, 192–3, 203
Mankiewicz, Tom 310
Mann, Abby
   The Judgment at Nuremberg 202
Mann, Daniel 221
Mann, Margaret 89
Mann, Michael 85
Mansfield, Jayne 204
Manslaughter (1922) 73–4, 83, 98
Manslaughter (1930) 74
Manson, Charles 240
Man That Corrupted Hadleyburg, The (1980) 294
Man-Thing (2005) 352
Mantrap (1926) 93, 105
Man Who Came to Dinner, The (1942) 119, 156
Man Who Knew Too Much, The (1956) 12
Man Who Played God, The (1932) 156
Man Who Shot Liberty Valence, The (1962) 203
Man Who Wasn't There, The (2001) 330
Man without a Country, The (1917) 83
Man with the Golden Arm, The (1955) 204, 207, 208
March, Fredric 174
March, Joseph Moncure
   "The Wild Party" 14
Marcus, James A. 95–6
Mark of the Whistler, The (1944) 177, 179
Mark of Zorro, The (1920) 106, **107**

Mark of Zorro, The (1940) 157
Markov, Margaret 273
Marley, John 252
Marlowe (1969) 258
Marlowe, Christopher 24
Marlowe, Philip 182–3, 258, 317
Marmont, Percy 105
Marnie (1964) 12
Marquand, Christian 247
Marquand, John P. 128, 132
   The Late George Apley 128, 193
   Point of No Return 202
   The Return of Mr. Moto 202
   Sincerely, Willis Wade 202
Marsden, James 356
Marshall, Herbert 167
Marshall, Tully 101
Marshall, William 273
Martha (1974) 178
Martin, Darnell 23
Martin, George R.R. 23
   Game of Thrones 348
   A Song of Ice and Fire 348
Martin, Skip 21
Martin, Strother 244
Marton, Andrew 261
Marvel Comics 363
Marvel Enterprises 352
Marvel Entertainment 352
Marvel Productions 352
Marvel Studios 359
Marvel Universe 28, 351–2, 355–8, 369
Marx Brothers 80, 119
Marx, Groucho 119, 138, **139**
Marx, Samuel 111, 112, 113, 120, 132, 135, 136, 141
Mary of Scotland (1936) 116
Mary of Scotland (TV, 1951) 202
Masculin féminin (1965) 171
M*A*S*H (1970) 257
Mask, The (1994) 313
Maslin, Janet 331
Mason, Perry 127, 131–2, 133, 134, 173
Masque of the Red Death (1964) 21, 293
Masterpiece Theatre (TV, 1971–2014) 24

Mast, Gerald 265 n.10
Matheson, Richard 262, 372
  I Am Legend 330
Mathews, Lester 20
Mathis, June 82
Matilda (1996) 2
Matlin, Marlee 281, **281**, 282
Matrix, The (1999) 362, 363, 365, 368
Matrix Reloaded, The (2003) 363
Matrix Revolutions, The (2003) 363
Matthiessen, F.O. 11
Maugham, W. Somerset 199–200
Mauldin, Bill 195
Mayer, Louis B. 113, 123, 129, 135, 141, 234
Mayo, Margaret
  Baby Mine 79
  Polly of the Circus 79
  Twin Beds 79
McAleer, John 152 n.29
McBain, Ed. *See also* Hunter, Evan
  Blood Relatives 171
  Fuzz 246
McCabe and Mrs. Miller (1971) 257
McCambridge, Mercedes 191, 250, 283
McCarthy, Cormac 327–31, 372
  All the Pretty Horses 328
  Blood Meridian 328
  Cities of the Plain 328
  The Crossing 328
  No Country for Old Men 328, 340
  The Road 330–1
McCay, Winsor
  Dream of the Rarebit Fiend 48–50, **49**
McCoy, Horace
  They Shoot Horses, Don't They? 175, 176, 250–1
McCraney, Tarell Alvin
  In Moonlight Black Boys Look Blue 340
McCrea, Joel 122
McCrum, Robert 361
McCulley, Johnson 106, 107
  "The Curse of Capistrano" 106
McCutcheon, Wallace 45
McFarlane, Brian 41, 120, 151 n.16

McGee, Vonetta 273
McGehee, Scott 322
McGovern, Elizabeth 288
McGrath, Douglas 320
McGregor, Ewan 342, 344
McGregor, Malcolm 102
McKee, Raymond 87, **88**
McKee, Robert 121
McKellan, Ian 356
McKim, Robert **107**
McMurtry, Larry 326–7
  Comanche Moon 327
  Dead Man's Walk 327
  The Desert Rose 261
  Horseman, Pass By 326, 327
  The Last Picture Show 326, 327
  Leaving Cheyenne 326
  Lonesome Dove 327
  Streets of Laredo 327
McPartland, John
  No Down Payment 217–18, 219
McQueen, Steve (actor) 253
McQueen, Steve (director) 309
Me and Earl and the Dying Girl (2015) 348
Mean Streets (1973) 279
Meeker, George 90
Meer, Sarah 68 n.22
Meet Joe Black (1998) 320
Meet John Doe (1941) 155, 292
Meet Nero Wolfe (1936) 127
Meighan, Thomas 73
Meikle, Kyle 36, 297, 298, 364
Melford, George 74
Méliès, Georges 50, 72, 301
Mellor, William 214
melodrama 15, 46, 75, 83, 85, 112, 140, 142, 145, 150, 171, 191, 192, 195, 221
Melville, Herman 6, 13, 14, 25, 79, 170
  The Confidence Man 15
  Moby-Dick 6, 8, 14, 37, 40, 239, 273, 304, 358
Memoirs of a Geisha (2005) 2
Men in Black (1997) 314
Menzies, William Cameron 149, 301, 302

Merchant, Ismail 13, 14, 322
Merci pour le chocolat (2000) 171
Meredith, Burgess 166, 309
Meredith, George 25
Meredith, Hal 39
Merimee, Prosper
    Carmen 297
Merrill, Sam 265 n.19
Merritt, Russell 108 n.1, 108 n.2
Merry-Go-Round (1923) 81
Merry Widow, The (1934) 116
Merry Widow, The (1952) 204
Merton of the Movies (1924) 119
Merton of the Movies (TV, 1947) 119
Mesmer, Otto 309
metafictionality 132, 342, 356, 358
Metalious, Grace
    Peyton Place 28, 214–15, 216–17, 349, 370
meta-sites 368
metatheatricality 148–9
Metro-Goldwyn-Mayer Studios (MGM) 23, 81, 83, 111, 112, 113, 114, 118, 120–1, 122, 123, 124, 130, 135, 136, 137, 138, 140–1, 145, 149, 150, 157, 158, 159, 163, 174, 180, 181, 185, 188, 190, 195, 204, 205, 206, 222, 234, 241, 271, 272, 274, 280, 286
Metropolis (1926) 301
Metzger, Radley 297–8
Metz, Walter 225
Meyer, Nicholas 342, 346
Meyer, Russ 298
Meyer, Stephenie 23
    Twilight 348
Michaels, Dolores 204
Micheaux, Oscar 143–5
    The Conquest 143
    "Jeff Ballinger's Woman" 144
Michelena, Beatriz 77–8
Mickey Mouse 309
microcultures 369
midcult 249–50
Midnight Cowboy (1969) 243, 245, 254
A Midsummer Night's Cream (2000) 297

Midsummer Night's Dream, A (1935) 156
Milar, Adolphe 95
Mildred Pierce (1945) 156
Mildred Pierce (TV, 2011) 180
Milestone, Lewis 186
Milk (2008) 284
Milland, Ray 252
Miller, Alice Duer
    Manslaughter 73
Miller, Arthur
    Death of a Salesman 193
Miller, Bennett 10
Miller, Carl 100
Miller, Frank 312, 318
    Batman: The Dark Knight Returns 316, 354
    Batman: Year One 316, 350
Miller, Henry 6
    Quiet Days in Clichy 171
Miller, J.P.
    Days of Wine and Roses (TV, 1958) 202
Miller, Neil 229 n.11
Miller, Renata Kobetts 42
Miller's Crossing (1990) 187, 329
Miller's Daughter, The (1905) 45–6
Miller, Tim 358
Miller, Wentworth 343, 344, **345**
Millet, Jean-François
    The Sower 62
Million Dollar Baby (2004) 292
Miltern, John 74
Milton, John 247
miniseries 25, 83, 180, 320, 321, 322, 327, 340, 370, 371
Minnelli, Vincente 174, 277
Minority Report (2002) 263, 308
Minority Report (TV, 2015) 308
minstrelsy 42–4, 72, 76, 91, 95, 102, 106, 123, 144–5, 160–1, 269, 276, 280, 287. *See also* blackface
    intertextual 44
Miracle, The (1948) 207, 208
Miracle on 34th Street (1947) 253
Miracle Worker, The (TV, 1957) 202
Miracle Worker, The (1962) 268, 280
Miramax 344

INDEX 427

Mirror Has Two Faces, The (1996) 278
mise-en-scene 183, 184
Misery (1990) 373, 374
Mishima: A Life in Four Chapters (1985) 261
Missing, The (2003) 329
Mississippi (1935) 118
Mississippi Mermaid (1969) 170, 178
Miss Lulu Bett (1921) 79, 93–4
Mister Roberts (1955) 190, 203
Mistress Nell (1915) 92
Mitchell, Cameron 218
Mitchell, David T. 280, 299
Mitchell, Erika. *See* James, E.L.
Mitchell, Margaret 14
   Gone with the Wind 23, 28, 149, 164, 213, 273, 331
Mitchum, Robert 175
Mix, Tom 101
Mizoguchi, Kenji 79
Moby Dick (1930) 11, 28
Moby Dick (1956) 203, 304
modernism 23, 139–40, 164, 219, 358
Moeller, Philip 324
Mogambo (1953) 203
Monogram Pictures 128
monster films 112, 151, 273, 303
monsters 43–4
monstration 33, 36–7, 42–4, 48, 50, 53, 59, 61, 62–3, 64, 66, 67 n.12, 69, 72, 84, 115, 119, 161, 167, 187, 280, 284, 285, 293, 294–5, 306, 357. *See also* display
   vs. adaptation 64, 187
   vs. immersion 66
   vs. narrative 33, 43, 167
Montgomery, Robert 183
Mooney, William H. 27
Moon Is Blue, The (1953) 207, 208
Moon Is Down, The (1943) 159, 165
Moonlight (2016) 339, 340
Moore, Clement Clarke
   "A Visit from St. Nicholas" 46
Moore, Demi 18, **18**, 19
Moore, Frank 55
Moore, Mary Tyler 288, **289**
Moore, Terry 214, **215**
Moran of the Lady Letty (1922) 81, 93

Morley, Christopher 195
   Kitty Foyle 188
Morning Glory (1933) 157
Morrell, Stanley 143
Morris, Glenn 124
Morrison, Toni 23
   Beloved 328, 361
Mortenson, Viggo **323**
Morton, Charles 90
Moscow, Alvin 261
Moses, Harry 120
Moskowitz, Joseph 206
Most Dangerous Game, The (1932) 135
Motion Picture Association of America (MPAA) 233, 234, 359
Motion Picture Producers and Directors of America (MPPDA) 122, 141
Moto, Mr. 128, 129, **129**, 132, 173
Movie Star, A (1910) 61
Mower, Jack 73, 95
Moxon, Lew 316
Mozart, Wolfgang Amadeus 251
Mr. and Mrs. Bridge (1990) 14
Mr. Blandings Builds His Dream House (1948) 155
Mr. Deeds Goes to Town (1936) 292
Mr. Moto's Gamble 129, **129**
Mr. Skitch (1933) 125, 126
Mr. Wong, Detective (1938) 128
Mrs. Miniver (1942) 165
Mrs. Parkington (1944) 174
Mulligan, Robert 204
Muni, Paul 147, **147**
Murder at the Vanities (1934) 148
Murder by Death (1976) 232
Murder, My Sweet (1944) 171, 175, 181–2, 184–5
Murder on a Bridle Path (1936) 131
Murders in the Rue Morgue (1932) 20
Murnau, F.W. 93
Murphy, Audie 166, 195
Murphy, George 167, 168
Murray, Kathleen 36
Murray, Simone 17
music 34, 36, 59, 115, 118, 138, 144–5, 160–1, 167, 168, 222, 239, 256, 271, 272, 273, 290

musicals 17, 53, 54, 56, 80, 112, 118–19, 146, 151, 173, 201, 290, 301, 302
Music Man, The (1962) 119
Music School, The (1974) 209
Musser, Charles 45
Mutiny on the Bounty (1935) 148
Mutt and Jeff 40, 53
My Darling Clementine (1946) 144
My Friend Flicka (1943) 155
My Sister's Keeper (2009) 348
Mysterious Mr. Wong, The (1935) 128
Mystery Train (1989) 319

Nabokov, Vladimir
  Lolita 18, 282
Naked Came the Stranger (1975) 298
Naked City, The (1940) 185
Naked Lunch (1991) 10
Nancy Drew and the Hidden Staircase (1938) 132
Nancy Drew ... Detective (1938) 128, 132
Napolin, Leah
  Yentl 278
Naremore, James 122, 175
narrative
  cinema 34
  competence 34–5
  and meta-narrative 66
Nashville (1975) 257, 293
National Association for the Advancement of Colored People (NAACP) 70
National Book Award 328
National Book Critics' Circle Award 328
National Book Foundation 372
National Broadcasting Company (NBC) 142
National Endowment for the Humanities (NEH) 296
Native Americans 85, 90, 92, 101, 102, 104, 236–7
Native Son (1951) 23, 274
Native Son (1986) 274
Natural, The (1984) 28
Neal, Patricia 326
Nebel, Frederick 128, 132

Neely, Richard
  The Damned Innocents 170–1
Negri, Pola 115
Negroponte, Nicholas 368
Negulesco, Jean 204, 219
Neill, John R. 56
Nelson, Kenneth 284, **285**
Nelson, Ralph 280
Nervous Wreck, The (1924) 80
Netflix 201, 359, 364, 368
Neumann, Kurt 302
Nevins, Francis M. 152 n.31
New Adventures of Tarzan, The (1935) 123
New Adventures of Wonder Woman, The (TV, 1977–9) 309
New Hollywood 243, 244, 246, 257
Newman, Paul 222, 244
Newmar, Julie 309
news 368–9
Newsome, Carman 144, **145**
Newsome, Nora 143
New Wave, French 170–2, 255, 256
New Wizard of Oz, The (1915) 58
niche markets and subjects 259, 264, 267, 284, 287, 319, 320
niche novelists 341
Nichols, Anne
  Abie's Irish Rose 80
Nichols, Mike 244, 256
Nicholson, Jack 21, 244, 297, 312, **313**, 327, **371**
Nick and Norah's Infinite Playlist (2008) 348
Nigh, William 76, 77
Night at the Opera, A (1935) 119
Night before Christmas, The (1905) 46, **47**
Night Flight (1933) 135
Night Has a Thousand Eyes (1948) 177
Nightmare (1956) 177
Nightmare Alley (1947) 158
Night of the Iguana, The (1964) 203
Nilsson, Anna Q. 96
9 to 5 (1980) 277
Nixon, Richard 344
Nobel Prize for Literature 19, 158, 341, 361

INDEX   429

No Country for Old Men (2007)
　328–30, **329**, 339
No Down Payment (1957) 217–19,
　224, 226
Nolan, Christopher 312, 316, 318,
　350–1, 354
Nolan, Lloyd 216
No Man of Her Own (1950) 177, 178,
　185
None but the Lonely Heart (1944) 117
No, No, Nanette (1930) 80
No, No, Nanette (1940) 80
Norden, Martin F. 299 n.10
Norman, Gertrude 88
Normand, Mabel 59, 277
Norris, Frank 79, 81
　McTeague 13, 81, 85
　Moran of the Lady Letty 93
　The Octopus 61
　The Pit 61
　The Wolf 61
Norris, Margaret 103
North (1994) 320
North by Northwest (1959) 12
North, Sheree 218
Northwest Passage (1940) 163–4, **164**,
　188
Norton, Roy 39
Nosferatu (1922) 172
Notorious (1946) 12, 137
Nouvelles de Henry James (TV,
　1974–6) 25
novelizations 253
novels, *vs.* plays 120–2, 134–5, 137
Now, Voyager (1942) 156, 185
Nugent, Elliott
　The Male Animal 202
Number One Son 129, **129**, 133, 134
Nuts (1987) 278

Oakland, Vivien 95
O'Brien, George 93, 101
O Brother, Where Art Thou (2000) 329
Obsession (1975) 261
O'Connor, Flannery 6, 14, 200
　"The Displaced Person" 294
　"Good Country People" 290
　"A Good Man Is Hard to Find" 294

Octavius 40
Odd Couple, The (1968) 232
Odets, Clifford 10, 16, 117, 148, 178,
　232
　Awake and Sing! 117
　The Big Knife 117
　Clash by Night 117, 202
　The Country Girl 117
　Golden Boy 117
　Paradise Lost 117
　Waiting for Lefty 117
Of Human Bondage (1934) 156
O'Flynn, Siobhan 362, 363, 364
Of Mice and Men (1939) 23, 158
Of Mice and Men (TV, 1968) 158
Of Mice and Men (TV, 1981) 158
Of Mice and Men (1992) 158
Of Mice and Men (2014) 158
O'Hara, George 37
O'Hara, John 200, 221–3, 227
　BUtterfield 8 221, 222
　"The Doctor's Son" 290
　From the Terrace 221
　Pal Joey 190
　A Rage to Live 222
　Ten North Frederick 221, 222
O. Henry Award 372
O. Henry's Full House (1952) 199–
　201, **200**, 292
Oh, Sailor Behave! (1930) 116
Oklahoma! (musical) 173
Oland, Warner 101, 127, 128–9, 133,
　134
Olcott, Sidney 50
Old Acquaintance (1943) 156
Old Boyfriends (1979) 261
Old Maid, The (1939) 156
Old Man (TV, 1958) 202
Oldman, Gary **18**, 19
Old Man and the Sea, The (1958) 19,
　203
Old Wives for New (1918) 81
Oliver, Edna May 127, 131, 162
Oliver's Story (1978) 253
Olivier, Sir Laurence 174
Omega Man, The (1974) 330
On a Clear Day You Can See Forever
　(1970) 278

Once in a Lifetime (1932) 119
O'Neal, Ryan 251, **253**
One Flew Over the Cuckoo's Nest (1975) 244–5, 254, 255, 280
O'Neil, Dennis 315, 318, 350
 "The Man Who Falls" 350
O'Neill, Eugene 6, 9, 16, 23, 116, 117, 232
 Anna Christie 79, 114, 206, 273
 Beyond the Horizon 79
 Long Day's Journey into Night 284
 Strange Interlude 138
O'Neill, Tatum 326
One Night in Lisbon (1941) 165
On the Town (musical) 173
On the Town (1949) 173
On Your Toes (1939) 118
Opening of Misty Beethoven, The (1976) 298
Oppenheim, James 39
Opper, Frederick Burr 38, 40
Ordinary People (1980) 288–90, **289**, 290
origin stories 316–19, 354
Orlandello, John 26
Orr, Mary
 "The Wisdom of Eve" 193, 292
Örümcek Adam (1966) 352
Orwell, George
 Nineteen Eighty-Four 7, 306
Osseana, Diana 326
Ossessione (1942) 172
O'Sullivan, Maureen 124, **124**, 132
Othello: Dangerous Desire (1997) 297
Otis, Ted 220
Our Town (1940) 148
Our Town (TV, 1950) 202
Outcault, Richard Felton 39, 40
Out of Africa (1985) 332
Out of the Past (1947) 175–6, 183
Out-of-Towners, The (1970) 232
Outsiders, The (1983) 347
Owens, Mitchell 229 n.20
Ox-Bow Incident, The (1943) 329
Oz Film Company 55

Pace, Judy **270**
Pacino, Al 254, 259, **260**, 309

Page, Anthony 280
Pagnol, Marcel
 Topaze 135
Palacio, R.J.
 Wonder 348
Palance, Jack 117
Pale Rider (1985) 327
Pal Joey (1957) 118, 190, 207
Pallette, Eugene 105
Pallotta, Frank 373
Palmer, R. Barton 26, 27
Palmer, Stuart 131
 The Penguin Pool Murder 127
Paltrow, Gwyneth 320
Panavision 224
Pangborn, Franklin 283
Paper Moon (1973) 326
Papp, Joseph 241
Paquin, Anna 355
Paradine Case, The (1947) 12
Paramount decree 156–7, 234, 268
Paramount Pictures 104, 112, 122, 127, 134, 136, 140, 156–7, 179, 186, 223, 234, 259, 260, 309, 313
Paris, Henry 298
Parker Adderson, Philosopher (1974) 294
Parker, Eleanor 186
Parker, Jane 124, 132
Parker, Peter 317, 352, 354
Parker, Suzy 219, 222
Parks, Gordon 271
 The Learning Tree 274
Parody, Claire 363–4
Parsons, Harriet 277
Passions of Carol, The (1975) 297
Patchwork Girl of Oz, The (1914) 55–6, 58
Paterson, Catherine
 Bridge to Terabithia 348
Pathé Frères 37, 127
Patinkin, Mandy **279**
Patsalidis, Savas 170
Patterns (TV, 1955) 201
Patterson, Elizabeth **160**
Patterson, Frances Taylor 52
Patterson, James 370
Patton (1970) 259

Patty Hearst (1988) 261
Pavlásková, Irene 342
Pawnbroker, The (1964) 207
Payne, Alexander 340
Payton, Lucy 98
Pearl, The (1947) 159
Pearson, Ridley 373
Pearson, Virginia 100
Peary, Gerald 26
Peck, Gregory 204, **205**, **208**
Pendo, Stephen 26
Penguin, the 309, 316
Penguin Pool Murder, The (1932) 127, 135
Penn, Arthur 242, 256
Pennick, Jack 90
Penn, Sean 284
Peppard, George 224
Percy, Walker
　The Moviegoer 261
performance 43, 44
　of sexuality 286, 287
Perks of Being a Wallflower, The (2012) 348
Perl, Arnold 269
Permenter, Brady 5
Perrine, Valerie 311
Perry, Eleanor 277, 292
Perry, Frank 277, 280, 292
Perry Mason (TV, 1957–66) 203, 305
Perry, Tyler 361
Persona (1966) 257
Peters, Brock 204, **205**
Peters, House 77
Petrified Forest, The (1936) 117, 156
Peyton Place (1957) 174, 204, 213–17, **215**, 218, 219, 220, 221, 224, 255, 349
Pfeiffer, Michelle 312, **325**
Phantom, The (1996) 313
Phantom Empire, The (1935) 301
Phantom Lady (1944) 177, 178, 179
Phantom President, The (1932) 118
Philadelphia (1993) 284
Philadelphia Story, The (1940) 142, 146, 157
Philco Television Playhouse (TV, 1948–55) 201

Philip K. Dick's Electric Dreams (TV, 2017–18) 308
Phillips, David Graham
　Old Wives for New 81
　Susan Lenox: Her Fall and Rise 145
Phillips, Gene D. 26
Phillips, Lee 214
Pianist, The (2002) 339, 340
Pichel, Irving 302
Picker, David 258
Pickett, Rex
　Sideways 339
Pickford, Mary 61, 62, 92, 105
Picoult, Jodi
　My Sister's Keeper 348
Pierce, Donn
　Cool Hand Luke 244
Pierson, Frank 278
Pierson, John 319
Pigeon Feathers (1988) 294, 295, **296**
Pike, William 78
Pinchon, Edgcumb
　Viva Villa! 135
Pinky (1949) 187, 188
Pinter, Harold
　The Birthday Party 284
Piper, Oscar 127, 132
Pit, The (1914) 81
Pit and the Pendulum (1961) 293
Pitkin, Walter B. 126
　Life Begins at 40 126
Pitts, ZaSu 81, 125, 131
Places in the Heart (1984) 62, 277
Platinum Blonde (1933) 292
Player, The (1992) 37
Playhouse 90 (TV, 1956–60) 202, 203
Play It as It Lays (1972) 280
Play Misty for Me (1971) 332
plays, *vs.* novels 120–2, 134–5, 137
Plaza Suite (1971) 232
Pleshette, Suzanne 223, **223**
Poe, Edgar Allan 6, 7, 8, 10, 11, 14, 15, 19–22, 39, 40, 65, 239, 294, 296, 297, 372, 374
　"Annabel Lee" 64, 65–6
　"The Bells" 65
　"The Black Cat" 65
　"The Cask of Amontillado" 63, 65

"The Haunted Palace" 293
"Hop-Frog" 21
"The Pit and the Pendulum" 20
"The Raven" 20–1, 64, 293
"The Tell-Tale Heart" 63, 65
"To One in Paradise" 64
Poeland 22
Point of No Return (TV, 1958) 202
Poitier, Sidney **232**, 245, 269, 273
Polanski, Roman 250, 257
Polito, Robert 175
Pollack, Sidney 250
Pollard, Harry A. 94, 95, 118
Polly of the Circus (1917) 79
Polly of the Circus (1932) 79
Polonsky, Abraham 211
Poole, Wakefield 298
Poor Little Rich Girl (1917) 92
Pope, Alexander
 "Epistle to a Lady" 223
Popeye (1980) 311–12
Porgy and Bess (1959) 80
pornography 297–8
Porter, Cole 118
Porter, Edwin S. 40, 43, 44, 45, 46, 48
Porter, Jane 123
Porter, Katherine Anne
 "Flowering Judas" 294
 "The Jilting of Granny Weatherall" 294
 "Pale Horse, Pale Rider" 290
Porter, Nikki 133, 134
Porter, William Sidney. *See* Henry, O.
Portis, Charles
 True Grit 330
Portnoy's Complaint (1972) 342
Portrait in Black (1960) 204
Portrait of a Lady, The (1996) 321, 323, **323**, 325
Poseidon Adventure, The (1972) 262
Postcards from the Edge (1990) 332
Postman, The (1997) 320
Postman Always Rings Twice (1946) 156, 180, **180**, 190, 204, 227
Postman Always Rings Twice, The (1981) 180
Post, William H.
 The Vagabond King 80
Potter, Andrew 264
Potter, Harry 22
Powell, Dick 183
Powell, Frank 61
Powell, Sandy 324
Powell, William 127, 129–30, **130**, 133
Power, Tyrone [Jr.] 157–8
Power, Tyrone [Sr.] 99
Practical Magic (1998) 2
Prague Orgy, The (2019) 342
Prana Film Gesellschaft 172
Precious (2009) 339, 340
Preer, Evelyn 143
Premature Burial (1962) 293
Preminger, Otto 204, 207–8, 209
Prentice, Keith **285**
Presley, Elvis 223
Prêt-à-Porter (1994) 293
Pretty in Pink (1986) 347
Price, Reynolds 375 n.1
Price, Vincent 21, 22
Pride and Prejudice (1940) 155, 174
Pride and Prejudice (TV, 1995) 320, 321, 324
Priest, Judge 126
Prime Time Emmy Awards 327, 370
Prince, Michael J. 265 n.18
Prince and the Pauper, The (1937) 209
Prince of Foxes (1949) 157
Prince of Tides, The (1991) 278
Princess Diaries, The (2001) 348
Prisoner of Second Avenue, The (1975) 232
Prisoner of Zenda, The (1922) 136
Prisoner of Zenda, The (1937) 136
Private Lives of Elizabeth and Essex, The (1939) 116, 156, 209
Prizzi's Honor (1985) 203
Proctor, William 377 n.31
Prodigal, The (1955) 204
Producers Guild of America 363
Production Code 206–8, 213, 216–17, 219, 221, 224, 225, 227, 228, 233, 234, 237, 243, 291
Production Code Administration 140. *See also* Hays Office
Prohibition 237
Project Moon Base (1953) 302

prosumers 362, 366
Proulx, E. Annie
   "Brokeback Mountain" 326, 340
Proust, Marcel 328
Pryor, Richard 275, 311
psychiatrists 185–6, 280, 288
Psycho (1960) 12, 353
Public Broadcasting System (PBS) 249, 294
Public Enemy (1931) 175, 185
Pueblo Romance, A (1912) 92
Puig, Manuel
   Kiss of the Spider Woman 283
Pulitzer Prize 23, 79, 80, 93, 116–17, 119, 128, 138, 146, 147, 154 n.57, 157, 190, 193, 202, 204, 327
Pulitzer Prize Playhouse (TV, 1950–2) 202
Pullman, Philip
   His Dark Materials 348
Punisher, The (2004) 352
Punnami Chandrudu (1987) 178
Push (2009) 340
Puss in Boots (1908) 37
Putney Swope (1969) 276
Puzo, Mario 309–10
   The Godfather 259, 309
Pyle, Ernie 166
Pynchon, Thomas 22, 372
   V. 358

Quartet (1948) 199
Queen, Ellery (author) 127, 132–3
   The Door Between 133
   The Roman Hat Mystery 132
   The Spanish Cape Mystery 127
   Ten Days Wonder 170
Queen, Ellery (character) 133, 134, 173, 175
Quiet Days in Clichy (1990) 171
Quiet Man, The (1952) 144, 203
Quillan, Eddie 127
Quinn, Patricia 242

Rabbit, Run (1963) 241, 256
racism 44, 69, 70, 100, 102, 188, 204, 245, 271, 341, 342
radio 141–2

radio adaptations 133, 193, 201
Radio-Keith-Orpheum (RKO) 112, 118, 124, 127, 131, 134, 136, 137, 146, 159, 173, 179, 187, 188, 309
Rado, James
   Hair: The American Tribal Love-Rock Musical 241
Rafelson, Bob 180
Raffles (1939) 156
Rage in Harlem, A (1991) 273
Rage in Heaven (1941) 165
Rage to Live, A (1965) 222, 223, **223**, 224
Raging Bull (1980) 261
Ragni, Jerome
   Hair: The American Tribal Love-Rock Musical 241
Ragona, Ubaldo 330
Rahv, Philip 237
Raiders of the Lost Ark (1981) 263, 267
Raimi, Sam 352, 354
Rain (1932) 116
Rainer, Luise 147, **147**
Rains of Ranchipur, The (1955) 204
Raintree County (1957) 190
Raker, James 222
Raksin, David 209
Ralston, Esther 104
Rambeau, Marjorie 161
Ramona (1910) 62–3, **63**
Randall, Alice
   The Wind Done Gone 273
Randall, Tony 218
Random Harvest (1942) 155, 165, 185
Random House 328
Rapf, Joanna E. 152 n.33
Raphaelson, Samson
   "The Day of Atonement" 114
   The Jazz Singer 114, 116
Rappaccini's Daughter (1980) 294, 295
Ra's al Ghul 350
Raskin, Victor 36
Rasputin and the Empress (1932) 121
Rathner, Harry 140, 153 n.47
Ratings Code 233–4, 319
Raven, The (1935) 20–1

Raven, The (1963) 293
Raw, Laurence 26
Ray Bradbury Theatre, The (TV, 1985–92) 305
Ray, Satyajit 263
Razor's Edge, The (1946) 157
Reagan, Ronald 167, 168
Rear Window (1954) 12, 177, 291
Rebecca (1940) 12, 136
Rebel without a Cause (1955) 235, 241, 243
reboots 316, 317, 319, 350, 351, 353–5, 359, 363
Red Badge of Courage, The (1951) 195–6, **196**, 203
Redford, Robert 288
Red Kimona, The (1925) 100
Red Planet (2000) 320
Red Pony, The (1949) 159
Reed, Peyton 359
Reed, Vivian 58
Reeve, Christopher 310, **310**
Reeves, Keanu 308
Reflections in a Golden Eye (1967) 203, 283
Regeneration (1915) 95–8, **96**, 100, 217
Reid, Hal 39
Reiner, Rob 373
Reinhardt, Gottfried 195
Reising, Russell 29 n.19
Remains of the Day, The (1993) 13
remakes 22, 74, 98, 107, 117, 128, 137, 143, 144, 146, 165, 177, 178, 180, 186, 187, 204, 206, 221, 267, 274, 278, 305, 307, 340, 353–4, 371
Rendezvous in Black (TV, 1956) 202
Renner, Jeremy 356
Renoir, Jean 172
Report from the Aleutians (1943) 195
Republic Pictures 132
Repulsion (1965) 257
Requiem for a Heavyweight (TV, 1956) 202
Return of Mr. Moto (TV, 1952) 202
Reunion in Vienna (1933) 117
Revenge of Tarzan, The (1920) 123
Revolt of Mother, The (1988) 294

Reynolds, Lynn 101
Reynolds, Ryan 358
Riaume, Helen 99
Rice, Elmer 16, 116, 148
   The Adding Machine 116
   Counsellor at Law 191
   On Trial 116
   Street Scene 116
Richard, Jean-Louis 171
Richman, Arthur
   The Awful Truth 146
Riddler, the 309, 316
Riders of the Purple Sage (1925) 101, 102
Riley, James Whitcomb 11
Rio Grande (1950) 203
Riordan, Rick 348
Rio Rita (1929) 80
Rio Rita (1942) 80
Rip Van Winkle (1896) 28, 31–3, **32**, 35–6
Rip Van Winkle (TV, 1950) 201
Rising of the Moon, The (1957) 203
Ritt, Martin 219, 225–6, 259, 274, 278
River Wild, The (1994) 332
Roache, Linus 323
Road, The (2009) 330–1
Robbe-Grillet, Catherine. *See* de Berg, Jean
Robbins, Harold 223–5
   The Carpetbaggers 223
   Never Love a Stranger 223
Robbins, Jerome 119
   West Side Story 241
Roberta (1935) 118
Roberts, Kenneth 163–4
Roberts, Theodore 93
Robertson, Cliff 352
Robin 309
Robinson Crusoe on Mars (1964) 302, 303
Robinson, Dorothy 111
Robinson, Henry Morton
   The Cardinal 1950
Robinson, Mabel 269
RoboCop (1987) 363
Robson, Mark 204, 213, 221
Rocketship X-M (1950) 302

Rodd, Marcia 249
Rodeo Dough (1936) 124
Rodgers, Mary
  Freaky Friday 348
Rodgers, Richard 118–19
  Carousel 119
  Flower Drum Song 119
  The King and I 119
  Oklahoma 119
  Pal Joey 190
  The Sound of Music 119
  South Pacific 119
Rodriguez, Robert 312
Roe v. Wade 277
Rogers, Ginger 118, 173, 185
Rogers, Rena 99
Rogers, Roy 122
Rogers, Will 112, 125–7, **126**, 136
Roiphe, Anne Richardson
  Up the Sandbox 278
Rolling Stones, the 235
Romance of Tarzan, The (1918) 123
romances 112
Roman Scandals (1933) 117
romantic comedy 105, 146, 233, 301
Romeo and Juliet (1936) 24
Romero, Cesar 309
Rooney, Mickey 122
Roosevelt, Franklin D. 119, 169, 341
Root, Lynn
  Cabin in the Sky 174
Roots (1977) 327
Rope (1948) 12, 283
Ropes, Bradford
  42nd Street 118
Roscoe, Alan 84, **84**
Roscoe, Albert. *See* Roscoe, Alan
Rose, Frank Oakes 50
Rose, Reginald
  Twelve Angry Men 202
Rosemary's Baby (1968) 250
Rosenberg, Stuart 244
Ross, Diana 275, **275**
Rossellini, Roberto 207
Rossen, Robert 191
Ross, Lillian 195, 196
Rossner, Judith
  Looking for Mr. Goodbar 280

Rosson, Richard 55
Ross, Ted 275, **275**
Roszak, Theodore 235
Roth, Philip 6, 8, 10, 14, 340–6, 347, 361, 369, 372
  American Pastoral 341, 343
  The Breast 340
  The Counterlife 341
  Deception 343
  "Defender of the Faith" 290
  The Dying Animal 341, 342, 346
  Everyman 341
  Exit Ghost 341
  The Ghost Writer 341
  Goodbye, Columbus 340
  The Great American Novel 340
  The Human Stain 341, 343, 346
  The Humbling 341
  I Married a Communist 343
  Indignation 341
  My Life as a Man 340, 343
  Nemesis 341
  Operation Shylock 341
  Our Gang 340
  The Plot against America 341
  Portnoy's Complaint 238, 340, 343
  The Professor of Desire 343
  Sabbath's Theater 341, 343
Roth, Veronica
  Divergent 348
Rotten Tomatoes 3, 5, 343, 368
Roundtree, Richard 271, **272**
Rouveroul, Aurania
  Skidding 122
Rowling, J.K. 348
Royal Family (TV, 1951) 202
Royal Family of Broadway, The (1930) 119, 146
Ruark, Robert C.
  Something of Value 221
Rubenstein, Hal 29 n.25
Ruffalo, Mark 356, **356**, 357
Ruffin, James D. 143
Ruggles, Wesley 324
Rule, Janice **242**
Rumble Fish (1983) 347
Run Silent Run Deep (1958) 165
Rush, Barbara 218

Rush, Richard 247
Russell, Jane 208
Russell, John (actor) 210
Russell, John (writer) 101
Russell, Nipsey 275
Russell, Raymond 55, 58, 59
Russell, Rosalind 133
Ryan, Cornelius
  The Longest Day 165–6
Ryan, Marie-Laure 363
Ryskind, Morrie
  Animal Crackers 119
  The Cocoanuts 119

Saboteur (1942) 12
Sacks, Michael 243
Sagal, Boris 330
Saidy, Fred
  Finian's Rainbow 259
Saint-Exupéry, Antoine de
  Night Flight 135
St. Jacques, Raymond 270, **270**
St. Johns, Adela Rogers 100, 135
Salem's Lot (TV, 1979) 370
Salem's Lot (TV, 2004) 370
Sale, Tim
  The Long Halloween 350
Salinger, J.D.
  "A Perfect Day for Bananafish" 290
Salkow, Sidney 330
Sally of the Sawdust (1925) 83
Salome 76, 77
Salomon, Mikael 370
Salomy Jane (1914) 76–9, **78**, 83
Salomy Jane (1923) 77
Sampson, Will 245
Samuel Goldwyn Productions 112
Sanctuary (1961) 225
Sanders, George 210, 212
Sanders, Steven M. 336 n.1
Sanger, Margaret 99, 100
Sarandos, Ted 368
Saratoga Trunk (1945) 146
Saroyan, William 16, 170
  The Human Comedy 174
  The Time of Your Life 193, 202
Sarrazin, Michael 250, **252**
Sarris, Andrew 259

Sartre, Jean-Paul
  No Exit 297
Satan Met a Lady (1936) 156, 181
satire 60, 119, 244, 247, 254, 259, 340, 358
Saul, Oscar 193
Savage (1973) 262
Saving Private Ryan (1998) 263
Savlov, Marc 321
Scanner Darkly, A (2006) 308
Scarface (1932) 175, 185
Scarlet Letter, The (1926) 83, 85–7, **86**, 115
Scarlet Letter, The (TV, 1950) 202
Scarlet Letter, The (1995) **18**, 18–19, 85, 320
Scarlet Pimpernel, The (1934) 117, 148
Schamus, James 342
Scharnhorst, Gary 76
Schary, Dore 195
Schatz, Thomas 151 n.6, 154 n.60
Schechner, Richard 260
Scheider, Roy **262**
Schenck, Joseph M. 195
Scheuer, Philip K. 217
Schickel, Richard 337 n.26
Schiffman, Suzanne 171
Schindler's List (1993) 263, 339
Schlesinger, John 243
Schneider, Rebecca 17
Schrader, Paul 176, 261
Schulberg, B.P. 140
Schumacher, Joel 350, 351
Schumann, Robert
  Piano Concerto 216
Schwab, Laurence
  Good News 80
Schwager, Jeff 198 n.24
Schwarzenegger, Arnold 312
science-fiction films 33–4, 301–8, 319, 340
Scorsese, Martin 38, 261, 279, 297, 324
Scott, A.O. 344, 346
Scott, Ridley 306, 307
Scott, Sir Walter 15, 25, 139
scripts 16–18, 19, 23, 26, 27, 36, 44, 59, 69, 87, 92, 126, 128, 137,

148, 158, 166, 168, 173, 175,
  181, 187, 192, 199, 201, 219,
  226, 227, 257, 268, 277, 284,
  288, 296, 309, 310, 318, 319,
  324, 327, 330, 331–5, 343, 344,
  346, 358, 372, 374
  and anti-scripts 312
Sea Beast, The (1926) 37
Sea Chase, The (1955) 165
Sealed Room, The (1909) 63
Searchers, The (1956) 13, 203
Searching Wind, The (1946) 165
Seastrom, Victor. *See* Sjöström, Victor
Seaton, George 253
Sebold, Alice
  The Lovely Bones 361
Second World War 141, 158, 161, 164,
  165, 166, 167, 168, 187, 190,
  195, 218, 236, 243, 244, 279,
  303, 326, 341, 357
  as adaptation of First World War
    167–8, 187
Secretary (2002) 298
Secret Hour, The (1928) 79
Seeger, Pete 235
Seff, Manuel 118
Segal, Erich
  Love Story 253
Seitz, George B. 85, 102
Selig Polyscope Company 54, 55
Selznick, Brian
  The Invention of Hugo Cabret 348
Selznick, David O. 11, 135–7, 138, 140,
  141, 145, 149, 159, 190, 234
Selznick International 136, 137
Selznick, Irene Mayer 135, 194
Semenza, Greg M. Colón 7, 8, 27, 274
Semon, Larry 59
Sennett, Mack 59, 60, 61
Sense and Sensibility (1995) 320, 339
sequels 37, 55, 107, 123, 126, 130,
  136, 163–4, 203, 253, 267, 271,
  278, 306, 311, 313, 314, 327,
  348, 349, 352, 354, 355, 356,
  359, 362
Sergeant, The (1968) 283
Sergeant Rutledge (1960) 203
Sergeant York (1941) 162, 166, 174

Series of Unfortunate Events, A (2004)
  348
Series of Unfortunate Events, A (TV,
  2017–19) 348
Serling, Rod 203
  Patterns 201
  Requiem for a Heavyweight 202
Serpico (1973) 245, 246, 254
Serra, Antônio 169
Servant, The (1963) 183
Seton, Anya
  Dragonwyck 193
Seven Blood-Stained Orchids (1972) 178
7th Heaven (1927) 91, 93
7 Women (1966) 203
Sewell, Anna
  Black Beauty 270
sex 19, 70–1, 77, 84, 86, 87, 105,
  179, 180, 182, 209–11, 212,
  214, 217, 222, 224, 225, 236,
  244, 245, 247–8, 249, 255, 258,
  272, 273, 274, 277, 278, 282,
  283, 284, 286, 287, 291, 293–4,
  297–8, 313, 315, 321, 322–3,
  324, 334, 343, 344, 346, 359
  as selling point 207
sex, lies, and videotape (1989) 319
Seymour, James 118
Shadow of a Doubt (1943) 12
Shaft (1971) 269, 271–2, 272, 274
Shainberg, Steven 298
Shakespeare in Love (1997) 10
Shakespeare, William 7, 9, 19, 22, 24,
  25, 39, 174, 239, 247, 297, 360
  Hamlet 227
  King Lear 227
  Romeo and Juliet 233, 241
  The Tempest 304
Shamroy, Leon 211
Shane (1953) 13
Shange, Ntozake
  *For Colored Girls Who Have
    Considered Suicide When the
    Rainbow is Enuf* 361
Sharknado (2013) 37
Shatzkin, Roger 26
Shaw, George Bernard 9
  Pygmalion 298

Shaw, Irwin 200
Shaw, Robert **262**
Shawshank Redemption, The (1994)
  292, 373, 374
Shearer, Norma 138, 286
Sheer, William 96
Sheik, The (1921) 93
Sheldon, Dyan
  Confessions of a Teenage Drama
  Queen 348
Shelley, Mary
  Frankenstein 44, 317
Shepherd, Cybill 326
Shepherd, Elizabeth 21
Sherwood, Robert E. 16, 116–17, 232
  Abe Lincoln in Illinois 116, 202
  Idiot's Delight 116
Shining, The 371, **371**, 373
Shining, The (TV, 1997) 371
Shoot the Piano Player (1960) 170
Short Cuts (1993) 292–3
short stories, adaptations of 3, 52, 113,
  114, 155, 178, 202, 290–6, 308,
  373
Show Boat (1929) 118
Show Boat (1936) 80, 118
Show Boat (1951) 80
Showtime 201
Shumlin, Herman 120–1
Shurlock, Geoffrey 225
Shurlock Office 206, 209, 233, 319
Shutter Island (2010) 261
Sideways (2004) 339
Sidney, Sylvia 140
Siegel, Bernard 103
Siegel, David 322
Siegel, Don 276
Siegmann, George 65, 95
Silence (2016) 261
Silence of the Lambs, The (1991) 27,
  339
Silverado (1985) 327
Silver, Joan Micklin 279
Silverstone, Alicia 320
Simenon, Georges
  Maigret's First Case 317
Simmons, Jerold L. 206
Simon, Neil 16, 232–3

Barefoot in the Park 232
California Suite 232
Chapter Two 232
The Gingerbread Lady 233
The Goodbye Girl 232
The Odd Couple 232
The Out-of-Towners 232
Plaza Suite 232
The Prisoner of Second Avenue 232
The Star-Spangled Girl 232
The Sunshine Boys 232
Sweet Charity 232
Sims, David 374
Sinatra, Frank 190, 297
Sincerely, Willis Wade (TV, 1956) 202
Since You Went Away (1944) 165
Sin City (2005) 312
Singer, Bryan 355
Singer, Isaac Bashevis
  "Yentl the Yeshiva Boy" 278
Sinise, Gary 344
Siodmak, Robert 16, 19
Sirk, Douglas 221
Sisterhood of the Traveling Pants, The
  (2005) 348
Sisters (1973) 261
Sisters, The (1938) 156
Six Feet Under (TV, 2001–5) 201
Sixteen Candles (1984) 347
Sjöström, Victor 83
Skin of Our Teeth, The (TV, 1951) 202
Sky Is Gray, The (1980) 294
Slashdot 368
Slaughter (1972) 273
Slaughterhouse-Five (1972) 242, 243,
  254, 255, 264
Slaves of New York (1989) 14
Slezak, Victor 333
Sling Blade (1996) 339
Sloan, A. Baldwin
  Tillie's Nightmare 59
Slumdog Millionaire (2008) 339, 340
Smalley, Phillips 99
Smalls, Charlie 274
Smart Blonde (1937) 128
smartphones 366, 367
Smash-Up: The Story of a Woman
  (1947) 213

Smight, Jack 305
Smith, Betty
   A Tree Grows in Brooklyn 174
Smith, Edgar
   Tillie's Nightmare 59
Smith, Kate 167
Smith, Lillian
   Strange Fruit 191
Smith, Paul Gerard
   Funny Face 80
Smith, Stephen 153 n.51
Smith, Will 314
Smith, Winchell
   Lightnin' 79–80
Smollet, Arthur 59
Smyth, J.E. 153 n.56
Snake Pit, The (1948) 157, 280
Snapchat 359, 366
Snicket, Lemony
   A Series of Unfortunate Events 348
Snipes, Wesley 313–14
Snows of Kilimanjaro, The (1952) 19, 203, 207, **208**
Snows of Kilimanjaro, The (TV, 1960) 202
Snyder, Sharon L. 280
Snyder, Zack 312
Sobchack, Vivian C. 160
So Big! (1932) 146, 156
Social Network, The (2010) 339, 340
social-problem films 187–8
Soderbergh, Steven 319
Softley, Iain 321, 323
Soisson, Joel 373
Soldier's Daughter Never Cries, A (1998) 14
Soldier's Home (1977) 294
Some Kind of Wonderful (1987) 347
Some Like It Hot (1959) 208
Somerset Maugham TV Theatre (TV, 1951–2) 200
Something Evil (1972) 262
Something of Value (1957) 221, 269
Something Wicked This Way Comes (1972) 305
Something Wicked This Way Comes (1983) 305

Sondheim, Stephen
   Merrily We Roll Along 119
   West Side Story 241
Song of Bernadette, The (1943) 136, 174, 187
Song of the Thin Man (1947) 130–1, **131**, 173
Son of Tarzan, The (1920) 123
Son of the Thin Man (1941) 173
Sontag, Susan 240
Sony Pictures 354, 355
Sophie's Choice (1982) 332
Sopranos, The (TV, 1999–2007) 201
So Red the Rose (1935) 116, 146
Soubirous, Bernadette 187
Sound and the Fury, The (1958) 225
Sounder (1972) 274
Sound of Thunder, A (2005) 320
soundtracks, multichannel 185
Southern, Terry 235
   Candy 244
Spacek, Sissy 370, **371**
Spanish Cape Mystery, The (1935) 127
Sparks, Nicholas 23, 348, 370
Spartacus (1960) 268
Spellbound (1945) 12, 280
Spider-Man 107, 317, 352, 354, 355, 357
Spider-Man (TV, 1981–2) 352
Spider-Man (2002) 352, **353**
Spider-Man 2 (2004) 352
Spider-Man 3 (2007) 352
Spider-Man: Homecoming (2017) 355
Spider's Web, The (1926) 144
Spielberg, Steven 261–4, 308, 331
Spook Who Sat by the Door (1973) 276
Squaw Man, The (1914) 31
Stagecoach (1939) 155, 162, 291
Stage Door (1937) 119, 146, 157
Stage Door Canteen (1943) 124, 166, 173
Stage Fright (1950) 12
Stahl, John M. 174, 209
Stallings, Laurence 163
   What Price Glory? 80
Stamp, Shelley 109 n.19
Stam, Robert 16, 18

Stand by Me (1986) 373
Stander, Lionel 127–8
Stanwyck, Barbara 176
Stardust (2007) 348
Star Is Born, A (1937) 136, 278
Star Is Born, A (1954) 278
Star Is Born, A (1976) 278
Stark, Richard 171
stars 3, 16, 22, 37, 91, 111–12, 115, 118, 121, 130, 131, 132, 133, 135, 136, 137, 156–8, 169, 173, 190, 195, 212, 216, 228, 235, 267, 277, 335, 344
and star personas 92–3
Star Spangled Girl (1971) 232
Star Trek: The Motion Picture (1979) 363
Star Wars (1977) 260, 263, 267, 306, 320, 365
State Fair (1933) 126
State Fair (1945) 119
Steamboat Round the Bend (1935) 127
Steele, Jessamy Harte 76
Steiger, Rod **232**, 245, 269, 305, **305**
Steinbeck, John 13, 23, 158–9, 170, 199–201, **200**
  East of Eden 199
  The Grapes of Wrath 158, 160
  In Dubious Battle 6
  The Moon Is Down 159, 165
  Of Mice and Men 158
  The Wayward Bus 204
Stella Dallas (1937) 120, 142
stereotypes 41, 43, 44, 72, 95, 102, 140, 170, 249, 269, 270, 271, 274, 284, 286
Sternberg, Josef von 140
Sterne, Laurence
  Tristram Shandy 319
Stevens, George 221
Stevenson, Robert Louis 6
Stewart, Michael 278
Stewart, Patrick 356
Stoker, Bram 172
  Dracula 274, 370
Stoker, Florence 172
Stolen Life, A (1946) 156

Stompanato, Johnny 227
Stone, Emma **355**
Stone, Lewis 136
Stong, Phil
  State Fair 126
Story of G.I. Joe (1945) 166
storyworlds 351, 362, 364–5
Stout, Rex 128
Stowe, Harriet Beecher 350
  Uncle Tom's Cabin 40–1, 43, 44–5, 94, 95, 139, 169, 204, 213
Strange Affair of Uncle Harry, The (1945) 185
Strange, Dr. 356, 357
Strange Fruit (1979) 191
Strange Interlude (1932) 116
Strangers on a Train (1951) 12
Stratemeyer, Edward 128
Strathairn, David 344
Strawberry Blonde, The (1941) 156
Strawberry Statement, The (1970) 246, 254, 255, 256
Streep, Meryl 220, 331–5, **334**
Street Angel (1928) 91, 93
Streetcar Named Desire, A (1951) 193–4, **194**, 195, 218
Street, Della 132, 133, 134
Street of Chance (1942) 177, 178, 179, 184, 185
Street Scene (1931) 116
Streets of Laredo (TV, 1995) 327
Streisand, Barbra 278, **279**
Stribling, T.S.
  Birthright 144
Stringer, Arthur
  "Womanhandled" 104
Stroheim, Erich von 81–3, 85, 88
Stromberg, Hunt 136
Strong, Austin
  7th Heaven 91
Stuart, Randy 212
Studio One (radio, 1947–8) 201
Studio One in Hollywood (TV, 1948–57) 202
Studio One Summer Theatre (TV, 1948–57) 201–2
Sturges, John 19
Sturges, Preston 91

subcultures 72, 83, 94, 96, 134, 160, 224, 226, 236, 238, 245, 268, 277–82, 290
subjectivity 65, 115, 134, 138, 140, 142, 143, 144, 145, 146, 150, 155, 161, 175, 181–6, 191, 269, 287
Sub-Mariner 352
Subterraneans, The (1960) 241, **242**, 246, 256
Such a Gorgeous Kid Like Me (1972) 170
Such a Little Queen (1914) 92
Sugar Hill (1974) 277
Sugarland Express, The (1974) 262
Suicide Squad (2016) 358
Sullivan, Pat 309
Summer Theatre (TV, 1948–57) 202
Sun Also Rises, The (1957) 19, 158, 203
Sunrise (1927) 93
Sunshine Boys, The (1975) 232
Sun Shines Bright, The (1953) 203
Supaidâman (TV, 1978–9) 352
Super Fly (1972) 273
superhero films 309–19, 348–58
Superman 28, 107, 312, 314, 315, 317, 318, 350, 351
Superman (1978) 309–11, **310**, 315, 330, 354, 358
Superman II (1980) 309, 311
Superman III (1983) 311
Superman IV: The Quest for Peace (1987) 311
Superman and the Mole Men (1951) 309
Susan Lenox (Her Fall and Rise) (1932) 145
Suspicion (1941) 12
Sutherland, Donald 288, **289**
Swarup, Vikas
  Q and A 340
Sweet, Blanche 61, 64, 79
Sweet Charity (1969) 232
Sweet Smell of Success (1957) 117
Sweet Sweetback's Baadasssss Song (1971) 269, 271, 272
Swicord, Robin 2

Swimmer, The (1968) 291
Switching Channels (1988) 186
Sylvester, Robert
  Rough Sketch 195
synchronized sound 80, 111, 114–16

tableaux 13, 21, 42, 43, 44, 45, 51, 293
Take Me Out to the Ball Game (1949) 173
Tale of Two Cities, A (1935) 136, 137
Tales of Terror (1962) 293
Taliaferro, Edith 75
Tamblyn, Russ 214
Taming of the Screw (1997) 297
Tan, Amy 373
  The Joy Luck Club 279
Tank Girl (1995) 313
Tarantino, Quentin 263
Targets (1968) 326
Tarkington, Booth 39, 40
  Alice Adams 157
  The Magnificent Ambersons 202
  Monsieur Beaucaire 202
Tarnished Angels, The (1958) 221
Tarzan 123–5, 129, 130, 132, 135, 145
Tarzan and His Mate (1934) 123
Tarzan and the Amazons (1945) 124
Tarzan and the Green Goddess (1938) 123
Tarzan Escapes (1936) 123
Tarzan Finds a Son! (1939) 123
Tarzan of the Apes (1918) 123
Tarzan's Desert Mystery (1943) 124
Tarzan's Magic Fountain (1949) 124
Tarzan's New York Adventure (1942) 123
Tarzan's Revenge (1938) 124
Tarzan's Secret Treasure (1941) 123
Tarzan the Ape Man (1932) 123, 124, **124**
Tarzan the Fearless (1933) 123
Tarzan the Mighty (1928) 123
Tarzan Triumphs (1943) 124
Taxi Driver (1976) 261
Taylor, Elizabeth 222
Taylor, Kent 125
Taylor, Mary Imlay 39

Taylor, William Desmond 81
Tea and Sympathy (1956) 207, 283
Technicolor 19, 163, 166, 174, 187, 205, 206, 211, 224, 302, 349
Teenage Mutant Ninja Turtles (1990) 313
Teenage Mutant Ninja Turtles II: The Secret of the Ooze (1991) 313
Teenage Mutant Ninja Turtles III (1993) 313
television 2, 3, 6, 7, 13, 24, 25, 27, 37, 38, 79, 116, 158, 169, 178, 199–203, 205, 206, 209, 213, 217, 220, 221, 223, 227, 228, 233, 234, 239, 240, 256, 257, 261, 262, 267, 274, 288, 301, 304, 305, 306, 307, 308, 309, 310, 314, 317, 319, 320, 322, 324, 327, 340, 344, 347–8, 349, 352, 357, 361, 366, 367, 370, 372, 373
Telotte, J.P. 336 n.3
Temblay-Leduc, Gabrielle 22
Temple, Shirley 112, 125
Ten Commandments, The (1923) 74
Ten Days Wonder (1971) 170
Tender Is the Night (1962) 225
Ten North Frederick (1958) 221, 222, 226, 227
Tennyson, Alfred, Lord 9, 10
  "Enoch Arden" 37
Terminator 2: Judgment Day (1991) 302, 314
Terms of Endearment (1983) 327
Tex (1982) 347
Thackeray, William Makepeace 24–25
  Vanity Fair 14
Thalberg, Irving 81, 113, 123, 135, 147
Thank You, Mr. Moto (1937) 132
Thank Your Lucky Stars (1943) 166
That Cold Day in the Park (1969) 257
That Was Then … This Is Now (1985) 347
theatrical models of screenwriting 121
Their Eyes Were Watching God (TV, 2005) 23
Them (1954) 303

Therese and Isabelle (1967) 298
These Three (1936) 191
They Had to See Paris (1929) 116, 125, 126, 127
They Knew What They Wanted (1940) 79
They Shoot Horses, Don't They? (1969) 250–1, **252**, 255
Thieves Like Us (1974) 257
Thing, The (1982) 307
Thing from Another World, The (1951) 302, 303
Things to Come (1936) 301
Think Fast, Mr. Moto (1937) 128
Thin Man, The (1934) 129–30, **130**, 131, 132, 133, 181
Thin Man Goes Home, The (1944) 173
Thin Red Line, The (1964) 261
Thirty Seconds over Tokyo (1944) 166
This Above All (1942) 157, 165
This Island Earth (1955) 302
This Is the Army (1943) 166–8, **168**, 169, 172, 173, 187
This Property Is Condemned (TV, 1958) 201
Thomas, Elton 106
Thompson, David 258
Thompson, Derek 359
Thompson, Emma 320–1
Thompson, Fred
  Funny Face 80
  Rio Rita 80
Thompson, Jim
  The Killer Inside Me 175
Thompson, Kay
  Eloise 202
Thompson, Kristin 264 n.6
Thor 352, 356, 357
Thoreau, Henry David 11
Thornton, Billy Bob 328
Thorpe, Richard 136, 204
Thorpe, Rose H.
  "Curfew Shall Not Ring Tonight" 40
Thor: Ragnarok (2017) 356, 357
Those Awful Hats (1909) 61
Three Came Home (1950) 166

Three Coins in the Fountain (1954) 219, 220
3-D projection 205, 208, 306, 349
3 Dev Adam (1973) 352
Three Faces of Eve, The (1957) 280
300 (2007) 314, 315
Three Musketeers, The (1948) 204
Three the Hard Way (1974) 273
3 Women (1977) 257
thrillers 112, 178, 258, 261, 370
Thurber, James
  "The Greatest Man in the World" 294
  The Male Animal 202
Thurman, Uma 312
THX-1138 (1971) 260
Tibbetts, John C. 26
Tidyman, Ernest
  Shaft 271
Tierney, Gene **160**
Tierney, Harry
  Rio Rita 80
Tillie's Punctured Romance (1914) 60
Timeline (2003) 320
Time of Your Life, The (TV, 1958) 202
Tobacco Road (1941) 159–61, **160**, 188
To Catch a Thief (1955) 12
Todd, Mike 222
Todorov, Tzvetan 324
To Each Her Own (1946) 157
Toffler, Alvin 362
To Have and Have Not (1944) 19, 155
To Hell and Back (1955) 166
To Kill a Mockingbird (1962) 27, 204, 205
Tolentino, Riccardo 169
Toler, Sidney 128
Tomb of Ligeia, The (1964) 293
Tomorrow (TV, 1960) 202
Tom Sawyer (1917) 81
Too Busy to Work (1932) 125, 127
Tooker, William H. 85
Too Many Girls (1940) 118
Topaz (1969) 12
Topaze (1933) 135
Top Gun (1986) 267
Topor, Tom
  Nuts 278

Torn Curtain (1966) 12
Torpedo Run (1958) 165
Torrence, Ernest 105
Torrid Zone (1940) 186
Tortilla Flat (1942) 158
Total Recall (1990) 291–2, 308, 369
Toth, Emily 216–17
Tourneur, Jacques 261
Tourneur, Maurice 83, 84, 85
Tovarich (1937) 117
Towering Inferno, The (1974) 262
Tracy, Spencer 19, 163, 164
Tracy, William **160**, 161
Traffic (2000) 339, 340
Transmedia Producers Credit 363
transmedia storytelling 363
Tree Grows in Brooklyn, A (1945) 155, 174
Trial of the Incredible Hulk, The (TV, 1989) 357
Trick Baby (1973) 272
Trilogy (1969) 292
Trilogy Studios 364
Trio (1949) 199
Trip to the Moon, A (1902) 301
Trollope, Anthony 24–5
Trotter, David 299 n.16
Trotti, Lamar 162
True Grit (1968) 330
True Grit (2010) 330
Truffaut, François 170, 171, 304
Tuck Everlasting (1981) 348
Tuck Everlasting (2002) 348
Tumin, Melvin 343
Turner, Lana 190, 204–5, 214, 227
Turner, Otis 54
Turow, Scott 373
Turturro, John 117
Twain, Mark 6, 11, 16, 25, 38, 40, 79, 81, 170, 174, 237
  The Adventures of Huckleberry Finn 14, 138, 237, 273
  The Adventures of Tom Sawyer 201, 203
  "The Man That Corrupted Hadleyburg" 294
Twelve Angry Men (TV, 1954) 202
Twelve Angry Men (1957) 202

INDEX

12 Years a Slave (2013) 339, 340, 369
Twentieth Century Fox 112, 124, 127, 128–9, 134, 137, 158, 159, 162, 166, 173, 174, 187, 192, 193, 204, 206–7, 208, 209, 211, 213, 216–17, 219, 221, 222, 234
Twentieth Century Pictures 112
20,000 Years in Sing Sing (1933) 156
Twilight (2008) 348
Twilight Zone, The (TV, 1959–64) 203
Twin Beds (1920) 79
Twin Beds (1929) 79
Twin Beds (1934) 79
Twin Beds (1942) 79
Twitter 366
Two Face 316
Two Kinds of Women (1932) 117
Two Rode Together (1961) 203
2001: A Space Odyssey (1968) 282, **283**, 306
Tyler Perry Productions 361

Uhry, Alfred
  Driving Miss Daisy 319
Ulmer, Edgar G. 20
Unbeliever, The (1918) 87–9, **88**
Uncle Tom's Cabin (1903) 40–5, **42**, 52
Uncle Tom's Cabin (1910) 52–3
Uncle Tom's Cabin (1927) 94–5
Under Capricorn (1949) 12
Under the Volcano (radio, 1947) 201
United Artists 105, 106, 112, 137, 158, 173, 179, 221, 223, 243, 258, 276
Universal–International Pictures 21, 22, 293, 306
universality 53, 91, 92, 160, 333, 366
Universal Pictures 20, 22, 81, 94, 112, 118, 127, 132, 135, 137, 179, 187, 190, 205, 221, 234
universes, fictional 315, 318–19, 350–2, 354, 364–5
Unstrung Heroes (1995) 332
Untamed (1955) 213
Updike, John
  "The Music School" 294
  "Pigeon Feathers" 294, 295
  Rabbit, Run 241

Up in Arms (1944) 80
Up in Mabel's Room (1926) 80
Up in Mabel's Room (1944) 80
Up Periscope (1959) 165
Upstairs, Downstairs (TV, 1971–5) 24
Up the Sandbox (1972) 278

Vagabond King, The (1930) 80
Vagabond King, The (1956) 80
Valenti, Jack 234
Valentino, Rudolph 93
Valley of Decision, The (1945) 174
Valley of the Dolls (1967) 221
Van Buren, Mabel 93
Vance, Philo 127, 130, 133, 173, 317
Van Dine, S.S.
  The Canary Murder Case 127
Vanessa, Her Love Story (1935) 136
Vanishing American, The (1925) 102, **103**
Van Peebles, Melvin 271
Van Sant, Gus 353
Van Upp, Virginia 277
Varsi, Diane 214, 222
Vasey, Ruth 113
Veiled Aristocrats (1932) 143
Veiller, Bayard
  Within the Law 83
Venable, Evelyn 125, **125**
Verevis, Constantine 376 n.15
Verhoeven, Paul 308
Verne, Jules 301
  From the Earth to the Moon 302
Vertigo (1958) 12
Vest, Jason P. 27
V for Vendetta (2006) 315
Vicas, Victor 204
Victim (1961) 283
videocassette recorder (VCR) 367
Vidor, Charles 19, 221
Vidor, King 163, 164
Vietnam War 165, 235, 236, 243, 247, 341
Vincendeau, Ginette 321
Virginian, The (1923) 83
Visconti, Luchino 172
Vitagraph Company 52

Viva Villa! (1934) 135
Viva Zapata (1952) 159
Vivre sa vie (1962) 171
Voight, Jon 243
Vonnegut, Kurt, Jr. 6, 243
Von Trier, Lars 344
von Zell, Harry 211

Wagner, Richard
   Tristan and Isolde 212
Waititi, Taika 356
Wakefield (2009) 3
Wakefield (2016) 1–3, **2**
Wakefield Variation, The (2013) 3
Walcamp, Marie 99
Wald, Jerry 213, 217, 218, 219, 221, 222, 225
Walker, Alice
   The Color Purple 263
Walker, Ellie Wood 309
Walk in the Sun, A (1945) 166
Walkman 367
Wallace, Edgar 135
Wallace, Henry 51
Wallace, Lew
   Ben-Hur: A Tale of the Christ 50–1
Waller, Robert James 23
   The Bridges of Madison County 28, 331
Walsh, Raoul 95, 187
Walthall, Henry B. 62, 64, 66, **66**, 69, 87
Wang, Wayne 279
Ward, Fannie 71, **72**
Ware, Irene 20
war films 161–8
Warhol, Andy 297
Warner, Jack L. 234, 259
Warner Bros. 36, 111, 112, 113, 114, 127, 128, 133, 134, 156, 159, 163, 166, 173, 174, 179, 186–7, 194, 204, 234, 241, 351, 354
War of the Worlds, The (1953) 302, 304
War of the Worlds (2005) 263
Warren, Robert Penn 195
   All the King's Men 190, 191
Warshow, Robert 291

Washington Square (1997) 321, 324, 325
WASP culture 288–9, 290
Watchmen (2009) 312, 314, 315, 358
Watch on the Rhine (1943) 156, 165
Waterloo Bridge (1931) 117
Waterloo Bridge (1940) 117, 165
Watermelon Man (1970) 271
Waterworld (1995) 320
Waxman, Franz 214
Wayne, Bruce 354
Wayne, John 280, 330
Wayne, Marie 55
Wayne, Martha 315, 316
Wayne, Thomas 315, 316, 317
Wayward Bus, The (1957) 204, 222
Wead, George 108 n.9
Webb, Marc 354
Webb, Millar 37
Weber, Lois 98, 99, 100
Webster, Jean
   "Daddy-Long-Legs" 83
Wedding, A (1978) 293
Weekend (1967) 239
Week-End at the Waldorf (1945) 204
Weidman, Jerome
   I Can Get It for You Wholesale 211, 212
   I'll Never Go There Any More 213
Weimar cinema 176, 184
Weinberg, Herman G. 108 n.10
Weinberg, Jack 233
Weiner, Matthew 220
Weird Science (1985) 347
Weissmuller, Johnny 123–4, **124**, 132
Weisz, Rachel 361
We Live Again (1934) 116
Welles, Orson 192, 193
Wellin, Arthur 169
Wellman, William 329
Wells, H.G. 301
Wells, Mai 59
Welsh, James M. 26
Welty, Eudora 6
Werfel, Franz
   The Song of Bernadette (1943) 187
Westcott, Edward Noyes
   David Harum 125

Westerns 13, 17, 33, 83, 101–5, 162, 301, 302, 323, 327–30
  and anti-Westerns 327, 329
Western Union (1941) 12
Westinghouse Studio One (TV, 1948–57) 201
Westinghouse Summer Theatre (TV, 1948–57) 202
West, Mae 157, 313
West, Nathanael 6
Weston, Maggie 95
West Side Story (1961) 119, 241, 245, 255
We Were Strangers (1949) 193
Wexley, John
  The Last Mile 121
Wexman, Virginia Wright 205
Whale, James 118
Wharton, Edith 27, 228, 324
  The Age of Innocence 26, 324
  "A Bottle of Perrier" 290
  The House of Mirth 13, 324
What Maisie Knew (TV, 1968) 322
What Maisie Knew (2012) 322
What Price Glory? (1926) 80
What Price Glory? (1952) 80
What Price Hollywood? (1932) 135, 136
Whedon, Joss 357
Wheeler, Harvey
  Fail-Safe 303
When Ladies Meet (1941) 174
When Worlds Collide (1951) 302–3, 304
Where Are My Children? (1916) 98–100, **98**
Where Love Has Gone (1964) 226
While the City Sleeps (1956) 12
White, Peter **285**
Whitman, Walt 9, 11, 237
Whitmore, James 195
Whittier, John Greenleaf 11, 12, 40
Who Framed Roger Rabbit (1988) 267
Who Killed Cock Robin? (TV, 1938) 116
Whoopee! (1930) 80
Who's Afraid of Virginia Woolf? (1966) 207

Why Change Your Wife? (1920) 81
Why Did I Get Married Too? (2010) 361
Wilcox, Collin 204
Wilde, Cornell 209, **210**
Wilde, Hagar
  "Bringing Up Baby" 157
Wilde, Oscar 9
Wilder, Billy 179
Wilder, Robert 221
Wilder, Thornton 16, 117
  The Bridge of San Luis Rey 154 n.57
  Our Town 148, 202
  The Skin of Our Teeth 202
Wild Girl (1932) 77
Wild Horse Mesa (1925) 102–4
Wild One, The (1954) 241, 243
Wild Party, The (1975) 14
Wiley, Hugh 128
Willeford, Charles
  Pick-Up 175
Williams, Ben Ames
  "Jubilo" 125
  Leave Her to Heaven 174, 188–9, 213
Williams, Cora 105
Williams, Jesse Lynch
  Why Marry? 79
Williams, Tennessee 6, 16, 232
  Glass Menagerie, The 273
  A Streetcar Named Desire 193–4
William, Warren 127, 131
Willis, Bruce 321
Wilson, Elizabeth 249
Wilson, Lois 73, 93, 102
Wilton, Eric 316
Window, the (1949) 177
Wings of Eagles, The (1957) 203
Wings of the Dove, The (TV, 1959) 202
Wings of the Dove, The (1997) 321, 323–4, 325
Winsor, Kathleen
  Forever Amber 209, 210, 217
Winter Dreams (TV, 1957) 202
Winter, Jessica 337 n.18
Winterset (1936) 116

Winters, Roland 128
Wire, The (TV, 2002–8) 201
Wise Blood (1979) 203
Wise, Robert 119, 241, 280
Wister, Owen
   The Virginian 83
Witch Queen, The (1914) 56
Withers, Hildegarde 127, 131, 132, 173
Within Our Gates (1920) 143, 144
Within the Law (1923) 83
Witness for the Prosecution (1957) 158
Wiz, The (1978) 274–6
Wizard of Oz, The (1925) 59
Wizard of Oz, The (1939) 149–50, 274, 325
Wolfe, Nero 127–8, 173, 317
Wolf of Wall Street, The (2013) 261
Wolverine 355
Wolverine, The (2013) 352
Women, The (1939) 286
Womanhandled (1925) 104–5
Woman in the Window, The (1944) 185
Woman on the Moon (1929) 301
Women's World (1954) 219
Wonder (2017) 348
Wonderful Wizard of Oz, The (1910) 54–5, 58
Wonder Woman 309
Wonder Woman (TV, 1976–7) 309
Wonder Woman (2017) 358
Wonder Woman: Who's Afraid of Diana Prince? (1967) 309
Wong, James Lee 128
Wood, Michael 142
Woods, Donald 132
Woods, Frank E. 69
Woodward, Fred 56
Woodward, Joanne 218
Woodward, Richard 337 n.22
Woolf, Virginia 23, 139, 344
   To the Lighthouse 139
Woolrich, Cornell 177–9, 181, 195, 200. *See also* Hopley, George; Irish, William
   Black Alibi 177, 179
   Black Angel, The 177, 179

   The Black Curtain 177, 179
   The Black Path of Fear 177, 179
   "The Boy Cried Murder" 177, 178
   The Bride Wore Black 170, 177, 179
   "Cinderella and the Mob" 178
   "Cocaine" 177
   "The Earring" 178
   "For the Rest of Her Life" 178
   "He Looked Like Murder" 177
   "Hummingbird Comes Back" 178
   "It Had to Be Murder" 177
   "The Mark of the Whistler" 177
   "Nightmare" 177
   Rendezvous in Black 177, 178, 179
   Savage Bride 177
   "The Shirt Collar" 178
   "Silent as the Grave" 178
   "Somebody on the Phone" 178
   You'll Never See Me Again 177
Wordsworth, William 9, 10
Workers Leaving the Lumière Factory (1895) 43
Wray, John Griffith 79
Wright, Richard 23
   "Almos' a Man" 294
   Native Son 274
Wright, Todd 59
Written on the Wind (1956) 221
Wu, Tim 366–7
Wyler, William 127, 191–2, 277
Wylie, Ida Alexa Ross 90, 174
   Mother Bernle Learns Her Letters 89
Wyllie, Barbara 26
Wyman, Jane 281

Xavier, Dr. Charles 356
X Hamlet (1995) 297
X-Men 132, 350, 356, 357
X-Men (2000) 352, 355–6, 357
X-Men: Apocalypse (2016) 359
X2 (2003) 352

Yagoda, Ben 152 n.28
Yankee Doodle Dandy (1942) 119
Yates, Peter 245
Yeats, William Butler 333

Yentl (1983) 278, **279**, 291
Yokum, Li'l Abner 309
York, Susannah 250, 257
You Can't Take It with You (1938) 119
You Can't Take It with You (TV, 1950) 202
Youmans, Vincent 118
   Hit the Deck 80
   No, No, Nanette 80
Young, Gig 251
Young Adult (YA) fiction 347–8
Young at Heart, The (1938) 136
Young Lions, The (1958) 165
Young, Robert 163
Young Romance (1915) 74–6, 83
Young Sherlock Holmes (1985) 316
Young, Stark
   So Red the Rose 146

You're a Big Boy Now (1966) 259
Your Show Time (TV, 1949) 202
youth demographic 228, 233, 235, 243, 253, 267, 306, 319–20, 321, 347–9, 358–60
YouTube 359, 360, 362

Zane Grey Theatre (TV, 1956–61) 305
Zanuck, Darryl F. 169, 188, 206–7, 209, 234
Zimbalist, Efrem, Jr. 226
Zimmerman, Paul D. 265 n.23
Zoetrope Studio 259
Zorro 106–8
Zuckerman, Nathan 341, 342, 343, 344
Zuckoff, Mitchell 265 n.25
Zukor, Adolph 234

www.ingramcontent.com/pod-product-compliance
Lightning Source LLC
Chambersburg PA
CBHW052111010526
44111CB00036B/1666